I attribute my success to this—I never gave or took any excuse.
- Florence Nightingale

The ACT Prep Black Book

"The Most Effective ACT Strategies Ever Published"

By Mike Barrett

Dedication

This book is dedicated to my friends and family—past, present, and future—and to my many clients and readers the world over, some of whom have become like friends and family themselves. Your steadfast support has been a blessing, and I am more grateful than I can say.

Free Video Demonstrations

If you'd like to see videos of sample ACT solutions like the ones in this book, please visit www.ACTprepVideos.com. A selection of free videos is available there for readers of this book.

TABLE OF CONTENTS

DEDICATION..4

FREE VIDEO DEMONSTRATIONS 5

NOT HARD—JUST UNUSUAL...8

GETTING THE MOST OUT OF *THE ACT PREP BLACK BOOK*...10

A NOTE TO CONCERNED PARENTS...12

FREQUENTLY ASKED QUESTIONS 13

"HOW WELL CAN I DO ON THE ACT?"..19

HOW TO TRAIN FOR THE ACT—MASTERING THE IDEAS IN THIS BOOK.....................22

UNDERSTAND YOUR MISTAKES..29

THE "NATURAL TEST-TAKER" 31

WHAT YOU MUST UNDERSTAND ABOUT THE ACT..34

THE TRUTH ABOUT THE ACT...39

THE ACT'S BIGGEST WEAKNESS..41

USING THE REAL ACT PREP GUIDE, 3RD EDITION (THE "RED BOOK").........................45

CARELESSNESS WILL COST YOU..48

HITTING A TARGET SCORE...49

THE GENERAL GAME PLAN FOR ATTACKING A SECTION OF THE ACT ON TEST DAY....51

TIMING ISSUES...55

READING PASSAGES ON THE ACT 58

ACT TRAINING 60

ACT READING 61

   How To Read Passages On The ACT Reading Section 68

   The General Process For Answering ACT Reading Questions...70

   Walkthroughs: The ACT Reading Process In Action Against Real Questions 73

   ACT Reading Quick Summary..114

ACT MATH...115

   ACT Math Toolbox..117

   Unwritten Test Design Rules Of ACT Math 166

   Testing Values..169

   ACT Math Answer-Choice Patterns 171

   The General Process For Answering ACT Math Questions 177

   ACT Math Closing Thoughts...181

   Walkthroughs: The ACT Math Process In Action Against Real Questions....................186

   ACT Math Quick Summary..264

ACT SCIENCE 265

   Unwritten Test Design Rules Of ACT Science 268

   How To Read Passages On The ACT Science Section...270

   Using Simple Trends To Make Predictions 271

   ACT Science Question Types..273

   ACT Science Answer-Choice Patterns..276

   The General Process For Answering (Most) ACT Science Questions 278

   Walkthroughs: The ACT Science Process In Action Against Real Questions 280

   ACT Science Quick Summary...322

ACT ENGLISH 323

   Commas In The ACT English Section 326

   ACT English Question Types...327

   How To Read Passages On The ACT English Section 355

   The General Process For Answering ACT English Questions 356

   ACT English Answer-Choice Patterns And Issues...358

   Walkthroughs: The ACT English Process In Action Against Real Questions 360

   ACT English Quick Summary..388

ACT WRITING TEST (THE ACT ESSAY)...389

   Unwritten Test Design Rules Of The ACT Essay (ACT Writing Test) 391

   Recommended Step-By-Step Approach To The ACT Essay..397

Example ACT Essay *399*

Analysis Of Sample Essays In The Real ACT Prep Guide, 3rd Edition...*402*

ACT Writing Test (The ACT Essay) Quick Summary..*406*

YOU HAVE TO PRACTICE 407

WHEN THINGS GO WRONG...408

4 ACT MYTHS...410

SHOOTING FOR A 36..412

IF AMERICAN ENGLISH ISN'T YOUR FIRST LANGUAGE 414

PARTING ADVICE 416

THANKS FOR READING!...417

APPENDIX: WRITING TOOLBOX..418

Not Hard—Just Unusual

"Every great and deep difficulty bears in itself its own solution. It forces us to change our thinking in order to find it."
- Niels Bohr

Millions of students worry over the ACT every year. They spend countless hours (and dollars) trying to cram scientific theories and obscure trig formulas into their heads so they can get the best possible score—and most of them just end up frustrated and unhappy with their results, despite all their work. If you're reading this book, it's probably because you're also unhappy with your performance so far on the ACT. (If you were happy with your score, you wouldn't need to keep preparing, right?)

Because so many people have such a tough time with the ACT (and with other standardized tests like it), the test has developed a reputation for being a difficult obstacle to overcome. A lot of people will tell you that the only way to "prepare" for the ACT is to read novels, study advanced math, take AP science classes, watch the Discovery Channel between practice essay sections, and do all kinds of other pointlessly rigorous things.

But those people are wrong. The ACT isn't hard because it's advanced. It's hard because it tests the *basics*—but in very strange ways. It's designed according to rules that are actually pretty simple, even though they're also pretty different from the rules that govern tests in high school and college.

That's a very important idea, so make sure you never forget it: the ACT is only challenging because it's a weird test of basic skills, not because it's an advanced test that rewards you for being a genius.

This book will teach you a simple and effective approach to the test, an approach that exploits the weaknesses created by the standardized nature of the ACT. You'll learn to take the knowledge you already have and apply it to the ACT in a way that the test will actually reward, so you can achieve your highest possible score.

The approach I'll show you in this book is one I've taught to many, many students who used it to get much better scores on the ACT than they originally thought possible. If you pay careful attention to the ideas and examples in this book, you can use this information to increase your score, as well—but that won't happen unless you actually make an effort to learn and practice these strategies.

Don't expect to read this whole book through once and then just automatically be able to find the correct answer to every single ACT question you ever see for the rest of your life. If you really want to maximize your performance, it isn't enough just to read what I've written. You actually have to apply it on your own by following the drills and exercises in this book, trying to figure out real test questions from ACT, Inc., and learning from your mistakes. Applying this method means adjusting to a different way of thinking about the ACT, which means you'll need to practice against real ACT questions until you get the hang of it. This does take a little time for most people, but not nearly as much time as the "traditional," mainstream approach—and the results are far better.

So if you want great results, give us both a fighting chance. Read this whole book with an open mind, follow along with the question walkthroughs to see how these ideas are applied to real ACT practice questions, go to www.ACTprepVideos.com to watch the free video demonstrations, and—above all else—stick to it when you run into something challenging, or something that doesn't seem to make sense at first.

I've done everything I can in this book to show you how the ACT really works, and how you can beat it.

Now, it's up to you to learn that material, practice it, and make it happen.

Let's get right down to it.

Remember The Rules, And Don't Give Up

There will be times in your practice (and even on test day) when you encounter a question that seems to break the rules that we'll talk about in this book. This happens to everybody—it even happens to me occasionally.

When it does happen, we must remember that *it's always because we've made a mistake.*

I know that sounds harsh, but I say the exact same thing to myself when I run into a question I can't figure out at first: "Okay, Mike—according to the way you've just read this question, none of the answer choices is correct. But you know that ACT questions are always written so that exactly one answer choice is valid according to the test's rules. That means you must have made a mistake and read the question wrong."

You see, the ACT is a standardized test that's carefully controlled. A standardized test must always follow the same rules, or else it wouldn't be standardized anymore. It's important that we never, ever forget that.

On a standardized test, there are limits to the ways questions can be asked, and there are rules and patterns that govern things like the relationships among answer choices, the relationship of the question to the relevant passage or diagram, and so on. If you understand these rules, and you understand how important they are, you'll do better on the test, because you'll know how to handle what you see on test day. If you don't appreciate the importance of the rules, then you'll start to feel lost pretty quickly, because it will seem like the ACT could ask you anything at all, and you might not know how to answer. This is why it's so important that you remember all those rules are still in effect, even when a question challenges you. Forcing yourself to evaluate each real ACT question in terms of the test's rules will give you the best chance of figuring out how to answer the question correctly.

The test's rules are never broken. All the questions you see on a real ACT (one that's written and published by ACT, Inc.) have been carefully edited and reviewed by many people to make sure they fit the ACT's design standards. If a question shows up on test day, then it's valid, and it's carefully designed so that it only has one valid answer choice, according to the rules of the ACT.

So if you see a real ACT question (one that was written by ACT, Inc., and not by some other company), and if that question seems not to have any valid answers, or if it seems to have more than one valid answer, then you can be sure the mistake is somewhere in your mind, and not on the actual page.

Remember, though, that part of what makes the ACT challenging is that it intentionally tries to present questions so they seem different from what they really are. This is why everybody, including me, will sometimes encounter questions that don't seem to follow the test's rules at first.

So when this happens—and it definitely will, I promise you—remember that the ACT is *intentionally* trying to get you to misread or misunderstand something.

Don't let it get away with that!

Getting The Most Out Of *The ACT Prep Black Book*

The best way for you to use this book will depend on the time you have between now and your test date.

If you're not in much of a time crunch, the very best thing to do is just to read the whole book, in order. Doing your best on the ACT, and doing that efficiently, is very much about developing an understanding of the way the entire test works, even if you feel like you only need help in one or two sections. Reading the whole book will give you the clearest overall picture of the special way this test operates, so my recommendation for anyone who isn't in a time-crunch is, again, to read this entire book in the order it's presented.

Of course, some people are short on time for their preparation. If you find yourself in that situation, then you should read the sections in this book that pertain to the sections and question types you find most challenging. Beyond that, though, you should be sure to read a few other important sections that don't relate to any specific question type. These sections are useful because they'll address training ideas and frequently asked questions related to the ACT, and they'll also give you a vital overview of the structure and function of the test—and that knowledge will make the specific strategies more intuitive and easier to apply.

That said, here are the sections you should still read, even if you're short on time:

- Frequently Asked Questions
- How To Train For The ACT—Mastering The Ideas In This Book
- Understand Your Mistakes
- What You Must Understand About The ACT
- Carelessness Will Cost You
- Hitting A Target Score

If you're reading this literally the night before the test, you may decide only to read the sections pertaining to the question types that give you the most trouble—but if at all possible, I'd recommend that you try to read the sections I just listed as well.

What's In This Book

We'll start our discussion of the ACT with some general information about the purpose of the test, how it's designed, and why. You may be tempted to skip or skim this information, but I would strongly recommend that you read it carefully instead. This information lays an important foundation that will help you understand why these strategies work, which will help you to apply them more effectively and consistently as you learn them.

After that, we'll look at each major question type on the ACT. We'll learn how each question type works, and the best way to approach it. Then we'll do a walkthrough of the most challenging and notable questions of each type that appear in the practice tests in your copy of *The Real ACT Prep Guide, 3rd Edition* (which I will affectionately refer to as the "Red Book," because it's red, and it's a book). That way, you'll be able to see my techniques in action against a wide variety of real ACT questions, which will help you master the strategies you'll learn in this book.

(I call those questions the most challenging and notable because they're either the ones that my private tutoring clients tend to ask about most frequently, or they're the ones that I consider to be excellent examples of particular concepts from this book.)

After we've gone through all the question types and seen the techniques in action against real practice questions of each type, we'll close with a few short articles covering other helpful topics, such as making an elite score (34+) and avoiding common ACT misconceptions.

The Real ACT Prep Guide, 3rd Edition (AKA The "Red Book")

By now I've already mentioned the so-called "Red Book." Its official name is *The Real ACT Prep Guide, 3rd Edition*, and it's made by ACT, Inc. I'll mention it many, many more times throughout the rest of this book. The Red Book is the only ACT prep book that's published by the same company that actually writes the ACT, which means it's also the only book that contains real ACT prep questions, which are absolutely essential to your preparation (more on that later).

If you want to prepare for the ACT effectively, you must have access to the Red Book. You can buy it online, and you can also find it in local bookstores. You can even borrow it from your school library or local library. No matter where you get it, though, you need a copy.

At the time that I'm writing this, the most recent version is the 3rd edition, so that's the one you should use to follow along with the walkthroughs in this book.

The Black Book that you're reading right now will teach you effective strategies for tackling every type of real ACT question, but you can only practice those strategies if you have real ACT questions to prep with—so let me say it one more time:

If you want to do a good job of preparing for the ACT, you *must* have a copy of *The Real ACT Prep Guide, 3rd Edition*!

Also, I strongly, strongly advise that you avoid practice questions from any other company; we'll get into the reason for that soon.

First, let me address a common concern I sometimes encounter from the parents of my students.

A Note To Concerned Parents

"If you are truly serious about preparing your child for the future, don't teach him to subtract—teach him to deduct."
- Fran Lebowitz

Every so often, I get an e-mail from a parent who is concerned about my method of preparing for standardized tests. Basically, the parent is worried that approaching the test in the way I recommend somehow corrupts the purpose of the test as a learning experience for his child. Let me take a minute to address this concern in the beginning, so we're all on the same page for the rest of this book and for the rest of your preparation.

As I've already mentioned, and as I'll continue to mention throughout the book, standardized tests like the ACT have very little in common with the tests you might take in school. In school, tests have a lot to do with your ability to memorize a lot of information ahead of time, and then recall that material on test day. But doing well on the ACT is much more about being able to understand a set of standardized rules and patterns, and then recognizing those patterns and rules in action and responding accordingly on test day, in a highly repetitive way.

In other words, preparing for (and doing well on) the ACT isn't a learning experience in the way you might think it should be. The skills that you need to do well on the ACT simply aren't the same skills you've developed in school, for the most part.

Let me be very clear here: I think learning is extremely important. I think it's a very big deal for students to be passionate about learning and understanding new material. It's essential for all of us to read novels, and learn history, and study science, and to develop and grow intellectually—not just in high school or college, but for our whole lives.

But if a high school student is trying to do her best on the ACT, then developing and growing in those ways simply isn't going to help much, because the ACT doesn't actually reward that kind of growth. So when I say things like "make up any examples you want for your essay," or "don't worry about exactly what this word means," or "there's no point in learning advanced math formulas for this kind of situation," it's absolutely not because I'm against learning stuff in general. It's only because the point of this Black Book is to help my readers get the best scores on the ACT that they possibly can, and doing that requires them to know how the test actually works—even if it seems like we're avoiding an opportunity to learn something.

If that's a surprise to you, bear with me, and we'll address all those issues more specifically in the coming sections.

Even though it might seem like preparing for a test as important as the ACT should necessarily involve sharpening the skills one would traditionally associate with being a "good student," it's probably best if you don't look at it this way. It's much better if we understand that doing well on the ACT requires a different set of skills from those required to do well in school, so that we can focus on developing those skills. The ACT is simply an obstacle we have to overcome so we can move on to the next step in the educational process.

Again, I'm a firm believer in doing well in school, reading widely, learning new words, and studying math and science . . .

. . . but if I told my readers to do those things *in order to improve their ACT scores,* I'd be wasting their time.

Since our only goal here is to get the highest score we can, and since that involves following all the rules of the ACT, we'll focus on learning and exploiting those rules for the duration of this Black Book.

Okay! Glad we covered that. If some of it didn't make sense, it'll probably be cleared up after you read the next few sections, when we discuss how everybody *thinks* the ACT works, and how it *actually* works.

Frequently Asked Questions

There are a few questions that I hear from almost everybody I work with on the ACT, so I thought it would be a good idea to address those here.

General Questions

How much time do I need to prepare for the ACT?

There is no universal answer to this question—some students will feel comfortable after studying for only a couple of days, while others will practice for a couple of months before they feel they've got the hang of it. Ideally, you should probably start at least a couple of months out from the test date to give yourself some extra time, but if you have less than that you can still see great improvement. Try to think less about "putting in the time," and think more about developing a better understanding of the test with each practice session.

How did you learn these strategies?

I developed these strategies through careful analysis of the test over the course of many years. I've been teaching them now for well over a decade through a number of different media, and in that time I've worked to refine the techniques—as well as the way I teach them—to make the whole process as effective and efficient as possible. To learn more about me and my background, take a look at my blog at www.TestingIsEasy.com.

What's the best way to get started?

As previously discussed, the best way to get started is just to read the material in the order it's presented. You'll start out with some general information about the test, then you'll learn the strategies for a given section in the abstract, then you'll see them in action against real ACT practice questions (be sure to follow along in your copy of the Red Book).

Of course, after that, it's incredibly important that you try these techniques yourself on real practice ACT questions, and then carefully review your practice. More on that later, especially in the section called "How To Train For The ACT."

Also, for a selection of video demonstrations of the ideas in this book, check out www.ACTprepVideos.com (free to readers of this book).

Do these strategies work on the SAT?

As we'll briefly discuss in another section, the SAT and the ACT are fundamentally the same. They're both internationally administered standardized tests for high school students that primarily test basic reading and math skills in ways that differ from those used by "normal" classroom tests. In fact, most of the questions that appear on either test could also appear on the other one, because most of the rules on the two tests allow the same types of questions in many situations. (There are exceptions to this, of course—each test also has question types that don't even appear on the other test, for one thing. But the principles underlying the design of individual questions on both tests are still largely similar.)

Still, it's important to realize that specific question types that might seem to be common to both tests are not perfectly identical! Each test has its own spin on reading, writing, and math, and of course the ACT has the Science section (although you'll see that this section mostly requires a combination of the skills used in the Reading and Math sections). So while all the underlying principles that you'll learn in this Black Book apply to both tests—the idea of testing simple concepts in unusual ways, the highly standardized structure, and so on—the specific strategies for specific question types aren't all the same. If you're familiar with my SAT preparation materials, you may find that some of the more general information in this book is similar to the general information in my SAT book, though the specific details related to the question types may vary quite a bit.

Some students are able to take the fundamentals of my approach to the ACT and modify them appropriately to be used on the SAT. If you'd like to test that out, simply try to attack some real SAT practice questions after you've become comfortable with the strategies in this book. If you find you can apply them effectively, great. If not, then you'll probably want to use some SAT-specific training materials. I recommend my *SAT Prep Black Book* for that—but, of course, I'm biased :)

What if I want to score a 36? Or a 22? Or 33? Or a 28? Or . . . ?

There's a common misconception that a student who wants to achieve a certain score should follow a certain set of strategies, while a student with a different target score should use different strategies. In reality, the test's design is constant, so you should use the same set of strategies, and the same basic approach, no matter what your target score may be. The only difference is that you'll need to be more accurate in your execution if you want to reach a higher target score.

So students who want higher scores or greater improvement should be using the same strategies and techniques as everybody else—they just have to train and practice a little more to make sure they're using those strategies and techniques more consistently and effectively, and making fewer mistakes. (Exactly how much more training is necessary will depend on the student's specific situation.)

The most direct answer is that you'll still use the strategies laid out in this Black Book, no matter what you've scored before or what you hope to score. The best approach is to learn these strategies and practice them until you can execute them accurately enough to be comfortably in your target score range. Of course, the higher your target score, the more accurate you'll need to be—for a perfect 36, you'll generally only be able to miss one question or so per section, at most.

What if I can't get the strategies to work?

At some point, almost everybody—myself included—runs into a practice question that they just can't seem to solve with the normal strategies. Although this sort of thing is always aggravating, it can be a very beneficial experience if you approach it in the right way.

When you run into a problem like this, the very first thing you should do is confirm that you're working with a real ACT question written by ACT, Inc. It's very important to work only with real practice questions from the test-maker, not from some third-party company (we'll discuss that in more detail later). If the question isn't written by the test-maker, then the strategies from this Black Book might not work against it, since fake tests usually don't follow the rules that the real test does.

After that, go back and make sure that you've read the answer key correctly. Many times I've talked to students who were completely baffled by a question they got wrong that they were sure they had solved correctly, only to have them realize afterwards that they *had* solved it correctly in the first place and had only misread the answer key.

If you know you're working with a real ACT question, and you know you've read the answer key correctly, and you're sure you can't figure out the question, then you're in a frustrating situation—but it's also potentially a very helpful situation.

Let me explain why.

The ACT is highly standardized. That means that questions on the ACT must be repetitive in a lot of ways—they have to do similar things in similar ways on every single test, or else there would be no standardization. You might (correctly) assume that having to ask the same kinds of questions over and over again would make the test too easy. For this reason, the people who make the test try to disguise the questions as best they can, so they don't seem to work the same way that all the other questions work.

That means you'll find real ACT practice questions that *can* be answered using the techniques and strategies in this book, but that *seem* at first like they can't, because the test-maker has done a good job of making it seem like a particular question is different from all the others.

This is one of the primary challenges you'll encounter if you want to beat this test: when you find yourself facing a question that seems to break all the rules, you have to make sure you don't get frustrated and assume that the rules must not work, or that the ACT must have messed up on this question, or that something else out of your control is going on. If you let yourself get frustrated, you'll probably give up, and ultimately your score will suffer. Instead, take the time to understand each question that frustrates you. Figure out what's going on with it, where you went wrong in your initial approach, and *what you can do to avoid getting stuck like that in the future.*

The more you do this, the more you'll begin to understand how the test really works and how it's written, which will make it harder and harder for the test-maker to trick you in the future. That's why getting stuck on a hard question can actually be a huge opportunity for improvement: since the test is standardized, every time you get unstuck from a difficult situation is a time that helps you avoid those kinds of situations on test day.

So how do you go about trying to figure out a question that stumps you? First, you'll want to make sure the strategy you're trying to apply is appropriate to the situation. For example, you might be accidentally applying an idea for ACT English to an ACT Reading question.

If you feel confident that the strategy you're trying to use is appropriate, then the most likely thing is that you've overlooked or misread some detail in the text. If it's a math question, you may have overlooked a labeled value on a diagram, or put a decimal in the wrong place, or mixed up your positive and negative signs. If it's a science question, you may have misread a long or unusual scientific term, or you may be looking at the wrong part of a graph, or at the wrong graph or diagram entirely. On an English question, you may have failed to notice a comma, or you may have misunderstood exactly what a certain pronoun refers to, or you might be looking at the wrong sentence or paragraph. On a reading question, you may be looking at the wrong passage, you may have missed a word like "not" or "no" or a prefix like "un-," or you may have misread an answer choice.

Of course, there are other details you might overlook or misread as well, and performing well on the ACT comes down to paying attention to all these little details. Catching any one of them isn't difficult, but trying to keep up with all of them throughout a whole test can be challenging, especially because a lot of mainstream education nowadays tends to focus less on details and more on the big picture.

Once you approach the test with the proper mindset, you should have no trouble training yourself to look for those details, but there will still be times when you overlook one and can't find the right answer. If it happens on test day, then move on and answer the questions you can answer more quickly before coming back to spend time on the difficult ones. If it happens in practice, then when you review your practice, spend as much time as you need to in order to be able to find out what went wrong on that question. Once you do that, you will have taken a large step forward in your training.

(You may also find it helpful to check out www.ACTprepVideos.com, where I've made some demonstration videos available for free to the readers of this book.)

Which practice books should I buy?

This book was written so that the only other ACT book you'd need would be the "Red Book"—*The Real ACT Prep Guide, 3rd Edition*. You should be able to get it from any major bookseller, either online or in a physical bookstore. Your school library may also have a copy. Be aware that if you get one from a library, it may have already been marked up by someone else, which isn't ideal—if possible, get a fresh copy.

Reading Questions

You say the correct answer to each question is always spelled out on the page, but I found a question where it isn't. What does that mean?

You may remember that earlier we talked about how the ACT tries to be tricky, and to make it seem like the questions are less straightforward than they actually are. I definitely know what it feels like to look at a question and feel certain that the answer isn't right there on the page, but this issue is always the result of an error made by the test-taker (that's you or me) and not an error made by the test-maker (ACT, Inc.).

(Of course, as always, this only applies if you're using real ACT practice questions made by the test-maker. If you're using questions written by some other company, then those aren't real ACT questions, and they can't be expected to work the same way as the real thing.)

The first thing you need to do is step back and accept that the error must be on your part, and realize that the answer to your problem must be somewhere in the passage, question, or answer choice. Then, try to clear your mind of anything you've thought about the question so far, and take a fresh look at it. Read the passage carefully, read the question carefully, and read all the answer choices carefully, and do your best to find the place in the text that spells out the answer choice—it's in there.

Taking the time to look carefully for the text that supports the right answer will give you a better understanding of how the test works, and will help improve your ability to spot the supporting text for other challenging questions. It's worth the time it takes.

I got a question wrong, but my answer is better than the answer choice the ACT says is correct—now what?

One big mistake that untrained test-takers make when they approach tests like the ACT is going through all the questions and just looking for the answer choices that seem best *to them*.

But it's very important for us test-takers to understand that the ACT doesn't care what we think. At all.

The ACT has its own system for deciding which answer choices satisfy its requirements, and which ones don't. For that reason, we have to stop looking at answer choices and thinking, "Which one do I like best?" Instead, we should think, "Which of these choices fulfills the ACT's requirements for a correct answer to this type of question?"

If you frequently find yourself feeling like your favorite answer choices are better than the ones the ACT says are right, take some time to review the advice in this Black Book and get a refresher on exactly what the ACT wants to see in correct answers to that type of question.

Math Questions

Which math formulas are most important for the ACT?

If I had to pick a single most important formula, it would probably be the Pythagorean Theorem, just because it shows up a lot in one form or another on the ACT. Beyond that, basic geometric formulas and rules (like the ones related to triangles, rectangles, circles, complementary and supplementary angles, and so on) also seem very common.

Still, you need to keep a few things in mind:

1. No matter what, you'll still need to be familiar with everything in the ACT Math Toolbox (in this Black Book) if you want to be ready for anything you might encounter in an ACT Math question.

2. Frequently, just knowing a formula isn't going to be enough to get you the right answer to an ACT Math problem—you'll also need to be familiar with the special characteristics of ACT Math questions, and you may have to get a little "creative" in your approach to a question.

3. To find out which topics tend to come up in ACT Math questions, one of the best things to do is to read the section of this Black Book on ACT Math questions, and then just practice with a lot of real ACT Math practice questions.

For further information about the ACT Math section, take a look at the relevant section of this Black Book.

Which type of calculator should I use?

This is a common question with a simple answer: use the type of calculator that you feel most comfortable with (assuming it's allowed, of course; most calculators are, but you should check to be sure). Remember that the most difficult part of finding the correct answer to an ACT Math question often lies in figuring out how to set up the problem, which is something a calculator can't do. The bottom line is that the most important part of your approach to this section is your own training, not your calculator.

If you're comfortable with graphing calculators, then you should probably use one, because they can sometimes help you answer math questions quickly and easily. We'll see this idea demonstrated in the question walkthroughs at the end of the Math section of this Black Book—the solution I provide for question 57 on page 178 of the Red Book is one good example.

But don't worry if you're not comfortable with graphing calculators, because they're not even useful on most real ACT Math questions, and there's always at least one way to solve every problem without a calculator. Don't try to use a calculator you're not comfortable with, because there's a good chance you'll make mistakes that can cost you time and points.

For more on the right approach to ACT Math, check out the ACT Math section of this Black Book.

For more on specific ways to use calculators on the ACT Math section, see the section of this Black Book labeled "Using A Calculator," as well as the walkthroughs in the Math section of this Black Book.

I tried to find the answer based solely on patterns in the answer choices, and it didn't work. Why not?

Always remember that patterns in the answer choices are simply hints at the issues we can expect to be important to the solution for that question. They'll *often* point to a likely correct answer, *but not always*. For that reason, you should never rely completely on answer-choice patterns in determining the correct answer to any question, unless you've given up trying to answer the question with math and you just want to guess.

The best way to use these answer-choice patterns is to let them guide your analysis if you're not sure what the best approach to a question might be, and/or to check your answer once you've finished the problem to make sure you didn't make a mistake. More on that in the ACT Math section later in this book.

English Questions
I found a correct answer that doesn't follow the rules of grammar I learned in school. How can that be?

Remember that the only thing that matters on the ACT is what the people who make the ACT say is right. In the context of ACT English, there are some grammar rules that the ACT likes to follow that may be different from the rules you're used to. In fact, they may even contradict each other directly, particularly where punctuation is concerned.

Don't worry! The grammar rules used in the ACT English section must be standardized, just like every other aspect of the test, so we can learn these rules and answer the questions accordingly. Don't be shocked if you come across a correct answer on the ACT that seems to break the grammar rules you're used to, or an incorrect answer that seems to follow them. Always learn what the ACT rewards and punishes, and answer questions accordingly. For more on this, check out the section of this book that deals with ACT English.

What if I can't think of good examples for the ACT Essay?

Remember that any example you come up with is fine as long as it supports your argument—it doesn't have to be literary or historical, or even factually accurate (as long as it would support your argument if it were true). Remember also that personal examples can be just as valid as any other type of example, as long as they support the thesis.

Since the essay prompt will be related to high school in one form or another, you should be able to think of personal examples (real or invented) that will fit the prompt if you practice with other prompts beforehand. For more on this topic, take a look at the section of this book that deals with the ACT Essay.

Science Questions
The Red Book says the ACT Science section covers things like botany, thermochemistry, oceanography, and optics, but I've never studied those. How am I supposed to get a good score on the ACT Science section?

As you explore the ACT, you'll see that the test is often not what it seems to be—and the ACT Science section is a prime example of this. Although we normally think of a science test as something that rewards us for learning scientific concepts beforehand, we'll see that almost every ACT Science question will ask about information that's provided by the test itself, right there on the page in front of you, in one form or another. On the rare occasions when you do need outside scientific knowledge, that knowledge will be basic—usually the sort of thing you might learn in elementary school or middle school. For more on this, check out the part of this Black Book that covers the ACT Science section.

"How Well Can I Do On The ACT?"

"Your present circumstances don't determine where you can go; they merely determine where you start."
- Nido Qubein

Sooner or later, almost every client I work with will ask me this question in one form or another:

"How well can I do on the ACT?"

Often they'll include their best score to date on a practice (or real) test, and then mention a target score:

"If I've already gotten a 23, would it be possible for me to get a 31?"

There's a pretty good chance you've asked someone this question, or at least thought it to yourself. It's understandable—the ACT is a big deal, and it can have a big impact on where you'll end up going to college, not to mention how much you might pay for your education.

Concentrating on this kind of question probably isn't a good use of your time, but here's the most complete answer I can give you without knowing you personally:

If you have the following skills, then you have all of the basic tools that you need to get any score on the ACT, including a 36:

- speaking and reading American English without much trouble
- knowing some *basic* science (like the idea that ice is frozen water)
- having a reasonable understanding of the basic principles of arithmetic, geometry, algebra, and trigonometry

This is true because finding the correct answer to every question on the ACT requires nothing more than the correct application of these skills, or of some combination thereof.

Notice that I said these are the "basic tools" you need to get any score—simply having the tools isn't the same thing as knowing how to use them properly, which will be the real focus of this book. As it turns out, most people who take the ACT have the necessary knowledge to score significantly higher on the test than they actually do, but they approach it the wrong way. The proper technique makes a much bigger difference than most untrained test-takers ever realize.

"Really, Though, How Well Can *I* Do On The ACT?"

You might feel like I haven't *really* addressed the question of how well you, in particular, can do on the ACT. Well, here's another way to look at the answer to that question: the only real way to know how well you can do is to prepare for the test correctly, take it, and then find out what the results are. All that matters here is the actual score you get—not what some tutor or diagnostic test says you *should* get. Anything else is just talk.

Besides, whether someone tells you that you should be able to get a 25 or a 35, you're still going to have to learn the right way to beat the test, and then practice those methods until you get them right. So knowing the score you "should" get (which is just speculation anyway) doesn't have any impact on the way you'll prepare for the test, which is what you should really be focusing on.

Anyone with the basic skills mentioned above has what it takes to score a 36. Really. The challenge everybody faces is that the ACT is very different from the tests you take in high school. The ACT rewards you for figuring out weird questions about basic concepts, and for paying careful attention to small details. Neither of those skills requires any advanced knowledge.

What they do require is that you make some deliberate effort—that you really work to get a better understanding of how the test works, and change the way you think about it. It means carefully reviewing your practice to see exactly what's stopping you from answering the questions you find challenging.

What if you only have limited time between now and test day? Even if you're short on time, your best bet is to focus on preparing and improving as much as you can, and let everything else work itself out. This is good life advice in general, and it's certainly true in test prep as well.

Putting Your Tools To Work

This Black Book will definitely cover the limited subject matter involved in ACT questions (such as basic math, how to form the possessive of a plural noun, and so on), but we'll spend much more time on helping you develop the ability to apply those tools correctly and consistently.

As I've mentioned repeatedly and will continue to mention, the ACT is fundamentally different from the tests you take in school. When something is tested in school, you typically study that thing for weeks leading up to the test, and when the test day arrives, you have a pretty specific idea of what'll be on the test and how it'll be tested.

But the ACT isn't about cramming facts into your head. The ACT is largely a test of your ability to know which basic skills to use in which situations.

Let's imagine that an ACT math question asks you to find the area of a strange-looking figure that's made up of several circular components. You might not realize at first that the figure you're looking at is made up of several circles. In that case, even if the formula for the area of a circle is the only formula you need to know, and even if you know that formula, you might still not be able to get the question right unless you eventually realize that the formula you know is relevant to the question.

In a case like that, the challenge would be simply to realize what you're looking at—once you can do that, the actual math is pretty straightforward.

The same general concept applies to other ACT questions as well, as you'll see later in this Black Book.

In addition to figuring out which skills to apply, the other main challenge is simply to use your skills correctly and accurately.

For example, there's a very particular way that you need to read individual phrases of ACT reading passages (we'll talk about it in detail later). This way of reading is almost totally different from the way we tend to read in school. In this situation, the challenge is to look at the passage in the way that the ACT rewards, and not to slip back into the habit of reading the passage the way you would in school. It's the sort of thing that isn't difficult to do a single time, after you've got the hang of it—but you have to train yourself (through practice) to do it correctly over and over again on test day.

The more you practice and train for the ACT, the more you'll see that it's a very repetitive test—it has to be, because if it weren't fundamentally the same every time, it wouldn't be standardized, and then there would be no reason for it to exist.

So if you want to beat the ACT, you'll have to train yourself to do strange, simple tasks over and over again. You'll need to be able to look at a question, determine which simple skills are required to figure out the answer, apply those skills correctly, make sure you haven't made any mistakes, and then move on to the next question. Then you'll do that over and over (and over) again until you've completed the test. It's very repetitive and very predictable once you know what to look for—which is what we'll be discussing in the rest of this Black Book.

Getting Better

Whenever you try to get better at something, it's a good idea to find some way to measure the progress you're making—it's encouraging to see improvement when you make it, and it's important to be aware if you aren't making any progress, so you can figure out what's going wrong.

Most people simply track their progress by scoring their practice tests or practice sections. This isn't unreasonable, since your ultimate goal will be to achieve a certain score, but I find it a bit one-dimensional, and not always helpful.

Instead, especially in the beginning, I like to recommend that you focus a little less on the result and a little more on whether you can refine the execution of the proper techniques.

In other words, instead of saying, "I want to score at least a 32 on this section," you might say, "I want to try to get through this entire math section without making a single *careless* error," or, "I want to do an entire English section without missing a single question related to pronouns."

When students make sure their goals are more focused on specific skills, and less arbitrary, their practice scores tend to rise higher and more quickly than when the goals are simply tied to achieving a certain score—especially when students tie those goals to known issues they might have in a particular section.

Of course, as you get closer to the test date and you get a chance to address any major issues, it may make sense to think more about the actual scores you're getting. But by that point you may already be performing well above your target range.

How To Train For The ACT—Mastering The Ideas In This Book

"The essence of training is to allow error without consequence."
- Orson Scott Card

It's very important for you to read this Black Book and learn all the strategies for each question type. But it's every bit as important that you actually apply that knowledge to real ACT practice questions in your training. After all, it's one thing to read along as I walk you through a solution to a problem, pointing out all the things to watch out for and be careful about . . . and it's something entirely different to answer questions on your own without any guidance, which is what you'll have to do on test day.

So you MUST learn to do these things on your own.

After questions about specific question types, the most common question I hear comes down to this: "How should I train for the test?" That question is usually followed by a string of questions about different specific training strategies and schedules. Because I hear these questions so often, I thought it would be a good idea to address them in the beginning of this Black Book, before we even get into the specific training for each section.

The bottom line is that there's no single training schedule or approach that works best for everybody. Every student has her own strengths, weaknesses, goals, attention span, scheduling issues, and so on. So instead of trying to put together a one-size-fits-all approach, I'll give you some general guidelines, and then I'll advise you on how to tweak them to fit you personally.

The Recommended Progression

Most people track their progress by looking at practice test scores, but I wouldn't recommend that, at least not in the beginning. The score on test day is what ultimately matters, of course, but evaluating yourself based only on that number isn't going to be very helpful at this stage.

Instead, my recommendation is that you track your progress based on your understanding of the test. This is more subjective, but more useful at this point in your training.

The first thing you want to do is develop a general understanding of each section of the test. You can do that by reading this Black Book in order, and then taking a look at the sample solutions until you feel like you understand how the different question types work.

Next, you want to develop the ability to recognize and understand your mistakes. Notice that we're not even trying to fix those mistakes yet; we're just trying to learn to *recognize* them. That means you need to be able to do some practice work, then take a second look at the questions you missed and figure out where you went wrong. You need to identify what you misunderstood or overlooked that stopped you from answering the question correctly, and what you could have done to avoid the mistake and get the question right.

After you know why you're making mistakes, you need to train yourself to fix them. This is extremely important. Take the knowledge you've gained so far and apply it in your practice, either to avoid errors in the first place, or to recognize them and resolve them once you've made them. Your goal at this point in your training is to avoid careless mistakes, so that the only time you miss a question is when it involves a concept you're not familiar with.

Once students train themselves to stop making careless errors, they're typically scoring in a range that they're quite happy with. If you get to this point and you still need to increase your score, then you'll need to take a look at what's stopping you from answering the remaining questions. Be careful, though—too often, students conclude that they're missing Math questions because they don't know some obscure formula, or missing Science questions because they don't know enough physics or chemistry. In almost every case, the real issue has to do with a failure to understand some principle or idea related to the structure of that question type. Take a close look and try to identify the real issue, so you can work on it.

Also, if you're having performance issues related to timing, be sure to take a look at "Timing Issues," the section of this book that deals with time management. Remember that when you're trying to work on your timing, your goal isn't to do the same thing more quickly, it's to find a different way to answer the question in front of you that's faster and simpler.

Order Of Attack

A lot of students like to start their preparation by focusing on the section of the ACT they have the most trouble with. That's understandable. If you've got the time, though, I'd definitely recommend you prepare for each section in the order laid out in this book. That way, you'll be able to build on the skills learned in each section as you progress through the training.

I almost always start students off on the Reading section, for a few reasons. The first reason is that careful, precise reading is the most important skill on the entire ACT (yes, even on the Math and Science sections), so it makes sense to start developing that skill directly, right from the beginning. The second reason is that it's usually easier to see how predictable and repetitive the Math, Science, and English questions are if we've already seen how predictable and repetitive the ACT Reading questions are.

The only two situations I can think of in which I wouldn't recommend that you start with ACT Reading would be the following:

1) You literally *never* miss *any* ACT Reading practice questions, or
2) You have very little time before test day, and you feel you need to spend that time working on other sections.

Unless one of these applies to you, I would definitely say that you should start your training with the ACT Reading section.

After you feel comfortable with the Reading section, I find it's usually best to work on ACT Math. As we'll discuss in the Math training section, excelling at ACT Math essentially comes down to being able to read a question, figure out which basic math concepts need to be applied to find the answer, and then apply them. Typically, the bigger challenge is just figuring out which math concepts to use; the actual math you do on most problems is pretty simple (but you still need to look out for careless errors at all times).

Because ACT Math problems appear on the surface to vary more than the questions in other sections, it might take a little more time for you to get comfortable with the approach to the ACT Math section, which is why I usually like to introduce it as soon as possible after the Reading training.

After that, I'd recommend that you take a look at the Science section. The skills you need to do well on the Science section are basically the same as the ones you will have learned for Reading and Math. Mostly, you'll be using the careful reading we'll talk about in the Reading section—only now it'll be applied to charts, graphs, and scientific texts. You may also need a little bit of basic math thrown in there, and a tiny bit of basic science, which is so minimal that it's almost irrelevant. We'll talk more about that in the Science training section.

Next you'll want to look at the ACT English section. Some of these question types will require skills that are similar to the ones from the Reading section, and of course we'll also talk about how to attack the other question types.

Last, we'll talk about the ACT Writing Test, also known as the ACT Essay. Before you spend any time on this, you should find out if your target schools even care about it, because many don't—just take a look at the schools' websites or call their admissions departments directly to find out. If they do, then of course you'll want to prepare for this section as you would for any other. If they don't care, then you don't want to spend much time at all worrying about this part of the test.

Drills And Exercises

What do you do to prepare for a test in school? You probably gather together all the notes and materials you've covered leading up to the test, and you sit down and memorize those specific concepts, because you know they'll show up on test day. This works pretty well for most people in a high school environment.

Well, many students try to do something similar when they prepare for the ACT. They review a lot of school material, and then they take the test—and they typically find that all their preparation has very little positive impact on their ACT performance, and they wonder what to do next.

Once you read the training sections of this Black Book that explain the proper approach to each question type, you'll see why the typical style of preparation isn't very effective. Preparing for the ACT isn't about memorization. There will be some limited amount of memorization as you internalize the material, but mostly you'll be learning and practicing skills that you can apply to real ACT questions.

In each training section of this book, you'll develop an understanding of how a particular part of the test works, and you'll learn about the standards and patterns that appear on each question type. Once you've learned that, you can read through the question walkthroughs in this book, and then spend some time working with real ACT practice questions on your own, possibly by doing some of the drills we'll discuss in just a moment. Eventually your goal is to be able to apply the correct techniques to real ACT questions without any help.

Let me reiterate that you shouldn't actually do the following drills until you've studied the training materials in this book; I'm just discussing them here because I often get asked about this when I first start working with a student.

With that in mind, here are my four favorite drills and exercises you can do with real ACT practice questions, when the time comes. These will help you develop the skills you'll need on test day.

(I've gone ahead and given them weird names so they'll be easy to remember.)

1. Semi-Structured Stare-And-Ponder

This is a great, low-pressure way to begin to apply your knowledge to practice questions, and it can also be a good option as you progress in your preparation if you feel like you need to spend some time on a relatively unstructured exercise.

All you need to do is flip through your copy of *The Real ACT Prep Guide, 3rd Edition* (the "Red Book") until you find a question you'd like to work on (any question will do).

Then, you just take all the time you need to read and think about the question, the answer choices, and any associated passage, diagram, chart, graph, or anything else.

Of course, you probably want to think about what the right answer is at some point, but, beyond that, you just want to think about everything else that could possibly be going on in this question. Your goal is to understand exactly what the writers and editors of the question were thinking about when they created it. Why is the question worded the way it is? Why was each wrong answer choice included—what kind of mistakes is the question trying to get you to make? How could somebody miss this question? Can you predict any common mistakes that test-takers might make when they attempt this question? Which specific design rules does the question follow? How could the elements of this question appear in future questions?

The things you could choose to ponder go on and on, though some ACT questions definitely give us more to ponder than others do. The point here is just to spend as much as time you need in order to think about every possible aspect of the question based on what you've learned from this Black Book. If you happen to get the answer wrong, then of course you'll want to think about why you got it wrong, what you missed or misunderstood in the question, and how you could avoid that mistake in the future. But the goal of this exercise isn't simply to get the question right—the goal is just to understand how the question was built, in terms of the concepts from this Black Book.

After you've thought about every aspect of a particular ACT question, just move on to another question and ponder it in the same way you pondered the first one. When you're done, move on to another question and repeat the process again. And so on and so on, for as long as you care to sit and ponder.

Of course, you don't want to try to look at a question this way on test day. On test day, your goal is to be efficient, accurate, and purposeful, because you're working with a time limit.

This exercise is very effective because it helps you to look at any given ACT question and then start to pull it apart and think about it effectively. That way, it'll be much easier for you to separate right answers from wrong answers, and it'll be much harder for the ACT to trick you.

2. Practice-And-A-Postie

In the title for this drill, the word "postie" stands for "post-mortem," and I included it in the title of the drill to make it very clear that simply doing a practice section or test isn't enough by itself if you want to see improvement. It's *absolutely essential* that you thoroughly review all of your practice work before you move on and do more practice work.

Let me be clear—when I talk about reviewing all of your practice work, I don't just mean checking the answer key to see what you missed. I mean going back over every single question you missed or were unsure about, and trying to figure out what was going on in each question that stopped you from being certain about the correct answer. That way you'll know how to overcome similar issues on test day.

Typically, the process of reviewing your work should take about as much time as the original practice takes (at least until you hit a point where you don't miss any questions at all). In other words, if you spend 30 minutes doing practice questions, you'll probably spend about 30 minutes doing a thorough review of everything you got wrong. It might take you even longer, especially in the beginning. Give it as much time as it takes to do a thorough job.

I just want to make sure we're very clear on the importance of the review. It's the most important part of this drill—and the most important part of all your training—because it's the part where you see what you did wrong and you figure out how to fix it in the future. Most people who try to prep for the ACT just take practice test after practice test without doing any real review at all, and they never figure out why they're not improving. You simply must review your work, or you'll never realize what you're consistently doing wrong!

So you'll do a practice section, or a whole practice test if you feel like it, and then thoroughly review your work afterward. You can do the practice timed, or untimed—it's not so important to work with a time limit in the beginning, but the real thing will be timed, of course, so you'll need to get comfortable with that as you get closer to the test date.

As with the other drills, don't bother doing this until you've digested the training material later in this book, because you'll just get frustrated otherwise, and you won't have much to go on when you try to review your mistakes. Above all, don't bother doing practice sections if you aren't going to review the outcome once you're done so you can figure out what's causing your mistakes.

3. The "Shortcut" Search

The "Shortcut" Search can be a drill on its own, or it can be part of the review you do in the previous exercise. Either way, in this drill you need to know the answers to the questions you're working with ahead of time. So this drill is something you should do with questions that you've already tried to answer for some other drill. That way, you don't burn through the limited number of real ACT practice questions available from ACT, Inc.

In this drill, your goal is to take as much time as you need to try to figure out any and all "shortcuts" you might have been able to use to arrive at the correct answer in the least amount of time possible. I'm putting the word "shortcuts" in quotation marks because I take issue with the idea that approaching questions in this way is lazy. Actually, it requires more creativity and training than any other approach, and the whole point of this Black Book is to get you to be able to identify and exploit those "shortcuts" as often as possible. There's nothing wrong with approaching the test in the most efficient and reliable way possible, even if that approach differs from the way we approach things in school.

For example, on a Math question, you might realize that some pattern in the answer choices gives you a hint at how to set up the problem. On a Science question, you might realize that several of the values in the answer choices are far too small or large to be possible answers, so they could be eliminated right away. On a Reading question, you might figure out which exact word or phrase makes the right answer right, and then you could think about the fastest way you could have figured that out. On an English question, you might realize that the sentence before the one you're being asked about has the same structure as one of the answer choices . . . and so on. The training sections and the walkthroughs in this Black Book will show you how to look for these kinds of solutions reliably and confidently.

When you practice looking for these alternative solutions in this kind of drill, you should feel free to take as much time as necessary to try to find solutions that could have been worked out in seconds if you had noticed them right away. In other words, if it takes you 10 minutes (or even longer) of thinking about a question to figure out a solution that would have taken 30 seconds, there's nothing wrong with that at this point. Of course, you probably won't have the luxury of staring at an individual question for 10 whole minutes on test day, but doing this kind of drill now, as part of your preparation, will help you identify these kinds of super-efficient solutions more quickly when it counts.

As with the other drills, you should wait to do this one until you're familiar with the training material, and then you'll know what to look for.

4. What Would Make It Right?

In this drill, you'll look at wrong answer choices and ask yourself, "What would make it right?"

For example, in a Science question that asks you about a value in Table 1, you might see a wrong answer choice that incorrectly uses the corresponding value from Table 2. In that case, the answer to "What would make it right?" would be "If the question asked about Table 2 instead of Table 1, then this answer choice would be right."

For another example, if a Reading question asks for the meaning of a certain phrase in the text, and one of the wrong answers gives a correct meaning for another phrase later in the text, the answer to "What would make it right?" would be "If the question had asked about the other phrase in the text, that would make it right."

As you'll learn later in this Black Book, the ACT will frequently offer wrong answer choices that are still relevant to the passage or problem—just not in the way that the question requires. Thinking about how the question could be changed to make wrong answer choices correct gives you another opportunity to think about how the test is designed from the standpoint of ACT, Inc., and it will also help you to identify wrong answers more quickly and reliably on test day.

Figuring Out Your Schedule

As I mentioned above, I've found that there's no single training schedule that works best for every student. So instead of trying to come up with one that would only work for some people, I'm laying out some ideas you should think about to determine the best approach for you.

Do You Need An Early Start?

When a teacher assigns a big project that's due in several weeks, some people rush home and begin right away, while others prefer to wait until the day or two before to get started. Neither approach is necessarily better, as long as you're happy with the results that you get.

The methods that I teach for the ACT can really be taught and learned in less than a week. But not everybody is comfortable with that, and if you aren't, then you should allow yourself more time—probably at least a month or two.

If you're used to doing work at the last minute, then you might feel okay with a lot less preparation time. I've seen both approaches work quite well, as long as the person in question felt comfortable with the approach he chose.

What's Your Attention Span?

Some people can't stand to work on their preparation for more than 20 minutes or so at a time, whereas others can go for a couple of hours or more and still be productive. If you're the sort of person with low test prep stamina, you're going to need to study more frequently to make up for it; if you can spend more time on each individual prep session, then you won't need to have so many sessions. This is something you need to be realistic about as you try to map out the time you'll spend preparing.

How Much Of A Score Increase Are You Shooting For?

As you might imagine, students who need larger score increases should probably plan to allow themselves more time to prepare than students who need smaller score increases.

How Much Will You Improve After Each Practice Session, On Average?

Unfortunately, there's no universal answer to this question: some students can take 20 practice tests and still not improve much (usually because they aren't trained well and they don't review their work sufficiently), while other people really take to the material quickly and make noticeable improvement in their first practice session. It will depend a lot on your confidence, and on how well you take direction. If you read this Black Book but don't make a conscious effort to implement what you learn, your improvement will be slower. If you make a wholehearted effort to implement the right approach, though, you'll probably progress more quickly, even if it's frustrating at first.

What determines your level of progress will be the quality of your practice, not the quantity, so don't go into it thinking that you just need to get through a certain number of practice tests in order to get the score you want. Instead, be prepared to go through as many practice questions as necessary in order to feel comfortable applying the correct strategies for each part of the test. This typically takes fewer practice sessions than people expect. But whether it's more or fewer doesn't really matter, as long as you make sure to focus on the quality of your practice. Make sure you pay attention to what you're doing, and make sure you really try to change the way you see the test.

Do You Really Even Need A Schedule?

Most people like the idea of mapping out a schedule, because it feels comfortable and productive. Even so, I would like to put the idea out there that maybe you don't need to try to establish any kind of rigid schedule for your preparation. Allow me to explain.

Because preparing for a standardized test like the ACT is so different from preparing for a normal high school test, it's hard to make an accurate prediction of exactly how much prep time you'll actually need. That means students who try to lay out a schedule might quickly find that some aspects of preparation take a lot more or a lot less time than they anticipated, which can throw off the whole idea of a schedule, and possibly create a stressful situation.

Here's what I would do instead, if I were in your shoes: start prepping (in some way) as early as you can—which is to say, now. The prep you do doesn't necessarily have to be torturous and mind-numbing.

If you're short on time, you'll probably want to get in as much preparation as you can between now and test day anyway. If you're not short on time, then starting now will let you prepare in a low-pressure environment without strict time limits. Just take an active interest in your progress, read through this book, and start trying to apply the strategies to real ACT practice questions in your copy of *The Real ACT Prep Guide, 3rd Edition*. Use these drills and exercises to practice in ways you find to be mentally engaging, and take breaks when you get bored or lose focus. Above all, after any work with real ACT practice questions, always thoroughly review any mistakes and/or issues you encounter in those questions.

If you notice that you're making good progress relative to your target score and your test date, then keep it up. If you feel like you're not making enough progress, then try to increase the amount of focus and energy you bring to your prep sessions; if that still doesn't work, then consider making more time to prepare.

It really is that simple—just stay motivated and keep at it.

Understand Your Mistakes

"Failure is the key to success; each mistake teaches us something."
- Morihei Ueshiba

A vital step in your improvement on the ACT is developing the ability to recognize and understand your mistakes and weaknesses so you can do what's necessary to avoid the mistakes and strengthen the weaknesses—and, ultimately, to improve your score.

But, as we've already discussed (and will continue to discuss in more detail), the ACT tests different types of skills from the skills tested in the classroom, and it does so in a highly structured and standardized way that's very unfamiliar to most students. This results in a lot of test-takers missing questions, but not understanding exactly why they're missing those questions.

This means that if you aren't careful when you try to figure out your weak points, you might end up focusing on skills that are irrelevant to the mistakes you're making, which can cause you to waste time without improving your score. Let me give you an example.

Let's say you miss a trig question while you're working on the ACT Math section. A lot of people might decide to respond to this by learning more trigonometry so their scores would improve. They might go to a math teacher and ask for help, or go online and find some trigonometry videos. Some people in this situation might spend hours, or days, or even weeks making time to study trig in the hopes of improving their performance on the ACT.

But hold on a minute—what if you take a closer look at the way you approached the trig question that started all of this? You might notice that you cross-multiplied incorrectly, or even that you misread the question, or had your calculator in the wrong mode, or bubbled an answer incorrectly.

In other words, just missing a trig question doesn't necessarily indicate that you need to learn more trig. One of the most important skills in ACT Math (whatever the specific subject matter) is the ability to execute simple mathematical operations consistently and correctly; in my experience, much of the aggravation that people experience on the ACT comes from a failure to do that. The simple fact is that most people just aren't used to being as careful with basic math as the ACT Math section requires them to be.

In this example, that means you could end up spending days or weeks on trigonometry when, in reality, you might just need to read more carefully, think more about the answer choices in the question, or even just remember to carry a 1 correctly.

In the context of the ACT Reading section, you might miss a question that involves an unfamiliar word, and then decide you need to learn what that word means. But closer inspection of the question often reveals that the meaning of the unknown word isn't directly relevant to finding the correct answer, and that a more careful application of the strategies in this book would have led you to the right answer anyway.

So whether you're evaluating your own practice, or you're looking at a diagnostic test from a tutor or test prep company (or even from ACT, Inc. itself), be careful. You might be told that you need to learn more math, grammar, or science—or who knows what else—but it's much more likely that your problem is related to executing some relatively basic skill in a consistent manner. Standardized tests like the ACT require a higher degree of precision and consistency (especially in executing basic skills) than normal classroom tests do, and this is the most common difficulty for most students.

When you look at a question you've missed, go back through your work so you can figure out exactly how you made your mistake. It might not have anything to do with subject matter. In fact, most test-takers can probably safely start with the assumption that they know enough subject matter to answer almost all (or even all) the questions on a real ACT.

Once you know the real issue that caused you to miss a question, you can work to fix it. It might take a little bit more time in the beginning, but it can save you a ton of time in the long run if it means you're not wasting energy trying to strengthen an area that isn't actually a weakness, or working to avoid a type of mistake you aren't actually making in the first place.

The "Natural Test-Taker"

"At one time I thought the most important thing was talent. I think now that the young man or the young woman must possess or teach himself, train himself, in infinite patience, which is to try and to try and to try until it comes right."
- William Faulkner

Some people are "natural test-takers." What does that mean?

It means they just seem to have a knack for scoring high on standardized tests. We've all encountered them. They may not be the most motivated students, they may not always get the highest grades, but, for whatever reason, they just seem to thrive on high-stakes tests.

It all has to do with having the right mindset and approach. If you understand what's really being tested, and you understand what it really takes to separate the wrong answers from the right ones, you can excel on test day with a lot less effort than your peers will need.

This is what "natural test-taking" is all about.

It's certainly not about cheating, and it's not about being lazy. It's about understanding the skills and choices that the test actually rewards, and then practicing them so you can execute them as well as possible on test day.

Because tests like the ACT are so widely misunderstood (even by educators who have only the best intentions), and because so many people spend so much time on drills and techniques that don't actually improve their scores, approaching the ACT as a natural test-taker would is much less time-consuming than the more common approach.

So that's our goal for this manual: to think and act like natural test-takers. We're going to take a little bit of time up front to understand the test, and that will save us loads of time drilling and cramming later. Then we'll be able to leverage our existing knowledge as much as possible, so we end up with the highest scores possible.

In this book, I'll often refer to the idea of a "trained test-taker" or an "untrained test-taker." When I mention a "trained test-taker," I'm talking about someone who might not be a natural test-taker, but who has studied and implemented the "natural" approach to standardized tests like the ACT—the approach we'll learn in this book.

An "untrained test-taker," of course, is the typical test-taker, one who isn't familiar with this approach.

The approach I teach in this book is the most direct and effective way I know of to prepare for the ACT, and it's the only way that I recommend. But sometimes it can seem a little too good to be true, so let me clear up some common concerns.

It's Not Magic

I've made a lot of big promises about the approach we're going to use. I've told you it's going to allow you to get a better score while probably spending less time studying. I've told you there's a hidden structure to the test, and that we can unlock it to maximize our performance on test day. Doesn't that seem a little over-the-top?

It might sound that way, but it's true. If you really take the time to understand these techniques, and then you practice them on real ACT practice questions, you'll see exactly what I'm talking about. But I should point out right now that it doesn't just happen by itself.

Sometimes I'll work with students who get very excited after just talking with me once, because they feel like they're really, finally understanding how it all works. Their earlier frustration seems unnecessary. They're ready to get in there and get a perfect score . . .

. . . and then they try out one or two questions and do no better than before.

That usually doesn't make those people too happy.

The problem is that simply reading this material isn't going to result in a perfect score for most people by itself.

You actually have to practice these techniques on real ACT practice questions until you can reliably apply them.

It usually doesn't take a ton of practice to see improvements, if you prepare in the ways I recommend in this book, but it does take *some* practice.

Until you do start practicing intelligently, you probably won't see much improvement in your scores.

In school, you often have tests where at least part of the test involves memorizing facts. Once you've memorized a fact, you don't need to practice knowing it, right? You just know it. If you need to know that the Battle of Waterloo took place in 1815, you read it a few times, and you know it. That's it.

Prepping for the ACT isn't like that. I like to talk about my approach to the test less in terms of *studying* and *memorizing*, and more in terms of *training* and *practicing*—more like playing a sport or learning a musical instrument than like cramming facts in your head for a typical high school test.

So it probably isn't enough just to read this book, understand the test, and understand my methods, without actually trying to implement them on your own. That's an important first step, of course, and it's great to read this book and have those moments when you feel like you're finally grasping how all of this really works, and what you need to do to get your best score.

Still, the only way to be sure you're improving your score is to practice the method until you can consistently apply it well. This can take some time. It should take a lot less time than what most people do to get ready for the ACT, and your results should be a whole lot better, but it still does take some time.

So don't be discouraged if you read this whole book, feel like you understand every ACT question you've ever seen, and then sit down and do exactly as well as you always do on a practice test on your first try. You still have to get the hang of things. Learn the method, put in the practice, and you'll see the results.

Repetition Is Good

We haven't even started talking about concrete techniques for attacking different question types on the ACT, and I've already repeated myself a few times in this book :)

And I'll continue to repeat certain concepts for the rest of this book.

If you start to get aggravated by all this repetition, you should direct your anger at the people who make the ACT, not at me.

You see, the ACT itself is very repetitive. It consistently rewards a certain small set of behaviors, and it consistently punishes another set of behaviors. If you want to succeed, you need to have (or develop) an instinctive awareness of what the test rewards and what it punishes. I've learned over the years that most students need to have these ideas repeated a lot of times before they become second nature.

This is another situation where we see that the ACT isn't like school. In school, we're encouraged to think creatively and use our imaginations. Some students try to carry this mentality over to the ACT, and they hope to use the process of preparing for the test as some kind of creative, intellectual exercise.

But the ACT doesn't reward you for thinking up your own answers. Once you see the test from the right perspective, you'll see that it's EXTREMELY repetitive. You'll find yourself looking for the same elements in the same types of questions over and over again. You'll see wrong answer choices trying to trick you in the same ways, over and over again. You'll encounter the same kinds of sentences, passages, charts, and graphs over and over again.

And over and over and over again.

I know it gets repetitive and boring, but we have to learn to see repetition as a good thing on the ACT! When things start to feel repetitive on the ACT—and when you're getting questions right, of course—it means you've really internalized the patterns and standardization of the test, and you're on your way to getting a great score.

So as you continue to read this Black Book, and as you see me going back to some of the same concepts and patterns over and over again, remember that I'm doing it because the ACT itself keeps going back to the same ideas over and over again. When you start to find the test incredibly repetitive, it means you're on the right track—and if my own repetitiveness starts to drive you a little crazy, I hope it's because whatever I'm repeating is so completely burned into your mind that you'll never forget it, through all your practice and review, all the way up to test day.

Why Is The ACT So Scary?

You may be wondering why people are so bothered by the ACT, if it's really as simple and beatable as I say. Why is ACT preparation such a scary, stressful, nerve-wracking experience for so many people? The reason, as we've discussed, is that people who struggle with the ACT are approaching it the wrong way. They're approaching the ACT as though it were a normal high school test, and it isn't.

But why are they doing that? This is a very, very important concept to understand. They approach the test the wrong way because they buy into the ACT's reputation. In fact, the people who make the ACT *desperately need* lots of people to misunderstand the test and approach it incorrectly; if everybody understood the test and scored well on it, there would be no point in having it, because it wouldn't help colleges weed out their applicants.

So how does ACT, Inc. encourage high school students to misunderstand the test?

Well, we'll address the company's specific techniques in more detail as we look at individual question types later in this book, but here are some of the things you'll run into, to give you an idea:

- ACT, Inc. tells you that high-scoring ACT essays show "good command of language" and are "effective essays that represent strong responses," but in reality the best predictor of an essay's score is its length.

- ACT, Inc. says that ACT Math questions are designed to measure "the knowledge, skills, and reasoning techniques that are taught in high school mathematics courses," but ACT Math questions tend to be unlike questions you'd have to answer in high school math courses.

- ACT, Inc. encourages the myth that the ACT Science section requires you to be familiar with dozens of fields of scientific study, even though very few questions per test require any outside scientific knowledge at all.

I could go on, and I will, in later sections, but for now you get the idea. The fact is that ACT, Inc. has two equally important jobs. One of them is continuing to make a repetitive, predictable, standardized test that's the same in all the ways that matter every time that it's administered, and that requires little or no outside knowledge. The other job is to continue to encourage the perception that their test is a subject-matter-oriented exam that rewards the types of skills and habits that succeed in high school and college classrooms.

That way, most people keep trying to prepare for the kind of test the ACT pretends to be, and they keep struggling when they try to perform on the test that the ACT actually is. The ACT seems mysteriously difficult, only a few students are able to "crack the code" and score well, and the ACT stays relevant.

That's why the ACT seems so scary, even though it's not—the people behind the test work hard to make it seem that way. But we can learn to see through all of that, and we can score well without wasting time.

What You Must Understand About The ACT

"Human beings, who are almost unique in having the ability to learn from the experience of others, are also remarkable for their apparent disinclination to do so."
- Douglas Adams

You've heard me say a few times already that if you want to beat the ACT in the most effective, efficient way possible, you'll need to understand it in a way that most test-takers never do. In order for us to understand the ACT, we'll need to take a step back and look at why and how the test was designed. That way we can understand the limitations of the test, how the test tries to make up for those limitations, and how we can take full advantage of the situation.

Let me say right now that even though it'll only take a few minutes and a few pages to discuss this, doing so is crucial to your success on the ACT. A lot of people may be tempted to skip this part of the book and get straight into the material for specific question types, but these next few pages are some of the most important pages in this whole Black Book, so please read them carefully and take the time to understand them.

Why are there standardized tests like the ACT? One simple answer might be that they provide a standard measure that allows schools to compare one student to another. When a college or university has applicants from different backgrounds with completely different educational experiences, it can be hard to compare their GPAs in a meaningful way, since those GPAs will reflect different classes taken at different schools. But if all the applicants take a test that's "standardized," so that the results of the test can be reliably compared to each other even when students take the test on different days in different places, then colleges can have some way to measure students against one consistent standard, which can (at least in theory) give us some idea about which students might be better suited to a particular college.

Let's think about that—just about every school considers both your GPA and your ACT (or SAT) score when you apply. This suggests (and many other details confirm) that schools consider your GPA and your standardized test scores to be measurements of *two different things.* If they both measured the same thing, there would be no need to track both of them, right?

So the first important thing to remember about the ACT is that it's a tool used by schools in the admissions process. Except in certain situations that might require a student to get a certain score to be considered for a scholarship or other award, the only reason people take the ACT is because they're applying to a college.

This evidence strongly supports something I've already said and will continue to mention throughout this book:

1. Doing Well On The ACT And Doing Well In School Are Two Different Things. The Skills That Get Rewarded On The ACT Are Not The Same As The Skills That Get Rewarded In The Classroom.

This is why we all know people with awesome grades in advanced classes who simply can't figure out how to score well on the ACT, not to mention other students who struggle in the classroom but who can get elite standardized test scores without really seeming to try very hard.

It's also why students who spend dozens of hours on the sorts of activities that might get rewarded in a classroom—like memorizing formulas, reading novels, and so on—often end up with scores that are no better than they were before all that work. For this reason, as previously discussed, we won't be spending our time on that kind of preparation.

(There is, of course, some overlap between the skills used in high school and the skills used on the test, but it's important for us to clarify early on that the most important skills needed in each scenario are actually very different).

So we've established that the skills required to get a good score on the ACT aren't the same as the skills required to get good grades in high school. Now we need to figure out exactly how they're different, so we know what kinds of skills to practice in order to do well on the test.

A Real Life Example

Let's begin by imagining you're in a typical high school classroom, and your teacher is going over a multiple-choice test he's just handed back to the class.

When the teacher mentions the answer for one particular question, half the students in the class raise their hands. It turns out that the wording of the question confused them, and many ended up marking a wrong answer choice that seemed to be right because they misread the question. One student in particular stands up and explains why she chose that answer, and why she believes it should be considered right based on the wording of the question. The teacher sees that the question was a little ambiguous, and decides to give credit for both answer choices, or even decides to give everybody credit because, in retrospect, the question was confusing.

This sort of thing happens every day in schools all across the country, and it's quite understandable. More often than not, high school teachers are overworked. They teach multiple classes, and—in addition to grading homework and projects—they have to make their own tests for each class.

So you can see how an overworked teacher who has to make his own tests, and who probably doesn't have as much time to proofread them as he would like, might occasionally make an error in the creation of a test question.

This sort of thing DOES NOT happen on the ACT. (I know that, every once in a long while, a question on the test is challenged and overturned, but that's so unusual that, for our purposes, it may as well never happen.)

The ACT isn't a test that one busy person wrote to use in one high school class. It's a product created by many people over a long period of time, and one of the most important elements of the test is that the correct answer choice for each question must be completely, 100% certain. The term I like to use is "bulletproof." On every real ACT question, the ACT can point to concrete, consistent reasons why the correct answer choice is correct, and why every other answer choice for that question is wrong.

Why is this so important? Well, think about what the ACT is. It's the backbone of an entire company whose purpose is, basically, to make the ACT. The company that makes the ACT (which is creatively called "ACT, Inc.") is a non-profit, but it still employs a lot of people, and those people's jobs depend on the test being relevant and useful to the college admissions process.

Well, how relevant or useful would the test be if the answers weren't bulletproof? If the questions were subjective, or if they frequently had more than one valid answer but only gave credit for one arbitrary choice, then there would be no correlation between ACT scores and college performance. If that were to happen, colleges would quickly realize that the ACT wasn't a reliable tool for evaluating students, and they'd stop accepting ACT scores on applications. That means people would stop taking the ACT.

This is why ACT, Inc. has people whose job is to make sure that the questions on the test are bulletproof. So here's our next important fact to remember:

2. The ACT's Very Existence Depends On Each Question Being Bulletproof. Every Question Must Have Exactly One Predictably Correct Answer, Or The ACT Would Have No Reason To Exist.

To explore further the inner workings of the ACT, let's think a little more about what it means for a test to be standardized. For one thing, it means that two people can take the ACT hundreds of miles apart, on different days, and their scores can still be reliably compared to one another.

How is that possible?

ACT, Inc. obviously can't administer the exact same test, every single time, with the exact same questions word for word. If it did that, pretty soon everybody would know those questions, and everybody would get a perfect score, and the ACT would be useless.

That means the challenge for ACT, Inc. is to make a *new* test with completely *different* questions (on the surface) for each test date—but the scores for each new test must still be consistently and meaningfully comparable to each other.

So how does ACT, Inc. do that?

Well, to start with, the basic structure for the ACT has to be consistent—it has to have the same number of answer choices for each given question type from test to test, the same amount of time for breaks in between sections, the same number of sections with the same number of questions on each section, and so on.

But that isn't enough by itself. After all, just answering 60 math questions in 60 minutes isn't automatically the same thing as answering any other set of 60 math questions in 60 minutes. The questions in each batch must test the *same concepts* in the *same ways*, without actually repeating each other. For that matter, the wrong answer choices themselves must be *wrong* in similar ways—if you made two versions of a test, both asking the exact same questions, but one test used wrong answer choices that were very tricky, and one only used wrong answer choices that were clearly wrong, then one test would be much harder than the other, *just because the answer choices were different*.

(This, by the way, hints at something very important that we'll get into later.)

You can probably see where I'm going here—every official ACT on every test date must test the same things in the same ways, with the same types of right answers and the same types of wrong answers, or else the results from different test dates couldn't be reliably compared to one another. Of course, the exact questions themselves have to be different on each test, as do the exact passages on the English, Reading, and Science sections, but the questions always have to follow the same rules and patterns, in the exact same ways, on every test.

Some of those rules and patterns are very obvious, like the number of questions in a section. The other standards are more subtle. They aren't directly stated in any official materials from ACT, Inc.; instead, they're the sort of thing you have to look for very carefully (or learn from this Black Book ☺). If these other standards were too easy to figure out, then everybody would realize exactly how to beat the test.

So all of this leads up to our next important ACT fact . . .

3. The ACT Must Be Exactly The Same In Every Important Way Every Time It's Given. It Must Always Yield To The Same Strategies. If You Know Those Strategies, You Can Beat The Test.

The standardization of the ACT means that if a set of strategies can beat the official tests that have been released in sources like the Red Book, then those strategies must be able to beat the test every time, because, again, the test has to be fundamentally the same each time it's given.

So if we can come up with strategies that always beat real practice ACT questions, then we know we can use those strategies to beat the real ACT on test day, so we can get the score we want, and move on with our lives.

Of course, I've already come up with those strategies, and this Black Book will teach them to you.

(I keep driving this point home because, almost every time I work with someone, there comes a point when the student says something like, "Okay Mike, I know your strategies are great most of the time, and they usually work, but I found a practice question where your strategies just don't work. This question must just be different." Literally every single time this happens, it's because the student has overlooked or misunderstood an important part of the question, or forgotten an important part of the strategy. Once we identify the mistake, it becomes apparent that the question is just another standardized question that we can beat using the strategies in this book.)

As you can see, much of the proper approach to the ACT relies on a deep understanding of the test's design. And that leads us to our next major point.

4. We Should Only Practice For The ACT With Real ACT Questions Written By ACT, Inc., And Not With Fake Questions Written By Any Other Company.

Because of the subtle standards that ACT, Inc. uses to design the ACT, we must only ever work with real ACT questions created by ACT, Inc. when we prepare. ACT, Inc. is the only company that we know we can trust to provide real ACT practice questions, because it's the only company that designs the real ACT.

A lot of other companies like to write their own practice questions for two main reasons: it gives them more stuff to sell you, and it's easier to get you to believe that their advice works when they're the ones who write the questions that you try the advice on.

It's essential that you only use real ACT practice questions when preparing for the ACT, for all the reasons we've just talked about. When you use real ACT practice questions, you're training yourself on a conscious level, as well as on an intuitive level, to recognize and respond to the standards in real ACT questions.

When you use some other company's tests, you're basically learning about how that particular company makes tests, not about how the actual ACT works. But on test day, when it really counts, you won't be taking a test made by that other company, will you? So why practice with those fake tests at all?

I'll say it one more time—never use anything besides real ACT practice questions if your goal is to do well on the real ACT.

What About Harder Practice Questions?

Some test prep companies have a reputation for making fake ACT practice questions that are supposedly harder than the real thing. Some people think it's a good idea to practice with these questions, because they think that practicing with something that's harder than the real thing will make the real thing seem easy by comparison.

But the same basic problem still exists—these are fake practice questions that aren't necessarily made according to the real standards of the ACT. If they don't challenge you *in the same ways that actual ACT questions would challenge you*, then it doesn't matter how challenging they are in other ways.

Imagine that you wanted to learn to make a grilled cheese sandwich. Would it help you to learn how to make your own cheese first? Probably not, even though making your own cheese is much harder than making a grilled cheese sandwich. Even though the two activities sound like they're kind of related, the bottom line is that learning to make cheese is a waste of time if your actual goal is to make a sandwich.

Similarly, any time you spend working on fake ACT practice questions, no matter how hard they are, is time you're not pursuing your actual goal of getting better at real ACT questions, because those fake questions could be breaking the ACT's rules if they require you to know and do things that the real test will never require you to know or do.

So if you want to improve your performance on the ACT, you need to work exclusively with real ACT practice questions written by ACT, Inc.

Summary

Okay! That should cover all the basic information you need to know about the ACT for now. If any of it's unclear, you may want to go back and read it over again. There's more to know about the test, of course, but most of what's left is specific to the different question types, so we'll cover that when we get to them. Let's quickly recap:

1. Doing well on the ACT isn't the same as doing well on a normal high school test.
2. Every question on the ACT must be bulletproof.
3. The ACT has to be the same in all the ways that matter every time it's administered.
4. You must always and only use real practice ACT questions to prepare for the ACT.

If you've read and understood this section, you're now armed with a better understanding of the ACT than probably 90% of the people who take the test—and we haven't even started talking about actual test items yet. Good for you! The key now is for us to build on that understanding and start applying it to individual questions. We'll explore how those questions are designed, and how to exploit that design, and then we'll practice with real ACT questions until we can apply the proper methods reliably.

First, though, we'll cover a few more important concepts.

The Truth About The ACT

"If you would be a real seeker after truth, you must at least once in your life doubt, as far as possible, all things."
- René Descartes

If you've been paying attention so far, you can probably tell that we're going to look at the ACT in a way that's a little different from the standard approach. For that reason, you can also probably imagine that there are more than a few common "myths" related to the ACT—we'll talk about those a little later. After all, many of the common strategies and pieces of advice related to test-taking are ultimately based on a poor understanding of the nature of standardized tests.

There's one particular myth that's very specific to the ACT that we should clear up in the beginning. Let's start with a tiny bit of background.

You're probably aware that the two major so-called "college entrance exams" in the United States are the ACT and the SAT.

The two tests are in direct competition with each other. The good people behind the ACT want more people to take the ACT, and the good people behind the SAT want more people to take the SAT.

The SAT comes under fire from time to time because of its various shortcomings, and because of our society's general dissatisfaction with standardized testing. The people behind the ACT seem to try to take advantage of the SAT's bad press by talking about how different the ACT is from the SAT.

They say the ACT is a more intellectual test. They say that it's a better test of real subject matter knowledge—after all, it has a Science section, and its Math section tests trigonometry. They try to overstate how different the ACT and the SAT are in the hope that people will think the ACT is the better test, and that it's the one everybody should be taking . . .

. . . and that's the myth.

You see, in spite of ACT, Inc.'s desire to convince us otherwise, the SAT and the ACT are largely the same test—not identical, by any means, but largely the same. Most of the individual questions that appear on one test could appear on the other (with the notable exception that most questions on the ACT have only 4 answer choices, while most questions on the SAT have 5—still, the answer choices are designed in largely similar ways on both tests). In fact, because of some of the strict rules that any truly standardized test must follow, the two tests basically MUST be the same in a lot of ways in order to fulfill their common role in the admission process.

Some of the specific details of approaching specific question types differ on each test, but the ACT and SAT are essentially the same "type" of test. One isn't more or less intellectual, or academic, or predictable than the other one is, in any way that matters.

You'll see more of the details of the ACT in the coming chapters focusing on each question type, but the fact is that both tests present many of the same challenges to test-takers. They both present simple math concepts in unusual ways. They both test a fairly predictable set of grammatical concepts in similar ways in their English/Writing sections. They both encourage the illusion of the need for interpretation in the Reading section.

And what about the dreaded ACT Science section—the one that's supposed to make a dramatic difference between the ACT and the SAT?

You'll see this in more detail when we talk about the Science section specifically, but for now let's just say that the Science section primarily requires a combination of the skills you use in the Reading section and Math section of both the ACT and the SAT. That's all. ACT Science is just a little reading, a little math and a *tiny* bit of actual scientific knowledge every once in a while. (Of course, we'll cover the details later in this Black Book.)

To be sure, there are a few other differences between the tests as well. The ACT has fewer sections, and just one section of each question type, unlike the SAT. There's no penalty for wrong answers on the ACT like there is on the SAT, but that actually shouldn't have much of an impact on your approach, if you know how the test works. (See the "Guessing On The ACT" section of "The General Game Plan For Attacking A Section Of The ACT On Test Day" in this Black Book.) The lengths of the sections of the two tests are different; different test-takers sometimes respond more positively to one test or the other for that reason. But those things don't make either test more or less similar to high school tests, or make either test more or less dependent on high school subject-matter.

Like I said, we'll cover all the specific strategies for the different question types later in this Black Book, but I just wanted to make it clear from the beginning what kind of test the ACT really is. It's a major standardized test for college admissions, basically just like the other major standardized test for college admissions.

It's important for us to clarify this early on, because too many test-takers have the idea that getting better at the ACT depends on learning "school stuff:" math, science, grammar, literary theory, and so on. But the ACT really doesn't reward that—as far as subject-matter knowledge is concerned, all the ACT really requires is a basic knowledge of math and a good general ability to read American English. Of course, there may be a moment when you need to learn how the ACT wants you to form a possessive on the English section, or how to find the area of a circle or something if you don't already know those relatively basic formulas. But for the most part, for most people, improving on the ACT is a question of learning how the test is designed, and then exploiting the weaknesses in that design.

The ACT's Biggest Weakness

"All men can see these tactics whereby I conquer, but what none can see is the strategy out of which victory is evolved."
- Sun Tzu

The ACT's single biggest weakness is probably the fact that it has to use the multiple-choice format—this causes a lot of problems for the test-maker, and trained test-takers can take advantage of those problems if we use the right strategies.

Why Is The ACT Multiple-Choice?

Let's take a second to discuss one of the most important (and also most easily overlooked) attributes of the ACT: except for the essay, every single question uses the multiple-choice format. Why is that? (We'll talk about the essay later in this Black Book.)

Think about it. If you were face-to-face with someone, and you really wanted to test whether she knew something, would you ask her a multiple-choice question, or would you just ask a regular, open-ended question without providing answer choices, and force her to demonstrate her knowledge by coming up with her own answer?

Of course, you'd just ask an open-ended question and then let her answer as best she could. That would be the best way to know if the student really grasped the material. That's why it's much harder to fake your way past an oral exam or an essay question on a high school test than it is to get lucky and answer a multiple-choice question correctly.

But the ACT is full of multiple-choice questions. (The test only includes one essay question, and, as we'll see later, that one essay question is unlike the questions you see on regular tests in school. It doesn't require us to know anything, since we can make up whatever proof we like when we answer it. Again, we'll cover how to handle the ACT Essay later in this Black Book.)

Why can't the ACT just ask us tons of open-ended questions and let us fill in the blanks with our own answers? Because it would be pretty hard to grade millions of tests every year *using the exact same standards of grading on every test* if people could just write down whatever random answers they wanted. Having to read and consider every single answer individually would be impossibly time-consuming and expensive. It would also require a looser grading structure, because different test-takers would write about different things in response to the same questions, and those responses would have to be evaluated by different graders. (This is why standardized tests with open-ended questions can only use broad grading scales like 1 – 5 or 1 – 6, while multiple-choice standardized tests can be much more precise in their grading scales.)

Instead, the ACT needs a format that allows it to grade tests efficiently and with a high degree of accuracy. It also needs a format that allows it to apply the exact same standards to every single test-taker, so each test-taker's results can be reliably compared to the results of every other test-taker with a high degree of precision.

These goals can only be achieved if the test questions provide answer choices to choose from.

Multiple-choice tests are obviously easier and more efficient to grade than free-response tests. They also allow a much higher degree of precision when it comes to applying standards: in addition to writing the question prompts themselves according to particular standards, the testing company can sculpt correct answers and incorrect answers to follow certain standards as well.

That's a major benefit to you as a test-taker, because it means that every single ACT question has to put the correct answer right in front of your face.

It also changes your job as a test-taker. Instead of needing to know the actual answer to a question on your own, all you need to do is select the right answer from four or five choices that are provided for you. That difference might not sound like a big deal, but it definitely can be. We'll come back to this idea over and over again.

The Importance Of Answer Choices

In this Black Book, we're going to do everything we can to take advantage of the information provided to us by the ACT in the test itself. We're going to pull Reading answers right out of the provided text, without interpretation or subjectivity. We're going to see through strange presentations of Math problems and use basic formulas (if we even need formulas at all) to find the right answers. We're going to take in all the scientific information built right into Science questions so we can find the correct answers to questions on scientific topics we've never heard of. And so on.

Still, it's easy to forget that there's an extremely important source of information sitting right in front of us on every multiple-choice question: the answer choices themselves.

This is why I emphasize that students must always, ALWAYS read each ACT question completely, including the answer choices, before they start to figure out the answer. Too many people just read the question prompt (the part that doesn't include the answer choices), then stop and try to solve the problem on their own, then check to see if their answer is reflected in the choices. This approach, though typical, will make life harder for you and cause you to miss hints and clues that are basically staring you in the face once you know how to look for them.

Of course, we'll talk more about those clues as we look at each question type specifically. For now, I just want you to get used to this idea right from the beginning.

So how can answer choices make a question easier? Let's take a look at an extreme example that I'll make up right now, just to illustrate the point. Imagine that you were taking a history test in school, and you saw this question:

Who was the King of Prussia during the Franco-Prussian War?

Unless you're a Prussian history buff, you'd probably start to sweat a little if you saw this question. (Of course, it could never appear on the actual ACT. Again, I'm just using it to illustrate a point.)

Now let's imagine that you see this on a test, instead:

Who was the King of Prussia during the Franco-Prussian War?

A. Wilhelm I

B. Purple

C. Wednesday

D. The Cleveland Browns

If we use our powers of deduction, we can probably pick choice (A) with confidence. Why is that? Well, it doesn't take much thought to realize that neither purple, nor Wednesday, nor the Cleveland Browns could ever be the king of something.

So even though we probably never would've been able to come up with "Wilhelm I" as an answer on our own, almost anyone could pick the right answer out of those four choices.

(Also note that if you had just read the question, realized you didn't know the answer, and then skipped on to the next question without taking a look at the answer choices, you'd be missing out on easy points.)

That was a ridiculous example, of course, but this exercise illustrates the way answer choices can hint at the correct answer when considered in the context of the original question.

Let's look at a slightly trickier version of the same question:

Who was the King of Prussia during the Franco-Prussian War?

A. Wilhelm I

B. Haloti Ngata

C. Thomas Jefferson

D. Nelson Mandela

In this version, all of the incorrect answer choices are people's names. This makes a strategic guess a little more difficult than it was the last time around. Let's consider each answer choice as though we don't already know the answer.

(A) sounds plausible. At the very least, there's no obvious reason to eliminate it. The name sounds like it could be Prussian, and a lot of names of kings have a Roman numeral after them.

(B) seems like it's probably wrong. We may have an idea that Prussia was a country in Europe, and this name doesn't sound European.

We probably know that (C) is someone from American history who was probably never the King of Prussia, since he kept pretty busy in America.

We may have heard of the person in answer choice (D) before, and, if so, we probably know he was a more recent figure in world history. If we know that the Franco-Prussian war didn't happen too recently, we can be pretty certain that (D) isn't right.

Taking all of that into consideration, we can be pretty certain that (A) is correct. (Even if we haven't heard of (D) before, the Roman numeral after the name kind of helps sell (A) in this case.)

Do you see what happened there? Even though we didn't necessarily know anything about kings of Prussia or about the Franco-Prussian war, and even though all four choices were people's names, we were able to apply some basic reasoning to the answer choices to come up with a pretty solid idea of which one was correct.

So, how might this concept actually help us on the real ACT? Well, imagine you're looking at an ACT Math question and you just aren't sure where to start—but you've read all the answer choices, and most of them have square roots in them. This might be a hint that the question will involve square roots, which means that it might involve triangles and the Pythagorean theorem. A little hint like that can push you in the right direction, so you can get to work on the problem instead of hesitating for a little while, wasting time, and possibly getting flustered.

Or you might see a different kind of ACT Math question, and you might be able to determine that the answer must be positive. If the answer choices are -9, -3, -1, 0, and 4, then you know that 4 must be correct. If you don't check out the answer choices first, you'd have to work through the whole problem to come up with the answer. But if you take the time to notice the characteristics of the answer choices, then as soon as you know the answer must be positive, you can mark 4 and move on.

This concept doesn't just apply to ACT Math questions. If you read the all the answer choices on an ACT English question and notice that the only differences among the answer choices have to do with the positions of commas, then you'll know to focus on comma placement instead of getting distracted by any other error you think might be in there. If you feel lost on an ACT Science question, and then you notice that every answer choice is in the same unit, then you know that you probably need to find a chart or graph with measurements in that unit.

These are just relatively basic applications of this idea on the ACT. As we'll see, individual ACT question types have certain wrong-answer patterns and rules that are specific to the ACT. Knowing these, and using them where appropriate, can make the test even easier. We'll explore this idea a little bit in just a moment.

Hopefully, you begin to get the idea. The answer choices can contain valuable hints and clues that can keep you on your game throughout the test, and if you don't take the time to read them for every question, you're making things harder on yourself. You won't find clues on every single question, but getting into this habit will certainly pay off on most of them.

So remember: always read the entire question every single time, including all the answer choices.

Wrong-Answer Choices Are Standardized, Too!

As we just learned, using different types of wrong-answer choices can have a huge impact on the difficulty of a question, even if the question prompt and the right answer are the same. For this reason, if ACT, Inc. wants its scores to be consistent and useful for colleges, it needs to keep its wrong-answer choices as standardized as the rest of the test.

Knowing that the wrong answer choices are standardized can be extremely helpful. The ACT tries to use wrong answer choices to lure you off track, and if you know in advance what sort of tactics the test will use, you're much less likely to fall for them.

Also, if you keep these wrong answer types in mind while you practice, you'll get better and better at spotting them, which will make you an even more efficient ACT-destroying machine—which is kind of the whole point of all of this, right?

This doesn't mean you'll have to classify every single wrong answer choice you see if you want to do well on this test, or even that it would be possible to do that if you wanted to. Not every single choice will fit one of the patterns we're going to talk about. But as we learn about each question type, we'll discuss the major answer-choice patterns you can expect to see on real ACT practice questions. If you keep these in mind while you practice, you'll be surprised at how obvious these wrongs answer choices will start to become.

Using Answer-Choice Patterns

We'll talk about specific answer-choice patterns at the end of our discussion of each section of the test. Those patterns can be extremely helpful, but it's very important that we understand the proper way to use them. It can be tempting to rely on them too heavily, but doing that is much more likely to hurt your score than it is to help it.

So the point of understanding the design of the answer choices isn't that they'll just tell you the correct answer if you know how to decode them. Instead, understanding how the ACT uses wrong-answer patterns will help you in two main ways:

1. If you look at a question and you're not sure what to do, the answer choices can often point you in the right direction, because they include concepts that the test thinks are relevant to the question.
2. Once you've found an answer choice that you like, the answer-choice patterns can help you confirm that you're probably correct—or they can help you catch a mistake if you were wrong.

This is a big deal, because it helps to prevent two of the main things that the ACT tries to do: it tries to present concepts in bizarre ways so we're not sure what to do, and it tries to get us to make simple mistakes without noticing them. So appreciating the value of answer choices can be a great weapon against the test.

We'll look at all of this in more detail when we talk about the different sections of the ACT, of course. I just want to make sure from the beginning that you understand how useful the answer choices can be. They won't always tell you the correct answer outright, but they can often point you in the right direction, and help keep you from making small mistakes that cost you points for no reason.

Using The Real ACT Prep Guide, 3rd Edition (The "Red Book")

"Whatever you would make habitual, practice it; and if you would not make a thing habitual, do not practice it, but accustom yourself to something else."
- Epictetus

The Real ACT Prep Guide, 3rd Edition (the "Red Book") is the book published by ACT, Inc. that contains real practice ACT tests. I've already mentioned it a few times, but I wanted to take an opportunity to discuss it in a little more detail.

First, let's talk about this book from the perspective of the test-maker: ACT, Inc. That company's job is to create and administer the ACT. It's also the company's job to keep the ACT relevant and useful for colleges. Part of that usefulness is making sure the test creates a spectrum of results—if everybody who took the ACT got roughly the same score, the test wouldn't help colleges rank their applicants.

In other words, it's not in the interest of the good people who make the ACT to tell us exactly how their test works so we can all ace it. In fact, it's in their best interest to keep most of the standards and patterns in the test as secret as possible, so that test-takers who know those standards or patterns will do well, and other test-takers will struggle, and the whole test-taking population will get a nice range of scores that colleges will find useful in their admissions processes.

So while *The Real ACT Prep Guide, 3rd Edition* is extremely valuable as a source of real ACT practice tests—which you MUST have if you hope to do well on this test—the ACT prep advice in the book is often less than helpful. You can read it if you like, of course, but I wouldn't recommend following it in most cases.

The most useful prep information in the Red Book appears on pages 5-8, and chapters 4 and 5. Pages 5-8 just contain general information about what you can bring to the test center, how you'll check in, what to do if you get sick during the test, that sort of thing. It's not a bad idea to review this, especially if you've never taken the ACT before.

Chapter 5 is important because it tells you how to score your practice tests, which is helpful if you'd like to know roughly where you stand with your practice work.

But Chapter 4 is the one that really counts. This is the chapter that contains real ACT practice tests, which are absolutely crucial to your preparation. Without having real practice questions—and ACTUALLY PRACTICING WITH THEM AND REVIEWING THEM—you can't hope to improve your performance on the test.

I've been teaching students the methods in this Black Book for a long time, and I know they're effective when used correctly. But even if you memorized every word in this book, it wouldn't help much if you didn't also practice applying the strategies to real questions. Reading and understanding this Black Book is only part of the equation. You MUST practice applying these strategies to real ACT questions on your own.

Sometimes I have parents complain to me that their child hasn't done as well as expected on the ACT. There are several questions I ask in this situation, to help me get an idea of where the problem might lie. One thing I ask is how well the student had been performing in practice sessions before the real test—was he getting questions right at home, but not on test day? Then I often learn that the student wasn't doing any practice at all.

You can't expect your score to go up if you don't practice at least a little bit. Just reading about the techniques and watching me walk through some solutions of real questions from the Red Book won't help you much if you don't get used to applying them on your own.

The other important part of chapter 4 is the answer explanations, but you have to be more careful with those. The people who make the ACT decided to include an explanation of every single practice question in *The Real ACT Prep*

Guide, 3rd Edition—you can find them at the end of each practice test. The explanations will tell you which answer choice is correct and why, and which answer choices are incorrect and why.

These explanations aren't always terrible—but they usually aren't great, either. There are some key weaknesses in the explanations for each question type, and we'll look at those in more detail for each question type later.

We've already talked about how the ACT wants you to see its questions in a way that's different from the way they really are. Among other things, the test doesn't want you to realize how the right answer choices are objectively correct, and how the wrong ones are objectively wrong. The ACT seems to want you to think there's some kind of gray area on the test, probably because that belief makes the test seem more challenging.

Unfortunately, this desire to seem mysterious often comes through in the Red Book's answer explanations. For example, most Red Book explanations start out by saying something like this: "Question X. The *best* answer is Y. [emphasis mine]" When the Red Book addresses the other choices, it introduces them by saying, "The best answer is NOT," and then it discusses the other choices.

Did you catch the subtle implication in those phrases? When the Red Book talks about a "best" answer, instead of talking about "right" or "wrong" answers, most readers will naturally make the mistake of assuming that more than one answer might be pretty good, but one of the choices is subjectively "best," and it's our job as test-takers to try to guess which answer the choice the ACT is going to reward—as opposed to the reality, which is that only one answer can possibly be right if we know the ACT's rules, while the other choices are all inarguably wrong if we know the ACT's rules.

You might think I'm harping on this too much, because it might seem like a minor point right now. But, as someone who has spent well over a decade focusing most of his working life on studying and understanding standardized tests, I can say without reservation that this point is very important. People who don't embrace it have a much harder time improving on the test—almost an impossible time, actually.

So when you look at the answer explanations in *The Real ACT Prep Guide, 3rd Edition*, it's very important that you don't fall for the ACT's trick of the "best" answer. For every question, there's one correct answer choice, and the rest are wrong, without exception. Don't get distracted from that fact.

Why Bother Explaining Questions From The Red Book?

You may have realized by now that the Red Book already contains explanations for every practice question in that book, and that this Black Book also contains a large number of explanations for those practice questions.

You may be asking yourself why I would bother writing out a ton of in-depth explanations for questions that are already described in the Red Book. It's an important question to ask, and it has a very important answer.

If you've read everything up to this point, you're probably getting the idea that this Black Book is going to approach the ACT very differently from the way most people approach this test. The approach you'll learn from me is certainly different from the way ACT, Inc. wants you to approach the test, because the ACT wouldn't be useful to colleges if every person who took it did very well on it.

At best, the Red Book explanations are frequently adequate. They'll generally point out the major issues involved in a question, and they'll occasionally point out something of value about a wrong answer choice. At worst, they can be unclear and even misleading. Sometimes they can even be wrong . . .

How Can The Red Book's Explanations Of Its Own Questions Be Wrong?

When I say that some question explanations from the Red Book are "wrong," I don't mean that they support the wrong answer choice for the question being explained. Instead, what I mean is that the explanation uses the wrong *reasoning* to justify why an answer choice is right or wrong. We can tell the Red Book's reasoning for an explanation is wrong if it would lead us to choose wrong answers for other questions.

In other words, the *real* reasoning behind all real ACT questions must be consistent, since the test is standardized. If a proposed explanation for a correct answer to a real ACT question could apply equally well to some wrong answers on other real ACT questions, then the explanation is wrong, and there must be some other reason behind the correctness of the right answer.

One example of this kind of issue appears on page 218 of the Red Book, in the explanation for question 23 on page 155 of that book. The Red Book's description of the correct answer (which says that it "provides the added detail asked for in the question") applies just as well to at least one of the wrong answers for that question, and arguably to all of the wrong answers. A test-taker who tries to rely on the Red Book's reasoning for this question will find himself drawn to wrong answers for other questions in the future.

But the explanation in this Black Book for the same question provides a way to understand the correct answer that *only* applies to the correct answer, and will reliably allow you to identify correct answers on similar ACT questions in the future.

(Of course, that particular Red Book explanation isn't the only one that I'd call "wrong." I just singled it out here because it happens to be wrong in a way that's relatively easy to understand without getting into the details of how different types of ACT questions actually work.)

Don't get me wrong—some of ACT, Inc.'s explanations are decent. The problem is that many of them aren't. We'll discuss plenty of other examples of bad Red Book explanations in the hundreds of walkthroughs in this Black Book.

In fact, one of the major benefits of this Black Book is that it spells out the *actual* reasoning behind the correct answers to ACT questions, and then demonstrates repeatedly how this reasoning should be applied to real test questions. That means the explanations in this Black Book are often very different from what the Red Book explanations say.

It probably seems odd to you that the Red Book isn't always consistent and accurate in explaining its own questions. It seemed strange to me when I first noticed it, too. I'm not sure why many of the explanations are wrong, but the fact remains that they are, as I'll demonstrate in more detail when we talk about specific questions later on. I think the people who write the explanations in the Red Book must not be the same people who write the actual questions—either that, or some of the Red Book explanations are deliberately intended to mislead us, which strikes me as unlikely.

At any rate, the walkthroughs in this Black Book will tell you definitively and objectively why the right answers to Red Book questions are right, and why the wrong answers are wrong. You'll see that the approach I recommend works on all the questions in the Red Book, as well as on any real ACT questions you'll see in the future, including on test day. My explanations will also tell you which errors might lead you to certain wrong answers, and they'll often show you multiple approaches to answer a given question, so you can decide which approach suits you best.

Carelessness Will Cost You

"Concentrate all your thoughts upon the work at hand. The sun's rays do not burn until brought to a focus."
- Alexander Graham Bell

One of the most important differences between the ACT and a normal high school test is the extreme importance of details on the ACT—and this means that careless mistakes on the ACT will be much more harmful to your score than they would be in a normal classroom situation.

In school, for instance, math teachers may give you partial credit on a test question if they can see that you tried to apply the correct formula, even though you made a small calculation mistake and arrived at the wrong answer.

But what happens if you set up an ACT Math problem correctly and do almost everything right, but make a small calculation error on the last step and choose a wrong answer?

Here's what happens: you get no credit on that question whatsoever. It's exactly the same as it would have been if you'd just left it blank and done no work at all.

Or imagine you're in a discussion in English class about a character in a book who was very unhappy, and you described that character as being "desperate." Your English teacher probably wouldn't think twice about this small discrepancy; she would see that you clearly had a general understanding of the mental state of the character, and she would appreciate that you were sharing your perspective on the book.

But on an ACT Reading question, you can't describe an unhappy character as "desperate" unless there's something in the text that specifically describes how that character was in a difficult situation and was feeling totally hopeless, because that's what the word "desperate" specifically means. A lot of desperate people are probably unhappy, but not every unhappy person is desperate, so if you chose an ACT answer that described someone as "desperate" without something in the text that specifically supported it, you'd be completely wrong. No partial credit for the question, no consideration for your other thoughts about the character—on the ACT, you're just wrong, exactly as though you'd left the question blank.

The same concepts apply to the other sections of the ACT as well, of course. One major reason that the ACT is so challenging for so many test-takers is that it's so highly detail-oriented, even though it limits itself to relatively basic subject-matter.

Noticing these details and avoiding carelessness is so important that most students could probably hit their target scores simply by training themselves to eliminate careless errors. Yes, really—it's that big of a deal.

So How Do We Avoid These Careless Errors?

The biggest thing you need to do to avoid careless errors is to realize that this test demands a different mindset from the one that most high school students have in the classroom. The ACT isn't about the big picture, or about advanced material. It's about simple ideas and simple tasks done exactly the right way . . . over and over and over again. If you let yourself make minor mistakes in that process, it'll hurt your score, *even if you actually do understand the major concepts involved.*

Embrace this different mindset when you're preparing for the ACT (and performing on test day). Review your practice carefully, and pay attention to the specific mistakes you make so you can make an effort to avoid them in the future.

Hitting A Target Score

"Setting a goal is not the main thing. It is deciding how you will go about achieving it and staying with that plan."
- Tom Landry

Very often, students who prepare for the ACT have a target score in mind, typically either for a scholarship program or for a certain school they'd like to attend.

The most common approach to this kind of situation is for students to work hard to improve one of their major "problem" areas—for example, if a student's Science score is his lowest one, he might spend a lot of time trying to improve that section, since it has the most room for improvement.

That might seem logical, and it might work for some people, but let me propose an alternative: if you're trying to hit a target score and you're not *too* far off, you might want to start by taking your strongest area and getting even better at that. This can be very effective for a few different reasons.

First of all, it's your strongest area, so you must be reasonably comfortable with the material, which means that improving your performance on it could be less stressful and more effective than trying to improve in a section you find difficult.

But there's another important angle to consider, and it has to do with the way the test is scored. When you take a section of the test—the English section for example—you end up with a certain number of questions answered correctly; on an English section, that number is somewhere from 0 to 75, since there are 75 questions on that section.

Of course, your final score for the section is somewhere from 1 to 36, so that raw score from 0 to 75 must be converted to a final score from 1 to 36—and the payoff for each additional correct answer isn't constant.

The closer you get to the top of the scoring scale, the more each individual correct answer tends to contribute to your score. To see what I mean, take a look at page 878 of your copy of *The Real ACT Prep Guide, 3rd Edition*. In the second column of that table, under "English," you can see the number of questions you have to get right to earn the scaled score in the first column on the left, under "Scale Score." So let's say you got 43 English questions right—that would correspond to a scaled score of 18. You could get 5 more questions right (for a total of 48), and you'd still only have a scaled score of 19—that's a 1-point improvement for 5 more correct answers.

Now, let's imagine you're higher up on the chart, and you've answered 68 questions correctly. That corresponds to a scaled score of 29. In this case, if you get 5 more questions right (for a total of 73 questions answered correctly), you'll have a scaled score of 34—that's 5 more points on your final score for that section, for only 5 more correct answers. At this end of the scale, almost every additional correct answer gets you another scaled point, whereas in the middle of the scale you could get several more questions right and only raise your scaled score for that section by a point or so.

Not every test has this exact conversion scale, because the conversion will vary slightly each time the test is administered, for reasons we don't need to address now. Still, we'll generally find that there's less payoff for each individual additional correct answer in the middle of the scale than there is toward the top of the scale.

So if you can improve on sections where you're already near the upper end of the scoring scale, you'll get a bigger payoff for each new correct answer, instead of struggling against questions on a section you're less comfortable with and getting a smaller payoff per question.

One more thought: if you happen to be getting a perfect score on your strongest section (good job, by the way!) then you can just move on to your next best section, and so on, as needed.

What If I Have To Improve On A Particular Section?

If your target score requires you to improve on a specific section, and you can't just pick which section you want to improve on, then you won't necessarily benefit from the scoring issue we just discussed, but you can still focus on the question types within that section that you do best on.

For example, if you need to improve your Reading score, and you do best on the questions with line citations, then you can work on line citation questions until you can reliably answer every single one of them correctly. If you need to improve your English score, and you're better at the English questions that have to do with reading comprehension, you can start by getting even better at those. And so on.

What If I Need A Significant Improvement In My Score?

If you need to increase your score by a large margin, it probably won't be enough just to work on your strongest areas. Instead, you'll likely have to improve in several areas. If you don't have a lot of time left before you have to take the test, then you can start your preparation by working on your strongest section first, then move on to the next strongest one, and so on. As you continue to hone your skills on each successive section, the odds are good that your overall understanding of the test will develop in such a way that the other areas of the test that used to give you trouble may become easier. If you do have a lot of time, then I'd recommend you consider following the "order of attack" that I recommend in "How To Train For The ACT—Mastering The Ideas In This Book."

The General Game Plan For Attacking A Section Of The ACT On Test Day

"We cannot make events. Our business is wisely to improve them."
- Samuel Adams

In the next chapter, we'll discuss specific strategies for dealing with time-management issues on the ACT. Before we do that, though, I want to make sure we're on the same page when it comes to the best way to attack a multiple-choice section of the ACT when the clock is running, because I've learned over the years that most test-takers have never learned how to do that.

The optimal basic approach to a section of the ACT relies on remembering three important things at all times:

1. Every question on a given section of the ACT is worth one raw point on that section, no matter how hard or easy the question is for you.
2. Every real ACT question is carefully designed so that it follows certain rules. The answer to a real ACT question is never arbitrary or unpredictable if we know the ACT's rules, and if we read and understand every word in the question.
3. You should answer every question before time runs out on the section.

For these reasons, the best approach to a section of the ACT involves making multiple passes through the section, so that you maximize the possibility of spending your time and energy figuring out the questions that will seem easiest for you, and minimize the amount of time and energy you spend on questions that you'll just have to guess on anyway. (Of course, as you continue to improve your understanding of the way the ACT works and your execution of the ideas in this Black Book, the number of questions you have to guess on will drop, until it ideally reaches zero.) As you near the end of the allotted time for the section, you should start thinking more about checking over your work and guessing on any questions you haven't answered yet.

On the first pass through the section, you look at each question in order, and decide whether to answer it or skip it for the moment:

- If you think you understand the question and you can answer it relatively quickly and easily, then you go ahead and answer it.
- If you think you understand the question, but that it might take you a relatively long time to figure out the answer, then you skip it. You'll save it for a later pass. If you want, you can mark that question in your test booklet in a way that lets you know you decided to skip it because you thought it would take a little too long to answer, not because you thought you wouldn't be able to answer it at all.
- If you don't think you can figure out the answer to the question, then you skip it. Again, if you want, you can mark the question with a quick symbol in your test booklet that indicates you thought the question was too hard the first time you saw it. If time permits, you'll come back to these questions later.

At the end of your first pass through the section, you will have answered all the questions that seemed fairly quick and easy for you. You will also have looked through every question in the section, and you'll have a pretty solid idea of which questions seemed like ones you would have been able to answer if you were willing to spend more time on them, and which questions seemed too hard for you to answer with certainty no matter how much time you were willing to spend on them.

(It takes some practice to figure out how aggressive you should be with skipping questions during the first pass. Some people like to skip a question as soon as they come to a word or a concept they're not familiar with; this saves time, but it might cause you to skip questions in the first pass that you could have answered correctly if you'd actually finished reading them. Other people prefer to read a whole question before deciding whether to skip it; this gives them a better idea of the question, but it can also take up more time. Play with different approaches during your practice and see what works best for you. Also bear in mind that your ability to answer questions quickly and correctly will improve as you practice the concepts in this Black Book on real ACT questions from the Red Book, as will your ability to spot questions that are going to be challenging for you.)

When the first pass is over, you immediately flip back through the section and begin the second pass. In the second pass, you attack the questions that seemed like ones you could answer with certainty if you spent a little more time. Ideally, you should try to attack the easiest of these questions first, and then the next easiest one after that, and so on. But don't worry too much about observing a strict order—the time you waste trying to figure out exactly which question is the next easiest one for you to answer is time you could be spending on answering questions.

If you come across a question during the second pass that seems a little harder than you thought, you can skip it again and save it for the third pass.

At the end of the second pass, you will have answered all the questions that seemed like ones you could figure out with certainty, whether those answers came to you pretty easily or you had to work a little harder for them.

At this point, if you have enough time left, you should make a third pass through the section and reconsider the questions you've been avoiding so far. You may discover that you actually can answer some of them now, because you realize what you had previously overlooked or misunderstood. You may also decide that those questions really are too challenging for you to answer, and you'll have to guess on them.

If you don't have enough time for a third pass, then you should shift your focus to guessing on the questions you haven't answered yet, and/or re-checking the questions you've already answered. (You may be wondering how much time is "enough time" for a third pass. The answer will depend on you, because different test-takers will work at different speeds and decide to skip different numbers of questions in the first two passes. You'll develop a sense of how much time you need as you keep practicing with real ACT questions.)

Let's spend a little time talking about guessing and re-checking on the ACT, because they're very important skills that most test-takers ignore.

Guessing On The ACT

Unlike the SAT, the ACT has no wrong-answer penalty. In other words, the ACT doesn't take any points away from you if you answer a question incorrectly (as opposed to leaving it blank). With that in mind, there's never a reason to leave a question blank on the ACT; you should always at least mark something, even if you're just randomly choosing an answer in under a second. It can't hurt you, and there's a small chance that it could help.

But guessing on ACT questions shouldn't be your default response!

Notice I'm not suggesting that you guess on any questions until you've gone through at least two passes in a section and answered the questions you could handle with certainty.

In contrast, most untrained test-takers just kind of float through the entire ACT without ever actually being certain about the answers they're choosing. These test-takers are basically guessing on every single question. They don't know how the ACT works, they don't have a game plan, and they suffer for it.

You need to maintain a disciplined approach to every real ACT question you encounter, because that's the only way to make sure you attack each question using the principles in this Black Book. The guessing mindset is a dangerous trap to fall into, and it harms a lot of ACT-takers.

Remember that every question and answer on the ACT must be bulletproof, and that there's always exactly one correct answer, and that correct answer is undeniably right, according to the ACT's rules—no matter how strange it might seem to an untrained test-taker.

It's absolutely important that you remember this at all times. If you don't, you may end up facing a challenging question that you can't quite figure out right away, and you may forget that every question has one clearly correct answer. You might decide that this one question is the exception, and that really two or three of the answer choices are all equally valid. Then you might start to deviate from the strategies you've learned from this Black Book as you go through the rest of the test, and you might end up with a much worse score than you could have achieved if you had just remembered the rules.

Of course, you're probably going to run into ACT questions on test day that challenge you so much that you skip them in your first two passes. In those cases, you should still mark the answer choice that seems most likely to be correct (either because of the content of the answer choice, or because it fits an answer-choice pattern that you've learned in this Black Book).

But if you do find yourself guessing on a particular question, you have to remember that it's not because the question can't be answered with certainty, and it's not because the strategies you've learned in this Black Book don't work. It's because there's something about this question that you just aren't seeing. It might be a word you don't really know, or it might be a math concept that you're overlooking, or a complicated sentence you don't quite understand, or it might just be that you're getting flustered and forgetting something about how the questions work.

That's fine. You can be totally stumped a few times on test day and still get a great score. The point is not to beat yourself up about it. You just have to make sure you don't lose faith in your ACT training simply because you're unable to execute that training sometimes. If you've got no other options, you should guess on a question before time runs out rather than leave it blank.

But guessing shouldn't be your game plan. Understanding the test and paying attention to the right details should be your game plan, and that's what you'll learn in this Black Book.

Re-Checking Your Answers

One of the major themes of this Black Book is that the ACT is a very detail-oriented test of relatively basic concepts. This means that a lot of test-takers cost themselves a lot of points just because they don't pay enough attention to what they're doing, not because they don't know enough to answer a question.

So it should come as no surprise that I highly recommend re-checking your answers on a section if you have time. (You should be constantly re-checking your work and your assumptions as you go through each question in the first place. You should also be using the knowledge of the ACT's design that you get from this Black Book to make sure you can account for each part of a question as you answer it, because that's another good way to make sure you haven't made a small mistake somewhere.)

The question is whether you should re-check your answers or guess on the questions you've skipped if you don't have enough time to do both.

Again, the answer comes down to your personal style and tendencies. If you do a good, careful job of checking your answers as you go, then you may not find any mistakes in your re-checking. On the other hand, you may also find that you're not very good at guessing correctly on the ACT, in which case it might make more sense to shift more of your energy towards re-checking the questions you actually understand.

The only way to know which activity is most likely to result in extra points for you is to experiment with both of them in your practice sessions. Of course, the most ideal scenario is one in which you have enough time to do both.

The Bottom Line

So here's the best general way to approach a section of the ACT. You'll notice that it bears little resemblance to what most people do on the test, which is simply to mark their best guess on each question as they encounter it.

1. Start by answering all the questions that seem relatively simple and easy for you. Skip the ones that seem too hard or too time-consuming for now.
2. After you've made your first pass through the section, go back on your second pass and do the questions that seemed like they would be time-consuming but still possible to figure out. Try to approach them in order from easiest to hardest, but don't obsess over getting the order exactly right. Skip any questions that turn out to be too hard to answer.
3. After the second pass, go back and revisit the questions that you've skipped so far. You may find that you can actually figure some of them out after all. If so, go ahead and answer them. Save the remaining questions for guessing.
4. Remember that a small mistake on a question can be all it takes to cost you that question. Depending on the results you obtain in your practice sessions, consider leaving yourself enough time to re-check the questions you felt you could answer with certainty.
5. Be sure to guess on all remaining unanswered questions before time runs out.

Attacking a section of the ACT in this kind of disciplined, focused way will allow you to make sure you answer as many questions as possible with total certainty. It will also ensure that you spend your time and energy where it will do you the most good.

One Final Note

This probably goes without saying, but make sure you bubble in your answer sheet correctly as you're going through each pass! It would be a shame to work through the section correctly and still lose a lot of points because you didn't pay attention to the numbering on the answer sheet.

Timing Issues

"Time is what we want most, but what we use worst."
- William Penn

One of the biggest causes of stress in standardized testing is the time limit. This is especially true on the ACT, which requires you to answer more questions with fewer breaks than most other standardized tests people take before college. Most of the students I work with are at least a little concerned about the timing aspect of the test before we start working together; some are extremely concerned.

When you keep running out of time before you've finished a section, it's understandable that you might get a little worried. Often, students who have this problem try to solve it by timing themselves as they do a bunch of practice sections; they hope to improve their time management without really doing anything in particular to change their approach. They're basically trying to do what they've always done, and just hoping they'll somehow get it done faster.

But in most cases, even students with major timing problems are best served by putting those issues aside temporarily and focusing on mastering the concepts presented in this book. If you can do that, you'll often find that your timing issues resolve themselves.

Let me elaborate on that a little.

Any single ACT question can be approached in a number of different ways. Some approaches will result in wrong answers, and some in correct answers; some take a long time, and some take only a matter of seconds. Not surprisingly, people with timing issues on the ACT usually approach questions in ways that are more time-consuming and complicated than necessary, instead of attacking questions in the easiest and most direct ways.

But the solution to this problem isn't to train yourself to do the complicated, time-consuming approaches more quickly, as though you were hitting fast-forward on a video. The solution is to learn a completely different approach—one that's better because it's less complicated and can naturally be completed in less time.

Usually, the more "academic" approach to an ACT question—the one that feels more like a solution to a normal high school test item—is the most comfortable and familiar approach for most test-takers. Unfortunately, it's also the approach that usually takes a lot more time than necessary.

Since most people don't appreciate the important differences between the ACT and a normal high school test, they also don't realize that this academic approach is unnecessarily slow and complicated when applied to most real ACT questions.

Students without timing issues usually aren't just doing the normal "academic" approach at super speeds. Instead, they're using an entirely different approach that simply doesn't take as much time.

To illustrate this idea, let's imagine that two people each have to chop an onion. One person uses a knife and a cutting board and takes five minutes to get the job done. The other person uses a food processor and takes 10 seconds.

Is the second person better at chopping onions than the first person? Of course not. She just knows how to use the food processor; she'd probably take just as long as the first person if she only had a knife and cutting board. Similarly, the first person could probably also chop the onion in ten seconds if he knew about the food processor.

So if you're worried about time management, your first step should be just to learn the most efficient ways to attack the ACT, which is what we'll cover in this Black Book, instead of trying to get faster at the approach you're already using. The odds are good that your time-management problems will no longer exist once you learn to attack each question the way a trained test-taker would. You'll be using the food processor instead of the knife, so to speak.

This is one of the reasons that people who excel on standardized tests like the ACT often finish sections with a ton of extra time. It's not because they're superhuman; it's because understanding the test goes hand-in-hand with answering questions more quickly—when you work on your understanding of the test, the average time you need per question will naturally go down considerably, even without special training to increase your speed.

All the same, there are a few little tips and strategies that might be helpful for some students, so let's talk about them here.

30 Seconds Or Less

When approached correctly, every single ACT question can be answered in 30 seconds or less, and many can be answered in less than 10 seconds. Again, this doesn't involve actually going through a bunch of complicated steps at lightning speed. It means using an approach with fewer, quicker steps in the first place.

When I talk about how it's possible to complete all real ACT questions in less than 30 seconds, I don't mean that you have to do each problem in less than 30 seconds in order to be successful. Even the best test-takers run into questions they just have a hard time figuring out at first, and even the quickest students get stuck occasionally. By the time you've got the right techniques down, though, you should be doing enough of the questions quickly enough that you aren't hurt by the ones that take a little more time.

Read A Little Faster

This one might seem a little obvious, but it helps. There are all kinds of speed-reading courses and related schools of thought out there, but most people can noticeably increase their reading speed by just making a point of reading faster. I like to compare it to walking; most people could walk faster than they normally do without much extra effort. They just don't, unless they think about it.

So, whether you're reading for pleasure, for school, or for test prep, just consciously think about doing it a little faster than normal. If you keep it up, you should be able to start automatically reading more quickly.

In general, if you can read fast enough to keep up with your classes in school, you shouldn't have anything to worry about on the ACT, but you might as well try this strategy out and see if it helps.

One more thing: if you have a serious issue with reading speed that's been diagnosed by a professional, you should look into contacting ACT, Inc. to request extra time on test day.

Dealing With Anxiety

Anxiety can be a big problem for a lot of students, and it can manifest itself in different ways. Some students freeze up, get confused, or second-guess themselves in practice or on test day because of it.

There are two main ways to deal with this issue that I like to recommend to my students. The first way is to make a conscious effort to channel this nervous energy into something productive. When you start to feel restless or nervous during practice, switch to a less-structured drill, like the Semi-Structured Stare-And-Ponder (we talked about this in the "How To Train For The ACT" section).

Even taking a little break from training to take a walk and get some fresh air can be productive, if it means you're able to relax and focus on the test when you get back.

The other way of dealing with anxiety is to take the time to understand where it comes from, and then explore those issues.

In the vast majority of cases in my experience, anxiety over the ACT comes from the fact that it's an important test that will have an impact on the college you attend, and most people aren't sure how to do well on it.

Let's address those ideas.

First of all, I should point out that your ultimate happiness and success in life will depend on a lot more than your ACT score. This single thing isn't going to make or break you, no matter how much it might feel like that's the case right now.

Secondly, if you plan to go to college, you're probably going to have to take this test (or the SAT). There's basically no way around it, so you may as well just commit to doing the best you can, and then see how it goes.

Finally, the test can also seem challenging because most test-takers and tutors don't understand how it really works. The odds are good that a lot of the advice you've received about the ACT isn't actually helpful, and may even be harmful. In that case, the best thing to do is just to start from square one and use the material in this book. You'll probably find that performing on the test will become much less stressful than it used to be.

Go Through Multiple Passes On Each Section
Approaching each section of the ACT in multiple passes will allow you to minimize the amount of time you waste on questions that you find more challenging. For a detailed discussion of this important strategy, see "The General Game Plan For Attacking A Section Of The ACT On Test Day" earlier in this Black Book.

Summary
Every student is different, but most time management issues come down to the things we discussed in this section. In my experience, the best way for almost anyone to deal with this problem is to learn and practice the techniques in this book, because most students will find that using the optimal techniques will allow them to answer questions much more quickly than they do on their own.

Reading Passages On The ACT

"It has been established beyond a shadow of doubt that readers in general waste a great deal of time and effort."
- Manya and Eric De Leeuw

Students frequently ask me how they should read things on the ACT. They don't only ask me how to read the passages in the Reading section—on the ACT, passages appear in the English and Science sections as well, and even the Math section includes several questions with multiple lines of text.

The basic issue is this: people often find it impossible to read a page or more of text, become thoroughly familiar with it, and then accurately answer a series of questions on it, all within the time limits for that section.

I understand where they're coming from, because this isn't the sort of thing we'd expect to do in almost any normal classroom situation. In school, if we're supposed to study a text, we get a little more time to do it before we have to take a test on it.

Yet again, though, we see a situation on the ACT that differs from what we'd expect in a normal classroom setting. It's very important that you understand this concept as early as possible so that you have the right mindset when you read a passage on the ACT—whether it's a Reading passage, a Science passage, or even an English passage.

When you read a passage on the ACT, you're not supposed to become an expert on the topic of that passage. All you want to do when you read an ACT passage is to get a rough idea of which concepts appear in which parts of the passage, so you can go back and find them later when a question asks about them. That's all.

We'll discuss this in more detail in the appropriate sections of this book, but for now I'll just say that any correct answer to a question about an ACT passage must be directly supported by a specific set of words in the text.

This means that, at any given moment, the only part of a passage that we need to care about is the part that supports the correct answer to the question we're working on.

Because we only care about those specific parts of the passage, we don't need any kind of "big picture" understanding of the text. We don't need to be experts on what the passage is talking about—we just need to know where we can find the correct answer to the question we're working on.

So when you read (or skim) a passage, you're not supposed to be absorbing and processing all the information on the page. You just want to create a rough "mental map" of where the concepts appear.

For example, imagine that part of a passage mentions someone who drives by a park on the way to school. Let's say the first mention of the park appears halfway down the first column of text. If you see a question that asks about the park, you just need to know that the relevant information from the passage should be about halfway down the first column of text. Then you can go back and read that part of the text more carefully, so you can find the answer you need, and then go on to the next question.

In other words, you only need to go back and read closely when you're hunting for the answer to a specific question. When you read or skim a whole passage at once, you're not trying to pick up enough information to answer questions—you're only reading to get a general idea of where different topics appear, so you can come back to them later if a specific question requires you to do so.

Searching through a passage to find answers is one of the most valuable skills you can have on the ACT, so you definitely want to make an effort to get better at it. One simple but powerful technique is to learn to scan for unusual characters that are related to a question. For example, on a Reading or Science question that asks about a proper noun, you might need to scan the text for capital letters. Depending on the question, you might also need to scan for italics or quotation marks. Or if the answer choices to an ACT Science question all involve a certain unit, like m^3/hr, then you can often save a lot of time by looking for places where that unit occurs in the passage.

Of course, we'll talk about all of these topics in the training and see them in the walkthroughs, so if this doesn't make total sense yet, just keep reading. The most important thing is that you understand that when you read a passage on the ACT, your goal is not to process and remember all the material that you see. You only want to be generally familiar with the location of different pieces of information so that you can go back and find that info as quickly as possible if a question asks you to do that. That's all.

ACT Training

Whew! Now we've gotten through the introductory material. It's a lot to cover, but believe me—understanding that material will save you a ton of time and frustration, because now you have a solid general understanding of how the ACT works, which puts you way ahead of the curve compared to all the other people out there who have to take the test.

This is the moment we've been waiting for—we're going to start learning the specific approach to each question type, starting with ACT Reading. Just bear a few things in mind as you learn about each question type:

1. This training (and especially the question walkthroughs) will probably seem repetitive, but repetition is good on the ACT. Once you drill these ideas into your head, it'll be that much harder for the ACT to trick you on test day.
2. The training in this Black Book is far more valuable when you see these ideas in action against real ACT practice questions from the Red Book. Make sure you read through the question walkthroughs after each training section in this Black Book, and follow along in your copy of *The Real ACT Prep Guide, 3rd Edition*.
3. You're almost guaranteed to run into a concept or idea that doesn't make sense to you right away. Don't get discouraged. Stick with it. If worse comes to worst, just move on and make a note to come back to the concept that's troubling you. It may make more sense as you read the rest of the material and look at some question walkthroughs.

Without further ado, let's get started with ACT Reading!

ACT Reading

"Tell me how you are searching, and I will tell you what you are searching for."
- Ludwig Wittgenstein

Overview and Important Reminders for ACT Reading Questions

ACT Reading is tough for a lot of students, and it kind of embodies a central complaint a lot of people have about this test: how can you pick *one* right answer to a question about a passage? How can a student be sure she's chosen the right answer, when anything a person reads might be interpreted in several different ways that are equally valid?

Don't worry. This is one of the many parts of the ACT that are nothing like their apparent counterparts in a normal high school situation. We're going to learn exactly how the ACT can design Reading questions with correct answers that are just as bulletproof and inarguable as correct answers on the ACT Math section.

After all, we've already learned that these questions and answers MUST be "bulletproof"—no matter what the subject matter—or else the ACT would be worthless to colleges.

In fact, the ACT Reading section is the best place to start understanding how the test really works. If we can see the standardization at work here, it'll help us understand the rest of the test.

The other reason that I always like to discuss the Reading section first is that the secret skill required to beat the ACT Reading section is the single most important skill on the entire test. If you can really, truly understand and master this skill, you'll be able to get a great score across the board, in every section.

The Big Secret Of ACT Reading

What is this secret skill that you need to beat the ACT Reading section?

Pssst—don't tell anybody else:

You have to be able to read.

That's really it. Well, to be more specific, you have to be able to read *carefully* and *precisely*. In other words, you have to hone the skill of reading exactly what's on a page, and taking in everything that's stated directly in the text, without taking in anything that's not.

That probably seems like it should be pretty straightforward. So why is this part of the ACT such a challenge?

Well, it turns out that the kind of reading you need to do on the ACT is almost the exact opposite of the kind of reading students are trained to do in high school. I'll show you what I mean.

A Real-Life Example

Let's imagine a typical English classroom discussion, and then consider how the skills developed during such a discussion might be incorrectly applied to a Reading question on the ACT.

Imagine you're in an English class discussing a passage from a book you're currently reading. In this passage, the main character is very upset. She's just learned that her cousin has a serious illness, and the passage describes how worried and concerned she is for his health. Your teacher asks the class for their opinions on the main character's emotional state.

You raise your hand and say something like, "I think the main character seems troubled and conflicted." Your teacher asks, "Conflicted? Why do you say conflicted?" You then go on to explain that you were in a position like this once and you remember feeling conflicted, so you think the character probably feels conflicted, too. Your teacher thanks you for your contribution, and probably agrees that, yes, it's possible the main character in this passage might feel conflicted.

This sort of open interpretation is often encouraged in a classroom, but it'll cause you to miss a lot of questions on the ACT.

We've talked about the idea that all ACT questions have to be "bulletproof" and objective in order for the test to serve its function in the admissions process. The only way for a correct answer on an ACT Reading question to satisfy this requirement is to avoid any kind of interpretation, because interpretation is always subjective.

And the only way for a correct answer choice to refer to a passage without interpreting it is to restate some element of the passage exactly. Any other description of the text would necessarily involve interpretation, and then the correct answer wouldn't be objectively correct anymore.

So if the same hypothetical passage we were just talking about appeared on an ACT test, and you chose an answer saying that the main character felt "conflicted," you'd get the question wrong, even though your English teacher would probably accept that analysis.

If an ACT passage describes someone in a difficult spot as upset, worried, and concerned, then we can choose any answer that means exactly the same thing as "upset," "worried," or "concerned" . . . but we can't pick a word like "conflicted" unless the text specifically states that a character feels two different emotions at the same time that seem to go against each other, because that's what the word "conflicted" literally means.

On the other hand, if the passage said something like, "I was worried about my cousin's illness, but I was also optimistic that he was strong enough to overcome it," then you could pick an answer choice that described the character as "conflicted," because being "worried" and "optimistic" are two conflicting emotions. Further, the ideas of those emotions would be connected by the word "but," which shows that the speaker considers them to be conflicting ideas. See how that works?

On the ACT, it's not enough that being worried or upset is a negative thing, and that feeling conflicted is typically a negative thing that could kind of go along with the idea of being upset and worried. It doesn't matter that *you* might feel conflicted if you were in the position described in the text, or that you think you could defend your reasoning in a classroom discussion.

The only thing that matters in ACT Reading is that the answer you choose is supported directly and specifically in the text, in a way that requires no interpretation. If an answer choice is supported by the text in that way, then it's right. If it's not, then it's wrong.

That's such an important concept that I'll say it again, with exclamation points:

The only thing that matters in an ACT Reading question is that the answer you choose is supported directly and specifically in the text, without interpretation! If it is, then you're right! If it's not, then you're wrong!

Just Trust Me—At Least Until You Read The Walkthroughs

It might not seem like what I'm saying is right. I'm sure that you're thinking, even now, of times when you've seen an ACT Reading question that seemed to require interpretation of the text.

But the reason you feel like you should be interpreting the text is that you've always been trained to do that in other situations, and because the ACT wants you to think that it's like a regular school test. The test specifically designs answer choices that are supposed to take advantage of your habit of interpreting everything you read in your own way, instead of just reading exactly what the text says and nothing more.

This is why a lot of people might read a passage about a character who feels "upset," "worried," or "concerned," and then wrongly mark an answer choice that says the character felt "conflicted." Students are taught to think of words in a passage as approximations that can be twisted and turned this way and that to accommodate a lot of different meanings. On the ACT, though, words can only mean exactly what they mean—nothing more, and nothing less.

This is what I'm talking about when I say that the only skill you need on the ACT Reading section is to be able to read carefully. Really, if someone reads about a character who feels "upset," "worried," or "concerned," and then decides that the character must feel "conflicted," that person hasn't actually read the passage carefully, at least not as far as the ACT is concerned. Instead, that person has read a passage that contained some information, and then made an assumption that some other information must also be true, even though the passage never said it was.

So this is what I mean when I talk about careful, precise, effective reading: I mean that you must train yourself to take in all the information in the text, without missing anything, and without adding in any of your own assumptions. Just because someone is "happy," you can't assume that person is "energetic." Just because someone is "sad," that doesn't mean the person is "anxious." We might think of these terms as being similar to each other in a certain context, but they aren't actually synonyms.

On the ACT we must get used to the idea that a word means only exactly what it says, and nothing more. Wrong answer choices will often try to get you to equate two different words that seem sort of related so that you'll make the kind of assumption you might make in an English class, and then get the question wrong.

Remember: wrong answer choices will try to exploit your English class instincts! Stay on your guard, and don't fall for their tricks.

Careful Reading At Work Against A Real Question

With that in mind, let's take a look at the very first Reading question on an ACT from the Red Book. You can find it on page 181 of the 3rd edition of *The Real ACT Prep Guide*. (As previously discussed, you need a copy of the Red Book if you hope to do well on the ACT, because it contains 5 real practice ACT tests.)

At any rate, we're going to walk through this question (number 1 on page 181), and the answer choices, and you'll be able to see a lot of the concepts in play that we've been discussing so far.

Let me point out right here that I'm going to take more time going through this first question than I will with other examples later, just to try to illustrate as much as possible with this example. Don't be intimidated by how long the explanation is, and don't think that you'll have to go through every detail of every answer choice the way I'm going to do it right now. The later explanations will be more indicative of a more "normal" thought process for a Reading question. This explanation is just longer and more involved in order to help you get into the proper mindset, and to demonstrate clearly what separates the right answer from the wrong answers.

So let's jump in.

Right off the bat, the prompt for this question includes the phrase "would most likely agree." This is a perfect example of how the ACT will phrase its concrete, bulletproof, 100% objective questions in terms that make them sound like a classic open-ended English class discussion kind of question.

The test could have started the question with a phrase like "Which of the following is a true statement about . . . ," because, really, that's what the ACT is going to reward—a true, concrete statement that's directly supported by the text. Instead, they talk about what Fran "would most likely agree" with.

Do you see how tricky the test is being? The ACT is trying to put you in the position of deciding what an imaginary character "would most likely agree" with. They want you to ask yourself something like, "How could I possibly know what Fran would most likely agree with? I only just heard about her, and she's not even real." But you have to remember that ACT questions can never be subjective or unpredictable. If they were, the test wouldn't be standardized. That means there must be a concrete reason in the text that one answer choice is right and the others are wrong.

(Sorry to go on about that. It's just really important that you learn to catch these things.)

When you see this kind of wording, you have to get used to reading it as something like "Which of the following is a true statement, based on the passage, about Fran's relationship with Linda Rose?" Now you're in the right mindset. You're not venturing your best guess—you're searching for concrete evidence to support a correct answer and to eliminate 3 incorrect answers.

Now we look at the first answer choice. We know that (A) is correct because it's directly supported by the text. It says their lives are "still connected." This idea is supported in the text by phrases like "homing pigeon" (line 3) and "human boomerang" (line 5), which Fran uses to describe the way that Linda Rose would come back into Fran's life. It's also supported by the fact that lines 30 through 34 describe how Fran has been "found" by Linda Rose after "waiting so long." In lines 68 through 70, Fran tells us that Linda Rose was a baby Fran gave up 24 years ago—a direct example of how their lives were once physically connected. So we're told that Fran gave up Linda Rose and then waited for decades for Linda Rose to find her, like a homing pigeon or a boomerang—two things that return to their starting points. The word "connected" can mean a lot of things—"linked," "interrelated," "interdependent," and so on. In fact, according to dictionary.com, one of the less common meanings for the word "connected" is "related by family ties," which directly describes Fran's relationship with her daughter, Linda Rose. Clearly, we can confidently conclude—based on the text—that Fran and Linda Rose "are still connected."

This answer choice also includes the phrase "despite long separations of time and distance," and that phrase is also reflected directly in the text. We know Fran thinks the separation has gone on for a long time, because she specifically uses the word "long" in lines 5 and 34 to describe the amount of time she's been separated from Linda Rose. We also know that distance is involved, because the letter from Linda Rose came from another state, as we can see in lines 9 and 10 (if Fran doesn't know anyone in Texas, then she must not live in Texas, because she knows her own mother, who is there with her). So Fran and Linda Rose clearly have a separation of time and distance.

And there you have it—every part of the correct answer choice is directly supported in the text, even though the ACT tried its best to make the question seem subjective and open-ended.

Now let's check out the other answer choices.

Choice (B) is wrong because nothing in the text mentions any *resentment* between Fran and Linda Rose. Even if it did, there's no indication anywhere that they won't be able to have a good relationship. It's true that Fran seems to be going through a lot of emotions that could be characterized as negative—in lines 30-33, she describes feeling like one of "those Nazis" who gets "arrested;" in lines 63-66 she's in "disbelief," and feels like she has "just shaken hands with Death;" in line 72 she says the situation is "not fair;" in line 81 she "bristle[s]."

These could all be seen as indicators of negative emotions, just as resentment is a negative emotion. But the text never specifically says that Fran *blames Linda Rose* for Fran's negative emotions, which is what the word "resentment" would require if it were going to be part of a correct answer on an ACT Reading question.

There's still more. Even if the text described Fran feeling resentful, which it doesn't, we'd still need to see some evidence of resentment *from Linda Rose*, because the answer choice includes the phrase "each other." Even if the entire passage were about how much Fran resented Linda Rose (which, again, it's not), we'd still need something to indicate that Linda Rose resented her back, and this passage doesn't say anything like that.

A lot of people might read this passage and just naturally assume there could be some negative emotions like resentment between an adopted child and her biological mother. In fact, if you were in an English class and you said you thought Fran and Linda Rose probably resented each other too much to have a good relationship, your teacher probably wouldn't tell you that you were wrong. But that doesn't matter on the ACT, because the passage never actually says that Fran and Linda Rose resent each other.

Choice (C) is wrong because it takes a concept that's briefly mentioned in the passage, and then gets it backwards and jumbled. It's true that Fran's mother suggests, in the last paragraph, that Fran might be "worried" that Linda Rose will be "disappointed," or that Linda Rose might have "had this big fantasy for all these years" about who Fran was. But that's a description of *Linda Rose's* dreams of a perfect *mother*; it has nothing to do with *Fran* having a dream of a perfect *daughter*. Of course, this phrase in the last paragraph also can't be relevant to Fran's feelings because the question asks what Fran thinks, and Fran never actually says she feels any of the things that her mother describes. That means we can be certain that this answer choice is incorrect, for several reasons.

Like choice (B), choice (D) is wrong even though it offers another fairly reasonable assumption based on the text. In lines 10 and 11, Fran says that Linda Rose's handwriting reminds her of her own, and in line 75 Fran's mother says Linda Rose "looks just like" Fran. So there are indications that Fran and Linda Rose have things "in common." But the text absolutely never says anything about whether it will or won't be "difficult for them to get close."

Now, if you're an optimistic sort of person, and you think a special bond exists between a parent and a child, and you notice how the text mentions Fran and her daughter having a few things in common, then you might feel like it's reasonable to assume the two women will become close once they get to know each other. But the text doesn't actually say that, so it's wrong. Again, it doesn't matter that the answer choice might seem plausible to us—it actually needs to be stated in the text to be the correct answer, and it isn't stated in the text.

There's one more aspect of this answer choice we want to be clear about. The choice says Fran and Linda Rose have "enough in common" that they should be able to have a close relationship. The text mentions they have a similar appearance, and similar handwriting.

This answer choice isn't wrong just because looking alike and having similar handwriting aren't *actually enough* to guarantee a close relationship with someone *in real life*. In other words, you can't just read the text and then think to yourself, "Well, personally, I don't think that's enough to create a close relationship between two people in real life, so (D) must be wrong."

This answer choice is ONLY wrong because *the text itself* doesn't specifically say that having these things in common is sufficient to lead to a close relationship.

This is a very important distinction.

In other words, you aren't expected to look at what Fran and Linda Rose have in common, and then decide whether that's enough to guarantee a close relationship in your opinion. When you evaluate this answer choice on the ACT, you're only supposed to look for two things:

- whether the text describes the two women as having things in common, and
- whether the text also tells you that having those things in common means it won't be difficult for them to get close.

You must not fall into the habit of making your own judgment calls about whether an answer choice is reasonable or unreasonable. You always have to look at what the text says. If the text contradicts the answer choice, or doesn't address whatever the answer choice says, then the answer choice is wrong, whether it makes sense to you or not.

Remember: all that matters is exactly what's stated in the text. So if you read the text about Fran and Linda Rose, and you read this question, and you read the answer choices, you can only conclude that choice (A) is absolutely the correct answer, because it's directly restated in the text; choices (B), (C), and (D) are absolutely wrong, because they differ from the text.

You MUST intentionally develop this black-and-white mindset about ACT Reading—and about the rest of the ACT—if you want to do your best on the test.

ACT Reading Answer-Choice Patterns

Let's consider some of the different answer-choice patterns on ACT Reading.

ACT Reading Answer-Choice Pattern 1: Reasonable Assumption

This is one of the most common and most dangerous wrong answer choice types. Basically, this type of wrong answer will make a statement about something related to the text that sounds reasonable, but isn't actually mentioned anywhere in the text.

A real-life example of this type of wrong answer choice is choice (B) from the question we just looked at (number 1 on page 181 of the Red Book). It makes a statement about an adopted daughter and a biological mother that might be completely reasonable, but isn't supported by the text.

This is an assumption, not a direct statement from the test, so it's wrong—it doesn't matter whether we might think the assumption can be defended.

So remember: an answer choice that makes an assumption that isn't directly supported by the text is wrong.

ACT Reading Answer-Choice Pattern 2: Confused Concept

This is another tricky wrong answer pattern. This type of answer will take a real concept directly out of the text, but it will confuse the way it fits into the text. If the text says that a student learned an important lesson from his teacher, the answer choice might describe how that teacher learned an important lesson from her student. If the passage describes an applicant who is nervous about going in for a job interview, the wrong answer might mention that the interviewer is nervous about talking to the applicant for the job, and so on.

A real-life example of this kind of wrong answer is (C) from the question we just looked at, question 1 on page 181 of the Red Book. The answer choice talks about "Fran's dreams of a perfect daughter" getting in the way of their relationship. This idea was mentioned in the text in lines 93 – 97, but it was Fran's mother, not Fran, who mentioned it—and she mentioned it as a suggestion of the way Linda Rose might feel about Fran, not the way Fran might feel about Linda Rose.

So the idea of having "dreams of a perfect" long-lost relative is mentioned, but not in the way the question describes.

Students might choose this type of wrong answer either because they're reading too carelessly and they don't take the time to realize their mistake, or because they aren't sure what's going on in the question, but they vaguely remember something like this from the text, so they go with it.

Remember: if you see a concept from the text mentioned in an answer choice, make sure that the answer choice describes the concept correctly, in a way that's consistent with the way it appears in the text. Don't get sloppy.

ACT Reading Answer-Choice Pattern 3: Exact Opposite

This is an interesting type of wrong answer choice that comes up a lot. You can probably guess how it works. Basically, the ACT will just stick in an answer choice that's exactly the opposite of what's stated in the text.

A real-life example of this type of wrong answer choice is (H) from question 4 on page 181 of the Red Book. The question asks what the main point of the first paragraph is. In that paragraph, Fran talks about how she always knew her daughter would get in contact with her again. It even says in lines 6-9 "I was not surprised when I walked down the gravel drive . . . and found the flimsy envelope . . . [from her daughter]."

In spite of the phrase "I was not surprised" in line 6 (in reference to getting the letter), choice (H) says that "Fran finds the arrival of a letter from Linda Rose surprising."

Why would the ACT offer a wrong answer choice that's such an obvious contradiction of the passage? The test is probably hoping that you'll read carelessly and overlook the word "not" in line 6, misreading the text as "I was surprised" instead of "I was not surprised."

See what an easy mistake that would be? This is why we always need to remember that the ACT does, in fact, offer us incorrect answer choices that directly and obviously contradict the text. Be on the lookout.

ACT Reading Answer-Choice Pattern 4: Completely Irrelevant

You'll also frequently see wrong answer choices that are completely irrelevant—just kind of random thoughts that get stuck in with the other answer choices.

A real life example of this kind of wrong answer choice is choice (D) from question 9 on page 181 of the Red Book. The question asks about a reasonable conclusion that can be drawn from the letter and the picture that Linda Rose sent to Fran. Although the other choices have at least some connection to something in the text, choice (D) says that Linda Rose "cares little about how she or her house looks." There's no mention anywhere in the text of anyone being concerned, or unconcerned, about her appearance or the appearance of her home, which makes this answer choice completely irrelevant to the passage.

Let's think about this one. Why would the ACT include completely irrelevant answer choices? Probably because the test-makers know that lots of test-takers will read the passage subjectively and try to give credit to any interpretation they encounter, just like they're taught to do in English class. An untrained test-taker might read choice (D) and think, "Wow, I don't even remember the passage mentioning Linda rose caring about her appearance or her home's appearance, but I guess that makes sense—I don't see anything to contradict it." Or an untrained test-taker might also think, "Wow—I must have missed a whole paragraph! I didn't see anything about this when I read the passage . . . ." Then that person might go frantically searching through the text for something that isn't there.

Of course, we know better. It's not enough for the text not to contradict an answer choice; the text must specifically say that the answer choice is correct. But a lot of people who take the ACT don't know that, and many people will choose an irrelevant answer choice because it feels "safe." Don't do that!

How To Read Passages On The ACT Reading Section

As a professional ACT tutor, I get asked a lot of questions about ACT strategy, as you might imagine. One of the most common is the question of how to read ACT Reading passages. Another popular question is how to take notes on the passages.

Let's talk about those things. My answers are pretty simple, really:

1. You can read the passage in any way you want, as long as it leaves you enough time to finish the section and mark answers with certainty. You can even skip reading the passage if you prefer, and then just refer back to portions of the text on a question-by-question basis. (We'll discuss this more below.)
2. You shouldn't take notes on the passage.

Like most good ACT advice, those two tactics contradict most of what you may have heard from teachers, tutors, and prep books, so let's explore them a little. (If you haven't already read my previous remarks on what separates right answers from wrong answers on ACT Reading questions, I'd recommend you go back and do that before proceeding.)

When I talked about correct answer choices for ACT Reading questions, I indicated that they restate elements of the relevant portion of the original text. This is necessary because ACT, Inc. needs to have an objective, legitimate reason to say that one choice is correct and the others are incorrect, and the only real way to do that is to have the correct answer be the only choice that restates the passage.

This means there are always specific words and phrases in the passage that correspond to the correct answer. It also means that, technically, the only portion of the text you would need to read for any question is the specific portion that contains the words restated in the correct answer choice for that question.

So, *in theory*, if it were somehow possible to know in advance which portions of the text were going to contain the key phrases restated in the correct answer, we could avoid reading the rest of the passage.

In other words, there's literally no benefit whatsoever in trying to get an overall impression of the passage, because there will never be a real ACT question that requires us to do that—even when a question seems to ask about broader concepts or large portions of the passage, there will always be certain specific phrases that support the correct answer.

(To be sure, there are some students who try to draw inferences from the text and still have some success, but it's not the most efficient or reliable approach, and it's never necessary. We can always find the answer for every question spelled out somewhere in the text, even when the question asks about the main idea of a paragraph or passage.)

For this reason, it doesn't really matter which specific method you use to read the text. All that matters is that you can locate the relevant portion of the text and figure out which answer choice restates it as quickly as possible, without sacrificing accuracy.

In general, there are three ways to do this, and I recommend you play around with them to see what works best for you. Again, you can mix, match, or modify these approaches as you see fit, so long as you come up with a system that lets you find the relevant portion of the text quickly enough to allow you to complete the entire section within the time limit.

The first approach is the old standard of simply reading the entire passage before attempting the questions. This is by far the most widely used approach. It can definitely work, as long as you don't read too slowly to finish the section before time is called. One note, though—if you read the passage first, don't worry about trying to understand it as an organic whole. Definitely don't take notes on it, for reasons we'll get into in a moment. Just give it a thorough once-over. You're going to have to come back to specific parts of it later to verify which answer choices are correct anyway, so just read it once and move on to the questions.

The second-most popular approach is to skip reading the passage and just move straight to the questions. Then, you start with the questions that have specific line citations. For each citation question, you go back to the relevant portion of the text, read that portion, and then consider the answer choices. When you've finished all the citation questions, you'll generally have a good idea of how the passage is structured. Then you move on to the questions with no citations. Many of those questions will mention key concepts that you'll recall from the citation questions, so you'll know where to go back in the passage and locate those portions of the text again. When a question has no citation and also doesn't refer to something that you've already read, you can simply skim the portions of the text that you haven't read yet to find the relevant key terms, and proceed accordingly.

That brings us to the third type of approach, which simply involves lightly skimming the passage before approaching the questions, in order to construct a rough mental map of where different terms and concepts appear in the passage. I want to stress that, so I'll say it again: in this type of skimming, you're just moving your eyes through the text quickly, NOT trying to understand the text, but trying to get a rough idea of where various concepts appear in the text so you can use your "roadmap" later. This way, if a question lacks a citation, you can look at the concepts in the question and in the answer choices and recall those concepts from your skimming, which allows you to zero-in on the relevant part of the text and then find your answers. Of course, you can always re-skim if you need to.

Again, it's important to be aware of these different approaches, and to be ready and willing to play around with them during your practice sessions, so you can figure out what works best for you personally. If my experience told me that one approach was best for everybody, I would recommend that approach—instead, my experience has repeatedly shown me that different students will prefer different reading approaches based on their personalities and skills.

You may be wondering why I'm opposed to the idea of taking notes on the text as well. The reason is simple, actually: taking notes involves interpreting the text, and interpreting the text isn't helpful on the ACT. As we keep discussing, the correct answer to every single question is spelled out somewhere on the page, so there's no need for you to interpret what you're reading. If all you're worried about is exactly what the text says, what's the point of taking a note? It'll either be an interpretation of the text, which we don't want, or else it will exactly restate the text, which is pointless, because then you're just copying down what the text already says.

The General Process For Answering ACT Reading Questions

Most ACT Reading questions can be answered with a fairly simple process, which we'll discuss now. Later, I'll show you how to answer other types of ACT Reading questions that might seem a bit harder—although the process we'll use for all ACT Reading questions is basically the same, with a few very minor, very occasional modifications.

For right now, let's assume that we're talking about questions with specific line citations.

1. Read or skim the passage if you want to.

There are a lot of ways to approach reading the actual passage, as we discussed earlier. Pick whichever approach works for you, whether it's one of the ones I explained or your own approach.

2. Read the question, noting the citation. Then read the citation.

Find the citation in the text that the question is referring to. Read it. If the cited line picks up in the middle of a sentence, go back up to the beginning of that sentence and start there. (It may also help to read the sentence before or after the sentences in the citation, but this often isn't necessary.)

3. Find three wrong answers.

It's generally easiest to find wrong answers first. For one thing, there are three of them in every question, as opposed to just the one right answer. For another, it's usually easier to identify ways that answer choices differ from the text than it is to feel confident that a choice says exactly the same thing as the text. Expect that most (and very possibly all) of the wrong answers you find on any one question will fit into one of the types we talked about earlier.

If you end up not being able to eliminate 3 choices, then you're making some kind of mistake. It might be that you've misread the text or the question, or didn't read enough of the surrounding text. It might be that your understanding of one of the words you read is slightly (or very) inaccurate. It's often the case that people who are left with 2 or 3 answer choices that seem to restate the text probably aren't being picky enough about sticking to exactly what each word means to ensure an accurate restatement.

If you end up eliminating all 4 answer choices from consideration, then, again, you've definitely made some kind of mistake, but it might be a different kind of mistake. You may have been referring to the wrong part of the passage, for instance. You might also have misread or misunderstood one or more words.

4. Confirm the remaining answer choice.

See if the remaining answer choice fits the right answer pattern (in other words, see if it restates concepts and relationships from the relevant portion of the text, without contradicting the text). If it does, that's great. You've found the right answer.

If you still can't identify one choice that clearly restates the passage and three choices that don't restate the passage, you should move on and come back to this question later. If you come back later and still can't come up with an answer, and/or if time is running out, you should just mark your best guess, since there's no penalty for wrong answers on the ACT—but remember that you're only guessing because you were unable to execute some part of the proper approach to ACT Reading questions, not because this question was just different somehow. It's very important that you maintain your awareness that every ACT Reading question must follow the same rules, even if you end up having to guess on some of them. (See "The General Game Plan For Attacking A Section Of The ACT On Test Day" earlier in this Black Book for more on this.)

And that's it, believe it or not—the process for ACT Reading questions typically isn't as complex as the processes for other question types can be. Take a look at the walkthroughs that begin in a few pages to see how this process can be used against real ACT Reading questions from the Red Book.

As I noted above, the simple process we just went through works on all line-citation questions exactly as described. In a broader sense, it also works on all other ACT Reading questions. But let's look at some specific, small adjustments we might make if the question isn't exactly a classic line-citation question.

What About Paragraph Citations?

Sometimes a question asks about a whole paragraph. These questions work the same way as line citation questions, except you should go ahead and read the whole paragraph. If a question asks about the "main point" of a paragraph, you want to choose the answer that describes whichever idea comes up most often in the paragraph.

What About Questions Without Citations?

When a question has no citation, very little actually changes in our approach to it. The answer to the question is still going to be spelled out somewhere in the passage, but now it might be anywhere in the passage, instead of being near a specific line mentioned in the question.

Let me say that again: even though there's no specific citation, the answer is still going to be spelled out somewhere. You should NOT try to answer a question like this by making a broad inference from the overall passage that isn't directly supported by actual phrases from the text.

The only challenging thing that separates a question like this from a question with a citation is that it can sometimes be harder to locate the part of the text with the answer—but *there is still a part of the text that spells out the answer.*

I'd recommend saving any general questions for last. In other words, I would skip around and do all the citation questions first, then come back and pick up the more general questions. I do this because answering the citation questions will typically cause me to go back through a lot of the text, and I'll often find that the answers to general, non-citation questions are right there in the citations for other questions. That way, I can save some time and energy by doing the citation questions first.

Even if answering the citation questions doesn't actually cause me to read the part of the text that contains the answer to a general question, I still haven't lost any time—I've just failed to *save* some extra time, that's all. Plus, it's still helpful to know that the answer to the general question isn't in the citations for the other questions, because I know I don't need to re-read or skim those areas of the text when I go back through to try to find the answers.

Sometimes the question will contain a citation of sorts, even if it's not a line citation or a paragraph citation. Question 7 on page 181 of your copy of *The Real ACT Prep Guide, 3rd Edition* asks about Fran's feelings "when she hands her mother the letter from Linda Rose." Even though it doesn't say which line this happens on, we know that this question is asking about a certain moment in the text, and if we've already answered some other questions and read some pieces of the passage then we might be able to use this detail to find the relevant text pretty quickly.

Again, the critical thing to remember with questions that lack citations is that the answer is always clearly spelled out in black and white somewhere within the passage, even though the question lacks a citation. There is literally never a moment on a real ACT in which the only way to answer a Reading question is to draw a general inference from the overall "feeling" of the text. If there were any questions that required those kinds of inferences, the reliability of the test would disappear.

What About Main Idea Questions?

Even though questions that ask about the main idea of a paragraph or passage don't provide specific line citations, we'll still find that the correct answer restates something directly from the relevant part of the text. It's just that we might have a harder time finding that restatement, since the paragraph or passage that we're asked about might be kind of long.

For that reason, I'll often save main idea questions until I've answered all the citation questions for a passage, especially if the main idea question is asking about a large stretch of text.

There's one other thing we need to know about main idea questions on the ACT, and it's pretty important, so pay attention: on these questions, we'll sometimes find TWO answer choices that reflect something in the text!

When that happens, the correct answer will be the one that appears more frequently.

For an example, let's check out question 4 on page 181 of the Red Book. It asks about the main idea of the first paragraph of the text. We see that choices (F) and (J) both include ideas that are directly in the text. (F) is reflected when Fran calls Linda Rose a "homing pigeon" and a "human boomerang" who Fran "knew would make a U-turn," all of which indicates that Fran expected Linda Rose to come back into her life. Fran also says she "was not surprised" to hear from Linda Rose, all in the first paragraph. (J), on the other hand, is only reflected in the last line of the paragraph.

In these situations, we know the ACT rewards the answer choice that appears in the text more frequently. That means (F) will be the correct answer, because the idea of Fran knowing that Linda Rose will contact her one way or another is mentioned multiple times, while the idea of the two women having similar handwriting is only mentioned once.

What About "EXCEPT" Questions?

Some questions take the normal question-answering process and turn it on its head, often by using the word "EXCEPT" or "NOT" in all capital letters. Such a question might say something like "all of the following are found in the passage EXCEPT . . ." For a question like this, we're still going to read the relevant portion of the text carefully, but now the correct answer is going to be the only choice that does NOT appear in the passage.

It's always important to make sure you read all four answer choices for every question (it helps you catch mistakes). It's ESPECIALLY important on these "EXCEPT" questions, because students often accidentally forget about the word "EXCEPT" and just choose the first answer choice they see that appears in the text—and they get the question wrong as a result. If you accidentally overlook the word "EXCEPT" but still read all four answer choices, you'll have a better chance of noticing your mistake, because you might notice that more than one answer choice seems to be right. That should make you re-evaluate the situation.

What About "Vocabulary In Context" Questions?

Some questions ask you how a word is used in the passage. They often read something like this: "As it is used in line 14, the word 'sad' means . . ."

For these questions, just like for all the others, we're ultimately looking for an answer choice that restates something from the passage—and not just one that restates the original word in the question, because several of the choices will probably do that in one sense or another. Instead, we need a word that restates an idea from the surrounding text. In the imaginary question above, if the text said, "The crumbling old warehouse was in a sad state by the time the inspector closed it for safety reasons," then the correct answer would be something like "worn out," because "worn out" means the same thing as "crumbling" in this context, and the warehouse that's "crumbling" is also described as "sad." You'll see examples of this concept in this Black Book's walkthroughs for this section of the ACT.

Walkthroughs: The ACT Reading Process In Action Against Real Questions

The best way to learn to use the ACT Reading strategies we've talked about is to see them in action against real ACT practice questions. I really can't stress enough how important it is for you to go through these walkthroughs and learn the process firsthand.

In order to do that, you'll need to follow along in your copy of *The Real ACT Prep Guide, 3rd Edition*. If you still haven't gotten your hands on a copy of that book, well, do it! The book contains five real ACT practice tests, and real practice tests are an essential element of your training.

We'll be looking at a selection of real questions from the practice tests in that book. These questions were selected for one or both of the following reasons:

- They're the questions I'm most often asked about when I work with students one-on-one.
- They're particularly effective at illustrating some of the concepts we talked about in the training.

(If you'd like to see some video demonstrations of these ideas, go to www.ACTprepVideos.com for a selection of demonstration videos that are free to readers of this book.)

Page 181, Question 4

This question asks about the "main point" of the first paragraph. A lot of students struggle with the idea of finding the "main point" of a passage on the ACT, because the phrase "main point" feels like it's open to some interpretation. But, as trained test-takers, we know that any correct answer to a "main point" question on the ACT must directly restate a phrase from the text; if more than one answer choice does this, then the correct answer choice will be the one that appears most frequently in the text.

With that in mind, let's take a look at the answer choices in this question to see which one is correct.

(F) looks like the correct answer. The narrator in the text, who is Fran, says repeatedly that she "knew" that a particular person would come back into her life (lines 2 and 3), and that she "was not surprised" to receive the letter (line 6). She describes this person as a "homing pigeon" and a "human boomerang" (lines 3 and 5). Later in the passage, in line 40, we find out that the person who wrote the letter, and the person referred to as "she" in the first paragraph, Is Linda Rose. Remember that the ACT sometimes requires us to combine information from two different areas of the passage, so it can often be helpful to have a general awareness of the concepts that appear throughout the entire text. (Of course, the correct answer to an ACT Reading question will always refer to some specific combination of words and phrases directly from the text.)

So (F) looks like it could be the correct answer choice at first blush—it appears in the first paragraph, and it's mentioned repeatedly. But, as trained test-takers, we know that we always have to read all of the answer choices for each question, to make sure we haven't made a mistake somewhere.

(G) will definitely be tempting to some test-takers who don't read carefully, because the paragraph does contain the phrase "wild little bird." But if we read carefully, we see that the paragraph actually says that Fran's mother *always thought of [Linda Rose]* as some wild little bird. [emphasis mine]" So the paragraph doesn't say anything about how Linda Rose acted; it only says how the mother thought of her. In fact, if we read the rest of the passage, we know that Fran gave up Linda Rose when Linda Rose was only a "baby girl" (lines 69-70), so neither Fran nor her mother would really have known Linda Rose "when she was young."

But we don't specifically need to be aware that Fran gave Linda Rose away when Linda Rose was a baby. All we really need to do is keep in mind that it's very important to read carefully, and then to notice the difference between how Mother "thought of" Linda Rose (lines 1 and 2), and how Linda Rose acted when she was young. That's enough for us to realize that this choice doesn't restate the passage exactly, so it must be wrong.

(H) is the exact opposite of what the text says. In line 6, Fran says she was "not surprised" when she received the letter. Be very careful of this kind of wrong answer! If you read carefully, you'll typically be able to notice when a wrong answer is an exact contradiction of the text. But if you don't read carefully, you can easily fall for a choice like this.

(J) does actually directly restate something from the end of the first paragraph. But, as trained test-takers, we know that it sometimes happens that a "main idea" question has two answer choices that restate some portion of the text. When that situation arises, we know that the correct answer will be the one that appears more frequently in the relevant text. The idea that Fran believed that Linda Rose would come back into her life is mentioned several times in the paragraph ("homing pigeon," "U-turn," "human boomerang"), but the idea of their handwriting being similar is only mentioned once.

This question provides a great example of a situation in which an untrained test-taker could easily fall for a wrong answer, or at least spend a lot of time debating between choices (F) and (J). But, once we know the rules of the test, we can say with certainty that the correct answer choice is (F), because it restates the idea that appears most frequently in the relevant text.

Note that the ACT's own explanation of this question on page 260 of the Red Book uses the subjective idea of something being a "main point" or a "supporting" "detail." This is a good example of the way the Red Book's own solutions to its questions don't give away the fundamental design of the test, as I've said many times before and will say many times again. The writers of the Red Book may use subjective terminology when providing their explanations for the masses, but trained test-takers like us know that there's always an objective, black-and-white explanation for each correct answer to a real ACT question—otherwise, the test would be useless for colleges. Keep this in mind at all times.

Page 181, Question 7

This question is another one that an untrained test-taker would probably have a very hard time with. It's also another example of a question whose official solution in the Red Book is a little misleading to the average person.

If we look at the text, we can see that Fran hands her mother the letter at line 55. The text immediately after the sentence that describes Fran handing her mother the letter says that the letter was "short" and "businesslike," but that Fran knows there are also "long letters [Linda Rose] must have written and crumpled into the wastebasket" (lines 57 and 58). Let's look at the answer choices.

(A) is the wrong answer that most people will choose if they miss this question, from my experience. The statement in this choice seems like a reasonable assumption, because most people could probably understand feeling disappointed by getting a short letter from someone after so much time. But our assumptions don't mean anything on the ACT! Nothing in the text actually *says* that Fran was disappointed in the letter's length, so this choice is incorrect.

(B) would be another reasonable assumption to many readers, and it's also incorrect on the ACT because it isn't actually stated on the page. Fran has just heard about the birth of her grandson, which most people would consider "good news." And the text even mentions "good news" in the first paragraph, when Fran describes painting her mailbox yellow. But the text never specifically says that Fran considers Blake's birth to be good news—nor does it say that she thinks the birth is bad news, neutral news, or any other kind of news. The text doesn't restate the idea in this choice, so this choice is wrong—even if it seems like a reasonable inference.

(C) is yet another reasonable assumption that turns out to be a wrong answer on the ACT. The text does describe the letter as "businesslike," but it never says anything about the letter being "cold," "icy," "distant," or any other word like that. The text also never mentions the idea that Fran is offended. (Some might argue that the text says Fran is generally upset in lines 63 through 73, but being upset isn't always the same thing as being offended—and, anyway, those lines don't say Fran is upset because the letter is "businesslike" or "cold." She's upset in those lines because she's just found out she's a grandmother without any prior warning.)

(D) is correct, because the text says that Fran could "see" all of the "long letters [Linda Rose] must have written and crumpled in the wastebasket" before she completed the letter that she mailed to Fran. Those "long letters" "crumpled in the wastebasket" whose "ghosts" are visible to Fran can only be previous drafts of the letter Fran is holding, so choice (D) directly supports the way Fran's thoughts are described in the paragraph that mentions her handing the letter to her mother.

Note that the Red Book's explanation for this question, which appears on page 261, repeatedly says that Fran feels "sympathy" for Linda Rose. *The text doesn't actually say that, though*—it only says that Fran is aware how much effort must have been involved, not that Fran feels sorry for Linda Rose, or that she feels the same way Linda Rose feels, which is what the word "sympathy" would require. It's important to be on the lookout for those kinds of distinctions, and this is one more example of the way we can be misled if we take the Red Book's solutions too much to heart.

Page 181, Question 8

This question will mislead a lot of test-takers because it asks us to infer something, but the key to the correct answer is actually spelled out on the page, as always. No inference is necessary.

(F) is irrelevant to the text, so it's wrong. There is nothing to indicate that Linda Rose left home to get married. Beyond that, in line 91 Fran specifically says that Linda Rose "didn't mention any husband at all," so there's no reason whatsoever to think that Linda Rose left home to get married, or even that she ever was married.

(G) is not supported by the text either—there is no mention of any argument between Fran and Linda Rose.

(H) is also not supported by the text—Linda Rose's father is never mentioned anywhere in the text.

(J) is the only answer choice supported by the text, which means it's correct. Fran specifically describes Linda Rose as "a baby girl" that Fran "gave up 24 years ago" in lines 69 and 70. That's all we need to read to be sure that (J) is correct, but the text also alludes to Mother wanting "to keep her," and includes Fran telling Mother her child's name. This indicates that Fran didn't already know her own daughter's name. There are plenty of other indications that Linda Rose was given up for adoption as well.

Let this question serve as one more reminder that we'll always find the correct answer spelled out on the page somewhere, even when the question includes a word like "Inferred!"

Page 182, Question 11

This is a challenging first question about the passage because it asks us about "one of the main points . . . in the passage." If you've read or skimmed the whole passage before looking at this question, then you may feel like you have enough of an idea of the passage's message to attack this question right away. On the other hand, if you prefer not to read the passage before tackling the questions, then you might decide to skip this question for now, try to answer some of the other questions that deal with smaller portions of the text, and then return to this question after you've got your bearings a little more. Either approach can work, depending on your personal inclination.

When you deal with a "main point" question, you have to remember that it's sometimes possible for there to be more than one answer choice that restates an idea from the text. If that happens, then the correct answer will be the one that restates the idea that appears most often.

Now, let's look at each answer choice in turn, and see what we come up with.

(A) is incorrect. The author does mention the idea that people can't understand government, and he does mention the idea of newspapers and television, but he never connects those ideas by saying that people are unable to understand government *because* they read *too many* newspapers or watch *too much* television. Lots of people mistakenly pick this choice because they know it's vaguely related to concepts they remember from the passage, but, as trained test-takers, we have to remember to pay attention to small details, and to look out for wrong answers that try to confuse us by jumbling together some ideas from the passage. This is also an example of a wrong answer that might seem like a decent interpretation of the text, but that doesn't matter on the ACT. What matters on the ACT is that the correct answer is directly restated in the text, and this answer choice doesn't meet that standard. So it's wrong.

(B) is correct. The idea that Americans have difficulty improving government because they don't understand the details appears multiple times in the text, most directly in the last sentence of the fourth paragraph (lines 58-61). In that sentence, the author says that "voters are unable" to tell "the rascals [politicians] how to do their jobs better," and the reason for this is that the voters themselves "don't understand the technical questions" of government. Notice how the phrase "do not understand the technical questions" in line 60 matches up with the phrase "do not understand the important details" in the answer choice, just as the phrase about getting the rascals to "do their jobs better" in the text matches up with the phrase "improving government" in the answer choice. (Just to be clear, the word "rascals" in the text must refer to politicians, because the rascals are people that can be selected or rejected for their jobs by voters, and the only people in that position are politicians, by definition.)

Notice that the Red Book's explanation for this question on page 263 is a bit misleading. It refers to a list of other quotations from the text that kind of go along with the idea of the correct answer, but don't actually restate it. The Red Book explanation talks about how the text describes voters as people who don't care very much about government, but those phrases aren't actually directly relevant to the correct answer, and you shouldn't rely on them when you answer this question. Being disinterested in something is different from being unable to understand it. (B) is correct because of sentences like the one we identified in lines 58-61, not because of sentences about voters being apathetic. I want to make sure this is clear to you, because the only way to proceed on the ACT with full confidence and accuracy is to insist on answer choices that restate ideas from the text, not on answer choices that kind of go along with ideas in the text.

(C) is wrong because it contradicts the text, which specifically states in lines 58-61 that "voters are unable to . . . tell [politicians] how to do their jobs better." Further, the author also mentions in lines 79-84 that the idea that "elected officials" are "democratically responsive" is "largely a myth." The text does draw a distinction between elected officials and bureaucrats in lines 74 through 76, but it doesn't say that the elected officials are any more responsive than the unelected ones. Remember, as always, how important it is to read everything carefully on the ACT!

(D) is wrong for several reasons, even though it might seem like it would be a reasonable inference to draw in a classroom discussion. For one thing, the text never actually says that government used to be more responsive, even though it does mention in the second and third paragraph that levels of political activity have changed. Those paragraphs describe things like the Lincoln-Douglas debates, but they never actually say that politicians were more responsive to voters—they only say that more voters used to listen to political speeches and debates, and that they used to be longer than forty-five seconds. Another problem with (D) is that the entertainment aspect of television is only mentioned in lines 51-53, which say that television does not "intend to lose [its] primary value as entertainment." This is not the same thing as saying that television has cut back on the news in order to offer more entertainment; instead, it's a statement that television's main reason for existence is entertainment, with no mention of a changing role for the news at all. These might seem like trivially small distinctions—in fact, most high school and college English teachers would have no problem if you offered a statement like choice (D) as a summary of this text during a classroom discussion. But we know that the ACT is a lot more demanding than high school or college English classes when it comes to noticing small details, and these kinds of differences between the text and an answer choice will always indicate a wrong answer on the ACT.

As it turns out, this was a "main point" question where only one answer choice restated an idea from the passage exactly. Notice, though, how easy it would be to misread a couple of key phrases in the answer choices or the passage, and end up missing the question for no real reason!

Page 183, Question 12

The answer choices for this question follow a very common pattern on the ACT. The four choices essentially mix-and-match the elements of being inexperienced, experienced, educated, uneducated, and young; the ACT does this because it wants to trick test-takers who don't pay very careful attention to the text.

So we need to find the relevant text, and then read it very carefully to see which answer choice matches it exactly.

The relevant part of the text starts on line 32 and continues to the end of the third paragraph. We can tell that this is the relevant part of the text because we see words like "reporter," "journalism school," and "inexperienced," which all relate to the concepts in the answer choices for this question.

So now we read carefully and see what's going on.

The first word we see in choice (F) is "inexperienced." We'll notice in the text that the first word the author uses to describe this person from the newspaper is exactly the same: "inexperienced" (line 34). (If you're reading very carefully, you may notice that the sentence in line 34 refers to a journalism school graduate, but a graduate of journalism school is not necessarily a reporter. Notice, though, that the author calls this same type of person a "reporter" in line 39.)

So the first parts of (F) and (G) work, since they use the exact same word that the text uses. We also see that (H) is wrong, because "experienced" directly contradicts the word "inexperienced" from the text. This is an example of the ACT trying to confuse you by offering an answer choice that is the exact opposite of what the text says.

The next part of choice (F) says "insufficiently educated." If we go back to the second half of paragraph three, we'll see that the author talks about how the reporter has never taken "advanced algebra, to say nothing of calculus."

That means the author specifically points out that the reporter's education didn't include certain classes, and that, as a result, it's hard for the reporter to understand the "program budget." That directly corresponds to the idea of being "insufficiently educated." Since both parts of choice (F) are directly reflected in the text, we know that (F) is the correct answer.

Of course, we'll need to check out the other choices to make sure we haven't made a mistake.

Choices (G) and (J) both say that the reporter is "well educated," but we know from the text that the author disagrees with this idea, for the reasons we just saw.

Note that many test-takers would see the references to the reporter being a "graduate" of "journalism school" and conclude that the reporter must be well educated. This might seem like a reasonable assumption if we were allowed to interpret the text on our own—but we aren't allowed to interpret the text on our own! We have to look at the author's words and figure out what the author thinks of journalism school graduates, and the author says that people who go to journalism school don't take advanced algebra or calculus, which makes it hard for them to understand the idea of "solving a grand equation" (lines 37 and 38).

Page 183, Question 13

The "description of the tax seminar" referred to in the question takes place in the fifth paragraph. The first sentence of that paragraph says that "government is so technical that even career civil servants cannot explain what is happening." This matches up almost exactly with choice (A), so (A) is the correct answer.

Choice (B), in contrast, says that *only* civil servants can understand it, which is obviously wrong, since the text specifically says that they can't. But a lot of test-takers who don't read very carefully will assume that people who work in the government must be able to understand it, so they'll choose (B) and get the question wrong.

(C) might be tempting to some test-takers, because (like the text) it mentions the Tax Reform Act, and it seems to go along with the general feeling in the text that issues related to government are getting more technical and difficult to understand. But nothing in the description of the tax seminar indicates that the Tax Reform Act has made things *more* technical *than they used to be*; instead, the text simply mentions that some IRS lawyers don't understand that particular act, as an example. There's no specific mention of things being less technical before the act, so we can't assume that they were.

(D) is similar to (B) in that it also claims that only a certain type of tax expert at the seminar could understand these technical issues, when in fact the text specifically says (lines 66-68) that they didn't understand an important technical issue.

There are probably two primary ways that the ACT is hoping to catch you with this question. First, it's easy to get mixed up on whether *only* a certain group of people can do something, or *not even* that group can do something, especially when the test-taker is trying to scan through the section quickly. Both (B) and (D) directly contradict the text in this way, and a test-taker could easily read either of those choices, see several ideas from the text, and get the details wrong.

The other way the ACT might catch you here is that (B) and (D) contain reasonable assumptions. Someone who didn't read the text carefully could easily come to the conclusion that *only* a "career civil servant" or "Internal Revenue Service tax lawyer" might understand the technical aspects of government, which makes either of those choices appealing. But we always have to remember that our own assumptions are irrelevant. The ACT will reward the statements that are directly restated in the passage, and choice (A) comes almost word-for-word out of the relevant text.

Page 183, Question 14

This question tries to mislead us by asking what the author "most likely" means. But we have to remember that the correct answer will still be the only choice that's directly stated in the text. Let's take a look.

(F) restates an idea that's repeated throughout the text, which makes it the correct answer. The relevant idea is stated in lines 78-79, when the author says that people "know little and care less about the technical functioning of their government." Notice how this idea of not caring in the text directly reflects the idea of being "not concerned" in the answer choice, and notice how the phrase "technical functioning of their government" restates the idea of "technical, but important, details of government" from the answer choice. There are many other places in the text that restate this idea as well, but we only need to find one of them to know we have the right answer.

(G) is incorrect. Many test-takers will be tempted by this choice because it mentions the same "myth" that the text mentions in line 84. But, unlike the text, (G) says that citizens are "completely taken in" by that myth. Remember that it's not enough for an answer choice just to mention something from the text! Everything in the correct answer must be echoed in the text. The text never mentions whether voters are "completely taken in" by this myth, or partially taken in, or not taken in at all, so this phrase is unsupported by the text, and (G) is wrong.

(H) is wrong because nothing in the text talks about citizens being responsive to officials or bureaucrats—the idea of officials or bureaucrats being "democratically responsive" to voters comes up in lines 83 and 84, but this answer choice tries to trick you by reversing the relationship in the text. The text discusses the concept of public officials being responsive, but this choice talks about citizens being responsive.

(J), like (G), mentions a concept from the text, but adds irrelevant details that aren't found in the text. In lines 81 through 85, the text mentions the idea of a government being legitimate because it was elected democratically. But (J) says that citizens are "not prepared to concede legitimacy to a government unless it is democratically elected." The text never actually says anything about democratic elections being a *necessary* element for voters to concede legitimacy, so the word "unless" in the answer choice is unwarranted. As trained test-takers, we know that an idea that isn't addressed in the text can't be part of a right answer.

Notice, once more, that the correct answer is the only one that's fully supported by the text, even though the prompt of the question deliberately includes the misleading phrase "most likely." Remember that those phrases should always be ignored, and we should always look for the answer choice that directly restates the text!

Page 185, Question 22

This question tells you to look at lines 1-33, and then asks you which answer choice accurately describes the author's girlhood and early adulthood. This is a great example of how the ACT looks much more closely at the details of a text than almost any high school English teacher does.

If you don't recall which parts of the text mention the various locations in the answer choices, or if you haven't read or skimmed the full text before attempting this question, then it might help to skim the text and look for the capital letters in key words from the answer choices, like "Calcutta," "United States," "England," "Irish," "Manhattan," "Bangladesh," and "Faridpur."

Now let's take a look.

(F) says the author grew up and was educated in Calcutta. We can see that Calcutta is mentioned in lines 3 through 5, where it says the author "attended a school . . . in Calcutta." That looks good so far. Then (F) says she moved to the United States. Line 26 mentions the United States, and says, "I have found my way to the United States . . ." So this answer choice still looks good. Finally, (F) says she lived in Manhattan; we see Manhattan mentioned in line 28, and referred to as the author's "'desh,'" which means "country" according to line 6. So choice (F) is correct, because every part of it matches up with the text.

Now let's look at the other choices. (Remember that you always have to give equal consideration to every answer choice on the test, instead of just deciding you like one choice and not even really reading the others. This way, you'll have a better chance of catching any mistakes you might have made.)

The biggest problem with (G) is that it says the author was educated in England by Irish nuns. The text actually says, in lines 3-5, that the Irish nuns at her school "regarded our walled-off school compound in Calcutta as a corner of England," which means that the compound itself was in Calcutta, but the nuns treated it like it was England. So (G) must be wrong.

(H) says the author was raised in Bangladesh, which isn't mentioned in the text. In fact, lines 5 through 8 describe a place in Bangladesh that the author has "never seen." This answer choice also mentions moving to England at one point, which isn't supported by the text; as we just saw, the only mention of England in the passage has to do with the nuns in Calcutta.

(J) says the author was born in Faridpur, but lines 5 through 10 refer to Faridpur as the birthplace of the author's father, and as a place that the author has "never seen." The author also refers to Faridpur as "unglimpsed" in line 27, which literally means that the author has never seen it. Even if we ignore those phrases, the text doesn't specifically say the author was born in Faridpur, which would still be enough to make (J) wrong.

Notice, once more, how an untrained test-taker could easily miss this question if he didn't read carefully enough. Remember that the ACT requires us to pay constant attention to small details!

Page 185, Question 25

There are two reasons I think it's important for us to discuss this particular question.

The first is that it asks *why* the author refers to Faridpur as a "phantom" in line 27. This type of question annoys a lot of people, because it seems to be asking you to read the author's mind and figure out her motivation for choosing a particular word, which seems unfairly subjective. But, as trained test-takers, we have to know that the answer to this question, like the answer to every ACT Reading question, is somewhere directly on the page and requires no subjectivity at all, no matter how the question is phrased.

The second reason is perhaps even more important: part of the ACT's own explanation for this question is at least incomplete and misleading, and arguably *wrong*. (Remember that when I say that a question explanation from the ACT is "wrong," what I mean is that the logic it follows won't always lead you to find correct answers on future ACT questions. In other words, such an explanation can't reflect the actual reasoning of the test, because the test is standardized and the Red Book's explanation wouldn't always lead to correct answers.) I'll explain more about why the ACT's explanation is bad after we take a look at each of the answer choices.

(A) is wrong because the text never makes any connection between Faridpur and the author's mother. This is an example of the type of wrong answer that jumbles ideas from the text (the author's mother's tales are referred to in lines 63 through 73).

(B) is wrong because lines 5 through 6 explain that "desh" means the author's "country," and in lines 27 and 28 she explains that Faridpur and Manhattan have merged together to become her "desh." In other words, the author's "desh," or "country," includes both places, not just Manhattan. You can probably imagine how easily a lot of test-takers could misread the text and accidentally choose this answer!

(C) is wrong, too. The text does say, in lines 7 and 8, that Faridpur "is now in Bangladesh." But the text never says that Faridpur was once a part of India. Remember that we always have to find supporting text for every part of an answer choice, not just for most of it! (By the way, if you really know your Bengali history, you might know that Faridpur was once part of the same political entity as the nation now called India, and you might be tempted to choose this answer because it seems factually accurate. Remember, though, that factual accuracy is irrelevant on the ACT Reading test! All that matters is what the author actually says, and the author never specifically says that Faridpur was ever a part of India.)

(D) is correct, but we may have to read very carefully to see why. The text mentions that Faridpur is the "ancestral home" of the author's father in line 7. But the answer choice says Faridpur is the ancestral home of the author herself. You may be wondering why this is okay, when I keep emphasizing repeatedly that we have to pay very careful attention to such small differences. The reason this is okay has to do with the meaning of the phrase "ancestral homeland." A person's "ancestors" are the people in her lineage—her parents, grandparents, great-grandparents, and so on. So, by definition, the "ancestral homeland" of the author's father must also be the author's ancestral homeland, because the author's father is one of the author's ancestors. The second half of the answer choice—which says that the author has never been to Faridpur—is restated when the text calls Faridpur a place she has "never seen" In line 6. This idea is restated in line 27, when the author says Faridpur is "unglimpsed."

Now let's talk about why the ACT's explanation on page 268 of the Red Book is bad. The ACT claims that (C) is wrong simply because "this isn't why she refers to Faridpur as a 'phantom'." In other words, the ACT's explanation just subjectively asserts that (C) is a true statement, but it's the wrong true statement, and a test-taker is magically supposed to know that. As we've discussed many times, though, this kind of explanation is never really the reason why an answer on the ACT is correct, even though we may be tempted to assume it is if we get frustrated with a particular question.

As I mentioned above, the actual reasoning behind (C) being a wrong answer—the objective reasoning that will continue to apply to all future official ACT questions, with no subjective interpretation necessary on our part—is that the text never actually says that Faridpur "was once part of India," as the answer choice claims. The text does say that the author thinks she "'belongs'" to Faridpur, and it does say that India is "the larger political entity to which [she] gave [her] first allegiance (lines 10 - 11)," but that doesn't mean by itself that Faridpur used to be a part of India. As a parallel example, I might say that I feel I belong to Ireland because it's my ancestral homeland, but that I gave my first political allegiance to the larger entity of the United States—both statements are true, but they don't necessarily mean that Ireland was ever part of the United States. So the historical fact that Faridpur was once part of India isn't actually directly expressed anywhere in the text.

So let me say it one more time, to be perfectly clear: (C) is wrong because the first part of that choice isn't found anywhere at all in the text. Also, the ACT's explanation of (C) on page 268 is (at least) misleading, because it makes it sound like you just have to guess that (C) is wrong for subjective reasons, which is something the ACT can never require us to do.

Let this be one more reminder of the importance of understanding how the ACT actually works, and of taking the Red Book's explanations with a grain of salt!

Page 185, Question 28

This is one more question for which the Red Book's own explanation is incomplete. Let's take a look.

(F) is wrong because it's not supported by the text. For one thing, the answer choice mentions cultural differences "among characters," while the text only talks about cultural differences between the characters and the audience, or between the author and the audience, but not among the characters themselves.

(G) is correct, but not exactly for the reasons that the Red Book gives on page 269. The Red Book says (G) is correct because the readers "never knew" that people from other cultures had an "inner life." This is partially correct reasoning, because the phrase "I never knew" in the text goes with the idea of not having realized something in the answer choice.

But the text never actually says that having an "inner life" means having something in common with the author's readers—the text never says that the readers have inner lives of their own, only that the readers are surprised at the inner lives of the characters. So the line in the text about the "inner life" isn't enough, by itself, to make (G) the correct answer. To find the part of the text where the author says that her readers have something in common with her characters, we have to look in the fourth paragraph, where the author says she struggles to "make the American readership . . . acknowledge [that] . . . the foreign-born . . . with non-European languages and appearance, can be . . . American." In that paragraph, the author specifically says that her writing makes American readers realize that people from non-European backgrounds can be American like them, and this is what the answer choice is referring to when it says the readers and the characters have "much more in common" than the readers realized. (Notice how the "non-European" people referred to in the fourth paragraph are the same people the author refers to in lines 52 and 53.)

(H) is incorrect because the text never says anything about the number of characters in any kind of story. This is a good example of an answer choice that's completely irrelevant, which is the sort of thing that might make you second-guess yourself and wonder if you missed something in the text.

(J) is incorrect. The text does mention the "inner life" of immigrants, but it never says their "inner life" is "stronger" than anyone else's. Watch out for answer choices like this, which take a fact from the text and then add a little extra information that isn't from the text!

As we've already seen many times, and as we'll continue to see throughout this Black Book, you have to be very careful with the solutions found in the Red Book, because they don't always fully explain the test's reasoning.

When you review a question, make sure you come up with solutions that require no subjectivity, and that use reasoning that could be applied to all real ACT questions. Then you'll know that you truly understand the test, and that you'll be able to find the correct answers to future ACT questions reliably.

Page 186, Question 31

This question asks us about the meaning of a certain phrase in the context of the passage. Notice that the question uses terms like "infer" and "most reasonable" to get you to think there's something subjective about the correct answer, when of course we know that there can't be anything subjective about an ACT Reading question. As always, only one choice will actually make sense in the context of the passage if we pay careful attention to detail and look for the answer choice that restates elements of the text.

(A) is wrong, even though it sounds like a reasonable inference if you only read lines 16 through 18 and don't read the rest of the passage. The quote might sound like it could be describing the evolution of a dinosaur, but the passage clearly indicates that we're talking about the evolution of the way researchers *think about* dinosaurs. Note, for instance, that lines 14 and 15 talk about the ways that "most paleontologists are now willing to view [dinosaurs]."

But if we read carefully, we can tell that the quote in lines 16 through 18 can't be about the evolution of dinosaurs anyway, even if we don't look at any other lines. The quote begins by referring to "the *Brontosaurus* that wallowed in its pond a generation ago," which doesn't actually make any literal sense, since actual dinosaurs have been extinct for millennia. So the sentence must not refer to dinosaurs evolving over the course of a single generation, because there were no dinosaurs one generation before the text was written, and the passage is talking about how *Brontosaurus* was "a generation ago."

Remember that it's always important to read everything on the ACT very carefully!

(B) is correct, because of the things we just discussed about choice (A). The passage clearly discusses changes in the way "most paleontologists are willing to view [dinosaurs]" (lines 14 - 15). Also notice how the phrase "within the last generation" in this answer choice matches up with the phrase "a generation ago" from the quote in the question.

(C) is wrong for a variety of reasons. The most obvious issue is probably that this answer choice mentions illustrations "inaccurately depict[ing]" dinosaurs' lifestyles, but the text doesn't actually try to describe what those lifestyles were like. Everything discussed in the text with regard to the Brontosaurus is theoretical, because the Brontosaurus is extinct. Several phrases from the text indicate that the author isn't claiming to know for certain what dinosaurs were really like; he's only explaining which view he agrees with. (See, for example, "have usually been reconstructed," in line 9; "many paleontologists now believe," in lines 22 and 23; "I regard it as," in lines 27 and 28; and "the revisionist interpretation, which I support," in lines 29-30.)

(D) is also wrong because it's not supported by the text. Again, nothing in the text discusses changes in the actual behavior or abilities of *Brontosaurus*. Instead, the text only discusses the change in the way researchers see the animal, as we discussed in the explanations for choices (A) and (B).

Remember, as always, that every correct answer to an ACT Reading question must be fully supported by the text, even if the prompt uses misleading phrases like "most reasonable to infer."

Page 187, Question 35

I singled out this question for discussion because of the relationships we can find among the answer choices here. Note that three of the four choices discuss the relative brain sizes of dinosaurs and humans. This type of pattern often strongly suggests two things on the ACT:

1. The correct answer will probably be one of the three choices that focus on brain size, because the ACT typically only chooses to repeat an idea in a lot of answer choices when the idea is related to the correct answer.
2. We'll probably need to read really carefully to make sure we don't accidentally misunderstand the passage and fall for a wrong answer, since the wrong answers will have a lot of similarities to the right answer.

When we look back at the fourth paragraph, which specifically describes "the revisionist interpretation" in lines 29 and 30, we see that lines 28 and 29 mention "the issue of stupidity and its correlation with size." So we can see that we've found the relevant part of the text for this question because the question mentions "the revisionist interpretation" and the "relationship between intelligence and physical size," just as this part of the text does.

The end of this paragraph, lines 31-33, says that the revisionist interpretation "does maintain that [dinosaurs] . . . had the 'right-sized' brains for reptiles of their body size." This matches up directly with the correct answer, (D), which says that the brains are "appropriately sized."

(A) is wrong because nothing related to the revisionist interpretation in the text actually says dinosaurs had relatively large brains, even if the theory does say dinosaurs "were not small-brained at all" (line 32). Many people who don't read carefully might accidentally equate the idea of not being "small-brained" with the idea of being "large-brained," but these ideas aren't exactly the same, because it's possible to have a brain that's "right-sized," according to the author (line 33).

(B) is the exact opposite of the text, which says on lines 30 and 31 that the author's view "does not enshrine dinosaurs as paragons of intellect." (Notice that we don't need to know what the word "paragon" actually means here—we just have to read the text and match up related phrases.)

(C) is an idea that's mentioned elsewhere in the text, but this paragraph about the revisionist interpretation is specifically arguing against the idea of dinosaurs being small-brained. A lot of test-takers will incorrectly choose this answer if they only have a vague sense of what the passage says, or if they happen to be familiar with the traditional view that dinosaurs have small brains.

Remember that all of our answers must be directly supported by the text, and remember that details can make all the difference, especially when the answer choices are so similar to one another!

Page 187, Question 39

This question simply asks us directly for a fact from the passage, and if we've already read the appropriate text for question 34, we should know to look back at the eighth paragraph where lines 74 and 75 say that dinosaurs "dominated the earth for so long" and "held sway for 100 million years." We can see right away that choice (D) must be correct. Choices (B) and (C) mention numbers that appear in lines 82 and 77, respectively. Choice (A) doesn't appear in the text, but it kind of sounds similar to the correct answer; this choice is probably included to trick people who don't bother to go back and re-confirm that the right number is one hundred million instead of one hundred thousand.

Now, this might seem like a fairly obvious question that's not really worth explaining. But I'm including it here because people actually do miss this question fairly often if they're not in the habit of reading very carefully at all times while taking the ACT. Remember that you really can't afford to make careless errors on questions like this! Most test-takers could hit their target scores if they would just eliminate these kinds of mistakes, and all it takes to do that is awareness and commitment on your part.

Page 321, Question 1

I singled out this question for discussion because it's one that a lot of people miss unnecessarily. If we just read carefully and pay attention to the details—like we always need to do on the ACT—we can figure out the answer.

One thing I would notice pretty quickly is that the first two answer choices refer to the narrator as an adult, while the last two refer to her as an adolescent. This means that the text must clearly indicate whether she's an adult or an adolescent. Since figuring that out will allow me to eliminate two answer choices in one shot, I'd probably start there.

At this point, I'd probably skim through the passage and look for words like "adult" or "adolescent," or any other reference to age. I would see that the word "adolescent" appears in line 57 and doesn't seem to show up anywhere else, so I'd probably start by focusing there.

That sentence talks about the author having to "forgo the luxury of adolescent experiments" in order to be able to help her mother.

Now, if you know the word "forgo," then you can understand that the author is saying she'll give up her right to adolescent experiments in order to help her mother. This means the author can't be past the adolescent stage of her life—otherwise, it would be too late to forgo anything from that stage.

But what if you don't know the word "forgo?"

On this question, you could actually work around that unknown word, as will often be the case on the ACT. No matter what the word "forgo" means, we can still tell from the sentence that the author is talking about making some kind of decision about adolescent experiments. If the author still has the chance to make any decisions about her adolescent experiments, then it must be the case that she hasn't passed through adolescence yet—which, again, means she must not be an adult.

(There's another way the word "forgo" can trip people up, actually. If you read that sentence from the text too quickly, you might think the word "forgo" is actually the word "forget," and then you might be in real trouble if you reasoned that only an adult could "forget" her adolescence. This is one more example of the extreme importance of reading carefully on the ACT!)

So we know (A) and (B) are wrong, because they refer to the author as an adult, not an adolescent.

If we consider the rest of (C) and (D), we can tell that (C) is also wrong, because the text doesn't say the author is "imagining" anything—she describes what actually happened.

(D) is correct because the author specifically says, in lines 58 and 59, that she would have to "scoop my mother out of harm's way and give her sanctuary," which matches up with the idea of "eas[ing] her mother's adjustment to life in the United States" from the answer choice.

I'd also like to point out that it's possible to answer this question even if we never figure out whether the author is an adult or an adolescent, because we can still focus on the other parts of the answer choices and read carefully.

(A) would still have to be incorrect because the text doesn't say that the mother and the narrator were only visiting the United States. In fact, the last sentence of the passage specifically mentions that the author and her mother "would not be returning" to their "former lives."

(B) has the same problem as (A), because the text never says that the author plans to return. In fact, as we just saw, the text says exactly the opposite.

Page 321, Question 4

People miss this question all the time, and it's usually just because they don't approach the question with discipline.

Go to www.ACTprepVideos.com.

First, it's absolutely critical that we notice the word "EXCEPT" in all caps. That word indicates that we're looking for the one choice that the narrator's mother doesn't find "troubling." In other words, the correct answer will be the choice that's not in the text, which is the opposite of the usual situation on an ACT Reading question.

(F) is wrong because lines 14 and 15 say, "My mother did not appreciate the exacting orderliness . . ."

(G) is wrong because lines 15 through 18 say, "She could not give in to . . . the absence of carcasses . . ."

(H) is correct because the text never mentions other shoppers being "hurried," so we have no evidence of how the narrator's mother might have felt about those kinds of shoppers, or whether they were even present in the store.

(J) is wrong because the author explains the checkout system in lines 69 through 71, and then the mother experiences "a few moments' hesitation" because of the "peculiarity of my explanation;" then, in line 84, the mother "grumble[s]" because of how the checkout clerk treats her.

Now, let me call your attention for a second to the Red Book's explanation of this question, which can be found on page 406. The Red Book says (H) is correct because of line 10 in the passage, which mentions that people "meandered" through the store. The Red Book points out that "meandered" is sort of the opposite of "hurried" in choice (H).

But the word "meandered" actually has nothing to do with (H) being correct, in the sense that the correct answer to an "EXCEPT" question on the ACT doesn't have to include a word that contradicts the text. The only thing needed to make (H) correct is the absence of any mention of the mother being "troubled" by "hurried shoppers." In other words, even if the word "meandered" weren't there, (H) would still be correct, because the text never mentions the mother having any negative feelings toward "hurried shoppers."

Again, it's important to take the ACT's explanations of its own questions with a grain of salt. If you read the Red Book's explanation for this question, you might get the wrong idea about how "EXCEPT" questions work on the ACT. The right answer to an "EXCEPT" question doesn't have to contradict the text, even though the Red Book says (H) is correct because of the word "meandered." The right answer to an "EXCEPT" question only has to fail to show up in the text in order to be correct.

There's one more thing I want to mention. You may remember that I constantly remind you to go through all the answer choices for every question, instead of just pouncing on a choice you like and then moving on to the next question without reading the other choices. This type of question is one of the main reasons that I insist you consider all the answer choices: if you overlook the word "EXCEPT" in the question, you'll probably think that choice (F) looks good right away, but if you keep reading through the other choices, you'll probably notice that (G) and (J) also seem decent. You might end up being pretty sure that more than one of the answer choices is directly in the text, even though you know that every ACT question can only have one correct answer. And that should make you realize that you've made a mistake at some point in your approach to this question—which would give you the chance to re-evaluate the question, and hopefully recognize that you had overlooked the word "EXCEPT." In that way, you could give yourself the chance to fix your mistake and pick up an extra question that you would otherwise have missed.

Remember that elite ACT-takers are usually just people who are very, very good at paying attention to detail, avoiding mistakes for the most part, and fixing whatever mistakes they do make. Learning to consider every answer choice as part of the question is a critical step in minimizing needless mistakes.

Page 321, Question 7

This question is another one that people often miss because they fail to read carefully enough.

The relevant portion of the text is in lines 54 through 68, when the narrator says, "all children eventually watch their parents' astonishing return to the vulnerability of childhood," but that "the process begins much earlier than expected" for "children of immigrant parents." The narrator also mentions "help[ing]" her mother in line 55, and in the rest of that paragraph.

These phrases match up exactly with the correct answer, which is choice (B). The text refers to the idea that all children eventually see something, which matches the idea of "the inevitable shift" in the answer choice. The idea of the "parent's . . . return to the vulnerability of childhood" from the passage is reflected in the phrase "the vulnerable parent" in the answer choice. The idea of "protecting" from the answer choice echoes the idea of keeping the mother "out of harm's way" and "giv[ing] her sanctuary" in lines 58 and 59. The phrase "takes place sooner for children of immigrants" from the answer choice matches up with the phrase "for us the process begins much earlier than expected." So all aspects of choice (B) are supported by the text.

Choices (A) and (C) both contain ideas that are related to those in the text, but the second half of (A) contradicts the text, while (C) includes details not mentioned in the text.

(D) introduces a totally unrelated, but plausible, concept that isn't addressed anywhere in the text, so it's wrong. As we keep seeing, the ACT will throw these answer choices in there sometimes, probably hoping you'll bite. Remember to stay disciplined in your approach to the ACT Reading section, and only mark an answer when you can see how it's supported in the text!

Page 322, Question 11

This question asks what can be "reasonably inferred from the passage." Remember that the ACT uses these kinds of subjective phrases to make it sound like you're supposed to interpret something or make a judgment call. But, as trained test-takers, we know we'll always find the correct answer indicated in the text, in an objectively verifiable way.

So let's take a look.

(A) is wrong because the author directly quotes Jefferson himself describing his works as not "aiming at originality" (line 38), which contradicts the phrase "attempts at originality" in the answer choice.

(B) is correct. We can say the author thought Jefferson was "brilliant," because in line 45 the text describes Jefferson's words as "ingeniously double-edged," and "brilliant" can be a synonym for "ingenious." We can also say the author thought Jefferson was "practical" because he describes Jefferson's approach to the Declaration of Independence as "the obvious practical course" (line 79). The author doesn't see Jefferson as a plagiarizer, because he specifically says in line 70 that his statement is not meant "to accuse [Jefferson] of plagiarism." We also know the author doesn't see Jefferson as a prophet, since he says in lines 29 through 32 that "no serious student . . . has ever claimed that [Jefferson] foresaw . . . consequences of what he wrote." Finally, we know the author saw Jefferson as a man "writing under pressure" because lines 75 through 79 list several factors of the "context" surrounding this document, including Congress "being overwhelmed."

Notice that this answer choice describes five aspects of Jefferson—that he was brilliant (1) and practical (2), that he was not a plagiarizer (3) or a prophet (4), and that he wrote under pressure (5). In order for the answer choice to be correct, all five elements need to be supported by the text, and we can see that they are.

(C) is incorrect because the text never says Jefferson should get more attention than he does.

(D) is incorrect because the author never describes Jefferson as "average."

Some ACT Reading questions, like this one, can require us to draw on words and phrases that are scattered throughout the text, instead of localized to a particular line or paragraph. Keep this in mind as you decide whether you prefer to read the text before answering the questions. You might find it easier to skip a question like this one when you first see it, and save it until you've answered all the other questions about this passage, which would allow you more of a chance to familiarize yourself with the passage while you gain points by answering other questions. Then, when you returned to this question, you would probably find it easier to pinpoint relevant phrases.

Of course, as I mention elsewhere in this Black Book, there is no single best way to approach reading or skimming a passage on the ACT Reading section that is guaranteed to be optimal for every test-taker. You'll need to experiment with your approach until you find something that works for you. Just make sure your approach allows you to accommodate questions like this one, where the key phrases in the passage appear many lines apart from one another.

Page 323, Question 14

This question is worth examining closely because it demonstrates a lot of the issues we need to be on the lookout for on the ACT Reading section.

First, the question asks us to find the statement that "best summarizes" Lincoln's comments, and many untrained test-takers might be worried that more than one answer choice could be a decent summary of these comments. But as trained test-takers, we know that the correct answer will be the *only* choice that accurately summarizes the comments.

The wrong answers for this question are also pretty sneaky, even for an ACT question. Each of the wrong answers is composed mostly of concepts taken directly from the text, but the wrong answers relate those concepts to one another in ways that differ from the way they appear in the text. This is why it's so important to make sure you choose an answer with the right concepts *and* the right relationships among those concepts, instead of just leaping at the first choice that seems to mention the same basic ideas from the text.

Finally, this question demonstrates a pattern that we'll see fairly often on the ACT, across all four multiple-choice sections. Two of the answer choices begin with the same phrase, while the other two choices begin with different phrases: both (H) and (J) begin with "even under pressure of war," while (F) starts with "even during the fight" and (G) starts with "even during a revolution." Conceptually, those three phrases are all pretty similar, but only (H) and (J) use exactly the same initial phrases. This will typically suggest—BUT DOES NOT GUARANTEE—that either (H) or (J) is correct, because the ACT often likes to repeat elements of the correct answer in one or more incorrect answers.

This also means we need to pay strict attention when evaluating the last two choices, since they start out very similarly. It would be easy to realize that you liked one of those choices, and then to think, "Oh, I liked the choice about the pressure of war," and then accidentally fill in the wrong answer, even if you correctly understood the question, just because you got confused going back and forth between the test booklet and your answer sheet.

Whew—that's a lot of stuff to mention before we even really get into the answer choices! Let's take a look at them now.

(F) is wrong because it says that Jefferson's statement has been used against revolutionaries, but Lincoln says the statement will be used against tyrants and oppressors. People often incorrectly choose (F) because they misread the phrase "against revolutionaries" in this answer choice as though it said "by revolutionaries." This is one more example of why it's so important to read carefully, and to read all of the answer choices. Reading carefully might help you avoid choosing (F) in the first place; if you did happen to misread (F), then reading the other answer choices might help you to realize your mistake when you got to choice (H) and realized that another choice also seemed to restate the passage.

(G) says that Jefferson predicted future tyrants, but Lincoln never said Jefferson actually predicted future tyrants; Lincoln only said that Jefferson's words would have an effect on the "harbingers of reappearing tyranny." In other words, Lincoln says that Jefferson's words would impact later tyrants, but Lincoln never says that Jefferson actually deliberately *predicted* there would be future tyrants. (Another issue is that the phrase "harbingers of . . .

tyranny" isn't exactly synonymous with the word "tyrants," since a harbinger is an indication that something is coming. But most ACT-takers don't know the word "harbinger," and anyway we can still tell that this choice is wrong because of the problem with the word "predicted," as I just explained.)

We can see that choice (H) is correct because every part of (H) is supported by Lincoln's words. The answer choice begins with the phrase "even under pressure of war," and Lincoln's statement mentions that Jefferson was "in the concrete pressure of a struggle for national independence" in lines 22 and 23. The answer choice also says that Jefferson's document "not only announced a revolution, but also spoke against oppression for all time," and Lincoln called the declaration a "merely revolutionary document" in which Jefferson "introduce[d] . . . a rebuke . . . to . . . oppression" (lines 24 - 28) that would stand for "all coming days." So, as always, we see that every phrase in the correct answer choice is directly restated in the relevant part of the text.

(J) says that Jefferson "dared tyrants to continually reappear," but Lincoln never described Jefferson issuing a dare.

There's a lot going on in this question, and in my explanation—it might be a good idea to review both of them a couple of times to make sure you don't miss anything.

Page 324, Question 21

This question asks us about the "main purpose" of this passage. A lot of test-takers have trouble answering questions that ask about a passage's "main purpose," but we find the answers to questions like these directly in the text, just as we would with any other ACT Reading question. The only extra consideration we might have to keep in mind is that "main purpose" questions sometimes include more than one answer choice that directly reflects the text. If this question turns out to be like that, then the correct answer will be the one that's restated most often in the passage.

(A) is correct because it describes a topic that comes up again and again in this passage. The author talks about "how" the show endured when he says the show "captured the imagination and viewer loyalty of millions of Americans" (lines 8 - 10), and when he mentions its "meteoric rise to popularity" (line 11), and when he says that "by 1977, *Star Trek* had become the most watched off-network series drama of all time" (lines 54 and 55). The author talks about "why" the show endured when he says it "benefited greatly from being the right show at the right time" (lines 17 and 18), and when he says the show "resonated with millions of idealistic and awestruck Americans" (lines 36 and 38), and when he says no other classic show "illustrate[d] the scope of America's cultural evolution as eloquently" (lines 69 and 70), and so on. The hows and whys of *Star Trek*'s success come up again and again in the passage, which is why (A) is the correct answer to this "main purpose" question.

(B) is incorrect, even though the author does use the third paragraph to discuss what American society was like when the original series was created. Remember that "main purpose" questions on the ACT Reading section can sometimes feature more than one answer choice that appears in the text, and the correct answer to such a question will be the choice that's restated most often in the passage. (B) is wrong because it doesn't come up as often as the topic of "how and why *Star Trek* has endured" as mentioned in choice (A).

(C) is incorrect because the text doesn't mention the storyline changing over the 30-year history of the show.

(D) is also incorrect, even though, like (B), it does actually restate an idea from the passage. The many different forms taken by the *Star Trek* story are mentioned in the seventh paragraph of the passage, and again in the last half of the last paragraph. Still, the hows and whys of *Star Trek*'s success are mentioned more often, so (A) is correct.

This question can seem very subjective and confusing to an untrained test-taker! Let this be one more reminder of the importance of understanding how the ACT really works, so that on test day you'll know exactly how to answer these apparently subjective questions with total certainty and objectivity.

Page 325, Question 22

Many students read a question like this and think, "How am I supposed to know how the author feels about this subject?" But trained test-takers know that the description in the correct answer choice will be directly supported by the text, and the descriptions in the wrong answer choices won't. And don't forget that each answer choice here involves two words—both words have to be directly supported by the text for the correct answer to be correct.

(F) is incorrect because neither word is supported by the text. For a word like "amused" to be accurate, the text would have to include a phrase like "it makes me laugh" or "I can't help but chuckle . . . " or something like that. For a word like "tolerance" to be accurate, there would have to be a phrase like "I guess such-and-such is okay" or "I have no choice but to go along with such-and-such" or something like that. We don't see any phrases like this in the text.

Some untrained test-takers might think that the author sounds intelligent, and they might be able to imagine that someone in the author's position could feel something like "amused tolerance" towards a TV show, so they might talk themselves into choosing this answer. But those kinds of considerations are irrelevant on the ACT—all that matters is whether an answer choice restates the text. This one doesn't, so it's wrong.

(G) is wrong. It's also kind of an odd answer choice because it mentions "detached interest," which sounds like a difficult balance to strike—how can an author be simultaneously detached and interested? Anyway, if we look at each word in this choice individually, we see that (G) must be wrong. We can't describe the author's attitude as detached, since he uses very positive wording to describe the show, like when he mentions the show's "insight and added perspective" (line 51), or when he says no other classic show "illustrates the scope of America's cultural evolution as eloquently" (lines 69 and 70), or when he mentions the show's "provocative insight" (line 78) and "reassuring comfort" (line 79). Since the author clearly has a positive emotional reaction to the show, the ACT won't let us describe his attitude as "detached."

(H) is the correct answer because we can see in a number of places the "warm" feeling the author has toward the show, which goes hand-in-hand with his "appreciation" for it—in fact, we could even argue that feeling warmly about something and appreciating it are synonyms in this context. The phrases I cited in discussing choice (G) clearly demonstrate the author's positive attitude towards the show.

(J) is incorrect because nothing in the text supports the idea that the author is "skeptical" about this show to any degree. In fact, the passage closes with the author's proclamation that "as America goes boldly into the next millennium, so will *Star Trek* in print, on television, and in formats yet to come." If "skeptical" were going to be part of a correct answer for this question, the passage would need to include statements like "I'm not sure if I believe in *Star Trek*," or "It's difficult to accept such-and-such about *Star Trek*," and so on.

Remember that the correct answer to an ACT Reading question must always be directly and objectively on the page, even when the question might seem subjective to untrained test-takers.

Page 325, Question 26

I chose this question for further discussion because it's another example of the Red Book giving a poor explanation of an answer choice—in this case, choice (H). It's important to make sure you understand what's really wrong with (H) in a way that will allow you to answer ACT questions correctly in the future.

Let's go through the answer choices in order.

Choice (F) is correct because the third paragraph describes the time of the show's creation as one of "social and political change" during which it was "difficult for people to unite in common purpose," and says that a number of topics "divided many Americans by race, gender, age, and politics." These phrases match up directly with the "unsettled social and political conditions" mentioned in choice (F), so (F) is right.

Choice (G) is wrong because the "general popularity of syndicated reruns" is never mentioned in the passage.

The Red Book's explanation on page 413 is completely incorrect with respect to choice (H). The Red Book says (H) accurately describes a portion of the text, but that (H) is still wrong because the question asks for the author's opinion, and the author believes the show "offered insight and added perspective." There are at least two major problems with this analysis. The first problem is that the question asks why the author thought the show was right for its time, not why the author himself liked the show, so the author's personal feelings on the show aren't relevant to the question—the only relevant issue is what the author says about *viewers in general* being ready to embrace the show. The second problem is that the Red Book's explanation is completely, objectively wrong when it says that "the author himself believes *Star Trek* was 'a window into current controversy' that 'offered insight and added perspective . . .'" The author clearly says that the show was such a window *"for those who saw the program"* that way (lines 49 and 50, emphasis mine), but the author never says whether he was one of those people—or, indeed, whether the author even existed at all when the show was launched.

So the Red Book's explanation is wrong about what the sentence in line 50 of the text means, and it's wrong about whether that meaning is more relevant to the question than the reference to escapism in line 29 of the text.

It's because of Red Book explanations like this that I'm pretty sure the people who write the ACT's explanations and the people who write the actual ACT are different people. (For more on this topic, see "How Can The Red Book's Explanations Of Its Own Questions Be Wrong?" earlier in this Black Book.) If you take the Red Book's explanation of choice (H) to heart, you'll probably answer some future ACT questions incorrectly, because the Red Book's explanation of this particular choice is based on a fundamental misreading of the prompt, the answer choice, and the passage.

At this point, you may be wondering what's actually wrong with (H), if the problem isn't what the Red Book says it is.

The real problem with (H) is the word "increasing." The text never says the demand for escapism was increasing (or decreasing, or staying constant, or anything else), so the word "increasing" makes (H) wrong. That's all there is to it. There are other problems with (H), too, but the word "increasing" is enough for (H) to be wrong.

Once more, we see that reading carefully and understanding how the test actually works will allow us to save time and answer more questions correctly, because it allows us to zero in on what actually matters.

One big problem with (J) is similar to the problem I just mentioned with (H). The text never says anything about a change in the level of power for the middle class, so the word "increasingly" in (J) is enough to make it wrong.

As this question amply demonstrates, you really do need to be careful when you work with the Red Book's explanations! In some cases those explanations are quite adequate, but in many cases they're inefficient, misleading, or flat-out wrong.

Remember that it's always important to understand the underlying reasoning behind a correct or incorrect answer choice in a way that will allow you to identify correct answers consistently in the future. That's why one of the primary goals of this Black Book is to teach you what the ACT actually rewards and punishes—so you can know what you're really up against, and how to beat it.

Page 325, Question 29

This question gives us an especially clear example of the importance of reading everything on the ACT very closely, with a literal mindset.

The question asks about the use of the term "visionary" in line 46, so we should go back and read the sentence that contains that term, as well as a sentence or two before and after, so we have an idea of the context.

(A) is incorrect because it says the issues addressed by *Star Trek* "weren't problems at the time," but line 45 calls them "contemporary social problems," which means they *were* problems at the time—the word "contemporary" means "happening at the same time." This answer choice contradicts the text, so it's wrong.

(B) is correct because it mentions the show's "complex themes" and "imagination and foresight." We see these themes listed in lines 46 and 47, and we see the imagination and foresight mentioned in lines 51 and 52, when the text mentions the show's "insight and added perspective." Notice the strong literal similarity among the roots of the key words in the question and the text: "*vision*-ary," "*imag[e]*-ination," "fore-*sight*," "in-*sight*," "per-*spect*-ive." If we look at the words on this fundamental level, we see they all revolve around the same idea of something visual, and then it becomes even clearer that the phrases including those words are also all talking about the same things.

Now, to be clear, I'm not saying that you have to notice the similarities in those roots in order to answer this question correctly. Plenty of untrained test-takers might be able to answer this question correctly, basically by luck; even a trained test-taker could realize that (B) is correct without stopping to reflect on the actual roots of the words involved.

And I'm certainly not saying that the correct answer to every single ACT Reading question will incorporate roots that are synonymous with the roots of the relevant words in the text.

I just wanted to point out the roots in this particular question so that I could reinforce the idea that we should always be on the lookout for phrases in the answer choices that restate phrases from the passage *exactly*. Even if the correct answer doesn't feature words whose roots are synonymous with the roots of words in the passage, we still want to approach each answer choice with a completely literal mindset, making sure we deal with what each word actually means, and not with our own interpretations or subjective assumptions about each word.

(C) is incorrect because the text never mentions that the show offered "dreamy" or "unrealistic" solutions to problems. Many untrained test-takers will be drawn to this answer choice, because they'll assume that any science fiction show must automatically be "unrealistic." But the text doesn't actually say anything about the solutions being realistic or unrealistic.

(D) is incorrect, but we need to read carefully to understand why. The text mentions *Star Trek*'s "wide appeal in syndication" in line 53, but this "wide appeal" is the appeal of the show in general. The question, on the other hand, specifically asks about the "visionary episodes" mentioned in line 46. The author doesn't explicitly say that every single episode of the show was visionary; he says that there were some visionary episodes in line 46, and then he says a few sentences later that, "either way," the show had "wide appeal in syndication." The difference between the idea of specific visionary episodes and the idea of the show in general is enough to make this choice wrong, and the phrase "either way" also indicates that the author isn't citing the "wide appeal" in connection with the "visionary episodes."

Yet again, we see that the key to answering an ACT Reading question correctly is to read carefully, and to be disciplined in our search for an answer choice that restates the relevant portion of the text.

Page 325, Question 30

This question asks us which answer choice expresses a paradox that the author sees. Most untrained test-takers will try to make a subjective assessment of the article and choose the paradox that makes the most sense to them, but we know that we have to look for phrases that the author specifically mentions as opposites in the text.

(F) is incorrect. The author does mention "cultural values" in lines 78 and 79, but he never mentions the idea of entertainment being opposed to those values, so there's no evidence in the text that the author thinks there's a paradox here.

(G) is correct because the author specifically describes "the paradox" of combining "changing cultural values" with "reassuring comfort" of "the 'known'" (lines 77 through 80). The phrase "changing cultural values" corresponds directly to the idea of "change" in the answer choice, and the phrases about the "reassuring comfort" of the "'known'" correspond to the word "familiarity" in the answer choice.

The notion that these ideas are "conflicting" is reinforced by the word "nonetheless" in line 81, which indicates that one idea is working against the other.

Further, if we look at lines 73 through 76, we see that the author talks about "bitter . . . change" being "sweeten[ed]" by "familiarity" on *Star Trek*. This sentence also explicitly positions "change" and "familiarity" as opposites, and would be enough for us to know that (G) was correct even without lines 77 through 80.

(H) is incorrect because the author describes the knowledge of the *Star Trek* universe as a "comfort," which means these two ideas are not in conflict in his opinion.

(J) is incorrect. Although the "survival" of the *Star Trek* universe and "being provocative" are both mentioned, nothing in the text indicates that these two concepts are conflicting in the author's opinion.

Notice in this question that even if we weren't sure of the meaning of the word "paradox," the question itself ends with the hint that you need to look for "conflicting ideas," in addition to the fact that lines 77 through 80 specifically use the word "paradox" to describe this situation.

Page 326, Question 31

This type of question often bothers untrained test-takers because it seems to be pretty subjective. But, as always, we know that the correct answer will have to restate something directly on the page.

I would probably attack this question by trying to find an area of the text with the words "Helmholtz" and "Goethe" close to one another. Line 7 has both words, so that might be a good place to start looking.

We can see in that line that "Helmholtz . . . gave admiring lectures on Goethe and his science." But the question asks how Helmholtz feels about Goethe's "color theory" specifically, so we need to see if the text equates the idea of Goethe's science with his color theory in order to tell if this is the right part of the text.

We see a direct reference to "Goethe's color theory" in line 1; in line 5, we learn that many saw Goethe's color theory as "pseudoscience;" in the next sentence, the author says that "science" and Goethe's theory had some things in common; then we read that Helmholtz gave admiring lectures on Goethe's science. So we can see that the idea of Goethe's science and his color theory are equated in the first three sentences of the passage.

This means the correct answer will have to match up with the word "admiring." Only choice (B) does that.

Untrained test-takers may be tempted to pick (A), (C), or (D), because of phrases like "dismissed by all his contemporaries," "whimsy," and "pseudoscience" in lines 3 through 5, but these phrases don't reflect Helmholtz's opinion. The question asks about Helmholtz's opinion, not about the general opinion of Goethe's unnamed contemporaries.

Once more, we see the importance of reading carefully and paying close attention to the text!

Page 327, Question 34

A lot of untrained test-takers miss this question because they never find the relevant portion of the text. They get overwhelmed by the relative complexity of this passage, and just try to guess their way to the right answer.

But we always need to remember that the correct answer is spelled out in the text somewhere. If we haven't found the place where it's spelled out, then we either haven't looked in the right place, or we haven't understood the passage.

In this case, the structure of the question tells us that the correct answer will appear in the passage somewhere word-for-word: since the question asks what Helmholtz calls something, the correct answer will have to be the phrase that Helmholtz actually uses in the text.

So we could try to find the relevant portion of the passage by looking for references to apples, redness, lighting, or any of the phrases in the four answer choices.

We would want to notice the phrase "color constancy" in quotation marks in line 10. Since that's one of the answer choice phrases, it might be a good idea to see how the text describes this term, so we can figure out if choice (J) is right or wrong.

If we read the entire sentence that starts in line 9, we do see that Helmholtz used the phrase "color constancy" for something. And if we read the following sentence, the text describes the way we "consistently see [an apple] as red" even when the "illumination" "var[ies]." This sentence even includes the phrase "for instance," which refers back to the "color constancy" idea in the previous sentence to tell us it's an example of that concept.

At this point, it looks like choice (J) is correct.

But I'd still want to check out the other answer choices, of course, just to make sure I haven't misread or misunderstood anything.

The next phrase I see from the answer choices is "sensory flux," which appears in choice (G) and in lines 25 and 26 of the passage. This sentence says that Helmholtz viewed color constancy as an "example of the way in which we achieve perceptual constancy generally" and "make a stable perceptual world from a chaotic sensory flux." If we read this sentence carefully, we can see that the idea of the "sensory flux" is described as something different from the "perceptual constancy" or "color constancy" earlier in the sentence. The sentence says that we somehow take the "chaotic sensory flux" and turn it into "constancy." Notice that the words used to describe the "constancy" and the "sensory flux" are antonyms: the perceptual constancy is "stable" in line 25, while the "sensory flux" is chaotic. All of this indicates clearly that "sensory flux" is not the same idea as always perceiving an apple to be red.

"Color separation," from choice (H), is the next phrase from the answer choices to appear in the text, in lines 44 and 45. Those lines, and the preceding sentences, make it clear that "color separation" was a tactic employed by James Clerk Maxwell (who is named in lines 30 and 31). Test-takers often fall for this answer choice because the idea of color separation appears next to a description of an "image taken through [a] red filter" in line 48, and lots of people desperately try to equate that to the idea of the red apple in the question. But, if we read carefully, we see that Helmholtz has nothing to do with color separation in the text.

The last phrase we need to check out is "split-beam filtering" from choice (F). If we skim for that, we see the word "split-beam" appearing in line 66, but not in connection with the idea of a filter, and not as an example related to Helmholtz. So this can't be the right answer, either.

Page 327, Question 35

Test-takers often miss this question because they don't read carefully enough.

The question uses the phrase "vary considerably," and the same phrase appears in lines 15 and 16 of the text, which talks about how the "actual wavelengths reflected by the apple" (lines 14 and 15) "vary considerably depending on the illumination" (lines 15 and 16).

So the "illumination" affects the "actual wavelengths reflected by the apple," according to the text. The word "illumination" refers to light, and the word "wavelengths" in this context is also referring to light. We know that the idea of "reflecting" off of something means striking that thing and bouncing off, so choice (D) must be correct when it mentions "variations in the source of light reaching the apple." Once again, we see that every phrase in the correct answer choice directly reflects the relevant portion of the text.

The rest of the citation makes no mention of the differences between the viewer's right and left eyes, or the distance between the apple and the eyes, so we know those choices must be wrong.

But wait a minute—the text does describe "the viewer's ability to perceive red in any light," as choice (C) describes. So why isn't (C) the right answer? Once more, it all comes down to the relationships of concepts in the passage. The question asks us *why* the reflected wavelengths vary. But the text doesn't say that the wavelengths vary *as a result of* people's ability to perceive red, which is what choice (C) would require; instead, the text says that people can always perceive red *even though* the wavelengths vary.

Remember that careful reading and attention to detail will help you avoid unnecessary mistakes like choosing (C)!

Page 327, Question 40

People often get frustrated by this question because they feel like it requires them to know the technical details of photography. But, of course, the ACT could never require us to know those kinds of things. No matter how technical or obscure the topic of an ACT Reading question might seem, the answer is always directly on the page somewhere, even if we have trouble finding it at first.

Since there's no line citation in this question, I would probably skim the passage for the name "Land" if I hadn't read the passage, or if I couldn't remember which part of the passage had that information.

We see the description of Land's photographic process in lines 65 through 69. There's no mention of anything like "a screen lit from the front and back" or "flickering light sources" being used to obtain the images, so (F) and (G) must be wrong.

That part of the text says Land made "two black-and-white images using a split-beam camera . . . taken at the same time . . . through the same lens." The word "a" in the phrase "a split-beam camera" means that only one camera was used, so (H) must also be wrong, and (J) is right.

Page 467, Question 3

This question seems extremely subjective to most untrained test-takers, but, as always, we'll find the answer with certainty by looking at the relevant part of the text and choosing the answer choice that matches it.

This question is also another example of the frequent shortcomings of the Red Book's answer explanations. The ACT's official explanation of this question on page 543 of the Red Book makes reference to the wrong parts of the text in trying to justify the correct answer; if you used that kind of reasoning on other ACT questions, you could very easily end up with a lot of wrong answers.

Let's take a look at the answer choices and see what's really going on.

(A) is correct because it describes the situation in both paragraphs quite literally.

This answer choice mentions people acting "carefully," which literally means that they act with care—they think about the possible consequences of their actions, and make a deliberate effort to behave in a way that will create a particular result. The twelfth paragraph describes how Vida chooses not to face Ted so that he doesn't "become silent and wander away." The thirteenth paragraph describes Ted making "slow and meticulous" cuts in the glass and being very diligent about not wasting the glass. In both cases, we see a character acting with care, making a deliberate choice to avoid a particular outcome.

The answer choice also mentions the idea of "shattering something precious." The word "precious" can have a lot of different meanings, and some of them are reflected in these paragraphs. In the twelfth paragraph, we see that Vida thinks it is "perfect" and "rare" to see Ted; if something is "perfect" and "rare," it could definitely be described as "precious." (At first, it may look like these remarks apply to the wild pheasants instead of Ted, but if you look carefully you'll see that the remarks apply to both Ted *and* the pheasants, because of the phrase "the same" in lines 64 and 65.) In the thirteenth paragraph, we see that Ted doesn't want to waste the glass, and that it's "special" to him, and those ideas certainly also reflect the idea of something being "precious."

The word "shatter" has multiple meanings. In a physical sense, it refers to the idea of violently breaking something fragile and rigid, like a piece of glass or pottery. But, in an abstract sense, it can also refer to the idea of damaging or destroying anything, like when we say an athlete shatters a record, or a crisis shatters people's confidence.

So both paragraphs clearly reflect the idea of a person acting with care to avoid damaging or destroying something they think is precious: Vida doesn't want a particular situation to end because of her actions, and Ted doesn't want to stray from his plan and waste his glass.

Notice that the Red Book's explanation on page 543 doesn't touch on most of those details. It doesn't specifically explain why Vida's actions in the twelfth paragraph could be called "careful," and it doesn't explain which phrase in that paragraph justifies the word "precious" in the answer choice. The Red Book's explanation hits on the phrase "wild thing at peace," but "wild thing at peace" isn't a definition of the word "precious!" "So perfect, so rare" is the phrase in the twelfth paragraph that justifies the word "precious" in the answer choice, and the Red Book's explanation never explicitly mentions it. The Red Book also doesn't explain why the word "shatter" is appropriate in the answer choice.

So the Red Book explanation ends up being incomplete, and seems to encourage a loose, subjective approach to the text. But if we really scrutinize the ACT Reading section, we'll see that official ACT questions always incorporate the type of literal, word-by-word approach that I'm teaching you in this Black Book.

As I've said repeatedly, it's important for us to appreciate the actual reasoning behind the test's design, instead of taking the Red Book explanations at face value.

Now let's examine the other answer choices.

(B) is wrong because we have no reason to think that either character is indignant or frustrated; further, the two relevant paragraphs don't say anything about success being out of reach. This is the kind of wrong answer that might appeal to an untrained test-taker who tries to interpret the passage as literature: it sounds like a plausible theory of the characters' motivations, but it has no direct literal support in the text.

(C) is also incorrect because the relevant part of the text doesn't describe either character losing interest at any point, for any reason.

(D) is wrong because neither of these paragraphs actually describes a strength or a weakness in literal terms. If an untrained test-taker tried to interpret this text in a literary way, he might arbitrarily decide that certain behaviors by the characters seem weak or strong to him. But the text never uses either of those words, nor any synonym of those words, so this choice is wrong.

Page 467, Question 4

If we go back and read the 12th paragraph (which contains line 69 with the term "wild thing"), we can see that Vida stands listening to Ted "in the same even breath and heart beat" she used when she saw wild pheasants; the next sentence says it was "so rare to see a wild thing at peace." The phrase "wild thing at peace" refers to both Ted and the pheasants, because of the phrase "the same" in lines 64 and 65.

So choice (F) is correct. The word "reverently" in the answer choice reflects the use of the words "perfect" and "rare" in line 69.

(G) is wrong because it reverses the idea of which character is thinking about the other, and because the text doesn't specifically mention that Ted gets physically near to Vida *at the fort*. Look out for these kinds of small mistakes on the ACT!

(H) is wrong because the paragraph describes Vida's feelings, not Ted's.

(J) is wrong because the text doesn't say that Vida wants Ted to be a different way.

Once more, we see how important it is to read everything on the ACT very carefully.

Page 467, Question 8

Many untrained test-takers would worry that they needed to have a deep understanding of the entire passage to answer a question like this, but, if we read carefully, we'll see that we can answer the question just by using the cited paragraph and sticking strictly to the text, and perhaps lightly skimming other parts of the passage.

Let's take a look at the answer choices.

(F) is wrong because this paragraph doesn't mention anything about Ted being discouraged, disheartened, dejected, or anything else like that, and neither does the rest of the passage. This answer choice is probably here to mislead test-takers who attempt to interpret the text on their own terms, because some people might read this and decide that Ted probably feels discouraged, even though the idea is never mentioned anywhere in the text.

(G) is wrong because the text never describes the tree house actually being dismantled, destroyed, undone, removed, or anything along those lines. The paragraph referred to in the question does mention the *possibility* of the fort having to come down if it harms the trees, but the text never tells us that the fort actually does come down.

(H) is the correct answer because it matches up directly with the text. The phrase "takes an interest" in the answer choice goes with the sentence "I'll be checking" in line 25; the idea of determining how the project should be carried out in the answer choice is reflected in the advice in the paragraph about "keep[ing] your nails together" and not damaging the trees; the idea of "avoiding problems" in the answer choice is reflected in the statement that the fort will "have to come down" if the "trees get damaged," and the advice not to damage them.

(J) is wrong because there is no indication of whose willingness is greater. Some untrained test-takers might be tempted by this interpretation, but it's not literally reflected anywhere in the text at all.

Notice, again, that we didn't really need to know much about the rest of the passage in order to answer this question. All we needed was the text in the cited paragraph, and perhaps a little skimming to make sure the text had no references to Ted being discouraged, the project being dismantled, or the willingness to accept responsibility.

Page 469, Question 11

In order to answer this "EXCEPT" question, we have to go through the passage and eliminate any answer choice that appears in the text as something that the company's emissions help produce.

This question is likely to require more work than most other ACT Reading questions, for two reasons:

1. It doesn't refer us to a particular line or paragraph, meaning that every word in the passage is potentially relevant.
2. It's an "EXCEPT" question, meaning that we can only answer it by successfully locating three of the four answer choices somewhere in the text, so we'll have to find three times as many things in the text as we normally would.

For these reasons, and because this is the first question that addresses the passage on page 468, I would probably skip this question when I first saw it, and try to answer other questions about the passage before returning to this one. If I did that, I might get lucky and run across some of the answer choices for this question while I'm trying to approach other questions, and that could save me some time when I try to answer this question. And even if I didn't get lucky and stumble across some of these answer choices in my reading for other questions, I still wouldn't lose any time by doing the questions in a different order. So I'd have nothing to lose, and potentially something to gain. (For more on these kinds of ideas, see the "Skip Hard Questions" section under "Timing Issues" earlier in this Black Book.)

So now let's take a look at our answer choices.

(A) appears in lines 27 through 29, which say that "waste steam . . . is used . . . to . . . produce insulin." So we know choice (A) is wrong, because this "EXCEPT" question requires us to find the one answer choice that's not in the text.

Then we see in line 32 that fertilizer is produced as part of the same process, so we can eliminate choice (C).

Finally, in lines 42 through 44, we can see that the power company "also squeezes sulfur from its emissions, but converts most of it to . . . (industrial gypsum)." So that eliminates choice (D).

Since (B) doesn't appear in the text, it must be the correct answer to this "EXCEPT" question.

Some people might get confused and eliminate (B) because lines 21 and 22 say that "waste steam" is used to "heat . . . homes," "eliminating the need for oil furnaces." Of course, "eliminating the need for oil furnaces" isn't the same thing as actually producing heating oil, but many people will accidentally see the words "heat" and "oil" in the same sentence and be misled because they aren't reading carefully enough.

(By the way, notice that question 13 tells us to look at lines 13 through 44 of the passage. When we do that, we'll end up going through all of the citations I referred to in this solution. So if you decided to skip this question at first and come back to it after attacking the other questions for this passage, your experience answering question 13 would have given you a pretty good idea of where to find most of the answer choices for this question, which would probably have saved you some time and frustration.)

Page 469, Question 13
We should re-read, or at least skim, the second, third, and fourth paragraphs to refresh our memories for this question. If we do, we'll see that they describe the way the Asnaesverket Power Company, Statoil Refinery, Novo Nordisk, and Gyproc all use each other's waste products to produce things, which means choice (A) is correct.

(B) is wrong, even though many untrained test-takers will be tempted to choose it when they read that the first sentence of this selection calls the town of Kalundborg "the world's most elaborate prototype of an ecopark." The fact that Denmark has "the world's most elaborate prototype of an ecopark" doesn't necessarily mean it's "one of the world's leaders in developing new sources of energy," as the answer choice requires. Having an ecopark that recycles waste products isn't necessarily the same thing as developing new sources of energy. This is yet another example of the extreme importance of reading everything on the ACT very carefully, and not allowing yourself to make assumptions!

(C) is wrong because the idea of eliminating the need for energy is never mentioned in the passage. Many untrained test-takers will fall for this choice because they don't read it carefully enough. This choice does seem vaguely related to the text, which talks about energy and recycling; we see in lines 21 and 22 that some "waste steam" is used to "heat thirty-five hundred homes in the town, eliminating the need for oil furnaces," but "eliminating the need for oil furnaces" in the text is not the same thing as eliminating a "town's need for energy" in the answer choice, because the text never says that oil furnaces are the only source of energy in the town.

(D) is incorrect because it's not supported by the text, even if it might seem reasonable to an uninformed reader. The text never mentions money at all, so the ACT won't accept this as a correct answer.

Page 469, Question 15

For this question, we need to find evidence in the text that each part of the pair in the correct answer choice provides some material or service to its partner. As always, this will require us to read carefully.

(A) is wrong. The text says Statoil provides purified waste gas to Gyproc (lines 35 through 38), but we don't see any evidence of Gyproc providing anything to Statoil.

(B) is wrong. Although we can see that the Asnaesverket Power Company provides heat to warm fish farms, the text doesn't mention the fish farmers doing anything for the Asnaesverket Power Company.

(C) is correct because Novo Nordisk provides fertilizer to farmers in lines 31 through 33, and the farmers' plants are then used "to feed the bacteria in the fermentation tanks" (lines 33 and 34) back at Novo Nordisk (note that the fermentation tanks are mentioned in connection with Novo Nordisk on line 28). So we can see that each element of this pair provides something to the other one, just as the question requires.

(D) is incorrect because the passage doesn't mention Statoil and Novo Nordisk providing things to one another.

Page 469, Question 19

A lot of untrained test-takers will be needlessly frustrated by this question, because they won't know the meaning of the word "offal," and they'll expect that to keep them from understanding the answer. But the question is written in a way that doesn't require us to know what the word means; all we have to do is find the relevant portion of the text and see what it describes.

So let's do that.

If we go back and read about "designed offal" in line 51, we can see that it refers to the concept described in the previous sentence, which says that some companies "design[] their processes" so "any waste . . . is valuable and can be used by someone else." This matches up almost word-for-word with choice (A), which says that "companies can design ways in which their waste products can be used," so we know (A) is the correct answer.

(B) will be a tempting choice because it talks about reducing waste, which seems to go along with the general theme of this passage. But if we look at the specific sentence in line 51, we see that the key idea is *re-using* waste, not *reducing* it. The text even says in lines 51 through 54 that "a process with lots of waste . . . may be better than one with a small amount of waste" under certain conditions. Remember that you always have to read carefully and avoid making assumptions about the text!

(C) is wrong because there isn't any discussion of whether technology has kept pace with waste disposal.

(D) is wrong because it doesn't restate the text; instead, it just jumbles together certain concepts from the text. The passage does mention design, and it also mentions landfills, but it doesn't talk about designing landfills. It talks about designing industrial processes so that less waste ends up in landfills.

Notice, again, that we were able to find the answer to this question with complete confidence even though we never had to think about the actual meaning of the word "offal." Remember that the ACT will often let you work around small gaps in your knowledge if you read carefully and stick to the approach laid out in this Black Book.

Page 470, Question 21

This is one of those ACT Reading questions that will seem unfair to many untrained test-takers, because it asks us to find the choice that "best characterizes the author's attitude." Most people will approach this question subjectively, but we trained test-takers know that the correct answer will be the one that objectively restates ideas from the text, no matter how subjective the wording of the question might seem to somebody who doesn't understand the test.

We also know that we don't have to answer this question first just because it's the first one in the passage. Since this question doesn't have a line citation, and since it seems like it might touch on many different portions of the text, it might be easier to work through some or all of the other questions about this passage first, and then return to number 21 after we have a little more familiarity with the concepts in the passage. It's up to you which order you choose to approach the questions in, but I'd probably skip this question the first time around and come back to it after I'd answered some of the others.

This is also, unfortunately, another striking example of a question whose explanation in the Red Book is (at best) needlessly complicated. The Red Book's explanation never explicitly refers to the key phrases in the passage that decide the correct answer, which is a serious problem for readers who want to learn how the ACT actually works so they can increase their scores.

Let's take a look.

(A) is correct because it's fully supported by the text. We can see right away that the author "welcomes" the CD-ROMs because he calls them "potentially the most important thing to happen to the texts of Shakespeare since the 18th century" in the first sentence of the passage

The answer choice also refers to the "original intent" of the playwright, and we find that referred to in three places in the passage: line 23, line 27, and line 64.

In line 23, the author says Shakespeare "intended [his plays] to be repeatedly performed." Line 27 says Shakespeare's "words were not meant to remain on the page" because they were "destined for the . . . human voice." Line 64 says the same words "were meant for our ears as well as our eyes."

Those last two citations are the other key phrases that make (A) correct, because the author specifically says in those citations that the works of Shakespeare were meant to be heard, not just read. The passage says repeatedly that CD-ROMs allow people to hear the plays as well as read them (see paragraph 4, for example).

But the Red Book's explanation for this question on page 550 never touches on those critical citations. Instead of explicitly pinpointing the phrases that actually make (A) correct, the Red Book offers a list of vaguely relevant phrases that don't contradict (A) but also don't explicitly support it. The Red Book's explanation points out that the CD-ROM allows viewers to imagine different versions of the play, but it never says this was Shakespeare's intent, because the passage itself never says this was Shakespeare's intent. (The closest the passage gets to that is in lines 22 through 26, when it says that Shakespeare intended the plays to be "repeatedly performed," and, *as a consequence* of that intention, the plays "would be continually cut . . . or even radically reconceived." But this isn't the same thing as saying that Shakespeare's intention was to have the plays reconceived. His intention was to have them performed, and their reimagination is presented as a by-product of the repeated performances, not an intended outcome in itself.)

To a lot of people, everything I've just said may seem like splitting hairs for no reason. But I have a very good reason for taking issue with the Red Book's explanation for this question: I want you to do well on the ACT, and this Red Book explanation doesn't lay a good foundation for you to do that.

If you want to answer ACT Reading questions with speed and confidence, and get them right, then you need to look at the text in the precise, literal-minded way that I teach in this Black Book. If you use the vague, subjective approach often found in Red Book explanations, you'll waste a lot of time on test day and get a lot of questions wrong.

The ACT is all about details and repetition, and that's why I repeatedly point it out when the Red Book gets the details wrong. I want you to succeed on the test, and these are the kinds of issues you need to be aware of in order for that to happen.

Now let's take a look at the other choices.

(B) is incorrect because the author never indicates that the CD-ROMs actually *verified* anything. The passage talks about people revising Shakespeare's plays, and it talks about CD-ROMs, but it never connects those two ideas in the way this answer choice does.

(C) is incorrect because, as described in the explanation of choice (A) above, the author praises the CD-ROMs in the first sentence of the essay. He never "bemoans their arrival" as this answer choice would require.

(D) is incorrect because the author never expresses any skepticism about the potential of CD-ROMs, and never discusses people who are intimidated by Shakespeare.

Page 471, Question 22

Because of the way this question is phrased, the correct answer must restate a concept that appears in the last paragraph but doesn't appear anywhere else in the passage.

It might be easier to go through the answer choices if we've read the passage beforehand, or if we've answered a few of the other questions before attacking this one (remember that we don't have to answer the questions in the order they're presented). Let's see what we find.

(F) is incorrect because the author offers specific examples of the way CD-ROM technology enhances appreciation of Shakespeare in the fourth and fifth paragraphs.

(G) is incorrect because the fifth paragraph discusses specific actors and actresses who have performed roles in Shakespeare plays. We could find their names by skimming the passage for capital letters close together in the middle of sentences.

(H) is incorrect, but the reasoning might be a little tricky. The specific reason why scholars started to view the plays as treasures isn't discussed anywhere in the passage, including the last paragraph. People often incorrectly choose (H) because they reason that a concept that's not anywhere in the passage would still be absent from the passage if the last paragraph were removed. To be honest, I can understand this type of reasoning, and I don't think the ACT should include these types of wrong answers on a question like this (which they do very rarely). But if we read the original question *extremely* literally, we see that the phrase "*would* contain no specific examples [emphasis mine]" is in the subjunctive, and technically indicates that the original passage *does* contain such an example as long as the last paragraph is included. Don't get me wrong—I'm not defending the ACT on this. I think this question is misleading in a way that transcends the normal misleading that happens on a standardized test like the ACT, and borders on flawed test design. But it's technically true that the wording of the question does require us to find a concept that appears in the last paragraph, rather than a concept that doesn't appear anywhere in the passage.

So here's the bottom line on something like this: if you ever see another real ACT question worded like this, just know that the test is going to require you to find a concept that does appear somewhere in the passage.

(By the way, this is one more very good example of the importance of considering all the answer choices. If you accidentally stopped at (H), thinking it was correct, you'd miss the question. But if you still looked at (J), as I teach you to do, you might have seen that (J) also seemed like a valid answer, and from there you would have been able to figure out that (J) is in line with the wording of the question while (H) is technically not.)

(J) is correct because the last paragraph ends with a specific example of an inconsistency in the text of *Romeo and Juliet*: the difference between "rest" and "rust." There are no other specific phrases from the text of a Shakespeare play in the rest of the passage.

Page 471, Question 27

This question often frustrates test-takers. But, as always, we'll find that the frustration and confusion disappear if we read carefully and take things one phrase at a time.

The question mentions that the passage refers to "efforts today by editors to assemble a final version" of a Shakespeare play. Using similar wording, choice (B) refers to the "final form" of Shakespeare's plays.

All of the other answer choices are wrong because they deal with the idea that Shakespeare's plays were "open" and "unfinished" (lines 22 and 23); that is, that they were open to interpretation and adaptable and changeable instead of being intended to exist in some "final" form.

That's really all there is to it: on a fundamental level, (B) is right because it talks about a "final form" that corresponds to the phrase "final version" in the original prompt.

So why do so many people struggle with this question?

I think the primary issue for most people is that the passage as a whole *rejects* the idea of a finalized form of Shakespeare's works, but this question asks about people trying to create such a finalized form. So if you waste time worrying about the overall theme of the passage, you can end up confusing yourself on this question. On the other hand, if you just keep it simple and notice that the phrase "final version" is pretty much an exact synonym for the phrase "final form," then this question isn't such a big deal.

This is a great demonstration of the point I've made repeatedly throughout these solutions: the ACT Reading section is all about reading carefully and paying attention to detail, not about trying to analyze or interpret anything in your own way.

Page 471, Question 30

This is another question that test-takers often miss because they don't focus on reading the relevant text carefully. The question asks about a statement in line 80. If we read the entire sentence that contains the citation, we see that (F) is correct because it directly restates the text.

The sentence starting in line 77 describes "a stage performance at its best" that "makes us . . . think . . . 'this *must* be so,'" which matches up directly with the idea of "an audience member's response to a high quality theater performance." The "audience" in the answer choice refers to "us" in line 79; the "response" in the answer choice refers to what we're made to "experience" and "think" in lines 78 and 79; the "high-quality theater performance" in the choice corresponds to "a stage performance at its best" in lines 77 and 78.

(G) is wrong because nothing in the surrounding text indicates this is a line from a play. This answer choice is probably intended to confuse people who don't go back to the passage to check that their answers match up with the text exactly, because such a person might mistakenly recall the two quotes in the final sentence of the passage, rather than the reaction that the question is actually referring to.

(H) is wrong because nothing in the text indicates that this is being said by a director; in fact, directors are only mentioned much earlier in the passage.

(J) is wrong because the text never says this quotation is part of any audio clip. This is yet another wrong answer on the ACT Reading section that tries to confuse us by combining unrelated concepts from the passage into one answer choice.

Page 472, Question 31

The prompt for this question combines two elements that will frustrate most untrained test-takers: a reference to the "author's purpose," and the phrase "most likely." Either phrase individually would be likely to make most test-takers try to interpret the passage subjectively, and combining them only tends to multiply that effect.

But, as trained test-takers, we know the correct answer choice will be supported directly by the text, no matter how subjective the wording of the question seems to be. It's important to remember, though, that when the ACT asks about the "purpose" or "point" of a passage, we might see that more than one answer choice restates an idea from the passage. If that happens, then the correct choice will be the one that is restated most frequently in the passage.

If you like to read or skim the passage before answering questions about it, you may be able to recall enough of the material to be able to work through the answer choices. If you prefer not to look at the passage before diving into the questions, then it might be a wise idea to skip this question at first and answer some of the questions with obvious line references in them before returning to answer this one.

Now let's take a look at the answer choices.

(A) is incorrect because the passage doesn't specifically say any differences are "irreconcilable," although it does mention some differences among theories. We may think that the differences seem difficult to reconcile, or even impossible, but the ACT doesn't care what we think—it only cares what's actually on the page. Since the text never says that the differences can't be reconciled, (A) is wrong.

(B) is incorrect. The passage does discuss the early history of Mars, but that discussion is never related to "other aspects of planetary science" as this answer choice would require.

(C) is wrong, but we need to be very familiar with the rules of the ACT to see why. The first paragraph does mention the idea of Earth's atmosphere maintaining a high pressure that makes it possible for rivers and oceans to exist (lines 8 through 10). It also mentions that data from Mars seemed to suggest that Mars once had a thick atmosphere and water on its surface (lines 4 through 8). So the first paragraph definitely mentions a difference between the atmospheric pressure levels on the two planets, and illustrates this difference by pointing out that surface water can exist on Earth but not on Mars. But when we look at the next answer choice, we'll see that it restates ideas that appear in the text far more often than this idea of illustrating differences in atmospheric pressure, which only occurs in the first paragraph. Remember that questions about the author's "purpose" can often have more than one answer choice that restates a part of the text, and the correct answer will be the one that is restated most often in the text.

(D) is correct because the entire passage mentions "recent theories" and "controversies" related to early Martian history:

- Line 11 talks about what "scientists proposed" to explain what Mars's atmosphere was like when it formed. This is a theory.
- Line 22 mentions "scenarios" that "researchers have suggested," and these are also theories.
- Line 25 mentions what some scientists have "hypothesized," and those hypotheses are also theories.
- The fourth paragraph explains the mechanics behind Melosh's and Vickery's theory about the loss of the Martian atmosphere, and the fifth paragraph describes how they tried to test their theory with computer modeling.
- Line 65 says "some researchers are questioning" whether there ever was an atmosphere on Mars like the one that Melosh and Vickery believe existed. This is a controversy—a disagreement between two sides.
- Lines 78 through 81 talk about a "suggest[ion] that the planet might have been covered by . . . ice," which is yet another theory.

- The last paragraph mentions Vickery "sticking by her original assumptions," which is another reference to Vickery's position in the controversy mentioned in the 6th paragraph.

So we can see that the "recent theories" and "controversies" mentioned in this answer choice come up much more often in the passage than the idea from choice (C) does, which makes choice (D) right and choice (C) wrong, according to the ACT's rules for Reading questions about the "author's purpose."

Page 473, Question 40

A lot of test-takers miss this question because they just don't bother to go back to the passage and double-check the numbers in the answer choices. Don't make that kind of mistake! Don't let laziness or haste keep you from correctly answering a relatively easy question.

When we look at the description of Vickery's and Melosh's work on the amount of time it took for Mars's atmosphere to change, we see that paragraph 5 describes their computer modeling. The last sentence of that paragraph, which goes from lines 58 to 62, features numbers that appear in three of the answer choices for this question:

- 3.7 billion
- 10,000
- 600-700 million

So which number is the correct answer? If we read the sentence carefully, we see that the researchers' model was "able to . . . grow a thick atmosphere in only 600 or 700 million years" (lines 60 through 62). So choice (G) is correct.

As it turns out, 3.7 billion is the number of years that Vickery and Melosh went back to determine the "impact rate" to use in their modeling, and 10,000 is the average number of years between impacts according to that rate.

The number in choice (J) appears in line 12 as the age of the planet Mars.

This question might seem pretty simple when we examine it calmly, but questions like this often prove troublesome for many test-takers, because they don't seize the opportunity to make sure they lock down a correct answer on a relatively easy question. Easy questions count just as much towards your score as hard ones do, so don't throw them away!

Page 605, Question 3

This is yet another ACT Reading question whose official Red Book explanation completely overlooks the key phrase in the passage.

The question talks about what the passage "strongly suggests," and the Red Book's explanation on page 685 talks about what the passage "implies," but the fact of the matter is that the passage directly and specifically states that the second set is the final set. There is no suggestion or implication involved. As we've seen repeatedly throughout this Black Book, there is never any suggestion or implication involved with the ACT, even if the Red Book tries to tell you there is.

The only mention of the sets in the show comes in the first paragraph, so let's look there.

In the very first sentence of the paragraph, we see that the "jazz show" was "winding down" when it was "nearing the end of the second set." This is all the Red Book's solution mentions when it justifies (A) as the correct answer, but this isn't actually enough to make (A) correct according to the ACT's rules for the Reading section. For instance, it might be possible that the show could consist of three sets: maybe the first two sets are 20 minutes each, and the last one is just 5 minutes. If that were the case, we could say that the show was "winding down" as it approached the end of the second set, because there would only be another 5 minutes of performance after that set, compared to the previous 35 or 40 minutes of performance—but in this hypothetical scenario, the second set wouldn't have to be the final one.

So why is (A) actually correct, then?

(A) is correct because of lines 10 and 11, which say that it was customary to invite a musician on stage "toward the end of the final set."

So the first paragraph says that Everett Payne was invited onstage "nearing the end of the second set." At the end of the paragraph, we're told that a musician is customarily invited up "toward the end of the final set." That means that the "second set" in the first sentence of the paragraph and the "final set" in the last sentence of the paragraph *must be the same set*.

So there's actually no suggestion or implication involved. The first paragraph says explicitly that the "second set" is the "final set," though we have to read carefully to catch it, and though the official explanation in the Red Book itself doesn't actually acknowledge it.

Let's check out the other choices.

(B) is tempting for a lot of test-takers, because the description of Everett Payne's playing certainly sounds like it would take a long time. But the text never explicitly says how long the playing actually takes, nor does it say anything about the length of the first set. Since there's no concrete way to know the length of either set, there's no way to compare their lengths, and no way to say that (B) is reflected in the text.

(C) is incorrect because the text never mentions a third set on Sunday night; in fact, the idea of a third set is ruled out by the phrases quoted in our discussion of choice (A).

(D) is wrong because the text says of the musicians in the bullpen that "one or two of" (line 11) the bandstand musicians were invited "to sit in with the band" "toward the end of the final set" (lines 10 through 12), which means the musicians in the bullpen played along with the band, and only did that toward the end of the set. The beginning of the set must have been played by the band. Some test-takers will be tempted to choose this answer if they don't read the text carefully enough, because the last few paragraphs make it sound like Everett Payne is playing *Sonny Boy Blue* by himself. But the 9th paragraph mentions that the bassist and drummer are playing with him.

Again, the main lesson to learn from this question is that the correct answer to every question on the ACT Reading section is *always* stated directly in the text, even when the Red Book's own explanation doesn't acknowledge that.

If you want to beat the ACT, you have to remember that the correct answer to every real ACT question is always objectively predictable if you know how the test works, and if you read carefully. Thinking about suggestions and implications while you take the ACT will only hurt your score.

Page 605, Question 6

Most untrained test-takers would try to approach a question like this by subjectively interpreting the text, but we trained test-takers know the correct answer will have to be directly restated in the text, even if the question seems subjective on the surface.

Also, notice that each answer choice for this question includes two descriptions of "the purists." Remember that we only need to find one incorrect description (of the two) to eliminate an answer choice, and that both descriptions in the right answer must be supported by the text.

Let's take a look.

(F) is wrong because we know "the purists" aren't "open minded," since we can see in line 37 that they showed "open disgust" after only a few chords of music, without giving Everett Payne a chance to show what he wanted to do.

(G) is correct because the text gives us examples of "the purists" being both "snobbish" and "intolerant." We can see that they're snobbish in line 87, which says that they "normally refused to applaud even genius," and we know that they're intolerant because line 37 says they showed "open disgust" when they heard Everett Payne begin to play.

(H) is wrong because nothing in the text supports the idea that they're either rational or educated. We might subjectively expect people who care a lot about jazz music to be "well educated," but that's not enough on the ACT; since the text doesn't explicitly state that the purists are rational or educated, (H) is wrong.

(J) is wrong because nothing in the text indicates the experience level of the purists, one way or the other.

Page 605, Question 10

This is a relatively easy and direct question if we correctly locate the key phrase in the text, but many test-takers give up on it and don't take the few extra seconds to make sure they've actually selected the right answer.

The text says Everett Payne's playing is "at a slower tempo" in line 41, which could mislead a lot of test-takers into choosing (F). And paragraphs 3 and 4 describe Everett Payne himself as both "deliberate" and "absentminded," which could make a lot of test-takers choose (G) incorrectly. On top of that, line 82 mentions "church," so some people could be misled into choosing (H), too.

The problem is that none of these incorrect answer choices specifically indicates what *Hattie* thinks about the *playing*. Only (J) does that, because we see Hattie's view of the performance in lines 78 and 79: "[Everett Payne] took them on a joyous, terrifying roller coaster of a ride [sic] it seemed to Hattie." Since this directly states that "it seemed to Hattie" to be a "roller coaster of a ride," we know that (J) is correct.

(F) describes how the playing seemed to the narrator. (G) describes how Everett Payne himself seemed to Hattie. And (H) describes the atmosphere after Everett Payne had finished playing.

Let this question be yet another reminder of the importance of reading extremely carefully on the ACT! If you miss one key phrase in the prompt or in the passage, or if you don't bother to look at all the answer choices in the text, you could very easily end up throwing this easy question away for no reason. That's exactly the kind of mistake that low-scoring test-takers often make. Don't do that.

Page 607, Question 14

This is an example of an "EXCEPT" question, so we have to find the one answer choice that is NOT present in the text. This will require us to locate three different answer choices somewhere in the text, which kind of means we have to work three times as hard on this question as we might for another question. (Remember that we should always consider every answer choice in a question, but it's usually easier to figure out why an answer choice *fails* to restate the text then to be certain that a choice actually restates the text.)

For a lot of test-takers, it might be easier to approach this question after answering most or all of the other questions in this passage, because doing that will usually help you familiarize yourself with most of the passage, which could make it easier to figure out which answer choice doesn't actually exist in the text.

Let's take a look and see what we find.

(F) is the correct answer. The author does say a lot about sprawl, but he never actually says how long it's been happening in U.S. cities.

(G) is wrong, because the author says specifically, in lines 17 and 18, that "development that destroys communities isn't progress," which answers the question in (G).

(H) is wrong because lines 67 through 72 describe zoning laws and codes, and then lines 73 and 74 say the codes are "a major reason why 82 percent of all trips in the United States are taken by car," which answers the question in (H).

(J) is wrong because the author offers an answer to this question in the final paragraph, though we have to read carefully to see it. This paragraph doesn't actually use the word "sprawl," but it does refer to the idea of shaping communities "by choice, not by chance," and the idea of making choices that encourage "alternatives to the automobile." In the rest of the passage, sprawl is equated with unplanned, chaotic development, and also with widespread reliance on cars for transportation. So we know that the steps in this paragraph that could be taken to fight bad development and the use of cars are also steps that would fight sprawl, according to the author.

Page 607, Question 18

The Red Book's explanation for this question makes no sense, and can only have been written by someone who either didn't read or didn't understand the question and the text. The first problem with the Red Book explanation is that it says the word "leapfrog" "means that there is open space between that urban fringe and the subdivisions in question." But the word "leapfrog" doesn't actually mean there must be open space between two things; in fact, its meaning doesn't indicate anything about spatial relationships (if anything, we might even argue that two people can only play leapfrog if they're right next to each other). The second problem is that the question and the text are talking about an individual house being "detached," while the Red Book explanation talks about the fact that space must exist between the urban fringe and the subdivisions in the text. Finally, the Red Book explanation assumes that all subdivisions must consist only of detached homes, but, in reality, subdivisions can feature townhomes and other non-detached housing—and, on top of that, the ACT Reading section would never require us to know about types of housing in order to answer a question. So the Red Book explanation for this question isn't much help if our goal is to learn to approach other questions in the future.

Let's talk about what's actually happening in this question.

The word "detached" is used in line 51, in the phrase "a detached home in the middle of a grassy lawn." If the home is "in the middle of a grassy lawn," then it makes sense to say that it must be "set apart" from other homes, since there is a grassy lawn all around it. That means (G) is the correct answer.

There's nothing in the text to support the idea that the home in the sentence would be "objective," and there's also nothing to indicate that the home has been "broken apart" or "taken away" from anything.

Remember that when you're choosing the meaning of a word used in context, there has to be something in the text that directly supports your choice—you can't just answer based on a feeling you get about the word, without verifying that your answer directly restates a concept that is explicitly stated in the passage. Here, for instance, we see the phrase "in the middle of a grassy lawn," which concretely supports the idea that the "detached" house must be "set apart" from other houses.

Page 608, Question 21

Like every ACT Reading question, this one will depend on key phrases found in the text. Since the question asks about the narrator's point of view and doesn't give a specific line citation or paragraph for us to refer to, we may need to be broadly familiar with the passage in order to know which parts we should look at more carefully to find the correct answer. For that reason, some test-takers might prefer to skip this question at first, and return to it after they've become more familiar with the passage from answering other questions.

(A) is correct. Line 1 describes how the author's interest in flowers began ("I was seventeen when it started . . ."). Paragraph 6 shows how her study of flowers became a bigger part of her life by describing her increasing use of the field guide: "over the next several years this field guide would become my closest companion . . ." Finally, the closing paragraph describes how her interest in flowers led her to "travel" down a "road" that included "geology, biogeography, evolutionary biology," which are all different disciplines related to the study of the natural world. This matches up exactly with choice (A).

Notice that we don't need to know the exact meaning of the words "quaternary" and "biogeography," because we can tell that words like "geology" and "biology" relate to the natural world; we might also notice that "bogs," "forests," "climate change," and "continental drift" are also part of the natural world, and are also mentioned as things the author studied after learning about flowers.

(B) is incorrect, but just barely. The author does begin by describing an event that led to a lifelong fascination, but this fascination is with flowers in general, not with asters in particular. It's true that the first flower she takes notice of is an aster, but the rest of the passage clearly indicates that the author is interested in all flowers. Remember that even one wrong word makes an entire answer choice incorrect.

(C) is incorrect for a couple of reasons, but we may need to read carefully to see how. First, the passage doesn't "review" any relationships; it only mentions them in passing. Second, the passage only explicitly mentions that the narrator loves flowers; it doesn't actually say that this interest is shared by the young man in the first paragraph or by Julie in the last paragraph. The young man in the opening of the passage happens to know what an aster is, but there's no indication that he's interested in flowers in general. In the closing paragraph, Julie is described as someone who also identifies individual plants, but that isn't the same thing as being interested in flowers.

(D) is wrong because the text never describes the author having any kind of career.

Notice, once again, how the question hangs on specific key words and phrases, and how critical it is to read the relevant parts of the text very carefully!

Page 609, Question 23

The answer to this question is (D), because the author never actually gives a name for the flower she's looking at. She does list the names of other flowers that are similar to the one she's looking at, but she never positively identifies it. She finishes her description of this incident in lines 48 through 51 by saying, "I noticed that there were six more pages ahead, each packed with five-petaled yellow flowers—St. Johnsworts, loosestrifes, puccoons." These names make up the first three answer choices for this question, but the author never says that one of them was the name of the flower she found.

Page 609, Question 27

I want to call your attention to this question because it's a perfect example of the way careless test-takers often miss ACT questions that they could have easily answered correctly.

The text contains many references to the idea of the Peterson's book in connection with vague references to time that might seem related to words like "days," "weeks," and "months" in the wrong answer choices. Line 31 mentions the author owning the book "for about a week," which could indicate a time period measured in days or in weeks. Line 67 indicates the author was using the book "by the time the next summer came," which could be a period of time measured in months from the events at the beginning of the text.

Careless, untrained test-takers might be tempted to try to guess the correct answer from those inconclusive phrases in the text. But disciplined, trained test-takers know that the correct answer must be spelled out somewhere directly on the page—if we haven't found the answer spelled out in black-and-white, then we haven't finished looking.

In this case, when we eventually locate the specific point in the text that describes the Peterson's as the author's "closest companion" in line 26, we see that the book became her companion "over the next several years" (line 25). That matches up exactly with choice (D), so we know we have the correct answer, with no ambiguity or hesitation.

This question is arguably more straightforward than many ACT Reading questions will be—the correct answer is always spelled out in the text, but in this case we're dealing with the exact same words and phrases in the prompt, the text, and the correct answer. Remember that this question counts towards your score just as much as every other question does! It would be a shame to miss this question just because you didn't force yourself to find the part of the text that was directly relevant to the question.

Page 611, Question 32

This question will be challenging for a lot of test-takers because this passage will bore most readers, and because the question has no citation, which means we may have a harder time locating the relevant portion of the passage.

The only direct mention of saving money comes in lines 71 through 72, which mentions the idea of "sav[ing] $38 million." If we look at the rest of the short paragraph that includes that phrase, we see that the money would be saved if the accuracy of the prediction were increased by 1 percent.

This seems to match up pretty closely with choice (G), which has words like "forecasters," "predict," and "accurately," which restate the words "forecasts," "prediction," and "accurate" in paragraph 10. So it looks like we're on the right track. But we have to be able to match up every phrase in the answer choice with a phrase in the text, so we have to make sure that the phrase "quantity of water in the snowpack" from the answer choice has a corresponding phrase in the text.

Paragraph 10 includes phrases like "the model" and "the prediction" that must be referring to concepts from earlier in the passage (we can only use the word "the" in the phrase "the model" if we've already discussed a particular model). So let's go back to the previous paragraph and see if we can figure out what's being predicted. Notice that paragraph 9 talks about how "scanning electron microscopy" is used to forecast "amounts of snowpack water." The phrase "scanning electron microscopy" in line 62 matches up with the exact same phrase in the prompt, which tells us that paragraph 9 is probably relevant to the question. And the phrase "amounts of snowpack water" in line 63 matches up with the phrase "quantity of water in the snowpack" from choice (G).

So we can see that paragraph 9 talks about using scanning electron microscopy to predict the amount of water in a snowpack, and that paragraph 10 talks about saving money by increasing the accuracy of that prediction. That means (G) is definitely correct, because it clearly restates the relevant portion of the text.

Notice that answering this question really doesn't require us to understand how scanning electron microscopy actually works, or even what a snowpack is. All we needed to do was match up the phrases in the prompt and choice (G) with the phrases from part of the text, and make sure that the relationships among those phrases were the same in the choice and in the text. In other words, it's enough to know that both (G) and the text talk about saving money by improving the accuracy of predictions about the amount of water in snowpack—we don't have to know what the technical terms actually mean, just how they relate to each other.

Let's look at the other choices now.

(F) is wrong. The passage mentions the possibility of an increased need for water in the future in lines 74 through 83, but it never connects that idea to the idea of saving money through the use of scanning electron microscopy.

(H) is wrong because the discussion of "agricultural researchers" in the sixth and seventh paragraphs makes no mention of saving money.

(J) is wrong as well. The text mentions that snowmelt accounts for "about 75 percent of the annual water supply" of those states, but that's not the same thing as saying that scanning electron microscopy will save money by increasing the water supply by 75 percent.

Page 611, Question 33

Many untrained test-takers will miss this question because they're too lazy to go back to the text and take a second look at the citation to make sure they don't make a mistake. Instead, they'll try to choose an answer based on their memory of the passage, and risk throwing away an easy question.

If we look back at the citation, we see very clearly that the phrase "metamorphosed conditions" is immediately followed by an explanation: "crystals often change once on the ground . . ."

That matches exactly with choice (C), the correct answer.

Let's take a look at the wrong answers.

(A) is incorrect. Temperature and humidity are mentioned in line 29, but not in connection with "metamorphosed conditions."

(B) is also incorrect. The text mentions dust in line 19, but not in connection with "metamorphosed conditions."

(D) is also wrong. The text mentions changing environmental conditions in the eleventh paragraph, but not in connection with "metamorphosed conditions."

Notice that all three of the wrong answer choices appear somewhere in the text—they're just not related to the phrase "metamorphosed conditions" that appears in the question. Because those terms appear in the text, many test-takers will accidentally choose one of them—they'll recall reading something about one of them at some point, but they won't take the extra 5 seconds to look back at the citation in the question and see what the text actually says about the key phrase. Don't make that kind of mistake!

Page 611, Question 37

I wanted to talk about this question because it's another great example of a relatively straightforward question that many untrained test-takers will miss unnecessarily, simply because they don't make an effort to read carefully.

The text explains the relationship between snowflakes and snow crystals in lines 16 through 17: "snowflakes are collections of two or more snow crystals." This matches up directly with the correct answer, (D), which says that snowflakes "are composed of more than one crystal."

(A) and (C) might be tempting choices for some test-takers who misread the question or the text, because both of these answer choices refer to snow crystals. They're both wrong because the question asks us for an attribute of snowflakes.

(B) is wrong because it reverses the relationship described in (D). This answer choice says that snowflakes combine to form snow crystals, when the text says that the crystals combine to form the flakes. You can probably see how easily a test-taker might choose (B) if he didn't read it carefully enough, and if he didn't look at all the other choices to make sure he hadn't made a mistake!

Even though this passage is one of the ones in the Red Book that students complain about the most, this particular question is actually pretty simple if we locate the relevant portion of the text and read it carefully. Keep that in mind the next time you see a daunting or boring passage on the ACT—no single question will require you to have a deep understanding of the entire passage.

Page 749, Question 1

This question might confuse a lot of test-takers at first, especially if they haven't really read much of the passage before they try to answer it.

All of the answer choices talk about how the narrator feels about going to college, but the idea of college only appears once in the entire passage, when the narrator mentions "going to the university that fall" in line 19. If you don't notice that phrase, then you'll end up concluding that all of the answer choices are totally unrelated to the text—which is impossible, of course, because one of them has to be the right answer.

The narrator says her family has to sell its wheat instead of holding it "if I was going to the university that fall" (lines 17 through 19). That means (A) can't be correct, because it mentions the narrator being "unsure" whether she wants to go to college. Some test-takers might be confused by the word "if" in the text, which might make the author sound uncertain if we don't read carefully enough. But in this case the word "if" only means that the author's desire to go to the university is the reason the wheat must be sold in September. This is confirmed by the next sentence, which says the family "couldn't wait for" the price to go higher "along toward Christmas" (line 20).

(B) is incorrect because nothing in the text supports the idea that the narrator believes she'll be prevented from going to college, and nothing in the text actually indicates the cost of attending.

(C) is incorrect because the narrator never says she's planning to stay on another year at the family ranch.

(D) is correct because lines 17 through 20 specifically say that the narrator wants to go to college in the fall, and that going to college depends on the money that would come from selling the wheat. Some trained test-takers might get caught up on the phrase "anxiously anticipating" in the answer choice, but it's justified by the next-to-last paragraph in the text, which says the narrator "felt so excited" about selling the wheat early so she could go to college that she "couldn't walk soberly."

Page 749, Question 7

This is another question that the Red Book explains poorly. The official Red Book explanation on page 827 says the answer to this question is (D) because of the phrase "blows dirt into your eyes and hair." But we know, as trained test-takers, that this explanation can't be the real one, because the ACT Reading section requires correct answers to restate elements of the text, and the idea of blowing dirt into someone's face isn't the same thing as the idea of power presented in choice (D).

Choice (D) is actually correct because of the word "roars" in line 3. According to the Merriam-Webster online dictionary, the verb "to roar" means to make a sound "with full force," and it's this idea of forcefulness that's restated by the word "powerful" in choice (D): if the wind roars, and roaring means doing something with full force, then the wind is forceful, and "forceful" is a synonym for "powerful."

It might seem like I'm needlessly splitting hairs here, especially if you haven't read "How Can The Red Book's Explanations Of Its Own Questions Be Wrong?" earlier in this Black Book, where I explain why the Red Book's explanations for its own questions are often bad. But I assure you that these small distinctions are actually very important if you want to maximize your ACT score—it's absolutely critical that you understand how the test actually decides which choices are correct and which choices are incorrect. If you approach all questions in the subjective way that the Red Book recommends for this question, you might occasionally get lucky and get a question right, but most of the time you'll end up talking yourself into a wrong answer, which is exactly what the ACT wants you to do.

If you want to be able to answer ACT Reading questions quickly, correctly, and confidently, then you have to look for the answer choice that directly restates the key words and phrases in the text. Always. No exceptions.

Page 749, Question 9

To answer this EXCEPT question, we need to decide which answer choice can't "reasonably be said to mean" the same thing as "fenced" does in line 30.

If we go back and read the use of the word "fenced" in context in line 30, we see that we get the following results when we try each of the answer choices in place of the word "fenced:"

(A) "Then I <u>shut</u> them in with my hand and poured off the water . . ."

(B) "Then I <u>penned</u> them in with my hand and poured off the water . . ."

(C) "Then I <u>committed</u> them in with my hand and poured off the water . . ."

(D) "Then I <u>held</u> them in with my hand and poured off the water . . ."

We can see that (A), (B), and (D) still make sense and mean the same thing as the original, whereas (C) doesn't really make any sense. The phrases "to shut in," "to pen in," and "to hold in" all sound natural to a native English-speaker, but the phrase "to commit in" is nonsense in this context. For all these reasons, we know that (C) is the correct answer to this question.

As with most "EXCEPT" questions, the ACT is probably hoping you'll misread the question and pick the answer choice that you think sounds the closest in meaning to the word "fenced," instead of picking the one answer choice that can't be a synonym for "fenced."

This is why it's so important to read everything carefully, and to make sure you briefly consider all the answer choices for every question, so you give yourself a chance to catch your own mistakes. Questions like this also demonstrate why it's so important to be aware of the ACT's rules, and to follow them with extreme discipline.

If you had overlooked the word "EXCEPT" in this question and thought that (A) or (B) seemed like the correct answer, you might still catch your mistake if you looked at all the answer choices and realized that two or three of the choices all seemed equally acceptable. An untrained test-taker in that situation would just randomly pick a single answer choice that seemed the best, but a trained test-taker knows that there's always exactly one valid choice, and three invalid ones. A trained test-taker knows she's made a mistake when she thinks that more than one answer choice is arguably correct. This discipline and awareness would lead her to re-evaluate the entire question, ultimately realizing that she had overlooked the word "EXCEPT," and that (C) was actually correct.

Training yourself to understand and implement the ideas in this Black Book will keep you from throwing away points on the ACT.

Page 751, Question 18

Most untrained test-takers will be frustrated by this question because the prompt seems to be asking us to interpret the passage subjectively. But, as trained test-takers, we know the ACT never asks us to do that—even when the question uses phrases like "most likely" and "in order to," the correct answer must still be the only choice that directly restates elements of the relevant portion of the text.

Let's take a look.

If we go back to read the context of the phrase "walking through" in line 6, we'll see that the relevant sentence contains the phrase "virtually 'walking through.'"

Because of the adverb "virtually" and the paragraph's reference to "three-dimensional computer modeling" in lines 5 and 6, it's clear that (J) is correct.

(F) is incorrect because the phrase "walking through" describes what "researchers" (line 7) did, not what actual Romans did.

(G) is incorrect because this sentence has nothing to do with tourists visiting the Colosseum. Some untrained test-takers will be drawn to this answer choice because it seems like common sense to them—it probably is true that the best way to take a tour of the Roman Colosseum is by proceeding at a leisurely pace. But the actual text has nothing to do with that, so (G) is wrong.

(H) is incorrect because there's no warning in the text, and because the text never indicates whether "researchers are just beginning to develop" these models.

As we can see, the correct answer to this question is spelled out in black and white on the page, just as it must always be for all official ACT Reading questions.

Page 752, Question 21

The key here is to notice the word "LEAST," all in capital letters. You might think to yourself, "How could someone miss a word in all capital letters like that?" Believe me, people do it all the time. I do it myself every once in a while, and I promise you that you'll do it at least once on your ACT journey.

This is why it's so important to make sure you read every question carefully, and to make sure you read through each answer choice—if you do overlook a word like "LEAST" or "EXCEPT" in the prompt, one of the best ways to catch your mistake is to look at all the answer choices and realize that more than one of them seem to describe the text, which isn't the case on a question without a word like "LEAST, "NOT," or "EXCEPT".

With all of that in mind, let's take a look at the answer choices.

(A) is mentioned several times throughout the text: in lines 31 through 38, lines 52 through 57, lines 61 through 63, and so on.

(B) describes a broad topic that comes up in almost every paragraph.

(C) mentions a topic that only comes up once, in the first sentence of the essay (lines 1 through 6).

(D) is another topic that comes up in almost every paragraph.

So we can see pretty clearly that (C) is the answer choice whose topic gets the least attention in the passage.

Page 753, Question 23

This question uses the phrase "most directly," which makes it sound like more than one of the people in the answer choices might have expressed this opinion *somewhat* directly, and our job is to make a subjective decision about who expressed it *most* directly. But, as trained test-takers, we know that it must be the case that only one person directly expresses the idea, and our job is to identify that person, without any subjective interpretation necessary.

I would probably attack this question by referring to the places in the text where Iyer, Rekha, Rahman, and Iyer's parents are quoted, to see which person expresses the idea that the hybrids have matured musically.

For choice (A), Iyer says some positive things about South Asian music in lines 32 through 38, but he never specifically says anything about "maturing musically." This is a great example of a situation in which ACT Reading is not like a normal high school English class; in most English classes, if a student read lines 32 through 38 and said that it mentioned maturity, the teacher would probably accept that phrase as a decent reaction to the text. But on the ACT, we need the correct answer to be directly supported by the text, and we don't have that with choice (A).

For (B), Rekha says in line 57 that "the music has come of age." Since "coming of age" is a synonym for "maturing," (B) is the correct answer because Rekha comes out and makes this statement directly.

(C) and (D) are both wrong because neither Rahman nor Iyer's parents say anything at all in the text.

Page 755, Question 39

Many test-takers will miss this question because they won't read enough of the relevant text. If we only read the sentence from the text that has the word "love" in it, we might be confused, because the sentence mentions submersibles and the squid, but it doesn't actually say that the man who made the video loved either of those things. In the next sentence, though, the text says clearly that the man filmed the squid because "his girlfriend was interested in marine biology" (line 52). That makes it clear that the love referred to in line 49 is for the man's girlfriend, so (C) is correct.

Let's take a look at the other answer choices.

(A) is wrong because the text never indicates that the man who made the film loved the new squid.

(B) is also wrong, but some test-takers might accidentally choose it if they don't read the passage carefully. The man who made the video of the squid did it for his girlfriend, as we just saw in our discussion of choice (C), and he did it because the girlfriend "was interested in marine biology." But that doesn't mean the man himself loved marine biology. (In fact, it doesn't even mean that the man's girlfriend loved marine biology—being interested in something and loving it aren't necessarily the same thing.)

(D) is wrong because nothing in the text indicates that the man who made the video of the squid loved submersibles.

Conclusion

You've now seen the ACT Reading approach put to the test against a large selection of real ACT Reading questions. You probably noticed that it was highly repetitive and detail-oriented, and that we were always able to find the correct answer somewhere in the text. Keep that in mind as you continue preparing!

Using The Question Explanations In *The Real ACT Prep Guide, 3rd Edition*

When you look at the question explanations in *The Real ACT Prep Guide, 3rd Edition,* you'll want to keep two main things in mind.

First, remember to ignore the way the Red Book refers to the correct answers as the "best" answers. As trained test-takers, we know there are only correct answers and incorrect answers, and correct answers will always be indisputably supported by the text, whereas incorrect answers will not be.

Second, although the Red Book's actual explanations aren't always great, they often do a decent job of highlighting the phrases from the text that either support or contradict an answer choice.

Video Demonstrations

If you'd like to see videos of some sample solutions like the ones in this book, please visit www.ACTprepVideos.com, where a selection of free videos is available for readers of this book.

ACT Reading Quick Summary

This is a one-page summary of the major relevant concepts. Use it to evaluate your comprehension or jog your memory. For a more in-depth treatment of these ideas, see the rest of this section.

The Big Secret: The answer to every question comes directly from what's on the page, without any interpretation or subjectivity.

The actual rules for attacking ACT Reading questions are simple. <u>The hard part is making sure you follow them carefully all the time</u>. Here they are:

- Correct answers are always directly supported in the text.

- Details make the difference—this is not like reading in high school.

- There is always one—and only one—correct answer per question.

Here are the most common wrong-answer patterns you'll see:

- Wrong answers might contain a <u>reasonable assumption</u> that isn't stated in the text.

- Wrong answers might mention concepts from the text but <u>confuse the relationship</u> between those ideas.

- Wrong answers might say the <u>exact opposite</u> of what the text says.

- Wrong answers might be <u>completely irrelevant</u> to the text.

Here's the general ACT Reading process:

- Skim, read, or skip the passage (experiment to find the method you prefer).

- Read the question, and note any citation.

- Read the relevant portion of the text (the citation if there is one, or the part of the text that involves similar concepts to those mentioned in the question).

- Find three wrong answer choices (make use of wrong answer patterns).

- Confirm the remaining answer choice.

- Mark the correct answer.

- Save general passage questions and more difficult questions for the end, and use the knowledge of the text you've gotten from answering the other questions to make these less challenging.

Go back through the ACT Reading walkthroughs and follow along in your copy of *The Real ACT Prep Guide, 3rd Edition* to see demonstrations of these ideas.

ACT Math

"In mathematics the art of proposing questions is more valuable than solving them."
- Georg Cantor

Overview and Important Reminders for ACT Math Questions

We just covered in some detail how the right way to handle the ACT Reading section isn't at all like the right way to handle a typical English class. In an English class, we get credit for being open-minded and imaginative, and for seeing multiple possible meanings in a passage. On the ACT Reading section, we must interpret the text to mean only and exactly what it directly says—no more, and no less.

In the same way that being successful on the ACT Reading section means we have to recognize it as different from the kind of reading we'd do in school, doing well on ACT Math means appreciating how very different ACT Math is from school math. (You'll also see this pattern repeated when we talk about ACT Science and ACT English.)

But, for now, let's take a minute to think about what the ACT Math section is and how it has to work. Then, we'll be in a better position to understand how to beat it.

The ACT is given to around 2 million American high school students each year. Those students go to lots of different schools with thousands of different teachers, and take lots of different kinds of math classes, like algebra, geometry, trigonometry, calculus, and statistics.

Some students go far into calculus and statistics, while others don't get past basic algebra. Some students have the choice to take advanced math, and others go to schools where those classes aren't even offered.

How would you test such a large, diverse group of test-takers, if you were in charge of the ACT?

If you came up with a very advanced test (with calculus, and statistics, and advanced trigonometry), the students who hadn't taken those subjects would have almost no chance at a good score—even if they were very good in the math classes they'd taken, they wouldn't know how to handle an ACT Math section loaded with advanced math they'd never seen before.

On the other hand, it seems that if you made a math test that just covered all the basic topics like simple algebra, geometry, and a little trigonometry, then everybody's scores would be too high. Simple math like that wouldn't be much of a challenge for most high school students, and a test that everybody scored well on wouldn't be of much use to colleges trying to rank their applicants.

So it seems like the test should only ask about relatively basic high school math . . . while still being hard enough that not everybody would do well on it. How could a test accomplish that?

Well, one way would be to test simple math ideas, but to present those simple math ideas in unusual ways that students aren't used to seeing. If the questions ask about basic math ideas in unexpected ways, then the test can simultaneously accomplish both goals: any student with a basic level of math knowledge could potentially answer the questions, since the questions would stick to a certain set of relatively simple math concepts, but the unusual presentation would cause difficulties for a lot of students, so scores wouldn't be high across the board.

As it turns out, that's exactly how the ACT Math section works.

That's why you'll find some students who get straight A's in advanced math courses but can't figure out ACT Math, while other students who've only ever done relatively basic stuff in math classes can do surprisingly well on the ACT. It's a different kind of test from what you'd expect in a normal high school math class, and it requires a different approach if you want to succeed.

The Big Secret Of ACT Math

At this point, you might not be convinced. You might ask yourself, "If the math really is so simple, how come so many people think it's so challenging?"

I would first respond by pointing out that many people think ACT Reading is impossible to master, and we've already discussed at length how the only thing you need to do to answer every question is just to read carefully and find the answer choice that directly restates the text. That's simple enough to do, but many people struggle because they don't know they're supposed to do it.

This is the same type of situation we see with ACT Math. Students don't know how to handle this kind of test, so they want to approach it like they approach high school math tests, which won't work. You're probably starting to understand why that approach fails—let's go into it a little bit more.

Think about the period of time leading up to a typical high school math test. Imagine that your math class is starting a new unit, which probably focuses on a handful of closely related mathematical ideas. For several days or weeks, you'll study those ideas. You'll get homework assignments in which you might do a few dozen problems at a time that all have you repeat basically the same solution with different numbers, over and over again.

Once you've done enough drilling and practicing of those concepts, you'll take a test. That test will ask you to do a few different types of questions—all the things you've been practicing and drilling for weeks. If you've been doing your homework, and paying attention in class, then the material on the classroom test will all be stuff you've seen a lot of times before, and every question will be basically the same thing over and over again. When the test is over, you'll start a new unit on a new topic and go through the whole process again with new material.

The ACT Math section is nothing like that. ACT Math questions will all seem different from each other. When you look at an ACT Math question, it may not be immediately obvious what you're even supposed to do, let alone how you should go about doing it. If you're good at following the format of a normal math test in school, then some ACT Math questions might feel completely foreign to you.

If you're like a lot of untrained test-takers, you'll get frustrated. You may even panic, and you'll probably conclude that ACT Math is way harder than normal math—which is exactly what the people who make the ACT want you to think. But people only think that because nobody has ever told them how the ACT Math section really works.

The Two Critical Components of ACT Math Success

We've learned that ACT Math is all about relatively basic math ideas being presented in unusual ways. That means there are two things we need in order to do well on this section:

- We need basic knowledge of the kinds of math that can appear on the ACT (arithmetic, algebra, geometry, and a tiny bit of trigonometry).

- We need an understanding of the ACT's unwritten rules, patterns, and standards that govern the way ACT Math questions can operate.

Once we're comfortable with the basic math concepts that can appear on the ACT, and we're familiar with the various ways those basic concepts can be presented, we've got everything we need to answer any ACT Math question we'll ever see, even if the question throws us when we first look at it.

We'll start off by covering all of the basic math ideas that can appear in ACT Math questions in the next section, the ACT Math Toolbox.

ACT Math Toolbox

In the coming section, we'll be discussing the best way to approach the ACT Math section. We'll talk about that in terms of patterns and strategies and standards, as we do with the other sections.

But before we do that, we need to be sure that we're familiar with all the math concepts that are allowed to appear in the ACT Math section—most of the math is pretty basic by high school and college standards, but we still need to go over it to make sure we're properly prepared.

The goal of this section is to review each important concept quickly and efficiently. If you need more of an explanation for any given topic, consider asking your math teacher for additional guidance.

You might notice that the material in this review actually seems to be easier than the questions you see in real ACT Math questions. That's because the challenge in the majority of ACT Math questions isn't the actual math you need to do; it's figuring out the proper way to set up the solution. Once you do that, the math is often quite simple (as we'll see in this Toolbox and in the walkthroughs).

Remember that you don't have to be an expert on every one of these concepts. You just need to be able to understand them, and to have an idea of how to work with them in order to be ready for this section of the test. Also, bear in mind that some of this material might seem unfamiliar when you first look at it—if that's the case, I strongly recommend you read through the whole Toolbox twice. Most students are more comfortable with the concepts on the second read-through.

This list is based on the "Content of the ACT Mathematics Test" section of *The Real ACT Prep Guide, 3rd Edition*, which you can find on pages 50 and 51 of that book. It also includes a couple of other ideas that aren't specifically mentioned in the Red Book, but that sometimes come up in real ACT Math questions.

Again, this section isn't about learning the strategic approach to the ACT Math section—that will come later. First, you just have to make sure you're familiar with a relatively dry, boring list of math ideas, and the best way to do that is to go over each one as completely (but quickly) as possible. Let's get started.

Number lines

A number line is a simple diagram that arranges numbers from least to greatest value on a line.

The positions on a number line can be labeled with actual numbers, or with variables.

Example:

This number line shows all the integers from -5 to 6:

-5   -4   -3   -2   -1   0   1   2   3   4   5   6

Absolute value

A number's absolute value is that number's distance from zero on the number line.

Example:

-4 and 4 both have an absolute value of 4. We signify the absolute value of a number with vertical lines on either side of the number: $|-4| = |4| = 4$.

We can create equations using absolute values and one or more variables.

Example:

$|x| = 4$

$x = 4$ or $x = -4$

Properties of integers

Any number that can be expressed without a fraction, decimal, or special symbol is an integer.

Integers can be negative or positive.

Zero is an integer.

Example:

These numbers are integers: -45, -2, 0, 11, 432

These numbers are NOT integers: π, 12.1, 2/3

Integers can be even or odd.

Only integers can be odd or even—a fraction or symbolic number is neither odd nor even.

Even integers can be divided by 2 with nothing left over.

Odd integers have a remainder of 1 when they're divided by 2.

Example:

These are even integers: -14, 8, 38

These are odd integers: -11, 47, 603

An even number plus an even number results in an even number.

An odd number plus an odd number results in an even number.

An odd number plus an even number results in an odd number.

An even number multiplied by an even number results in an even number.

An even number multiplied by an odd number results in an even number.

An odd number multiplied by an odd number results in an odd number.

Some integers have special properties related to addition and multiplication:

- When you multiply or divide any number by 1, the number is unchanged.

- When you multiply any number by 0, the result is 0.

- It's impossible to divide a number by 0 on the ACT Math section.

- Adding or subtracting 0 to or from any number leaves that number unchanged.

Digits

A digit is the individual number character used to write a number.

Example:

These are one-digit numbers: 3, 7, 2

These are two-digit numbers: 93, 28, 11

Special characters are not digits.

Example:

These numbers don't involve digits: π, i

We can refer to digits by the order they appear in the number, starting from the left.

Example:

The third digit in the number 3,920 is 2.

The first digit after the decimal in the number 5.19 is 1.

Rational numbers versus irrational numbers

A rational number is any number that can be expressed as a ratio of two integers.

Examples:

4 is rational because it's equal to $\frac{4}{1}$.

3.9 is rational because it's equal to $\frac{39}{10}$.

0.428 is rational because it's equal to $\frac{428}{1000}$.

Irrational numbers cannot be expressed as a ratio of two integers.

Examples of irrational numbers:

$\sqrt{5}$, π, $\sqrt{19}$

Basic operations

You'll have to do basic operations (addition, subtraction, multiplication, division) with integers, fractions, and decimals.

These are examples of basic operations on integers:

$$3 + 4 = 7$$

$$5 - 2 = 3$$

$$3 \times 7 = 21$$

$$8 \div 4 = 2$$

These are examples of basic operations on fractions:

$$\frac{1}{2} + \frac{3}{2} = 2$$

$$\frac{4}{3} - \frac{2}{3} = \frac{2}{3}$$

$$\frac{3}{2} \times \frac{1}{2} = \frac{3}{4}$$

$$\frac{7}{4} \div \frac{1}{4} = 7$$

(These are discussed in more detail in the "Fractions" section.)

These are examples of basic operations on decimals:

$$2.3 + 3.19 = 5.49$$

$$9.3 - 6.3 = 3$$

$$1.24 \times 3.5 = 4.34$$

$$8.7 \div 10 = 0.87$$

Multiples

A "multiple" of an integer is a number that can be reached when the integer is multiplied by another integer.

Example:

21 is a multiple of 7 because $7 \times 3 = 21$, and 3 is an integer.

The multiples of 7 are 7, 14, 21, 28, 35, 42, and so on.

Every integer is the smallest multiple of itself.

The "least common multiple" of a set of numbers is the smallest multiple common to each member of the set.

Example:

The least common multiple of 4, 5, and 6 is 60, because 60 is the smallest number that's a multiple of 4, 5, and 6.

Factors

A "factor" of an integer is an integer that can be multiplied by another integer to arrive at the original integer.

Example:

7 is a factor of 21, because $7 \times 3 = 21$, and 7 and 3 are integers.

The factors of 21 are 1, 3, 7, and 21.

The "greatest common factor" of a set of numbers is the largest factor common to each member of the set.

Example:

> **The greatest common factor of 24, 60, and 72 is 12, because 12 is the largest number that's a factor of 24, 60, and 72.**

1 is a factor of every integer.

Every integer is its own greatest factor.

A "prime number" is an integer with only two factors: itself, and 1.

1 is not a prime number.

Order of Operations (PEMDAS)

When an expression involves multiple types of operations, the rules of math require us to perform them in a certain order, called the order of operations. Many students learn the proper order by memorizing the acronym **PEMDAS**, which stands for **P**arentheses, **E**xponents, **M**ultiplication, **D**ivision, **A**ddition, **S**ubtraction.

This is the order in which we must perform the operations in an expression. Any PEMDAS operations that don't appear in an expression are omitted when we evaluate that expression.

Example:

$1 + (9 - 3) \times 7 - 6^2 \div 2$

First we do the operation within the parentheses:

$1 + \underline{(9 - 3)} \times 7 - 6^2 \div 2$

Next, we address the exponent expression:

$1 + 6 \times 7 - \underline{6^2} \div 2$

Then we do any multiplication in the equation:

$1 + \underline{6 \times 7} - 36 \div 2$

Then we do the division:

$1 + 42 - \underline{36 \div 2}$

Next we do any addition:

$1 + 42 - 18$

Finally, we do any subtraction that might be in the equation:

$43 - 18$

That gives us the simplified value of the expression:

25

Word problems

In general, ACT word problems are descriptions of either real-life situations or abstract concepts.

Example of a word problem about a real-life situation:

> "Ann buys two sandwiches for four dollars each. She also buys a few bottles of water. Each bottle of water costs seventy-five cents. Ann pays with fifteen dollars and gets four dollars and seventy-five cents in change. How many bottles of water did she buy?"

Example of a word problem about an abstract concept:

> "If y is the arithmetic mean of 5 consecutive even numbers, what is the median of those 5 consecutive even numbers, in terms of y?"

In order to solve ACT word problems, we have to turn them into math problems.

To do that, we note all the numbers given in the problem, and write them down on scratch paper. Then, we identify key phrases and turn them into mathematical symbols for operations and variables. Finally, we use these to relate the numbers we wrote down in the first place.

Example:

> In the phrase "two sandwiches for four dollars each," the word *each* tells us we have to *multiply* the two sandwiches by the four dollars so that we can find out how much money was spent on the two sandwiches: $2 \times 4 = 8$. Eight dollars were spent on the two sandwiches if they cost four dollars each.

> If Ann paid with 15 dollars and got back $4.75, we know that the total cost of the sandwiches and water was $15.00 - $4.75, or $10.25. If we know that the sandwiches cost $8.00, that means the three water bottles cost $10.25 - $8.00, or $2.25.

> If the cost of the water bottles was $2.25, and we know that each water bottle is $0.75, then we can find the number of water bottles by dividing the total cost by the cost of each one: $2.25 / $0.75. Seventy-five cents goes into $2.25 three times, so we know that Ann bought three water bottles.

As you can see, once we've converted the word problem into a math problem, we can solve it like any other question. We'll talk more about the general approach to ACT Math questions in our discussion of the "Math Path."

Fractions

A fraction is a number that represents parts of a whole.

Fractions look like this:

$$\frac{\text{number of parts represented in the fraction}}{\text{number of parts the whole is divided into}}$$

Example:

> **Peter and Jane are sharing a pack of gum. There are 8 sticks of gum in the pack, and Peter takes 3 of them. Since Peter has 3 of the 8 sticks in the pack of gum, he has $\frac{3}{8}$ of the pack of gum.**

The number above the fraction bar is the *numerator*.

The number under the fraction bar is the *denominator*.

If the value of the numerator is less than the value of the denominator, the value of the fraction is less than 1.

If a fraction's numerator is greater than its denominator, then the value of the fraction is greater than 1.

Example:

> $\frac{2}{5}$ **is the same as two fifths, which is less than 1.**
>
> $\frac{8}{2}$ **is equal to 4, which is more than 1.**

Any integer can be seen as having the denominator 1 underneath it.

Example:

> **9 is the same as $\frac{9}{1}$.**

The "reciprocal" of a fraction is what we get if we switch the numerator and denominator of the fraction.

Example:

> **The reciprocal of $\frac{2}{9}$ is $\frac{9}{2}$. The reciprocal of 4 is $\frac{1}{4}$. (Remember that all integers can be thought of as having the denominator 1.)**

Multiplying fractions requires two steps. First, we multiply the numerators to find the numerator in the product fraction. Second, we multiply the denominators to find the denominator in the product fraction.

Example:

> $\frac{3}{8} \times \frac{5}{7} = \frac{?}{?}$
>
> **In step 1, we multiply the numerators to determine the product numerator. In this case, 3 x 5 = 15. So we write 15 as the numerator of the new fraction.**
>
> $\frac{3}{8} \times \frac{5}{7} = \frac{15}{?}$
>
> **In step 2, we multiply the denominators to determine the product denominator. In this case, 8 x 7 = 56. So 56 is the denominator of the product.**
>
> $\frac{3}{8} \times \frac{5}{7} = \frac{15}{56}$

To divide one fraction by another, we simply multiply the first fraction by the RECIPROCAL of the second fraction.

Example:

$$\frac{3}{10} \div \frac{2}{3} = \frac{3}{10} \times \frac{3}{2} = \frac{9}{20}$$

Notice that, to divide $\frac{3}{10}$ by $\frac{2}{3}$, we multiplied $\frac{3}{10}$ by the reciprocal of $\frac{2}{3}$, which is $\frac{3}{2}$.

If you multiply a non-zero integer by a fraction that's smaller than 1, the result will have a smaller absolute value than the original number did.

Examples:

$$4 \times \frac{3}{7} = \frac{12}{7}, \text{ and } \frac{12}{7} \text{ is closer to 0 than 4 is.}$$

$$-9 \times \frac{1}{5} = -\frac{9}{5}, \text{ and } -\frac{9}{5} \text{ is closer to 0 than -9 is.}$$

Fraction a is equal to fraction b if you could multiply the numerator and denominator of fraction a by the same number to get the numerator and denominator of fraction b.

Example:

$$\frac{2}{3} \text{ is equal to } \frac{24}{36}, \text{ because } \frac{2}{3} \times \frac{12}{12} = \frac{24}{36}$$

Since $\frac{12}{12}$ is the same as 1, and we can multiply $\frac{2}{3}$ by $\frac{12}{12}$ in order to get $\frac{24}{36}$, we know that $\frac{2}{3}$ is equal to $\frac{24}{36}$.

"Simplifying" or "reducing" a fraction is the process of dividing the numerator and denominator of the fraction by their greatest common factor.

Example:

$$\frac{15}{20} \text{ is equal to } \frac{3}{4}. \text{ The greatest common factor of 15 and 20 is 5;}$$
when we divide both the numerator and the denominator by 5, we're left with $\frac{3}{4}$.

In order to add or subtract fractions, they must have the same denominator. That means we have to find the "least common denominator" of the fractions, and then convert the fractions so they all have the least common denominator as their denominators. The least common denominator of two or more fractions is the least common multiple of their denominators. That might sound confusing, so let's look at an example.

Example:

$$\frac{1}{2} + \frac{1}{3}$$

We can't add one half and one third in these terms, because they have different denominators.

What's the least common denominator of these two fractions? It's 6, because the least common multiple of 2 and 3 is 6.

We need to put both fractions in terms of sixths in order to be able to add them.

One half is the same as three sixths, and one third is the same as two sixths.

Now our expression looks like this:

$$\frac{3}{6} + \frac{2}{6}$$

Once both numbers have the same denominator, we just add the numerators, keep the same denominator, and we're done:

$$\frac{3}{6} + \frac{2}{6} = \frac{5}{6}$$

Now let's look at an example involving subtraction.

$$\frac{5}{6} - \frac{1}{4}$$

In this case, we can put both numbers in terms of twelfths, which looks like this:

$$\frac{10}{12} - \frac{3}{12}$$

Now we just subtract the second numerator from the first, and keep the same denominator:

$$\frac{10}{12} - \frac{3}{12} = \frac{7}{12}$$

Exponents

When we multiply a number by itself a certain number of times, the result is an exponent of that number.

Example:

$y \times y \times y \times y = y^4$ is an example of an exponential expression. In this example, the y is called the "base," and the 4 is the exponent.

Exponents can be either positive or negative.

To evaluate a positive exponent, we multiply the base by itself as many times as the exponent tells us to.

We evaluate a negative exponent the same way we evaluate a positive exponent, except that we take the reciprocal of the end result.

Example:

$$y^4 = y \times y \times y \times y$$

$$y^{-4} = \frac{1}{y \times y \times y \times y}$$

We can multiply exponent expressions if they have the same base. In that situation, we just add the exponents.

Example:

$$(n^3)(n^4) =$$

$$(n \times n \times n)\,(n \times n \times n \times n) =$$

$$n \times n \times n \times n \times n \times n \times n =$$

$$n^7$$

It's also possible to divide exponent expressions with the same base by subtracting the exponents.

Example:

$$(n^5)/(n^2) =$$

$$\frac{(n \times n \times n \times n \times n)}{(n \times n)} =$$

$$n \times n \times n =$$

$$n^3$$

We can also raise an exponential expression to another exponent by multiplying the two exponents:

Example:

$$(n^4)^5 =$$

$$(n^4)\,(n^4)\,(n^4)\,(n^4)\,(n^4) =$$

$$n^{20}$$

Raising any number to an exponent of zero results in the number 1.

Example:

$$n^0 = 1$$

Logarithms

A logarithm is an expression that tells us how many times we multiply one number by itself to get another number. The expression $\log_x(y) = z$ means that if you multiply x by itself z times, the result is y. In that expression, we would call x the "base" of the logarithm, as in "the logarithm of y with base x is z." Let's look at an example with real numbers.

Example:

$\log_2(32) = 5$, because we would have to multiply 2 by itself 5 times to get 32: $2 \times 2 \times 2 \times 2 \times 2 = 32$

Logarithms don't come up often on the ACT, but they do show up sometimes, so we need to make sure we understand them.

Squares and square roots

The square of a number is that number multiplied by itself.

Example:

Four squared is equal to 4×4, or 16.

The square root of a number is the amount that must be multiplied by itself to result in that number.

Example:

The square root of 16 is the number that results in 16 when multiplied by itself. That number is 4, so the square root of 16 is 4.

Squared numbers are always positive. This is true because a positive number multiplied by a positive number has a positive result, and a negative number multiplied by a negative number also has a positive result.

Keep in mind that you can easily find the square or the square root of a number with your calculator if necessary.

Ratios, proportions, and percentages

We can express a relationship between two numbers using ratios, proportions, and percentages.

A ratio is expressed as a pair of numbers with a colon between them.

Example:

If you walk 4 miles for every 1 mile Jake walks, then the ratio of *the distance you travel* to *the distance Jake travels* is *4 : 1*.

A proportion is typically written as a fraction.

Example:

If you walk 4 miles for every 1 mile Jake walks, then you can compare the distance you travel to the distance Jake travels with the proportion 4/1. (Also, the proportion to compare how far Jake walks to how far you walk would be 1/4.)

A percentage is a type of proportion that compares one number to 100.

To find a percentage, first create a proportion or fraction. Then, divide the numerator by the denominator and multiply the result by 100.

Example:

> If Jake walks 1 mile for every 4 miles you walk, then the proportion that compares the distance Jake travels to the distance you travel is 1/4. If we divide 1 by 4 and multiply by 100, we see that Jake walks 25% as far as you walk.

Ratios can be set equal to each other and "cross-multiplied." (Don't worry if you don't already know how to do this—it's just an algebraic shortcut, and you don't specifically have to know how to do it for the ACT.)

If two quantities have a relationship such that increasing one quantity causes a consistent, predictable, proportional increase in the other quantity, we say those two quantities "vary directly" or are "directly proportional."

Example:

> Imagine that you're driving a car that can go 20 miles on one gallon of gas. If you have one gallon of gas, you can drive 20 miles. If you have 3 gallons, you can drive 60 miles. If you have 10 gallons, you can drive 200 miles. The distance you can travel "varies directly with" or is "directly proportional to" the amount of gas you have, since every additional gallon of gas increases the distance you can drive in a predictable way.

If x and y vary directly, then their relationship can be expressed by the equation $x = vy$, where v is a constant.

Example:

> If x and y vary directly and x is 60 when y is 3, then $x = 20y$. We can see that increasing either variable automatically increases the other variable. For example, we see that x is 200 if y is 10.

If two quantities have a relationship such that increasing one causes a consistent, proportional decrease in the other, we say those two quantities "vary indirectly" or are "inversely proportional."

Example:

> Imagine that you are riding your bike for a distance of 20 miles. If you ride your bike at 5 miles per hour, you will cover the distance in 4 hours—4 hours of traveling at 5 miles per hour means you cover 20 miles. However, if you speed up to 10 miles per hour, you will cover the same distance in 2 hours—2 hours of traveling at 10 miles per hour means you cover 20 miles. When you double your speed, you cut the travel time in half. We can say that speed and travel time "vary indirectly" or are "inversely proportional," since increasing one value causes the other value to decrease in a consistent, predictable way.

If x and y are inversely proportional, then $xy = v$, where v is some constant.

Example:

> If x and y vary indirectly and x is 4 when y is 5, then we know xy
> = 20. Increasing either variable creates a decrease in the other;
> for example, x is 10 if y is 2.

Simple probability

The probability of a possible event tells us how likely that event is to happen. It's expressed as a fraction with a value between 0 and 1. The closer a probability fraction is to 1, the more likely the event is to happen; the closer a fraction is to zero, the less likely the event is to happen.

To create a probability fraction, you first figure out the total number of possible outcomes and make that number the denominator of the fraction. Then, you figure out the number of desired outcomes that satisfy the requirements of that event, and you make this number the numerator of the fraction.

Example:

> What's the probability of a flipped penny landing tails-side up?
> There are 2 possible outcomes when the penny is flipped: heads
> or tails. So 2 goes in the denominator of the fraction. Out of
> those 2 outcomes, we're only interested in one (tails), so 1 goes
> in the numerator of the fraction. That means the probability of
> the coin landing tails-up is $\frac{1}{2}$.

To find the probability of two or more events happening in a row, we just multiply the probability of the first event by the probability of the second event.

Example:

> What's the probability of a penny landing tails-side up twice in a
> row? We know that the probability of a penny landing tails-side
> up one time is $\frac{1}{2}$. That means the probability of a penny landing
> tails-side up twice in a row is $\frac{1}{2} \times \frac{1}{2}$, or $\frac{1}{4}$.

Probability fractions can be manipulated just like any other fractions—for example, a probability of 2/8 is equivalent to a probability of 1/4.

"Counting problems"

What I call a "counting problem" on the ACT is a question that asks you to figure out the total number of ways that two or more events could happen.

You may have studied these problems in math class; if so, you probably called them "permutation and combination" problems.

Here's the general rule for these problems: if the first of two events could happen in any one of x ways, and the second of two events could happen in any one of y ways, then the total number of ways that the events could happen together is given by xy.

That might sound a little complicated, so let's do an example and you'll see how it works.

Example:

> Imagine you have to buy one fruit and one vegetable. There are 4 kinds of fruit and 5 kinds of vegetables. How many possible combinations of one fruit and one vegetable can you pick?

> Well, there are 4 kinds of fruit, so there are 4 possibilities for the first event (choosing a fruit). There are 5 kinds of vegetables, so there are 5 options for the second event (picking a vegetable).

> So the total number of possible combinations of one fruit and one vegetable is 4 × 5, which is 20.

Often, the biggest challenge in this type of question is making sure you correctly count the number of possible outcomes for each event.

Example:

> Imagine you have to select two different kinds of fruit from a single produce section that offers 4 different types of fruit. How many possible combinations of two *different* fruits can you get?

> In this case, the answer is 12 combinations, because the first selection has 4 possible outcomes, and the second selection has *only 3* possible outcomes, and 4 × 3 = 12. The second selection has only 3 possible outcomes because we've already chosen one of the 4 original options in the first event, leaving only 3 options for the second event, because the question specified that the two types of fruit must be *different*, which means we can't re-pick the same fruit for both events.

Charts, tables, and graphs

Charts, tables, and graphs are three ways to represent data. To use charts, tables, and graphs, we simply read the labels of each section to find the information we need. The following chart shows the number of days spent on vacation of three different age groups for five different months.

Example chart:

Average Number Of Days Spent On Vacation

AGE	March	April	May	June	July
21-25	2	3	4	3	4
26-30	1	1	3	1	1
31-35	2	4	3	2	2

> From this chart, we can see that people 21 - 25 years of age spend an average of 4 days on vacation in May, and people 31 - 35 years of age spend an average of 2 days on vacation in June, and so on.

The following table shows the scores of Student 1 on four different math tests.

Example table:

Student 1's Math Test Scores

Test Number	Score
1	79
2	78
3	86
4	90

From this table, we can see that Student 1 scored an 86 on math test 3, and a 79 on math test 1.

The following graph shows the average number of siblings of students in 4 classes.

Example graph:

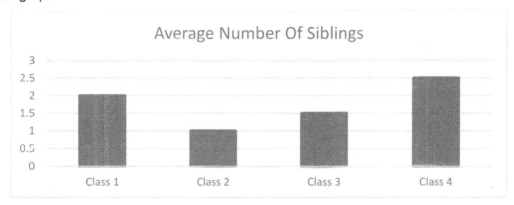

From this table, we can see that the average number of siblings for students in Class 2 was 1, and the average number of siblings for students in Class 3 was 1.5, and so on.

Simple statistics

There are three main concepts you'll need to be familiar with when it comes to statistics on the ACT: average (arithmetic mean), median, and mode.

The arithmetic mean of a set of numbers is what you get when you add the numbers together and then divide the result by the number of things that you added together. (This is also called the "average" of the set of numbers.)

Example:

The mean of {7, 18, 23} is 16, because $\frac{7 + 18 + 23}{3} = 16$.

The median of a set of numbers is the number in the middle of the set when all the numbers in that set are ordered from least to greatest.

Example:

> **The median of {7, 18, 23} is 18, because when those numbers are ordered from least to greatest, 18 is in the middle.**

If the set has an even number of elements, then the median of that set is the average of the two numbers that end up in the middle of the set when the elements of the set are ordered from least to greatest.

Example:

> **The median of {7, 12, 18, 23} is 15, because there's an even number of elements in the set, and 15 is the arithmetic mean of the two numbers in the middle of the set when the numbers are ordered from least to greatest (12 and 18).**

The mode of a set of numbers is the number that appears in the set more frequently than any other.

Example:

> **The mode of {16, 17, 18, 19, 24, 24, 95} is 24, because 24 appears more often than any other number in the set.**

Expressing relationships with variables

You can use variables to express a relationship between two quantities.

Example:

> **If one quantity is equal to three times another quantity, we can represent them with x and y respectively, and write this: $x = 3y$.**

If you have a value for y, you can plug it to find a corresponding value for x.

Example:

> **If $x = 3y$, and we know $y = 4$, then we can write $x = 3(4)$, so $x = 12$.**

Equations

On the ACT, an equation is a statement with an equals sign and at least one algebraic expression.

Example:

> **$3y = 15$ is an equation, because it has an algebraic expression ($3y$) and an equals sign.**

When we solve an equation for a variable, we find the value of the variable in that equation. We do this just as you've learned in your high school math classes—by carrying out the same operations on both sides of the equation until the variable is alone on one side of the equals sign, and its value is on the other side.

Example:

$$3y = 15$$
$$\frac{3y}{3} = \frac{15}{3}$$
$$y = 5$$

If an equation has multiple variables, we can solve the equation "in terms of" one particular variable. To do this, we just isolate the target variable on one side of the equation.

Example:

Solve this expression in terms of z.

$$2z + 5y = 3x$$

$$2z = 3x - 5y \qquad \text{(subtract 5y from both sides)}$$

$$z = \frac{3x - 5y}{2} \qquad \text{(divide both sides by 2)}$$

A system of equations is a group of two or more equations that have the same variables.

Example:

This is a system of equations:

$$a - b = 3$$

$$4a + b = 27$$

Solving a system of equations means identifying the values of the variables in the equations. One way to do this is to solve one of the equations in terms of a particular variable, like we did in the last example. Then, we substitute that value into the other equation and obtain a numerical value for the other variable.

Example:

To solve the system of equations above, we'll begin by isolating the a in the first equation.

$$a - b = 3$$

$$a = 3 + b \qquad \text{(add } b \text{ to both sides)}$$

Now that we know a is equal to $3 + b$, we can plug that in to the other equation:

$$4a + b = 27$$

$$4(3 + b) + b = 27 \qquad \text{(substitute } 3 + b \text{ for } a\text{)}$$

$$12 + 4b + b = 27 \qquad \text{(distribute the 4)}$$

$$12 + 5b = 27 \qquad \text{(combine like terms)}$$

$$5b = 27 - 12 \qquad \text{(subtract 12 from each side)}$$

$$5b = 15 \qquad \text{(combine like terms)}$$

$$b = 3 \qquad \text{(divide both sides by 5)}$$

Since we know b equals 3, we just plug that back into the first equation, and solve for a:

$$a - (3) = 3 \qquad \text{(substitute 3 for } b\text{)}$$

$$a = 3 + 3 \qquad \text{(add 3 to both sides)}$$

$$a = 6 \qquad \text{(combine like terms)}$$

Operations on polynomials

A polynomial is an expression that includes multiple terms, at least one of which contains a variable.

Examples:

$$5x + 3$$

$$x^2 - 2x + 9$$

$$4ab^2 + 5a$$

When we write a polynomial, we list the terms in decreasing order of the exponent of the variable. That sounds complicated, so let's look at an example:

$$x^4 + 3x^3 + 5x^2 - 2x + 4 = 0$$

We started with the x-term raised to the fourth power, then followed with the one raised to the third power, then the one that was squared, then the x-term without an exponent (which is the same as x^1), then the constant with no x-term (which as the same as an x^0 term, since any number raised to the power of zero is equal to 1).

Polynomials can be added, subtracted, multiplied, and divided, but sometimes there are special considerations.

When we add or subtract polynomials, we simply combine like terms.

Example:

Let's add the polynomials $5x + 3$ and $x^2 - 2x + 9$:

$5x + 3 + x^2 - 2x + 9$	(original expression)
$x^2 + (5x - 2x) + (9 + 3)$	(group like terms)
$x^2 + 3x + 12$	(combine like terms)

As you can see, we combined the x^2 terms (there was only one, in this case), the x terms (5x and -2x), and the constants (3 and 9).

Notice that you can only add or subtract like terms during this process.

Example:

Let's add the polynomials $2x^3 + 4x^2$ and $x + 7$:

$$2x^3 + 4x^2 + x + 7$$

In this case, nothing can be combined, because there are no like terms. So we just write the sum as shown above.

We can multiply a polynomial by another quantity by multiplying each term in the polynomial by that term.

Example:

$3y(5x + 6)$	
$(3y \times 5x) + (3y \times 6)$	(distribute the 3y)
$15xy + 18y$	(multiply)

Go to www.ACTprepVideos.com.

A binomial is a polynomial with two terms.

We can multiply one binomial by another binomial using the FOIL technique, which you've probably encountered in your math classes. Here's how it works:

Example:

Let's multiply $2x + 5$ by $x - 1$:

$(2x + 5)(x - 1)$

First, we multiply the first two terms of each polynomial together (the "F" in FOIL stands for "first"). That gives us $2x(x)$, or $2x^2$.

Next, we multiply the outer two terms together (the "O" in FOIL stands for "outer"). That gives us $2x(-1)$, or $-2x$.

Next, we multiply the two inner terms together (the "I" in FOIL stands for "inner"). That gives us $5(x)$, or $5x$.

Last, we multiply the last two terms of each polynomial together (the "L" in FOIL stands for "last"). That gives us $5(-1)$, or -5.

Now that we have all the terms, we simply add them together (combing like terms, as always):

$2x^2 + (-2x) + 5x + (-5)$

$2x^2 + 3x - 5$

On the ACT, we can also divide a polynomial by another quantity if each term of the polynomial has a factor in common with the quantity we're dividing by. Simply divide each term of the polynomial individually.

Example:

Let's divide $14ab + 2b$ by $2b$:

$\frac{14ab + 2b}{2b}$

$\frac{14ab}{2b} + \frac{2b}{2b}$

$7a + 1$

Factoring polynomials

On the ACT, factoring polynomials means taking a polynomial and breaking it into two expressions that can be multiplied together to get the original polynomial.

On the ACT, there are three possible factoring situations you'll need to be able to recognize:

1. common factors
2. "FOIL" in reverse
3. difference of squares

Recognizing common factors comes down to noticing that each term in a polynomial has a common factor that can be factored out.

Example:

> If we have a polynomial like $(3x + 9)$, we can see that both $3x$ and 9 are divisible by 3. That means we can divide a three out of each term in the polynomial and end up with the factors 3 and $(x + 3)$, because $3(x + 3) = 3x + 9$.

Factoring polynomials means doing the steps of FOIL backwards. It can be a little intimidating, but it's easier than it looks when you get used to it.

Example:

> Suppose we're asked to factor the trinomial $6x^2 - 7x - 3$ into two binomials.
>
> We'll need to reverse-FOIL the trinomial. We can see the product of the first terms of each polynomial will have to be $6x^2$. So we'll just pick two x terms to try out, like $3x$ and $2x$:
>
> $(3x + ?)(2x + ?)$
>
> We also know the last terms will have to multiply together to equal -3, so they must be either -1 and 3 or 1 and -3. We'll just try one pair (reverse-FOILing often involves a lot of trial and error).
>
> $(3x + 1)(2x - 3)$
>
> Then we multiply out our binomials to see if we've reverse-FOILed correctly:
>
> | | |
> |---|---|
> | $(3x + 1)(2x - 3)$ | (our guess for the factorization) |
> | $6x^2 - 9x + 2x - 3$ | (FOIL the two binomials) |
> | $6x^2 - 7x - 3$ | (combine like terms) |
>
> In this case, we got it on the first try; if you don't, of course, you can look at what didn't work and try other pairs of factors. Problems like this on the ACT aren't too common, and the factors usually aren't too hard to figure out. This gets a lot easier with a little bit of practice.

There's a special case in factoring binomials called a "difference of squares." You can recognize a difference of squares because both terms in the binomial will be squares, and the second term will be subtracted from the first (this is why it's called a "difference" of squares; this special factoring shortcut doesn't work when the squares are added together). When we see this situation, the two factors are the following:

- the square root of the first term *plus* the square root of the second term

- the square root of the first term *minus* the square root of the second term

Example:

> $4x^2 - 25 = (2x + 5)(2x - 5)$

Remember that 1 is a square, and that x^2 is the same as $1x^2$. That means something like $x^2 - 9$ is a difference of squares as well, with factors of $(x + 3)$ and $(x - 3)$.

Simple quadratic equations

A quadratic equation involves three terms. On the ACT, the three terms are usually the following:

1. a variable expression raised to the power of 2, like x^2.
2. a variable expression not raised to any power, like $6x$.
3. a constant (a regular number with no variable), like -5.

Example:

> $x^2 + 6x = -5$ is a quadratic equation because it involves a term with x squared, a term with x, and a constant.

On the ACT we solve quadratic equations by factoring, as discussed in the previous section on factoring polynomials. To do that, we have to set one side of the equation equal to zero first.

Example:

$x^2 + 6x$	$= -5$	(original equation)
$x^2 + 6x + 5$	$= 0$	(add 5 to both sides)

Once we have the equation equal to zero, we factor the polynomial.

$x^2 + 6x + 5 = 0$

$(x + 5)(x + 1) = 0$ (reverse FOIL)

Since the product of the two factors is zero, we know that one of the factors must be equal to zero, but we don't know which one. So solving a quadratic equation usually results in two possible values for the variable: one value causes one of the factors to equal zero, and the other value causes the other factor to equal zero.

$(x + 5) = 0$	or	$(x + 1) = 0$
$x = -5$	or	$x = -1$

If we want to test our solutions, we just plug them back into the original equation to see that they work:

$x^2 + 6x = -5$

$(-5)^2 + 6(-5) = -5$	$(-1)^2 + 6(-1) = -5$
$25 - 30 = -5$	$1 - 6 = -5$

Inequalities

An inequality is a statement that tells us that two quantities are not equal. An inequality makes use of one of the following signs:

- $<$ means "less than."
- $>$ means "greater than."
- $\leq$ means "less than or equal to."
- $\geq$ means "greater than or equal to."

Inequalities are solved the same way that equations are solved, with one important difference: when you multiply by -1 to solve for a variable, you also have to switch the direction of the inequality symbol.

Example:

$$-\frac{x}{3} = 4 \qquad\qquad -\frac{x}{3} \leq 4$$

$$-x = 4(3) \qquad -x \leq 4(3) \qquad \text{(multiply both sides by 3)}$$

$$-x = 12 \qquad\; -x \leq 12 \qquad\; \text{(simplify)}$$

$$x = -12 \qquad\; x \geq -12 \qquad\; \text{(multiply both sides by -1)}$$

Some inequalities involve only one variable.

Examples:

$$x > 3$$

$$y \leq 1.2$$

Some inequalities involve more than one variable.

Examples:

$$y \geq x - 19$$

$$n < 14r + 2$$

Inequalities can be solved for a particular variable, just like equations can.

Example:

Let's solve $3y - 11 > 9x + 4$ for y:

$$3y - 11 > 9x + 4 \qquad \text{(original inequality)}$$

$$3y > 9x + 15 \qquad\quad \text{(add 11 to both sides)}$$

$$y > 3x + 5 \qquad\qquad \text{(divide both sides by 3)}$$

We can also represent an inequality on the coordinate plane by shading in the region of the graph that satisfies the inequality.

Example:

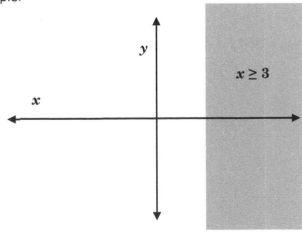

Radicals

If we take the square root of an imperfect square, the result is a radical expression.

Example:

The square root of 2 is equal to $\sqrt{2}$.

Radical expressions can be multiplied together.

Example:

$$\sqrt{2} \times \sqrt{7} = \sqrt{14}$$

Radical expressions can also be factored.

Example:

$$\sqrt{12} = \sqrt{4 \times 3} = \sqrt{4} \times \sqrt{3} = 2\sqrt{3}$$

Imaginary numbers

Imaginary numbers involve the imaginary quantity i. The quantity i represents the square root of -1.

Example:

$$\sqrt{-25} = \sqrt{-1 \times 25} = \sqrt{-1} \times \sqrt{25} = i \times 5 = 5i$$

Complex numbers

A complex number involves a real number and an imaginary number. On the ACT, a real number is any number that doesn't involve i or the square root of a negative number, and an imaginary number is any number that does involve i or the square root of a negative number.

Examples of real numbers:

$\sqrt{5}$, 19, π, –4

Examples of imaginary numbers:

$\sqrt{-7}$, $14i$, i

Examples of complex numbers:

$4 + i$
$6 - 3i$

To do operations involving i, just treat i like its own variable, except that any time you get an i^2, it becomes a -1.

$3i(2 + i)$
$6i + 3(i^2)$
$6i + 3(-1)$
$6i - 3$

Sequences

A sequence is a series of numbers that follows a rule, so that if you know any number in the sequence, and you know the rule that governs the sequence, you can figure out any other number in the sequence.

Typically, a sequence on the ACT will depend either on addition/subtraction or multiplication/division.

A sequence that relies on addition or subtraction to generate the next term is called an arithmetic sequence.

Example of an arithmetic sequence:

2, 7, 12, 17, 22...   (each term is 5 more than the term before it)

A sequence that relies on multiplication or division to generate the next term is called a geometric sequence.

Example of a geometric sequence:

3, 12, 48, 192, 768... (each term is 4 times the term before it)

You may have studied "series" in your math classes. ACT questions about sequences aren't as complicated as a high school math question about a series can be. For example, there's no sigma notation on the ACT. (If you've never heard of sigma notation, or you've never studied formal mathematical series, don't worry about it.)

Sequences on the ACT can either go on forever or stop at some point, depending on the setup of the question.

The ACT Math section might ask you to figure out any of the following:

- The sum of a certain set of terms in a sequence.
- The average of a certain set of terms in a sequence.
- The value of a particular term in a sequence.

Common Difference and Common Ratio

The "common difference" of an arithmetic sequence is the difference between two consecutive terms.

Example:

In this sequence, the common difference is 9, because the difference between each term and the term before it is 9:

5, 14, 23, 32, 41, 50, 59...

The "common ratio" of a geometric sequence is the ratio of any one term to the term before it.

Example:

In this sequence, the common ratio is 5, because each term is 5 times the term that comes before it.

1, 5, 25, 125, 625...

Matrices

A matrix is a set of numbers displayed in a grid format. (The plural of "matrix" is "matrices.") Matrix questions are rare on the ACT, and tend to be relatively simple.

Examples of matrices:

$$\begin{bmatrix} 3 \\ -1 \end{bmatrix} \quad \begin{bmatrix} 25 & -2 & 16 \\ 8 & 5 & 7 \end{bmatrix} \quad \begin{bmatrix} 87 & 4 \end{bmatrix}$$

You can add or subtract matrices of the same size by adding or subtracting corresponding elements (add the first terms to get the first term in the answer, the second terms to get the second term in the answer, and so on):

Example:

$$[6 \quad 3 \quad -5] + [-2 \quad 2 \quad 4] = [4 \quad 5 \quad -1]$$

You can multiply one matrix by another only when the number of rows in the first matrix is equal to the number of columns in the second other. The result will have as many rows as the first matrix and as many columns as the second matrix.

Example:

$$\begin{bmatrix} a \\ b \\ c \end{bmatrix} \times \begin{bmatrix} x & y & z \end{bmatrix} = \begin{bmatrix} ax & ay & az \\ bx & by & bz \\ cx & cy & cz \end{bmatrix}$$

You can also multiply a matrix by a number. To do that, just multiply each element by that number.

Example:

$$4\begin{bmatrix} 3 & 1 \\ 7 & 2 \end{bmatrix} = \begin{bmatrix} 12 & 4 \\ 28 & 8 \end{bmatrix}$$

Geometric notation

The ACT likes to use the following notation to describe lines, rays, angles, and so on. You've probably seen this notation in your classes, but don't worry if you haven't—it's not hard to learn.

AB describes the distance from *A* to *B*.

$\overleftrightarrow{AB}$ describes the line that goes through points *A* and *B* (the little arrows on the ends indicate an infinite extension into space in both directions).

$\overline{AB}$ describes the line segment with endpoints *A* and *B* (the lack of arrowheads on the symbol indicates that the given segment doesn't continue on to infinity).

$\overrightarrow{AB}$ describes the ray with endpoint *A* that goes through *B* and then continues on infinitely.

$\overrightarrow{BA}$ describes the ray with B for an endpoint that goes through A and continues on infinitely.

∠*ABC* describes the angle with point B as a vertex that has point *A* on one leg and point *C* on the other.

∠ *ABC* = 60° indicates that the measure of the angle with point B as a vertex and with point *A* on one leg and point *C* on the other is 60 degrees.

Δ*ABC* describes the triangle with vertices *A*, *B*, and *C*.

▱*ABCD* describes the quadrilateral with vertices *A*, *B*, *C*, and *D*.

$\overline{AB} \perp \overline{BC}$ indicates that the line segments *AB* and *BC* are perpendicular to each other.

Angles in a plane

Degrees are the units that we use to measure angles.

Examples:

The measure of this angle is 45 degrees:

This angle is 90 degrees, also called a "right angle:"

This is a 180-degree angle, which is the same thing as a straight line:

_____

Angles can have special relationships. The two special relationships that will come up frequently on the ACT are called vertical angles and supplementary angles.

When two lines intersect, the pairs of angles that lie opposite each other are called vertical angles. The two angles opposite each other in a pair of vertical angles have the same degree measurements.

Example:

Angles ∠VWX and ∠YWZ are vertical angles, so they have the same degree measurement. Angles ∠VWY and ∠XWZ are also vertical angles, so they also have the same degree measurement.

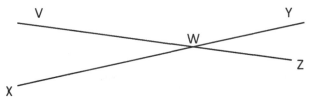

Pairs of angles whose measurements add up to 180° are called supplementary angles. When two supplementary angles are next to each other, they form a straight line.

Example:

∠VWX and ∠VWY are supplementary angles: their measurements add up to 180 degrees. They form the straight line $\overline{XY}$.

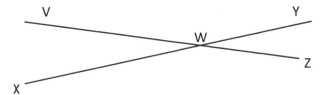

Triangles

A triangle is a three-sided figure. Triangles show up frequently on the ACT Math section.

The measures of the three angles in any triangle add up to 180 degrees.

The area of a triangle is equal to one half of the base times its height, or $\frac{1}{2}bh$.

Example:

This diagram shows how base and height are determined so they can be used to find the area of a triangle in the formula $\frac{1}{2}bh$.

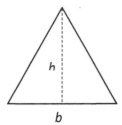

The longest side of any triangle is always opposite the biggest angle, and the shortest side of any triangle is always opposite the smallest angle.

An "equilateral" triangle has sides that are all the same length, and its angles measure 60 degrees each.

Example:

In the equilateral triangle ΔJKL below, all the sides are of equal length, and all the angles are 60 degrees.

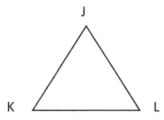

An "isosceles" triangle has two sides that are the same length as each other, and two angles that are the same size as each other.

Example:

In the isosceles triangle ΔXYZ below, side $\overline{XY}$ is the same length as side $\overline{XZ}$. Also, $\angle XYZ$ and $\angle XZY$ have equal measurements.

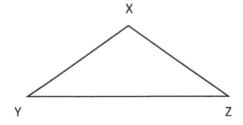

A "right" triangle includes a ninety-degree angle as one of its three angles.

There's a special relationship involving the measurements of the sides of a right triangle: If you square the lengths of the two shorter sides, and then add those two squares together, the result is the square of the length of the longest side, or hypotenuse.

Example:

In the right triangle below, $a^2 + b^2 = c^2$

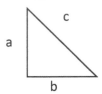

This formula, $a^2 + b^2 = c^2$, is called the "Pythagorean Theorem," and it comes up a lot on the ACT.

We call a set of numbers that satisfies this formula a "Pythagorean Triple." There are four of these in particular that you'll want to know on the ACT:

{3, 4, 5} is a Pythagorean triple because $3^2 + 4^2 = 5^2$.

{1, 1, $\sqrt{2}$} is a Pythagorean triple because $1^2 + 1^2 = \sqrt{2}^2$

{1, $\sqrt{3}$, 2} is a Pythagorean triple because $1^2 + \sqrt{3}^2 = 2^2$

{5, 12, 13} is a Pythagorean triple because $5^2 + 12^2 = 13^2$

When we multiply each number in a Pythagorean triple by the same number, we get another Pythagorean triple.

Example:

We know that {3, 4, 5} is a Pythagorean triple, so we also know that {6, 8, 10} is a Pythagorean triple, because {6, 8, 10} is what we get when we multiply each number in {3, 4, 5} by 2.

A {1, 1, $\sqrt{2}$} right triangle has angle measurements of 45°, 45°, and 90°.

A {1, $\sqrt{3}$, 2} right triangle has angle measurements of 30°, 60°, and 90°.

Examples:

The following two "special" triangles will show up on the ACT. You should be familiar with their angle measures and side length ratios.

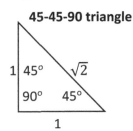

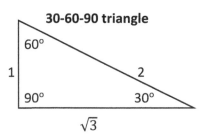

Two triangles are called "similar triangles" if they have all the same angle measurements.

Between two similar triangles, the relationship between any two corresponding sides is the same as between any other two corresponding sides.

Example:

> Triangles ΔPQR and ΔWXY below are similar. Side $\overline{PQ}$ has length 3, and side $\overline{WX}$ has length 6, so every side measurement in ΔWXY must be twice as long as the corresponding side in ΔPQR.

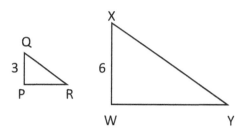

The length of each side of a triangle must be less than the sum of the lengths of the other sides. (Otherwise, the triangle wouldn't be able to "close," because the longest side would be too long for the other two sides to touch.)

Example:

> You can see in this diagram that the longest side is longer than the two shorter sides combined, which means the two shorter sides are too far apart to connect and "close" the triangle.

Parallelograms

A parallelogram is a four-sided figure with two pairs of parallel sides. Each side is parallel to its opposite side.

In a parallelogram the measures of all four angles add up to 360°, and opposite angles are equal.

Example:

> In $\square$STVU below, the sum of the interior angles is 360°, and opposite angles have equal measurements.

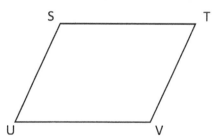

Rectangles

Rectangles are parallelograms whose internal angles each measure 90°.

The area of a rectangle is equal to its length times its width.

Example:

> **The rectangle below has a length of 24 and a width of 10. That means the area is 24 × 10, or 240.**

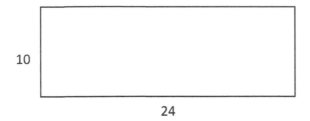

If you know the lengths of a rectangle's sides, then you can use the Pythagorean Theorem to figure out the length from one corner to the opposite corner, which is called the "diagonal."

Example:

> **In the rectangle below, the Pythagorean Theorem tells us that diagonal $\overline{EG}$ must have a length of 26, since $10^2 + 24^2 = 26^2$.**

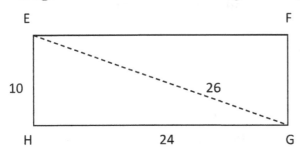

Squares

A square is a special kind of rectangle with sides of equal length. Like a rectangle's area, a square's area can be found by multiplying its width by its height. Since all the sides are the same length, this is the same as squaring the length of any side of the square.

Example:

> **The square below has sides of length 4. To find its area, we simply square the length of a side, which gives us 16.**

Trapezoids

A trapezoid is a four-sided figure with one pair of opposite sides that are parallel. In a trapezoid, all the internal angles add up to 360. The area can be found by averaging the lengths of the parallel sides and multiplying the result by the height. This formula is given as $\frac{a+b}{2}h$, where a and b are the lengths of the parallel sides and h is the height.

Example:

In the trapezoid below, the parallel sides are of length 8 and 10, and the height is 3. That means the area is $\frac{8+10}{2} \times 3$, or 27.

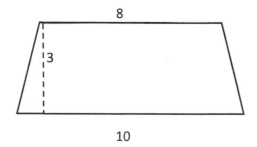

Perimeter

The perimeter of any non-circle object on the ACT can be found by adding up the lengths of all its sides.

Example:

In the rectangle below, there are two sides of length 10, and two sides of length 3. That means the perimeter is 10 + 10 + 3 + 3, or 26.

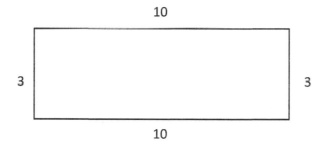

Circles (diameter, radius, arc, tangents, circumference, area)

A circle is defined as the set of points in a plane that are all equidistant from a single point, called the center. A circle has the same name as its center point.

> Example:
>
> **Circle _C_ below consists of all the points in one plane that are 7 units away from the center, point _C_:**

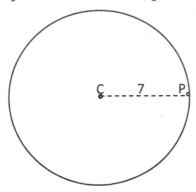

A radius is a line segment drawn from the center of a circle to the edge of that circle.

> Example:
>
> **In circle C above, the line segment $\overline{CP}$ is a radius of circle C because it stretches from the center of the circle (_C_) to the edge of the circle (in this case, point _P_).**

All points on the edge of a circle are the same distance from the center point, so all radii of a circle have the same length.

A diameter is a line segment that starts at one edge of a circle, passes through the center, and continues all the way across to the opposite edge of that circle.

> Example:
>
> **$\overline{WP}$ is a diameter of circle C because it starts at one edge of the circle, passes through the center of the circle, and stops at the far edge of the circle.**

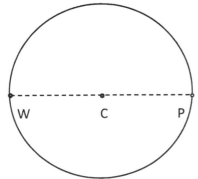

A diameter is basically made up of two opposite radii, so a diameter of a circle is always twice as long as a radius of that circle.

Go to www.ACTprepVideos.com.

A diameter of a circle is the longest line segment that can be drawn through the circle without extending outside the circle.

A line is "tangent" to a circle when it lies in the same plane as the circle and intersects the circle at only one point. A tangent line is perpendicular to the radius of the circle that ends at the point shared by the tangent line and the circle.

Example:

Circle C has a tangent line $\overleftrightarrow{OQ}$ that intersects the circle at point P, and is perpendicular to radius $\overline{CP}$.

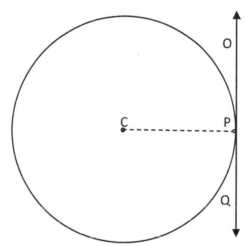

An arc is a portion of a circle. We can measure an arc by drawing one radius to each of the endpoints of the arc, and then measuring the angle formed by those radii at the center of the circle.

Example:

Circle C has a 90° arc $\overarc{BD}$. The measure of that arc is the same as the measure of the angle formed by radius $\overline{BC}$ and radius $\overline{CD}$.

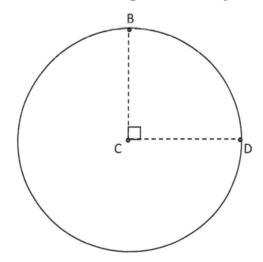

The length around a circle is its circumference; this is similar to the perimeter of a polygon.

You can find the circumference of a circle by multiplying π by the diameter. Since the diameter is two times the radius, the circumference can also be expressed as two times π times the radius, or $2\pi r$.

Example:

> $\overline{CP}$ is a radius of circle C with a length of 3. The circumference of circle C is equal to 2π(3), or 6π.

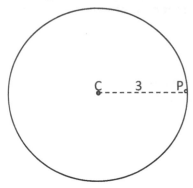

The area of a circle is equal to π times the square of the radius, or πr^2.

Example:

> $\overline{CP}$ is a radius of circle C with a length of 3. The area of circle C is equal to π(3)², or 9π.

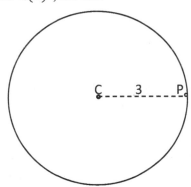

Translations, rotations, and reflections

The words "translation," "rotation," and "reflection" all describe ways that an object can be moved in a plane.

If an object is translated, that means it's sliding from one place to another. It doesn't spin, flip, or rotate.

Example:

> In this diagram, the letter "B" is being translated in the direction indicated by the arrow. Notice that it doesn't spin, flip, or rotate.

If an object is rotated, then it's turned, or spun. We have to know what point it is being turned with reference to, and we say that it's being rotated "about" that point.

Go to www.ACTprepVideos.com.

Example:

In this diagram, the letter "B" is being rotated about the given point.

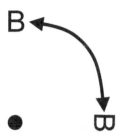

If an object is reflected across a line, then the object is flipped so that it appears as a mirror-image on the other side of that line.

Example:

In the following diagram, the letter "B" is reflected across the dashed line.

Three-dimensional geometry

You might occasionally encounter an ACT Math question that involves finding the volume of a three-dimensional object. Finding that volume will be a simple matter of knowing and applying the volume formula for that type of object, so let's take a look at those here.

The volume of a rectangular prism can be found by multiplying its length times its width times its height: $V = lwh$

Example:

The rectangular prism below has a length of 8, a width of 3, and a height of 4. That means its volume is equal to 8 × 3 × 4, or 96.

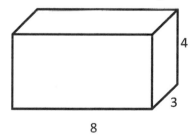

A cube is just a rectangular prism whose height, length, and width are all equal. We can find the volume of a cube by cubing the length of any side of the cube.

Example:

> **Each side of the cube below is 5 units long. That means its volume is equal to 5 × 5 × 5, or 5³, or 125.**

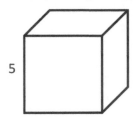

The volume of a cylinder is equal to the area of the circular face of the cylinder multiplied by its height. Since the area of the circular face is equal to πr^2, the volume is equal to $\pi r^2 h$.

Example:

> **The circular face of the cylinder below has a radius of 2, and the cylinder has a height of 6. That means its volume is equal to $\pi(2)^2(6)$, or 24π.**

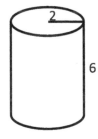

The volume of a sphere is equal to $\frac{4}{3}\pi r^3$.

Example:

> **The radius of the sphere below is 4. That means its volume is equal to $\frac{4}{3}\pi(4)^3$, or $\frac{256}{3}\pi$.**

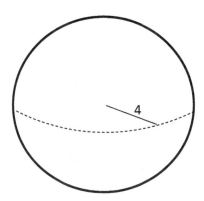

Points and lines in a plane

Any two points in a plane can be connected by a unique line.

Given any two points in a plane, there is a midpoint halfway between them.

Any set of three or more points may or may not lie on the same line. If they are on the same line, we say the points are "collinear."

We can graph a point on a coordinate plane by finding the intersection of the vertical line corresponding to its x coordinate and the horizontal line corresponding to its y coordinate.

Example:

The point (3,2) is located at the intersection of the vertical line $x = 3$ and the horizontal line $y = 2$.

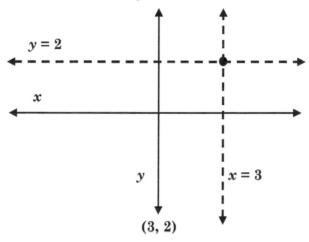

We can graph a line by connecting all the points whose (x, y) coordinates are solutions for the equation of that line.

Example:

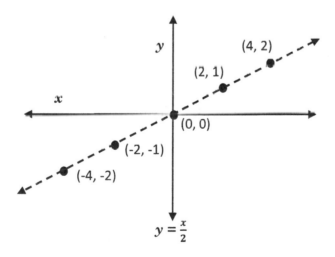

You can find the distance between two points in a coordinate plane by creating a right triangle on the coordinate plane with the distance between the two points as the hypotenuse (this is essentially an application of the Pythagorean Theorem, or the distance formula).

Example:

> Let's find the distance between the points (-1,-3) and (3,2). We'll begin by plotting them and then constructing a right triangle whose hypotenuse will be the distance between the points.

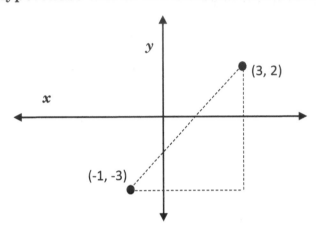

> The length of the horizontal leg is the distance between the two x coordinates, and the length of the vertical leg is the distance between the two y coordinates.
>
> In this case, the horizontal length is 3 – (-1), or 4, and the vertical length is 2 – (-3), or 5. Once you have the lengths of the two legs, you can plug them in to the Pythagorean Theorem and solve for the hypotenuse.
>
> $a^2 + b^2 = c^2$ (Pythagorean Theorem)
>
> $4^2 + 5^2 = c^2$ (substitute lengths of legs)
>
> $16 + 25 = c^2$ (square 4 and 5)
>
> $41 = c^2$ (add 16 and 25)
>
> $\sqrt{41} = c$ (take square root of each side)

So the distance between (3,2) and (-1,-3) is equal to $\sqrt{41}$.

The midpoint between two points in a coordinate plane is the coordinate pair whose x coordinate is the average of the x coordinates of the two points, and whose y coordinate is the average of their y coordinates.

Example:

> The midpoint between (-2, 4) and (3, 7) is $(\frac{-2+3}{2}, \frac{4+7}{2})$,
>
> or $(\frac{1}{2}, 5\frac{1}{2})$

Functions

A function can be thought of as a formula that tells you how to start with one value and generate another value.

Functions are often written in $f(x)$ notation, also called "function notation."

>   Example:

>   **$f(x) = 2x^2 + 1$ is a function written in function notation.**

This notation can be written with other variables besides f and x (like $h(j)$, $y(z)$, and so on).

Be sure not to confuse $f(x)$ with an expression like $(f)(x)$, which would mean "f times x" !

To find the value of a function for a certain x, we plug the x into the function and solve for $f(x)$. In other words, we insert our value for x everywhere the function has an x, and then we do the math described in the function.

>   Example:

>   **In the function $f(x) = 2x^2 + 1$, we can find the value of $f(x)$ where $x = 3$ like this:**

> | | |
> |---|---|
> | **$f(x) = 2x^2 + 1$** | **(original function)** |
> | **$f(3) = 2(3)^2 + 1$** | **(substitute $x = 3$)** |
> | **$f(3) = 2(9) + 1$** | **(square 3)** |
> | **$f(3) = 18 + 1$** | **(multiply 2 by 9)** |
> | **$f(3) = 19$** | **(combine like terms)** |

>   **So in this function, when x equals 3, we see that $f(x)$ equals 19.
>   In other words, $f(3) = 19$ for this function.**

Every function has a "domain" and a "range."

The domain of a function is the set of the numbers on a number line that generate a defined value when they're plugged into the function for x.

>   Examples:

>   **In the function $f(x) = 2x^2 + 1$, the domain is all the numbers on the number line, because we can plug in any value for x and get a valid result for $f(x)$.**

>   **In the function $f(x) = \dfrac{9}{x-5}$, the domain is all numbers except 5, because when $x = 5$, the denominator is equal to zero, and dividing by zero gives an undefined result.**

The "range" of a function is the set of numbers that $f(x)$ can possibly equal.

Examples:

> The function $f(x) = x^3 - 3$ has a range of negative infinity to positive infinity, because it's possible to get any number for $f(x)$ when we plug in all possible x values.

> The function $f(x) = x^2$ has a range from zero to positive infinity, because any value we use for x can result in any non-negative value for $f(x)$, but cannot result in a negative value for $f(x)$.

For every x value in a function, there can be no more than 1 corresponding y value. If an equation yields multiple y values for the same x value, then that equation isn't a function.

We can check the graph of an expression to see if it's a function by using something called "the vertical line test."

In order for the graph of a function to pass the vertical line test, we must be able to draw a vertical line anywhere on the graph of the function without crossing the function more than once.

Here's the graph of a linear function:

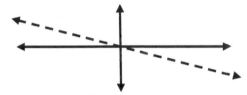

We can see that the function represented by the dashed line passes the vertical line test because we could draw a vertical line anywhere on the graph and never cross the dashed line more than once with each vertical line:

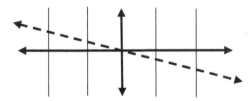

Here's an example of a graph of an expression that *fails* the vertical line test, so it's not a function:

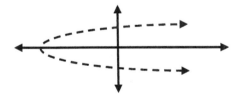

As we can see, there are a number of places where we can draw in vertical lines that would cross the graph of the expression more than once:

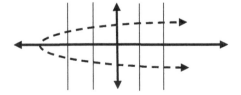

Again, this means the dashed line on this graph is not the graph of a function.

Even though one *x* value of a function can't have multiple *y* values, one *y* value can be shared by multiple *x* values in the same function—there is no "horizontal line test" that we need to worry about.

Linear equations with one variable

On the (*x*, *y*) coordinate plane, a vertical or horizontal line can be expressed as a linear equation with one variable.

Example:

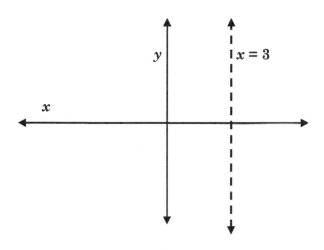

Also:

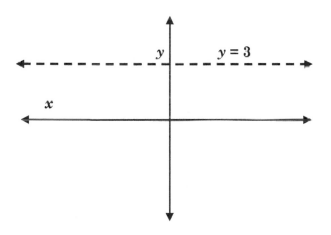

Linear functions

A linear function is a function such that all the (x, y) value pairings form a straight line when they're plotted as points on a graph.

Example:

> $f(x) = x - 1$ is linear, because all the (x, y) pairings that it generates form a straight line when plotted on a graph.
>
> Here are some (x, y) pairings for the function $f(x) = x - 1$:

x	y
-2	-3
-1	-2
0	-1
1	0
2	1
3	2

When we plot the (x, y) pairings from a linear function, we can see they fall in a straight line:

Example:

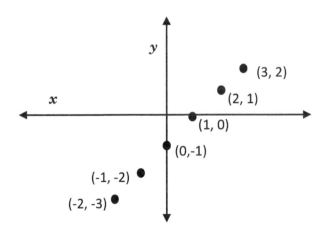

> As you can see, we've only plotted six specific points based on the (x, y) coordinates we got for six specific values of x. But we can see that the domain for $f(x) = x - 1$ must be all numbers from negative infinity to infinity, because any x value we plug in will result in a defined y value. So we can draw a line connecting these plotted points, and the line will represent all possible (x, y) pairs that satisfy $f(x) = x - 1$.

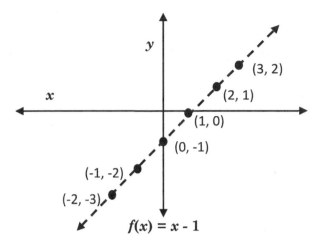

$$f(x) = x - 1$$

The slope of a linear function is a measure of how much the function rises or falls as it moves from left to right across the grid. A positive slope means that the line rises as it moves from left to right, and a negative slope means that the line descends as it moves from left to right.

The slope of a line is expressed as a fraction. The numerator of the fraction is the vertical separation of a pair of points on the line, and the denominator is the horizontal separation of the points. This ratio is always constant for any two points on a given line.

Example:

One way to calculate the slope of the linear function $f(x) = x - 1$ is to choose two points on the line and compare their vertical and horizontal separation. We'll use the points (1, 0) and (3, 2).

The numerator of the slope fraction will be the vertical separation between the two points. The y coordinates of these points are 0 and 2. Since 0 – 2 = -2, the vertical separation is -2.

After we know the vertical separation between the two points, we put that value in the numerator of the fraction that describes the slope of the line, like this:

$$\frac{-2}{?}$$

Now we have to find the denominator of the slope. That number is the horizontal separation between the two points, which is the same as the difference between the x coordinates.

The x coordinates of these points are 1 and 3. 1 – 3 is -2, so the horizontal separation between the points is also -2, coincidentally.

Now we put this value for the horizontal separation in the denominator, to get our slope fraction:

$$\frac{-2}{-2}$$

So the slope of the line $f(x) = x - 1$, which contains points (1, 0) and (3, 2), is $\frac{-2}{-2}$, which is the same as 1.

(Note that it doesn't matter which order we subtract the x and y values in, as long as we use the same order for both calculations. In this example, we subtracted the (3, 2) values from the (1, 0) values both times.)

You'll often see linear functions written in something called "slope-intercept format," which looks like this: $y = mx + b$. (Remember that $f(x)$ is the same as y in this context.)

This $y = mx + b$ form is called "slope-intercept format" because it lets us easily determine two things about a given line:

- Its slope.

- Its y-intercept (that is, the y value at which the line crosses the y-axis).

In slope-intercept format, m corresponds to the slope fraction, and b is the y-intercept.

Example:

The function $f(x) = x - 1$ is in $y = mx + b$ format.

According to $y = mx + b$ format:

- y represents the $f(x)$ value.

- m represents the slope, which is the coefficient of x. In the case of $f(x) = x - 1$, the coefficient of x is 1, which means the slope is $\frac{1}{1}$. In other words, from any given point on the line, moving one unit up and one unit to the right will leave us at another point on the line.

- x represents the x value.

- b represents the y-intercept, which in this case is equal to -1. We saw on the graph of the function on the previous page that the line does indeed cross the y-axis at $y = -1$.

Another example:

$f(x) = \frac{x}{3} + 17$

In this function, the slope, or m, is equal to $\frac{1}{3}$. (Remember that $\frac{x}{3}$ is the same as $\frac{1}{3}x$.)

The y-intercept, b, is equal to 17.

Another example:

$f(x) = -3x + 4$

In this function, the slope is equal to -3.

The y-intercept is equal to 4.

Two linear functions with the same slope and different y-intercepts are parallel.

Two lines are perpendicular when their slopes are the negative reciprocals of one another (for example, 2 and $-\frac{1}{2}$).

You'll never have to graph a linear function on the ACT. Instead, you might have to use your understanding of graphs to figure out a value, or to pick one graph out of several others as the correct graph of a particular function. (Your calculator may come in handy for that—see "Using A Calculator" later in our discussion of the ACT Math section.)

Graphing quadratic functions

In a quadratic function, the x term is squared when the function is expressed in its most simplified form.

Example:

$y = x^2$ is a quadratic function.

Quadratic functions are NEVER linear—instead, they're represented by a curved line on the x-y coordinate plane.

You'll never have to draw the graph of a quadratic function on the ACT. You'll only have to use provided graphs to answer questions, or choose which graph is correct for a given function. (Again, your calculator may be useful in those situations. See "Using A Calculator" later on in our discussion of the ACT Math section for more on that.)

Quadratic functions always extend infinitely either up or down.

Examples:

The graph of $y = x^2$ extends "up" infinitely. It looks like this:

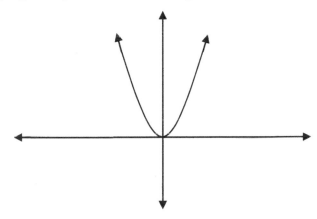

The graph of $y = -x^2$ extends "down" infinitely. It looks like this:

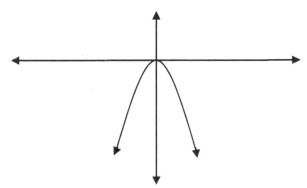

You can also think of the "direction" of the graph of a quadratic equation in terms of its range. When the range extends to negative infinity, the graph "opens down." When the range extends to positive infinity, the graph "opens up."

The highest point of a quadratic function that "opens down" is the (x, y) pair that has the greatest y value.

The lowest point of a quadratic function that "opens up" is the (x, y) pair that has the lowest y value.

The "zeroes" of a quadratic function are the points where the graph of the function touches or crosses the x-axis. To find the zeroes, set $f(x)$ equal to zero, then solve the resulting equation.

    Example:

To find the zeroes of $f(x) = 2x^2 - 8$, we set $f(x)$ equal to zero and then solve for x:

$0 = 2x^2 - 8$	(substitute 0 for $f(x)$)
$8 = 2x^2$	(add 8 to both sides)
$4 = x^2$	(divide both sides by 2)
$x = 2$ or $x = -2$	(take square root of both sides)

So the zeroes of $f(x) = 2x^2 - 8$ are 2 and -2.

Trigonometry

The trigonometry that you need on the ACT is relatively basic and limited. The most important things you need to know are the three basic trigonometric ratios and their inverses.

You've probably learned the three basic ratios in math class with the acronym "**SOHCAHTOA.**"

"**SOH**" stands for **S**ine = **O**pposite / **H**ypotenuse

"**CAH**" stands for **C**osine = **A**djacent / **H**ypotenuse

"**TOA**" stands for **T**angent = **O**pposite / **A**djacent

Given a right triangle:

The "hypotenuse" is the side that's opposite the right angle.

The "opposite" side is the one across from the angle whose sine, cosine, or tangent we're evaluating.

The "adjacent" side is the side that's next to the angle we're evaluating (the one that isn't the hypotenuse).

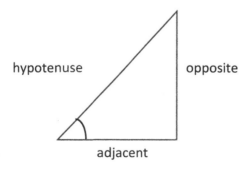

You can use these ratios to solve for the lengths of sides or the measure of angles.

Example:

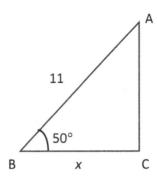

In this figure, we're given the measure of an angle and the length of the hypotenuse. We can set up an expression for *x*, the adjacent side length, because we know that the cosine of an angle is equal to the length of the adjacent side divided by the length of the hypotenuse.

In this example, $\cos 50° = \frac{x}{11}$, so that means $11(\cos 50°) = x$.

You should be able to recognize the graphs of sine, cosine, and tangent:

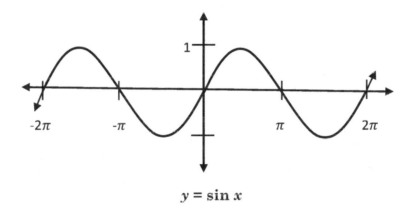

$$y = \sin x$$

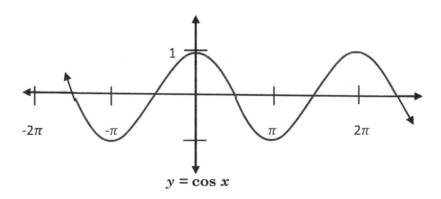

$$y = \cos x$$

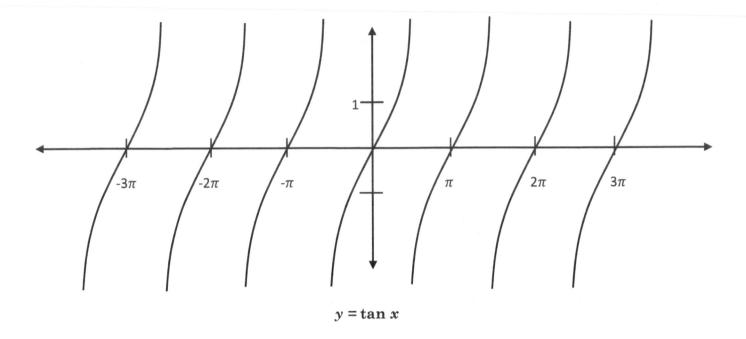

$$y = \tan x$$

The period of a graph is the smallest section of the graph that you could "copy and paste" over and over again to make the graph.

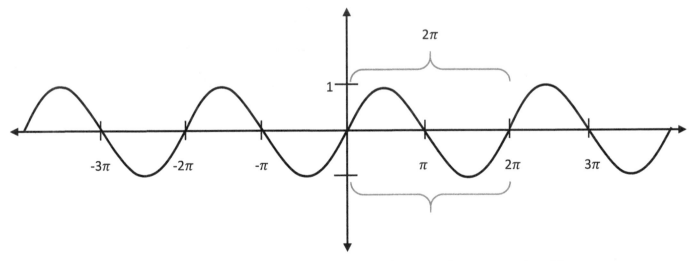

The period of $y = \sin x$ is 2π, because the graph repeats itself every 2π units.

You may also see the terms cosecant, secant, and cotangent, which may be written as csc, sec, and cot, respectively.

Cosecant is the reciprocal of sine.

Secant is the reciprocal of cosine.

Cotangent is the reciprocal of tangent.

Cosecant = Hypotenuse/Opposite

Secant = Hypotenuse/Adjacent

Cotangent = Adjacent/Opposite

The ACT Math section doesn't allow itself to ask questions that require you to understand advanced trig concepts. It can only test you on the six basic trig functions: sine, cosine, tangent, and their reciprocals (cosecant, secant, and cotangent, respectively).

NOTE: If you've studied trigonometry in school, you may be familiar with the idea of trigonometric identities. Although the ACT sometimes designs questions in a way that makes untrained test-takers think they need to understand how to use these trig identities, you never actually need to know them for the ACT. We'll cover this in more detail when we talk about the unwritten rules of the ACT Math section, and the walkthrough section of this Black Book also includes solutions for questions like this. (If you've never heard of trig identities, or if you don't remember any of them, don't worry—they're not something you need to know for the ACT).

Conclusion

If you're familiar with all the concepts in this toolbox, then you have the basic math knowledge necessary to answer any real ACT Math question. Of course, it's important to remember that simply knowing these concepts isn't enough to guarantee a good ACT Math score. It's equally important—perhaps *more* important—to focus on the design of the ACT Math section and to learn how to take apart challenging questions.

After all, the difference between people who score high on the ACT Math section and people who don't usually has very little to do with math knowledge. Generally speaking, people who score higher on the ACT Math section have a better understanding of how the test works, and pay more attention to small details—*that's* what actually sets them apart from the average test-taker.

On the next page, we'll start talking about the tactics that trained test-takers use when they apply their math knowledge to the ACT . . .

Unwritten Test Design Rules Of ACT Math

Now that we've talked a little bit about how ACT Math works, and we've covered the concepts that can appear in ACT Math questions, let's talk about the unwritten rules of ACT Math.

ACT Math Rule 1: You Have To Know The Words And Symbols

In the walkthroughs we looked at for the ACT Reading section, it was often possible to find a correct answer choice for a question even if we didn't know a few words in the question or in the relevant portion of the text. But it will usually be difficult to work around unknown terms on the ACT Math section: if an ACT Math question asks about the greatest common factor of two numbers, you have very little chance of getting that question right if you don't know the definition of the term "greatest common factor."

Fortunately, you shouldn't have a problem with math terminology on the ACT if you're comfortable with the concepts from the Math Toolbox in this Black Book. Just remember that you need to get familiar with any unknown math terms you might run into while you're preparing. It's very likely that you'll see those terms again on other ACT Math questions, possibly on test day.

ACT Math Rule 2: No Advanced Formulas

You'll need to use some formulas on the ACT, but the formulas will be relatively simple and largely repetitive. The real challenge is usually figuring out exactly what the question is asking, and then deciding which simple formulas to apply.

Don't spend any time working through advanced math concepts, because they won't help you on this test. Instead, familiarize yourself with the ideas in the ACT Math Toolbox in this Black Book, and, once you've read all the training, start working through the ACT Math walkthroughs later in this section.

By the way, roughly once per test you'll run into a math question I call the "note" question. The note question is a trig question that seems fairly advanced at first, but then provides a note that explains the advanced trig formula necessary to answer the question. These questions often intimidate test-takers who don't read the note, because the questions seem to require advanced trig formulas if we don't realize that those formulas have been provided for us in the question. If we do read the question carefully, we can see that these questions actually just require us to read the provided formula and substitute the provided values in the appropriate places—a relatively basic math skill. We'll see examples of these "note" questions when we do the question walkthroughs in a few pages.

ACT Math Rule 3: Calculations Are Relatively Simple

As you work through real ACT Math practice questions, you'll find that the calculations you'll do are relatively easy. The real challenge is often in knowing how to set the problem up—the final calculation you'll need to do will frequently be along the lines of "4 + 7" or "2 - 0" or something like that.

In fact, if you find yourself writing out a very complex expression while trying to solve a question, that can often be a warning sign that you're on the wrong track. You'll see this idea in action once we start going through the ACT Math question walkthroughs.

ACT Math Rule 4: Limited Subject Matter

As we've discussed, there's a limit to the math concepts that can come up in ACT Math questions, and all of those concepts are discussed in the ACT Math Toolbox in this book. Once you feel good about those concepts, you know all the math ideas you need to know for the ACT Math section. All that's left is to learn how to deal with the unusual presentation of those ideas in real questions.

This is important because most untrained test-takers will panic when they see a challenging ACT Math question, because they assume they don't know the math involved. But trained test-takers are confident they know all the math necessary to answer any question on the ACT, so they don't panic when they see a strange question. Instead, they remain calm and follow the "Math Path," which is a rough outline for solving challenging ACT Math questions that we'll discuss in a few pages.

ACT Math Rule 5: 30 Seconds or Less

This is an important concept, and it may seem hard to believe right now: every ACT Math question can technically be solved in 30 seconds or less if you find the most efficient approach to it.

But this doesn't mean that your answer must be wrong if it takes you longer than 30 seconds to find it!

As we'll see in the ACT Math walkthroughs in a few pages, we can always find multiple valid approaches to every ACT Math question. An approach that takes longer than 30 seconds isn't necessarily any worse than one that takes less than 30 seconds, as long as you still have enough time overall to finish the ACT Math section and get the score you need.

But it's very important to understand, strategically, that every question *can* be answered in less than 30 seconds. This is important because the ACT likes to make simple things seem complicated so that untrained test-takers won't know what to do. The test will go out of its way to make you think that some questions require 2 or 3 minutes of complicated calculations—but if you remember that every real ACT Math question can actually be answered in less than 30 seconds, you'll be motivated to try to view the question in simpler terms.

These under-30 second solutions often involve unorthodox ways of looking at questions; in many cases, they'll involve techniques your teacher wouldn't let you use in a math class. For example, you might have to rely on the scale of a diagram or plug an arbitrary value into a variable expression—we'll talk about these techniques, and others, over the coming pages.

ACT Math Rule 6: All Necessary Information

Unless there's an answer choice that says the correct answer can't be determined from the given information, every single question must provide all the information you need to find the answer. Sometimes it might seem like a question is leaving something out—if it seems that way, then you're forgetting some math idea, or overlooking something. In this case, we have to try to look at all the information in the problem in a different way and generate a solution.

Again, we'll expand on this idea when we talk about the general process for answering ACT Math questions, and when we do the math walkthroughs in a few pages.

ACT Math Rule 7: Scale Is Pretty Much Always Accurate

The instructions for the ACT Math section specifically state that "illustrative figures are NOT necessarily drawn to scale" (emphasis in original). In other words, the test is telling us that we shouldn't assume the diagrams and graphs on the ACT Math section are drawn to scale . . .

. . . but literally every single diagram I've ever seen in a real ACT Math section has been drawn to scale. That means their angle measurements are consistent with what the question describes, and the relative lengths of lines are accurate, as well. (For example, if one side of a rectangle is labeled 6 units long and another side is labeled 3 units, the ACT's diagram will accurately show the longer side being twice as long as the shorter side.)

This can be very helpful, because the ACT often provides us with wrong-answer choices that are much too large or too small to be correct when we consider them in terms of the diagram's scale, leaving the correct answer as the only choice that seems plausible relative to the scale. In other words, we might see a question that asks us to find the measure of an angle in a diagram, and we may be able to tell that the angle is slightly larger than 90° just by looking at the diagram, because we know that a 90° angle is a perfect right angle, and the angle in the diagram is slightly larger than that. Then we might find that the only answer choice that's slightly larger than 90° has a value of 96°, and the other four values in the answer choices are 42°, 48°, 84°, and 135°. In that case, we could know that 96° must be correct, without even doing any actual math.

So keep your eyes open for opportunities to use a diagram to your advantage like this. They don't come up on every single question, of course, but when you do encounter them they can often get you quick, easy points. It's not uncommon for a real ACT Math section to offer us 3 or 4 opportunities to answer questions this way.

(One important note: even though I've never seen an ACT Math diagram that wasn't to scale, I always double-check that a diagram seems to be to scale before I rely on the scale to choose my answer. I usually do this by making a rough comparison of two labeled lengths on the diagram, to confirm that their relative lengths seem consistent with the labels. You'll see this technique in action for some of the walkthroughs in a few pages.)

ACT Math Rule 8: Answer Choices Are Important!

The answer choices for each ACT Math question aren't randomly generated—they're constructed as carefully as the rest of the question.

Let's think about this—imagine that you were doing an ACT Math question and you came up with an answer of 10, but 10 wasn't an answer choice. If that happened, you'd be getting a free shot to try to do the problem again, because you would know you'd made a mistake.

The ACT doesn't want that to happen, so it tries to provide wrong answers that anticipate the mistakes it thinks you're likely to make. That way, if you make one of those mistakes, you'll find an answer choice that reflects it, and you'll be likely to choose that wrong answer without realizing you're wrong.

These cleverly positioned wrong-answer choices might seem like they would make it harder to get ACT Math questions right, but they can actually work to our advantage if we know how to exploit them. Depending on the context of the question, we can use a set of answer choices to give us hints about which concepts are involved in the solution to the question, or even about which answer choice is likely to be correct.

We'll talk more about this in the section called "ACT Math Answer-Choice Patterns," and you'll see these concepts in action in the ACT Math section walkthroughs.

Testing Values

We've already seen how some of the weaknesses of the multiple-choice format can be used to our advantage on the ACT Math section. But there's another way we can sometimes exploit the multiple-choice format, as well: we can sometimes test values from the answer choices instead of having to solve a math question on our own.

There are two general types of situations on the ACT Math section in which you can find the correct answer by testing values in a variable expression:

If a question asks us to solve for a variable and the answer choices don't involve variables, we can often just plug each answer choice back into the expression from the question.

If a question has a variable (or variables) in the answer choices, we can often assign an arbitrary value to that variable (or those variables) and then evaluate each expression in the prompt and the answer choices.

Both of these concepts might make a lot more sense once if we consider some examples. We'll look at both of them now, starting with the easier one:

Plugging values from the answer choices into an expression from the question

Sometimes you'll see a question that presents some kind of expression with a single variable, and then asks you for the number that makes that expression true.

If such a question only has numbers in the answer choices, then the most straightforward (and fastest) approach is sometimes just to plug each answer choice into the variable expression to see which one works. Let's look at question 23 on page 169 of the Red Book to see this idea in action.

This question asks us which value "is a solution to the equation $x^2 - 36x = 0$." Then it gives us five numbers to choose from.

Some test-takers will start trying to factor out the equation to find a solution, as though they were taking an algebra test in high school. This approach will work if you do it correctly, but a lot of people don't like to factor expressions with variables. Since we know that one of the values in the answer choices must be a solution for the equation, we can just plug each answer choice into the equation and see which one makes it true:

(A) $(72)^2 - 36(72)$ $5184 - 2592 = 2592$

(B) $(36)^2 - 36(36)$ $1296 - 1296 = 0$

(C) $(18)^2 - 36(18)$ $324 - 648 = -324$

(D) $(6)^2 - 36(6)$ $36 - 216 = -180$

(E) $(-6)^2 - 36(-6)$ $36 + 216 = 252$

(Remember you're free to use a calculator to do this, in case you don't want to evaluate something like $(72)^2 - 36(72)$ in your head.)

When we plug each answer choice into the equation from the prompt, we can see that only one of them results in a value of zero, as described in the question. That means we know the correct answer is (B), 36.

Now let's talk about a slightly more advanced way to answer an ACT Math question by testing values.

Using arbitrary values to test answer choices containing variables

If the answer choices for a question involve a variable, we can sometimes solve the question by assigning a value to the variable and then evaluating the expressions provided in the prompt and in the answer choices.

I know that might sound a little confusing, so let's check out a real-life example of this technique in action by looking at question 21 from page 169 in the Red Book.

This question asks us which answer choice is equivalent to $\frac{x}{y}$ for all positive integers x, y, and z. All of the answer choices are fractions with different combinations of the variables in the denominator and the numerator.

To apply this technique to the question, we would just choose some values for x, y, and z, then plug them into the answer choices and see which one results in an expression that's equal to $\frac{x}{y}$. The question said that x, y, and z were all positive integers, so we MUST pick positive integers to make this work. Let's say that $x = 3$, $y = 5$, and $z = 6$.

That means we want to find an expression in the answer choices that would be equal to $\frac{3}{5}$ (remember that we picked 3 for x and 5 for y, and the question asked for a value that is equal to $\frac{x}{y}$).

Let's plug these values into each answer choice.

(A) $\frac{x*z}{y*z} = \frac{3*6}{5*6} = \frac{18}{30} = \frac{3}{5}$

(B) $\frac{x*x}{y*y} = \frac{3*3}{5*5} = \frac{9}{25}$

(C) $\frac{y*x}{x*y} = \frac{5*3}{3*5} = \frac{15}{15} = 1$

(D) $\frac{x-z}{y-z} = \frac{3-6}{5-6} = \frac{-3}{-1} = 3$

(E) $\frac{x+z}{y+z} = \frac{3+6}{5+6} = \frac{9}{11}$

We can see that only (A) can be correct, since it's the only choice that can be reduced to our target value, $\frac{3}{5}$.

Most people will approach a question like this by manipulating the variables without substituting any actual numbers. If you're comfortable doing that, go right ahead—just remember that this type of question always gives us the option of coming up with values and then actually testing each variable expression. Just remember that the values you choose must satisfy the terms of the question (in this case, they needed to be positive integers because the prompt demanded it).

A Couple Of Important Notes

There's one very important thing to be aware of when you use this technique. It's possible, through sheer chance, that you might pick variables that result in more than one answer choice coincidentally matching the expression from the question. If that ever happens, just pick new values for the variables and re-evaluate everything. It's extremely unlikely that such a coincidence will happen on the second try as well, so there should only be one choice left that satisfies the question.

You can decrease the likelihood of this kind of coincidence by avoiding certain values when you make your substitution. I'd advise you not to choose the values 0 or 1 for any question, because of their unique properties; I also try to avoid picking any values that already appear in the prompt or in the answer choices.

It's also important to keep in mind that you don't have to use this approach if you don't want to. There are always other ways to approach a question, but it can sometimes be helpful to remember that this option exists if you can't figure out a quick algebraic solution to the question.

You'll see this approach in action against other real ACT practice questions as you go through the ACT Math walkthroughs later in this section.

ACT Math Answer-Choice Patterns

Earlier in this book, we discussed the importance of answer choices in general. We've also talked about different types of answer choices on the ACT Reading section. Now, let's take a look at some of the answer-choice patterns you'll see on the ACT Math section.

You know by now that wrong-answer choices can contain valuable information if we know how to exploit them. Well, some of the special characteristics of answer choices on the Math section can be especially useful.

Now, I should point out that some people sort of intuitively just "get" some of the concepts that we're about to talk about. Even if you feel like you already know some of this stuff, I still recommend that you read this section carefully. It can be very valuable to see these strategies spelled out in black and white—and you may also discover some tactics you've never thought about before.

In order to understand how the sets of answer choices on the ACT Math section are designed, let's imagine we're actually in charge of writing a math question that's going to be used on the ACT. We've got the beginning of the question all ready to go, but we need to add in some wrong-answer choices to complete it.

Our main goal is to provide choices that might trap someone who made a mistake in solving the question, or who didn't understand the question in the first place and just wanted to take a guess.

As we discussed earlier, in "The ACT's Biggest Weakness," if the wrong-answer choices are unrelated to the question, it'll be too easy for test-takers to identify the right answer without understanding the question. So we might try to provide "decoy" answers that a confused person could accidentally pick. Let's look at a fake sample question to illustrate this concept (of course, this question is too simple to be an ACT Math question, but we're just using it to illustrate a basic concept):

$$176 \times 4{,}673 = y$$

What is the value of y?

Now, that's not something most test-takers can do in their heads. But most test-takers could pick out the correct answer in just a few seconds if these were the answer choices:

(A) 1

(B) 0

(C) -11

(D) 822,448

(E) $\frac{1}{12}$

These answer choices make the correct answer instantly obvious. The only number that's remotely large enough is choice (D), and (D) is the correct answer. Beyond that,

- (A) is obviously too small.

- (B) is impossible since we're multiplying two numbers and neither number is zero.

- (C) is impossible since it's negative and neither of the two numbers being multiplied is negative.

- (E) is impossible since it's a fraction and we're multiplying two whole numbers.

In other words, the wrong answers make this fake question very easy for any test-taker who knows the basics of multiplication and who bothers to read the answer choices.

This is an extreme and unrealistic example designed to illustrate a point, but you see what I mean. Coming up with some plausible incorrect answer choices is every bit as important as any other part of the design of the question.

Now, let's think a little more about how we might try to come up with those incorrect answer choices if we were trying to write an ACT Math question.

Imagine the question we're creating involves solving for x in this equation:

$$2x^2 = 50$$

and then plugging x into this equation to solve for y:

$$y = 3x + 2$$

For the first step, a test-taker on the right track would figure out that x = 5, because $2(5)^2 = 50$. Then she'd plug x into the second equation, and get y = 17, because 17 = 3(5) + 2.

You can probably see that one really good wrong-answer choice for us to include would be 5. Some test-takers might figure out that x = 5 in the first part of the problem, and then forget that we actually asked them to solve for y, and they still have another step left.

So we'd definitely want to include 5 as a wrong-answer choice. That way, we'd catch anybody who managed to do the first part of the question correctly, but who lost track of what the question actually asked for, and failed to finish it.

Another good wrong-answer choice for us to include might be 77. Some test-takers might realize that $2x^2 = 50$, but then accidentally plug x^2 into the second equation instead of x. Really, x is 5, but x^2 is 25; if a test-taker accidentally plugged x = 25 into the expression y = 3x + 2, he'd end up with 77 as the answer, because 77 = 3(25) + 2.

There are other set patterns the ACT often uses to generate wrong-answer choices on the Math section, and we'll discuss them below. For now, though, you get the idea: the ACT puts a lot of thought into the wrong-answer choices for each question.

It's very clever of the test to include these tricky wrong answers in order to catch as many people in their mistakes as possible. But, if we're paying attention, we can use these patterns to our advantage.

If the ACT has to include wrong answers that are closely related to things going on in the question, and if we know how to look for those relationships in the answer choices, then the set of answer choices can become like a set of clues to help us realize which math concepts are related to the question—in some cases, the answer choices can even offer strong hints of which answer choice is likely to be correct.

Not every single question will have answer choice clues exactly like that, but almost every real ACT Math question will have something in the answer choices that can help us out if we know to look for it. With that in mind, let's discuss a few of the most common wrong answer types in real ACT Math questions. (Of course, you'll see ample demonstrations of all of these concepts in use against real ACT questions when we do the math walkthroughs in a few pages.)

ACT Math Answer-Choice Pattern 1: "On-The-Way" Answer

This is the sort of thing we were just talking about. Sometimes you'll see a wrong answer choice with a number that you need to find in order to answer the question, but that number itself isn't the right answer.

You can see a real-life example of this wrong answer type in choice (E) of question 3 on page 164 of *The Real ACT Prep Guide, 3rd Edition*. This question asks you how much less the school board would pay if it pays a substitute teacher for one day's work, while the regular teacher takes a day off without pay. The question provides the teacher's annual salary, the number of days in the school year, and the amount the substitute gets paid for one day's work.

In order to solve this question, you first have to find out how much the teacher gets paid for one day's work. To do that, you must divide his salary ($22,570) by the number of days he works (185) to get his pay for one day, which is $122.

But the question doesn't ask how much the teacher gets paid for a day's work! It asks how much *less* the school board pays the substitute for one day's work ($80) than it would pay the full-time teacher ($122), and the correct answer is $42, because $122 - $80 = $42. So (A) is correct.

But choice (E) is there to offer $122 as an option in case someone figures out the first part of the problem, and then forgets to do the rest.

This type of wrong-answer choice shows up frequently. Before you select an answer, always check to make sure you've done the whole problem, and that what you've selected is actually the answer to the question being asked, and not just a number you need to find along the way. Don't make the mistake of thinking that you must be right because you arrived at a number that appears in one of the answer choices.

ACT Math Answer-Choice Pattern 2: Calculation Mistake

As you can imagine, another extremely common type of wrong-answer choice simply involves making small, predictable calculation mistakes.

This sort of thing might involve multiplying when we're supposed to divide, or finding the area of a figure instead of the perimeter. It might reflect forgetting how to do FOIL or add fractions correctly. Basically, the ACT likes to give you chances to make tiny mistakes in the execution of a solution—this way, you can still arrive at a wrong answer even if you figure out the correct overall approach to the question.

A real-life example of this type of wrong answer can be found in choice (B) of question 1 on page 164 of *The Real ACT Prep Guide, 3rd Edition*. This question asks us to find the total distance run by Kaya in two days, which requires us to add $1\frac{2}{5}$ and $2\frac{1}{3}$.

To do this correctly, of course, we'd need to find a common denominator so that both fractions could be added together. (Incidentally, we'd do this by converting both fractions to fifteenths, which would give us the numbers $1\frac{6}{15}$ and $2\frac{5}{15}$. Adding them together would give us $3\frac{11}{15}$).

But if we forgot how fractions worked, we might just try to add the corresponding numbers in the expressions: 1 plus 2 to give us 3 for the whole number, then 2 (in the first numerator) plus 1 (in the second numerator) to give us 3 for the numerator, and 5 (in the first denominator) plus 3 (in the second denominator) to give us 8 for the denominator.

That would mistakenly give us $3\frac{3}{8}$, which is choice (B), which is incorrect.

We'll see many more wrong-answer choices that give us the opportunity to make these kinds of mistakes in the walkthroughs.

ACT Math Answer-Choice Pattern 3: Most Like The Others (Or *Almost* Like The Others)

Being aware of this pattern can give us a significant advantage on the ACT, but we should take care not to rely on it too much.

You should never select an answer choice based purely on this pattern alone—unless you've given up all hope of understanding the question, and you're just marking an answer as a best guess. (For more on this, see "Guessing On The ACT" in "The General Game Plan For Attacking A Section Of The ACT On Test Day" earlier in this Black Book.)

The basic idea behind this pattern is that the ACT likes to incorporate some elements of the correct answer into the incorrect answers, so that test-takers who can only figure out part of a complicated question will still see more than one answer choice that seems like it might be correct. Because of this, we'll frequently find that the correct answer to a question is the answer choice that has the greatest number of features in common with the other answer choices.

That abstract description probably sounds a little strange, so let's look at a concrete example of this concept. Please check out question 22 on page 169 of the Red Book.

You can see that all the answer choices for that question share a few obvious characteristics:

- They all have a y term.
- They all have an x term with a coefficient of either 8 or 6.
- They all have either a plus sign or a minus sign after the x term.
- They all end with either 6 or 8.

Let's try to figure out why the ACT would make the answer choices for this question be so similar to one another. Wrong answer choices are often designed to attract untrained test-takers, right? On a question like this, the ACT might want the wrong answers to share as many features as possible with the correct answer. That way, for instance, a test-taker who correctly figured out that the coefficient of x should be 8 would still have to figure out whether (H) or (J) were correct. On top of that, even if a test-taker correctly determined that the right answer was $y = 8x - 6$, he might still misread the answer choices if he were in a hurry, and accidentally bubble the wrong letter anyway. (Untrained test-takers do that kind of thing all the time. It's one of the reasons people often feel like the ACT is going well when they're taking it, only to be disappointed when they get their results.)

For these kinds of reasons, we'll often find that the ACT uses wrong answers that include elements of the right answer, whenever the correct answer to a question is complicated enough to make these kinds of wrong answers possible.

And this means the correct answer will often (but not always!) be the answer choice that has the most characteristics in common with the other answer choices.

With that in mind, let's take another look at the choices in question 22 from page 169 of the Red Book. Let's see if we can figure out which answer choice has the most in common with the other choices.

All of the answer choices start with "$y =$," so we know the right answer must also start with "$y =$."

After that, 2 out of 5 choices have a minus sign, while 3 out of 5 don't. That means we'd expect the right answer not to have a minus sign in that position, because the majority of the answer choices don't.

Next, we see that 4 out of 5 choices have an 8, while only one has a 6. So we'd expect 8 to be part of the correct answer, because it appears most frequently in the answer choices at this position.

All of the answer choices then have an x.

After that, 3 of the answer choices have a minus sign, while 2 don't, so we'd expect the correct answer to have a minus sign in this position, in order to side with the majority.

Finally, 4 answer choices feature a 6 in the last position, while only one has an 8 in that position.

Taking into account all of the most common features in the answer choices, we'd expect the correct answer to be $y = 8x - 6 \ldots$

. . . and it is.

Before you get too excited over this kind of approach, I want to stress that this approach is NOT, under ANY circumstances, the only thing that I would recommend you rely on when answering an ACT Math question.

The reason I tell you not to rely on this pattern exclusively isn't that I want you to learn actual math. As far as this test is concerned, I don't care if you know any math—and neither does the ACT, really. All the ACT cares about is whether you fill in the right bubble when you answer the question (without cheating), so that's all I care about, too (at least for the purposes of this Black Book).

The reason I tell you not to rely exclusively on this pattern is that it doesn't work 100% of the time. Sometimes a set of answer choices seems like it's set up to follow this pattern, and the right answer ends up not being the one we'd expect. In fact, sometimes the right answer is the one with the most common characteristics *in all but one place*!

We can call this related pattern the "*Almost* Like The Others" pattern.

You can see this answer-choice pattern in question number 2 on page 164 of the Red Book. For this question, you might expect the right answer to have the following elements:

- a first term of 24 (since 3 out of 5 choices have 24 in this position)
- a second term of x^{12} (since 3 out of 5 choices have x^{12} in this position)
- a third term of y^2 (since 4 out of 5 have y^2 in this position)

But the right answer is actually (H), $24x^7y^2$, which sides with the majority of the other answer choices on the first and third terms, but not on the second one. It's *almost* like most of the other choices, but it includes the less common option for the *x* term.

As I said, this kind of thing can happen on the ACT. So if our goal is to answer every question correctly, we have to consider other things in addition to these patterns. The point of being aware of these patterns isn't to depend exclusively on them—the point is to use them as guides, and as tools for evaluating a given question from multiple perspectives.

These patterns can also be hints that help us find non-traditional solutions to a question. If we have no idea where to start on a question, we might see if any patterns in the answer choices suggest that certain elements are likely to be part of the correct answer, and then try to work backwards from there. Or if we solve the question but come up with an answer that seems unlikely to be correct according to a pattern, then we might take a second to think carefully back through our reasoning to make sure we haven't made a wrong turn somewhere.

You'll see several examples of these kinds of tactics discussed in the walkthroughs in a few pages.

ACT Math Answer-Choice Pattern 4: Half Or Double

There are many ACT Math questions that involve multiplying or dividing by two. For whatever reason, it's just some arbitrary pattern the ACT likes to follow sometimes, even when it doesn't seem particularly relevant to a specific question that incorporates it.

At any rate, you'll often see incorrect answer choices on the ACT Math section that are half of the right answer, or double the right answer.

For a real-life example, look at question 6 on page 165 of your copy of *The Real ACT Prep Guide, 3rd Edition*. The correct answer is (J), 700, but choices (G) and (K) are 350 and 1,400, respectively—one is half the correct answer, the other is twice as much as the correct answer.

In this case, the question gives you the length and width of a figure and asks for its perimeter. As you can imagine, some people might just add the length and width (instead of twice the length plus twice the width), not remembering that there are four total sides of the figure. This would give them half of the correct answer. It might also be possible that someone who knew to account for all four sides would end up multiplying by two again accidentally, and incorrectly end up with twice the correct answer. These are the types of predictable mistakes that the ACT is apparently trying to anticipate with these wrong answers.

But, as I just mentioned, we'll sometimes see this pattern even in questions that don't really involve the concept of doubling or halving anything. For example, check out question 4 on page 450, which involves finding the length of a side of a triangle. The correct answer is 6, and one of the wrong answers is 3, even though no likely mistake on the question could lead a test-taker to divide the correct answer by 2 accidentally. (The other wrong answers to the question all involve more understandable mathematical errors—for a complete discussion of them, see this Black Book's walkthrough for the question.)

So this is another important pattern to remember: if you see two answer choices, and one is twice the other, or even if you see three or more in a series that keeps multiplying or dividing by two, then one of those choices is disproportionately likely to be correct—not *guaranteed* to be correct, by any means, but likely to be.

ACT Math Answer-Choice Pattern 5: Series

This is another common pattern that can be related to the one we just discussed. We talked about a possible series of two or more answer choices that starts with one number and then keeps doubling or halving that number. You might also see several other different kinds of series.

Often, the correct answer to a question like this is a middle term in the series, or is at least a member of the series.

You can see a real-life example of this pattern in question 44 on page 174 of your copy of *The Real ACT Prep Guide, 3rd Edition*. The first three answer choices are 280, 300, and 320. This is a series of three terms, and you can see that the numbers are increasing by 20 with each term. The correct answer is (G), 300, the middle term in the series.

Let me stress again that these patterns aren't enough, on their own, to determine a correct answer with complete certainty! It can be very tempting to see a series in a set of answer choices and just pick the middle term, but this isn't how the test always works. This is just a trend that can frequently help you think about a question from a different perspective if you get stuck.

You might see answer choices forming a series in which each number increases by a set quantity—like the series 10, 17, 24. This might give you a clue that adding or subtracting 7 is part of finding the right answer. You might also see choices forming a series that involves multiplying by a certain number—like 0.89, 8.9, 89. 890. That might tell you that multiplying or dividing by ten is a part of finding the correct answer.

As with any other answer-choice pattern, it's also occasionally true that the correct answer won't be a part of a series in the answer choices. But it can still be helpful to be aware of these series, and with practice you'll be able to use them to help you solve questions more quickly and accurately.

We'll see examples of this idea in the walkthroughs.

The General Process For Answering ACT Math Questions

I've said before that the ACT is basically one big reading test, and that's as true on the Math section as it is anywhere else. If you can train yourself to read carefully and precisely—just like you do in the Reading section— you'll be able to "decode" what's going on in any ACT Math question, so you can see through the unusual presentation to the simple math concept underneath.

How do we do that? We follow something I call the "Math Path!" (I just call it that because it rhymes. Unfortunately—or maybe fortunately—I haven't been able to come up with good rhyming names for anything else in this Black Book . . .)

The Math Path

The Math Path is what I call the steps you should take when you're confronted with a challenging ACT Math question:

1. Note the words.
2. Consider the answer choices.
3. Determine the relevant math domains.
4. Try to figure out a 30-second solution.
5. Carry out your solution.
6. Check everything!

Before I explain these steps in more detail, I just want to point out that you are, of course, free to modify them as you see fit—as long as your method consistently yields correct answers and allows you to complete the section within the time limit. You should also feel free to ignore these steps completely on easier questions if you see what to do right away. The Math Path is simply one way to organize your thoughts when you can't figure out how to attack a question.

Now, let's look at each step in turn.

1. Note the words.

As I've said repeatedly, the entire ACT is a reading test, and reading accurately will do wonders for your score on every section, including this one.

The first step in solving any math question is to read the entire question carefully, paying attention to the specific math terms and concepts that appear.

In school, you usually don't need to read math questions so carefully, because school tests ask us to use the same math techniques over and over again in questions that are basically identical to one another. But ACT Math doesn't work like that. We never know precisely which combination of basic math concepts will be thrown at us in a particular question, so we have to pay attention to each question from the very beginning.

2. Consider the answer choices.

Most untrained test-takers will read the prompt of an ACT Math question, then try to answer the question on their own. When they have a solution they like, they'll try to see if it matches one of the answer choices; if it does, they pick it and move on without another thought.

That approach *can* lead to a great score—as long as the test-taker is good at figuring out what every ACT Math question wants her to do, and as long as she never makes a mistake in reading the question or performing her calculations. Few people fall into that category.

We trained test-takers know that it's much smarter and easier to consider the answer choices along with the prompt from the very beginning. We know the answer choices can contain clues and useful information, just like the question prompt does.

Concepts that appear in the answer choices can show you what the ACT expects test-takers to think about when they approach the question. If all of the answer choices include π, that's a clue that circles or radians are probably involved. If there are a lot of square roots in the answer choices, then you might be dealing with right triangles, or possibly with exponents, or with taking the square root of something for another reason. If the answer choices involve lots of numbers with unique properties like 0 and 1, or if two choices have quantities that are reciprocals or opposites of each other, then the question might be focusing on other specific mathematical concepts or properties. And so on.

You might also be able to identify relationships among the answer choices that fit some of the patterns we discussed in "ACT Math Answer-Choice Patterns." Noticing those patterns can give you insight into which choices might be likely to be correct.

3. Determine the relevant math domains.

Now that you've read the question stem and answer choices, think about what areas of math might possibly be related to the question. Sometimes, when untrained test-takers come across a question they can't answer right away, they have an instinct to try to throw all their math knowledge at it just to see what happens. This usually just gets confusing and wastes time, leaving them more frustrated than they were before.

So in this step, instead of panicking and thinking in broad terms about all the math you know, you want to narrow your focus to the areas of math that are directly related to the question.

How do you do that? By thinking about the terms, concepts, and relationships you've identified so far.

Remember that the ACT Math section can only test you on a certain limited inventory of math concepts—that's an inherent limitation of its standardization.

If you understand the math concepts from the Math Toolbox in this Black Book, then you technically know enough math to answer every ACT Math question you'll ever see, as long as you can figure out how to combine those relatively basic math concepts in different ways to solve the ACT's questions.

Toward that end, it's important to remember that math always proceeds logically, by small steps—not just on the ACT, but everywhere. This means the correct approach to the question must be closely related to the concepts and relationships that are included in the prompt and the answer choices (and the diagram, if there is one).

For example, key concepts in the question and the answer choices will let you know what kind of math you need to think about. If you see words like "radius" and "diameter," you know the question is related to circles, which means you need to look for opportunities to apply the few circle-related ideas the ACT allows itself to test (radius, tangent, arc length, circumference, area, and so on). If a question mentions sine, then it's obviously related to basic trig, and you need to start thinking about right triangles, "opposite over hypotenuse," and so on.

As trained test-takers, we try to get a very specific idea of the individual math concepts that might possibly be related to the things we see in the question. In the next step, we'll try to fit those individual concepts together in a way that lets us find the simplest, most direct solution to the question.

4. Try to figure out a 30-second solution.

Once you've taken note of the concepts and relationships in the question and thought about what types of math are related to the question, it's time to try to fit all of those puzzle pieces together into a solution.

Remember that all ACT Math questions can be answered in 30 seconds or less, and many can be answered in less than 10 seconds. (If you don't believe me now, you'll see what I mean later, when we walk through some real ACT Math practice questions from the Red Book.)

As I mentioned in "Unwritten Test Design Rules Of ACT Math," your solutions can still be perfectly valid even if they take longer than 30 seconds. But I still encourage you to look for a 30-second solution to each ACT Math question you encounter, because looking for those kinds of solutions will encourage you to approach the section in non-traditional ways.

These non-traditional approaches will vary depending on the subject matter of the question, as you'll see when we do the walkthroughs in a few pages. But here are some general ideas for discovering these simplified, quick solutions:

- Look out for the answer choice patterns we discussed in "ACT Math Answer-Choice Patterns." They can often help you pinpoint the key concepts to address in a given question.
- Look for expressions from the prompt that are equivalent, or that cancel each other out.
- Look for ways you might plug answer choices into an expression, or use a calculator, or eliminate choices that are much too small or much too large.
- In general, don't rely on formulas. (The ACT Math section does occasionally test your knowledge of a formula directly, but you'll find that most real ACT Math questions don't have formulaic solutions.)
- In general, look for the solution to be simple, and don't feel limited by the things your math teacher in school would accept.

The ability to identify fast, efficient solutions to ACT Math questions is a skill you'll have to develop with practice. Going through the walkthroughs that appear in a few pages will be a big, big help with that. If you read and understand all of this material, and you work with real ACT Math questions, and you stick with it even when it's frustrating, you'll learn to cut through the bizarre, unpredictable presentations of the questions so you can see the predictably simple math concepts that are hidden underneath.

5. Carry out your solution.

Now that you've read the question and the answer choices, focused on the relevant math domains that are allowed to appear on the ACT, and thought of the most efficient solution you can, your job is just to execute the solution.

Obviously, it's important not to make any small mistakes at this point, so be sure you guard against any small miscalculation or misreading at this point.

Notice that actually doing the calculation is one of the *last* steps in properly approaching a challenging ACT Math question. It's much more important to spend a few seconds in the beginning reading carefully, observing relationships among the concepts present in the question, and then thinking deliberately about the most efficient approach you can come up with. If you do those things well, then the calculation itself becomes a lot easier to do—sometimes, you'll find you can answer the question without even doing a calculation at all!

6. Check everything!

This is the last step, and perhaps the most important.

Once you've done everything else, you MUST take a moment to re-evaluate your solution.

There are a lot of different ways to do this—but, as usual, the normal ways of doing it aren't really that reliable.

What I would NOT recommend would be to go back through everything you just did, and see if you can catch any mistakes. Most people who do this will find that they just re-make the same mistakes they made a few seconds before, since no real time has passed after their initial solutions, and they haven't given themselves a chance to see the question differently.

Instead, I like to evaluate the question from a fresh perspective. This will be more likely to help me identify any mistakes I might have just made, because I'm not just rushing back through the same steps I just did.

The easiest way to evaluate the question from a fresh perspective is to look at the answer choices and try to figure out why the ACT included them in the question, since most wrong-answer choices reflect mistakes that could have been made in solving the question. It's not necessary to find an explanation for every single answer choice, but we'll often see that some of the wrong answer choices will point to errors we might have made in our solution.

I also look to see if I can observe any common ACT patterns among the answer choices, and whether those patterns indicate that the answer choice I like is probably correct.

Both of these approaches to the question allow me to see it from another perspective, which gives me a better chance of catching any small mistakes I might have made.

You'll see several examples of these ideas in action during the walkthroughs in the next few pages.

ACT Math Path Conclusion

It may seem like this Math Path is a little complicated, especially when I've told you that all real ACT Math questions can be answered in 30 seconds or less. But if we think about it, we'll see the first half of the process is just reading the whole question and the answers, and matching up some of the words to math ideas you know about. This is something that can be done very quickly, with practice. The remaining three steps are coming up with a solution, executing that solution, and then checking your work. These steps can also be done quickly if you practice looking for efficient solutions to ACT Math questions.

You don't have to consciously map out each step, and slowly do them one-by-one. I just recommend that you get in the habit of considering these six points if you want to answer questions as quickly and effectively as possible. Thinking about the problems in this way will keep you focused and help you work through the test, while still giving you a good opportunity to catch your mistakes, which is vital to getting a good score.

Now that we've discussed the general approach I recommend for challenging questions on the ACT Math section, let's take a look at some other issues that might come up on specific types of questions.

ACT Math Closing Thoughts

We've covered all the main issues that are generally related to the ACT Math section. In this section, we'll explore a few concepts that apply more to certain sub-types of ACT Math questions. After that, we'll put these strategies to the test against real practice ACT Math questions in the walkthroughs.

Using A Calculator

Calculators can definitely come in handy on the ACT Math section—but not as often as many untrained test-takers might expect. The trick is to know when to use the calculator, and when not to.

Most of the difficulty in *most* ACT Math questions involves simply understanding a question in the first place and setting it up correctly. As I've said repeatedly in this Black Book, the entire ACT is primarily a reading test, and that includes the Math section. You'll see a lot of questions that combine basic concepts in ways you've never thought of before, and the major challenge with those questions will involve close reading and careful thinking. Of course, calculators aren't much help when it comes to reading questions and setting up solutions to them. (In fact, that's probably why calculators are allowed on the ACT in the first place. Remember that the test is standardized, which means it tries to provide the same testing experience to all test-takers, so the results from their tests can be compared to each other in a meaningful way. But the ACT doesn't mandate that all test-takers use a particular calculator, nor does it provide a standard calculator for all test-takers. This strongly suggests that the people who write the ACT don't think that a calculator is likely to help you too much.)

But there are four situations you could encounter on the ACT in which you may find a calculator to be useful:

- simple calculations

- evaluating more advanced numerical expressions

- generating graphs for some questions about functions

- evaluating expressions with variables

We'll talk about each of these situations in order.

Simple calculations

Some test-takers just aren't confident doing any math in their head at all—either because they dislike math in general, or because the ACT Math section in particular makes them very nervous. For these test-takers, the calculator can be a welcome crutch. They might even feel the need to use it on almost every question, because they don't even trust themselves to add or subtract single-digit numbers.

There's nothing wrong with using a calculator on every question, of course, as long as it works for you in your practice sessions. You should do whatever you have to do on test day to make sure that you don't make any careless mistakes, and if a calculator helps you prevent those mistakes, then you should use it.

But you still have to be careful! Certain kinds of mistakes are arguably *more* likely to be made on a calculator, and many test-takers are less likely to check their work carefully if they use a calculator on a question. When you use a calculator, you might accidentally press the wrong button, causing you to execute the wrong operation at the wrong time, or possibly even execute an operation on the wrong numbers in the first place. Some questions will include wrong answer choices that reflect those mistakes, which means that a lot of untrained test-takers will never realize they might have used their calculators incorrectly. (This is more likely to happen with mistakes that involve executing the wrong operations, or executing the right operations in the wrong order.)

So don't let your guard down on a question just because you decide to use a calculator when you answer it. You still have to check back over every question by reviewing the steps you followed, and you still need to evaluate the rest of the answer choices to see if you can figure out what kinds of mistakes in the solution might have led to those choices, as we discussed in the Math Path.

Evaluating more advanced numerical expressions

The ACT occasionally asks us questions that reward us for evaluating numerical expressions with things like radical signs or logarithms. When this happens, it can be useful to enter the expression into a calculator, and let the calculator give you back a simple decimal approximation of the expression.

In most cases, simply entering the expression into your calculator won't be enough to find the answer, but it can help you. These kinds of situations often arise if a question involves taking a square root of a number that isn't square, or finding a third root of some number. If you'd like to see some walkthroughs of such questions in this Black Book, check out the following:

- my walkthrough for question 10 on page 166 of the Red Book.

- my walkthrough for question 45 on page 174 of the Red Book.

- my walkthrough for question 45 on page 598 of the Red Book.

The ACT might also ask you to evaluate a numerical expression involving something like a matrix or a logarithm, but these questions come up even more rarely than questions that reward you for coming up with the decimal approximation of a radical expression. For an example of a calculator-based walkthrough of a logarithm question on the ACT, please see my explanation for question 49 on page 599 of the Red Book.

It's also occasionally possible to use this technique on an expression involving a trig function like sine or cosine. See the calculator portion of my walkthrough for question 60 on page 179 of the Red Book for an example of how this can work.

Outside of this small handful of questions, very few Red Book questions actually reward us for using a calculator to evaluate a numerical expression. This is a good indication of how rarely you should expect to see this kind of thing on test day.

Generating graphs for some questions about functions

Some graph-related questions on the ACT Math section can be successfully attacked with graphing calculators, especially the ones that ask us to identify which answer choice contains an accurate graph of a given function, or that ask us to describe the graph of a given function.

In these kinds of situations, it can be helpful to enter the function in your graphing calculator so you can see what it actually looks like—sometimes, that's all you have to do in order to figure out the correct answer. (Of course, you still have to make sure you read the question carefully and enter the function correctly.)

Unfortunately, these kinds of questions don't come up very often on the ACT, and the Red Book explanations for these questions are unlikely to mention that they can be solved with graphing calculators in a matter of seconds.

But I'll be happy to tell you when graphing a function on your calculator would be the easiest way to solve a question, of course. For an example of a calculator-based solution to a Red Book question that asks us to identify the correct graph of a function, see this Black Book's walkthrough for question 57 on page 178 of the Red Book. For an example of a calculator-based solution to a Red Book question about the behavior of a graph, see this Black Book's explanation for question 42 on page 597 of the Red Book.

You may also be interested in this Black Book's walkthrough for question 48 on page 744 of the Red Book.

In each of those walkthroughs, you'll notice that I still go through the rest of the Math Path, even though I show you how to answer the question with a calculator. You'll also notice that I discuss other solutions to the questions that don't rely on calculators, because the ACT never *requires* us to use a calculator to solve a question.

Finally, you'll also notice that there aren't a lot of questions in the Red Book that would reward us for graphing a function besides the ones I mentioned here. As I said, the ACT Math section really doesn't provide us with a lot of opportunities to answer questions correctly simply by graphing a function. So don't be surprised if you don't see any questions on test day that allow you to do this—on the other hand, if you do see one, make sure you seize the opportunity to get it right!

Evaluating expressions with variables

The calculator can also occasionally come in handy when an ACT question asks us to evaluate expressions with variables, especially when the question is asking us to find the value of a particular variable.

(We already discussed this general idea in the section called "Testing Values," but I want to re-visit this concept because a calculator can sometimes make this approach easier to use.)

There are two general ways in which this can be done:

- If the answer choices for a question don't have any variables, then we may be able to use the calculator to plug each answer choice into an expression from the question and determine which choice is correct.

- If some of the answer choices include variables, then we may be able to assign arbitrary values to the variables and then use our calculators to evaluate each answer choice and see which one expresses an amount equal to the expression in the original question. (That might sound a little complicated, but it will probably make a lot more sense once you see me do it in the walkthroughs in a few pages.)

For an example of the first type of question, please see my walkthrough in this Black Book for question 18 on page 453 of the Red Book. In that question, the calculator makes it much easier to evaluate expressions like $2^{4.5}$ and 2^7.

For an example of the second type of question, please see this Black Book's walkthrough for question 34 on page 739 of the Red Book. In that case, the calculator might make it easier to evaluate expressions like $\frac{2(5)+3}{12(5)^2}$.

Keep all of these possible uses for calculators in mind as you read through the walkthroughs in this Black Book, and as you do your own practice on real ACT Math questions—but remember that most real ACT Math questions can't be solved by a calculator, and that you still need to be careful not to make mistakes when you use one.

You Can't Always Solve For Every Variable

One of the things the ACT likes to do best is to take advantage of your "school math" instincts. The test does this in a lot of different ways, and one of them is to present you with a math problem that involves several variables. In a school setting, we'd probably start trying to find the values of each variable; on the ACT Math section, we'll often find that some variables can't be solved for individually.

For example, if the ACT tells us $(x + y)^3 = 8$, and then asks for the value of $3x + 3y$, a lot of test-takers would waste their time trying to solve for the actual values of x and y individually . . . which literally can't be done in that situation. Either variable can have an infinite number of valid solutions.

But we can still figure out that $x + y = 2$, since $(x + y)^3 = 8$, and $2^3 = 8$. Since $3x + 3y$ is the same as $3(x + y)$, that means $3x + 3y$ is the same thing as 3 times 2, which is 6.

Do you see how much easier that was once we let go of the idea of trying to solve for each variable, and instead thought about what the question was actually asking?

One big hint that you don't need to solve for individual variables on a certain question is when that question asks for the value of an expression with more than one variable in it, like $3x + 3y$, instead of just asking for the value of an individual variable, like x.

Question 34 on page 172 of the Red Book is an example of this concept (on page 194 of this book). This question asks us to find the value of $(b - a)^4$. In this instance, it isn't possible to solve for the value of b or a individually, but we can manipulate the first expression in the question to find out that $b - a = -2$. Once we know that, we know that $(b - a)^4$ must be the same as $(-2)^4$, which is 16, choice (K).

You'll see more examples of this sort of thing in the question walkthroughs in a few pages.

Your Work Doesn't Matter

This is another example of how ACT Math differs from school math—your work doesn't matter on the ACT, in the sense that nobody is going to know how you arrived at your answers. A lot of test-takers lose a lot of time on the ACT Math section because school has conditioned them to do math in a very formal manner.

But there's no need to approach math formally on the ACT! In fact, we'll often run into situations in which trying to follow the formal approach to an ACT Math question makes finding the right answer harder and more time-consuming.

Of course, if you prefer using formal math for some reason, and if you can do it quickly enough to finish the ACT Math section in the time allotted (and you get the questions right), then there's nothing inherently wrong with that. But if you have trouble with the ACT Math section, then you shouldn't feel obligated to approach the section in a way that would please your high school math teacher. As I've mentioned repeatedly, and as you'll see when we go through the walkthroughs, the easiest and fastest solutions to many ACT Math questions involve tactics that are only possible because of the standardized, multiple-choice nature of the test. Don't be afraid to embrace that.

Finding The Areas Of Odd-Looking Shapes

Some ACT Math questions will ask us to find the area of a figure. This can be particularly challenging when the figure doesn't look like any of the familiar shapes whose area formulas we know.

But if the ACT asks us to find the area of an odd-looking shape, then that odd-looking shape must consist of some combination of "normal" shapes like rectangles, triangles, circles, and trapezoids. We can find the area of the odd-looking shape by finding the individual areas of the "normal" shapes and combining them.

If you'd like to see an example of this concept, take a look at this Black Book's walkthrough of question 24 from page 593 of the Red Book.

Let this be one more reminder that the best thing to do when you're confronted with an unfamiliar situation on the ACT Math section is to keep a level head and remember that ACT Math questions can always be solved relatively quickly, using only the concepts from the ACT Math Toolbox. Instead of panicking like an untrained test-taker would, your job is to figure out which concepts from the Toolbox are relevant to the question, and how to combine them so that the question can be answered as simply and directly as possible.

Don't Think About The "Order Of Difficulty"

A lot of test-takers believe they'll see harder ACT Math problems towards the end of a section, and easier problems toward the beginning of a section. Even though there might be some general truth to this concept (depending on how we define the words "harder" and "easier"), I'd strongly advise you to ignore this idea, because it doesn't actually help you do better on the ACT Math section.

First of all, what's difficult for you isn't necessarily the same thing as what's difficult for other test-takers—even if everybody else who takes the ACT struggles with question number 55 on test day, that doesn't mean you will, too. Different people can see different, equally valid solutions to the same ACT Math question, and those equally valid solutions can involve different levels of complexity and challenge. So the notion that each individual question has a universal amount of "difficulty" that will be constant for all test-takers is ridiculous.

Secondly, regardless of any general, overall "difficulty" trend, you can still encounter relatively difficult questions near the beginning of a section, and relatively easy questions near the end of a section, especially as you improve your understanding of how the test works.

My major concern here is that I don't want you to make any assumptions about how hard an ACT Math question is likely to be until you've actually read it and thought about it a little. It's also important to remember that questions can pose different types of challenges, and any of those challenges might lead you to miss a question. Some questions seem pretty simple, but offer a lot of opportunities to make careless mistakes; others might seem very challenging at first, but then offer a very simple solution to a trained test-taker who knows how to spot it.

Just approach each ACT Math question with an open mind—some will take more time and energy, and others will take less time and energy. It doesn't do any good to think about whether a question is supposed to be easy or hard for other people, or whether a question is easier or harder than the ones before or after it. Either way, our job is always to look at each question, read it carefully, try to figure out the most efficient solution we can, implement that solution, and check for mistakes.

That won't change based on where the question appears in the section.

When we do the walkthroughs in a few pages, you'll see several examples of questions that appear earlier in a section but can still be very tricky, and questions that appear later in a section but can still be answered in a few seconds by a trained test-taker.

"NOT" And "EXCEPT" Questions

The ACT loves to use "NOT" and "EXCEPT" questions to get you to choose wrong answers. We saw this on the ACT Reading section, and we'll see it in the ACT Math section as well.

In these questions, there will be four answer choices that *do* satisfy whatever the question is asking about, and one that doesn't. The people who make the ACT are hoping you'll overlook the word "NOT" or "EXCEPT" in the prompt. That way, you can notice one of the four answer choices that seem to satisfy what the question is asking about, and then choose that answer without realizing you were supposed to find the one choice that *doesn't* satisfy whatever the question is talking about.

This is one more reason why it's so important to review all the answer choices in a question before you move on to the next question. If you overlook the word "NOT" or "EXCEPT" and choose the first answer choice that seems valid, you can still catch your mistake if you look at the other answer choices, because you'll notice that several of them seem to be equally valid. This gives you the chance to go back over the question and realize that you misread it.

We can see an example of this type of trap by looking at question 19 on page 308 of the Red Book. The question asks us which choice "does NOT represent a line." If we accidentally overlook the word NOT, we might think we're looking for the one answer choice that DOES contain the equation of a line. A lot of test-takers in that position would just choose (A) and move on. But if we read carefully, we know that we need to find the only choice that is NOT the equation of a line, which means (E) is correct.

Again, if we had missed the word NOT, reading all of the answer choices should still tip us off that more than one choice seemed valid, which should have prompted us to re-evaluate the question and fix our mistake.

The ACT always puts the words "NOT" and "EXCEPT" in capital letters on these kinds of questions, but you'd be surprised how often people completely overlook those words. Always consider all your answer choices, and always read carefully!

Walkthroughs: The ACT Math Process In Action Against Real Questions

Now that we've talked about the best way to approach ACT Math questions, we're going to go through a selection of real ACT Math practice questions that you can follow along with in your copy of *The Real ACT Prep Guide, 3rd Edition*.

As was the case with the ACT Reading questions, these have been selected either because they're questions that my one-on-one tutoring students tend to have the most trouble with, or because they're good representations of the concepts we've talked about in the training.

Once more, I can't overstate the importance of reading through these walkthroughs and seeing these ideas in action against real ACT Math questions from the Red Book. This part of the process is absolutely critical if you want to internalize these strategies and score as high on the ACT as possible.

(If you'd like to see some video demonstrations of these ideas, go to www.ACTprepVideos.com for a selection of videos that are free to readers of this book.)

Page 164, Question 2

This question demonstrates a lot of the ACT's favorite tactics on the Math section. It focuses on fairly basic math concepts, and it offers a variety of very similar answer choices to try to confuse you. As trained test-takers, we know that we need to attack this question very carefully and pay strict attention to details.

We're asked to multiply three terms together. Each term has a numerical component, an x term, and a y term.

Right off the bat, we can multiply the coefficients together (3, 2, and 4). Multiplying those numbers gives us 24, which will be the first term in the correct answer. We know that only (H), (J), and (K) can be right, since (F) and (G) start with 9 instead of 24. (Why do (F) and (G) start with 9? Because some test-takers will accidentally find the *sum* of 3, 2, and 4, which is 9. But we're looking for the product, so we want 24.)

After that, we have to know how to multiply terms that include exponents. First we have to multiply x^3, x^2, and another x^2.

When you multiply variable expressions with exponents, all you have to do is add the exponents on the terms that have the same base. That means that $x^3 * x^2 * x^2$ is the same as $x^{(3 + 2 + 2)}$, or x^7.

It may help to rewrite $x^3 * x^2 * x^2$ like this:

$(x * x * x)(x * x)(x * x)$

This is the same as $x * x * x * x * x * x * x$, which is the same as x^7.

So we know that the x term in the correct answer must be x^7. (Some test-takers would actually stop right here, since there's only one answer choice that includes both 24 and x^7. But let's take a look at the y term, just to make sure we haven't made a mistake.)

There are only two y terms being multiplied, and they're both just y. Since $y * y = y^2$, the final piece of the correct answer must be y^2. This confirms that the correct answer is choice (H), $24x^7y^2$.

This is an example of the "Almost Like The Others" answer choice pattern. Of the three terms that show up in the problem (coefficient, x term, y term), the correct answer has two of the three terms in common with the majority of the other answer choices. In other words:

- 3 out of 5 answer choices started with 24
- 4 out of 5 ended with y^2
- only 2 out 5 had x^7 for an x term

Again, this is a great example of a question that a lot of students will struggle with because it's not the sort of math untrained test-takers expect to see on an important test like the ACT.

Page 165, Question 6

This question is a great example of the types of relationships that frequently exist in the answer choices of real ACT Math questions. As trained test-takers, we can use those kinds of relationships to check our understanding of the question and to help reassure ourselves that we haven't made a mistake. We'll talk about these relationships in a moment, but first let's talk about the solution to the question.

One small difficulty in this question is that a perimeter question in a math class would typically include a diagram, but this one doesn't. This question just describes a rectangle that measures 150 feet by 200 feet. That would look something like this if we diagrammed it:

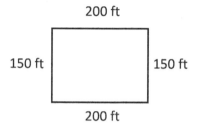

If we add up the lengths of all the sides of the rectangle, we get 150 + 200 + 150 + 200 = 700. So the answer is (J).

Now let's talk about the wrong answers, and how they demonstrate some common ACT patterns.

(F) is what you would get if you just multiplied the 150-foot dimension by two, ignoring the 200-foot dimension.

(G) is what you would get if you just added 150 feet and 200 feet, forgetting that the correct answer requires you to add each value twice, since the perimeter of a rectangle is the sum of all four sides, not just two of them.

(H) is what you would get if you just multiplied the 200-foot dimension by two, ignoring the 150-foot dimension.

(K) is what you would get if you accidentally doubled the correct answer. This could happen if you added 150 and 200, realized that you needed to double that number to get the perimeter, and then you got confused and accidentally doubled the resulting number.

As you can see, this question is actually pretty simple, at least when you compare it to the math that the average high school senior does in school. Still, I'm certain that many people who know how to find the perimeter of a rectangle would still get it wrong due to carelessness.

It all comes back to something we've already talked about several times: the ACT is a *reading* test, first and foremost. The people behind the ACT aren't really trying to see if you know what a perimeter is, because they know that pretty much everybody who takes this test knows that concept.

Instead, they're really testing whether you'll read the question carefully, take the time to understand it, and then execute the correct approach without making mistakes.

Notice, too, how an awareness of the relationships among the answer choices can help us to be sure we haven't made any small mistakes in our approach. Knowing that the correct answer is 700, we can see why the ACT thought it could fool us with the other choices. But if we accidentally thought the correct answer was (A), for instance, then looking at the other answer choices might make us realize that most of them would be irrelevant to the question if our understanding of the question were correct—which should lead us to re-evaluate the question, and hopefully notice our mistake.

I realize, of course, that this isn't exactly the hardest ACT question you'll ever see. But it's often easiest to understand these ideas once you've seen them at work with simpler concepts. Remember that doing well on this test comes down to reading carefully and correctly applying the knowledge you already have.

Page 166, Question 10

A lot of students will see this question and immediately start to sweat a little, because it doesn't really look like the sort of thing you'd normally see in a math class. But as trained test-takers, we know that the ACT can only test us on basic math ideas in the Math Toolbox, and we know that all ACT Math questions can be answered in 30 seconds or less.

Armed with that knowledge, we'll just try to go through the question one step at a time.

The question starts by telling us that $x^3 = 64$. Then it asks us to solve an equation that includes only x terms. So we'll definitely need to figure out what x is.

Most people who take the ACT won't be comfortable trying to take the cube root of a number, because few people are taught to memorize cube roots in school.

But if we're well-trained, we should notice the answer choices are all whole numbers. This means that x can't be a number that requires a decimal or a fraction bar, because a number like that would probably lead to a final answer that also required a decimal or a fraction bar.

Since 64 is a whole number, and the answers are all whole numbers, we know that the cube root of 64 is likely going to be easy to figure out. We can probably just start by cubing some small numbers until we find the one that 64 is the cube of.

Here's what we'd get:

$1^3 = 1$

$2^3 = 8$

$3^3 = 27$

$4^3 = 64$

There you go. Since $4^3 = 64$, we know that x must be equal to 4.

If you prefer to use a calculator that can find the third root of a given number, that would be another way to determine that x is 4 (assuming you use the calculator properly).

But be careful—4 isn't the correct answer to the question, even though it appears in choice (F)!

(F) is an example of an "On-The-Way" wrong answer, like we saw in our discussion of answer choice patterns on the ACT Math section. We just did a little bit of work and figured out *part* of the problem that might have seemed intimidating, and the ACT deliberately provided a wrong answer choice that reflects our work up to this point. This is exactly the kind of thing you have to be careful about—when you pick an answer choice, take a second to look at the actual question being asked, and make sure that your answer addresses the question. In this case, the expression we're asked to evaluate is this:

$x^2 + \sqrt{x} = ?$

So now that we know x is 4, we just plug 4 into that expression for x:

$x^2 + \sqrt{x} = ?$

$4^2 + \sqrt{4} = ?$

16 + 2 = 18

So the answer is 18, choice (H).

Now let's take a look at the other choices.

As we said before, choice (F) is the value for *x*, but it's not the correct answer.

(G) is what you might get if you multiplied 4 by 2, instead of squaring it.

(H) is the correct answer.

(J) is what you'd get if you added 4 to 16, instead of adding $\sqrt{4}$ to 16.

(K) isn't related to the question in any obvious way that I can see.

Do you see the analysis we were able to do there? We didn't have to notice all those things about the answer choices to get the question right—but if we did notice them, it would help us navigate the question more quickly. We'd have a better idea of what the question is asking, how the question asks it, and how the test is trying to trick us.

If you try to understand as much as you can about each question and its answer choices at a glance, you can learn to see right through what the ACT is doing in a lot of cases, which makes it almost impossible for the test to fool you.

Analyzing answer choices like this is kind of a higher-level concept, but it seemed like a good place to point it out. If this part of the explanation isn't making a ton of sense right now, don't let it bother you too much. Just keep reading through these explanations and try to see some of the helpful information that can be hiding in the answer choices.

Page 166, Question 12

Simple probability is almost guaranteed to show up somewhere on the ACT, and when it does, a lot of people get nervous about it.

If you feel rusty on this, you definitely need to revisit the Math Toolbox and get more comfortable with this concept, or follow along with this walkthrough and see if the process makes sense.

To solve this question, you just need to know that your answer will be a fraction: the number above the bar will be the number of desired outcomes, and the number below the bar will be the total number of possible outcomes.

So let's take a look.

The question asks for the probability that the selected marble will NOT be white. Let me point out here that even though the word "NOT" is in all capital letters, I regularly tutor very intelligent students who will completely overlook that word, do the rest of the math correctly, and then come up with the wrong answer—not because they don't understand the math, but because they didn't read carefully enough.

If you want the best possible ACT score you can get, you have to make the effort to pay close attention to what's on the page! (You've probably noticed that I repeat this idea a lot. There's a reason for that . . .)

Since we want to know the probability of picking a non-white marble, the top number in our fraction will be the number of non-white marbles, since each non-white marble is one of the possible desired outcomes. There are 14 marbles that aren't white (8 red marbles and 6 blue marbles), so 14 will be the number above the bar.

Now we need to figure out the number below the bar—the number of total possible outcomes.

There are 20 total marbles in the bag (8 red, 6 blue, and 6 white), so that means there are 20 different possible outcomes—20 individual marbles that could be selected. So the number below the bar must be 20.

That means the answer is 14/20. Of course, we can reduce that to 7/10 by dividing the top and bottom of the fraction by 2, so choice (K) is the correct answer.

We'll notice right away that one of the tricky things going on in this question is the fact that all the answer choices are reduced, so none of the denominators is 20. The ACT probably set the question up this way to make us panic and doubt ourselves while doing something that's relatively simple. Of course, as trained test-takers, we won't let this bother us, because we know how to reduce fractions.

The other tricky thing, as we mentioned before, is the word "NOT" in the prompt, which tells us that we have to find the probability of choosing any non-white marble, instead of a white marble. In fact, we might suspect the question would include an answer choice designed to trick anyone who missed the word "NOT" and accidentally worked out the probability of picking a white marble, instead of a non-white marble. Sure enough, (J) does exactly that.

Now let's take a look at the other wrong answers.

(F) is what you'd get if you didn't know what to do, and just put one of the sixes from the problem over the eight, and reduced it to 3/4.

(G) is the probability of selecting a non-*red* marble. This reflects yet another possible misreading of the question.

(H) is what you'd get if you accidentally accounted for 8 blue marbles instead of 6 when figuring out the number of desired possible outcomes (giving you 8 red marbles plus 8 blue marbles above the fraction bar).

Let's think about how you might look over the answer choices to check your answer.

You should feel pretty good about choosing (K), because the most likely mistake is probably missing the word NOT, and you can see that answer choice (J) is there to catch anyone who did that. In fact, (J) and (K) make up the only pair of answer choices that are complements of each other (which basically means they add up to one), and it's a good bet that the ACT would include the probability that is the opposite of the correct answer on a "NOT" question like this—in other words, the probability that represents the opposite outcome from the one the problem is asking about. And if you get really comfortable with the way the ACT likes to use answer choices, you might even notice that four out of the five choices are greater than 1/2, which would strongly suggest that the correct answer is also going to be greater than 1/2—and it is.

Remember that there's often more to an ACT Math question than a simple calculation!

Page 167, Question 16
I can almost guarantee that no high school student would see anything like this in a normal math class. But this is exactly what the ACT loves to do on the Math section: ask about easy math in a weird way, so it can trick you into giving up or making a mistake. As always, the way to beat this question is simply to stay calm, read carefully, find out what the test actually wants you to do, and do it.

This question tells us that the center cell must contain an expression which will make the sums of each row, column, and diagonal equivalent.

That might sound weird or scary to an untrained test-taker who's never seen a question like this before, but a trained test-taker just takes those instructions at face value and tries to follow them closely.

If the sum of each row, column, and diagonal must be equivalent, and if we're trying to replace the question mark with a value that follows those rules, then it will be helpful to figure out the sums of the existing rows and columns.

To find out what that value is, just pick any of the complete rows (the top or bottom ones) or the complete columns (the left or right ones), and add up the terms in that row or column. And since it's always very important to guard against the possibility of making small mistakes on the ACT, I'd probably recommend double-checking the sum by looking at another complete row or column.

I'll take the top row, for no particular reason. If we add *x*, *8x*, and *-3x*, we get *6x*. Just to check, I'll also pick one other set of terms to add up. Let's look at the bottom row, which is *7x*, *-4x*, and *3x* . . . yup, those add up to *6x* also. So each row, column, and diagonal must add up to *6x*. (Again, why did I double-check that? Is it because I'm not sure how to add simple algebraic terms? Of course not. I double-checked it because I've deliberately developed the good habit of being constantly on guard against any small mistakes that might come up. It would be stupid and pointless to risk throwing away a relatively easy question because I was too lazy to verify that *6x* is the proper sum of each row.)

Now we know that the question mark must make all the sets of 3 terms it's involved in add up to *6x*. Here's the thing—because these are all just *x* terms with coefficients (no exponents, absolute values, or anything tricky like that), we don't have to create a whole system of equations to figure this out. Any term that works with one row, column, or diagonal has to work with all of them.

So let's pick the row right across the middle. You've got *6x* and *-2x*, which add up to *4x*. What do you have to add to *4x* to get *6x*? Well, *6x - 4x* is *2x*, which is choice (H). Again, it can't hurt to check by looking at another set of terms to make sure. Let's look at the middle column. If the question mark is *2x* like we think it is, that gives us *8x*, *2x*, and *-4x*. Those also add up to *6x*, just like everything else. So we can be sure that (H) is correct.

On this question, some test-takers will try to set up a whole system of equations because they only feel comfortable using a math approach that would be approved by their teachers. But setting up such a system would involve introducing another variable to take the place of the question mark, and then doing a lot more algebra than necessary. It's much easier just to look at a row and think, "What do I get if I add up *x*, *8x*, and *-3x*?"

This is exactly what I'm talking about when I say that we should generally try to avoid formalized math solutions on the ACT, because they're often pointlessly messy. If you're working on an ACT Math solution and it starts to seem really complicated, and it looks like it's going to take more than 30 seconds to work out, then you're probably not on the right track. Either you'll end up wasting time on your way to the right answer, or you'll end up wasting time and arriving at the *wrong* answer . . . or maybe not even arriving at any answer choice at all.

It's also worth noting that it's impossible to solve for *x* in this question, because *x* can have any value. This is one more example of how the ACT Math section tries to take advantage of our school math instincts: a lot of untrained test-takers will dive right in and try to solve for *x* as soon as they see this question, because they don't know that they should look carefully at the question before trying to solve it, as we learned from the Math Path.

Now let's take a look at the wrong answers.

Notice that choice (F) is *6x*, which is an "On-The-Way" wrong answer. *6x* is what each column adds up to, but that's not what the question asked for. (G) is *2x* more than the right answer, (J) is the opposite of the right answer, and (K) is the opposite of (G). You can see how these wrong answer choices reflect the simple arithmetic mistakes that many careless test-takers could make on this question.

When we look at the set of answer choices by itself, our initial expectation would probably be that (G) is most likely to be correct, because it satisfies the greatest number of ACT Math answer-choice patterns:

- It's positive, like three out of the five choices (choices (F), (G), and (H)).
- Its opposite is present in another answer choice, like four out of the five choices (choices (G), (H), (J), and (K)).
- It's the middle number in the series *2x*, *4x*, *6x*.

So when we solve the problem and conclude that *2x* seems to be correct, rather than *4x*, we'd definitely want to double-check our work one last time to make sure we hadn't made a mistake. But when we do that quickly, we see once more that 2x must be right. And 2x still follows two of the three patterns mentioned above, so it's not completely out of line with the patterns on the ACT Math section anyway.

Remember that these ACT Math patterns can be helpful in a lot of ways, but they should never take the place of actual math! If you double- and triple-check your work and you're convinced that the correct answer breaks a pattern, then choose the correct answer and break the pattern. Remember that these are just general patterns that will tend to describe the correct answers, not absolute rules that can never be broken.

Once more, I want to point out that the challenge here is really in reading and understanding the question, not in doing the basic algebra. Once you know what the ACT is asking you to do, the math itself is generally pretty easy by high-school standards.

Page 168, Question 20

This is another simple geometry question that will require you to read carefully and do what is asked of you. It's also an example of a question that the ACT will let you solve without doing any actual math, if you notice the answer choices.

The question describes a rectangle with sides of 54 meters and 72 meters. Then it asks how long the diagonal of the rectangle is.

(Notice that you can't answer this question if you don't know that the word "diagonal" means a straight line from one corner of the rectangle to the opposite corner. This is one example of why it's so important to have a solid command of the basic math concepts that can appear on the ACT Math section.)

We can recognize that the question is talking about finding the hypotenuse of a triangle with sides of 54 and 72:

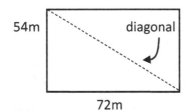

Most test-takers will probably approach this by just plugging it into the Pythagorean Theorem, which will look like this:

$a^2 + b^2 = c^2$	(Pythagorean Theorem)
$54^2 + 72^2 = c^2$	(plug in lengths of legs for a and b)
$2916 + 5184 = c^2$	(square 54 and 72)
$8100 = c^2$	(add 2916 and 5184)
$\sqrt{8100} = c$	(take square root of both sides)
$90 = c$	

That gives us (H) as the correct answer.

There's nothing wrong with this solution, and if you can apply it without making any mistakes, you can get the right answer in relatively short order and move on.

Still, there are a couple of interesting things to note in this question. For one thing, you might notice that 54 and 72 are both divisible by 18, then you can realize that those side lengths correspond to the legs of a 3-4-5 right triangle. That means the length of the diagonal must be equal to 18 x 5, which is 90.

(If that sounds confusing, or if it sounds harder than just using the Pythagorean Theorem, don't worry about it—just stick with the Pythagorean Theorem. Either approach can get you the right answer pretty quickly. It's a matter of personal preference.)

But there's another way to solve this question that almost doesn't involve calculating anything at all, and it's only possible because of the answer choices the ACT has provided for this question.

Notice that choices (F) and (G) are each too small to be the length of the diagonal, because the diagonal must be longer than either of the sides of the rectangle. (By the way, the idea of the diagonal being longer than either side isn't a geometry fact that I've memorized, and I'm not recommending that you memorize it. It's just something that kind of makes sense if you think about it—if the diagonal were the same length as one of the sides, then it couldn't reach all the way to the opposite corner from its starting corner. So the diagonal must be longer than either side.)

Now notice that (J) is what you get if you just add the two side lengths together, so it's too big to be the diagonal. (The diagonal is the shortest distance from one corner to the opposite corner, so it has to be less than the sum of both side lengths together.) Finally, (K) is what you get if you double (J), or if you misread the question and find the perimeter of the rectangle, instead of its diagonal. This is even bigger than (J), so it must also be wrong.

So if we pay attention to how the answer choices relate back to the quantities in the question, we can actually see that two choices are too small, two choices are too big, and only (H) is even a possible candidate for the correct answer. In that way, we can solve the question in a few seconds and never even pick up a pencil—not because of the math involved in the question, but because of the answer choices the ACT gives us.

I'd be pretty surprised if the Red Book ever showed us that kind of an approach to a math question!

Again, what counts here is reading, paying attention, and being aware of how ACT Math questions try to fool you. Doing the actual calculation is almost secondary.

Page 169, Question 23

This question asks for a solution to the equation $x^2 - 36x = 0$. The algebraic path to the answer is pretty straightforward:

$x^2 - 36x = 0$

$x^2 = 36x$ (add $36x$ to both sides)

$x = 36$ (divide both sides by x)

That gives you a correct answer of 36, choice (B).

Why is this question hard for some people? For one thing, the question is probably set up to make you think of a parabola or some other kind of quadratic equation, which might make an untrained test-taker worry about graphing things, finding zeroes, and getting bogged down in all kinds of other worries before actually trying the question and realizing how straightforward it is. In other words, the question is set up to take advantage of the fact that most untrained test-takers expect the math to be complicated. The ACT is simply trying to make you panic for no reason, because that's one of its favorite things to do.

Another reason people might miss this question is that the coefficient of x is 36, which is the square of 6, which is one of the wrong answer choices. If you're in a hurry, you might glance at this question and just see x^2 and 36, and then think, "Oh, that's easy, x squared equals 36, so x must be 6 or -6." Sure enough, choice (D) is 6 and choice (E) is -6, to take advantage of those kinds of mistakes.

Notice also that the correct answer, 36, is in the middle of a kind of halves-and-doubles series, with 72 and 18 on either end. As we've already discussed, multiplying or dividing the correct answer by two is a common way that the ACT comes up with wrong answer choices. Like any other answer choice pattern on the ACT Math section, it's not going to be accurate on every single question, but seeing it in this case can help reassure us that 36 is, indeed, probably correct.

Before we finish with this question, I want to point out that there's another way to approach it if you're handy with your calculator: you could just use the calculator to evaluate the expression with each answer choice plugged in for x, and then choose the answer that results in a value of zero. So you'd enter the following expressions in your calculator:

- $(72)^2 - 36(72) =$
- $(36)^2 - 36(36) =$
- $(18)^2 - 36(18) =$
- $(6)^2 - 36(6) =$
- $(-6)^2 - 36(-6) =$

Then you just see which one causes your calculator to return a value of zero, and that's the correct answer. Remember that you can do those kinds of things on the ACT sometimes—people often forget that such easy approaches are possible, because they wouldn't be allowed in some math classes.

Page 172, Question 34

It would be perfectly fine to approach this question in either of the ways suggested by the Red Book on page 245, so I won't spend time discussing the actual solution here. But this question still deserves our attention, for two reasons.

For one thing, the question uses two variables, which is often a deliberate ploy to make untrained test-takers panic over nothing. In school, most questions with two variables would require you to solve for each variable individually, but the ACT often likes to set up multi-variable questions that make it literally *impossible* to identify the values of individual variables. We should be alert to the possibility that it might be impossible to solve for either variable individually when we see that the question is ultimately asking us about an expression that involves *both* variables. The ACT Math section usually does that when it's only possible to determine a value for an expression that involves both variables, not for either variable on its own.

If we keep that in mind and use one of the approaches in the Red Book for this question, we'll see that the answer is actually pretty easy to find. All we have to do is pay careful attention to what the question actually says, and remember the kinds of standardized tricks that the ACT likes to play.

This question is also interesting because the correct answer satisfies a lot of the common patterns that frequently mark correct answers on the ACT Math section:

- It's similar to three out of five of the answer choices, in that it's positive.
- It's twice as much as one of the wrong answers.
- Its opposite is present in another choice, like four out of five of the choices.

All of these patterns would tend to support our conclusion that 16, choice (K), is the correct answer.

Untrained test-takers assume that the ACT Math section is like a high school math test. They never realize that the ACT Math section will often require them to deal with the ambiguity of unsolvable variables, or that the answer choices often demonstrate relationships that can help us find the correct answer or check our work. But we, on the other hand, know that questions on the ACT Math section will often try to trick us in standardized ways, and we practice outsmarting the test so we can do it with confidence on test day.

Page 173, Question 38

This is another relatively basic math question that the ACT has tried to present in a complicated way, in this case by combining two geometric figures and hoping you'll either get confused about how to start, or make a mental error in your solution.

The Red Book's solution to the question (which appears on page 246) is adequate, as far as it goes: If the radius of the circle is 7, then its diameter is 14, which means that the side length of the square is 14, which means the area is 14^2, or 196. So choice (K) is the correct answer. Fine.

But notice how hard this question is working to make us think about the circle rather than the area of the square!

For one thing, the diagram shows the radius at an upward angle, rather than showing a perfectly horizontal or vertical radius. I suspect that the ACT didn't want to make it too obvious that the radius could be used to establish the width or height of the square.

Further, (J) is the area of the circle, and (F) is the area of the circle if you forget about π.

Can you see how a lot of test-takers might misread the question, think they were supposed to find the area of the circle, and then choose (J) without a second thought? This is exactly the kind of mistake that you have to make sure you never, ever make on the ACT!

Along similar lines, (G) is what you would get if you solved for the square's perimeter (14 + 14 + 14 + 14) instead of its area—yet another possible misreading that the ACT is trying to take advantage of!

Also notice that (H) is what you would get if you squared the radius and then multiplied it by 2, instead of multiplying it by 2 and then squaring it. It's also half of the correct answer, which is a common wrong-answer pattern on the ACT Math section, as we've discussed for several questions.

This question is just one more piece of evidence to prove that the ACT deliberately tries to mislead and confuse you. Don't let yourself get distracted from the simple math concepts that make up the backbone of each question, and don't forget to read the question and all the answer choices carefully—it can help you avoid simple mistakes that will cost you points for no reason!

Page 174, Question 45

This is another question that has a much simpler solution than the one the Red Book provides on page 250. But let's go through the traditional approach first, just to make sure you understand the solution.

Personally, I prefer to draw a diagram when the question describes a physical relationship among points or lines but doesn't provide its own diagram. Of course, the diagram we draw doesn't have to be scaled accurately. Its purpose is just to help us quickly visualize the situation in the question. It might look like this:

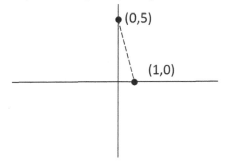

We're asked to find the distance between the two points, which I've indicated with a dotted line in my diagram.

As you probably know, there's a distance formula that is tailored exactly to this kind of situation. You can find it on page 250 of the Red Book, in the ACT's official explanation of this question.

Since the distance formula is just a specific application of the Pythagorean Theorem, and since the Pythagorean Theorem is easier for me to remember than the distance formula, I'd rather just use the Pythagorean Theorem. If you prefer the distance formula, please feel free to use that.

We can see from the diagram that we can make the point (0,0) be the right angle in our triangle. The horizontal leg of the triangle has a length of 1, and the vertical leg has a length of 5. The unknown distance will be our hypotenuse. So we plug our leg lengths into the Pythagorean Theorem, and solve for the hypotenuse:

$a^2 + b^2 = c^2$	(Pythagorean Theorem)
$5^2 + 1^2 = c^2$	(substitute leg lengths)
$25 + 1 = c^2$	(square 5 and 1)
$26 = c^2$	(add 25 and 1)
$\sqrt{26} = c$	(take square root of both sides)

So choice (E) is correct.

Like I said, that's the traditional way to approach the question—essentially what the ACT tells you to do on page 250 of the Red Book.

But we can answer the question much more easily and directly if we consider the answer choices from the beginning, and place them in context with the quantities in the question (the diagram may help us to grasp these relationships more easily, by the way).

If we do that, we see that (A) is too small to be the distance, because it's shorter than the vertical separation between the two points.

We also see that (B) is too large to be the distance, because it's the sum of the vertical separation and the horizontal separation, but the straight-line distance between the two points must be shorter than that sum.

Since (B) is too large, we can see that (C) and (D) are also too large, since they're bigger than (B).

(E) is expressed as a radical, but we can tell it must result in a value between 5 and 6 because 5^2 is 25 and 6^2 is 36, and 26 is between 25 and 36. (You could also just put $\sqrt{26}$ in your calculator, and you'd see it's roughly 5.1.)

So basically, if we can notice that (E) is the only answer choice that's greater than 5 (which is the vertical separation between the points) and smaller than 6 (which is the sum of the horizontal and vertical separations), we can tell it has to be correct, without even worrying about the Pythagorean Theorem or the distance formula.

And here's an even faster approach to this question, if you're up for it: if you realize that finding the distance will ultimately involve taking the square root of a non-square number (because you'll have to add 1 to a square number and then take the square of that sum), then that's another way to realize that (E) must be correct, without lifting your pencil.

Just to be clear, I'm not saying that either of those last two approaches is necessarily *better* than the approaches in the Red Book on page 250. If you feel more confident using a formula to approach this question, there's nothing wrong with that. I'm just trying to point out that there's often more going on in an ACT Math question than just the math itself.

With that in mind, let's take a look at some mistakes that could lead to the various wrong answers.

(A) is the difference between 5 and 1. It's what you'd get if you mistakenly thought the two points were connected by a horizontal or a vertical line, instead of a diagonal one, which could happen if you misread them as (0,1) and (0,5) or (1,0) and (5,0).

(B) is the sum of 5 and 1. It's what you'd get if you made the mistake from the previous choice AND you also thought one of the points was negative.

(C) is the square of (5 - 1), which you could get if you applied the distance formula incorrectly.

(D) is the square of (5 + 1), which you could also get by applying the distance formula incorrectly.

Page 175, Question 49

This question will intimidate a lot of untrained test-takers, because its appearance seems so different from anything you'd be likely to encounter in a classroom setting. But, as always, we trained test-takers know that ACT Math questions must rely on basic concepts, no matter how strange their presentations may be. We also know the importance of reading carefully at all times on the ACT.

So we just read the question carefully and find out what it wants from us.

The question just tells us to choose the answer that accurately describes the total number of dots in the first n rows. That's kind of a weird request, but we should be used to weird combinations of basic ideas on the ACT Math section by now. (Notice that we don't have to figure out that relationship on our own—we just have to recognize the correct description of that relationship from a set of answer choices.)

The Red Book's explanation on page 251 suggests that you make a table to relate the row-numbers to the number of dots, and then try to figure out the relationship on your own using the table. But I wouldn't do that if I were you. I think it's a much better idea to keep an open mind and just test out each answer choice to see if what it says is true. That will be a lot less frustrating for most people.

(A) says the sum of the number of dots is always equal to 25, no matter how many rows you count. We can disprove this by looking at just the first row—in other words, looking where $n = 1$, according to the wording in the prompt. We see there's only one dot in the first row. One dot isn't the same thing as 25 dots, so this choice is pretty obviously wrong if we understand what the prompt means when it mentions "the first n rows." But if you don't quite understand that phrase in the prompt, you might think this answer choice was valid because the number of dots actually on the page is 25. In that case, if you looked at the other answer choices, you might eventually realize that (C) also seems to be correct, which would indicate a mistake in your reading of the question or the answer choices.

(B) says the total is always the same as twice the number of rows. But if we look at the first row (where $n = 1$, to use the terminology from the prompt), we see it has only one dot. One is not twice as many as one. We can check out the next row too, just to see what happens. At two rows, there are four dots. This does fit the pattern in this answer choice, but only for the second row (where $n = 2$). The answer choice doesn't work for other rows, though. To be extra sure, we can try the third row (where $n = 3$). At 3 rows, there is a total of nine dots. Nine isn't twice as much as three, so we see once again that this choice doesn't accurately describe the relationship between the number of rows and the sum of the dots.

(C) tells us that the total is equal to 5 times the number of rows. As I mentioned in my explanation of choice (A), this is clearly incorrect if we understand what the prompt means when it uses the phrase "in the first n rows." For example, the first row has only one dot, not 5 dots. But if we don't quite understand that phrase, we might think (C) is correct, since there are 25 dots on the page and 5 rows on the page, and 5 * 5 = 25. But, again, we can only reach this incorrect conclusion if we misread the question, and that misreading would also lead us to think that (A) is correct. Since we know that only one answer choice can be correct, we should be able to realize that we must have misread the question, and need to re-evaluate it.

(D) says that the running total at each row is always equal to the square of the number of rows. Let's try this one out: at one row, there is one dot. One is equal to one squared, so that checks out. At two rows there are four dots, and four is equal to two squared. Then we have 3 and 9, 4 and 16, 5 and 25 . . . this pattern does work at every row in the diagram, so this must be the correct answer choice. (Of course, as trained test-takers, we know we have to check every answer choice to help us make sure we're not making a mistake.)

(E) must be wrong because we just saw that there is a relationship between the number of rows and the total number of dots.

Traditional math classes often leave us with the feeling that we have to be told exactly how to do something before we can do it ourselves. The ACT Math section tries to take advantage of that programming by showing us questions like this, with concepts we've probably never seen before. The ACT knows that most test-takers will get very frustrated with novel questions like this.

But trained test-takers like us always remember that the ACT Math section has to rely on very basic math concepts presented in weird ways, so we don't panic when we see something strange. Instead, we read carefully, keep the ACT's standard tricks in mind, and get to work.

Page 177, Question 55

This one might seem a little tricky, especially for people who aren't comfortable with graphing inequalities. But, as trained test-takers, we know that ACT Math questions don't necessarily require knowledge of the math concepts they seem to involve—in fact, we know the ACT often likes to try to mislead us by making questions look harder or more advanced than they really are.

It's always important to read the answer choices when you're looking at an ACT Math question, but it's especially important when we're not sure exactly how to proceed. In this case, when we check the answer choices, we see that each answer choice has the following elements:

- a relationship between y and $-2x$
- the word "and" or the word "or"
- a relationship between x and 3

Noticing these patterns in the answer choices actually makes this question a lot easier for us. We don't have to figure out the slopes of either of the lines in the figure, because we can tell from the answer choices that the slanted line must have a slope of $-2x$. Instead, all we have to do is figure out which answer choice describes the shaded region accurately.

There are at least two ways we can do that, depending on how comfortable we are with math.

If we're familiar with the actual math principles involved in the question, then we already know that the "greater than" inequality corresponds to shaded areas above or to the right of a line, while the "less than" inequality corresponds to shaded areas below or to the left of a line. We also know from the diagram that the shaded area must fall to the right of the vertical line $x = 3$, *and* to the left of the slanted line $y = -2x$. So choice (A) will be correct. This is basically the logic used in the Red Book's official explanation on page 255.

But there are other ways to approach this question without necessarily understanding all of the math involved in the Red Book's explanation. (Remember that ACT Math questions aren't always what they seem!)

If we're less comfortable with math concepts, then it might be easier just to pick some values in different regions of the graph, and test their x and y values against the answer choices until we find a single answer choice that accurately defines only the shaded region.

For this type of approach, I'd definitely want to make sure the correct answer accurately describes the value (4, -9), because that point is clearly inside the shaded region. So let's see which answer choices would include that point:

(A) does.

(B) does.

(C) doesn't.

(D) does.

(E) doesn't.

So we can tell that (C) and (E) must be wrong, because they don't work with the point (4, -9), which is a point that falls in the shaded region.

Now we should test some points that are NOT supposed to work, and eliminate any answer choices for which the test point would be valid. I'll pick the point (1, 1) to start, since the values of 1 and 1 should be relatively easy to test out (for that matter, any value is probably going to be pretty easy to work with on this question, since we're just comparing values to other values).

If we try the value of (1, 1), these are the results we get:

(A) isn't valid for the point (1, 1).

(B) is also not valid for the point (1, 1).

(C) was already eliminated when we tested (4, -9).

(D) is valid for the point (1, 1).

(E) was also already eliminated when we tested (4, -9).

Remember that the diagram in the question doesn't have shading in the region that includes (1, 1). That means we're looking for a correct answer that isn't valid for the point (1, 1). So (A) and (B) are still in the running, while (D) has been eliminated.

At this point, we would need to test a point in another region to see if we can eliminate either (A) or (B). An easy point to test would probably be (4, 0). That point isn't in the shaded region of the graph, so it should not be valid for the correct answer. Let's test it for (A) and (B):

(A) isn't valid for the point (4, 0).

(B) is valid for the point (4, 0).

The shaded region includes the point (4, -9), but doesn't include (1, 1) or (4, 0). So the correct answer should be valid for (4, -9), and it should be invalid for (1, 1) and for (4, 0). Only one answer choice meets all three of those criteria, and that's choice (A).

Of course, if this idea of testing different points to eliminate answer choices seems too confusing or time-consuming, then you don't have to do it—you could always just use the first approach if you want, or you could skip this question and come back to it later. I just wanted to walk through this second approach because some readers might prefer it.

(Also, just to be clear, it isn't necessary to test any of the three specific points that I tested; in order to follow this approach, it was only necessary to test points in different regions of the graph, and it just happened that those three points in different regions are the ones I chose. You could have achieved the same results by testing the points (5, -11), (2, 2), and (6, 0), for instance.)

This question also involves the "*Almost* Like The Others" pattern, because the correct answer agreed with the majority of the answer choices in all but one respect: 3 out of the 5 choices have "and" instead of "or," and 4 out of 5 have "$x \geq 3$" instead of "$x \leq 3$." But only 2 out of 5 started with "$y \leq 2x$" instead of "$y \geq 2x$."

Again, these patterns are never enough on their own to give you the correct answer, but they can point you in the right direction and help you check your work.

Page 178, Question 57

This question is worth discussing for a couple of very important reasons. For one thing, it's a question that follows a couple of ACT Math patterns, but in some very subtle ways. For another thing, it's a classic example of the way the ACT Math section likes to make questions seem harder than they are. And to top it all off, it's yet another question for which the Red Book's official explanation is more complicated than it needs to be.

So let's dive in.

The ACT is trying to give you the impression that the correct graph is going to be a parabola or some other quadratic function. That's why the function in the question includes the expression x^2, and some of the answer choices feature a parabola.

But the question is really just asking you to simplify the expression and then choose the answer with the appropriate graph. (Remember that the ACT can never really ask you to graph something on your own—because it's locked into the multiple-choice format, it can only ask you to identify the correct graph from a set of options.) When you simplify the fraction in the function, you'll see that it reduces to $2x + 1$, exactly as the Red Book's explanation on page 256 describes. Using the classic $y = mx + b$ format, we can see that the correct answer must have a slope of 2 and a y-intercept of 1. That's the graph shown in choice (A).

(The Red Book's explanation on page 256 adds that the correct answer must have a hole at the point (0, 1). This is true, but since every graph in the answer choices also has a hole at $x = 0$, it doesn't really matter if you notice it or not.)

If you're not too comfortable with graphing lines and parabolas, you could take advantage of a much faster way to solve this problem, assuming you have a graphing calculator. If you simply tell the calculator to graph the function described in the prompt, the correct result will appear on the screen, and you'll see that it matches choice (A). The Red Book never mentions that a graphing calculator can give you the answer to this question in a few seconds, even if you don't know the math.

Finally, let's talk about the answer choice patterns involved in this question.

As trained test-takers, we'd want to notice that three of the answer choices feature straight lines, while only two feature parabolas. This isn't a guarantee that the correct answer will feature a straight line, but it's a pretty strong indication that the correct answer *probably* features a straight line.

Another interesting thing is that four of the five choices go through the point (1, 3), which also strongly suggests (but doesn't guarantee) that the correct answer choice goes through that point.

What about the y-intercept value? We can see that choices (A) and (D) feature a y-intercept at (0, 1). We can also see that (B) and (E) each feature a y-intercept at (0, 0). Those two y-intercept values appear the most frequently in the answer choices—twice each—so we'd expect that one of them is probably correct. And here's where things get subtle, because the ACT is using its sequence pattern in choices (A), (B), and (C). If we look carefully, we'll see that the three choices feature y-intercepts at (0, 1), (0, 0), and (0, 2), respectively—three values in an evenly-spaced series. We'd expect that the value in the middle of the series is most likely to be correct, and that's (0, 1).

All of that strongly reinforces that (A) is probably correct.

Once more, we see that there's a lot more going on in this question than most test-takers will ever realize, or than the ACT itself will tell you about. Keep that in mind as you continue to prepare—the ACT Math section isn't always what it seems!

Page 179, Question 60

This question will fool most untrained ACT-takers. At first glance, it might look pretty ugly: it has four different Greek letters, a table, and an unfriendly-looking expression.

But we know better than to take an ACT Math question at face value. For one thing, we know that trig questions on the ACT can only require us to know the basic definitions of sine, cosine, tangent, and so on—the ACT doesn't allow itself to ask us trig questions that rely on things like the complicated identities you might have learned in a high school trig class. We also know that trig questions on the ACT that include a "note" are always just exercises in careful reading and substitution, no matter how complicated they look at first.

In the next paragraph, we'll start going through the substitution-based approach to the question, which is basically the one that the Red Book uses on page 258. After that, though, I want to show you a faster, easier approach to the question that relies on a calculator—an approach the Red Book doesn't tell you about.

Here's how the substitution approach works. The question asks us for sin ($\pi/12$), and then it tells us the following:

$\pi/12 = \pi/3 - \pi/4$

It also tells us this:

$\sin(\alpha - \beta) = \sin(\alpha)\cos(\beta) - \cos(\alpha)\sin(\beta)$

The key to the substitution approach is to realize that the expression "$\pi/3 - \pi/4$" can be plugged in for the "$(\alpha - \beta)$" portion of the expression "$\sin(\alpha - \beta)$." In other words, $\pi/3$ will be our value for α, and $\pi/4$ will be our value for β.

That means we can take our new values for α and β and plug them into the trig equation provided in the question. Here's the original equation as it appears on the page:

$\sin(\alpha - \beta) = \sin(\alpha)\cos(\beta) - \cos(\alpha)\sin(\beta)$

When we plug in our values for α and β, we get this:

$\sin(\pi/3 - \pi/4) = \sin(\pi/3)\cos(\pi/4) - \cos(\pi/3)\sin(\pi/4)$

That might seem a little intimidating, because we probably don't know the values for things like "$\sin(\pi/3)\cos(\pi/4)$" off the tops of our heads. But this is yet another moment when being trained in the ACT will help you avoid needless worry, because trained test-takers know that the ACT doesn't require you to memorize different sine and cosine values. So if the question is asking for $\sin(\pi/3)\cos(\pi/4)$, it has to provide you with a way to figure that out.

Sure enough, we see a table at the end of the question that includes a variety of sine and cosine values for given angle measurements. We see the following:

$\sin(\pi/3) = \frac{\sqrt{3}}{2}$

$\cos(\pi/4) = \frac{\sqrt{2}}{2}$

$\sin(\pi/4) = \frac{\sqrt{2}}{2}$

$\cos(\pi/3) = \frac{1}{2}$

Now we just plug those values in, according to the equation provided in the question. Remember that the original equation was this:

$\sin(\alpha - \beta) = \sin(\alpha)\cos(\beta) - \cos(\alpha)\sin(\beta)$

And then we plugged in $\pi/3$ for α and $\pi/4$ for β, and we got this:

$\sin(\pi/3 - \pi/4) = \sin(\pi/3)\cos(\pi/4) - \cos(\pi/3)\sin(\pi/4)$

And now we plug in the sine and cosine values from the table, and get this:

$\sin(\pi/3 - \pi/4) = (\frac{\sqrt{3}}{2})(\frac{\sqrt{2}}{2}) - (\frac{1}{2})(\frac{\sqrt{2}}{2})$

At this point, we can probably start to see that our work is beginning to look like the answer choices, which is a good sign. All we need to do from here is simplify the right-hand side of the equation and see which answer choice it matches:

$\sin(\pi/3 - \pi/4) = \frac{\sqrt{6}}{4} - \frac{\sqrt{2}}{4}$

$\sin(\pi/3 - \pi/4) = \frac{\sqrt{6} - \sqrt{2}}{4}$

So we can see that (K) is correct.

(K) also fits the "*Almost* Like The Others" pattern, because we can see that three of the five choices have radical expressions, three of the five have a denominator of 4, and (K) is the only choice to include $\sqrt{6}$. All of this suggests that our choice has a very good likelihood of being correct, in terms of the patterns the ACT likes to use on the Math section.

Notice that the table contains information about $\pi/6$, which has nothing to do with the question—it just clutters up the table in an attempt to make you wonder if you should be doing something with $\pi/6$ in the formula somewhere.

As I mentioned above, this substitution approach is essentially the one that the Red Book provides. It's a bit long and tedious, but it doesn't actually involve knowing any trigonometry, if you really think about it: all we had to do was recognize that $\pi/3$ corresponded to α and that $\pi/4$ corresponded to β, and then plug the given values into the given equation.

Now let's take a look at a much, much faster way to answer this question, if you're comfortable using your calculator.

The question is basically asking which answer choice is an expression equivalent to $\sin(\pi/12)$. So we could sidestep all of the substitution by just finding $\sin(\pi/12)$ on our calculator, and then evaluating each answer choice with the calculator to see which one matches the value of $\sin(\pi/12)$.

Our calculator tells us that $\sin(\pi/12)$ is roughly equal to 0.2588. (Remember that we have to use the "RAD" or "radians" mode when evaluating this expression, since it's a trig expression that uses π, and the ACT treats such expressions as radian expressions.)

Now we just plug each answer choice into our calculator to express them all as decimals. The one whose value is essentially 0.2588 will be the right answer. So let's take a look:

(F) gives us 0.25.

(G) gives us 0.5.

(H) gives us roughly -0.066987

(J) gives us roughly 0.1589.

(K) gives us roughly 0.2588.

So we can see that the expression in (K) is equivalent to $\sin(\pi/12)$, which shows again that (K) must be correct.

I want to say very clearly that I'm not endorsing either of these two approaches over the other. The calculator approach will be much faster and easier for test-takers who know how to use their calculators to evaluate trig expressions, but the calculator approach will seem not to work if a test-taker doesn't use the "RAD" or "radians" mode. On the other hand, the substitution approach can be used by anyone who reads carefully and pays attention to detail, whether that person has a calculator or not. So it's all a matter of finding the approach that works best for you. I just wanted to point out that the calculator approach exists for this question, because it's exactly the kind of useful shortcut that the Red Book will never tell you about, and it will be useful in other questions you might see in the future.

Page 304, Question 2

This question is a perfect example of how the ACT can take a fairly straightforward math concept and turn it into a question that will still confuse a lot of test-takers, especially if they don't pay attention. Let's take a look.

The question tells us that 12 vases cost $18, and it asks us how much one vase costs. To find the cost of one vase, we divide the total cost by the number of vases, which is $18/12, or $1.50. So choice (J) is the correct answer.

By itself, that isn't so bad. But, as usual, the ACT deliberately positions some of the wrong answers to try to encourage you to make a careless mistake.

One of the more obvious mistakes a person could make in this situation would be to divide 12 by 18, instead of the other way around. $12/18 would give you $0.66666, or $0.67, which is choice (F).

(One way you can quickly confirm that you should divide 18 by 12, rather than dividing 12 by 18, is to note that the cost of each vase must be more than $1. We know this because 12 vases would cost $12 if each individual vase cost $1; since the 12 vases cost more than $12, each individual vase must cost more than $1.)

Another easy mistake here would be to misread choice (G)—if you just reverse the last two digits in $1.05, you could think you were looking at $1.50 instead.

Choice (H) results from another potential misreading, because it's what you would get if you divided 16 by 12, rather than dividing 18 by 12.

It might seem like a waste of time to spend so much space discussing this question, which is relatively simple. But I really want to drive home the point that *most* ACT Math questions are actually pretty simple—what you really have to look out for are small mistakes like misreading, switching two numbers, and so on. As I keep saying, most test-takers could hit their target scores if they would just approach every single question with discipline and eliminate unnecessary mistakes on questions like this one.

Page 306, Question 10

This is yet another example of the ACT trying to make something more complicated than necessary. Many untrained test-takers will try to solve for a and b individually, but that's literally impossible here—either variable can have an infinite set of values. Instead, we have to take the fact that $a + b = 6$ and just plug in 6 everywhere we see the expression $a + b$. It sounds like a pretty simple task once we realize what we're actually supposed to do, but the ACT is trying to prey on your instincts from high school math, because it knows that most test-takers will instinctively try to solve for every variable in a question.

Once we plug in 6 for each instance of $a + b$, we get this:

$$2(6) + \frac{6}{6} + (6)^2 - 2$$

Now we have to be very careful to follow the correct order of operations when evaluating this expression.

Some test-takers will be so familiar with the order of operations that they have no problem following it automatically. For others, it can be useful to remember the acronym PEMDAS, which stands for the following:

1. Parentheses
2. Exponents
3. Multiplication
4. Division
5. Addition
6. Subtraction

If we follow that order to evaluate our expression, we get the following:

1. Parentheses
   There are no unresolved parenthetical expressions, so we can skip this step.

2. Exponents
   There's one exponential expression: $(6)^2$. 6^2 is 36, so we can sub 36 in for 6^2:
   $2(6) + \frac{6}{6} + 36 - 2$

3. Multiplication
   There's one multiplicative expression, 2(6). That's equal to 12, so now our expression looks like this:
   $12 + \frac{6}{6} + 36 - 2$

4. Division
   There's one expression with division, and it's $\frac{6}{6}$. That equals 1, so now our expression looks like this:
   $12 + 1 + 36 - 2$

5. Addition
   Now we have three terms being added: 12, 1, and 36. If we add them, our expression looks like this:
   $49 - 2$

6. Subtraction
   Finally, we have one expression with subtraction. When we resolve that, we see that the equation is equal to 47.

So the answer is (K).

As you can see, this question is actually pretty basic once you break it down. As is typically the case, the ACT isn't trying to trick you with advanced math concepts on this question; instead, the test is trying to overwhelm you with small details in the hope that you'll make a mistake. This is why trained test-takers always make it a point to pay very close attention to every detail in a question!

Page 309, Question 24

The ACT occasionally includes math questions that ask how many possible arrangements or combinations of something could be created in a particular situation, based on a set of rules.

In most high school math classes, these kinds of questions are referred to as "combination and permutation" questions. You may have encountered these types of questions in a pre-calculus class, or perhaps in a statistics class. These questions can often be very complicated when you cover them in school, but the ACT never makes them as complicated as they can be in school. Instead, the ACT follows its normal game plan: it asks a fairly basic version of a question, and hopes your school instincts will kick in and make the question seem harder than it really is.

This item is also a good example of the role that answer choices can play in answering an ACT Math question—but we'll get to that in a minute. First, let's talk about the solution to the question.

As the Red Book kind of explains on page 387, we ultimately find the answer to this question by multiplying 125 and 100. We do this because the question tells us to select one student from a group of 125 juniors, and another student from a group of 100 seniors. For any individual junior that we would select, there would be 100 possible seniors we could select. So that means there are 100 possible partners for each junior. Since there are 125 possible juniors, we need to multiply 125 by 100 to account for all the possibilities of starting with any individual junior and pairing them with any individual senior.

So the answer is (K). If you've ever covered combinations and permutations in school, I'm sure you'll agree that this question is actually pretty simple relative to most questions of that type—all we had to do was multiply two numbers together, without getting into factorials or anything else complicated like that.

But let's say we don't realize that we can just multiply the number of juniors by the number of seniors to find the correct answer, and we want to see if we can answer the question anyway.

We could start by imagining that we select one junior. How many different pairs can we make with that one junior? Well, that one junior could be paired with each of the 100 different seniors to make 100 different pairs. That's 100 so far.

Then imagine that we pick a different junior. That's 100 new possible pairs, because this new junior can also be paired with each of the 100 seniors, just like the first one could. So we're up to 200 total pairs so far.

Now imagine we select a third junior, instead. That would give us 100 more new possible pairs, because this third junior can be combined with all 100 of the seniors, just like the first two juniors. At this point we have 300 pairs, and we've only considered three juniors out of 125, so we know there are more. Only one answer choice is greater than 300: the correct answer, (K).

See how that worked? Even without knowing the formula right away, we could find a way to reason through the question and eliminate four of the answer choices because they were too small.

In fact, let's talk about the answer choices in more depth. When we think about how the answer choices relate back to the quantities in the question, we notice the following:

(F) represents the difference between the two numbers in the question.

(G) is the number of seniors.

(H) is the number of juniors.

(J) is the sum of the two numbers in the question.

(K) is the product of the two numbers in the question.

If you were pretty sure that you knew how to handle the question originally, then these answer choices would probably be very reassuring, because you would know that (F), (G), (H), and (J) don't make any sense in the context of the question.

But what if you weren't sure how to approach the question before you read the choices? Well, in that case you might still be able to use the answer choices to get an idea of how to answer the question. You might be able to reason that (G) and (H) don't make much sense, since each number is just the number of students in one of the two groups—there's no reason why the number of students in one group should be the correct answer as opposed to the number of students in the other group, so we could probably eliminate both of these choices from consideration. We could probably also eliminate (F), for two reasons: it doesn't make a lot of sense that subtraction would be involved in this question, for one thing, and it also probably doesn't make a lot of sense for the final answer to be a number that's much smaller than the number of students in either group. You may also be able to eliminate (J) if you reason that the sum of the two groups can't be the number of different two-person combinations, even if it's the number you get when you combine all the people in each group. (K) might make sense to you if you realize that none of the other numbers is large enough, or if you recall that combination questions typically involve multiplication.

In fact, I would even say that if I saw this question on test day and couldn't solve it on my own because I didn't remember the specifics of combination questions, I would still be sure that (K) was correct if I could recall that combination questions involve multiplication, or if I could recall that combination questions don't involve addition or subtraction.

This type of approach to the question is only possible because the question is multiple-choice, and because the answer choices happen to be set up in such a way that the answer is obvious if we remember that multiplication has to be involved.

So this question reinforces three important points when it comes to ACT Math. First, it's important to keep in mind that ACT Math questions tend to be relatively simple—even when a concept might be from pre-calculus, the ACT will ask about a basic application of the idea, not an advanced one. Second, we need to remember that the answer choices often give us a lot of information about different ways to attack the question, and that it's often (but not always) possible to arrive at a correct answer by disqualifying answer choices with rough reckoning. Finally, and most importantly, we always need to remember that there can be lots of ways to attack any given ACT Math question—not just the one your math teacher might recommend!

Page 309, Question 25
This is a question that rests on your understanding of the concept of slope, and on your ability to pay careful attention to detail. Like nearly any ACT Math problem, there are a few different ways to look at it.

The Red Book's explanation on page 387 is decent, but not great—it's a bit too formal for me. If you get in the habit of approaching every question with that much formality, you'll probably run into problems with the time limit.

Here's how I'd probably approach the question instead. I'd start out by noting that the ratio given for the ramp says that it rises 5 feet for every 100 horizontal feet. The question then says that the ramp only rises a total of 2 feet, and asks about the horizontal distance of the ramp.

A lot of people would set up a proportion here, like the one in the Red Book on page 387. But we could also take advantage of the fact that the question is multiple-choice, and try to see if we could eliminate any choices as being too large or too small. Since 2 is a little bit less than half of 5, we want the correct answer to be a value that's a little bit less than half of 100—in other words, since the height of our ramp is a bit less than half the 5-foot height of the example ramp, the length of our ramp must be a little less than half of the 100-foot length of the example ramp. The only answer choice in the proper range is 40, choice (C), which is the correct answer.

We also see a couple of common patterns in the answer choices for this question. For one thing, the fact that three of the answer choices involve a 4 probably indicates that the correct answer will involve a 4. We can also see a series at work in those three answer choices: 4, 40, 400. We know that the ACT likes to make the middle number in such a series be the correct answer, because it gives the test-taker a chance to make a mistake in two different directions: in this case, if you set up a proportion like the one suggested on page 387, you might accidentally handle the zeroes incorrectly and end up with either a 4 or a 400 instead of 40.

Once more, we see the extreme importance of reading carefully, keeping things simple, and paying attention to the answer choices.

Page 310, Question 30

If you look at ACT, Inc.'s explanation for this question, which appears on page 389 of the Red Book, you'll find a fairly straightforward mathematical treatment of the question. That treatment is technically correct, but it leaves out two important strategic points that well-trained test-takers will want to be aware of for future questions.

The first of those strategic points is that the ACT can only ask you to find the areas of rectangles, squares, trapezoids, and circles; if a question asks about any other shape, like this one does, then it must be possible to find the area of the specified shape by adding or subtracting the areas of squares, rectangles, trapezoids, and circles that make it up. In this particular question, we can see that the shaded region whose area we need to find is just the area of the larger circle after the area of the smaller circle is subtracted from it. As the Red Book explains on page 389, the formula for the area of a circle is $A = \pi r^2$. The radius of the bigger circle is 10, so its area is 100π.

For the smaller circle, the *diameter* (NOT the radius!) is 10. Half of the diameter is the radius, so the radius is 5. That means that the area of the small circle must be $\pi(5^2)$, or 25π.

Subtracting the smaller area from the larger gives us this:

$100\pi - 25\pi = 75\pi$

So the correct answer is (K), 75π.

And that leads me to the second point of strategic importance that I wanted to emphasize: a well-trained test-taker who's paying attention to this question doesn't even need to do all the calculating that we just did.

We can avoid almost all of that calculation by realizing that the area of the shaded region must be greater than 10π, and must involve π somehow because it would be the difference between the areas of two circles.

If we can realize both of those things, then we know right away that 75π must be the correct answer, because it's the only answer choice that satisfies both of those requirements.

But how do we know that the answer must be greater than 10π, and must still include π?

Well, we know the area of the smaller circle must be larger than 10π, because its radius is 5, and 5^2 is bigger than 10. And we can also see that the area of the shaded region must be greater than the area of the smaller circle, using the scale of the diagram.

And we would know that the correct answer must include π because it's the difference between the areas of two circles, and each circle must have an area measure that includes π if the radii are integers. (We could also tell that the correct answer is likely to include π because the majority of answer choices include it.)

When you practice ACT Math questions, remember that your goal isn't just to find the correct answer choice. Your goal is to practice finding the correct answer choice *as efficiently as possible*, so you'll be able to have enough time to finish the entire section with confidence and precision. As I keep pointing out in these solutions, ACT Math questions often offer us little "shortcuts" that allow us to complete a question or check our work very quickly and with total certainty, and these shortcuts often have very little to do with formal math.

So here are the two key things to learn from this question:

1. You find the areas of weird shapes on ACT Math questions by adding or subtracting the areas of familiar shapes (like circles) whose area formulas you can find in the Math Toolbox in this Black Book.

2. It's always important to pay attention to the relationships among answer choices and the quantities and concepts in the question, because an awareness of those relationships can often let you answer a question much more directly—without spending time and energy on formal math.

The specific idea of subtracting the area of one circle from the area of another circle isn't likely to come up on the ACT Math section too often, but the two general principles I just described will come In handy very frequently, which is why you should focus on them.

Page 311, Question 34

This question isn't really like anything you'd see in the average high school math class (do you notice how often I have to say that, by the way? :)). High school math classes might give you questions with diagrams, or questions with curves, or questions about the area of a triangle, and those are all concepts that appear in this question. But this question combines those ideas in a way you've probably never seen, and the ACT designs answer choices to trick you in specific ways that high school math teachers generally don't use.

For that reason, it will be extremely important to read the question very carefully (that's another thing I say all the time, isn't it?).

We're told that Tran wants to approximate the area under the curve. To do this, he finds the area of the triangle created by the origin and the points F and G. We have to figure out which answer choice describes the relationship between the area Tran found and the actual area under the curve.

If we look at the diagram and take the time to understand what the question describes, we can see that the area of the triangle created by F, G, and the origin is greater than the area under the curve. We can even see a little light-colored sliver between F and G that is part of the triangle and not part of the curve. So we know that the area of the shaded region is less than 20,000 units, which is the area of the triangle.

That leaves us only choices (F) and (G), since these are the only two that say the area of the shaded region is less than 20,000 square units. The only difference between these two answers is that one says the curve lies under $\overline{FG}$, and one says the curve lies over $\overline{FG}$.

The diagram clearly shows that the curve is under $\overline{FG}$, so that means (F) is correct.

But notice the other answer choices. Choices (F), (G), (J), and (K) offer us every possible combination of the following two ideas:

1. "less than" versus "greater than"
2. "under $\overline{FG}$" versus "over $\overline{FG}$"

And choice (H) is sort of a 'neutral' choice, because it says that the area of the triangle and the area under the curve are equal.

The ACT sets up a group of choices like (F), (G), (J), and (K) when it wants to confuse you—it knows that a certain percentage of test-takers will get confused by the high degree of similarity, and it also knows that many test-takers will simply misread one of the wrong answers and choose it based on their misreading, even if they actually understood the question.

So whenever you see a question with answer choices like this, you need to identify which concepts you're being tested on. You also need to pay *extremely close attention*, because it would be a shame to miss a relatively easy question like this one simply because we couldn't be bothered to read the answer choices carefully.

Page 312, Question 35

This is another example (like question 60 on page 179) of what seems to be a big, scary trig question that actually requires no trig knowledge at all. In fact, on this one, you don't even need to do the math. You just need to set up the problem correctly, which you do by using the formula provided in the question, and by reading everything extremely carefully—including the answer choices, of course.

As is often the case, there are at least two ways to approach this question:

- the traditional mathematical way, which involves actually doing math, and
- the way I would do it, which involves paying close attention to the question and thinking in terms of the ACT's design.

Let's talk about the more traditional approach first, which is essentially the one provided on page 390 of the Red Book.

To use that approach, we need to figure out how to take the values from the question and plug them in to the formula that's also provided in the question. Here's the formula:

$c^2 = a^2 + b^2 - 2ab \cos C$

Most test-takers won't know which values to substitute for the different variables, but we need to remember that the ACT can only test us on the definitions of the basic trig functions (sine, cosine, tangent, and their reciprocals). Since the formula in this question goes beyond those basic definitions, there must be enough information provided in the question for us to be able to figure out which values correspond to which variables.

We know from the note that the side lengths are given as the lowercase letters a, b, and c. We also know that the capital letters A, B, and C correspond to the vertices that are opposite the sides a, b, and c.

Further, we know that we're looking for the distance from the ship to the boat, and that the angle opposite that side of the triangle is a 5° angle.

Since we're looking for that unlabeled distance from the ship to the boat, and since that distance is opposite a 5° angle, we'll make that unlabeled distance be our lower-case c variable, and our upper-case C variable will 5°. The only other values we have in the question are the distances 4.2 and 5.0, and those will be our values for a and b. (For our purposes, it doesn't matter which one is a and which one is b, because the equation is set up so the result is the same either way.) Plugging those values into the equation from the note gives us the following:

$c^2 = 4.2^2 + 5.0^2 - 2(4.2)(5.0)(\cos 5°)$

To solve for c, we just take the square root of each side, and get this:

$$c = \sqrt{4.2^2 + 5.0^2 - 2(4.2)(5.0)(\cos 5°)}$$

So choice (B) is correct.

Now let's talk about how we might approach this question by taking advantage of the ACT's design.

We always want to be aware of the answer choices, especially if a question seems challenging to us at first glance.

In this case, we'll notice that four out of the five choices are almost identical. Choices (B), (C), (D), and (E) all have the following components in common:

- a radical symbol (also called a "square-root symbol")
- $4.2^2 + 5.0^2$
- $2(4.2)(5.0)$

The only differences among those four choices are the following:

- Whether there's a minus sign or a plus sign before the 2 in the middle of the expression
- Whether the expression refers to cos 5° or cos 85°

So there are really only three things we need to figure out if we want to find the right answer:

1. Is choice (A) correct, or is one of the other four choices correct?
2. If the correct answer is found in choices (B), (C), (D), or (E), then do we want a minus sign or a plus sign before the 2?
3. If the correct answer is found in choices (B), (C), (D), or (E), then do we want the cosine of 5° or of 85°?

First, let's see if choice (A) can be correct. Because we know the ACT often likes to make the wrong answers imitate the right answers, it's unlikely that (A) is going to be right, even if we ignore the rest of the question. When we pay attention to the question and notice that the expression in the note includes a lot of elements that aren't present in (A), such as a plus sign and a cosine expression, it becomes pretty clear that (A) lacks several critical elements from the note in the prompt, so it can't be right, since there's no reason to think those missing elements would have canceled each other out.

That means that (B), (C), (D), or (E) must be correct. When we take a look at those choices, we see they're all very similar to one another, with only the small differences we noted above.

So now our only real job is to figure out which combinations of those options is correct, and then pick the answer choice that includes the right features.

Let's start by figuring out if the right answer choice should have a plus sign or a minus sign in front of the 2 in the middle of the expression. If we look back at the note in the question, we can see that the sign before the 2 should be a minus sign. So choices (C) and (E) must be wrong, because they have plus signs in that position, and there's no reason to think we're subtracting negative values (which would effectively turn the minus signs into plus signs).

Finally, we need to determine whether the correct expression should involve the cosine of a 5° angle or an 85° angle. If we look carefully, we see that the only angle measurement anywhere in the question is a 5° measurement. So choice (D) must also be wrong. (Some test-takers might incorrectly assume that an 85° angle measurement is still relevant to the question, since 5° + 85° = 90°, and the idea of a 90° angle is often relevant to trig questions on the ACT. But there's no mention of a 90° angle in this question, so we have no reason to believe that an 85° angle would be relevant to the question.)

Since (A), (C), (D), and (E) are all wrong, and since (B) has all the same elements as the expression in the question, we know that (B) is correct.

So in this analysis, all we needed to do was to find the similarities and differences among the answer choices, and then think about how those things related back to the concepts in the question. In fact, you could argue that this question requires no knowledge of trigonometry whatsoever—the question does mention cosines, but we never need to know what a cosine is, as long as we can read carefully and see which choice matches with the formula provided in the question!

Once again, we see that careful reading is essential on the ACT Math section. We needed to read carefully to notice the note at the end of the question. We needed to read carefully to identify which values in the question corresponded to particular variables in the equation provided by the question. We needed to read carefully to note the similarities and differences among the answer choices. Finally, we needed to read carefully to make sure we chose the correct answer from a set of highly similar expressions.

Page 313, Question 40

Here, again (again, again, again . . . again . . . . . . *again*), we see an ACT Math question that asks about something we'd probably never encounter in any kind of high school or college math class.

As we always do in these situations, we'll figure out the correct answer by relying on careful reading, relatively basic math, and an awareness of the ACT's design.

Of course, as always, the first thing we must do is read the question carefully to make sure we understand what we're being asked to do.

The question refers to "a certain perfect square" that is "an integer between 1,000 and 9,999." Then it asks how many digits the square root of that number must have. In order to answer this question, we'll need to know the definitions of the following terms (all of which are in the Math Toolbox in this Black Book):

- Integer
- Digit
- Square

If we know those terms, then we should be able to test out a few different scenarios and determine which answer choice is correct.

I would probably start to approach this question by testing out some different numbers as examples of the options in each answer choice. For instance, I would test (F) by squaring 1 and 9, since 1 is the smallest one-digit number and 9 is the largest. 1^2 is 1, and 9^2 is 81. That range doesn't overlap with the range from 1,000 to 9,999 that appears in the question. So (F) must be wrong.

I'd test (G) by squaring 10 and 99, since 10 is the smallest two-digit number and 99 is the largest. 10^2 is 100, and 99^2 is 9,801. That range of numbers *does* overlap with the range from 1,000 to 9,999, so this looks like a promising answer choice. But it's always important to check every answer choice when we're trying to test out numbers like this, just to make sure we haven't made a mistake. So let's try the others.

We can test (H) by squaring 100 and 999, because they're the smallest and largest 3-digit numbers. 100^2 is 10,000, and 999^2 is 998,001. Those numbers are outside of our target range of 1,000 to 9,999.

Finally, we can test (J) by squaring 1,000 and 9,999—the smallest and largest 4-digit numbers. $1,000^2$ is 1,000,000, and $9,999^2$ is 99,980,001. Those squares also fall well outside our target range of 1,000 to 9,999.

What about (K)? We know that (K) must be wrong, because we tested the smallest 2-digit number, the largest 2-digit number, and the smallest 3-digit number, and we found that all the perfect squares between 1,000 and 9,999 had to have 2-digit roots, because squaring the smallest 3-digit number (which is 100) gives us a result of 10,000, which is outside the target range of 1,000 to 9,999. And we also know that squaring the largest 1-digit number, which is 9, gives us a result of 81, which is less than our target range of 1,000 to 9,999. So it wouldn't be true to say that the answer can't be determined, because we've determined that 2 must be the answer.

So we know that (G) is correct.

Notice how we found the correct answer by thinking about the definitions and properties of basic terms, and by testing out a few possibilities. Most untrained test-takers who have difficulty with this problem will make the mistake of expecting future ACT Math questions to focus on the number of digits in a particular kind of square number, but that would be a huge mistake—you'll probably never see a real ACT Math question exactly like this one ever again. Instead, you'll see other questions that ask about fundamental properties of basic math concepts in weird ways, and that's why it's so important to grasp the general process of working through bizarre ACT Math questions: you can't predict the strange questions that will appear on test day, but you do know that those questions will follow the rules and patterns that we keep talking about in this Black Book.

Page 314, Question 44

Here's another problem of the type that we wouldn't normally see in math class. As always, we'll simply read it carefully and reason through it, and we won't panic just because we're being asked to do something strange.

This question asks us how many prime numbers exist over a certain interval. Notice that the interval is fairly small—only 19 numbers, really. In fact, the interval is small enough that we could just go ahead and list every number in that interval and see which ones are prime.

We can leave out all the even numbers, because any even number is automatically divisible by 2, which means it can't be prime (except for 2 itself, but 2 isn't between 30 and 50). With that in mind, we'd get this list:

31, 33, 35, 37, 39, 41, 43, 45, 47, 49

Now I'd go through and eliminate the multiples of 3, since we've already eliminated multiples of 2:

31, ~~33~~, 35, 37, ~~39~~, 41, 43, ~~45~~, 47, 49

There's no need to eliminate multiples of 4, since we've already eliminated multiples of 2, and every multiple of 4 is also a multiple of 2. (For the same reason, we wouldn't need to eliminate multiples of 6, 8, 10, and so on—they're already accounted for in the multiples of 2 that we removed.) But we could still eliminate multiples of 5:

31, ~~35~~, 37, 41, 43, 47, 49,

And we could eliminate multiples of 7:

31, 37, 41, 43, 47, ~~49~~

From there we could try eliminating multiples of 11, 13, and so on. If you try that, you'll see that none of the numbers on the list is affected.

So that leaves 31, 37, 41, 43, and 47. These numbers are small enough that we can try to think of any factors for them that we might have missed, realize there aren't any, and be confident in that conclusion. Since there are five numbers left in the list, the correct answer is (G).

Notice that this problem is really just checking to see if you know what a prime number is, and whether you can carefully check through a short list to find them. The Red Book explanation mentions the idea that the largest prime number that needs to be checked as a factor is 7. This is true, but it's not something you need to figure out when you answer the question; if you accidentally check for factors like 11, 13, and 17, you might waste four or five seconds but otherwise there's no harm done.

Another common approach to this question is simply to go through each number in the set and try to think of factors for it, noting all the numbers that don't seem to have factors. I've seen this approach work well for many test-takers, but people often forget about one or two factors and end up missing the question unnecessarily. (By far, the most common mistake of this type on this question is thinking that 39 is prime.)

Remember that the size of the range of numbers is a good indication of how the ACT wants you to approach the question. If the range is relatively small, like this one was, then the easiest thing is probably just to make a list and go through each number. On the other hand, if the range had been something like the numbers between 1,000 and 10,000, there would be no way to go through each number in the allotted time, and you would know that the ACT expected you to find some pattern or apply a formula to find the relevant values without considering every single value in the range.

Another extremely telling detail on this question is the set of answer choices. Notice that the answer choices cover every integer in the range from 4 to 8, instead of being a more scattered set of numbers like 3, 5, 8, 9, 13. This tight cluster of values in the answer choices indicates that the ACT is hoping we'll make a careless mistake, either in finding the prime numbers or in counting them up after we've found them. As trained test-takers, we should take this set of answer choices as a strong signal that we absolutely MUST double-check (or even triple-check!) our work on this question, to make sure we haven't fallen into a trap for no reason. As I've said many times, and will say many more times, the first thing we should focus on to increase your score significantly is the idea of looking out for the little things, and becoming obsessive about handling them correctly. People who score 36 on the ACT

Math section don't do it because they know a set of special prime number formulas that you don't know; they score 36 in part by making absolutely certain that they don't make little mistakes that can be avoided. Keep that in mind at all times.

Page 315, Question 49

The Red Book's explanation for this question reads more like a formalized proof than like a practical solution to an ACT question that the average test-taker would be capable of putting together in a few seconds. So let's talk about this question from a practical standpoint.

There are two ways to look at this sort of problem: you can approach it in the abstract by thinking through it in terms of the principles of algebra, or you can evaluate the question concretely by plugging numbers in for each scenario and seeing what happens. Let's look at the concrete way first, since the concrete approach is usually the one that's favored by test-takers who are less confident in their math abilities.

Let's pick the numbers 3 and -3. I'm picking both a positive and a negative number because the question clearly deals with negative numbers, and I want to make sure I don't miss something important by only plugging in a positive number.

(I'm deliberately avoiding numbers like 0 and 1, because they have unique properties that may result in strange outcomes if I plug them into certain expressions. In this particular question, plugging in 1 would still produce a result that would be valid for all real numbers, but plugging in 0 wouldn't. Generally speaking, students who are drawn to the idea of plugging in numbers aren't usually very good at identifying cases that will result in strange outcomes, because identifying those cases requires thinking in the abstract, and most people who prefer plugging in numbers don't like to think abstractly. So, as a general principle, avoid plugging in the numbers 0 and 1 when a question asks what could be true for all real numbers.)

If I plug in 3, I get the following results:

I. $\sqrt{(-3)^2} = \sqrt{9} = 3$

II. $|-3| = 3$

III. $-|3| = -3$

And if I plug in -3 for x, I get this:

I. $\sqrt{(-(-3))^2} = \sqrt{3^2} = \sqrt{9} = 3$

II. $|-(-3)| = |3| = 3$

III. $-|-3| = -3$

So we can see that both 3 and -3 resulted in Roman numerals I and II having equivalent outcomes, while III had a different outcome. This indicates that (A) is correct.

Now that we've seen a couple of concrete examples, let's look at the question in the abstract.

The expression in Roman numeral I will always result in the absolute value of x (in other words, it will always result in a "positive version" of x). That's because it involves squaring x, which must be a real number according to the question. The square of x must be a positive number if x is a real number. Then we take the square root of that squared value—and square roots of positive numbers are always positive on the ACT.

The expression in Roman numeral II will also always result in the absolute value of *x*, because it involves taking the absolute value of -*x*, and the absolute value of *x* is always equal to the absolute value of -*x*. This value must be positive, too, because absolute values are always positive.

On the other hand, the expression in Roman numeral III will always result in the opposite of the absolute value of *x*—in other words, it will always result in a "negative version" of *x*.

Once more, we can see why Roman numerals I and II will always result in the same expression, while Roman numeral III will result in a different outcome, as we saw earlier.

As you can imagine, there are a lot of ways to mess this up. You might mess it up by plugging in zero for *x*. You might mess it up by misreading the expressions in the Roman numerals, or by misreading the answer choices. You might mess it up by forgetting the proper order of operations.

But you can also mess it up by misreading the original prompt itself, which is something many test-takers do. The original question asks you to find the expressions that always come out equal *to each other*, no matter which value is entered for *x*. As we've seen, those expressions are found in Roman numerals I and II. But lots of people misread the question and think they're looking for the expressions that will always come out equal *to the original value for* x, no matter which value we enter for *x*. If we misread the question that way, then we'll end up thinking that Roman numerals I and II work when *x* is positive, while III works when *x* is negative; in that case, we'd incorrectly choose (E). If we did that, it wouldn't be because we don't know how to do math—we'd be choosing the wrong answer because we had misunderstood what the question wanted in the first place, because we'd misread the question.

Yet again we see that this question, like so many others, is ultimately all about reading carefully and executing basic math ideas carefully. It doesn't require any super-advanced math knowledge. It just requires us to pay close attention at all times.

Page 317, Question 53

This question frustrates a lot of test-takers. It seems like the kind of thing you would need a formula for—indeed, if this question were to appear on a test in high school or college, you could be pretty sure that the teacher was trying to see if you knew the formula for the sum of an arithmetic series.

But we have to remember that this is an ACT Math question, and we can always find an alternative approach to challenging math questions on the ACT.

The Red Book describes several valid approaches to this question on page 400. As usual, though, the Red Book solutions don't address the things that a well-trained test-taker would notice when approaching this question.

One thing we'd want to realize is that it would probably be a little time-consuming to figure out the number of calls made on each of the twenty days and then add those numbers up. If the question had only wanted us to find the total after six or seven days, it might have made more sense just to list the totals for each day and add them up, but finding the total for twenty days would take a good bit longer if we did it that way. So I probably wouldn't approach the question that way. (Still, it wouldn't be totally impossible to list the totals for all twenty days, especially if we've been able to save time on other questions in the section. So if you had the extra minute or two that you'd need to list the calls for all 20 days, that wouldn't actually be a bad approach. It might not be optimal, but sometimes we just have to do whatever we can think of to solve a weird question—assuming there isn't an easier question somewhere in the section that we could handle in less time or with more confidence.)

Another approach to the question is to remember that it's a multiple-choice question, like all other ACT questions. That means we don't necessarily need to produce the answer on our own—it might be possible to rule out some of the answer choices through rough estimation, without actually using any memorized formulas.

If we take that approach, we could realize that Marshall must make at least 480 total calls, because he makes at least 24 calls per day for 20 days, and 24 x 20 = 480. That's not enough for us to be able to rule anything out yet, since every answer choice is greater than 480. But let's keep pursuing that line of reasoning.

The "extra" calls that Marshall makes every day will quickly add up. By day 6, Marshall will be making more "extra" calls than "original" calls—in other words, on day 6 he'll make his "original" 24 calls, plus 25 "extra" ones (since he started making 5 extra calls per day on day 2). For all the days from day 6 until day 20, Marshall will only continue to make an increasing number of calls. That means the total number of "extra" calls will have to be greater than the total number of "original" calls.

So that means (A) and (B) must be much too small to be correct answers. Marshall's "original" calls will be 480, and his "extra" calls will be at least that many, so he must make at least 960 calls. That means that answers in the 600s are far too small.

For that matter, (C) must also be too small. 960 would be the number of calls if the "extra" calls were exactly equal to the "original" 480 calls, but we can tell that the number of "extra" calls would have to exceed the number of "original" ones by an amount greater than 14. So 974 is too small. We can also tell that the correct answer must end in a zero or a five, because it will be the sum of 480 "original" calls and some multiple of 5, since Marshall makes 5 "extra" calls each day. So it's impossible for the total number of calls to end in a 4, which is another reason that 974 must be wrong.

That tells us that the total number of calls will be either 1430 or 1530, since those are our only remaining choices.

There are a couple of things we could do at this point to determine which value is correct. One thing that comes to mind for me is that 1430 is a little bit less than 3 * 480, while 1530 is a little more than 3 * 480. (Just in case you're wondering, I don't have the times table for 480 memorized, of course. Instead, I just mentally rounded 480 to 500, because 3(500) is exactly 1500. Then I could tell easily that 1430 must be a little less than 3 * 480, and 1530 must be a little more than 3 * 480.)

So now the question is whether the number of "extra" calls would more than double the number of "original" calls, so that the total number of calls would be more than three times the number of "original" calls. Some test-takers may be able to tell that the number of "extra" calls would be less than twice the number of "original" calls, but most won't feel comfortable making that judgment without actually doing a calculation.

But there's something else we might notice, if we're trying to think like the ACT. The difference between the value in choice (D) and the value in choice (E) is exactly 100—why is that? The ACT clearly thinks there's some kind of mistake we could easily make that would cause us to be off by 100. What mistake could that be?

We might notice that 100 is the product of 5 and 20, two numbers that play a significant role in this question. And then we might realize something very important: the question says that the extra 5 calls per day begin on the *second* day, not on the first day. In other words, the first day has 24 calls, the second day has 29 calls, the third day has 34, and so on. But a test-taker could easily misread the question and think that the extra calls began on the *first* day. In that scenario, the first day would have 29 calls, the second day would have 34, the third would have 39, and so on. If we misread the question in that way, we would end up counting an extra five calls for each of the twenty days—for a total of 100 extra calls.

Now we understand why choice (E) is exactly 100 calls more than choice (D). (E) anticipates the result we would get if we mistakenly started adding five calls per day from day 1, instead of from day 2. (D) is the right answer, and reflects the result if we correctly start adding five extra calls per day on day 2.

In my experience, most test-takers will be very frustrated by this question. So this is a good moment to redirect your attention to two sections of this Black Book: "The General Game Plan For Attacking A Section Of The ACT On Test Day," and "Timing Issues." Those considerations are very important if you want to maximize your score.

Page 317, Question 54

As usual, there are a lot of ways to answer this question. Also as usual, I like to look for the quickest one.

The Red Book's explanation on page 400 is mathematically correct, of course, but it approaches the question in a time-consuming way, as usual. The Red Book shows you how to generate the correct answer on your own, ignoring the fact that this is a multiple-choice question. It's often much faster and easier to take the entire set of answer choices into account, and approach the question with the goal of identifying the correct answer from the options provided by the test, rather than by trying to generate the right answer on our own.

If we're thinking in terms of mathematical fundamentals, one thing should jump out at us right away when we see the answer choices: the question tells us we're trying to graph a function, but three of the answer choices can't be graphs of functions, by definition. Choices (J), (G), and (H) all fail something called the "vertical line test," which says it's impossible for a vertical line to intercept the graph of a function in more than one point at a time. (This is just another way of saying that a real function is set up so that no single x value in the function has more than one y value associated with it.) Choice (J) has multiple y values for each x value from $x = 0$ to $x = 1$. Choice (G) has multiple y values for each x value from $x = 0$ to $x < 5$. Choice (H) has multiple y values for each x value where $1 < x \leq 2$.

So that means either (F) or (K) is correct. Let's see how we can identify the right one.

Choices (F) and (K) are completely identical except for two things:

1. (F) starts with a portion of a parabola that "opens downward," while (K) starts with one that "opens upward."
2. The middle piece of (F) has a filled-in point at $x = 5$ while the piece to the right has an empty endpoint at that value, and the middle piece of (K) has an empty endpoint at $x = 5$ while the piece to the right has a filled-in point at that value.

So if we can identify the correct option for either of those two differences, we can find the right answer.

If we remember the basics of parabolas, we could quickly identify that the parabola in the question has a positive x^2 value, so it must "open upward." That makes (K) correct. You could also test the difference between (F) and (K) by evaluating the parabola in the question at $x = 1$, to find that the correct y value at that point is -1, again making (F) wrong and (K) right. We could also be strongly reassured that the parabola should "open upward" because three of the five choices begin with parabolas that "open upward," and we know that the ACT often likes to repeat elements of the right answer among a majority of the answer choices. And, of course, if you have a graphing calculator, you can simply graph the equation $y = x^2 - 2$ and see whether it looks like the part of a parabola that appears in (F), or the part of a parabola that appears in (K).

Alternatively, you could note that the question uses a simple less-than sign ($<$) to define both ends of the range for the middle piece of the function, which means that the middle piece of the function should have two identical types of endpoints, and they should both be empty dots. That, again, identifies (K) as the correct answer. Once more, we can be strongly reassured that the middle piece of the function should have an empty dot for its left endpoint because three of the five answer choices show an empty left endpoint on the middle piece of the function.

Notice that we never actually needed to graph anything on our own to find the answer to this question. Instead, we could use our knowledge of the fundamental principles of graphing to figure out that four of the answer choices were flawed, and that only choice (K) contained certain necessary features of the right answer. Notice, also, that it was very important to pay careful attention to the answer choices, and to note the small similarities and differences among them—that allowed us to save a lot of time because we could find the differences between (F) and (K) and focus exclusively on them, without worrying about a lot of unnecessary elements of the question. Finally, notice that the correct answer follows the common ACT pattern of incorporating all the elements that appear most frequently in the set of answer choices. This question is an excellent example of the way a well-trained test-taker can exploit the weaknesses of the ACT's design and find the correct answer with minimal time and effort.

Page 318, Question 57

Most test-takers panic when they see this question, because they think the ACT is testing their ability to write the equation for a given circle, and most test-takers don't remember how to do that.

But we always have to remember that the ACT can't really test our ability to generate anything, since it's a multiple-choice test. All it can ever really test is our ability to identify the correct answer from a set of options. (Sometimes the fastest way to identify the correct answer is to generate it yourself, of course. But it's often faster and easier to identify the relevant elements of the answer choices and use them to eliminate the wrong answers.)

We know that one of the answer choices must be the correct equation for the given circle, and we know that the equation for a circle shows the mathematical relationship between the x and y values for any point on the circle. That means we can take the x and y values for a few points on the circle and try plugging them into the different answer choices. When we find the one choice that accurately reflects the relationships among all the points we've tested, we'll know that it must be the correct answer.

So let's pick some points and try them out. The four easiest points to identify are the ones where the circle touches the square:

- (3,0)
- (6,3)
- (3,6)
- (0,3)

So let's plug the first point into the first equation in the answer choices, and see what happens:

$(x - 3)^2 + (y - 3)^2 = 9$	(begin with the given equation in the answer choice)
$(3 - 3)^2 + (0 - 3)^2 = 9$	(test the values for x and y by plugging them in)
$0^2 + \text{-}3^2 = 9$	(simplify the expressions in parentheses)
$9 = 9$	(simplify the expression on the left)

So we can see that the expression in choice (A) is valid for the point (3,0). So far, so good. Let's try another point on the circle, (6,3). This one should also satisfy the correct equation, since it's the right-most point on the circle. Let's plug it in and see what happens:

$(x - 3)^2 + (y - 3)^2 = 9$	(begin with the given equation in the answer choice)
$(6 - 3)^2 + (3 - 3)^2 = 9$	(test the values for x and y by plugging them in)
$3^2 + 0^2 = 9$	(simplify the expressions in parentheses)
$9 = 9$	(simplify the expression on the left)

So the expression in choice (A) also works for the point (6,3), as it should.

Let's try another point that lies on the circle to see if it satisfies choice (A). I'll pick (3,6):

$(x - 3)^2 + (y - 3)^2 = 9$	(begin with the given equation in the answer choice)
$(3 - 3)^2 + (6 - 3)^2 = 9$	(test the values for x and y by plugging them in)
$0^2 + 3^2 = 9$	(simplify the expressions in parentheses)

$9 = 9$ (simplify the expression on the left)

That means the expression in choice (A) works for the point (3, 6), as well. Since a circle can be defined by any three of its points, we know that (A) must be correct because it correctly describes three of the points on the circle.

In this case, we happened to get lucky and find the right answer on the first try. But we can see that if we tried to substitute the same points into choice (B), none of them would work, since the left side of the equation is the same as in choice (A) but the right side is 3 instead of 9. The other choices would also fail to describe all of the points on the circle.

When we look at the other answer choices, we might be a little concerned to see that three out of the five choices have a plus sign inside the two parenthetical expressions, while only two out of the five choices have a minus sign inside them—that means (A) is in the minority, which we know is often a sign that it might be wrong on the ACT. Once the pattern calls my attention to that issue, I would definitely make sure to recheck my calculations, especially because it can be so easy to make a small mistake and end up switching a sign like that. But when we do recheck the calculation, we'll see for sure that the minus sign is correct. Remember, as always, that the patterns you learn in this Black Book can be useful for a lot of things, but they should never take the place of actual math if you can do it!

One last thing on this question before we move on. Once more, we see that an ACT Math question can be answered very easily if we simply read carefully and rely on basic math, even when the question seems to be testing our recall of an obscure kind of equation. In this case, all we had to do was identify a few points that lay on the diagram of a circle, and then plug a few values into some relatively simple equations and do calculations like "0 + 3" and "3^2." I would bet that over 95% of the test-takers who saw this question on test-day knew enough math to do each of those steps individually, but most of them didn't stop to realize the correct answer could be identified with such a simple approach. Keep this kind of thing in mind the next time you run into an ACT Math question that seems difficult for you.

Page 319, Question 60

Test-takers frequently miss this question because they misread it, or because they forget a fundamental property of percentages. But if we pay careful attention and remember to think of the answer choices as part of the question, we can actually identify the correct answer in only a few seconds.

The most common mistake people make on this question is to assume that increasing a number by 10%, and then increasing the new number by 20%, is the same thing as increasing the original number by 30%. If that were correct, choice (G) would be the right answer.

But (G) is wrong because the second increase is actually a 20% increase over the *increased* 1991 value, not over the *original* 1990 value. The 1991 value is 10% greater than the 1990 value. In other words, the second increase is a 20% increase from a value that's bigger than the original number from 1990, so the overall increase will be more than 30% larger than the 1990 value.

The Red Book demonstrates this in its explanation on page 404, and provides a couple of ways that you can calculate the correct answer as 32%. And those solutions are mathematically valid, of course.

But there's a much faster way to address the question if we just think about the relationships among the answer choices and the concepts in the question.

We know right away that (H), (J), and (K) must be wrong, because the correct answer must be greater than 20%, since the distance in the question had two separate increases and one of them was 20% on its own. So each of these choices is too small to be the correct answer.

If we think about the properties of consecutive percentage increases, we can realize that the correct answer can't be a flat 30%, for the reason we just discussed.

Only (F) is large enough, so (F) must be correct.

Most test-takers will miss this question because they don't think about it carefully enough, and simply choose (G). Once more, we see the importance of paying attention to small details, and of thinking about the answer choices as part of the question from the very beginning.

Page 450, Question 4

This question can be approached in a variety of ways. The Red Book describes one valid approach, which is to use the Pythagorean theorem, since the triangle is a right triangle according to the diagram:

$a^2 + b^2 = c^2$ (the Pythagorean theorem, where a and b are the legs of a right triangle and c is the hypotenuse)

$a^2 + 8^2 = 10^2$ (plug in values for one leg and the hypotenuse, according to the diagram)

$a^2 + 64 = 100$ (calculate the squares)

$a^2 = 36$ (subtract 64 from both sides)

$a = 6$ (take the square root of both sides)

So (H) is correct, of course.

As usual, there are other approaches we can use as well. Another mathematical approach is to remember the Pythagorean triple {3,4,5}, and to notice that this right triangle is just taking that Pythagorean triple and multiplying each side length by 2.

But the fastest approach in this case might be to think about the relationships of the answer choices to the diagram. We can tell the diagram in this question is basically drawn to scale, as we expect it to be on the ACT Math section. We can tell the diagram is roughly to scale because the wall does appear to be 80% as long as the ladder, and the angle between the two legs in the diagram is definitely a right angle. So let's think:

If we pick 2 or 3, we'd be saying the unlabeled side is *less* than half as long as long as the wall.

If we pick 6, we'd be saying the unlabeled side is a bit *more* than half as long as the hypotenuse or the vertical leg, but still shorter than either.

If we pick $\sqrt{2}$, we'd be saying the unlabeled side is basically 1 unit long, because $\sqrt{2}$ is a little bit more than 1. (You can use your calculator to find a decimal approximation of $\sqrt{2}$ if you want.)

If we pick $\sqrt{164}$, we'd be saying the unlabeled side is roughly 13 units long, because $\sqrt{164}$ is roughly 13 (again, use a calculator to find that value if you want to).

When we look at the diagram, it's pretty clear that the unlabeled side is more than half as long as either of the other two sides, but not roughly 13 units long, so (H) must be the correct answer.

At this point, we can probably also see which mistakes would lead to the wrong answers:

(F) is the difference between 10 and 8. We can imagine that some test-takers might make the mistake of thinking the unlabeled side should be as long as the difference between the other two sides, since it connects them.

(G) is half of the correct answer.

(J) and (K) represent mistakes a person could make in trying to apply the Pythagorean Theorem: (J) is the square root of the difference between 10 and 8, while (K) is the square root of the sum of the squares of the other sides—

in other words, (K) is what you'd get if you mistakenly thought the unlabeled side was the hypotenuse of the triangle, instead of its short leg.

So the only real way to arrive at (J) and (K) as wrong answers is to try to use a formula. On the other hand, if we just use the scale of the diagram to answer the question, we can't possibly be tricked into choosing either of those answers. Still, let me be absolutely clear on something here: I'm not saying the diagram-based approach is necessarily better than the mathematical approach. All that matters is that you get to the correct answer in a reliable way. I'm simply using this question to point out, once again, that the ACT Math section isn't strictly about knowing mathematical formulas or doing complicated calculations. In many cases, like this one, the ACT makes it possible to arrive at the correct answer without really doing any calculations. Keeping this in mind can help you find very fast solutions to a lot of questions on the ACT, even when those questions might seem difficult or nearly impossible for untrained test-takers.

Page 451, Question 9

The first thing to notice about this question is that it doesn't ask us to attempt to add these fractions, or actually manipulate them in any way. This is why it's so important to read a question all the way through before you start to work on it. Many test-takers are in such a frenzied state when they actually sit down on test day that they'll try to start working on a question before they even know what's being asked.

The question asks us to find the least common denominator for the set of fractions that it gives us. As trained test-takers familiar with the basic math concepts that can appear on the ACT, we need to know that asking for the least common denominator in a case like this is the same thing as asking for the least common multiple of the numbers in the denominators. The least common multiple is exactly what it sounds like: the smallest number that's a multiple of every number in the set. So we need to find the least common multiple of 2, 3, 9, and 15.

There are two main ways we can try to do this on an ACT Math question. The Red Book explanation shows one way to do it on page 521. That explanation involves deriving the prime factorization of each number and then constructing a new prime factorization that incorporates all the elements of the original numbers. The new prime factorization will be the prime factorization of the least common multiple.

If that sounds unnecessarily confusing, you're right—it is :)

The Red Book's explanation for this question is the kind of explanation that only makes sense if you already understand what's being explained. In other words, it's not a very useful explanation, and the approach that the Red Book recommends is unlikely to be helpful to test-takers who couldn't answer the question on their own in the first place.

So let's talk about the other way to approach this question, which is to go through each answer choice and see if it's a multiple of each denominator in the question. Since we're looking for the least common multiple, we'll start with the smallest answer choice and then work our way up from there.

45 is a multiple of 3, 9, and 15, but not a multiple of 2. So it can't be the least common multiple, since 2 is one of the numbers that needs to factor into the correct answer.

90 is a multiple of 2, 3, 9, and 15, so it's a multiple of each number in the denominators. It's also the second-smallest number in the answer choices. Only 45 is smaller, and we already know that 45 can't be the correct answer. So 90 must be the correct value for the least common multiple, which is the same thing in this case as the least common denominator. So (B) seems to be correct.

We always want to check back over our solutions on the ACT Math section, but it can be especially important to do that on questions like this one, where we can easily imagine that the tiniest mistake in basic arithmetic will result in a wrong answer. In this case, for instance, if you accidentally overlook the fact that 90 is a common multiple, you might think that 270 or 810 is the correct answer, since both of those choices are also common multiples for the numbers in the set. Or you might misread the original list of fractions and overlook the 2 in the first denominator, in which case you'd end up thinking that 45 was the correct answer. And so on. So we should definitely make sure to pause for a moment and be certain we haven't messed up, because it would be a shame to throw away a relatively simple question like this one just because we made a small mistake and couldn't be bothered to find it and correct it.

Once we double-check, we can confirm that (B) is, in fact, the correct answer.

As is often the case, we see that the easiest way to approach this question is simply to work through the answer choices, rather than to use the purely mathematical approach suggested in the Red Book. Remember that the fastest and easiest way to approach an ACT Math question often involves little or no formal math at all!

Page 452, Question 14

A lot of test-takers who don't take care to think in terms of mathematic fundamentals might be confused by this question, and they might even miss it if they don't read it carefully enough.

If we do read carefully, we see that the question refers to the possibility of multiple values for the expression $a + b$. We then see that a^2 is 49 and b^2 is 64. The first thing we need to figure out, then, is how there can be more than one possible outcome for the expression $a + b$.

Looking at the answer choices should give us a clue, because four of the five answer choices have their opposites in the choices as well. We see 15 and -15, and we see 1 and -1. That should help us remember that a and b can each be either positive or negative, because $(-7)^2$ and 7^2 are both 49, and $(-8)^2$ and 8^2 are both 64. This accounts for the pairs of opposites in the answer choices:

- -15 is the sum of -7 and -8
- -1 is the sum of 7 and -8
- 1 is the sum of -7 and 8
- 15 is the sum of 7 and 8

But there's no way to add any two of those four numbers together and arrive at 113, so (K) is the correct answer.

113, by the way, is the sum of $a^2 + b^2$ in this question, so there might be some way to misread the setup and arrive at 113 by adding the wrong things together.

The only math involved in this question is fairly basic arithmetic and algebra, but I've seen untrained test-takers miss this question far more often than you might think. When they do miss it, most of them choose (J), because they don't pay enough attention to the question—they think the question is asking them for the value of $a + b$, instead of asking for the only choice that can't possibly be the value of $a + b$. In other words, they end up missing this ACT Math question because of poor reading, not because they don't know the necessary math.

As I've said repeatedly, and as I'll continue to say throughout this Black Book, most test-takers could hit their target scores if they would simply eliminate these kinds of mistakes! One of the main reasons I keep pointing these things out to you over and over again is that you need to learn to become obsessive about these kinds of small details.

Page 453, Question 15

There are several things we can learn from this question that will help you on future ACT Math questions.

One of the first things I'd like to point out is that the Red Book's explanation for this question isn't very useful. The Red Book advises you to draw a number line and plot the points -5 and 17 on it, and then find the point in the middle of your number line. This is technically a valid approach to the question, but it's far more time-consuming than necessary.

The fastest way to approach the question is to realize that the midpoint of two points on a number line is the same thing as the average of the values of those two points. In other words, this question is simply asking for the average of -5 and 17. We can calculate that this way:

$\dfrac{-5 + 17}{2}$ (definition of "average:" the sum of a set of numbers, divided by the number of things in the set)

$\dfrac{12}{2}$ (simplify the numerator)

6   (simplify the entire fraction)

So the correct answer is choice (B).

The Red Book warns you that you might accidentally confuse the formula for the average with the formula for the distance from the midpoint to the end point, but I've never seen a person make that mistake. I actually doubt that many test-takers would have that formula memorized, since it comes up very rarely in high school or college math classes.

(To be clear, I'm not saying that the idea of drawing a number line is necessarily a bad one. If you do it correctly, you'll arrive at the correct answer. I'm simply saying that the number line approach is more complicated and time-consuming than the averaging approach.)

I'd also like to talk about the other answer choices, because analyzing those choices might help you figure out how to approach the question if you were stuck on it. Such an analysis can also help you check your work after the fact.

Choice (E) is the total distance from -5 to 17, while choice (C) is the distance from -5 or 17 to the midpoint. (This makes sense, since (C) is half of (E).)

Choice (D) is the sum of -5 and 17, so it follows the common ACT pattern of being "on the way" to the right answer—choice (D) is the sum of the two points that must be divided by 2 to find the average of the two values. (B), the correct answer, is half of (D).

So this set of answer choices clearly demonstrates that the people who wrote the question expect you to do something along the lines of adding or subtracting the given values, and then possibly dividing by 2. Again, noticing these relationships can give you added insight into which concepts are being tested.

This is just one more example of the ACT asking you to do simple math but presenting a question in a weird way. If the test had simply asked for the average of -5 and 17 rather than the midpoint, the easiest approach would have been far more obvious.

Page 453, Question 18

This is another question for which the Red Book's explanation is unnecessarily complicated and formalized. If we feel pretty confident with exponents, then we might naturally come up with the Red Book's approach, which appears on page 525.

But many test-takers aren't very comfortable with exponents, and won't be able to execute the Red Book's approach with confidence. Luckily for them, they don't need to—since the ACT is a multiple-choice test, we can find the answer to this question just by going through each of the answer choices and plugging it in for x in the original equation. (You'll probably want to use your calculator for that, of course.)

If we do that, we'll see that 7 is the only value that works for x, because $(2^7)(4) = 512$, and $8^3 = 512$. So (K) must be correct.

Of course, you'll want to make sure you enter each expression that you're testing into your calculator correctly! If you key in an expression incorrectly, you're likely to end up choosing the wrong answer. But if you can enter the expressions correctly, then you can answer this question without ever knowing the proper way to solve equations with exponents in them.

Page 455, Question 23

People often miss this question because they don't read it carefully enough, even though this is another one of those ACT Math questions that doesn't actually require you to do any calculations if you don't want to.

The Red Book explanation on page 527 shows two different mathematical approaches to the question—one using algebra and one using an arbitrary concrete value. (The Red Book explanation also includes the bizarre instruction "when you pour, be sure to get it all out of the smaller bottle," as though the author of the explanation thinks you might try to solve this question by using actual bottles of catsup for reference, even though I'm pretty sure you can't bring catsup bottles into the testing center with you. I have no idea how that command found its way onto page 527, but at this point I can no longer be surprised by anything I read in a Red Book explanation.)

But let's talk about how we might approach the question without using any real math, and without having access to catsup bottles.

We know the big bottle starts out 2/3 full, and that Angela is going to add catsup to it from the small bottle. That means that choices (A) and (B) can't possibly be correct, because they're both smaller than the starting amount of catsup in the bottle.

We can also work out that (D) can't be correct, because one bottle is 2/3 full and the other bottle is 1/3 full, but the bottles are different sizes, so there's no way that combining the two bottles can result in either bottle being perfectly completely full.

Instead, if we read carefully, we can see that the contents of the *smaller* bottle (which is 1/3 full) are being added to the contents of the *larger* bottle (which is 2/3 full). So the larger bottle will be more full than it was, but not totally full, and certainly not overflowing. The only answer choice in that range is (C), so (C) must be the correct answer.

As trained test-takers, we always want to try to figure out the mistakes that the ACT wants us to make. For this question, I think one of the easiest mistakes for a lot of test-takers to make is to get the bottles mixed up, and to think that the *larger* bottle is being poured into the *smaller* one, and not the other way around. If we make that mistake—which is essentially an issue with misreading the question, rather than a math-related issue—we end up choosing (E) and being wrong. For that matter, choice (D) is also the result of a reading error, because we'd end up choosing (D) if we didn't catch that the bottles in the question are different sizes.

Choices (A) and (B), meanwhile, are what we would get if we attempted a calculation and then made a mistake with it. (A) represents the product of 2/3 and 1/3, which has nothing to do with the question, and (B) represents the portion of the larger bottle that would be left if 1/2 of 1/3 of the larger bottle were removed from it, rather than added to it. In other words, both answer choices represent what you might get if you tried to set up an expression like (2/3) + 1/2(1/3) and then messed up the arithmetic somehow. These types of answer choices serve as one more reason why it's often best to ignore formalized math solutions on the ACT Math section, especially if you're not a very strong math student—some questions, like this one, are written so that you can work out the answer more easily without actually doing any math if you just pay attention to the details and think about them a little bit.

Page 456, Question 27

The Red Book's explanation for this question leaves a lot to be desired, so there are a few things I'd like to point out here.

The most important thing to keep in mind for this ACT Math question—and for many other ACT Math questions—is that you're not being tested on something you were supposed to have known in advance. Nobody is going to answer this question by recalling some fact they memorized off a flashcard once. The only real way to answer this question is to understand the properties of the concepts involved (in this case, the concepts of absolute value and inequality), and then use them to figure out what's going on in the question.

So it's very unlikely that you'll ever see another ACT Math question that directly tests the exact same ideas being tested in this question in the exact same way. Instead, you'll see some other question that asks about some other basic math property in some other strange way. That's why it's important for us to generalize our discussion of each ACT Math question as much as possible.

Now, in this particular case, we're asked to figure out what must be true about a and b if $|a| > |b|$. Some untrained test-takers might try to come up with a list of statements that would have to be true in this scenario, and then try to find an answer choice that matched one of their generated statements. That kind of approach could work, technically, but it would probably be very time-consuming—in fact, if you thought of true statements that were different from the true statement the ACT placed in the answer choices, then coming up with your own statements beforehand would be a total waste of time. For example, you might look at the given statement that $|a| > |b|$ and conclude, correctly, that $a \neq 0$, which is true—but it's not one of the answer choices, so you would have wasted your time in figuring that out.

So the smarter way to approach the question is probably to work through the answer choices and see which one must be true given that $|a| > |b|$.

(A) doesn't work. If $a = b$, then $|a| = |b|$, which means it's impossible for $|a|$ to be greater than $|b|$. You can easily test this with a concrete number—I'll randomly choose 3. If $3 = a = b$, it's NOT true that $|3| > |3|$, because 3 is not greater than 3.

(B) will turn out to be the correct answer. If $|a| > |b|$, it must be true that a and b are different numbers, because they have different absolute values—if they were the same number, they would have the same absolute value as one another, as we just saw when we thought about choice (A). So (B) is the correct answer. Of course, as trained test-takers, we want to make sure we look at the other answer choices so we can be more certain that we haven't made a mistake somewhere.

(C) gives us a statement that *could* be true, but it doesn't *have* to be true. It's possible to think of numbers that would satisfy the inequality, like $a = -5$ and $b = 3$. In this example, it's true that $a < b$, and it's also true that $|a| > |b|$. But you could also have $a = 5$ and $b = 3$, and it would still be true that $|a| > |b|$, even though $a > b$. There's another problem with this choice, from a test-design perspective: if (C) were correct, then (B) would automatically have to be correct also. In other words, if it MUST be true that $a < b$, then it also MUST be true that $a \neq b$. Since only one answer choice can be correct per question, (C) must not be correct for that reason, as well.

(D) is the same situation as (C), just in reverse: it can be true in some scenarios, but it doesn't have to be true in every scenario. Further, if (D) were a true statement, then (B) would also be a true statement, and the ACT only allows one correct answer per question, so (D) must be wrong for that reason, too.

(E) is a lot like (C) and (D) in that it's possible to find values for a that are greater than 0 that satisfy the inequality $|a| > |b|$, but it's also possible to find values for a that aren't greater than 0 but still satisfy the inequality as well. So it *can* be true, but it doesn't *have* to be true.

This question only provides further proof that the main challenge of the ACT Math section is to work carefully through strange questions about basic math concepts.

Page 457, Question 32

Most test-takers will want to draw their own diagrams for this question, and I would probably be no exception if I saw this question on test day. The challenge, as we'll soon see, is that we don't know the distances between any two points; we only know the order of the points. Based on the description in the question, the order of the points should be ABDC, and our drawing might look like this:

A   B   D   C

Or like this:

A   B D   C

Or this:

A   B D C

Or any number of other possibilities so long as the order is still ABDC.

Since we weren't given any information about scale, we have to figure something out based on the order of the points.

Once more, we find a situation where it's probably going to be easiest to go through each answer choice one-by-one and see if it has to be true, rather than trying to come up with a true statement on our own.

(F) doesn't have to be a true statement because we don't know anything about the distance from B to C, or from A to B. Either distance could be any value, and neither distance has any impact on the other.

(G) is essentially the same as (F): we weren't told anything about the distance from B to D, or from A to B, so we have no basis for trying to make a universally true statement about the relationship of those distances.

(H) is another answer choice that might or might not be true, for all we know. Since B and C are on opposite sides of D and no other information is given, there's no way for us to know the relative lengths of either distance.

(J) has the same problem that all of the other choices have had so far. We're not given any information about the distance from C to D, nor about the distance from A to B, and neither distance has any impact on the other, so we can't say if this statement is true or not.

(K) is a little bit different from the other choices, if we look carefully. (K) compares two distances that *do* have an impact on one another, because the distance from B to C *includes* the distance from C to D, since D is between B and C. (You may need to read that sentence again for it to make sense.) In other words, even though we don't know the actual distances between B, D, and C, we do know that the distance from B to C will always include the distance from D to C, plus some extra amount to cover the distance from B to D. So it must always be true that BC is greater than CD, which means (K) is correct.

When people miss this question, they generally make one or both of the following mistakes:

1. They write the points down in the wrong order (usually as ABCD).
2. They assume that the points are evenly spaced.

I'm sure you'll agree that neither of those mistakes really has to do with actual math in the way that most people think of math. Instead, both mistakes are the result of misreading the question or not paying enough attention to small details. As we've seen repeatedly, the ACT likes to turn basic math concepts into challenging questions by introducing bizarre details that don't normally appear in high school or college math questions. Don't let the test fool you.

Page 459, Question 38

As usual, the Red Book explanation on page 532 covers the basic mathematical approach to the question, which is to use the distance formula or the Pythagorean Theorem. To do that, you plot the two given points and construct a right triangle so that the distance between the two points is the hypotenuse, the vertical separation between the two points is one leg, and the horizontal separation between them is the other leg. Again, you can see what that looks like on page 532 of the Red Book.

But there's a faster way to attack this question. As usual, this faster approach relies on considering the answer choices from the very beginning, rather than trying to solve the question on our own and then looking for an answer choice that matches our answer.

We can see that the two dots have a separation in the x-axis of 7 units (since 4 − -3 = 7), and a separation in the y-axis of 6 units (since 5 − -1 = 6). So the horizontal (x-axis) separation of the two points is 7 units, and the vertical (y-axis) separation is 6 units.

With that in mind, let's take a look at our answer choices.

(F) works out to a number between 3 and 4, because $3 = \sqrt{9}$ and $4 = \sqrt{16}$. This is too small to be the distance between the two points, because it's even smaller than just the separation in the y-axis, which is 6.

(G) works out to a number between 4 and 5, because $4 = \sqrt{16}$ and $5 = \sqrt{25}$. This is also smaller than the separation in the y-axis, just like (F) was, so it must be wrong, too.

(H) works out to a number between 9 and 10, because $9 = \sqrt{81}$ and $10 = \sqrt{100}$. This seems like a plausible value for the distance between the two points if we just kind of think about it on a gut level, because we know the distance has to be bigger than either the x-axis separation or the y-axis separation by itself, but smaller than the sum of both separations together, which is 13.

(J) is 13, which is the sum of the separations between the two points in the x-axis and in the y-axis. That means it's too big to be the direct distance between the two points.

(K) is even bigger than 13, so it can't possibly be the straight-line distance between the two points.

So we can see that (H) is the only answer choice that's even plausible, given the context of the question. That means it must be correct.

Notice that the values in (F), (J), and (K) all come from mistakes that a test-taker could very easily make by accident if he tried to set the question up formulaically, without pausing to think about the question in common-sense terms. (F) comes from trying to apply the distance formula and accidentally taking the square root of the *sum* of the separations in the two axes, rather than taking the square root of the *sum of the squares* of those two distances. (J) comes from a compound mistake: forgetting to square the separations in the two axes before adding them, and then forgetting to take the square root of that sum. And (K) comes from forgetting to take the square root of the sum of the squares of the separations in the two axes. (For that matter, (G) seems to come from accidentally squaring the x and y values for the second point and adding them together for some reason, then taking the square root, which would be a severe misapplication of the Pythagorean Theorem.)

It would have been much harder to estimate the correct answer to this question with total confidence if there had been more than one answer choice in the neighborhood of $\sqrt{85}$. For instance, if the ACT had included wrong answers like $\sqrt{87}$ and $\sqrt{92}$, it would have been impossible to identify $\sqrt{85}$ as the only answer choice that wasn't too small or too big to be the right answer without applying the distance formula or the Pythagorean Theorem. But the ACT didn't make us do that—instead, the test made it possible for us to eliminate all the wrong answers just by using basic math to realize that they were too small or too large to be correct.

In fact, the wrong answer choices clearly show that the ACT sets out to trap the test-takers who rely on formulas, because the wrong answers can only be reached if a test-taker uses a formula incorrectly. This is one more reason why we often see that top-scoring ACT-takers don't rely very much on formal math.

Page 461, Question 46

This is another great example of an ACT Math question that asks about very basic mathematical concepts in strange ways. It's also a great example of a question that requires us to pay very careful attention to small details.

This question involves trigonometry, but the only real trig knowledge we need is the basic SOHCAHTOA acronym, which tells us that tan A in the question will be equal to a/b (opposite over adjacent), while sin B in the question will be equal to b/c (opposite over hypotenuse). If we multiply those two values, we get this:

$$\frac{a}{b} * \frac{b}{c}$$

The b variables in the numerator and denominator cancel out, and we're left with a/c. So (F) is correct.

Again, this is pretty basic math, and so far my analysis doesn't really differ from the Red Book's explanation on page 535. But I want to point out some relationships in the answer choices that we'll want to be aware of, so we can make sure we haven't made a mistake on the question.

Notice that choice (K) is the reciprocal of the correct answer. We can probably imagine why the ACT thinks somebody might pick that choice by accident: all you'd have to do to arrive at (K) is accidentally flip your starting fractions upside-down, so that you multiplied b/a and c/b instead of the other way around. Notice, also, that (F) and (K) are the only two answer choices that are reciprocals of one another. Because this question is one where it would be pretty easy to imagine a test-taker flipping the fractions upside-down by accident, the fact that (F) and (K) make up the only pair of reciprocals should serve as a strong indication that one of them is probably correct.

Further, if we pay careful attention to the answer choices we'll see that choice (F) follows the common right-answer pattern of being "Almost Like The Others," because three out of the five choices have a in the numerator and four of the five have c in the denominator. ((F) is one of the only two choices without b anywhere in the fraction, so it's in the minority in that respect.) This pattern strongly suggests that (F) is more likely to be correct than (K).

So this high degree of similarity among the answer choices sends two signals to a trained test-taker. The first signal is that it would be *very* easy to misread this question or make some small mistake and end up with a wrong answer, even if we understand what the question is asking about. The second signal is that (F) is probably the right answer.

Now, many untrained test-takers would consider a lot of the analysis I just did to be unnecessary. They would only be interested in getting the question right, and they wouldn't care about trying to understand why the ACT designed the question the way it did. But a top-scoring test-taker knows that these kinds of small details are absolutely critical on the ACT, and willingly looks out for those kinds of details on every single question. People who score a 26 on the ACT Math section usually know enough math to score a 31, or even a 36—the problem is that they don't pay attention to things like the answer choice patterns in this question, so they make a lot of unnecessary mistakes. Make sure you get in the habit of thinking like the ACT, so you'll be able to avoid losing points needlessly!

Page 461, Question 47

This is a perfect example of the importance of reading on ACT Math. This whole question comes down to reading everything carefully and thinking in terms of basic math principles.

The graph shows a change in slope at point *a*: after that point, the graph is still increasing, but it's increasing at a slower rate. Then we're asked which of 3 different events could have caused this to happen.

Of course, there's no formula we can possibly apply to figure out which Roman numerals are valid. In fact, there's no calculation we can do at all, because we have no numbers to work with. So all we can do is read and think: which scenarios in the answer choice could cause the depth to continue to increase, but not as quickly?

Let's look at each of the three possibilities.

Event I says the flow of water into the pool was increased. If the flow were increased, the depth would accumulate at an increased rate, because more water would be flowing in. So this Roman numeral doesn't work, because there's no way it could account for what we see in the graph: if the only change that happens to the pool is an increase in the flow of incoming water, then there's no way for the depth to start climbing at a slower rate.

Event II says the flow of water into the pool was *decreased*. If the flow were decreased, the depth would still be growing, but at a slower rate, which matches up with what we're seeing in the graph.

Event III says the drain was opened. This is a bit more difficult to think about than the first two events were, because we don't know how big the drain is or how much it might affect things. It may be that opening the drain causes the water to drain so quickly that the overall depth of the pool would decrease until it was empty. It could also happen that water might drain out at exactly the same rate it was entering the pool, in which case the depth would remain unchanged. But it could also happen that the water might drain out at a rate that was slower than the rate of the water still entering the pool—in other words, maybe water is coming into the pool at 10 gallons per minute, and then the drain opens and starts draining water at 5 gallons per minute. In that case, the depth would still increase after the drain was opened, but at a slower rate, which is exactly what we see in the graph. So this Roman numeral *could* account for what we see in the graph.

Since both II and III *could* explain the change in the graph at point *a*, the correct answer is (E).

Many untrained test-takers will see this question and assume that the ACT likes to ask questions about the rate at which water flows into pools, so they'll practice answering those kinds of questions. Don't make that mistake! By now we should know that the ACT can combine basic math concepts in any bizarre way it chooses—the key thing for us trained test-takers is to make sure we read carefully and pay attention to details.

Page 463, Question 50

This question is a good example of the way the ACT sometimes tries to intimidate you by trying to make you think you need to be familiar with a certain concept even when the question can be answered without it. In this case, the test wants you to get nervous if you've never heard of a family of parabolas before. In fact, even if you *have* heard of a family of parabolas before, your familiarity with that concept might make you think this question is going to be a lot harder than it actually is—remember that the ACT can never actually ask us to *create* a graph or an equation, because it's a multiple-choice test. All the ACT can ask us to do is to *identify* the correct expression from a set of options.

With that in mind, let's take a look at the graph, and at our answer choices.

When a multiple-choice question asks us to identify the correct function for a given curve, we can often choose a point on that curve with clearly identifiable values for *x* and *y* and then plug those values into each answer choice, and see which choice is a valid expression for those two values. But that would be hard to do for this question, because the only point on the curves that's easily identifiable is $(0,1)$. If we plug in $x = 0$ and $y = 1$ for each answer choice, the only one that doesn't work is (H), and we're still left with four possible answer choices.

So what else can we try?

If we still want to try to eliminate answer choices based on the properties of their features, we could notice that (J) and (K) would both produce some negative y values, since they involve multiplying x^2 by negative numbers. (This is another way to say that both (J) and (K) would produce graphs that "open down.") Since the parabolas in the graph don't open down or include any negative y values, we know (J) and (K) must be wrong.

From there, we need to see if we can figure out a way to tell whether (F) or (G) is correct. The only difference between them is that (F) multiplies the x^2 value by n, while (G) multiplies it by $1/n$. So now we need to decide which of those is an accurate description of what we see in the graph from the question. The graph shows that the curves become narrower when n is greater—in other words, when n is greater, the y value is higher for a given x value than it is when n is lower. This indicates (F) is the correct answer, because (F) will give us a bigger y value for any single x value as n gets bigger, since we'll be multiplying x^2 by a larger value when n is larger. On the other hand, (G) would have us multiplying by smaller and smaller fractions as n gets larger, because 1/3 is less than 1/2, and so on.

If that last part about (F) and (G) didn't make a lot of sense to you, don't worry! There are other ways to approach the question, and we'll talk about them now.

If we have a graphing calculator, one other approach is to try graphing some of the functions in the answer choices to see which choice creates the appropriate curves. We could try graphing each function in each answer choice with each possible value of n, but that seems like an awful lot of work. I'd rather just pick one value for n and graph that for each answer choice. That might show me enough of a difference between curves for me to be able to pick the right answer choice; if not, I can always come back and graph the other curves later.

I'll choose to graph each answer choice function with the n value set to 3, for two reasons:

1. I know the number 1 has unique properties that might cause more than one answer choice to seem okay if I use $n = 1$ for each choice.

2. I have a feeling that using $n = 3$ will really accentuate the differences among each answer choice, since 3 is the largest value for n that we have in our diagram.

So here's what we get if we graph each answer choice with $n = 3$:

(F) This graph of $3x^2 + 1$ looks exactly like the graph for the $n = 3$ parabola in the original question. We can see that it looks like it goes near the point (2, 13), for instance.

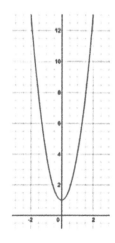

(G) This graph of $(1/3)x^2 + 1$ doesn't look like the graph of the $n = 3$ parabola in the question. This graph goes near the point (4, 6), for instance, while the $n = 3$ parabola in the original question clearly doesn't go near that point.

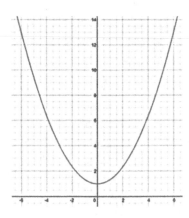

(H) This graph of $x^2 + 3$ clearly isn't the same as the graph of the $n = 3$ parabola in the question, because its y-intercept is $y = 3$, while the graph in the original question has a y-intercept of $y = 1$.

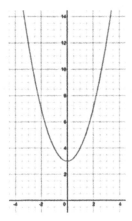

(J) This is the graph of $y = -3x^2 + 1$, which clearly isn't the same as the $n = 3$ parabola in the original diagram. It doesn't even extend in the right direction.

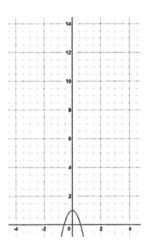

(K) This is the graph of $y = (-1/3)x^2 + 1$, and it also opens in the wrong direction, just like the graph in choice (J) does.

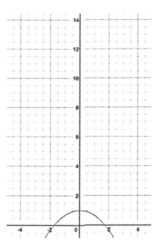

So our calculator makes it clear that only the function from (F) produces a graph that looks like the original $n = 3$ graph when we plug in 3 for n and graph it. That means that (F) must be the correct answer.

Here's another way to think about the question. If we look at the diagram in the original question, we see that, as the n value increases, the y values get higher and higher—in other words, all the points on the $n = 3$ parabola are higher than the points on the $n = 2$ parabola, which are higher than the points on the $n = 1$ parabola (except for where $x = 0$, which is the same point for all three parabolas). We also see that there's no limit to how high the y values can go in the original diagram. So we could also go through the functions in the answer choices and see which ones would reflect these features.

For (F), we can see that increasing n would always result in a higher value for y, since we'd be multiplying x^2 by a larger number. So (F) still seems to describe the situation in the question correctly.

(G) doesn't work. If we increase n in this function, we'll be multiplying x^2 by a smaller and smaller fraction—1/1, 1/2, 1/3, and so on. That means that increasing n will give us lower y values, not higher ones, so this choice is wrong.

(H) also doesn't work, because changes to n in the function from (H) will change the y-intercept of the parabola, but all the parabolas in the original diagram have the same y-intercept.

(J) has a problem because it opens "down," meaning that its y values extend towards negative infinity as the absolute value of x increases, because of the negative sign on the x^2 term. This differs from the graph in the prompt, which shows the parabolas opening "up."

(K) has the same problem as (J): it opens "down," while the parabolas in the original graph open "up."

Again, that leaves only choice (F), the correct answer.

Once we think we've arrived at an answer, it's always important to check our work, and one of the best ways to do that on the ACT, especially on the Math section, is to look at the relationships among the answer choices and see if they seem to indicate anything. In this question, (F) seems to be following the "Most Like The Others" pattern, which is a good sign that (F) is likely to be correct:

- (F) has a positive coefficient for the x^2 term, like three out of the five choices.
- (F) involves multiplying the x^2 term by a term involving n, like four out of the five choices, instead of just adding a term with n.
- (F) avoids any fraction bars in the function, like three out of the five choices.

As I always say, the fact that (F) fits this pattern isn't enough by itself to guarantee that (F) must be correct. But it's a very good sign for us that we've probably thought about the question correctly and that (F) is very likely to be correct, because we can see that the ACT is trying to make sure the wrong answers bear a lot of similarity to the right answer, which is something the test often likes to do.

Now, we can learn a lot from this question, just as we can learn a lot from any bizarre ACT question. Notice that it's possible to attack this question in at least two ways that don't actually involve any real calculations. The calculator-based approach that we went through doesn't even really require us to understand anything about parabolas, apart from being able to enter a function into a calculator, and then being able to compare the calculator's screen to the diagram in the question. Also note that the question refers to the idea of a "family of parabolas," but we don't actually need to know anything about what that phrase means in order to answer the question. Instead, all we have to do is read carefully, pay attention to details, and be willing to think about basic math ideas in a way that might be new to us.

Remember that it's very unlikely you'll ever see another question exactly like this on a real ACT in the future. But you'll definitely see other weird questions that will focus on the fundamental properties of math ideas in ways you've probably never thought of before. When that happens, your job will be to remain calm, read carefully, and be ready to analyze the question in terms of the ideas we keep discussing and demonstrating in this Black Book, just as we've done with this question.

Page 464, Question 55

This question seems very challenging to a lot of test-takers, because it involves factoring a trinomial expression. You probably have some experience with factoring from algebra class. Factoring a trinomial into two binomials is really just a matter of reversing the FOIL process (First, Outer, Inner, Last). You're probably more comfortable factoring polynomials where the coefficient of the x^2 term is 1. In this case, though, the coefficient is 2, which can make the reverse-FOILing a little more challenging.

If you look at the Red Book explanation on page 539, you can see the way your math teacher would approach this question if it weren't a multiple-choice question on the ACT. But it *is* a multiple-choice question on the ACT, of course, which means there's probably an easier way to tackle it. As usual, this approach to the question will involve working with the answer choices from the very beginning, instead of using the Red Book's approach, which tells you to ignore the answer choices until you've finished doing some pretty complicated algebra, at which point you just find the answer choice that matches the expression you came up with on your own.

Whenever we get stuck looking at a complicated algebraic expression on the ACT, we have to remember that algebraic expressions, by definition, demonstrate relationships *that are true for any number*. In other words, this question is telling us that we could plug *any* number into x, and then $x - 7$ would be a factor of $2x^2 - 11x + k$, where k is one of the numbers from the answer choices. So, if we want, we can just pick a number for x, plug it in, and then see which answer choice could be a value for k that would make $2x^2 - 11x + k$ be a multiple of $x - 7$.

So let's plug in a number for x. As usual, we want to try to avoid any number that might have a weird property relative to the question, or that appears in the question, because numbers with weird properties might result in a situation where more than one answer choice seems to work, and then we'd just have to repeat the process with another number to see which answer choice still worked. So we can potentially save ourselves a lot of work if we just plug in a "safe" number from the beginning. In this case, I feel like plugging in the number 100, since it seems to have no connection to anything in the question and should, therefore, be "safe." (We could also really choose any other number that wasn't 0, 1, 2, 7, 11, 17, 21, or 28, since those are the numbers we want to avoid because they appear in the prompt or in the answer choices.)

If I plug in 100 for x, then my $x - 7$ expression has a value of 93.

When I plug in 100 for $2x^2 - 11x + k$, I get this:

$2x^2 - 11x + k$	(original expression)
$2(100)^2 - 11(100) + k$	(plug in $x = 100$)
$2(10,000) - 11(100) + k$	(square 100)
$2(10,000) - 1,100 + k$	(multiply 11 by 100)
$20,000 - 1,100 + k$	(multiply 2 by 10,000)
$18,900 + k$	(combine like terms)

So now all I have to do is see which answer choice results in a multiple of 93 when I plug it in for k in the expression $18,900 + k$:

(A) gives us $18,900 - 21$ when plugged in for k, for a total of 18,879. 18,879 divided by 93 is 203—a whole integer value with no decimal and no remainder. So this value of k does result in a multiple of our expression for $x - 7$. This is exactly what I want to see in the right answer, but we still have to check out the other choices to make sure that only one answer choice works—if we accidentally chose a value for x that has unique properties relative to this question, then we could end up accidentally concluding that more than one answer choice might be equally right.

(B) gives us $18,900 - 17$ when plugged in for k, for a total of 18,883. 18,883 divided by 93 is approximately 203.04, which means that this value of k does NOT result in a multiple of our expression for $x - 7$.

(C) gives us $18,900 - 7$ when plugged in for k, for a total of 18,893. 18,893 divided by 93 is approximately 203.15, which means that this value of k does NOT result in a multiple of our expression for $x - 7$.

(D) gives us $18,900 + 7$ when plugged in for k, for a total of 18,907. 18,907 divided by 93 is approximately 203.301, which means that this value of k does NOT result in a multiple of our expression for $x - 7$.

(E) gives us $18,900 + 28$ when plugged in for k, for a total of 18,928. 18,928 divided by 93 is approximately 203.5, which means that this value of k does NOT result in a multiple of our expression for $x - 7$.

So we can see that when $x = 100$, only choice (A) makes the expression $2x^2 - 11x + k$ into a multiple of $x - 7$. That means (A) must be correct.

To be clear, I'm not saying that the Red Book's approach is wrong and that this approach is right. The Red Book's approach to this question on 539 is perfectly mathematically correct. As I said above, the Red Book's approach is what an algebra teacher would do if this question were posed in a lecture. But the Red Book approach will be far too complicated and challenging for most test-takers to execute on test-day, which is why I wanted to share this other approach with you. If we just plug in a number for x and then see which number works for k after that, we can arrive at the correct answer with just a little work on the calculator. Most test-takers will find it easier to use a concrete approach like this, rather than the generalized algebraic approach recommended by the Red Book.

(Of course, this approach assumes that we know the meaning of the word "factor." If we don't know that $x - 7$ being a factor of $2x^2 - 11x + k$ means that we can divide $2x^2 - 11x + k$ evenly by $x - 7$, then it will be impossible to use the approach above.)

Remember that there's always more than one way to attack an ACT Math question, and you can often make questions much easier by keeping the answer choices in mind from the very beginning!

Page 465, Question 58

This is a really bizarre question for most people, even if they understand the basic trig ideas involved, because most math teachers don't ask questions like this, especially with those weird Greek letters involved.

The Red Book's explanation of the question (which appears on page 540) is mathematically correct, as always, but it might be somewhat confusing. There are other ways we could choose to attack the question.

Before we get into that, let me explain something that a lot of test-takers might not understand when they see this question. The Greek letters α and β (pronounced "alpha" and "beta," respectively) aren't any kind of fancy mathematical symbol or anything; they're just variables that the ACT is using to represent unknown angle measurements. The ACT could just as easily have used a and b, or x and y, to indicate those angle measurements, but it chose to use α and β because the classic way to indicate trig variables is with Greek letters. So don't be thrown off by it.

One thing that a trained test-taker would want to notice about this question is that it contains a lot of text, so we'll want to make sure we read it carefully, of course. When we do that, we'll see that $\overset{\frown}{BA}$ is the same length as $\overset{\frown}{DC}$. This means that the angle AOB is the same degree measure as the angle COD (though it goes in the other "direction" according to the question). So if we found the angle measure of AOB, it could be relevant to finding COD.

Another *very* important thing to notice is that the answer choices are all given in terms of α and β, not in terms of actual concrete numbers. This is because it's not possible to arrive at concrete numerical values for the quantities in this question, since the setup of the question only deals in terms of variables, with no concrete reference point. (That doesn't automatically mean that (K) is the right answer! It might still be the case that one of the expressions in the answer choices will always give the proper value for angle COD in terms of α and β.)

We can also tell that the diagram is drawn close to scale, because angles AOB and COD are the same size in the diagram, just as the question (indirectly) tells us they are. So maybe we can use that, too.

At this point, there are two major types of approaches we might take to this question if we don't want to use an approach like the one the Red Book recommends on page 540. If you've been paying attention to the ideas in this Black Book, you probably know what they are before I even write them:

1. We can plug in some concrete values for α and β and see which answer choice makes sense in light of those.
2. We can take a look at the answer choices and see what we can figure out from them, based on how they relate to one another and how they relate to the concepts in the question.

So let's take a look at each kind of approach. We'll start with the approach of plugging in actual values for α and β, because doing that first might help make the second approach clearer for some readers.

When I look at the diagram, it seems to me that α (which is the measurement of angle AOC) looks like it's about 70°, and β (which is the measurement of angle BOC) looks like it's about 45°. That makes angle AOB about 25°, and we know that angle AOB is the same measurement as angle COD, so COD would also be about 25° based on our estimation.

Now we take a look at the answer choices, plugging in 70° for α and 45° for β, and see what happens:

(F) becomes -45°.

(G) becomes -115°.

(H) becomes -25°.

(J) becomes -70°.

So (H) looks pretty similar to our target value of 25°, except that (H) is a negative number. What do we make of that?

If we look carefully at the question, we see that we actually *want* a negative number for the correct answer, because the question says that angle measurements in the direction of α and β on the diagram are positive numbers, but our unknown measurement for angle COD has an arrow pointing in the opposite direction of the arrows for α and β—which means that our angle measurement should be a negative number. So -25° is appropriate, and we can see that (H) is correct.

Now let's try approaching the question by working backwards from the answer choices, to see what that method might look like. We'll rely heavily on the fact that ACT Math diagrams always seem to be drawn to scale. (Actually, in this particular question, as long as the circle is really a circle and the angles are all drawn with straight lines from the center of the circle, it's impossible for the relationships among the angles in the diagram not to represent their own relative scales accurately. But don't worry about that. Just remember that all ACT diagrams seem to be drawn to scale—see our discussion of scale in "Unwritten Test Design Rules Of ACT Math" earlier in this Black Book for more on that.)

(F) doesn't seem to work because angle COD clearly isn't the same size as angle BOC, which is the one labeled with the β symbol in the diagram.

(G) also doesn't work, but we may have to pay careful attention to see why. The expression -β – α basically means that we're taking the opposite of the β value and then subtracting the α value from that. Since the original values for both β and α are positive, this expression would be the same thing as turning them both into negative numbers and then adding them together. If we look at angle COD in the diagram, though, it appears to be smaller than either AOC (which is α) or BOC (which is β), so it can't possibly be the same size as both of them added together.

(H) is the right answer, as we can see if we look carefully at the diagram. Angle COD is the same size as angle AOB, and angle AOB is clearly the difference between α and β. The only issue is that this answer choice is a negative number, but, as we saw above, the question explains that angles measured in a clockwise direction should be measured with negative numbers, as this one is.

(J) is clearly incorrect because α isn't the same size as angle COD in the diagram.

(K) is wrong because we can see that (H) is a valid expression for angle COD in terms of α and β.

Yet again, we find that the ACT has deliberately tried to make a question look much harder than it actually is, and that the Red Book explanation doesn't describe the most straightforward solution. Remember the importance of reading carefully, noting details, and refusing to panic just because a diagram looks strange at first.

Page 589, Question 6

Like most ACT Math questions, this one relies on pretty simple math, and our job is to read carefully and not make mistakes. The Red Book explanation for this question, which appears on page 662, does a good job of explaining the math: the perimeter of a rectangle is equal to the sum of its sides, and there are two sides of 15 cm and 2 sides of 6 cm, so the perimeter is 42, because 15(2) + 6(2) = 42. So (H) is the correct answer.

But I want to spend some time taking a look at the wrong answer choices, because questions like this one make it especially easy to see how the ACT tries to catch you in a mistake. These relatively simple questions also make it easier to see how well-trained test-takers can use the wrong answers to help make sure they haven't made any mistakes in the question. And once you start to understand how these things work on relatively simple questions, it's easier to apply the same ideas to more challenging questions.

So let's take a look.

(F) is what you'd get if you just added the length and the width without realizing that there are two sides with each of those lengths. You can probably imagine that a lot of careless test-takers might make this mistake, especially if they were trying to speed through the question.

(G) is just twice the length, instead of being twice the length plus twice the width. This seems like a less likely mistake, but my experience over the years tells me that a small percentage of test-takers will accidentally forget about the width when calculating the perimeter, especially if they're in a hurry.

(J) is the area of the rectangle, which you would get if you multiplied 15 by 6. Finding the area is a classic mistake that a relatively large percentage of test-takers will always make on any question that asks about the perimeter of a rectangle. And, as you might imagine, when questions *do* ask for the area of a rectangle, a relatively large percentage of people will accidentally find the perimeter instead. These kinds of mistakes have nothing to do with math, and everything to do with reading carefully and paying attention.

(K) is twice the area of the rectangle, which is what you would get if you multiplied the length by the width and then multiplied that by two for some reason.

Do you see how thinking about where each answer choice comes from can help us make sure that we've answered the question correctly? Let's imagine that we accidentally calculated the area instead of the perimeter. When we go back through the answer choices and notice that (H) is the sum of the four sides of the rectangle, or that (F) is the sum of the width and the length, or that (G) is the sum of the two lengthwise sides, we might start to realize that a lot of the answer choices seems to reflect the idea of adding the side lengths together instead of multiplying them—and that should trigger us to go back and double-check the question, which would hopefully make us realize our mistake.

I know it may seem like we don't need to spend a lot of time thinking about this question in practice, but we really do. The majority of ACT Math questions are a lot more similar to this question than most test-takers think, which is why being very good at advanced math is unlikely to help much with the ACT Math section. In fact, when I've worked with test-takers who are pushing for an elite score like a 35 or a 36, if they miss one or two questions on a test, those questions tend to be relatively simple ones like these. Test-takers who are doing well often get cocky and assume they don't need to think very much about certain questions, and that's when the ACT manages to trick them with an answer choice that reflects a simple mistake.

Page 590, Question 12

The Red Book explanation for this question is on page 664. As always, it's mathematically correct; as usual, it's also more complicated than necessary.

For a question about the least common multiple, I would probably just check through each of the answer choices, starting with the smallest one, until I found an answer choice that was a multiple of each of the necessary numbers.

(F) and (G) don't work right off the bat, because they're both less than 70, so they can't possibly be multiples of 70.

(H) doesn't work because it isn't a multiple of 70 either.

(J) is the correct answer. 30 goes into 420 exactly 14 times, 20 goes into it 21 times, and 70 goes into it 6 times. Since it's a multiple of all the numbers, and since all the answer choices with smaller numbers are wrong, this must be the smallest common multiple.

(K) is the product of the 3 numbers multiplied together. So it's definitely a common multiple of all three numbers, but it's not the *least* common multiple, so it's not the right answer.

Note that this approach only works because the question is multiple-choice. If we had to generate the answer on our own, then one of the approaches recommended by the Red Book would be our only real option. But we don't have to generate the answer—if we want, we can just pick through the options in the answer choices to find the one that works.

Also note that choices (G) and (K) seem to be set up to take advantage of mathematical mistakes we might make if we did try to approach the question in a formalized way. If we tried to list the prime factors of each number and then multiply them together as the Red Book describes, we might end up somehow overlooking 2 and 5 because they appear as factors of 30, 20, and 70, which would give us 42 as a result; alternatively, we might forget that we only need to incorporate 2 and 5 once each when finding the least common multiple, in which case we'd arrive at 42,000. Once more, we see that the ACT deliberately tries to catch people who make mistakes in formal math, which is why it's often best to ignore formal math completely and just work through the answer choices!

Page 591, Question 18

This is yet another question that demonstrates the importance of *reading* on the ACT Math section, because answering this question is essentially a matter of reading everything very carefully—the setup *and* the answer choices.

The correct answer is (F), and the Red Book provides a decent explanation for this on page 666.

But I want to point out what's going on in the other answer choices, and how a trained test-taker might use those answer choices to keep himself from making an unnecessary mistake on this question.

In this question, the correct answer follows the common ACT pattern of incorporating the elements that appear most frequently in the entire set of answer choices. The expression $8(n + 4)$ appears on the left-hand side of the equation in three out of the five choices, and the expression $2n - 10$ appears on the right-hand side of the equation in three out of the five choices; we see that the correct answer choice is the only one that incorporates both of these most common expressions.

As always, the presence of this pattern isn't enough by itself to guarantee that (F) is the correct answer, but it strongly suggests that (F) is probably right.

The Red Book solution on page 666 tells us that the most common wrong answer was (H), which is the result of misreading either the setup or the answer choice, and accidentally choosing $10 - 2n$. If the many people who made that mistake had taken a moment to scan the other answer choices and notice that $2n - 10$ appeared more often than $10 - 2n$ (in other words, if those people had done what I'm training you to do), there's a good chance most of them would have been prompted to re-evaluate their decision to make sure that they weren't making a mistake.

Each little mistake like this will result in a wrong answer, and each wrong answer can cost anywhere from a quarter of a point (on average) to a full point on the final scale of 36 points for the Math section. If you want to maximize your score, you simply can't afford to let these little things slip past you. That's why I keep pointing out these small details over and over, and giving you tools to help you stay alert to them. If you want a great score on the ACT, you have to become obsessive about these kinds of things.

Page 593, Question 24

The Red Book explanation on page 668 adequately covers the two geometric approaches to this question: you can think of the figure as a 15 x 15 rectangle attached to a 5 x 10 rectangle, or you can think of it as a 15 x 25 rectangle with a 10 x 10 rectangle cut out of it. Either approach can lead you to the correct answer, choice (H), as demonstrated on page 668 of the Red Book.

As usual, I want to point out what's going on with the answer choices, and how a trained test-taker could use them to help avoid any mistakes in the question.

First, we should realize that (F) and (G) are each too small, because even the area of the large portion of the diagram is 15 x 15, which is much larger than 80.

By similar logic, we can realize that (K) must be too large, because 450 is 15 times 30, and our figure isn't even as big as 15 times 25 (since it has a chunk missing that prevents it from being a 15 x 25 rectangle).

With choices (H) and (J), we may be able to identify a common ACT Math pattern at work, because 375 is an answer you could arrive at on the way to the correct answer, if you proceed by finding the area of a 15 x 25 rectangle and then subtracting a 10 x 10 rectangle from that area. 15 * 25 is 375, so (J) represents the result you would get if you forgot to remove the 10 x 10 rectangle before marking your answer.

(Incidentally, (G) represents the perimeter of the figure instead of the area. The ACT knows that a lot of test-takers will find the perimeter when they're asked for the area, or find the area when they're asked for the perimeter. (F) represents the perimeter of the 15 x 15 rectangle that some test-takers will find if they approach this question by adding the area of the two smaller rectangles together.)

Do you see how this quick mental rundown of what's going on in the answer choices helps reassure us that we've thought about the question correctly? I'm sure a lot of test-takers miss this question because they choose (G) or (J). If they would only skim back over the other options and quickly try to get an idea of the thought processes that might lead to the other choices, they would have a very good chance of realizing their mistakes. Someone who accidentally found the perimeter, and liked (G), might realize that most of the other answer choices seemed a lot larger, and that might make the test-taker wonder if the question was really asking for the area, not the perimeter. Someone who liked (J) might find it odd that (H) was exactly 100 less than (J), and that might remind her that she was supposed to remove a 10 x 10 rectangle from the area of the 15 x 25 rectangle.

These little details make the difference between maximizing your score and continuing to be frustrated.

Page 593, Question 27

This is another great example of how using the answer choices and thinking like the ACT can help you find the answer to a problem, or at least double-check your work. (For the straightforward mathematical approach, see the Red Book's explanation on page 670, which involves factoring the expression $x^2 + x - 12$ into the binomials $x - 3$ and $x + 4$, and then setting each of those equal to zero and solving to get $x = 3$ or $x = -4$, and then adding those two possible values for x.)

This question asks us to find the sum of the two solutions to the equation $x^2 + x - 12 = 0$.

Knowing how the ACT likes to do things, we might reasonably expect that some of the wrong answers will be the values of the individual solutions. That way, if someone worked out one solution and forgot what the question was asking, he would have an answer choice to pick.

Since the sum of the solutions must be present in the answer choices (because it's the right answer), there should be one answer choice that is the sum of two other answer choices, if our theory about the individual solutions appearing as wrong-answer choices is correct.

Sure enough, we see that (C) is -1, which is the sum of -4 from (B) and 3 from (E). No other set of three answer choices demonstrates this relationship.

Of course, I always say that recognizing a pattern like this isn't enough for us to be certain we have the right answer, and this question is no exception. But we can easily check out -4 and 3 now that we think we've identified them as solutions. All we have to do is plug in each one individually for x and see if our original equation is valid:

$(-4)^2 + (-4) - 12 = 0$ (substitute $x = -4$)

$16 - 4 - 12 = 0$ (simplify)

$0 = 0$ (combine like terms)

If you substitute 3, you get this:

$(3)^2 + 3 - 12 = 0$ (substitute $x = 3$)

$9 + 3 - 12 = 0$ (simplify)

$0 = 0$ (combine like terms)

So both solutions check out, and they add up to -1, which means we know that (C) must be correct.

Once more, we see the value of learning to think like the test and considering all the answer choices as well as the actual math involved in the question.

Page 594, Question 30

The Red Book's solution for this question is, as usual, the straightforward approach your math teacher would use if you asked this question in school. But there are other aspects of this question we'd want to consider, as trained test-takers.

For one thing, if you don't feel comfortable dealing with the algebra, you could always just take each answer choice and test it out against the teacher's statement from the question to see which choice works.

If you do that, these are the results:

(F) doesn't work, because $23^2 - 23(23)$ equals 0, not 50.

(G) works out perfectly, because $25^2 - 23(25)$ does equal 50, just like the teacher said it needed to. So (G) is correct. Of course, as trained test-takers, we know we still need to check out the remaining answer choices, to help reassure ourselves that we haven't made a mistake.

(H) is incorrect because $27^2 - 23(27)$ equals 108, not 50.

(J) is wrong because $46^2 - 23(46)$ equals 1,058, not 50.

(K) is wrong because $50^2 - 23(50)$ equals 1350, not 50.

So there's an approach that doesn't require you to factor a quadratic expression, if you prefer not to do that.

We'd also want to notice the common ACT patterns at work in the answer choices here. (F), (G), and (H) form a series, and we know that the correct answer is often the number in the middle of a series if there's a series in the answer choices. We also see that (K) is twice as much as (G), which is another pattern indicating that (G) is likely to be correct. All of those things would help reassure us that we've probably thought about the question correctly.

There's one more thing I want to mention here. The reason that (F) and (H) both differ from the correct answer by 2 is probably that the two algebraic solutions to this question are 25 and -2, as the Red Book explains on page 671. The ACT probably thinks that some people will try to add those two solutions, which would give you 23, or add their absolute values, which would give you 27. These mistakes can only be made by someone who attempts a formulaic solution to the question without bothering to plug the values back into the teacher's statement—if you just plug the different answer choices into the statement, it never occurs to you that 23 or 27 might be correct. This is one more example of how formal math can actually cause more difficulty on the ACT than attacking questions less formally.

Page 594, Question 32

Many test-takers will be thrown off by the phrase "geometric sequence" in this question, and it's true that it would be helpful to know the meaning of that term in order to answer the question. (A "geometric sequence" is a series of numbers in which each term is multiplied by the same quantity to generate the next term in the sequence).

But we don't necessarily need to know the phrase "geometric sequence" when we approach this question. If we know that a "sequence" is a set of numbers governed by some rule or pattern, we can just look at the terms in the sequence and see how they're changing.

So let's look at the terms:

bcd, abc^2d, a^2bc^3d, ...

If you look closely, you might notice that b and d are the same in every term—they're just b and d. What about the other variables?

Well, a goes from not being present in the first term, to being a in the second term, to being a^2 in the third term. It seems like we're multiplying by one more a with each new term, which means the next term should have a^3 in it.

And how about c? It goes from being c in the first term, to c^2 in the second term, to c^3 in the third term. It seems like we're just multiplying by an additional c each time as well, so the next term should have c^4 in it.

So we want a^3, b, c^4, and d. That corresponds to the correct answer, choice (F), which is a^3bc^4d.

Incidentally, this correct answer follows the common ACT Math pattern of incorporating the elements that occur most commonly in the set of answer choices:

- three out of five choices have a^3
- three out of five choices have b
- two out of five have c^4 (which appears more than any other option for c)
- four out of five end in d

Again, the fact that (F) follows the pattern of being the choice that has the most in common with the greatest number of answer choices does not, by itself, mean that (F) is correct, but it's a very strong indication that (F) is probably correct, and it should be reassuring to us.

Remember that we didn't really need to know what a geometric sequence was to answer this question; all we had to do was observe the changes from one term to the next. Of course, that required us to stay calm, notice details, and avoid small mistakes—three things the ACT always rewards.

Page 597, Question 42

This question is very confusing for a lot of test-takers who don't read it carefully. The Red Book explanation is very formulaic, which doesn't help—it assumes you have an intimate knowledge of parabolas, which is not the case for most test-takers, and which isn't necessary at all on this question.

Most test-takers will simply assume that the smallest value of y will be listed on the table. But it we look at the table, we see that the lowest y value is 3—and it appears twice. Further, choices (G) and (J) both reflect x values that correspond to that y value.

So we might seem to have a bit of a problem here. We know there can only be one correct answer per question, and we also know that it looks like two answer choices are equally valid. That means we need to figure out what's going on.

At this point, I'd notice that the *x* values in the table increase by 2's, so numbers like *x* = 1, *x* = 3, and *x* = 5 aren't represented in the table, even though they appear in the answer choices.

Now it starts to click—there has to be an *x* value that isn't listed in the table, and it has to have a *y* value lower than 3.

One way I could find that *x* value would be to graph the parabola and take a look at it. That would make it very obvious which *x* value had the lowest corresponding *y* value. And I don't have to graph the parabola myself, if I don't remember how to do that—all I have to do is put $y = (x - 3)^2 + 2$ into my graphing calculator and look at the result. If we do that, we'll see that the lowest point of the parabola occurs at *x* = 3.

Another approach would be to take the *x* values from each answer choice and plug them into the equation to see what the corresponding *y* values were. If we do that, we get this:

(F) results in $(1 - 3)^2 + 2$, which is $(-2)^2 + 2$, which is 4 + 2, or 6.

(H) results in $(3 - 3)^2 + 2$, which is $(0)^2 + 2$, which is 2.

(K) results in $(5 - 3)^2 + 2$, which is $(2)^2 + 2$, which is 4 + 2, or 6.

I didn't need to test (G) and (J) because their *y* values are already in the table. (By the way, since they both have the same *y* value, and they can't both be right, they must both be wrong.)

This makes it clear, again, that (H) is correct, since 2 is the smallest *y* value out of all the values we've come up with.

A third approach is just to look at the table and think about how parabolas work. We know that parabolas are symmetrical, and we can see a symmetry in the *y* values for the last four rows on the table: 11, 3, 3, 11. That tells us that the *y* values are getting lower as the curve approaches *x* = 2, and then higher again after *x* = 4. We know that a parabola can't include a flat line from *x* = 2 to *x* = 4, and we know that the *y* values are symmetrical and descending as we approach *x* = 2 from the left and *x* = 4 from the right. That means there must be a point between them, at *x* = 3, with a lower *y* value.

Each of these three approaches to this question is faster, more intuitive, and less formal than the approaches recommended by the Red Book on page 676. Try to keep these kinds of approaches in mind as you practice for the ACT Math section, and remember that they typically involve reading carefully, paying attention to details, and taking advantage of the presence of the answer choices.

One more thing—remember that the ACT often likes to make the correct answer be the middle number in a series, if the answer choices contain a series of numbers. In this case, the five answer choices contain an arithmetic series (1, 2, 3, 4, 5), and the correct answer is the choice directly in the middle of the series, exactly as we might expect.

Page 598, Question 45
This question looks very strange and intimidating to most test-takers, and the Red Book's solution on page 677 is a fairly complicated, unimaginative approach using pure trigonometry and ignoring the design of the ACT.

Of course, as trained test-takers, we can find a much faster, easier solution.

For one thing, we can note that the diagram in the question is apparently drawn to scale. We can tell this because the length of the line segment representing 30km does seem to be about 3/4 of the length of the segment representing 40km, and the length of the 40km segment is a little less than half as long as the 100km segment. Further, the indicated angle measurements seem to be pretty accurate—the 30° angle looks like it's 30° off of vertical, and the 45° angle looks like it's 45° off of vertical.

Since the diagram is drawn to scale, we know the vertical line segment with the question-mark in it must also be to scale. We can eyeball it and see that it looks to be a little more than 4 times as tall as the vertical line segment labeled 30km. It's definitely not more than 5 or 6 times as tall as the 30km segment, so it can't have a height of 170 or 190, which means (B) and (C) must be wrong.

Using similar logic, we can also tell that (A) is too short, because the vertical line with the question-mark is definitely longer in the diagram than the angled line segment that's labeled a 100km line segment.

That leaves us with (D) and (E). There are two things we could use at this point to identify the right answer.

One approach is to realize that the correct answer must have three components, if it's not written as a decimal approximation: a 30km component to represent the vertical part of the trip, an expression to represent the part of the trip that happened at a 30° inclination, and an expression to represent the part of the trip that happened at a 45° inclination. We can see that (E) is the only choice with all those components (remember that expressions with $\sqrt{3}$ are related to 30°-60°-90° triangles, and expressions with $\sqrt{2}$ are related to 45°-45°-90° triangles).

But another, more concrete approach is just to use the calculator to approximate the value of (D) and the value of (E), and then use the scale of the diagram to figure out which choice is appropriate. If we do that, we see that (D) is approximately 106, while (E) is approximately 136. As we noted when we looked at (A), the vertical line with the question-mark in it is clearly a good bit longer than 100, which means it's a good bit longer than 106, too. But it does look like it could be about 135 units long—that even fits with our initial observation that the question-mark line was a little bit more than 4 times as tall as the 30km segment of the flight. So we can confirm that (E) is right with this approach, too.

Finally, if we think like the ACT a little bit, we can understand why (D) would be an attractive wrong answer for a lot of test-takers if (E) is the right answer. Test-takers who try to apply formal trig to this question will have to do some work to figure out that the two slanted portions of the flight have distances of $20\sqrt{3}$ and $50\sqrt{2}$. Many test-takers will forget there's a 30km component of the flight, and simply choose (D). Once we re-confirm that the 30km component of the flight must be taken into account, we can be even more certain that (E) is correct.

Most test-takers probably can't solve this question at all; even if they do, most of them will take a pretty long time to do it. But we just found a couple of ways to solve the question without doing any real math at all. Instead, we noted the details of the questions, thought about the answer choices, and exploited the ACT's design—all things that the Red Book's sample solutions don't really cover . . .

Page 598, Question 46

The Red Book's solution for this question, like its solutions for most other questions that involve conic sections (like parabolas and circles), requires us to know certain formulas that most test-takers will have long forgotten. Fortunately, there are other ways to approach the question that rely more on the fundamentals of graphing equations, as will always be the case on the ACT.

But if you do happen to recall the different formulas for identifying features of circles from their equations, and if you recall that the formula for the area of a circle is $A = \pi r^2$, then you can actually tackle this question very, very quickly. Let's get that out of the way first, and then discuss the way the rest of us would have to find the answer :)

In the standard equation for a circle, the constant value at the end of the equation is equal to the square of the radius. In other words, it's already equivalent to r^2. So in the equation $x^2 + y^2 = 16$, we can already see that 16 is r^2 for this circle.

If we plug that into the formula for the area of a circle, we get this:

$A = \pi r^2$ (formula for the area of a circle)

$A = \pi(16)$ (substitute $r^2 = 16$)

$A = 16\pi$ (simplify)

This corresponds to the correct answer, which is (H).

As I said, though, there's still an approach available to those of us who might have forgotten how to work with the equations for circles.

All we have to do is figure out some values for x and y that satisfy the equation, and then we can work out the radius of the circle from there, and plug it into the area formula.

The easiest place to start will probably be with an x or y value of zero. Let's see what happens if we make x equal zero:

$x^2 + y^2 = 16$ (equation for the circle)

$0^2 + y^2 = 16$ (substitute $x = 0$)

$y^2 = 16$ (simplify the left-hand side of the equation)

$y = 4, y = -4$ (take the square root of both sides)

So there are two y-values for this equation when $x = 0$. That gives us two points for the circle so far: (0,4) and (0,-4).

Now let's make the y term zero and see what happens. That gives us:

$x^2 + y^2 = 16$ (equation for the circle)

$x^2 + 0^2 = 16$ (substitute $y = 0$)

$x^2 = 16$ (simplify the left-hand side of the equation)

$x = 4, x = -4$ (take the square root of both sides)

Again we've got two values, which give us two points: (4,0) and (-4,0).

If we graph those 4 points and draw in the circle they define, we get this:

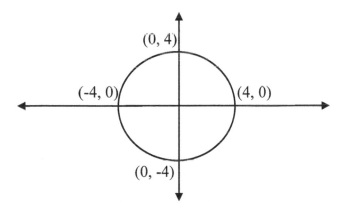

It looks pretty clear that our circle is 8 units all the way across, which means its diameter must be 8, and its radius must be half of that, or 4. If we plug in that radius for r, we get this:

$A = \pi r^2$ (the formula for area of a circle)

$A = \pi(4^2)$ (substitute $r = 4$)

$A = 16\pi$ (simplify)

Again, this gives us (H), the correct answer. So we can see that it's possible to determine what this circle looks like and what its area must be without remembering how to work with the classic equation for a circle. Instead, we can just plug in some values to plot some points, and work out the size of the circle that way.

Now let's take a look at the answer choices, to see if we can reassure ourselves that we're probably right, based on the common patterns of the ACT Math section. If we keep in mind that we needed to square a radius to find the answer to the question, we might expect a lot of squares to appear in the answer choices. Sure enough, in the answer choices we find 4 (which is 2^2), 16 (which is 4^2), and 256 (which is 16^2). In the middle of that series is the correct answer, just as we would normally expect on the ACT Math section.

It also makes sense to see 4π for another reason. It would appeal to test-takers who found that the radius was 4, and then stuck a π on the 4 and marked that answer, forgetting that the radius needed to be squared.

Here's one more thing to consider when looking at these answer choices. The formula for the area of a circle requires us to square the radius. But a common mistake people might make would be to double the radius instead. Only one number has its square and its double in the answer choices—that number is 4, which is the radius of the circle.

In this case it doesn't mean 4 is the correct answer, but the bulk of the math in this problem has to do with finding that number and then squaring it and multiplying it by π to get the correct answer, which is 16π. These are the sorts of thing you want to look out for whenever you look at a question and its answer choices.

Seeing all of these relationships among the answer choices can help reassure us that we've probably thought about the question the right way.

Page 599, Question 47

This question's setup looks very scary to a lot of test-takers, because they've never seen questions like this in math class. The ACT is really laying it on thick here, throwing all kinds of math terms at you and essentially trying to make you give up before you even find out what the question is asking. But trained test-takers like us don't fall for that kind of thing!

Instead, we'll read carefully and try to figure out what's going on.

Once we read the description and look at the diagram, we see that the question is asking us to find an algebraic expression for the area of the rectangle, in terms of a.

Looking at the answer choices confirms that the test doesn't want us to find an actual numerical value, just an algebraic expression with a.

Okay. So how do we do that?

Remember that we always want to think in the simplest terms possible, and we want to focus on definitions and properties of basic math concepts whenever we can. This question asks us to find the area of a rectangle. By definition, the area of a rectangle is found by multiplying the height of the rectangle by its width.

That means we need to know the height and the width of the rectangle. If we look at the diagram, we see that the height is $6 - 2a^2$. Okay, that's not so bad. For the width, we can see that *half* the width is a. That means the *entire* width must be $2a$.

So all we have to do is multiply those two values. Here's what we get when we do that:

$2a (6 - 2a^2)$ (multiply the width of the rectangle by its height)

$12a - 4a^3$ (simplify)

This is equivalent to choice (A), which is $-4a^3 + 12a$. So (A) is correct.

See how quick and easy that actually was, once we focused on the relevant details? The parabola actually never had anything to do with anything.

Let's take a look at the other answer choices and see if we can figure out some mistakes that might lead to them.

(B) is what we get if we mistakenly think the width of the rectangle is a, instead of $2a$.

(C) is what we get if we mistakenly find the perimeter instead of the area.

(D) is half of the perimeter, for people who add the height and the width instead of multiplying them.

(E) is the square of the height of the rectangle.

Being able to figure out where the wrong answers are coming from makes us even more certain that we've correctly found the area.

Another approach we could take would be to plug in a value for a. That would let us calculate a value for the area of the rectangle without really doing any algebra, if we don't like algebra.

The question tells us that a must be less than $\sqrt{3}$. Normally, I don't like to pick 1 as a value to plug in, but in this case I will, because there aren't other integers between 0 and $\sqrt{3}$. So if $a = 1$, then the height of the rectangle is this:

$6 - 2(a)^2$	(expression for the height of the rectangle in terms of a)
$6 - 2(1)^2$	(substitute $a = 1$)
$6 - 2(1)$	(square 1)
$6 - 2$	(multiply 2 by 1)
4	(subtract 2 from 6)

The width of the rectangle becomes 2, because it's $2a$ and a is 1.

That means the area of the rectangle is 4 * 2 when $a = 1$. So the area is 8 in our scenario.

Now we just go through each answer choice and substitute 1 for a. We're looking for an answer choice that equals 8 when a is 1. If there's only one choice with an expression that works out to 8 when a is 1, then it must be the right answer.

(A) gives us -4 + 12, which is 8. This is what we're looking for, but we still have to remember to check all the other answer choices, so we can make sure we didn't accidentally pick a value for a that results in more than one answer choice seeming to work.

(B) gives us -2 + 6, which is 4. So this must be a wrong answer.

(C) gives us -4 + 4 + 12, which is 12. So this is also a wrong answer.

(D) gives us -2 +2 + 6, which is 6, so this is another wrong answer.

(E) gives us 4 − 24 + 36, which is 16, so this is another wrong answer.

So we can see that plugging in $a = 1$ allows us to find the area of the rectangle with minimal work.

Let this be one more reminder to you that the "math" on the ACT Math section isn't nearly as complicated or advanced as most people think!

Page 599, Question 49

A lot of test-takers dislike logarithm questions because they never really learned how to manipulate logarithms in school.

If you know how to work with logarithms, this question is fairly simple, as the Red Book explanation on page 679 makes clear. Let's talk about that simple approach, and then we'll talk about how to answer the question with a calculator, if you don't feel comfortable with logarithms.

When we have $\log_5$(something), we're saying, "How many times do we multiply 5 by itself to get (something)?" In this case, with $\log_5 5^{(13/2)}$, we're saying, "How many times do we multiply 5 by itself to get $5^{(13/2)}$?"

Of course, if we're raising 5 to the power of 13/2, then that automatically means we're multiplying 5 by itself 13/2 times, since that's the definition of an exponent. The number 13/2, or 6.5, is between 6 and 7, so choice (D) is correct.

If that doesn't make any sense, you may want to head over to the Math Toolbox in this Black Book and review the brief section on logarithms.

If you have a graphing calculator (which occasionally comes in handy on the ACT), then all you have to do is enter the expression from the question, and the calculator's display window will show you that $\log_5(5^{13/2})$ is 6.5. Again, that's between 6 and 7, so the answer is (D).

In this question, there aren't really any patterns or anything that we can observe in the answer choices, so we should just make extra sure that we haven't made any small mistakes. Re-checking yourself on your graphing calculator would be a good way to do that.

Page 601, Question 55

Like many ACT Math questions, this one ultimately depends on the definition of a term that many test-takers might not use very often in math class. In this case, the term is "rational." A rational number is a real number that can be expressed as a ratio between two integers. An irrational number is any real number that can't be expressed in such a way. For instance, the number 3.885 is rational because it could be expressed as 3885/1000, and both 3885 and 1000 are integers. But the number $\sqrt{2}$ is irrational, because it can't be written as the ratio of any two integers.

With that in mind, let's take a look at the question.

We can eliminate choice (A) right away, because the question asks for an irrational number, and (A) is rational.

From here, we could choose to solve the equation in the classic algebraic way, as the Red Book recommends on page 681. But a lot of test-takers don't like using formal algebra to solve equations involving absolute value brackets. If that's how we feel, we could just take each answer choice and plug it into the given equation until we find the choice that works:

(B) gives us $|(\sqrt{2})^2 - 12| - 4$, which is the same thing as $|2 - 12| - 4$, which works out to $10 - 4$, which isn't 0. So this is a wrong answer.

(C) gives us $|(2\sqrt{2})^2 - 12| - 4$, which is the same thing as $|8 - 12| - 4$, which works out to $4 - 4$, which is 0. So this choice is the correct answer. Of course, we trained test-takers know we still have to keep checking the remaining choices to help us make sure we haven't made a mistake somewhere.

(D) gives us $|(4\sqrt{2})^2 - 12| - 4$, which is the same thing as $|32 - 12| - 4$, which works out to $20 - 4$, which isn't 0. So this is a wrong answer.

(E) gives us $|(2\sqrt{3})^2 - 12| - 4$, which is the same thing as $|12 - 12| - 4$, which works out to $0 - 4$, which also isn't 0.

So we can see that (C) is the correct answer.

Notice that (C) is the middle number in the series $\sqrt{2}, 2\sqrt{2}, 4\sqrt{2}$. As trained test-takers, we know that's a good sign that (C) is likely to be correct, so that's reassuring.

The overall key here, other than understanding the concept of absolute value, is noticing the word "irrational" in the question. If you overlooked that word, or if you misread it as "rational," you could easily do all the math correctly, arrive at 4 as a solution to the equation, and then pick choice (A)—but you'd still have the wrong answer, because you read the question incorrectly.

But if you read carefully, noticed the word "irrational," and then found that 4 was a solution (either by doing the algebra or by accidentally testing 4 in the equation), you would know that you were missing something, which would give you a second chance to correct your mistake by solving for the other solution. Never underestimate the value of reading carefully on the ACT!

Page 602, Question 56

This is definitely a weird-looking math question, and the solution in the Red Book on page 682 includes a pretty big table that's not going to help a lot of test-takers understand the question any better. Still, if we pay attention to the details in the question, we'll find it's nothing we can't figure out.

We're presented with a graph showing the distance between Malika and the motion sensor. Then we're supposed to pick 3 events from the 5 provided, and put them in an order that describes what's happening in the graph. Kind of weird, but it doesn't sound too complicated.

As always, we want to take a look at the answer choices before we get started, and see if we notice any relationships among the choices and the concepts in the question that might be useful in figuring out the answer.

As it turns out, there's a pretty massive shortcut hiding in the answer choices—a single thing we could figure out that would automatically show us the correct answer. Do you see what it is? Take a look at the set of answer choices again before you read the next line, and see if you can find the shortcut that would keep us from having to think about all three events in all five answer choices.

Here's the shortcut: the five answer choices each have a different first event—numbered I, II, III, IV, or V. That means all we have to do is figure out what the first event is, and then we just pick the choice that correctly reflects that first event. (Of course, even if we take advantage of this shortcut, we still have to check over the other choices and make sure we're not making a small mistake somewhere.)

Event I mentions standing still. But we can clearly see that the distance is changing in the first part of the graph, so she can't be standing still. This one is out.

Event II mentions walking away from the sensor. If Malika did that, the distance would *increase* on the graph. But it's decreasing instead. So this can't be the right description of the first part of the graph, either.

Event III correctly describes Malika walking toward the motion detector, but it gets the speed wrong. The first section of the graph lasts for a span of 4 seconds. The change in feet over that time is 8. That makes 8 feet per 4 seconds, which reduces to 2 feet per second, not 4 feet per second. So Event III is wrong.

Event IV has the same problem that Event II had, because it also says Malika was walking away from the sensor. So Event IV isn't a good fit with the first part of the graph, either.

Event V is a good description for the first part of the graph because it describes Malika walking toward the motion detector, and it uses the correct rate, 2 feet per second. Since we know for sure that this is the right first event, we know choice (K) is correct, because (K) is the only option that starts with Event V.

Still, just to be sure we haven't made a mistake, we should look quickly at the other elements of choice (K) and make sure they're accurate. The second part of choice (K) is Event I, which involves standing still for 5 seconds. That fits with the flat part of the graph, because Malika's distance would remain unchanged if she stood still for 5 seconds. The final part of choice (K) is Event II, which has Malika walking away at 4 feet per second. That fits with the third part of the graph, which shows an increase in distance of 4 feet in just 1 second.

So we can see for sure that (K) must be correct.

Do you see how noticing the answer choices allowed us to focus on the critical details, so we could answer the question correctly in a very efficient way? Most test-takers would just slog through each answer choice, testing out each description and getting frustrated or confused. We were able to avoid that by noticing that all we had to do first was figure out which event described the first part of the graph. Never forget how important it can be to notice the answer choices and the relationships among them!

Page 603, Question 59

This question presents a very odd, confusing situation involving three separate variables, among other headaches. The ACT is definitely trying to scare us away from this question. But, as trained test-takers, we know that we should simply read carefully and work through the concepts in the question as they're presented.

The very first sentence tells us to "consider all pairs of positive integers w and z whose sum is 5." That sounds like a weird request—something we'd never be asked to do in school—but let's think about those numbers. If we write them down, we get a list like this:

w, z

1, 4

2, 3

3, 2

4, 1

That's not a lot of pairs. In fact, there are only four of them. That means (D) and (E) are eliminated immediately, since they're greater than 4.

The small number of possibilities for this question is a very strong signal from the ACT that we're just supposed to list out each pair and test it individually, rather than trying to come up with some abstract, formal approach to the problem. The reason the ACT has made the number of pairs so low is probably that the test wants us to be able to try out all the pairs without needing an unreasonable amount of time. (Remember that every ACT Math question is designed so that it can be answered in under 30 seconds if we find the most efficient approach.)

Once we decide to plug in each pair and see what happens, we get these results:

$2^w = x$ $x^z = ?$	(original expression from the question)
$2^1 = 2$ $2^4 = 16$	(plug in values from $w = 1$ and $z = 4$)
$2^2 = 4$ $4^3 = 64$	(plug in values from $w = 2$ and $z = 3$)
$2^3 = 8$ $8^2 = 64$	(plug in values from $w = 3$ and $z = 2$)
$2^4 = 16$ $16^1 = 16$	(plug in values from $w = 4$ and $z = 1$)

We can see the two pairs in the middle result in a final number of 64 when we follow the given formula. So the correct answer is two pairs, choice (B).

This is a very strange question that probably bears no resemblance to anything your math teachers would ask you to do in high school or college. But that doesn't mean we can't figure out the answer if we pay attention to details, read carefully, and keep the test's design in mind—remember that one of the key indicators that we needed to check each pair of values manually was the fact that there were only four pairs to check. Most test-takers wouldn't realize the significance of that low number, so they'd search in vain for some kind of formalized way to approach the question.

Page 603, Question 60

The ACT loves to hide right triangles in other objects, and then invent ways to ask you to find them. In this case, the triangles are hidden in a cube inside a sphere, in a diagram that's supposed to make you cower in fear.

Still, if we can read through the question carefully and set it up correctly, we'll find that the math is no more challenging than it has been for any other ACT Math question.

We need to find the radius of the sphere, and we're given the length of one edge of the cube. How can we do that, using only the basic geometry and trig that are allowed on the ACT?

Well, we know the radius is the distance from the center of the sphere to any point on the sphere. And we can see there are eight points on the cube that touch the sphere—the eight corners of the cube. If we could find the distance from the center of the sphere to any one of those points, we'd know the radius, because the center of the sphere and the center of the cube are the same point.

We already know the side-length of the cube, and the sides of the cube do touch the corners of the cube. But the sides of the cube don't pass through the center of the cube/sphere. So we'll need to come up with something else.

At this point, it would be good to realize that the diagonal of the cube and the diameter of the sphere are the same distance. In other words, the measurement from one corner of the cube, through the center of the cube, and out to the very opposite corner of the cube is the same as the diameter, because the corners of the cube are points on the sphere:

diameter/diagonal

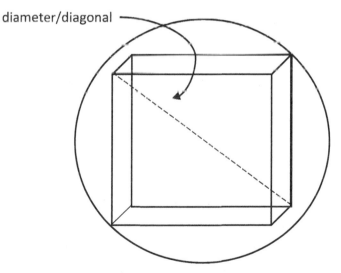

But how could we set up a right triangle to find that length? We'd have to know the length from one corner of one face of the cube to its opposite corner, like this:

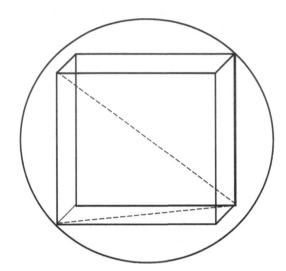

If we could figure out the length of that second dashed line, we could use it (along with one vertical side of the cube) to create a right triangle with the diagonal/diameter line as the hypotenuse.

So let's figure out the length of the line running diagonally across the bottom face of the cube. We know that the cube has a side length of 4, so we can use the Pythagorean Theorem to find the diagonal:

$a^2 + b^2 = c^2$ (Pythagorean Theorem, where a and b are legs and c is the diagonal)

$4^2 + 4^2 = c^2$ (substitute leg lengths of 4 for each leg)

$16 + 16 = c^2$ (simplify the left-hand side of the equation)

$32 = c^2$ (combine like terms)

$\sqrt{32} = c$ (take square root of both sides)

$\sqrt{16} * \sqrt{2} = c$ (simplify radical expression)

$4\sqrt{2} = c$

Now we know the diagonal across the bottom face of the cube has a length of $4\sqrt{2}$. (Note that this number is the incorrect "On The Way" answer choice (J), and that halving it would give us another incorrect answer: choice (G).)

As I said before, we can now use the diagonal across the bottom face of the cube as a leg in a new right triangle. The hypotenuse of this new right triangle will be the diagonal of the cube (also a diameter of the sphere), and the other leg will be a vertical edge of the cube.

Applying the Pythagorean Theorem to this new right triangle gives us the following result for the cube's diagonal:

$a^2 + b^2 = c^2$ (Pythagorean Theorem, where a and b are legs and c is the hypotenuse)

$4^2 + (4\sqrt{2})^2 = c^2$ (plug in lengths of the vertical edge of the cube and the diagonal across the bottom face of the cube)

$16 + 32 = c^2$ (simplify)

$48 = c^2$ (combine like terms)

$\sqrt{48} = c$ (take square root of both sides)

$\sqrt{16} * \sqrt{3} = c$ (simplify radical expression)

$4\sqrt{3} = c$

So the hypotenuse from one corner of the cube to the opposite corner of the cube is $4\sqrt{3}$. Notice that this is the incorrect "On-The-Way" Answer (H). Remember that the question asked us for the *radius* of the circle, not the diameter!

Since the radius is half the diameter, the correct answer is this:

$$\frac{4\sqrt{3}}{2}$$

Which can be simplified to $2\sqrt{3}$, which is the correct answer, choice (F).

This solution involved a bit more math than I generally like to do on the ACT Math section, but sometimes that can't be avoided. I wanted to go through this solution because the Red Book's approach on page 684 uses a formula for the diagonal of a rectangular prism, and I wanted to show that it's possible to find the answer without memorizing that formula (because I'd wager that 99% of test-takers have never even heard of the formula, let alone memorized it, and because the formula is basically a derivation of the Pythagorean Theorem anyway).

Notice, once more, all of the little traps the ACT left for us in the answer choices. (H) is the diameter instead of the radius. (J) is the diagonal of a face of the cube, and (G) is half of that distance, in case you accidentally got confused between the diagonal of the *face* of the cube and the diagonal of the *cube* itself. (K) is half the edge of the cube, in case you got really confused and thought that would be equal to the radius for some reason. I'm sure that many test-takers who missed this question probably understood how to approach it, but accidentally chose an answer like (H) because they forgot to pay attention to what the question actually said. Don't throw points away like that!

Page 732, Question 3

This question asks us to plug a value into a function to find the result; more specifically, we need to plug in the value $f(10)$ in the function $f(x) = (x^2 + 12)/(x - 6)$. As the Red Book tells us on page 803, that looks like this:

$(x^2 + 12)/(x - 6)$ (original function expression)

$(10^2 + 12)/(10 - 6)$ (substitute $x = 10$)

$(100 + 12)/4$ (square 10 in the numerator, subtract 6 from 10 in the denominator)

$112/4$ (simplify the numerator)

28 (divide)

So the answer is 28, choice (B).

If you don't feel like doing that math yourself, you could just plug the expression $(10^2 + 12)/(10 - 6)$ into your calculator, and it would tell you the expression was equal to 28.

This is a pretty straightforward question, but there are a couple of things in the answer choices that we should talk about. Choice (A) is the value of the numerator, and it's there to catch people who might find that number in the process of solving the question, notice it in the answer choices, forget the rest of the question, and then mark their answer and move on without realizing their mistake. In other words, it's a classic example of a wrong answer that's "on the way" to the right answer.

(D) is what you might get if you ignored the 12 in the numerator and the 6 in the denominator, which would leave you with x^2/x, or 100/10, or 10.

Also note the series 12, 10, 8 in choices (C), (D), and (E). As trained test-takers, we know that we'll often find the correct answer is the middle number in a series, if a series appears in the set of answer choices. But that pattern isn't an absolute rule; it's just a general pattern. Sometimes it doesn't indicate the right answer, and this question is one of those times.

Page 733, Question 7

This question gives us a relatively basic equation in a slightly awkward format. As always, there are multiple ways to approach it. The Red Book's approach is something like this:

$2(x - 6) + x = 36$	(initial expression)
$2x - 12 + x = 36$	(distribute the 2)
$3x - 12 = 36$	(combine like terms)
$3x = 48$	(add 12 to both sides)
$x = 16$	(divide both sides by 3)

So the answer is 16, choice (B).

But there's another approach we can take here, if we don't really like solving things algebraically, and that is to take each answer choice and plug it into the given equation, to see which one makes it true. The choice that makes it true is, of course, the correct answer.

Three of the wrong answers in this question result from various algebraic errors, which is typical for an algebraic ACT Math question. The last wrong answer seems to be an example of a common pattern on the ACT Math section, rather than a miscalculation.

(A) is what you get if you ignore the x outside the parentheses in the original equation because you didn't read the question carefully enough.

(C) is the result if you incorrectly distribute the 2 and end up with $2x - 6$ instead of $2x - 12$.

(D) is the result if you make the mistake in (C) and also eliminate the 6 on the left-hand side of the equation, then accidentally *subtract* 6 from 36, rather than adding 6 to both sides.

(E) is half of the right answer, which is a common ACT Math pattern for a wrong answer.

I know this question is probably relatively easy for most test-takers, so it may seem strange that I want to discuss it with you. But, as I've said repeatedly, these "simple" questions are the real key to hitting your target score. That's why it's so critical that we constantly go over all the little mistakes the ACT is trying to get you to make, and how you can avoid them. Top-scorers on the ACT are obsessive about these little details.

Page 734, Question 10

The Red Book's explanation on page 805 covers the math involved in this question, but I also want to call some of the answer choice patterns to your attention. This question is also worth talking about because many test-takers feel uncomfortable with averages.

As always, we want to try to approach this question in terms of definitions and properties of basic math concepts. So what is an average, by definition? Averaging a set of quantities is the process of adding up all the quantities, and then dividing by the number of quantities.

In this case, where the quantities are test scores and the target average is 85, our basic formula for the average will look like this:

$$\frac{\text{sum of the test scores}}{\text{number of test scores}} = 85$$

There are six test scores being averaged: the five already taken, plus the one that Mele is going to take. So we can plug 6 into the denominator:

$$\frac{\text{sum of the test scores}}{6} = 85$$

Now, what about the sum of the test scores—how do we express that? We know the first five test scores add up to 429, and the question tells us to use the variable s for the missing score. So the sum of the scores must be $s + 429$. When we plug that into the numerator of the fraction, we get this:

$$\frac{s + 429}{6} = 85$$

That's what choice (J) says, so (J) is correct.

Now let's talk about how we could approach this question by incorporating the answer choices into our analysis. Notice that choice (J), the correct answer, follows the common ACT pattern of incorporating all the most common elements from the set of answer choices:

- Three out of the five choices have $s + 429$ in the numerator, instead of s being added outside the fraction.
- Three out of the five choices have 6 in the denominator.
- Four choices are set equal to 85.

As I always say in these situations, it's important to keep in mind that (J) isn't guaranteed to be right just because it fits this common ACT pattern; sometimes we'll find that the answer choice that incorporates all the most common elements from the set of answer choices is actually the wrong answer. But answer choices that fit this pattern will often be correct, and seeing that an answer choice fits this pattern can help reassure us on test day that we've thought about the question correctly.

We could also use the similarities and differences among the answer choices to help us focus our thinking, if we weren't sure how to approach the question mathematically. By comparing the answer choices to one another, we can notice there are only three issues that need to be addressed in order for us to determine the correct answer. Here they are, in no particular order:

1. Whether the right-hand side of the equation should be 85 or 85/100.
2. Whether s should be outside of the fraction or added in to the numerator of the fraction.
3. Whether the denominator of the fraction should be 5 or 6.

Even if we don't feel confident doing the math in this question on our own, we can still think through each of these issues individually to help us figure out what the right answer should look like.

For the first issue, we can tell from reading the question that no mention is made of percentages, and the question specifically says that the average would be "exactly 85 points." That means that the expression for the average should be set to 85, not to 85/100. Again, the fact that the majority of answer choices have 85 rather than 85/100 on the right-hand side of the equation also strongly reinforces the idea that 85 is probably part of the correct answer.

When we think about the second issue, we might want to realize that s represents the score of another test that must be averaged; if we know that averaging involves adding things up and then dividing, then we know that s needs to be divided by something somehow. That means we'll want to choose an answer choice with s in the numerator, not one with *s* by itself. The fact that the majority of answer choices have *s* in the numerator of the average also strongly suggests that we're probably correct in our thinking.

To decide whether the denominator in the fraction should be 5 or 6, we need to think about what the denominator represents. In this case, it's related to the idea of averaging the scores—specifically, the denominator represents the stage in the averaging process where we take the sum and then divide it by the number of quantities that were added. So we're basically trying to figure out whether the sum being averaged is the sum of five things, or of six things. If we look carefully at the question, we see that it's talking about the average of "all 6 tests." So we need to divide by 6. Yet again, we see that most of the answer choices have 6 in the denominator, which strongly tends to support our conclusion that 6 is correct.

When we look at the answer choices, we see that only one option incorporates all three of the elements we've decided upon, and that option is (J), the correct answer.

So in this last approach, we're identifying the similarities and differences among the answer choices, and then using them to help us figure out which issues the question requires us to think about. Then we sort through those issues one at a time, and then we look for an answer choice that incorporates the elements we've decided on. This can be a very useful approach for questions that don't make sense to you at first, because it can help you gain a mental foothold on the question.

Now, I know it might seem like we've discussed this question a lot more than we needed to. But I really want to drive home the importance of incorporating the answer choices into your approach to each question, especially when the questions seem difficult to understand at first. These kinds of techniques can help you find very quick, simple solutions to questions that other test-takers will struggle with. There's a reason I keep repeating these ideas :)

Page 736, Question 19

This question basically asks about scientific notation. If you're familiar with scientific notation, you can tell pretty quickly that the correct answer is -4, choice (B). Alternatively, you could also enter this into a calculator and test the value for *n* from each answer choice to see which one results in the correct answer, but you'd have to be very careful about typing in the right numbers, and then be very careful about accurately counting up the resulting zeroes and decimal places.

Outside of those two approaches, the Red Book explanation on page 809 gives us a decent explanation of the underlying math, if you're not familiar with scientific notation or don't feel like using a calculator.

But the main reason I want to talk about this question is that it provides yet another example of a question that can be easily missed by someone who isn't paying careful attention, even if that person understands the concepts involved. When you see a question that involves a certain number of decimal places, or that involves anything else that requires careful counting, you need to make absolutely certain that you don't miscount—*especially* when the answer choices involve numbers that differ by one, as we see in this case. It would be very, very easy to miscount the four decimal places as three decimal places, and then choose (C) and miss the question for no good reason. It would also be possible to get confused about what the question is asking and choose one of the answer choices related to 7, because the number 0.0001056 has seven decimal places. Keep an eye out for these kinds of things, and don't let yourself be fooled!

Page 737, Question 22

The Red Book solution to this question, which appears on page 810 of the Red Book, reads like it was written by a lonely math professor trying to impress a date. There's absolutely no need to involve formal mathematical notation for sequences, because this is just a multiple-choice question on the ACT—it's not an actual math question that would require us to solve the problem on our own.

If I saw this question on test-day, I'd approach it in a much simpler way than the Red Book does. The question tells us that the angles of the triangle have degree measures that form a sequence, with a "common difference" of 10°. (In order to attack the question, we need to know that the phrase "common difference" refers to the difference between any two consecutive terms in the sequence—in other words, the question is telling us that the angles in the triangle form a series like 15°, 25°, 35°; or maybe 82°, 92°, 102°; or whatever.)

So we need to find a series of three angle measurements that increase by 10° each time and add up to 180°. The correct answer will be the first number in the series, because that's what the question asks for.

The easiest thing to do here is just to go through each answer and see if it works as the first number in a series like that.

(F) doesn't work because the series would be 80°, 90°, 100°, and that adds up to 270°, but the angles of a triangle must add up to 180°.

(G) doesn't work because the series would be 60°, 70°, 80°, which adds up to 210°, so those three values also can't be the angle measurements of a triangle.

(H) is the correct answer, because the series would be 50°, 60°, 70°, and those three numbers add up to 180°. Of course, as trained test-takers, we know we have to keep checking the other choices.

(J) is wrong because the sequence would be 40°, 50°, 60°, which only adds up to 150°.

(K) is wrong because the sequence would be 30°, 40°, 50°, which only adds up to 120°.

Remember that we don't have to approach ACT Math questions the way a teacher would make us approach them in school. Instead, keep in mind that the most effective approaches on the ACT are usually the least formal. Make it a habit to find the simplest, most direct solutions available.

Page 737, Question 26

Many untrained test-takers accept the ACT's claim that it tests what people learn in school. When those test-takers see a question like this, they assume they were supposed to have memorized a list of properties of even and odd numbers before attempting the test. When they realize that they've never memorized such a list, they tend to panic, and wrongly assume that they can't possibly answer the question correctly.

But we trained test-takers know that every ACT Math question can be worked out using relatively basic math principles and careful attention to detail. Instead of expecting to know all the properties of even numbers and odd numbers beforehand, we know that we can just test out each answer choice and figure out which one works. So let's do that.

The question asks which statement "is true." Since we want to know which statement "*is* true [emphasis mine]," not which one *might* be true or *could* be true under special circumstances, all we have to do is try to come up with one example to disprove each statement—if we can disprove the statement, then we can eliminate its answer choice. The correct answer will have a statement that's impossible to disprove. Let's take a look.

In the interest of keeping things simple, I'd probably start out by using the numbers 1 and 3 for examples with odd numbers, and 2 and 4 for examples with even numbers, since those are the first odd numbers and the first even numbers I thought of.

(F) says the sum of any two even numbers is odd. But 2 + 4 = 6, which is even, so this isn't true. So (F) is wrong.

(G) says the sum of any two odd numbers is odd. But 1 + 3 = 4, which is even, so this isn't true. So (G) is wrong.

(H) says the quotient of any two even numbers is odd. But 4/2 = 2, which is even, so this isn't true. So (H) is wrong.

(J) says the quotient of any two even numbers is even. 4/2 = 2, which is even, so this might be the right answer. As always, when we approach a question by trying to test out the answer choices, we have to check ALL the answer choices, to make sure that only one is valid—if we ended up plugging in a value that makes more than one answer choice seem to be valid, then we need to choose another to value to test until only one answer choice is shown to be valid for all tested values.

(K) says the product of any two odd numbers is odd. 1 * 3 = 3, which is odd, so this might be the right answer, too.

At this point, we see that (J) and (K) both passed our initial test. We know that there can only be one correct answer for every ACT question, so that means we must have done something wrong. Since our approach to the question involved creating examples with specific numbers that we chose at random, the problem probably comes from the fact that we accidentally chose numbers with abnormal properties relative to the answer choices. If we pick different numbers and re-test, we'll probably find that only one of the answer choices still holds true.

So let's do that. I'll pick 4 and 6 for my next pair of even numbers, and 3 and 5 for my next pair of odd numbers.

If we retest (J), we see that 6/4 = 1.5, which isn't even an integer, so it's neither odd nor even—which means it's not even, and (J) can't be the right answer.

If we retest (K), we see that 3 * 5 = 15, which is odd, just as (K) says. So (K) still holds up, and it must be the correct answer, since we've found examples that disprove all the other answer choices.

Let this solution remind you of the importance of testing EVERY answer choice if you decide to approach a question by eliminating answer choices!

Page 739, Question 30

This is another ACT question with a diagram that seems to be to scale—notice that the father's height does seem to be about 50% bigger than the son's height, and the horizontal line with a distance of 120 does seem to be a bit more than twice as long as the line representing the son's height. As trained test-takers, we know that some ACT questions with scaled diagrams are written so that only one of the answer choices is remotely possible if we just eyeball the relative dimensions of the figure. So we should check to see if this is one of those questions.

Sure enough, it is! We're asked to find the distance between the two people, and we can see that the distance is a little bit less than the height of the son. Since the son's height is 50, we need an answer choice that's a little bit less than 50. Only one choice is in that range, and it's choice (G). So (G) must be correct.

We might be tempted by choice (F), but (F) can only be correct if the distance between the two people is exactly half the height of the son. If we look closely, we see the distance is greater than that. So (F) can't be right.

Of course, we can also approach this question using actual math if we feel like it. For more on that, see the Red Book's solution on page 812. But notice that the mathematical solution involves finding the distance from the son to the end of the father's shadow, and that distance is 80—which is one of the wrong answers, choice (K). We can easily imagine that many test-takers who approached this question with the proper math might forget which distance they were asked for, and choose (K) even though they understood all the geometry involved. As we've seen many times, then, it can actually be more dangerous sometimes to approach an ACT Math question using actual math! If we just eyeball the diagram and take advantage of the scale, we're left to conclude that only (G) could possibly be correct—but if we try to approach the question mathematically, we might accidentally get tricked into picking choice (K) if we're not careful.

To be clear, I'm not saying that it's necessarily wrong to use formal math on the ACT. If you use it correctly and pay strict attention to what's going on in each question, you can answer every question correctly, of course. I'm just trying to make the point that formal math isn't the only way to go, and is arguably not the best way to go, at least for some questions. High-scoring test-takers use the most expedient approach they can think of for each question they run across.

Page 739, Question 31

The Red Book's solution for this question does a decent job of explaining the straightforward mathematical approach to the question, as we'd normally expect. The question can be approached either with the Pythagorean Theorem or with the distance formula (which is really just a modified version of the Pythagorean Theorem).

But there's another way to approach this question, as is often the case on the ACT Math section. If we consider the answer choices in the context of the setup, we can tell pretty quickly that three answer choices are clearly too small, one is clearly too large, and the only remaining choice must be correct.

The horizontal separation between the two points is 8 units, because the x-coordinate of one point is -3 and the x-coordinate of the other point is 5, and 5 − -3 is 8.

The vertical separation between the two points is 7 units, because the y-coordinate of one point is -2 and the y-coordinate of the other point is 5, and 5 − -2 is 7.

The straight-line distance between the two points must be less than the sum of the horizontal and vertical separations, but more than either the horizontal or vertical separation itself. So the straight-line distance must be bigger than 8, but smaller than 15.

If we look at the answer choices, we can see right away that 5 is too small (because it's less than 8), and 15 is too big (because the distance must be less than 15, since 7 + 8 = 15). So that gets rid of choices (D) and (E).

But what about choices (A), (B), and (C)?

If we estimate the value of the expression in choice (A), we see it must be between 3 and 4, since $\sqrt{9}$ is 3 and $\sqrt{16}$ is 4, and $\sqrt{13}$ is between those two values. That's too small, so (A) must be wrong.

If we estimate the value of (B), we see that it's also between 3 and 4, because $\sqrt{15}$ is also between $\sqrt{9}$ and $\sqrt{16}$. So (B) is also too small.

If we estimate the value of (C), we see that it's between 10 and 11, because $\sqrt{100}$ is 10 and $\sqrt{121}$ is 11, and $\sqrt{113}$ is between those two values. A value between 10 and 11 would be larger than 8 and smaller than 15, so it's the only answer choice that satisfies the requirement of being longer than the individual horizontal and vertical separations and shorter than the sum of those two separations. That means it's the only choice that could possibly be correct—and it is the correct answer.

Now let's consider some of the wrong answers. Choice (E) is a wrong answer that tries to take advantage of people who misapply the distance formula or the Pythagorean Theorem, and end up just adding the horizontal and vertical separations together. Choice (B) is the square root of choice (E), for people who make a different mistake in the formal mathematical approach, and simply take the square root of the sum of 8 and 7, instead of the square root of the sum of 8^2 and 7^2.

The ACT frequently writes questions with sets of answer choices like this, and I can only assume the test does this so repeatedly because it wants to reward test-takers like us who pay attention. If we can occasionally notice and take advantage of these built-in shortcuts, we can save ourselves a lot of time and frustration.

Page 739, Question 34

The Red Book explanation for this question, which appears on page 814, relies on an understanding of algebra and fractions. But many test-takers won't be able to find the answer to this question quickly enough if they try to use a formal approach like the one recommended by the Red Book, because they won't be able to reverse the process of adding two algebraic fractions.

An easier approach for many test-takers would be to choose a number to plug in for x, and then evaluate the original fraction and each answer choice using that value for x. Whichever answer choice matches the value of the original fraction must be the correct answer.

For this question, I would probably choose $x = 5$, because 5 is a small number that doesn't appear anywhere in the question, so it's unlikely to have any special properties relative to this question. Of course, we could choose to resolve these expressions by doing our own work, or we could plug them into a calculator (being very careful about not hitting the wrong buttons, of course). I'll show the work here, but if you want to use a calculator instead, there's nothing wrong with that.

If we plug 5 in for the original fraction, we get this:

$\dfrac{2x+3}{12x^2}$ (original fraction)

$\dfrac{2(5)+3}{12(5)^2}$ (substitute $x = 5$)

$\dfrac{10+3}{12(25)}$ (simplify 2(5) in the numerator and 5^2 in the denominator)

$\dfrac{13}{300}$ (add the terms in the numerator and multiply the terms in the denominator)

(If we plug $\dfrac{2(5)+3}{12(5)^2}$ into a calculator, we get 0.04333… . So, if we're solving the question with a calculator, our goal would be to look for an answer choice that also equals 0.04333… when we plug in that $x = 5$.)

Now we just plug in $x = 5$ for each answer choice, and see which one comes out to $\dfrac{13}{300}$ or 0.04333… .

(F) doesn't work because $\dfrac{1}{3}$ isn't equal to $\dfrac{13}{300}$ or 0.04333… .

(G) is wrong because it would give us $\dfrac{1}{5}$, which isn't equal to $\dfrac{13}{300}$ or 0.04333… .

(H) is wrong because it would give us $\dfrac{1}{10}$, which isn't equal to $\dfrac{13}{300}$ or 0.04333… .

(J) is wrong because it would give us $\dfrac{6}{50}$, or $\dfrac{3}{25}$, which isn't equal to $\dfrac{13}{300}$ or 0.04333… .

(K) would give us $\dfrac{1}{30} + \dfrac{1}{100}$ if we worked it out by hand. Is that equal to $\dfrac{13}{300}$? There are two ways we could figure that out. One way would be to recognize that the least common denominator for those two fractions is 300, and then convert them both and add them together—but we just said that we're trying to approach this question from the standpoint of a test-taker who isn't comfortable with manipulating fractions. So let's try another approach. We could convert both of these fractions to decimal expressions with our calculator, and then add them and compare them to the decimal equivalent of $\dfrac{13}{300}$. The decimal equivalent of $\dfrac{1}{30}$ is 0.03333… . The decimal equivalent of $\dfrac{1}{100}$ is 0.01. If we add them together, we get 0.04333… . The decimal equivalent of $\dfrac{13}{300}$ is also 0.04333… . So we can tell that (K) is actually equivalent to the original expression, which means it's the correct answer. (Of course, if we'd just started out by using a calculator to evaluate this answer choice, we would have seen that it was equal to 0.04333… right away.)

To be clear, I'm not suggesting that there's anything wrong with using formal math on this question, or on any ACT Math question. My goal is simply to demonstrate once more that the ACT's multiple-choice design allows us to take advantage of non-formalized approaches to a lot of the questions if we're not comfortable with the formal approach, or if we wouldn't be able to devise a formal approach to the question in the limited time provided by the ACT. Remember that we can always find an alternative solution to questions on the ACT Math section!

Page 740, Question 36

The Red Book's solution to this question appears on page 815. It takes the approach of sub-dividing the cake into 8 rows and 6 columns, for a total of 48 pieces. That approach is absolutely valid, but there are a couple of other mathematical approaches we could follow. Instead of calculating the number of rows and columns that the principal cuts the cake into, we could divide the area of the top of the cake by the area of the top of one slice. We could also divide the *volume* of the entire cake by the *volume* of one slice.

For the first approach, we'd find that the cake itself is 16 inches wide and 12 inches long, which means its area is 16 * 12, or 192. Each slice of cake is 2 inches wide and 2 inches long, so the top of each slice of cake has an area of 4.

Dividing the area of the top of the cake by the area of the top of each slice gives us this:

192/4 = 48

So our answer is 48 slices, choice (J).

We could reach the same conclusion if we divided the volume of the cake by the volume of each slice. The volume of the cake is 16 * 12 * 3, or 576. The volume of each slice is 2 * 2 * 3, or 12. Dividing 576 by 12 also gives us 48 as an answer.

One thing we have to make sure NOT to do is to use the volume of the cake and the area of the slice, or the area of the cake and the volume of the slice. If we accidentally divided the *area* of the top of the cake by the *volume* of the slice, we'd get this:

192/12 = 16

16 is choice (F), an incorrect answer.

(K) is what you would get if you misread the question and thought the area of each slice was 2, instead of 2 * 2.

As usual, we see that this ACT Math question can be attacked in a variety of ways, but they all require us to pay careful attention to detail as we do the appropriate basic calculations.

Page 743, Question 44

The Red Book's solution for this question on page 818 isn't bad, but there are a couple of other considerations I'd like to point out. As you might have guessed by now, they have to do with the set of answer choices to this question, and what those choices can tell us trained test-takers about the things we need to look out for when we choose our answer.

The high degree of similarity among the answer choices is a very strong signal from the test that we need to make sure we read the prompt *and* the answer choices extremely carefully, because the ACT clearly thinks it can fool us into making some small mistake and then accidentally choosing a wrong answer that's very similar to the right answer. As the Red Book explains, the correct answer is (G), but we can probably imagine that many test-takers will accidentally find the perimeter of the entire figure in the diagram, which is (J). Some might also find the perimeter of the quadrilateral AZBC, which is represented by choice (F). Each of these mistakes is quite minor, but each can be easily made by a test-taker who's in a hurry or who misreads the question, and each will lead directly to a wrong answer. When a trained test-taker sees a situation like this, she knows to be even more careful than usual about double-checking that she hasn't made a careless error.

The high degree of similarity also suggests that the correct answer is likely to follow the pattern of incorporating all the most common elements from the set of answer choices. In a way, we could argue that (G) does, indeed, follow that pattern. The most common version of the a term is just a by itself, with no coefficient. The most common versions of the b term are $2b$ and $3b$, which each appear twice in the set of answer choices. The most common version of the c term is $2c$. As it turns out, only one answer choice includes a by itself, $2c$, and either $2b$ or $3b$, and that choice is (G), the correct answer. Seeing this should reassure us that we've probably thought about the question correctly.

These may seem like unnecessary details, but they're actually quite useful things to notice, because they help us make sure we haven't made a careless error and thrown points away for no reason. If you want to maximize your score, these are the kinds of things you have to incorporate into your routine.

Page 744, Question 48

I expect that the Red Book's explanation for this question (which appears on page 819) will only make sense to people who already understand the question, which means it's not a very helpful explanation. If you've ever studied the ways that parabolas can be shifted around a coordinate plane through changes made "inside the parentheses" or "outside the parentheses," perhaps in a pre-calculus class or an algebra class, then the Red Book's explanation may jog your memory. Basically, adding a positive number inside the parentheses shifts the graph to the left, while adding a negative number inside the parentheses shifts it to the right; adding a positive number outside the parentheses shifts the graph up, while adding a negative number outside the parentheses shifts the graph down. If that doesn't make sense to you, or if you just don't like remembering it, there's an easier way to approach a question like this:

Just graph the answer choices on your calculator.

If you do that, you'll see that only choice (K) results in a parabola with a vertex at (3,-2), which is what the question asked us to find. So (K) must be correct.

There's even another way you could approach this question, and it doesn't require you to remember anything specifically related to parabolas, or to use a graphing calculator. This other kind of approach involves thinking about the vertex of the new parabola, and then finding an answer choice that would have the correct vertex by plugging values in for x and checking them. Let's see how that would work.

The problem describes a graph of the parabola $y = x^2$. It also shows us the graph itself, with a vertex clearly at (0,0). Then it asks us to find the equation of this parabola if it were moved 3 units to the right and 2 units down.

If this graph were moved 3 units to the right, and 2 units down, where would that vertex go? Well, right now it's at (0,0). If the x value moved three units to the right, it would be 3. If the y value moved 2 units down, it would be -2.

So the new graph must have a vertex at (3,-2). That means that if we plug in an x value of 3 to the correct equation, we should get a y value of -2. Let's give it a shot and see what happens.

(F) is $y = (x + 3)^2 + 2$. If we plug in 3 for x we get $(3 + 3)^2 + 2$, which is $6^2 + 2$, which is 38, and not -2. This one can't be right.

(G) is $y = (x + 3)^2 - 2$. If we plug in 3 for x we get $(3 + 3)^2 - 2$, which is $6^2 - 2$, which is 34, and not -2. This one also can't be right.

(H) is $y = (x - 2)^2 + 3$. If we plug in 3 for x we get $(3 - 2)^2 + 3$, which is $1^2 + 3$, which is 4. Wrong again.

(J) is $y = (x - 3)^2 + 2$. If we plug in 3 for x we get $(3 - 3)^2 + 2$, which is $0 + 2$, or 2. This isn't what we're looking for.

(K) is $y = (x - 3)^2 - 2$. If we plug in 3 for x we get $(3 - 3)^2 - 2$, which is $0 - 2$, or -2. That means this graph has a point at (3,-2). Since it's the only answer choice that goes through (3,-2), we know this must be the correct answer.

Let me point out something very important, though. It's important to realize that (K) isn't correct just because it goes through (3,-2)! An infinite number of parabolas also go through that point, and they wouldn't all be valid answers to this question. Instead, it was just that the correct graph would have to go through that point, and only one answer choice happens to do that. Since we know (K) is the only choice that satisfies a condition that the correct answer must satisfy, we know that (K) must be right.

If we had found that more than one answer choice went through the point (3,-2), then we'd need to test another point as well, or else attack the question in a different way. But it turned out that wasn't necessary here. The ACT could have included more than one answer choice whose graph ran through (3,-2), but it didn't. The fact that the ACT repeatedly makes questions vulnerable to these kinds of approaches strongly indicates that the test is deliberately designed to reward trained test-takers who think critically about the best ways to attack each question. Remember that you aren't bound by the limits of formal math when you take the ACT, especially when you see a problem and aren't sure how to solve it right away.

Page 745, Question 51

This is a great example of an ACT Math question that bears absolutely no similarity to anything that most test-takers would encounter in high school or college. The ACT sometimes likes to ask us about the logical implications of certain statements. While there are formal rules for these situations, most people do better with these questions if they just go through each statement and evaluate it on its own, without trying to remember any formal logical rules.

(By the way, as the Red Book points out on page 820, every true statement of the form "If x, then y," has a variant that's also true, and takes the form "If not y, then not x." This second form is called the "contrapositive" of the first form. You don't need to know that, really, but, if you want to, there it is :) .)

(A) says, "If a cat is female, then it is tricolor." But the original statement doesn't say that all female cats have to be tricolor, it just says that tricolors have to be female. So you could have a female cat that's only one color, and it wouldn't contradict the original statement. So this answer choice is wrong.

(B) says, "If a cat is not a female, then it is tricolor." This contradicts the original statement directly, because this statement describes a non-female tricolor cat, while the original statement says a tricolor cat must be female. So this answer choice is wrong, too.

(C) says, "If a cat is not a female, then it is not tricolor." In other words, if you know a cat is not female, you know it must not be tricolor, because all tricolor cats are female, as we are told in the original statement. This is the correct answer. Of course, we have to check out every answer choice to help make sure we haven't misread or misunderstood anything.

(D) says, "If a cat is not tricolor, then it is a female." But we aren't given any information about non-tricolor cats; they could be male or female without contradicting the original statement. This one doesn't have to be true, so it's wrong.

(E) says, "If a cat is not tricolor, then it is not a female." But the original statement never said that non-tricolor cats can't be female, it just said that all tricolor cats *are* females. This one doesn't have to be true, so it's not right.

So we know that (C) is the correct answer. Notice the importance of the part of the question that says, "would also *have* to be true [emphasis mine]." This is especially important in this question because some of the wrong answers *could* be true, but don't necessarily *have* to be true. Only (C) has to be true if the original statement is true.

As always, we see the importance of careful reading and careful thinking on the ACT Math section.

Page 747, Question 60

This question looks very intimidating to most test-takers, largely because it asks us to do something most of us have probably never seen before. The idea of applying a function to a pair of values separated by commas is something that most high school and college math classes don't address.

But, as trained test-takers, we need to remember the importance of reading carefully and trying to work through the question without getting overwhelmed by parts of the question that might seem odd.

We're told that $f(a, b) = b^2 - a$. Then we're asked to find $f((x^2 + y^2),(x - y))$.

There are two main ways we can approach something like this, as usual. One is to use a strict algebraic approach, as the Red Book solution does on page 824. The other approach is simply to pick a couple of numbers for x and y and plug them into the original expression and each answer choice, and see which answer choice matches the original expression after we do that. Most test-takers who are initially confused by this question will find the second approach easier, but let's take a look at both, starting with the algebraic approach.

We can see that the expression corresponding to a in the original function will be $(x^2 + y^2)$, and the expression corresponding to b in the original function will be $(x - y)$. Now we need to plug that in to $b^2 - a$. That gives us this:

$(x - y)^2 - (x^2 + y^2)$

So let's work it out algebraically:

$x^2 - 2xy + y^2 - (x^2 + y^2)$	(FOIL expression on the left)
$x^2 - 2xy + y^2 - x^2 - y^2$	(distribute -1 to parenthetical expression on the right)
$-2xy$	(combine like terms; x^2 terms and y^2 terms cancel out)

So the correct answer is choice (K), the expression $-2xy$.

There are a number of mistakes you could make here that would lead you to the other answer choices. Some common ones include FOILing out $(x - y)^2$ incorrectly, and failing to distribute the negative sign to y^2. These types of mistakes are one reason that the pure algebraic approach might not be the best idea for test-takers who are uncomfortable with algebra. Even if we do feel comfortable with algebra, though, it's still very important to make sure we proceed with great caution and don't make any mistakes, because we can be sure the ACT will position wrong answer choices to trap us if we do.

Now let's talk about the more straightforward approach, which involves choosing numbers for x and y and then plugging them into each expression in the question to see which answer choice has the same value as the original expression. This is a strategy that we can use pretty frequently on the ACT Math section, and by now you've seen us do it a lot in this Black Book.

The question doesn't place any restrictions on x or y, but we know that we should choose values for x and y that are unlikely to exhibit any abnormal properties relative to the question. That usually means avoiding 0 and 1, and any numbers in the question or the answer choices. So let's choose 3 for x and 4 for y. (If it turns out that we've chosen badly, and more than one answer choice seems to be equivalent to the original expression, then we can just re-choose and re-test until only one choice remains equivalent. So it's not the end of the world if we've chosen bad numbers—it just might cost us some extra time.)

Substituting 3 for x and 4 for y gives us this for the original expression:

$f((3^2 + 4^2),(3 - 4))$	(substitute $x = 3$ and $y = 4$)
$f((9 + 16),(-1))$	(square x and y terms in the first expression, simplify the second expression)
$f((25),(-1))$	(simplify the first expression)

 Go to www.ACTprepVideos.com.

Now we take these values and plug them into the $f(a, b)$ function. Our a is 25, and our b is -1:

$f(a, b) = b^2 - a$	(begin with original function)
$f(25, -1) = (-1)^2 - 25$	(substitute $a = 25$ and $b = -1$)
$f(25, -1) = 1 - 25$	(square -1)
$f(25, -1) = -24$	(simplify)

So $f((x^2 + y^2), (x - y)) = -24$ when $x = 3$ and $y = 4$.

Now we plug those x and y values into each answer choice, and see which one results in a value of -24:

(F) gives us $2(4)^2$, which is the same as 2(16), which is 32. So it's wrong.

(G) is 0, which isn't the same thing as -24, so it's wrong, too.

(H) is just the opposite of (F), so it'll work out to be -32, which isn't the same thing as -24.

(J) works out to be $-2(3)(4) + 2(4)^2$, which is the same thing as -24 + 32, which is 8. So this choice is also wrong.

(K) is -2(3)(4), which is -24. So we see once more that (K) is correct.

As always, I'm not endorsing one approach over the other. Some test-takers will prefer the algebraic approach, and some will prefer to pick numbers and plug them into each expression. The important thing to keep in mind is that the multiple-choice nature of the ACT often makes it possible to approach an ACT Math question in ways that wouldn't be possible in a math class. Keep this in mind the next time an ACT Math question has you momentarily stumped!

Conclusion

Whew! We just looked at a lot of questions together. You'll notice that in all of the work we just did, there weren't many particularly challenging mathematical concepts, or advanced math formulas, or intimidating calculations. Also, any trigonometry that came up actually ended up being fairly basic.

In general, the hard part of these questions was just figuring out what the test was actually asking us to do—and then making sure we carried out our solutions in the most efficient and effective ways possible, taking care not to make small mistakes.

Using The Question Explanations In *The Real ACT Prep Guide, 3rd Edition*

The ACT Math question solutions in your copy of *The Real ACT Prep Guide, 3rd Edition*, will typically show you how your math teacher might approach a question. This can be somewhat helpful, in that it can point out some concepts you might need to use when solving a problem, but you'll probably find that the Red Book's explanations are often unnecessarily long and technical.

The Red Book may also tell you which errors would lead to some of the wrong answer choices, but most wrong answer choices won't be fully explained.

If you do find yourself consulting the Red Book's explanations for its questions, try to remember to also keep your eyes open for more efficient solutions that exploit the ACT's weaknesses, like the solutions we just came up with in these Black Book walkthroughs.

Video Demonstrations

If you'd like to see videos of some sample solutions like the ones in this book, please visit www.ACTprepVideos.com, where a selection of free videos is available for readers of this book.

ACT Math Quick Summary

This is a one-page summary of the major relevant concepts. Use it to evaluate your comprehension or jog your memory. For a more in-depth treatment of these ideas, see the rest of the section.

The Big Secret: The ACT Math section tests simple math ideas in unusual ways. We need to get used to reading the problems carefully so we know what exactly we're being asked to do.

The concepts tested in ACT Math questions are limited. All of those concepts can be found in the ACT Math Toolbox in this book.

ACT Math questions can all be done in 30 seconds or less. (Of course, that doesn't mean you'll be wrong if you take longer.) Remember that the most efficient solutions to ACT Math questions often involve non-traditional techniques like considering the scale of a diagram or paying attention to answer choices from the beginning.

Wrong answer choices contain valuable information. They're just as important as any other part of the question, so read them carefully. Think about concepts they might involve, and how quantities in different answer choices might relate to one another.

Here are some of the most common answer choice patterns you'll see:

- A wrong answer choice contains an "On The Way" answer that's involved in the solution to the problem, but isn't the solution itself.
- A wrong answer choice is the result of an easy mistake a test-taker might make when solving the problem.
- A wrong answer choice is half or double the correct answer choice.
- A correct answer choice has characteristics that are similar to most of the wrong answer choices.
- A correct answer choice is part of a series with other answer choices.

Here's an abbreviated version of the general ACT Math process, or "Math Path," recommended for use against challenging questions:

- Words: Read the question carefully and consider the specific words that are used.
- Answer Choices: Read and consider the answer choices. Note concepts and relationships.
- Math Domains: Think about what areas of math are involved based on characteristics of the question and the answer choices.
- Speed: Think of a solution to the problem that will take 30 seconds or less. The best ACT Math solutions are often unorthodox. They might involve testing the answer choices, graphing something on a calculator, observing patterns in the answer choices, and so on.
- Solve: Do the solution you came up with in the previous step.
- Check: Check your work, preferably by trying to identify the ACT's reasoning behind the wrong answer choices. Remember that high-scorers can't typically avoid all mistakes; they're just able to catch their mistakes after they make them.

Go back through the ACT Math walkthroughs and follow along in your copy of the Red Book to see demonstrations of these ideas.

ACT Science

"Science is the belief in the ignorance of experts."
- Richard Feynman

Overview And Important Reminders For ACT Science

A lot of people worry about the ACT Science section—they think it makes the ACT more like an advanced high school test than like a regular standardized test, because they think it really requires a wide range of subject-matter knowledge.

The reality, of course, is very different. Just as you need relatively basic reading and math skills to beat the ACT Reading and ACT Math sections, you only need basic scientific knowledge for the ACT Science section—and even that basic level of knowledge only comes into play on a small handful of questions on any given ACT (typically fewer than 4 questions). All of the other questions on the section (roughly 37 to 39 of them, depending on the day) require only careful reading of text, charts, graphs, and diagrams with a little bit of simple math occasionally thrown in.

In other words, the vast majority of ACT Science questions require no scientific knowledge at all, even though they sometimes talk about obscure areas of science; they're just reading comprehension questions that involve charts, graphs, and diagrams.

If you think about it, it would be very difficult to make a meaningful standardized science test that used any challenging scientific subject matter, because students all across the country take different science classes taught by many different teachers. So ACT Science can only test very basic scientific skills or knowledge that any high school student could be expected to have, regardless of which specific types of science classes that student had taken. That's the only way to ensure that as many test-takers as possible have the potential to score extremely well on the section. (This is the same issue we identified when we discussed the design of the ACT Math section.)

The Big Secret Of ACT Science

For the large majority of the questions, all the information you need to answer the question will be right there on the page, just like on the Reading section. You'll see that the ACT tries to mix in as much scientific terminology as it can, often from sciences most students would never study in high school, in order to make you panic because you're unfamiliar with the material. But you never actually have to know any of those terms, except to match them up with phrases on a related chart and/or graph.

There's even more to it than that, though—being scientifically knowledgeable can actually be harmful to your score on the ACT Science section in some instances, if you don't know what the ACT Science section actually rewards.

Why is that?

The reason most people struggle with any area of the ACT is that they're approaching it the wrong way. Test-takers who prepare for the ACT Math section by studying advanced trig will have trouble seeing the simple math at the core of any ACT Math section. People who prepare for ACT Reading by really trying to develop their skills in literary analysis and note-taking won't realize that all they have to do is just find the answer choices that restate the passages exactly. Similarly, people who get ready for ACT Science by studying actual science might try to apply some scientific knowledge or bias on questions where it seems relevant, instead of just realizing that the information they need to answer the question is right there on the page, staring them in the face. Then they run the risk of misremembering or misapplying what they think they know, instead of simply reading the correct answer off the page.

So please, by all means, avoid studying actual science in preparation for the ACT Science section. Instead, you should learn the test-taking techniques in this Black Book, see them in action in the question walkthroughs, and practice them against real ACT Science questions from the Red Book, just as you would with any other question type.

Remember that this section of the test is like any other. It must test simple concepts in order to be useful for colleges and remain standardized, but it has to make those questions *appear* as complex and difficult as possible. So instead of rewarding a vast expanse of scientific knowledge, the ACT Science section actually rewards flexible thinking and attention to detail, just like the rest of the ACT.

The way the ACT tries to make Science questions complex is by filling them with a lot of scientific terminology and odd-looking diagrams, often from sciences like ecology and astronomy—things most high school students never get to study. The test will show you complex-looking diagrams you've never seen before, and ask about hypothetical experiments you've never heard of before.

The goal of all of this is to make you think, "Oh, no! I've never studied this stuff before. I bet every other kid in this room has done this experiment, or built this model, and I'm the only one who's sitting here, totally lost, feeling like an idiot. I'll never get into college at this rate . . ."

That might be a slight exaggeration, but it's basically an accurate depiction of what goes through a lot of untrained test-takers' minds. The ACT wants you to panic and feel unprepared, and it doesn't want you to realize that everybody else in the room feels just as lost as you do, because no high school student has previous experience with all the concepts in an ACT Science section.

For a quick example, just look at page 188 of the Red Book, at the very first paragraph of the first Science passage of the first practice test in that book:

> *Flood basalt plateaus* are large areas of Earth's surface covered with thick
> hardened lava. It has been hypothesized that the huge outpourings of lava that
> formed these plateaus were produced by *plumes* of molten material . . .
> (emphasis in original)

How many high school students (or college students, for that matter) have ever heard of flood basalt plateaus? Almost none. But it doesn't matter, because the questions in this passage don't require you to understand what the plateaus are or why anyone cares about them; the questions simply reward you for reading information right out of the passage.

Why Some People Struggle With ACT Science

At this point, you might be wondering why so many people struggle with the ACT Science section, if it just requires us to read carefully and find information in charts and diagrams.

Here's the answer: people struggle because they're not used to seeing unfamiliar material on tests.

In school, a test covers the material you've already been studying for weeks. On the ACT, you'll be asked questions about all kinds of scientific areas you've never studied before, and maybe never even heard of—ecology, astronomy, nuclear chemistry, meteorology, and who knows what else. Most untrained test-takers see these unfamiliar topics and assume they're unprepared for the ACT Science section.

But, again, the ACT Science section doesn't expect the average high school senior to be an expert in ecology, astronomy, nuclear chemistry, meteorology, or any other scientific specialization. The material you need to answer the questions will be right in front of you . . . even if it uses terms and units you've never seen before. Let's talk about that.

Dealing with strange terms and units

You must remember that any new concept you encounter on the ACT Science section will fall into one of three groups:

1. It will be explained in the text.
2. It won't be explained, and it won't be relevant to answering any of the questions.
3. It won't be explained, but you'll be able to match a concept in a question with the same concept somewhere in the passage, like on a chart or a graph.

The first two situations are probably clear enough, but let's elaborate on the third one for a moment—the idea that a concept might not really be explained, but that you can still work around it by matching up a concept in a question with the same concept in a chart or something.

Imagine we see this imaginary question on the ACT:

"According to Table 1, which group has the most blarg groupings?"

(Of course, that's not a real ACT question. The world isn't ready to learn the truth about blarg groupings . . .)

We don't know what blarg groupings are. But then we notice that Table 1 has this information:

Table 1: Grouping values (in blargs)

Group A	14
Group B	7
Group C	23
Group D	29

The answer to the made-up question would be Group D, because the table shows that Group D has 29 blarg groupings, which is more than any other group.

So the question is actually very straightforward if we just ignore the fact that we don't know what blargs are. Even though you've never heard the term "blarg" before in your life, and even though you'll probably never hear it again, the answer is completely clear, based on the information in front of you.

On the Science section of the ACT, you will definitely have to deal with concepts you've never heard of before. Expect it. Welcome it. The important thing isn't to know a lot of science in advance; the important thing is just to get used to reading carefully and finding the relevant parts of texts, charts, graphs, and figures. In the next pages, we'll learn more about how to do that, and then we'll see examples of it in action when we do our walkthroughs.

Unwritten Test Design Rules Of ACT Science

By now it should be clear that the ACT Science section has little in common with the kind of science tests you might take in a normal high school class. The majority of this section of the test comes down to being able to read questions carefully, then being able to find the information you need to answer questions in the text, charts, graphs, and so on that make up the passage you're working on.

These are the rules you need to remember as you train for the ACT Science section.

ACT Science Rule 1: Every Part Of The Answer Is Almost Always On The Page In Front Of You

Each ACT Science section will have approximately 3 questions (or fewer) that test actual scientific knowledge. (That knowledge is always relatively basic, by the way—we'll talk about that in a little bit.) For the rest of the 40 questions, everything you need to find the answer will be on the page in front of you—either in the text, in a chart or graph or diagram, or even in the question itself (or in some combination of those things).

The ACT never requires you to know about obscure branches of science; the necessary information related to those branches of science will always be somewhere on the page.

ACT Science Rule 2: Labels Are Important

You'll often need to find information on a chart, graph, or table. Get used to identifying the labels on these kinds of figures and matching them up to the words and phrases in the question and answer choices to find the information you need. Look for labels on the top, bottom, left, and right sides of graphs and diagrams, as well as within the graphs and diagrams themselves. We'll see examples of this throughout the walkthroughs in a few pages. (This might sound like a very obvious piece of advice, but you'd be surprised how often test-takers mistakenly think they can't answer a question because they failed to locate a label on an axis of a graph or something.)

ACT Science Rule 3: Be Sure To Use The Right Data

Most questions will require you to look somewhere in the passage for some kind of information. *Make sure you're looking in the right place.* There may be more than one experiment, or table, or chart, or graph in a given passage, and they often use similar (or even identical) labels for their data.

So when you refer back to a figure or table in the passage, make sure the one you check is actually the one the question is asking about. Again, I know this might sound kind of obvious, but we have to remember that one of the ACT's most effective tactics, on any section, is to give untrained test-takers the opportunity to make small, simple mistakes. As trained test-takers, we have to make ourselves look out for those small mistakes at all times. On the Science section, accidentally looking at the wrong piece of data is one of the easiest ways to fall for a wrong answer.

ACT Science Rule 4: Don't Get Intimidated By Vocabulary

The ACT loves to try to intimidate untrained test-takers with scientific vocabulary that sounds advanced.

Think about it. In school, any time we see a strange word in a science class, we have a teacher there to tell us what it means. We aren't used to reading a strange scientific term and having to figure it out on our own or just work around it. The ACT knows this, and it will intentionally make very straightforward questions seem intimidating simply by sticking in scary, unfamiliar words and phrases, like "stratopause" and "flood basalt plateau."

Don't let this throw you. Remember our hypothetical discussion of blarg groupings from a couple of pages ago. In the walkthroughs, you'll see several examples of effective solutions to ACT Science questions that involve working around unknown terms and concepts.

ACT Science Rule 5: You'll Need To Know BASIC Science A Few Times Per Test

There will be a few times per test when actual scientific knowledge will come into play. This could happen as many as four or five times in the whole 40-question section, but probably one to three times. This scientific knowledge will be very basic—something like knowing which elements water is made up of, or where a cell membrane is located (the answers are "hydrogen and oxygen" and "on the outside of a cell," respectively).

But these questions often won't seem so basic on the surface! The ACT will try to dress them up in complicated sentences to make them sound more advanced and specialized than they really are. We'll talk about this in more detail later, and you'll see a few examples in the ACT Science walkthroughs.

And remember—even if you somehow mess up every single one of these basic knowledge questions, you can typically still score above a 30 on the Science section, depending on the day, if you pick up all the questions that don't require any outside knowledge. (In fact, you can often score a 35 or 36 on the Science section if you miss every basic knowledge question but get all the other questions right.)

How To Read Passages On The ACT Science Section

Just as a lot of people ask about the best way to read ACT Reading passages, a lot of people ask about the best way to read ACT Science passages—and the answer is basically the same. There's no single "best" way to do this. There are three basic ways to approach it, and you should try each one in practice to see what works best for you.

Option 1: Read the whole passage first.

This is probably the most popular approach with untrained test-takers. In this method, you just read the entire passage before looking at the questions. When you get to any tables or figures, you don't need to read all of the values, but you should take note of any labels on axes, headings on columns, and so on. This way, you'll know which parts of the passage to refer back to when a question asks about a specific type of data.

Don't bother trying to grasp everything you read if you take this approach. The point isn't to understand everything that's going on in the passage—the point is just to see generally which parts of the passage talk about particular concepts, so you'll know where to look in more detail when a question asks about those concepts.

Option 2: Skip the passage and go right to the questions.

In this method, you don't even look at the passage first; you just start in with the first question. This method is a little easier with ACT Science passages than it is with ACT Reading passages, because ACT Science questions tend to refer to specific parts of the passage more clearly.

For example, imagine that a question says something like, "In Figure 1, what was the regromination index of thappentonium?" (I know that "regromination" and "thappentonium" aren't actually words. I'm using them in my imaginary question to demonstrate once more how we can often work around unknown words on the ACT Science section.) To answer this imaginary question without reading the passage first, we'd just find Figure 1, find a column with a label like "Regromination Index," and then locate the value for thappentonium. At no point in that process would we need to know anything about the rest of the passage. Then we could just repeat the process with the next question—we'd identify the key terms and values in the question, and then locate those terms and/or values in the passage and find the answer.

You'll see several examples of this idea in the walkthroughs.

Some people find this approach helpful because they can just focus on the relevant part of each passage with a given question in mind; other people just find this technique confusing, because it means skipping around in the passage. Try it out and see how it works for you.

Option 3: Skim the passage, then read the questions.

This method combines the previous two methods, and it's the one I generally prefer (though, again, you should give each one a shot and see which one you personally like best). In this method, we're going to start out by *quickly* skimming the passage. Take note of any unusual technical terms, formulas, or italicized phrases. Glance at any figures, read the labels on charts and graphs, and so on. In just a minute or so, you can have a reasonable idea of where different pieces of information are in the passage.

Then, you'll be in a better position to find the relevant information in the passage after you've read an individual question, even though you only invested a minimal amount of time skimming beforehand.

Conclusion

As I said, this is basically the same as reading passages for ACT Reading, except that ACT Science passages can include charts, graphs, and so on, and the Science questions will tend to direct you more specifically to the relevant areas of the passage. Just try out the different methods and see what you prefer.

Using Simple Trends To Make Predictions

On the ACT Science section, you'll occasionally need to make simple predictions based on clear trends in data from the passage. That data might be found in a chart, graph, table, diagram—basically anything with numbers.

The predictions will essentially require you to determine whether a number should be greater than or less than a number already in the data, or between two numbers already in the data.

The best way to discuss this is to use a real example from the Red Book. Let's look at question 5 on page 474.

As always, we want to figure out where we need to look in the passage based on the phrases in the question. The question mentions "Table 1, or Figure 1." Since it says, "or," we can look at either one. Let's start out by looking at Table 1. (There's no particular reason I chose to look at Table 1 instead of Figure 1. I just had to pick one to look at first, so I picked one.)

The question also mentions an "initial speed of 90 mi/hr." We can see that the first column of Table 1 is labeled "Initial speed (mi/hr)." So far, so good. Next, the question asks us what D will be, "according to Method 2." We can see that the last column in Table 1 has two labels: "Method 2," and "D." So we definitely seem to be looking in the right place for the information we need.

But the question asks for the value of D at 90 mi/hr, and that value isn't in the table. So what are we supposed to do now?

Well, first of all, we should notice that the answer choices don't give specific values. Instead, they give ranges. This tells us we don't need to calculate an exact value for D; instead, we just need to have a general idea of what it should be (remember how important it is to consider answer choices when answering any ACT question!). Secondly, we can see a clear trend in the data that allows us to make a simple prediction: in Table 1, as the initial speed increases, D (according to Method 2) increases.

The highest value for initial speed in Table 1 is 80 mi/hr, and we're asked what D would be at an initial speed of 90 mi/hr. Since higher values of D always correspond to higher values of initial speed in the data, we should expect a D value above 236 ft when the initial speed is 90mi/hr, because 236 ft is the D value for 80 mi/hr, according to Method 2.

Only two answer choices include values above 236 ft: (C) and (D). We know (D) is the correct answer because when we look at the values for D according to Method 2, we can see that they increase by about 60 ft for every 20 mi/hr increase in initial speed. That means we can expect the D to be bigger than 250 ft when the initial speed is 90 mi/hr, since the D value was 236 ft when the initial speed was 80 mi/hr.

So far we've only even considered Table 1, but this question also mentions Figure 1. When we look at Figure 1, we can see that initial speed in mi/hr is across the x axis, while D is measured in the y axis. The key tells us that the dashed line shows the D values for Method 2.

When we look at that dashed line, we see a pretty steady increase in D as initial speed increases (just as we saw in Table 1, since it's the same data). If we guess at the value of D according to Method 2 at an initial speed of 90 mi/hr, based on the trend in the graph, we would again have to come up with a value greater than 250 ft, since we can see that the dashed line in the graph seems to increase by more than 25 ft for every 10 mi/hr increase in initial speed. Once again, we see that (D) is the right answer.

A lot of questions will ask you to look at either a table or a graph; this one happened to provide both. As you can see, we were able to come up with the same answer either way.

Notice that the answer choices don't include values like 265 ft and 267 ft—that is, values that would both seem like reasonable estimates of what D might be for an initial speed of 90 mi/hr. If the answer choices had included values like that, there would have been no way for us to make a distinction between them and decide which one was right. Instead, the ACT had to give us broad ranges, and it was our job to identify the range that would clearly include the value we were looking for. Whenever you see a question like this, there will be only one clearly correct answer choice supported by the data—just like there is on any other real ACT Science question.

In this question, we were asked about an initial speed that was greater than any shown in the table or graph. On another question, we might be asked about a value that's *less* than any value in a given table or graph—the same principle would apply, and we would just answer based on a clear trend in the data.

It's also possible for the ACT to ask us about a value that falls *between* two of the values provided in the data. For example, what if this question had told us to look at Table 1, and asked us what D would be for an initial speed of 50 mi/hr, according to Method 2?

Well, 50 mi/hr isn't in the table, but we can see a value for 40 mi/hr and a value for 60 mi/hr. Based on the trend of the D value increasing as initial speed increases, we can see that the D value for 50 mi/hr would be between the D values for 40 mi/hr and for 60 mi/hr, since 50 mi/hr is between 40 mi/hr and 60 mi/hr. So the correct answer to that kind of question might have been something like "between 120 ft and 170 ft."

Again, if we saw a question like this based on a trend in the data, we wouldn't see answer choices like 146 ft, 147 ft, and 148 ft, because there wouldn't be enough data provided in the table to allow us to determine a precise value as the correct answer. The test would have to give us ranges of values to choose from, so there could only be one answer choice that could possibly be correct based on the information in the passage.

This is an important concept on the ACT Science section, and you'll definitely see it on test day.

ACT Science Question Types

I like to think of the ACT Science section in terms of four main question types and one minor question type. I'm not advising you to take the time to classify each question before you do it, since the basic approach to each type will still be the same. I'm just breaking them into groups like this so we can discuss what kinds of questions you should expect to see on this section of the test.

Let's take a look.

"Pure Data"

Many of the questions you'll see will be what I call "Pure Data" questions. These questions are exactly what they sound like—they ask you a relatively simple, straightforward question about the provided data, and you'll need to read the data accurately and choose the appropriate answer.

This process is essentially the same one you use for ACT Reading. The only difference is that you'll usually be reading tables, graphs, and diagrams instead of sentences or paragraphs. If you're comfortable with ACT Reading, and if you can get comfortable applying the same basic technique to charts, graphs, and diagrams, you'll be fine. Like everything else on the ACT, it just takes some careful thought and some careful practice, and then you'll get the hang of it and find it very repetitive. (Remember that it's good for the ACT to be repetitive, because that means we can predict its behavior and use that predictability to answer questions correctly and score high.)

"Pure Paragraph"

The next type of question we'll talk about is what I call the "Pure Paragraph" question. As you might guess, this type of question is based purely on what you read in a paragraph in the passage. These are just reading comprehension questions, and we'll approach them the same way we approach questions on the ACT Reading section. These questions can appear in any passage on the Science section, but they'll usually appear in the heaviest concentration on the "Scientist 1 vs. Scientist 2" or "Student 1 vs. Student 2" type of passage.

Just like we do on the ACT Reading section, we'll pick the answer choice that restates the relevant part of the text without contradicting it. We'll read carefully, and we won't be thrown off by scientific terms we're not familiar with.

"Data Plus Paragraph"

As you might imagine from the name, the "Data Plus Paragraph" questions will ask us something that combines information from a paragraph in the passage with data found in a chart, graph, diagram, etc.

Again, we'll just look carefully at the information that's relevant to the question, and then we'll apply what we find to answer the question.

"Data Plus Data"

Finally, there are the "Data Plus Data" questions. These will require us to use two different data sources from the passage—for instance, we might have to combine a data point from a line graph with a separate data point from a table in the same passage.

These types of questions are often a little harder than other questions on the Science section, just because they involve processing a little more information than other questions do. But, as with every other major question type on the ACT Science section, all we really have to do is read carefully and use the available information to answer the question.

The Minor Question Type

Now let's talk about the final and least important question type—namely the small number of "Actual Science" questions on each ACT Science section.

Roughly 1 to 4 times per Science section, you'll see a question that requires you to use real scientific knowledge. You'll typically be able to spot these questions because they'll involve terms that don't appear anywhere else in the passage, especially in the answer choices. When this does happen, the question will depend on very basic science, the kind of thing that almost any high school student would have a good chance of knowing. (Remember that a standardized test like the ACT is only useful if it tests skills that almost all test-takers could be expected to have. That means any outside scientific knowledge required by the test must be pretty basic.)

As we've seen with other question types, the ACT will often try to make these questions appear more advanced and challenging than they actually are, so you'll need to be prepared for that.

An example of an "Actual Science" question is question 31 on page 622 of your copy of *The Real ACT Prep Guide, 3rd Edition*. The question states that, in osmosis, water moves through a semi-permeable barrier. It then asks through which structure the osmosis in the passage occurs.

If we look back at the passage, the first and only mention of osmosis comes in the first bullet-point, which describes "a net movement of H_2O between the cytoplasm of the plants' cells and the environment via osmosis."

First of all, we have to remember that ACT Science questions can never require us to *produce* an answer on our own. They can only require us to *choose* the correct answer from a provided set of options. That means we don't have to come up with our own answer out of thin air. We just have to pick the correct answer from a set of 4 possibilities.

The answers, as we might expect, are appropriately scientific-sounding and intimidating, just as we know the ACT wants them to be. We have "Chromosomes," "Nuclear envelope," "Cell membrane," and "Rough endoplasmic reticulum."

At this point, most untrained test-takers would be wondering if their science teachers ever taught them about tomato plants growing in high-salt environments (since that's what the passage for this question is about). Or they might be struggling to guess what a rough endoplasmic reticulum is. That's exactly what the ACT wants us to do, so we won't notice how simple the question actually is.

Let's look at it again. What does the text describe? It describes water moving "between the . . . plants' cells and the environment via osmosis."

So we know that osmosis involves moving water between the cells and the environment.

If we think about it, that means the water must be moving from inside the cells to outside the cells, because "the environment" of the cells must, by definition, be an area outside of the cells, surrounding the cells.

If you remember anything about cells, you probably remember that a cell, by definition, is enclosed in some sort of membrane, which is a structure that selectively lets some stuff through and keeps other stuff out.

There's no way that water can pass from inside a cell to the cell's environment without going through that membrane, so the answer must be (C).

Even though that question might have seemed intimidating, it actually came down to some relatively basic science. We had to know that the phrase "the environment" described something outside of a cell, and we had to know that a cell membrane is the barrier between the inside of the cell and the outside of the cell. That's all.

We never needed to know what the term "osmosis" meant, because it was described in the passage for us. We never needed to know what a rough endoplasmic reticulum was, because another answer choice ended up being correct.

It was just a matter of cutting through the unnecessary information in the question to see the relatively simple concept the test was actually asking about.

". . . but what if I didn't know that?!"

Don't worry if you didn't know what a cell membrane was, and you don't think you could have answered that example question correctly. In fact, you don't really need to worry very much if you never answer a single "Actual Science" question correctly on the ACT, because the number of questions like this on any given test is relatively small. On most days you can miss all of the "Actual Science" questions and still score above 30 on the Science section (usually a 33, 34, or 35, and sometimes even a 36) if you get everything else right. (Remember that all the other questions only require you to find the relevant information in the provided text).

If you read an "Actual Science" question and its answer choices carefully, and you still aren't sure which choice to go with, just pick the one that seems most closely related to the subject matter in the question. You'll probably be right, and, even if you aren't, staring at a question whose answer you don't know means you're wasting time that could be spent on questions whose answers are right there in the passage. Since there's no penalty for wrong answers on the ACT, you may as well pick the one that looks best to you, and then move on.

If you want to score high on the ACT Science section, it's going to be far more important for you to focus on the questions that don't require any outside scientific knowledge, because there are a lot more questions like that, and because it's impossible to guess which topics will be covered by the "Actual Science" questions anyway, so there's no real way to prepare for them.

One more thing: remember that the few "Actual Science" questions on the test *must* be limited to relatively basic subject matter. If you see a question that's clearly asking about some obscure scientific concept, and neither the answer choices nor the terms in the question include anything that the average ACT student has ever heard of before, then it's important to remember that the answer to that question must appear somewhere in the passage.

Now that we've explored the most common question types, let's talk about some general ways to approach these questions. (Again, we'll see specific examples of how to approach all of these question types when we do the walkthroughs in a few pages.)

ACT Science Answer-Choice Patterns

Let's take a look at some common answer choice patterns on the ACT Science section.

ACT Science Answer-Choice Pattern 1: All Of One Type

On ACT Science questions, you'll often see a set of answer choices that includes the full range of possible values from a table or chart. In other words, the question might refer to groups 1, 2, 3, and 4, and the answer choices for a given question might be:

(A) Group 1

(B) Group 2

(C) Group 3

(D) Group 4

Similarly, a passage might talk about four periods of time, and your answer choices might just be those four time periods.

In a situation like this, it might seem like you're not going to get much use out of analyzing the answer choices.

But this kind of answer choice set is still helpful, because it can point you to a certain part of the data being presented to you.

For example, if the set of answer choices only includes the four time periods mentioned in the passage, and there's a graph that gives information about those different time periods, then that graph is probably where you should start looking to find the answer. The answer choices can help make that extra clear.

Similarly, if all the answer choices are different types of metal, and those metal names match up to labels on one of the charts, then that's a good indicator that you'll probably find that chart to be useful in answering the question.

If the answer choices are all names of gases, there's probably a chart or a graph somewhere that talks about those different gases.

You get the idea. As in ACT Math, ACT Science answer choices can give you an idea of the sorts of thing you might need to consider when finding the answer for a question. Basically, one of the biggest possible challenges on any ACT Science question is to find the relevant information in the given passage, and the answer choices can provide a set of relevant keywords or values that can help you find what you're looking for.

ACT Science Answer-Choice Pattern 2: Exact Opposite

You may remember this answer-choice pattern from the ACT Reading section. Sometimes you'll see a wrong-answer choice that's the opposite of the correct answer. It may describe the opposite of a relationship that appears in the passage, or it may rank some values in the opposite order from the way they're ranked in the correct answer, and so on. The ACT probably does this to make you second-guess yourself and wonder if you got something backwards in the passage.

So if you see two answer choices that are opposites of one another, don't get thrown off. Double-check the question, the passage, and the answer choices to make sure you're picking the right one.

ACT Science Answer-Choice Pattern 3: Completely Irrelevant

This is another answer-choice pattern that we saw in the ACT Reading section: sometimes you'll see an answer choice that's completely irrelevant to the passage. Again, the ACT is probably just trying to catch you off-guard and make you wonder if you overlooked something in the passage. Just double-check everything to make sure you're on the right track, and don't get flustered.

ACT Science Answer-Choice Pattern 4: Yes Yes No No

This is an answer-choice pattern that shows up on other sections as well, but it's probably most prevalent on the ACT Science and ACT English sections.

You'll see a question that asks which of two possibilities might happen in a given situation. The answer choices will feature two choices that support one possibility and two choices that support another possibility, and every choice will offer a different reason to support that possibility.

That might sound confusing, so let's make up an example. Imagine a portion of the text says this:

> "It was very cloudy Tuesday night. When there is a very cloudy night, it always rains the next day."

Now imagine a question that says:

> "Based on the text, will it rain on Wednesday?"

You might see answer choices like this:

> **(A)** Yes, because it always rains on Wednesdays.
>
> **(B)** Yes, because it was very cloudy on Tuesday night.
>
> **(C)** No, because Wednesday night wasn't cloudy.
>
> **(D)** No, because it didn't rain Tuesday.

Notice that there are two answer choices to support each possibility (two "yes" answers and two "no" answers), but just knowing whether the answer is "yes" or "no" isn't enough, because each question offers its own support that must be taken into consideration.

Here's the thing: in most cases, you can rule out three answers by ignoring the yes/no part of the answer and just checking whether the rest of the answer choice is supported by the text.

In this case, we can rule out (A), because there's no indication that it always rains on Wednesdays. We can rule out (C) because the text doesn't say anything about whether Wednesday night was cloudy. Also, (D) must be wrong because there isn't any mention of whether it rained Tuesday.

Once you've done that, you can see that the only choice left is (B), and we can confirm that this answer is supported by the text.

You can often rule out all incorrect answers just by checking to see whether the passage supports the reason given for each answer. If you eliminate the unsupported answers and you're still left with more than one answer choice that describes something in the passage, then you can eliminate the remaining choice that cites reasoning unrelated to the question. If this doesn't make any sense yet, don't worry—you'll see examples of this sort of thing when you read the ACT Science walkthroughs.

One more thing—I call this the "Yes Yes No No" pattern, but the two choices aren't always "yes" and "no." You might see a question that asks whether something increases or decreases, in which case there will be two choices that say "increase" and two that say "decrease," each with its own supporting reason. There might also be a question that asks whether Group 1 or Group 2 from a passage will do something, and there will be two choices that say "Group 1" does it and two choices that say "Group 2" does it, each for different reasons. You'll get used to recognizing the pattern as you work with practice ACT Science questions.

The General Process For Answering (Most) ACT Science Questions

Now that we've discussed all the important aspects of ACT Science questions, we can take a look at the recommended step-by-step process for answering most of them—that is, all of the questions that involve material presented in the passage, which will usually be 37 to 39 out of the 40 questions on any given Science section.

The "Actual Science" questions, as I call them, don't really call for a methodical approach. We simply recognize that we're dealing with one of those questions when we see that the answer choices aren't reflected anywhere in the passage, and then we do our best to answer them based on our outside scientific knowledge. Again, each ACT Science section will only feature a small handful of "Actual Science" questions.

So the following approach is intended for use on the majority of ACT Science questions—the ones that don't require any outside knowledge because all the relevant information is present in the passage. As always, you can see examples of this process in the walkthroughs in a few pages.

1. Read, skim, or skip the passage.

As we discussed a few pages ago, you'll want to either read, skim, or skip the passage, according to your preference.

2. Read the question carefully, noting key terms.

We've covered this over and over again, and it never stops being important: you must take the time to read the question carefully. Notice any key scientific terms—in other words, any technical-sounding terms that aren't part of most people's everyday conversation. Don't worry if you don't know what a term means: either the passage will explain it, or none of the questions will require you to understand it.

3. Read the answer choices carefully.

This step is very important, because reading the answer choices will tell you where to look in the passages and/or which options to consider while you look for the answer to the question.

4. Find the relevant part of the passage.

Once you've read the question and the answer choices carefully, you know what information you need to find.

If the text mentions a specific area of the passage, like "Study 2" or "Table 1," then look there.

If there are no specific indications of tables or figures to look at in the passage, you can still match up technical terms from the question and answer choices with key phrases in the text, or in labels on a chart, graph, or table.

Again, we'll see plenty of examples of this in the walkthroughs.

5. Find the correct answer, or eliminate three wrong answers.

Some questions will lend themselves to eliminating wrong answers, and in some cases it'll be easier just to find the right answer. Either way, use the information in the passage to select a correct answer. In most cases, you'll either be matching a specific value from the data to a specific value in an answer choice, or you'll be treating "Pure Paragraph" questions from the passage the same way you would treat ACT Reading questions. Either way, actually finding the answer is a relatively minor step (in terms of difficulty) once you've taken the time to locate the relevant part of the text in the previous steps.

Remember to read carefully.

6. Double-check your answer.

Once you've done everything and found your answer, take another look at the question. Did you refer to the right study? Did you find the right chart? Did you look at the right date range or temperature or depth (or whatever) on the right chart or graph? Did you overlook a word? Can you look at the answer choices you think are wrong and figure out which mistakes the ACT wants untrained test-takers to make to arrive at those answers?

Remember that high-scoring test-takers still make mistakes—they're just better at catching them afterwards. Get in the habit of double-checking yourself after you pick an answer.

Once you're satisfied with your answer, mark it on your sheet and move on.

Closing Thoughts

Doing well on the ACT Science section comes down to a few things:

- Read carefully. Make sure that you read only what the text says. Don't make any assumptions about what isn't explicitly mentioned.

- Don't be intimidated. You WILL see unfamiliar scientific terms; you'll probably see a lot of them. Don't let them scare you. Either they don't matter, or their meaning will be made clear enough in the passage for you to answer the questions.

- Rely on the passages. The information you need to answer almost every question is on the page in front of you. Match up key terms and units from the question and the answer choices to figure out where to find the answer in the passage.

- Seriously: read carefully. Reading carefully is the way to approach every single question on the ACT, so I'll list it here again. Read carefully at all times—and practice reading carefully—and you won't go wrong.

Walkthroughs: The ACT Science Process In Action Against Real Questions

Now that we've talked about the best way to attack ACT Science questions, let's attack some ACT Science questions! As always, you'll want to follow along in your copy of the Red Book—*The Real ACT Prep Guide, 3rd Edition*.

I keep saying this, but it's because it's really important: you need to see how this approach works against real ACT Science practice questions, so please be sure to read these walkthroughs. Once more, these particular questions were selected either because they're the questions that my one-on-one tutoring students ask me about most often, or because they do a particularly good job of illustrating some of the ideas we've talked about in this Black Book.

(If you'd like to see some video demonstrations of these ideas, go to www.ACTprepVideos.com for a selection of demonstration videos that are free to readers of this book.)

Page 189, Question 1

This question is a great example of what the ACT hopes to do with its Science section. It's a question about "mantle plumes," which is sure to be an unfamiliar term to the overwhelming majority of the test-takers who see this question.

Terms like this are used intentionally to make us panic, but we have to remember that most high school students don't study mantle plumes in school, so nobody else taking the ACT has any prior experience with this topic. The test must provide all the information we need to answer the question correctly.

And, of course, if we look at this question and the material provided, we'll see that it does contain all the information we need. All of the answer choices (remember to read the answer choices!) compare the head to the tail, and if we look at Figure 1, which is part of the "plume model in Study 1," we can see that the head and the tail are clearly labeled, so we know we're looking at the right part of the page.

The first three answer choices all mention the diameter, and we can see that the bottom of Figure 1 is labeled "diameter." Let's take a look at the answer choices and see which one describes the relationship accurately.

(A) says the heads are about half the diameter of the tails. If we look at the figure, we can see that head is wider than the tail, not narrower, so this answer choice isn't right. Some people might choose this answer if they thought they were measuring the head and tail against the scale on the left, because the tail is about twice as *tall* as the head. But the question clearly asks about the diameter, which is labeled on the bottom axis. People might also pick this choice by accident if they were in a hurry and switched the head and tail of the plume in their minds. These are both classic examples of the type of minor mistakes that the ACT tries to get us to make.

(B) says the heads are about twice the diameter of the tails. We can see in the figure that the diameter of the head is clearly larger than that of the tail, and we can reasonably approximate that it's about twice as wide. So (B) is the correct answer.

(C) says the head and the tail are the same diameter, but Figure 1 clearly shows the head is wider than the tail.

(D) talks about density, which isn't mentioned anywhere in Study 1 or Figure 1, so this choice is irrelevant and wrong.

This question is pretty simple once we actually attempt it, but that doesn't mean we can take it for granted! If you're not careful, you'll run the risk of misreading something and picking a wrong answer.

Page 189, Question 3

Don't worry if you've never seen the term "flood basalt plateau" or heard of a "Myr" unit. Remember that we don't need to know what those things mean, or why any scientist would actually care about them. All we have to do is read the question carefully and look at the given information, and we'll find the answer laid out in front of us.

The question asks about the results of Study 2, and Study 2 says that its results are in Table 1. Table 1 provides a variety of data, and the different parts of the table are clearly marked. The question mentions a "flood basalt plateau that produced lava for a period of 1.8 Myr." We can see a label on Table 1 that says "Length of time lava was produced (Myr)," so we can tell that's going to be relevant to our answer. The question also asks about "lava volume," and we can see that "Lava volume" is a label on the table as well, further reassuring us that we've correctly located the relevant information to answer the question. The answer choices also include quantities like 1,440,000 km^3 and 1,500,000 km^3, and these are quantities that appear in the "Lava volume" column.

So we're definitely looking at the right part of the passage. Now our job is just to figure out what the answer is.

The question asks about 1.8 Myr, but that quantity doesn't appear in the "Length of time lava was produced" column—only the quantities 1.6, 1.3, 1.2, and 1.7 appear. So there are two possibilities here: either we're looking at the wrong information and there's a data point for 1.8 Myr somewhere else, or else this is one of those ACT Science questions that wants us to identify a trend in the data and then make a simple prediction based on that trend.

There are two major ways we can tell that the second possibility is the scenario we're dealing with. One is that all of the details we mentioned before (the names of the columns and the correspondence between the units and the numbers in the answer choices and the table) indicate that we're looking in the right place. Another important detail is that the question uses the phrase *would most likely have* a lava volume [emphasis mine]. On the ACT Science section, that phrase indicates that we're being asked to make a prediction, rather than being asked to read a value directly off the page.

So what trend can we identify that tells us what kind of value would probably go in the "Lava volume" column if there were another row of plateau data with a value of 1.8 in the column labeled "Length of time lava was produced (Myr)?" If we look at the existing data, we can see that the lowest Myr value is 1.2, corresponding to a "Lava volume" of 1,440,000. The next-lowest Myr value is 1.3, with a corresponding "Lava volume" of 1,500,000. The second-highest Myr value is 1.6, which corresponds to a "Lava volume" value of 2,000,000. The highest Myr value is 1.7, and it corresponds to a "Lava volume" value of 2,125,000.

So we can see that lava volume increases as Myr increases, without exception.

Since the question asks us about 1.8 Myr, which is higher than any other Myr value listed on the table, it makes sense that the corresponding "Lava volume" value would also be greater than the largest number listed in the "Lava volume" column. The largest value in that column is 2,125,000 km^3, so the correct answer to this question is (D), "over 2,125,000 km^3."

The other answer choices are just the ranges among the other values from the "Lava volume" column in Table 1.

Notice that we were able to find the answer without having any idea at all about lava production, flood basalt plateaus, or anything else involved in the question. All we had to do was identify the part of the passage that included key words and quantities that appeared in the question, and then pay careful attention to the data.

There's one other thing I'd like to point out. If we tried to think logically about the situation in the question, it might make sense that the volume of lava produced would be greater if the length of production time was greater—the longer the lava's produced, the more lava there should be, right? But it's very important to realize that we can get the correct answer without having to think about the actual real-world scenarios that generated this data. In fact, it's actually better if we DON'T try to think about the practical application of the concepts in the passage, because it sometimes happens that people can get confused when they do that. It's much safer, and much faster, to focus exclusively on the data on the page.

Page 189, Question 4

We're asked about the relationship between the age of a flood basalt plateau and the length of time lava was produced at that plateau. The first thing we want to do (after reading the whole question and the answer choices, of course) is find the information we need to analyze.

As with the last question, this question deals with Study 2, the results of which are laid out in Table 1. We can see that the "Age" column is the second one, and the "Length of time lava was produced" is the fourth column.

We can see in the "Age" column that the numbers increase as we move down the column: 60, 67, 135, and 192. The corresponding "Length of time . . ." numbers are 1.6, 1.3, 1.2, and then 1.7. While the first set of numbers increases from beginning to end, the second set decreases from 1.6 to 1.2, but then increases at the end to 1.7.

Now let's take a look at the answer choices and see which one accurately describes the relationship.

(F) says that both columns increase together. That's clearly not the case, as we just saw.

(G) says that the "Age" column increases as the "Length of time . . ." column decreases. That's *almost* true—the "Length of time . . ." column decreases as we read down the first three rows, but then it increases at the very end, from 1.2 to 1.7. The ACT won't accept this as the correct answer choice because the sentence doesn't perfectly describe the data. You can probably imagine how a lot of untrained test-takers will be tempted to choose this, either because they don't bother to look at all the numbers in the "Length of time . . ." column, or because they figure it's okay for the answer choice to be generally accurate even if it's not perfectly accurate.

(H) is also wrong, because it gets the relationship between the two columns backwards. It says that the values in the "Length of time . . ." column *increase* and then *decrease* as we read down the rows, but actually they *decrease* and then *increase*. This is another thing the ACT loves to do with wrong answers on the Science section: provide an option that directly contradicts the data, in the hope that some test-takers will get things backwards in their heads.

(J) is the correct answer. As we've seen, there's no real relationship between the two sets of numbers—as one increases steadily, the other decreases and then jumps up at the end.

A lot of people will feel uncomfortable saying there's no relationship, because in a real science class, you almost never bother investigating a possible relationship unless your teacher already knows that you should find one. So it can feel weird to be told to find a relationship and then realize there isn't a relationship to find.

Remember, though, that the people who make the ACT want to make you doubt yourself if they can. Also remember that the ACT is ultimately a test of reading and paying attention to small details.

Page 191, Question 9

This question directs us to Figure 1, and it asks which period saw the biggest increase in net productivity. We can see in Figure 1 that net productivity is measured on the vertical axis, so the higher the lines goes, the greater the net productivity.

Some people might start by trying to approximate the actual numerical increase indicated in each answer choice. That would be one way to go, but it could get time-consuming, and might prove difficult. The ACT Science section usually doesn't require us to figure out specific numbers like that. So we can probably start by just doing a quick check of each time period to see if anything jumps out at us.

(A) covers the end of Year 2 to the end of Year 4. The period from 2 to 4 on Figure 1 shows a pretty flat line without much change in net productivity. Let's look at the next one.

(B) covers the end of Year 4 to the end of Year 14. Again, the line remains pretty flat.

(C) covers the end of Year 14 to the end of Year 50. This period includes a dramatic jump in net productivity. Clearly this is the largest increase of any answer choice we've seen so far.

(D) covers the end of Year 50 to the end of Year 200. Again, in Figure 1, this period is pretty flat.

We can see that choice (C) is the clear winner, because the other 3 choices show little or no increase in net productivity and (C) shows a big jump.

In my experience, people who miss this question usually choose (D). There are two reasons people might do this. One reason is that they might think the question is asking which period has the highest *amount* of net productivity, instead of the largest *increase*. The period from Year 50 to Year 200 in Figure 1 shows a level of productivity at 1,200, but there's no actual *increase* during that period. The other reason for the mistake is that people often look at Figure 2 instead of Figure 1. In Figure 2, the period from Year 50 to Year 200 contains the largest increase in the graph—but the question told us to look at Figure 1, so the graph in Figure 2 is irrelevant.

Situations like this remind us that it's always important to read carefully! It would be a shame to miss this question just because we weren't paying attention to the test.

Page 193, Question 12

The question asks at which temperature all of the liquids had the same volume in Experiment 2. If we look at Experiment 2, we see that it involved tracking how far different liquids rose up a capillary tube when they were exposed to different temperatures.

The only graph associated with Experiment 2 is Figure 2. In Figure 2, temperature is measured across the x axis, and the rise of the liquid is measured on the y axis. Based on the question, we need to find a value for which all of the liquids had the same temperature and the same *volume* (we'll discuss the connection between volume and rise in a moment).

We can see that the only place on the graph that shows the same value for all the liquids at a given temperature is the bottom left corner of the graph, at 20 degrees Celsius. So (F) is correct. None of the other choices can be correct because at any other temperature, the liquids have different values for the "rise of liquid" along the vertical axis.

It may not be immediately clear to some test-takers that the "volume" referred to in the prompt corresponds to the "rise of liquid" on the vertical axis of Figure 2. If we have a little awareness of scientific fundamentals, we may come to recognize that an increase in volume from the rising heat of the water bath is the reason that the liquid samples rise up the capillary tube. But even if we don't realize that, we can still notice that the question refers to the temperatures of liquid samples, and that the only indication of anything having to do with temperature in Experiment 2 appears in Figure 2—in fact, the horizontal axis of Figure 2 is the only part of the entire passage that mentions the numbers 30 and 50, which are answer choices for this question. So we know that Figure 2 is what we should be looking at when we answer this question. From there, we can notice that the only temperature value in Figure 2 that shows common values for the liquid samples is the 20° temperature, so volume must be related to "rise of liquid." Remember that the ACT Science section only requires very little knowledge of science—if we pay close attention to the passage and make sure we're reading our data from the right place, we can see that it's possible to answer this question without really knowing what's going on in the experiment at all.

Page 195, Question 18

This question asks us to find the upper boundary of the thermosphere in "the data provided." But the only data we're provided is the bizarre diagram at the bottom of page 194, along with the one-paragraph write-up at the top of the page. If we look at all of that information, we'll find that a certain range of the diagram is labeled with the word "thermosphere." But nothing indicates the upper boundary of the thermosphere.

If we look below the "thermosphere" label in the diagram, we'll see labels for the mesosphere, stratosphere, and troposphere. Between those labels, we'll see dashed horizontal lines with the labels "mesopause," " stratopause," and "tropopause." We might be tempted to think that those horizontal lines indicate the upper boundaries of the mesosphere, stratosphere, and troposphere—and perhaps they do, for all we know. But the passage never actually says that those lines represent the boundaries, or that the "-pause" suffix on words like "mesopause" indicates a boundary.

Even if we did assume that the "pauses" were boundaries (and, again, they might actually be boundaries—the page doesn't explicitly say one way or the other), there's no "thermopause" anywhere on the page.

We might also try to approach the question by looking at the answer choices. They all indicate measurements in kilometers. If we look at the diagram, it's pretty clear they're all referring to values on the left-most vertical axis, which is labeled "altitude" (note that the label matches up with the word "altitude" in the prompt). Near the top of that axis line, we can see the values 250, 200, and 100, which correspond to the three answer choices in the question.

But there's nothing at any of those markers that indicates the upper boundary of the thermosphere. So the answer is (J).

In my experience, a lot of people who get this wrong choose (H), 250 km, because that's the largest value listed on the altitude axis. But there's no indication that this is where the upper limit of the thermosphere is, as we just saw. It's just that the axis has to stop *somewhere*, and whoever made the graph decided not to continue the altitude axis past 250 km.

As usual, we don't need to have any idea what the words "thermosphere," "mesosphere," "stratosphere," or "troposphere" mean in order to answer this question. All we have to do is locate the word "thermosphere" in the diagram after seeing it in the question, and then search for some indication of an upper boundary and realize that there isn't one on the diagram.

Page 195, Question 22

This question gives us a little extra information, and then asks us a question based on that information. As it turns out, the answer to the question is actually contained within the question itself, if we think carefully about it. This specific situation doesn't arise very often on the ACT, but it's still a very good demonstration of the general importance of reading closely and thinking carefully.

The question tells us that atmospheric boundaries are higher than usual over areas with *more* direct solar radiation. Then it asks what would most likely be true if there were *less* solar radiation than there currently is.

Let's stop and think about that for a moment. If *more* solar radiation leads to *higher* boundaries, then *less* solar radiation automatically leads to *lower* boundaries if we consider the situation logically. The passage and the diagram don't say anything explicitly about atmospheric boundaries or changes in the amount of solar radiation, but the conclusion is inescapable if we're told that more solar radiation leads to higher boundaries. The ACT's solution to this question sort of hints at this on page 280 of the Red Book, but it doesn't explain the reasoning behind this conclusion. So let me show you why it has to be true.

The terms "more" and "higher" are relative terms. They only make sense when they're used in comparison to things that are smaller or lower in some way. So if we're told about an area with "more direct solar radiation," we have to ask ourselves, "more than *what*?" The answer, of course, is that it's more than the solar radiation in an area with *less* direct solar radiation. Similarly, if we're told that more radiation leads to "higher" "atmospheric boundaries," we should ask ourselves, "higher than *what*?" The answer there is that they're higher than atmospheric boundaries that are *lower*. If it sounds like I'm just talking in circles, that's because I am—and that's the whole point: if we say that more radiation leads to higher boundaries, that's automatically the same thing as saying that less radiation leads to lower boundaries. You can't have one situation without the other. It would be a logical impossibility.

So (G) is the correct answer.

Choice (F) is the exact opposite of the correct answer, which might sound silly if we've understood the question correctly, but it's exactly the kind of wrong answer that a lot of people will pick if they accidentally miss a word somewhere in the question or in the answer choice. The ACT frequently includes a wrong answer that's the direct opposite of the right answer, and it does so very deliberately, because it knows that a certain percentage of test-takers will make some small mistake on any given question. Never forget that the ACT is primarily a reading test, and careful reading is the most important skill you can develop no matter what section you're working on. (How many times have I repeated this idea by now? It must be important or something . . . ;))

Page 197, Question 25

This might sound like an intimidating question to most test-takers. We might read this and wonder how there can even be any undiscovered shrimp species left in the 21st century, or why it's okay to assume that the shrimp are only limited by temperature (instead of by currents, or by the presence of a predator, or just by their individual shrimpish preferences). But we trained test-takers know that the ACT is deliberately trying to make the question sound as scientific and technical as possible just to scare off the untrained test-takers. We also know that none of that stuff really matters to us as test-takers.

We're told to look at Figure 1. We're given a depth of 200 m, and we need to find a corresponding temperature.

That might sound simple enough before you actually try to do it, but many test-takers simply can't find the temperature data on Figure 1, at least not when they first look for it. So they give up and just guess . . .

. . . which is a mistake, of course.

We must *always* remember what the ACT Science section is really testing. It's not a standardized test of your shrimp-related knowledge—if it were, it might make sense for a graph about shrimp to leave out some important information. Instead, the ACT Science section is a test of your ability to find information that's laid out for you in texts, graphs, charts, and diagrams. So if this question tells you to look at Figure 1 and draw a conclusion about temperature, then there *must*—and I mean MUST—be some kind of information about temperature in Figure 1. If we don't see it when we first look for it, then we need to look more carefully, because it MUST be there.

As it turns out, most test-takers ignore the top horizontal axis on the graph in Figure 1, which is where the temperature information appears. They also ignore the key above the graph, which also mentions temperature. So they hunt in vain for a set of numbers in the same scale as the numbers in the answer choices.

That's the reason I want to discuss this question. The Red Book solution on page 281 simply says that the temperature curve (which is the one with solid black dots on its data points) has a temperature value of 7.5°C corresponding to an ocean depth of 200 m. That's true, but it doesn't address the fact that most test-takers who struggle with this question do so because they can't locate the temperature information in the first place, because they're not conditioned to look at horizontal axes that are above a graph instead of below it. The Red Book also doesn't bother to explain the test-taking psychology we need to have in order to keep from abandoning a question that might seem impossible at first.

And those are the two real lessons to learn from a question like this:

1) Remember that graphs can have more than one horizontal axis or vertical axis (see the diagram on page 194 of the Red Book for an example of multiple vertical axes in the same graph).

2) Remember that every ACT Science question on some obscure topic like the maximum temperature that could be withstood by a hypothetical shrimp is going to be written so that the answer is directly on the page in front of you—even when it seems not to be at first.

In the end, this question really just boils down to the following: "Which of the answer choices contains a temperature-related number that corresponds in some way to a depth of 200 m on Figure 1?" Once we notice that the curve with the filled-in dots represents temperature, and that the horizontal axis at the top of the graph indicates temperature, it's pretty clear that 7.5°C, choice (B), must be correct.

So we never had to know anything about shrimp to find that answer. It just took practice and careful reading.

Probably the most common problem that people run into here is that they fail to notice the "temperature" label on the top of Figure 1. Always remember to look at the entire graph, chart, or whatever the passage directs you to in order to make sure you're getting all the information! Otherwise, it's very easy to miss a question that you could otherwise have answered correctly.

Page 197, Question 27

This question is a bit more misleading than most ACT Science questions will be, because it seems to incorporate only data from Table 1 when we first read it; in the end, it turns out that Table 1 doesn't have all the information we need. Most test-takers will need to consult both Table 1 and Figure 1 together, though it's arguably possible to answer the question using only Figure 1.

First, let's talk about how to approach the question using both Table 1 and Figure 1, which is the approach that most test-takers seem to follow when they answer the question correctly. After that, we'll discuss a way to approach the question that relies only on Figure 1.

The question uses phrases like "Table 1" and "vm 2 and vm 3," all of which seem to indicate that Table 1 will contain the answer to the question, which is ultimately about "oxygen partial pressures below 25 mm Hg." But when we look at Table 1, we don't see anything at all about oxygen partial pressure, or anything measured in units of mm Hg.

Many untrained test-takers would panic at this moment, but we know the key to the correct answer must be explicitly stated somewhere on the page, so we just keep looking for something related to oxygen partial pressure and/or the mm Hg unit. There are only two other places to look: the paragraph at the beginning of the passage, and the graph in Figure 1. We'll see that "oxygen partial pressure (mm Hg)" is the name of the bottom horizontal axis on Figure 1. This looks promising. Now our job is to figure out how the oxygen partial pressure values from Figure 1 relate to the vm 2 and vm 3 values from Table 1.

The only data that's common to both Table 1 and Figure 1 is the data that has to do with ocean depth, measured in meters. The label on the vertical axis in Figure 1 is "ocean depth (m)," and Table 1 has a column with the heading "Depth range (m)." This common data is the only thing connecting Table 1 to Figure 1, which means it's the only thing that can possibly connect the idea of vm 2 and vm 3 (which appear in Table 1) to the idea of oxygen partial pressure (which appears in Figure 1).

If we look at the "Depth range" values for vm 2 and vm 3, we see that both have ranges that end with 400 m. If we look at 400 m on the vertical axis of Figure 1, we see that it corresponds to an oxygen partial pressure around 25 mm Hg (the curve showing oxygen partial pressure is the one with the empty boxes at the data points, as the key at the top of Figure 1 indicates).

So we see that there's a correlation between 400 m of depth and an oxygen partial pressure of 25 mm Hg. That means choice (C) is correct, because it states that vm 2 and vm 3 can't go beyond 400 m in depth because they can't stand more than 25 mm Hg of oxygen partial pressure.

As I mentioned above, it's arguably possible to answer this question without ever looking at Table 1. We can do that if we focus on the answer choices from the very beginning, and notice that three of the four choices are related to temperature or depth, and that Figure 1 relates oxygen partial pressure (which appears in the prompt) to temperature and depth (which appear in the answer choices).

From there, we just look at each of the answer choices:

(A) is wrong because Figure 1 doesn't relate the temperature value of 10°C to an oxygen partial pressure of 25 mm Hg. Instead, a temperature of 10°C (found on the upper horizontal axis) corresponds to an oxygen partial pressure of about 60 mm Hg (found on the lower horizontal axis).

(B) is wrong because oxygen partial pressure (which is mentioned in the question) only appears in Figure 1, and Figure 1 doesn't say anything about water content, so this answer choice is irrelevant to the data. (This choice is also incorrect because Table 1 shows that vm 2 and vm 3 have water content levels roughly in line with all the other species, but for purposes of this demonstration we're approaching the question using only Figure 1.)

(C) is correct because Figure 1 does show that an oxygen partial pressure of 25 mm Hg corresponds to a depth of 400 m.

(D) is wrong because Figure 1 shows that a depth of 100 m corresponds to an oxygen partial pressure of roughly 80 mm Hg.

In this second approach to the question, we're literally treating the entire question as though it simply said, "Which of the following answer choices contains a number that's related to 25 mm Hg in the provided data?" It may sound ridiculous, but the ACT Science section actually rewards this kind of approach in a lot of cases. It's just one more manifestation of a principle that we've seen played out over and over again across the entire ACT: a multiple-choice test can never test your ability to generate answers on your own. Multiple-choice tests can only evaluate your ability to identify a correct answer from a set of provided choices. On the ACT Science section, that typically just means figuring out which answer choice contains a number that's related to something in the prompt.

Finally, I'd like to address the answer choices for this question. Notice that (A) talks about temperature, (B) talks about water content, and (C) and (D) both talk about depth. As we've often seen, the ACT likes to include wrong answers that mimic elements of the right answer, so if we see two answer choices with one thing in common (depth) and then two other answer choices that each discuss their own unique concepts (temperature and water content), there's a very good chance that one of the choices related to depth is going to be correct. It's not an absolutely certain guarantee, but it's a very strong likelihood. Keep that in mind as you work through future ACT Science questions.

Page 198, Question 29

This question is from one of the ACT Science passages that's basically a reading comprehension passage.

(As we've seen, the key skill for the ACT Science section is the same as the key skill for the ACT Reading section: paying careful attention to specific words and phrases so we can find the answer spelled out directly on the page. But while most ACT Science passages incorporate graphs, diagrams, or tables, others dispense with those graphical elements altogether and include only text, much like a passage from the ACT Reading section. The passage with question 29 is one of these text-only ACT Science passages.)

Many test-takers are frustrated by the lack of numerical data in passages like this one. But, as trained test-takers, we know to ignore those kinds of concerns and focus simply on identifying the relevant parts of the passage that will contain the phrases that appear in the correct answer choice.

Towards that end, I'd approach this question by noting any concepts that stand out as probable examples of jargon or technical terminology related to the passage. One thing that leaps out at me right away is the idea of one chimney being "more efficient" than another chimney, which appears in the prompt. This is a pretty strange phrase, since people in everyday life don't normally talk about chimneys being efficient or inefficient. That means it's probably something that appears directly in the text, and finding it in the text will probably give me a good indication of where I can find the answer.

I'd also want to notice similarities and differences among the answer choices, and think about how those things might be relevant to the concepts in the question. Each answer choice talks about one of the chimneys being taller than the other, and whether the students would agree on which one should be taller.

So it looks like the concepts I want to find in the passage are going to be related to chimneys being efficient and/or tall. With that in mind, I'd take a look at the statements made by the different students.

I don't see anything in the first paragraph of Student 1's statement about chimney efficiency or height. But the first sentence of the second paragraph of Student 1's statement says, "As chimney height increases, efficiency increases." The first sentence of the second paragraph of Student 2's statement contains the exact same sentence: "As chimney height increases, efficiency increases." So both students explicitly state that increased chimney height and increased efficiency go together. That matches with the correct answer, choice (B).

Notice that this approach doesn't really give us any idea what the students mean when they talk about chimney efficiency. Also notice that it doesn't matter whether we understand chimney efficiency at all—the only thing that matters is that we can clearly identify sentences in the passage that relate chimney efficiency to height.

Also notice all the ways we could mess this question up if we're not careful with our reading! We might misread the word "increases" as "decreases." We might misread Chimney Y as Chimney X, or vice versa. Any one of those mistakes would cause us to answer the question incorrectly. The ACT deliberately sets up questions with several small details like these and then positions the set of wrong answers to anticipate small mistakes in reading or comprehension, as we've seen countless times by now. Keep this in mind every second you're taking the ACT, so you can make sure you don't fall for any of the test's traps.

Page 199, Question 34

This question often bothers test-takers because it seems totally unrelated to the passage at first, since Student 2's explanation is all about smoke going up a chimney, not about planes flying. But we can see that the common element is the idea of air moving over something, and something rising up. For the chimney, it's wind blowing over the top of the chimney causing smoke to rise up the chimney—so what would that mean for an airplane?

Let's look at exactly what Student 2 says:

"When air at the top of the chimney moves at a higher speed than air at the bottom of the chimney, the pressure difference between the bottom and the top of the chimney is so great that air is forced upward, carrying smoke with it."

So when the air on top is moving faster than the air on the bottom, air is forced upward, and it carries the smoke with it. How would that fit into the explanation for an airplane staying up in the air? In the case of an airplane, the airplane is behaving like the smoke does—it's rising because the air underneath it is rising. So we want the answer choice that describes something similar to what causes the smoke to rise—specifically, the one that describes air moving faster over something than it moves at the bottom of something, and causing that thing to rise as a result. That means choice (F) must be correct.

As always, let's take a moment to notice the rest of the answer choices and think about how they relate to the answer choice we think is correct. The first two choices relate to a difference above the wing as opposed to below it, and the last two choices relate to a difference in front of the wing as opposed to behind it. We can be sure the last two choices are wrong, since nothing in Student 2's statement has anything to do with things in front of the chimney or behind it. Within the first two choices, we see another common answer-choice pattern on the ACT Science section: each choice is the exact opposite of the other. As trained test-takers, we know that the ACT is hoping we'll misread or misinterpret the text or the question and end up choosing an answer that's exactly the opposite of the correct one. So we just have to make sure we read very carefully, to keep from getting confused between (F) and (G). If we do, it's clear that (F) is correct.

As you've probably noticed by now, the ACT gives us the opportunity to be wrong because of some trivial mistake like this on *almost every single question*. If you want to maximize your score, you really have to become obsessive about not making these small mistakes, which is why I keep pointing them out for every single explanation.

Page 201, Question 38

The Red Book's solution for this question on page 285 ends with the phrase "all other experimental procedures would be held constant." That's an awfully science-y (but not actually scientific :)) phrase, and those kinds of phrases often lead test-takers to think they have to understand actual science in order to do well on the ACT Science section. While I encourage everyone to study and understand science in real life, actual science has practically no bearing on the ACT whatsoever. We don't need to know what it means for a procedure to be "held constant," even though the Red Book's solution uses that phrase—we can still answer the question just by reading the passage and finding the answer choice that repeats the same concepts from the passage.

This question often intimidates test-takers who've never taken chemistry before, because they assume it's the kind of thing they should have learned in school. But we trained test-takers know that the answer to a fairly technical question like this must be somewhere on the page. So our job is just to find it.

The question mentions changing a coloring agent in the experiment, and then making a change to the procedure of the experiment, as well. Again, this will be a totally foreign concept to most test-takers, even if they've taken chemistry in high school. To find the answer, we need to see what the question says about the significance of the coloring agent in these experiments, and we need to see which answer choice reflects concepts that appear in the passage. For that, we need to go back to the part of the passage that mentions this coloring agent and what it does.

Note that the tables and the figure don't say anything about the function of the coloring agent in the experimental procedure. They do mention the concept of "absorbance," but they don't specifically say anything about the procedure. Since the tables and figure don't have any relevant information, we'll have to look in the actual text to find out how the coloring agent is involved in the procedure.

When we do that, we see that the coloring agent is first mentioned in the description of Experiment 1, which says that the coloring agent forms a "purple compound that strongly absorbs light of a specific wavelength." The text says the coloring agent is added to all the sample solutions. Then a colorimeter is used to measure the absorbance. The text explains that a colorimeter is "a device that measures how much light of a selected wavelength is absorbed by a sample."

Now let's see how the answer choices match up against the text:

(F) doesn't match the text, because the original coloring agent was added to all the samples, not just to the blank solution. There's nothing in the prompt that indicates a reason why the new coloring agent should be used any differently, so (F) is wrong.

(G) doesn't make any sense in the context of the prompt itself. The prompt says that the experiments will be repeated "using a different coloring agent." But this answer choice refers to using both agents together, so it must be wrong.

(H) contradicts the text, because the last sentence of the paragraph for Experiment 1 talks about *subtracting* the absorbance of the blank solution, but (H) talks about *adding* that quantity. This is another example of the ACT Science section's common pattern of including an answer choice that directly contradicts the passage.

(J) is the correct answer, because the text indicates that the colorimeter measures "light of a selected wavelength," and that the coloring agent absorbs "light of a specific wavelength." That means that changing the coloring agent to one that produces a different color will require us to change the colorimeter so it measures a different specific wavelength (to match the new color).

So this ends up being an example of a question that relies on the textual elements of the passage, rather than on tables and figures. In passages that incorporate tables and figures, it's more common for questions not to involve the textual elements of the passage much (or even at all), but sometimes we'll run into questions like this. Don't worry, though—as long as we keep constantly reminding ourselves to focus on what's spelled out on the page, we can answer any technical question the ACT Science section throws at us.

Page 201, Question 40

This is another example of how the ACT tries to make questions sound more technical and difficult than they actually are. But trained test-takers know that the ACT doesn't actually test our knowledge of advanced or obscure areas of science, so we'll just read carefully and figure out what's going on. Unfortunately, this is also an example of a question that the Red Book explains pretty poorly (see its commentary on page 286, which essentially restates the idea that absorbed light leads to a higher measurement three or four times, instead of actually explaining why). Let's take a look and see what's going on.

In order to understand how the scenario in this question would affect the measurements, we need to make sure we understand how the measurements work. This is spelled out in the paragraph for Experiment 1. That paragraph says we can test the amount of NO_2^- in a sample by adding a chemical that turns purple when it binds with NO_2^-, and then measuring how purple each sample is with a colorimeter. So the thing that we're actually measuring with the colorimeter is the "purpleness" of each sample (which the passage calls "absorbance"), and then we're correlating the amount of purpleness with the amount of NO_2^-, because NO_2^- is the stuff that binds with the coloring agent to turn the sample purple.

Now let's think about how that relates to the scenario in the question. The question talks about some other stuff in the samples from Experiment 2 that would also absorb the same kind of light as NO_2^-, and would therefore also register on the colorimeter as the same kind of purple as the coloring agent. In other words, according to the question, this other stuff in the meat samples is the same purple color as the NO_2^- after the coloring agent is added, even though the other stuff isn't actually NO_2^-.

If we think about it, that means the samples will seem to be "extra-purple," because there will be extra stuff in the samples that's the same purple as the NO_2^- compound. So it'll seem like there's more NO_2^- in the samples than there really is, because we're equating purpleness with NO_2^-, and there will actually be some purpleness in the samples that isn't coming from NO_2^-.

So (F) is correct.

Notice that the ACT gives us an answer choice for every conceivable way that we could mess this up—we can choose that the readings will be higher, lower, sometimes higher and sometimes lower, or the same. So there's not much we can glean from the set of answer choices in this case, unfortunately, except that we need to pay careful attention to how the passage describes the relationship between purpleness and NO_2^-. (But we already knew we needed to do that anyway, right?)

Go to www.ACTprepVideos.com.

Page 328, Question 2

This question just asks us to what decimal point the weekly average air temperatures were measured in Table 2. If we look at Table 2, we can see that all the numbers go to the hundredths place, which is two digits to the right of the decimal. That means the right answer is (F), 0.01°C.

This is a great example of a question that some test-takers will miss simply because they don't read it carefully enough or take the time to double-check themselves. Notice, for instance, that if you misread the question and look at Table 1 instead, you'll think the answer is (G). On the other hand, we might misread the question in another way and choose (J) because each value in Table 2 is between 10 and 100. As questions like this demonstrate, we simply *must* develop the habit of double-checking everything we do and being constantly on the lookout for these small mistakes, so we can make sure they don't cost us points.

Page 329, Question 5

This question asks us about the "efficiency of illumination," which seems to be an invented term just for this question. As trained test-takers, we know that the ACT has to define the terms that it invents, so we're not concerned when we run into a question with an invented term—we just read carefully to find out what it means.

In this case the efficiency of illumination is the intensity of the light absorbed by the plants divided by the intensity of light provided to the plants. So if we want to find the efficiency of illumination in Section 1 and compare it to the other sections, we need to know these two factors for each section:

- intensity of light absorbed
- intensity of light provided

When we look through the answer choices to see what our options are, we find that (A) and (B) indicate the conclusion is justified but cite two different reasons for the justification, while (C) and (D) indicate the conclusion is not justified and cite two different reasons for the lack of justification. It's particularly interesting that (D) says there's not enough information to draw a conclusion. That means that we might not find some of the data we're looking for when we go back to the passage to see which answer choice is correct.

If we look at the information in the passage, we see the idea of "average light intensity," but we don't see anything about two separate values for light absorbed and light provided. So the correct answer is (D), because we don't have enough information available to us to calculate efficiency of illumination as defined by this question.

In general, a lot of people will hesitate to say there's not enough information to determine something, but if we've read the question and the passage carefully, and we still can't find the information, we can be confident in saying that the information provided is insufficient.

One more thing—this question is a great example of the importance of reading all the answer choices before we start trying to find an answer. Otherwise, in this case, we might have wasted several minutes trying to hunt down an answer that didn't exist, because we might not have realized there was an option to say that finding the answer was impossible.

Page 330, Question 6

To answer this question, we just have to look at the data in Table 1 and see which answer choice describes what we see there. We know that's where we should look because the question refers to "the results from Experiment 1," and all of those results are in Table 1.

So let's take a look at the answer choices and see what's going on.

Choice (F) is wrong, because the highest percent of CO was recorded for the 1978 Model Y. This measurement is found in Table 1, at the 7th minute after starting. We can kind of tell it's the largest measurement at a glance, because it's the only measurement with two digits to the left of the decimal point.

Choice (G) is correct, because it's true that every row of data shows lower values for the 1996 models than it does for the 1978 models, *and* because the 1996 models are the "newer cars" referred to in the hypothesis in the prompt.

Choice (H) will be tempting for a lot of test-takers, because the second half of the choice is factually correct: it's true that the 1978 Model Y had the single highest reading. But the first half of the answer choice is wrong, because it's a bad interpretation of the data: the data *does* support the hypothesis in the question. (While we're on the subject, I should point out that the observation in this answer choice isn't enough to *prove* the hypothesis on its own, because the hypothesis is about comparing older cars to newer cars, so a single data point can't prove it. But the fact that an older car had the highest recorded percentage does *support* the hypothesis, since it's consistent with the hypothesis.)

Choice (J) is wrong because the observation in the second half of the choice says the opposite of what the table shows. The 1978 models had uniformly higher percentages, not lower ones. This answer choice will also be tempting for some test-takers who misread the data or remember it incorrectly and don't think to double-check before they answer.

This is yet another example of an ACT Science question that wants to trick us by giving us the chance to make a variety of small mistakes. As always, reading carefully and paying attention will let us find the correct answer.

Page 331, Question 11

To be able to answer this question, we need to re-read the description of exactly how the syringe was used to measure the percentages of CO. If we do that, we can see that the syringe was used to extract the exhaust from the plastic bag around the tailpipe, and then to inject that exhaust into a gas chromatograph, which is the thing that measures the percent of CO, according to the passage.

So if the syringe were contaminated by "CO-free air," that would mean that the sample getting measured would contain some air that had no CO in it at all. Adding something that has no CO to the sample would decrease the percentage of CO in that sample. As a result, all of the percentages that were measured would be lower. That means that choice (C) is the correct answer.

Notice that you don't need the information provided in parentheses in this question ("the composition of air is 78% N_2, 21% O_2, 0.9% Ar, and 0.1% other gases"). The ACT just threw in that information to make the question seem more complicated, which is something the test likes to do when it can. All you need to know is that the air contaminating the sample has no CO, which will bring down the percent of CO in each sample. It doesn't matter what the composition of the air is beyond that.

Page 332, Question 12

This question might look like it requires you to do some calculating. And you could do a calculation here, if you wanted to—that's what the Red Book advises in its explanation on page 422. But it isn't necessary. Let's look at the other way we could approach this question if we don't feel like doing the calculation.

The question mentions Activity 2, and Activity 2 contains Table 2. Table 2 has a column with the heading "Image size," which matches with the phrase "image size" that appears in the prompt for this question, so we know that we're looking at data that's relevant to the question. The "Image size" column in Table 2 has the following values: 4, 10, 20, 40. The corresponding values in the "M" column of Table 2 are 40, 100, 200, 400. So we can see a simple trend: as the image size increases, the M value increases.

The prompt asks about an image size of 30, which is between 20 and 40. That means that the M value for an image size of 30 must be between 200 and 400, because those are the M values for image sizes of 20 and 40. Only one answer choice falls in that range, which is (H). So (H) is correct. (Of course, when we notice that one of the wrong answers, (F), only differs from the correct answer by a single zero, we'll want to make extra sure we've read the table carefully and haven't somehow ended up being off by a factor of 10. But the fact that more answer choices end with two zeroes than with one zero or three zeroes is a good sign that two is probably the correct number of zeroes for the right answer.)

Again, we could always choose to use the formula for M from the passage, as the Red Book solution does. I happen to prefer looking at the data in this case, but either approach is fine. (If you were to do the calculation instead, I think you'd run a greater risk of miscalculating and being off by a factor of 10, which might lead you to choose (F) accidentally.)

Notice that answering the question doesn't require us to understand anything about Activity 2, or even what an objective lens is, or why anybody would care about calculating M. Understanding those things doesn't contribute to answering this question at all. Keep this kind of thing in mind the next time you see an ACT Science question that might seem a little strange.

Page 332, Question 13

This is one example of an ACT Science question that actually does seem to require us to do a basic calculation, unlike questions 12 and 16 from the same passage. The Red Book's solution is pretty decent here. It correctly explains that we need to find the image size for each answer choice, and that this requires us to use the formula in Activity 2 that relates image size to M and object size, because M and object size are the two values we have in each answer choice. That formula is here:

M = image size / object size

So finding the formula for image size, which is the same thing as isolating it on one side of the equation, requires us to multiply both sides of the equation by object size, which gives us this:

M × object size = image size

So all we have to do is multiply the given object size by the given M to get the image size for each answer choice:

(A) 40 × 0.7 mm = 28 mm image size

(B) 100 × 0.6 mm = 60 mm image size

(C) 200 × 0.5 mm = 100 mm image size

(D) 400 × 0.4 mm = 160 mm image size

We can see that the greatest image size is found in choice (D), so that's the correct answer.

As I noted above, this particular Black Book explanation doesn't really add anything to the Red Book explanation for the question. I'm only addressing this question because I want to distinguish it from questions 12 and 16 in the same passage. To untrained test-takers, it will seem as though each of these three questions requires us to do some math, but only this question actually does. (Some might argue that it's possible to do this question without a real calculation as well, because they might be able to notice that the M on objective lens 4 is so much larger than the M values for the other lenses that it will more than compensate for the fact that the object in (D) is the shortest object. In my experience, though, most test-takers would be better off simply doing the calculations, rather than trying to think in those abstract and relativistic terms.)

Page 333, Question 16

This question is similar to question 12 from the same passage, in the sense that both questions might seem to require us to do some kind of calculation, but we can actually determine the correct answer just by looking at the relevant data. The Red Book explanation on page 423 mentions that R in the given equation is inversely proportional to one value and directly proportional to another, but we don't need to think about any of that to answer the question.

The question mentions Activity 3, and Activity 3 includes Table 3. Table 3 has a column with the heading "NA," and another column with the heading "R." These two concepts match up directly with the concepts of "NA" and "R" that we see in the prompt, so we know that Table 3 is where we're supposed to be looking.

When we look at Table 3, we can see two simple trends:

1. The R values decrease as we move from lens 1 to lens 4.
2. The NA values increase as we move from lens 1 to lens 4.

(This is what the Red Book solution is getting at when it mentions that the given formula shows R varies directly with λ and indirectly with NA. But we don't need to know about direct and indirect variation to answer this question, and we definitely don't need to know how to read an equation and tell which variables will vary in which way with which other variables. That's all unnecessary. All we have to do is look at the given data and notice that one value is consistently going down and the other value is consistently going up.)

The question mentions that the fifth lens has an R value of 1,830. This R value falls between the R value for lens 1 (which is 2,750) and the R value for lens 2 (which is 1,100). Because of the trends we just noticed in the chart, we know that the NA value for this fifth lens must also fall between the NA values given for lenses 1 and 2 as well. That means the NA value must be between 0.10 (the NA value of lens 1) and 0.25 (the NA value of lens 2).

Only one answer choice is in that range, and it appears in choice (F), so (F) is the correct answer.

When we look at the other choices, we see that (G) is the same NA value as for lens 2, which has a different R value from the R value of lens 5, so (G) must be wrong. We also see that (H) falls between the NA values of lens 2 and lens 3, while (J) falls between the NA values of lens 3 and lens 4. Neither of those ranges works for the R value of the fifth lens, though, which is clearly between R values for lens 1 and lens 2. So we can be sure that (F) is correct.

Page 334, Question 19

A lot of test-takers have a very hard time with this question because they can't figure out where to find the answer. They don't know which part of the figure corresponds to a temperature of 300 K or a wavelength of 30×10^{-6} m, and they can't figure out why all the answer choices have "10^6 watts per m^3" in them.

As we trained test-takers know, all of these problems must come from not noticing key details of the figure, since the question specifically mentions the figure, and since there's no way the ACT could possibly expect all test-takers to know something about the brightness of a blackbody (or even why anybody would care what a blackbody was in the first place).

So let's inspect the figure. When the figure is a graph, it's pretty much always a good idea to take a look at the labels on the axes, so let's start there.

The vertical axis is labeled "brightness," which matches up with the word "brightness" in the question prompt. So that's promising. If we keep reading after the word "brightness" on the vertical axis label, we see that brightness is measured in units of 10^6 watts per m^3, which is the phrase that keeps appearing in all the answer choices. So that helps solve the apparent mystery of the answer choices. Now let's keep looking at the figure and see what else we can find.

The horizontal axis is labeled "wavelength," which is good for us, because "wavelength" was another word that appeared in the question prompt. The rest of the horizontal axis says the wavelength is measured in units of 10^{-6} m, which is also useful for us to notice because it matches up with the part of the prompt that mentions a wavelength being measured in units of 10^{-6} m.

But we still haven't found the part of the figure that mentions anything being 300 K. And we're running out of places to look :)

At this point, we should remember that we always have to make sure we've read any footnotes, legends, keys, or other surrounding information that might not have initially drawn our eye when we looked at the figure.

In this case, the key above the figure indicates that the dotted line corresponds to 300 K. That's great, because we can now understand that the question is asking us to look at the dotted line when we answer the question. We can also see that the note in parentheses below the figure indicates that the brightness values continue to decrease above wavelengths of 25×10^{-6} m. That's also useful for us to know, because the question asks about a wavelength of 30×10^{-6} m, which is greater than 25×10^{-6} m; now we know that the brightness level will be lower at 30×10^{-6} m than it is at 25×10^{-6} m.

When we put all of this together, we see that the question is asking us to look at the dotted line and figure out what value it would have on the vertical axis if it extended all the way to 30 on the horizontal axis.

(A) is the correct answer, because we can see that the dotted line is already below 5×10^{6} watts per m^3 on the vertical axis when the horizontal axis is at 25. We know that the curve will only continue to decrease from that point, for two reasons:

1. The note we just saw below the figure says so.

2. As trained test-takers, we know that the ACT Science section only asks us to extrapolate from simple trends. So if the curve has been steadily decreasing for a long time as it approaches 25 on the horizontal axis, it would have to keep decreasing as it approached 30 if the ACT is going to ask about it.

The other answer choices are all too large.

(In the end, it actually doesn't matter which curve we end up looking at, because all three of the curves in the figure are already at values below 5 on the vertical axis by the time they reach 25 on the horizontal axis. But it's still important to be in the habit of identifying where all of the numbers and key phrases in each prompt are coming from, so it's a good thing that we figured out which part of the figure corresponds to the concept of 300 K that appears in the prompt. Some small detail like that might be the difference between a right and a wrong answer on a future question.)

Notice that we were able to answer this question without understanding anything about blackbodies, K, brightness, wavelengths, joules, or anything else scientific. Ultimately, the question simply boiled down to this: if the horizontal axis went out to 30 instead of stopping at 25, roughly what value on the y-axis would the dotted curve have at that point?

As usual, we were able to answer the question by looking carefully at the figure and matching up phrases and numbers in the question to the things we saw in the figure. Remember this the next time you see an ACT Science question that seems to be asking you to find something that isn't in the figure—if the test is asking you to find something, it's on the page somewhere.

Page 334, Question 20
The Red Book's explanation for this question, which appears on page 424, is technically correct, but I've been asked about it so many times by so many people that I'd like to address this question here.

The question tells us that the radiation from a star can be graphed the same way as the radiation from a blackbody of a similar temperature. All this means is that we need to find the answer choice that follows the same patterns as the graph of the blackbody curve in the figure.

We don't need to understand what a blackbody is, or what a star is, or *why* the graph for a star looks the same as the graph for a blackbody, or what the graph represents. We just need to find the graph that behaves the same way the one in the figure does, because the question told us to do that.

If we look at the answer choices, we see that they follow a very common pattern on the ACT Science section: they offer us every possible combination of two different pairs of options:

1. One of the options is whether the highest curve on the graph is labeled 3,000 K or 9,000 K.

2. The other option is whether the peaks of the graphs are more to the left (very close to the origin of the graph) or to the right (separated from the origin by many data points).

Realizing that these are the only differences among the answer choices lets us focus our attention on them and ignore everything else (for instance, every answer choice has a vertical axis labeled "brightness" and a horizontal axis labeled "wavelength," so we don't need to think about whether that feature is correct).

Since we know that we're supposed to find the answer choice that's most similar to the original figure, all we have to do is identify the two options that reflect the original figure, and then find the choice with those two options.

In the original figure, the curve that goes the highest also has the highest K value, according to the key above the figure. So the curve that goes the highest in the correct answer choice should also have the highest K value (in this case, 9,000).

The original figure shows all the peaks of the three curves more to the left of the figure, so we also want an answer choice with that feature.

The only answer choice that includes both of the elements we want is (J), so (J) is the correct answer.

If you read the Red Book solution on page 424, it refers to the fact that the correct answer should show "that the wavelength with the maximum brightness . . . increases as the temperature . . . decreases." This is technically correct, but unnecessarily complicated—it just means that if you look carefully at the graph in the figure, and at (J), you'll see that the three peaks in the three curves don't line up perfectly on the same vertical line, because the peak for the highest temperature curve is a little to the left of the peak for the temperature curve in the middle, which is a little to the left of the peak for the lowest temperature curve. Even though the Red Book solution notes this, it's a bit too technical to be the real basis for the ACT's reasoning on this question. A much more generalized observation, like "all the humps in the original graph are pushed over to the left instead of the right," is just fine for ACT purposes.

Page 337, Question 24

Once again, we see that the Red Book's explanation for an ACT question is far more complicated than necessary. The Red Book solution, which can be found on page 426, launches into a discussion of the forces exerted by various fluids in Experiment 1, but we don't need to understand any of those—in fact, we don't even really need to read Experiment 1, except to make sure that the liquid referred to in the question is the hexane referred to in the passage.

Instead, all we have to do is notice that Figure 1 contains a diagram with a drawing of the experimental setup, and that diagram shows the "manometer" with a lower fluid level on the left and a higher fluid level on the right. There's also an arrow pointing to that part of the diagram with the phrase "height of Hg after addition of hexane."

We can also see in the answer choices that the column on the left shows the manometer "before liquid was added," while the column on the right shows the manometer "after Hg level stabilized." The description of Experiment 1 tells us that the Hg level stabilized after the liquid hexane was added—in other words, that the manometer in Figure 1 should correspond to the manometer in the right-hand column in the correct answer choice, because they both show the manometer after the liquid hexane was added.

Only one answer choice has an image in the right-hand column that matches up with the image of the manometer in Figure 1, and that's choice (G). So (G) is correct.

Notice that (J) is the opposite of (G)—it gets the images in the two columns reversed. This is a common type of wrong answer for the ACT to include, because some test-takers will get confused as to the proper order of the images.

Also notice that answering this question didn't require us to know what a "manometer" actually measures, or why some of the hexane evaporated, or what hexane even is. As trained test-takers, we know that we need to attack each question in the most direct and simplified way possible; on the ACT Science section, that usually (but not always) means we just find a relevant figure or table and then match it to one of the answer choices.

Page 337, Question 27

This question requires us to read closely—and it also requires us to know what a test tube is! (Well, kind of . . . keep reading.)

As we discussed in the Science training section of this Black Book, the ACT sometimes includes a question or two that actually does require you to have some scientific knowledge that doesn't appear directly on the page, but that knowledge is always fairly basic. For instance, there might be a question that requires you to know that water contains hydrogen and oxygen, or that dogs are mammals, or something else that's pretty elementary.

This particular question seems to require us to know what a thermometer looks like. We also need to know that a test tube is basically a cylinder that's sealed on one end and open on the other. Some people might argue that we don't really need to know what a test tube is to answer this question, because the passage tells us that the triangular thing in Figure 1 is a flask, so the triangular things in choices (C) and (D) must also be flasks. That's a valid point, I think, but we would still need to know that a flask is not a type of test tube, or another word for test tube.

With all of that in mind, let's look at the question.

As the Red Book points out on page 427, if we read Experiment 2 carefully and know what a test tube looks like, it's pretty clear that (B) is correct, because only (B) shows a test tube with a thermometer inside it, which is part of the description in Experiment 2. (In contrast, (A) shows a test tube next to a thermometer, with both of them inside something else, and (D) shows a flask—not a test tube!—with a thermometer in it.)

Some test-takers might think that the apparatus in Experiment 2 needs to resemble the thing from Figure 1, so they might be tempted to pick (A) or (C). But Experiment 2 never mentions a manometer, so we can eliminate choices (A) and (C), since they both have one.

Don't be too upset if you would have missed this question because you didn't know the difference between a test tube and a flask. It's only one question on the Science section, so it can't impact your overall ACT score too heavily by itself. In fact, you could technically still make a 35 on the Science section and a 36 on the test overall if this were the only question you missed on the entire test. Don't expect future ACT Science sections to ask questions about the difference between a test tube and a flask, because they probably won't—instead, you'll probably see some other basic scientific concepts being tested in the few questions per test that require you to have some outside knowledge.

It's because of questions like this that we need to make absolutely certain that we get questions right when they only require us to read the answers directly from the page—which is what the vast majority of ACT Science questions will do.

Page 337, Question 28

The Red Book solution on page 427 tries to explain this question the way a scientist might think of it, not the way a test-taker should think of it.

The best way to attack this question is probably to read the description of Experiment 1, and then go through each answer choice and consider it in light of what the experimenter did in Experiment 1.

(F) doesn't make any sense, because there's never any mention of H_2O vapor being in the flask, or coming out of it.

(G) doesn't make sense either. The 5 minutes of waiting happened *before* there was any liquid in the flask to evaporate, so it doesn't make sense for the experimenter to wait in order to allow something in the flask to evaporate when that something isn't there yet.

(H) is incorrect, because the experimenter doesn't wait for the Hg to stabilize until several steps after he waits 5 minutes.

(J) is correct because it's the only thing that makes sense in the context of the experiment. The text says that the experimenter waited five minutes immediately after it describes how the experimenter put the flask in the H_2O bath. We don't need to be aware of the scientific reasoning provided in the Red Book's explanation on page 427, because (J) is the only answer choice that's even possible, given the sequence of steps in Experiment 1.

Remember that the ACT Science section doesn't require you to have a strong scientific background! It just requires you to read carefully and pay attention.

Page 338, Question 29

To answer this question, we'll need to see what the passage says about protein shapes with relatively low energy, since that's what the prompt mentions. We don't need to worry if we don't know anything about proteins, or about energy, or why a protein would have a certain type of shape. We just need to find the relevant information in the passage and match it to the correct answer.

The passage specifically says that "lower-energy shapes are more stable than higher-energy shapes." The word "stable" means something like "unchanging," and the only answer choice that reflects this idea of stability is (D), which talks about maintaining (or holding) a shape. So (D) is the correct answer.

Let's take a look at the wrong answers:

(A) is wrong because the text specifically describes random coils as "high-energy shapes," but the question asked about shapes with low energy.

(B) is wrong because nothing in the passage mentions any protein lacking a primary structure.

(C) is wrong because the text specifically states that "a relatively high-energy shape may *denature*," but the question asks about a relatively low-energy shape.

This question ends up being one more example of something we can answer on the ACT Science section without really understanding the science behind it.

Page 338, Question 30

In order to answer this question, we need to understand the terms in the question and in the answer choices. The text tells us that when a protein is "completely denatured," it must be completely *unfolded*, since the text parenthetically defines "denature" as "unfold." So when the question asks which type of structure from the answer choices is not impacted by the protein denaturing, it's really asking which structure isn't impacted by the protein unfolding.

The description for "primary structure" in the passage doesn't say anything about folding.

The descriptions of "secondary structure" and "tertiary structure" both mention "folding patterns," so they would be affected by a process of unfolding.

The description for "quaternary structure" mentions "clustering between more than 1 folded polypeptide," and the first sentence of the passage tells us that a polypeptide is part of a protein. So, if the quaternary structure has to do with folded parts of a protein, then completely unfolding a protein must impact the quaternary structure as well.

So we can see that only the primary structure is unaffected by folding or unfolding, which means that (F) must be correct.

Notice that we didn't need to understand any of the actual science of proteins or amino acids to answer this question, even though the Red Book solution on page 428 refers to both things. All we really had to do was read the passage to realize that denaturing was the same thing as unfolding, and then pick the answer choice that didn't involve folding, according to the passage.

Page 339, Question 34

In order to answer this question correctly, we must (as always) read the whole question and look at all the answer choices. But it's important to realize that checking out the answer choices, in this case, also involves looking at the key below the answer choices, which helps us to realize that we're really being asked to compare the energy levels of a randomly coiled shape, the active shape, and the most stable shape of a protein in a way that is consistent with Scientist 2's assertions about the energy of proteins, but NOT consistent with those of Scientist 1.

Neither scientist addresses the randomly coiled shape specifically, so we can rely on the information given to us in the first half of Passage VI, which says that a random coil is both unstable and high-energy. So we would expect that the white bar should have relatively higher energy, not low energy. Choices (F) and (G) both show the white bar having the lowest energy, so they must be wrong.

That leaves us with (H) and (J). The difference between these two graphs is that one shows the active shape and the most stable shape at the same energy level, and one shows the active shape at a higher energy level than the most stable shape.

Scientist 1 says that "the *active shape* . . . of a protein is always identical to the protein's lowest-energy shape." Choice (H) reflects that view, because it shows that the active shape is tied for the lowest level of energy.

Since (H) is consistent with Scientist 1's assertions, it must not be the correct answer. But let's look at (J) to make sure that it fits with Scientist 2's view, so we can make sure we haven't made a mistake.

The final sentence of Scientist 2's statement says that a protein can have "an active shape that has more energy than its lowest-energy shape." This is certainly consistent with choice (J), which shows an active shape (the gray bar) at a higher level of relative energy than the lowest-energy shape. So we can confirm that (J) is the correct answer.

Page 341, Question 38

At first, this question might seem to be asking something that requires some scientific knowledge outside of what's provided in the passage. But it tells us to look at Figure 1, and if we take a minute to look at the answer choices, only one of them agrees with what Figure 1 says, while the other three directly contradict the figure.

Figure 1 clearly shows the saturation curve for $CaCO_3$ being to the right of the dashed vertical line that indicates saturation when we're looking at a depth less than 1 km. The saturation curve is solidly in the area labeled "supersaturated." Only choice (H) says that seawater is supersaturated with $CaCO_3$ at this depth, so (H) is correct.

If you've studied chemistry, you may know that supersaturation often leads to precipitation, even without looking at the figure. But it's important that we always look at the data provided by the ACT, because we may sometimes find that our understanding of advanced scientific concepts differs from what the ACT's data shows, or from what the ACT is actually asking us about. Notice that this question doesn't require any understanding of what would cause $CaCO_3$ to precipitate out of seawater in less than 1 km of water. All we had to do was read the question and the answer choices carefully, realize that we were being asked about Figure 1, and then find the only answer choice that actually agreed with Figure 1.

Page 475, Question 10

The Red Book's explanation for this question, which appears on page 561, is unnecessarily complicated. Nothing new there, of course. The Red Book talks about using specific gravity and density to determine the correct answer. While that approach isn't wrong, it ignores an approach that's much simpler for most test-takers. Let's talk about the easier approach.

This question might seem difficult at first, because it doesn't specifically refer to any particular table, and it doesn't use any units or key technical terms that might give us more of an idea where to look. Each answer choice does refer to a specific sample from one of the tables, but when we look at the information in those samples we don't see any information that clearly indicates a weight. But we know we must be looking at the right part of the passage, because each answer indicates a particular sample and the information for those samples only appears in the two tables.

So what's going on?

As I mentioned above, I'll address the question as though we don't understand what the prompt means when it asks about "weigh[ing] the most."

Here are the data for each sample mentioned in the answer choices:

(F) Volume: 260 mL. Color: 5. Specific gravity: 1.016. Solids: 42.56.

(G) Volume: 385 mL. Color: 2. Specific gravity: 1.006. Solids: 15.96.

(H) Volume: 150 mL. Color: 7. Specific gravity: 1.024. Solids: 63.84.

(J) Volume: 305 mL. Color: 3. Specific gravity: 1.020. Solids: 53.20.

The prompt specifies that we're only going to be using a 1 mL amount of each sample, so the volume data isn't really relevant to answering the question. In other words, it doesn't matter that the sample in choice (F) was 260 mL and the one in choice (G) was 385 mL, because the prompt tells us that we're just looking at 1 mL of each sample.

So that leaves us with only color, specific gravity, and/or suspended solids to consider when we try to figure out which sample should weigh the most.

Notice that the sample in choice (H) has the highest values in all three of those categories!

So, whether the weight of the 1 mL sample is determined by color, specific gravity, or suspended solids, choice (H) must weigh the most, no matter what, which makes (H) the correct answer.

You may be thinking, "Isn't it possible that there could be a complicated formula that could give us a calculation we could use to determine the weight of student urine, and that this formula might make it so that a 1 mL measure of the sample in (H) isn't actually the heaviest?" If we were actual scientists who were actually studying the actual urine of actual students, you'd be right to wonder about that. But we're just well-trained ACT-takers answering a multiple-choice question, and we know that the ACT Science section doesn't require us to do complicated calculations—*especially* if the passage doesn't even mention a formula for that calculation to follow. We also know the ACT Science section has to provide us with any formulas it wants us to use, and we know that there is no formula in the passage for determining the weight of student urine.

So this question can be answered with total confidence even if we don't understand that density and specific gravity are relevant to weight.

The Red Book solution, on the other hand, relies on the fact that weight is a measurement of the force of gravity on a specific object, and that force is the result of the amount of mass in the object. The density of an object is the ratio of its mass to the space it takes up, and specific gravity is a ratio of the density of an object to the density of water. That probably sounds pretty complicated if you've never studied those things before, but it all boils down to this: the higher an object's specific gravity, the greater the weight of a given volume of that object. But, again, you don't need to know ANY of this to answer this question correctly. All you have to do is look at the samples in each answer choice, ignore the volume data (since the question specifies a constant volume for each sample), and then notice that one sample has the highest numbers in all the other categories. No actual science required.

Now let's talk about the ways that we could mess this question up if we're not paying attention, because there are a lot of them.

One way to mess the question up is to try to find the sample with the greatest weight on your own, rather than comparing the given answer choices to see which of those weighs the most, as the question asks you to do. If you look at the tables and try to find the single sample that would weigh the most, you'll see that it's actually the 8 a.m. sample from Student A (again, this is true whether you use the Red Book's method of considering specific gravity, or the faster and more general method of noticing that the sample has the highest values in every category except volume, and that volume is irrelevant to the question). The problem here is that no answer choice includes the 8 a.m. sample from Student A, so finding that sample on your own would be a waste of time.

Another potential mistake would be to choose the sample with the greatest volume. If the question had asked for the heaviest sample overall, then the volume of each sample could be relevant. But, as we saw above, the prompt specifically asks about 1 mL of each sample, rather than the entire sample itself.

Yet another mistake might come from the fact that the students aren't listed in alphabetical order in the answer choices. I've seen test-takers miss this question in practice because they figured out that Student A's sample was the heaviest and then accidentally marked (F) anyway, since it was the first answer choice bubble in the question and they automatically associated the idea of "A" with the first bubble.

So this question ends up reinforcing a lot of the points that I've emphasized repeatedly through this Black Book. It doesn't actually require us to know anything about science, even though the Red Book would like us to think otherwise. But it does require us to read carefully and correctly navigate several potential traps that are deliberately built into the question.

Page 476, Question 14

In order to answer this question, we need to compare the following sets of things:

1. the freezing point of H_2O without NaCl to the freezing point of H_2O with 0.2 mole of NaCl

2. the boiling point of H_2O without NaCl to the boiling point of H_2O with 0.2 mole of NaCl

After we compare them, we'll find the answer choice that accurately describes their relationships.

In order to make this comparison, we'll need to know the boiling point and freezing point of H_2O without any NaCl in it. That information doesn't appear in either table, but it does appear in the last sentence of the very first paragraph in the passage, which says that H_2O freezes at 0°C and boils at 100°C.

(You might already know that pure water boils at 100°C and freezes at 0°C at standard pressure, but it's always best to check the passage for this type of information because you might remember it incorrectly, or the test might use different values or different units from what you're used to. Remember that you want to rely on information straight out of the passage or question whenever possible.)

So H_2O with no NaCl freezes at 0°C. We can see in Table 1 that with 0.2 mole of NaCl added, H_2O freezes at -6.9°C. That means there's a difference of 6.9°C between the two.

Now we can look at the difference in boiling point. H_2O boils at 100° C with no NaCl, and Table 2 tells us that it boils at 102.0°C with 0.2 mole of NaCl added, which is a difference of 2.0°C.

Since adding 0.2 mole of NaCl drops the freezing temperature by 6.9°C, but only raises the boiling temperature by 2.0°C, we know that (J) is the correct answer choice, because it says that the freezing point is lowered more than the boiling point is raised.

The ACT gives us the usual assortment of ways to mess this question up, all having to do with various ways that we might misread the prompt, the answer choices, or the data. For instance, if we get confused between the change to the boiling point and the change to the freezing point, we might end up choosing (F), which is an exact reversal of the correct answer. As always, we have to make sure we read carefully and don't let these kinds of mistakes happen.

Page 477, Question 16

If you've ever studied chemistry, you might think that this question requires you to understand how molecules of $CaCL_2$ and NaCl break into ions when mixed with water. But that's far too advanced to be required knowledge for an ACT Science question. Instead, we just have to know what the question tells us directly, which is that $CaCl_2$ breaks into three particles for every particle dissolved, while NaCl breaks into two particles for every particle dissolved.

The text in Experiment 1 tells us that 1 mole of NaCl produces 2 moles of solute particles when dissolved. If $CaCl_2$ produces the same effect on the freezing point per particle dissolved, but it produces 3 moles of solute particles, whereas NaCl produces only 2 moles of solute particles per mole dissolved, then we know that a given amount of $CaCl_2$ should have about 3/2 the impact on the freezing point of H_2O compared to a similar amount of NaCl.

Or, to put it another way, a given quantity of $CaCl_2$ should have a larger impact on the freezing point than the same quantity of NaCl, but the impact of the $CaCl_2$ should still be less than twice as large as that of NaCl.

Given that, we can check the chart to see what 0.1 mole of NaCl does to the freezing point of water, since that's the amount that the question asks us about. We can see that it lowers the freezing point by 3.4°C. If that's the case, we can expect $CaCl_2$ to have about 3/2 that effect when 0.1 mole is added to H_2O. So the change should be greater than 3.4°C, but less than 6.8°C. (H) is the answer choice that covers that range, so (H) is correct.

This question may seem a little tricky at first, but it really doesn't require any knowledge of chemistry, and it only requires a small amount of mental math—enough math to be able to tell that 6.8 is twice as much as 3.4. Remember that ACT Science questions will always turn out to be fairly simple if we remember to approach them correctly.

Page 479, Question 19

This question might sound like it requires us to make an actual scientific inference about the studies described, but if we read the answer choices, only one of them is actually supported by the text.

(A) can't be right, because Figure 1 shows the average air temperature by month for the year, and it's not below -25°C year-round.

(B) is the correct answer, because we know for sure there were glaciers present at many different locations since the text describes glaciers at 25 locations in the Arctic and 25 locations in the Antarctic.

(C) can't be right because the text never says there were several months during the year with no precipitation. In fact, the write-up for Study 1 says that containers were placed at the locations to collect snowfall for an entire year, without ever mentioning that there would be a period without snowfall, rain, or other precipitation.

(D) can't be correct because there is no mention of "large areas of bare soil and rock present" anywhere in the passage. The passage routinely mentions drilling ice cores, with no mention of rocks or soil present in the cores.

The Red Book's explanation for this question, which appears on page 564, makes it sound like we have to know something about science in order to be able to understand why the studies were carried out at these sites. But, as we just saw, we didn't actually have to do any scientific analysis here: we can know that (B) is the correct answer because it's the only one that reflects a fact supported in the passage. The other choices are clearly not mentioned in the passage. Don't make these ACT Science questions harder than they actually are!

Page 479, Question 22

This question is a little confusing for most people. Part of the intimidation comes from the notation itself, which most test-takers won't be familiar with. The wording is also a little awkward. But if we read carefully and focus on one part at a time, we can get through it.

Instead of the "$\delta^{18}O$" symbol, I'm going to use the phrase "O-18 index," which appears in the passage, because I think it's easier to understand—for a lot of test-takers, every time they read "$\delta^{18}O$," their eyes glaze over and it means nothing. I also don't want to keep using the phrase "$^{18}O/^{16}O$ ratio" for the same reason—people tend to read right over that without actually noticing it. Instead of saying, "$^{18}O/^{16}O$ ratio," I'm just going to say, "the ratio," and you'll know what I mean. Normally, I wouldn't bother coming up with special phrases for things in an ACT Science question—I'd just use the same phrases the ACT used. But in this case, I've had so many test-takers tell me they were so confused by "$\delta^{18}O$" and "$^{18}O/^{16}O$ ratio" that I've decided to re-name them something easier on the eyes.

Now, with that in mind, if we unravel the first sentence in the prompt, we see that it's asking us how "the ratio" of one sample must compare to "the ratio" of the standard, if the O-18 index for the sample is zero. Then the answer choices give a list of possible relationships.

There are a lot of ways we could approach this. The Red Book's solution is fairly straightforward: it notes that the O-18 index can only be zero if the numerator in its formula is zero, and the numerator can only be zero if "the ratio" for the sample and "the ratio" for the standard are identical, because the numerator is found by subtracting "the ratio" of the standard from "the ratio" of the sample, and the only way to subtract one number from another number and end up with zero is for the numbers to be identical. So (G) would have to be correct. But this is a bit more abstract than many test-takers will feel comfortable with.

If we wanted to think a bit more algebraically, we might approach the question like this:

$$\delta^{18}O = \frac{(^{18}O/^{16}O)_{sample} - (^{18}O/^{16}O)_{standard}}{(^{18}O/^{16}O)_{standard}} * 1{,}000 \qquad \text{(initial formula for the O-18 index)}$$

$$0 = \frac{(^{18}O/^{16}O)_{\text{sample}} - (^{18}O/^{16}O)_{\text{standard}}}{(^{18}O/^{16}O)_{\text{standard}}} * 1{,}000 \qquad \text{(set it equal to 0, as specified in the prompt)}$$

$$0 = \frac{(^{18}O/^{16}O)_{\text{sample}} - (^{18}O/^{16}O)_{\text{standard}}}{(^{18}O/^{16}O)_{\text{standard}}} \qquad \text{(divide both sides by 1,000)}$$

$$0 = (^{18}O/^{16}O)_{\text{sample}} - (^{18}O/^{16}O)_{\text{standard}} \qquad \text{(multiply both sides by “}(^{18}O/^{16}O)_{\text{standard}}\text{”)}$$

$$(^{18}O/^{16}O)_{\text{standard}} = (^{18}O/^{16}O)_{\text{sample}} \qquad \text{(add “}(^{18}O/^{16}O)_{\text{standard}}\text{” to both sides)}$$

This is really just a more formalized way to arrive at the same conclusion found in the Red Book, which is, again, that "the ratio" for the sample must be equal to "the ratio" for the standard.

A third way to approach the question is to borrow a technique we would normally use for the ACT Math section, and actually plug numbers in to the formula for the O-18 index according to the different relationships described in the answer choices, until we arrive at an answer choice that generates an O-18 index of zero.

For instance, to test choice (F), we could say that "the ratio" for the sample was 5, and "the ratio" for the standard was 10. If we plug those values in, the O-18 index doesn't equal zero.

To test choice (G), we could say that "the ratio" for the sample was 10, and "the ratio" for the standard was also 10. Plugging those numbers in (or any pair of identical numbers) does create an O-18 index of zero, because (G) is the correct answer.

To test choice (H), we could plug in 15 for "the ratio" of the sample and 10 for "the ratio" of the standard, and it wouldn't generate an O-18 index of zero.

Finally, to test choice (J), we could plug in 20 as "the ratio" for the sample and 10 as "the ratio" for the standard. Again, we'd see that the O-18 index wasn't zero.

Just to be clear, I'm definitely NOT recommending that you go through all of this substitution or algebraic manipulation if you don't feel like it. I'm just trying to show that it's possible, if you don't feel comfortable approaching the question in any other way. The most direct approach is probably some combination of noticing that the numerator in the fraction needs to be zero, and noticing that one of the answer choices suggests making the two values for "the ratio" identical. But some test-takers won't notice that right away, which is why I wanted to point out the other approaches that could be taken.

Page 480, Question 26

To answer this question correctly, we need to find something that both scientists agree caused the ocean to be oxygen-poor. One good way to do this is to skim the statements of both scientists, looking for phrases like "oxygen-poor," "having little oxygen," "without oxygen," and so on.

If we do that, we see that the phrase "oxygen-poor" appears directly in both statements.

Scientist 1 only describes ocean water as "oxygen-poor" once, at the end of her statement, which says that changing temperatures were "slowing ocean circulation and causing ocean water to become oxygen-poor."

Scientist 2 also only describes ocean water as "oxygen-poor" one time, with the following claim in relation to vertical circulation: "since this circulation was absent 250 Ma, the ocean water was stagnant and oxygen-poor."

So we can see that both scientists talk about ocean water being oxygen-poor when the circulation of ocean water "slowed, stopped, or was absent." That means that choice (G) is correct.

The wrong answers for this question are somewhat similar to the wrong answers we might expect to find in the ACT Reading section.

(F) talks about circulation reversing, but neither scientist mentions that, so (F) is wrong.

(H) talks about oceanic organisms, but neither scientist mentions organisms as factors that affect circulation—Scientist 2 does say that circulation affected organisms, but not that organisms affect circulation. So (H) is wrong.

(J) has the same basic problem as (H), which is that Scientist 1 doesn't mention organisms at all, and Scientist 2 only mentions them as things that are affected by circulation.

Page 482, Question 30

At first glance, this question definitely looks like something you might be asked in chemistry class when learning how to balance reactions. In fact, two of the wrong answers—(G) and (J)—are incorrectly balanced, so a lot of untrained test-takers with experience in chemistry will leap to the incorrect assumption that they should approach this question from that perspective.

But we trained test-takers know there must be something in the passage that will show us what the reaction should look like.

If we look at the very bottom of the first column of text in the passage, we see this reaction:

$2 H_2 + O_2 \rightarrow 2 H_2O$

And if we go back and read Experiment 1, we see that it describes basically the opposite of what the question is asking about. Experiment 1 talks about combining H_2 and O_2 to form H_2O, while this question is talking about H_2O breaking down to form H_2 and O_2. Since $2 H_2 + O_2 \rightarrow 2 H_2O$ describes the formation of water in Experiment 1, we want the answer choice for this question that reverses that process, which is (H). In other words, we want

$2 H_2O \rightarrow 2 H_2 + O_2$

instead of

$2 H_2 + O_2 \rightarrow 2 H_2O$

Furthermore, just from reading the description in the question, we should know that we're talking about H_2O breaking down into H_2 and O_2, so H_2O should be on the left side of the arrow and H_2 and O_2 should be on the right side of the arrow. That eliminates choices (F) and (G) immediately.

Then, reading carefully will show us that (J) is wrong, because it puts the 2 in front of the O_2 rather than in front of the H_2, where it is in the passage. (If we know chemistry, we might also realize (J) is wrong because it's not a balanced reaction—it has 4 H and 2 O on the left, but 2 H and 4 O on the right. But, again, it's always better to rely on what's in the text than to rely on outside knowledge.)

For all of these reasons, we know that (H) is the correct answer.

Page 483, Question 35

The Red Book explanation for this question on page 568 is pretty thorough, and quite valid from a scientific standpoint. But I'd like to point out an approach to the question that I think is probably a lot faster and easier for many test-takers, and which doesn't require much scientific reasoning at all.

Notice that (B) talks about a contamination with "*reactive* impurities [emphasis mine]," and (D) talks about "other reactions occurring" separately from the reaction being studied. Since both choices talk about extra things reacting in the experiment, both choices must be wrong. Think about it: there can only be one correct answer for each question, and both of these choices talk about the potential for extra reactions; since they can't both be correct (because that would require the question to have two correct answers), they must both be wrong.

We can also notice that (C) is incorrect if we look back at the description of Experiment 2 and realize that the "changes in the masses of the tube sections containing . . . $CaCl_2$ were used to calculate . . . the mass of H_2O formed." So if it were possible for H_2O to leave the experiment without being absorbed by the $CaCl_2$, then the change in the mass of the $CaCl_2$ wouldn't be an accurate indication of the amount of H_2O formed, and the results would be misleading. So (C) is also something that would impact the outcome.

Only choice (A) talks about a contamination with "*nonreactive* impurities [emphasis mine]." Since the word "nonreactive" means that the impurities wouldn't react with anything in the experiment, their presence couldn't affect the outcome at all, which means they wouldn't interfere with the interpretation of the results. So (A) is correct.

Notice the importance of the word "NOT" in the question—if we didn't catch that word when reading the question, and if we didn't check all of our answer choices, we might end up thinking we were looking for a single answer choice that *would* cause an error in interpreting the results, and then we might have chosen (B) as soon as we read it, and moved on to the next question without catching our mistake. Untrained test-takers do that kind of thing all the time, and it can cost them lots of points. Read carefully and think carefully, and you'll find the ACT to be an extremely repetitive test of extremely basic ideas, sometimes presented in strange ways, just like I keep saying it is.

Page 485, Question 38

This question asks us for the horizontal length of the chain on the tabletop before the chain was released. If we're not sure where to start with this, we get a hint from the answer choices, because all the answers are in terms of L and/or Y_0.

If we look back at the passage, we see that L is equal to the total length of the chain, and that Y_0 is the length of chain hanging over the table. It makes sense, then, to say that the horizontal length of the chain on the tabletop is equal to the total length of the chain, L, minus the length of chain that is hanging over the edge, Y_0. That matches up with the correct answer, choice (G).

Even if we had difficulty reasoning out the answer that way, we should still be able to arrive at the correct answer once we realize that all the answers are in terms of L and Y_0, and that L is equal to the total length of the chain, and that Y_0 is the length of chain hanging over the table.

We can eliminate (F), because this answer choice would take L (remember that L is already the total length of the chain!) and then add Y_0 (the part of the chain hanging vertically) to it. In order for this to be correct, the horizontal length of the chain would have to be the total length of the chain *plus* the vertical part of the chain, which would result in a length that was greater than the total length of the chain, which isn't possible. Of course, the inclusion of this answer choice follows a very common wrong answer pattern on the ACT, because this choice can be seen as the exact opposite of the correct choice, which involves subtracting Y_0 instead of adding it.

We can also eliminate (H), because there is nothing in the text to support the idea that Y_0, the length of chain hanging vertically over the edge of the table, is equal to the horizontal length of the chain lying on the tabletop.

Finally, we can eliminate (J), because we know that it's equal to the total length of the chain. Since we know a portion of the chain (Y_0) is hanging vertically off the edge of the tabletop, we know that the horizontal length on the tabletop cannot be equal to the full length of the chain.

So there are at least two ways to see that (G) is the correct answer—but both depend on reading the question, thinking about the answer choices, and getting the information you need directly from the passage. Always remember the importance of carefully reading the question, answer choices, and passage.

Page 485, Question 39

The Red Book's explanation for this question on page 569 is good as far as it goes, but it doesn't address the most common mistake that a lot of test-takers will fall for on this question.

Basically, the Red Book points out that a fall time of 0.7 seconds on Earth corresponds to a Y_0 of approximately 10 or 12 cm or so in Figure 3 (make sure you look at the key to realize that the Earth-related values are the ones with darkened boxes).

Then the Red Book shows us that the Y_0 value that corresponds to a fall time of approximately 0.7 seconds on the moon is 45 or 47 cm or so (the Moon-related values are denoted with plus signs).

Now that we know the Y_0 value on the Moon would be 45 or 47 cm or so, and the corresponding Y_0 value on Earth would be 10 or 12 cm or so, we can confidently choose (A), which says that the Y_0 value on the Moon's surface would have to be approximately 35 cm greater than the one on the Earth's surface.

The mistake that many test-takers will make is to choose (C), which mentions a distance of 47 cm. As we just saw, 47 cm is roughly the Y_0 value that corresponds to a fall time of 0.7 seconds on the Moon according to Figure 3— but the question asks for the *difference between the two chain lengths*, not the length of the chain on the moon itself. Can you see how a lot of test-takers will ignore the rest of the words in choice (C) and choose it because it has the number 47 in it?

The key thing here is to bear in mind that the answer choices are given in terms of the two values relative to each other. When people choose (C) because it has the number 47, they don't make that mistake because they don't understand science, or because they can't read graphs, or because they're not cut out for college. They make the mistake because they're not paying attention to the question. They don't read all of the words in all of the answer choices and realize that the question isn't just asking for the value on the graph that corresponds to a certain Y_0 value. This is why, on any section of the ACT, you always have to make sure you read the answer choices carefully, and that the answer you're providing actually answers the question you were asked.

Page 613, Question 2

The Red Book solution for this question appears on page 701. It makes the same tactical mistake that most test-takers will make on this question: it actually finds the mathematical average of the values in both figures. While this approach will lead to the correct answer if you execute it correctly, it will also take more time and energy than necessary.

Since the question asks which sites had the higher averages—and since this is the ACT Science section, which never requires us to do much math—we can probably figure out which values have the highest averages by glancing at the data.

Sure enough, both graphs show significantly more black than they do grey. Since black is associated with Site 1, we know that Site 1 has the higher average values in both figures, so choice (F) is correct.

That's all there is to it. Since the question doesn't require us to find the actual averages, there's no need to spend the time or energy doing it. That time is probably better spent on answering more questions!

The answer choices for this question follow a standard pattern for ACT Science questions, in that they offer every possible combination of two pairs of options. So all we have to do is make sure that we read carefully—for instance, make sure the question is asking for the *higher* average values, and not the *lower* ones.

Page 613, Question 3

The Red Book explanation for this question on page 702 is decent, as far as it goes, but there are a few things I'd like to point out about this question that the Red Book doesn't address.

First of all, notice that the ACT only mentions the stone fly larvae and the phrase "aquatic invertebrate" in this question to help it sound more scientific. All the question is really asking is whether the water quality is better at Site 1 or at Site 2.

And that's another interesting point—many test-takers might naturally assume that an increased number of larvae would correspond to a *lower* level of water quality, because most people would be unhappy to find larvae in their water. But the question specifically says that an increased number of larvae corresponds to a *higher* level of water quality. If you don't read carefully, and with an open mind, you could easily make a small mistake that would prevent you from answering the question correctly.

Finally, I'd like to point out that the question itself only refers us to Table 2, which has a column titled "Average BI," and that column only has numerical values—but the answer choices don't have numerical values for BI. Instead, they feature words like "poor" or "excellent," which might seem very subjective to us at first.

When that kind of thing happens on the ACT Science section, it means that we're not looking at the right part of the passage. In this case, we need to notice that Table 1 gives us a way to correlate BI values with the words "excellent," "good," "fair," and "poor."

Now we can see that Site 1's average BI of 6.3 from Table 2 would be rated "excellent" according to Table 1. Further, we can see that Site 2's average BI of 2.5 corresponds to a rating of "fair" on Table 1.

With this information, we can confidently choose answer choice (B), which says the information in Table 2 does support the idea that Site 1 would support more larvae, and that Site 1's rating was excellent and Site 2's rating was fair.

This is yet another great example of an ACT Science question that's actually very simple, but that offers a lot of opportunities for small mistakes that could cause us to answer the question incorrectly if we're not reading carefully and paying attention to details.

Page 615, Question 9

It's easy to look at this question and be a little intimidated, because it sounds like it requires some outside scientific knowledge. But we trained test-takers know that the ACT Science section can't require us to know something as technical as the details of the reaction referred to in the passage, which looks like this:

$$2Al + 6H_2O \rightarrow 2Al(OH)_3 + 3H_2$$

So that means there has to be some way to figure out the answer even if we only have a very shallow grasp of what's going on in the passage

We probably know that the arrow in the middle of the reaction equation indicates the process of reaction, which means that this reaction produces $Al(OH)_3$ and H_2. (If we don't know what the arrow indicates, we can still answer the question—I'll get to that approach in a minute.)

When we look at the answer choices, we see something interesting: they all refer to the idea of one chemical compound being converted into another, but only one of the answer choices shows anything being converted into one of the products from the reaction in the passage:

(A) mentions H_2O turning into Al. But the given reaction shows Al and H_2O both on the left side of the arrow, being converted into other things, not one being converted into the other. So this choice can't be right.

(B) is the same as (A), just in reverse, and it has the same problem: the reaction from the passage shows Al and H_2O both being converted into other things. So this choice is also wrong.

(C) talks about something from the left side of the reaction from the passage being converted into something that appears on the right side of the reaction from the passage. So this one might be correct—at the very least, it talks about something that's actually happening in the reaction from the passage.

(D) is the reverse of (C), because it describes $Al(OH)_3$ being converted to Al. But the reaction in the passage clearly shows Al on the left side of the equation and $Al(OH)_3$ on the right side of the equation, so actually Al is being converted into $Al(OH)_3$, and not the other way around. So this choice must be wrong as well.

That means (C) must be correct, even if we don't really understand what the question is talking about, because only (C) actually matches what's going on in the passage.

Now let's talk about how we could approach the question even if we didn't know that the direction of the arrow in the reaction indicates that Al and H_2O are coming together to form $Al(OH)_3$ and H_2. If we look for other parts of the passage that mention H_2, we can see that Table 1 refers to H_2 being "produced." The paragraph above Table 1 also refers to H_2 being "produced." This means that the reaction in the passage must be producing H_2. Since H_2 is on the same side of the arrow as $Al(OH)_3$, we know that $Al(OH)_3$ is also being produced by the reaction, which means that stuff is being converted into $Al(OH)_3$ and H_2.

Notice what happened there! We didn't have to spend any time thinking about what rate "the experimenters were able to monitor" "by measuring the volume of H_2." We didn't really have to understand any chemistry, or know what the different chemical symbols in the question refer to. When we actually looked at the answer choices and compared them to the passage, only choice (C) was even possible, because the other three choices all showed the wrong things being produced.

Always remember to keep the answer choices in mind from the very beginning, because they often offer strong clues about the best way to approach a question. And remember not to get intimidated when the ACT tries to make a question look more technical than it is!

Page 617, Question 13
The Red Book's explanation for this question, which appears on page 705, is decent and straightforward. But it leaves out one important detail I'd like to address, which is the concept of potential energy.

Potential energy is energy that's stored or trapped in some way, so that it can be released later. A compressed spring has potential energy, because the spring will exert a force when it returns to its original position after the compression is stopped. This definition of "potential energy" is a fairly basic scientific concept, and knowing it would make answering this question easier to do.

But some test-takers won't know the definition of potential energy. In that case, we could probably still work out that a greater weight and greater compression would probably result in more energy being involved, especially since the situation in Trial 1 leaves the spring totally unchanged, since the scale is empty. So we could still choose the correct answer, choice (C), with a high degree of confidence.

Again, we needed a little bit of outside information here, but it was pretty basic—we only needed to know (or be able to infer) that a compressed spring with weight on it is storing more potential energy than an uncompressed spring without weight on it. We didn't need to know any related formulas or anything else more advanced than that.

Page 617, Question 16
This question might seem like it's asking us to analyze the procedure in the experiment from a scientific standpoint. But, as usual, if we pay close attention to the passage, we'll find that only one answer choice makes sense.

If we read the text, we see that the students put a pencil on each scale, and then laid a board on top of the pencils so that it spanned the distance from one scale to the other. After that, they set the dials to zero.

So what was the impact of setting the dials to zero? Well, before the dials were set to zero, they must have showed some kind of reading, because the two pencils and the board were on the scales. (On top of that, if they weren't showing any reading, there would be no need to reset them to zero—they'd already be at zero if there were no reading.) If the students hadn't set the dials to zero at this point, then the scales would show the weight of the pencils and the board that were already on there, *plus* the weight of any additional object.

By setting the scale to zero, they removed the weight of the pencils and board from the reading, so that when other objects were added to the scales, the scales would only show the weight of the new objects.

That means any measurement they took after setting the dial to zero would be made *without* the weight of the pencils and board. That matches up with the correct answer, choice (J), which says it was done to "subtract" the weights of the board and pencils from each measurement.

Another way to tell that the weight of the pencils and the board is being subtracted from the overall weight measurement is to look at Trials 4, 5, and 6 in Figure 4. In each trial, a 10 N weight sits on top of both scales, and the measurements on the two scales add up to a reading of 10 N (we know this because we know from Study 1 that each 90° rotation on the dial of the scale corresponds to a 5 N weight). Since the scales are only showing the weight of the 10 N block, they must not be including the weight of the board and the pencils.

Choices (F) and (H) must also be wrong because they're talking about the weights of the scales themselves, but Trials 4, 5, and 6 don't show anything weighing the scales themselves.

Once again, we see that a question on the ACT Science section seems to require us to understand the scientific process, but closer inspection reveals that only one of the answer choices reflects what we see directly on the page, and that choice is automatically correct. Keep this kind of thing in mind when you run into challenging ACT Science questions in the future!

Page 619, Question 19

This question can be intimidating for some people because it looks like we're expected to derive some kind of complicated formula, which is something that a real scientist might have to do. But if we work backwards from the answer choices and just use some of the data from Table 1, we can nail down the correct answer pretty quickly.

The most straightforward way to attack this question is probably just to start plugging values from Table 1 into each answer choice. Let's just use the first row of values in Table 1 and see what happens.

The first row of data from the Table shows that when the volume of heptane is 0 mL, the volume of isooctane is 100 mL and the octane number is 100.

If we plug those values into choice (A), we'll notice that we end up dividing by zero, since the value for "volume of heptane" is zero, and that's the only thing in the denominator for (A). So we know that (A) must be wrong, because it's mathematically impossible to divide a number by zero.

If we plug the same values into the formula in choice (B), we'll find that it has the volume of heptane by itself in the numerator. That means the expression in choice (B) would have us divide zero by whatever is in the denominator, and then multiply by 100, which must produce a result of zero. Since we need an octane number of 100 to go with the numbers we're plugging in from the first row of data in Table 1, we know (B) is also wrong.

Choice (C) offers us an expression that won't be undefined or equal to zero, even when we plug in zero for the volume of heptane. When we plug in the values we've been using from the first row of data in Table 1, we get this:

$$\frac{100}{0 + 100} \times 100 \qquad \text{(plug in the data from the first row of Table 1)}$$

$\frac{100}{100} \times 100$ (simplify the denominator)

1×100 (simplify the fraction)

100 (multiply)

So when we take the values for the first row of data in Table 1 and plug them into choice (C), we get a result of 100, which is the octane number from the first row of Table 1. That means this equation works, at least for the first row of values. Now let's look at the final answer choice.

Choice (D) has heptane alone in the numerator again, like choice (B) did, so it will have to come out to be zero as well, which means it can't be correct since we're looking for a final result of 100.

If more than one expression had worked for the first set of values, we would have had to try the next row of values until we found that only one expression worked for all the values in the table. But we were able to rule out three of the four choices just by testing the first row of values in Table 1. Since only choice (C) worked for those values, we know that (C) is the correct answer. If we feel like it, we can test another set of values to make sure we haven't made a mistake and that (C) works for those values, as well.

Notice that if we just look at the table and glance through the answer choices, and if we realize that plugging in 0 for heptane has to be able to produce a result of 100, we can rule out (A), (B), and (D) immediately since a heptane value of zero in those expressions results in either zero or an undefined result no matter what the value for isooctane is. Since we trained test-takers know that the ACT Science section doesn't like to make us do much actual math, we can understand why the test included data points with a value of zero: they're much easier to plug into this set of answer choices.

Page 619, Question 21

This question asks us which of the 2 fuels from Experiment 3 would be "better" in an engine that runs between 1,500 and 3,500 rpm. If we look at Experiment 3, we can see there is a table laying out some information about Fuel A and Fuel B.

At first it might not be clear how we're supposed to determine which fuel is "better," but if we read the answer choices, we'll see that every single one makes reference to the EOR. Of course, EOR isn't anything we're supposed to know about already—it must be information we can find in the passage. The text for Experiment 3 tells us that EOR is "the minimum octane number of a fuel required for an engine to operate without becoming damaged."

If EOR is the minimum number that can be used without damage, then we obviously want the fuel to have a higher octane number than the EOR. Since we want to figure out which fuel is best at all speeds between 1,500 and 3,500, we need to see how the octane numbers of both fuels compare to the EOR at each engine speed in Table 2.

When we do that, we'll see that the octane number of both fuels is over the EOR in all but one case—the octane number of Fuel B is less than the EOR at 1,500 rpm. Since only Fuel A has an octane number above the EOR at each speed, we know that (B) is correct.

Notice that we could also just eliminate choices (A), (C), and (D) based on the supporting information in each choice.

(A) says that Fuel A's octane number was lower than the EOR at each speed, which isn't correct.

(C) says that Fuel B's octane number was lower than the EOR at each speed, which also isn't correct.

(D) says that Fuel B's octane number was higher than the EOR at each speed tested, which isn't correct, either.

That approach would also have left us with (B) as the correct answer.

Page 620, Question 25

The Red Book's explanation for this question on page 709 is okay as far as it goes: the introduction says that short-period comets have inclinations of 30° or less, and only choice (D) falls outside of that range, so it must be correct.

I just wanted to point this question out because it's one more good example of an ACT question that's very basic but very easy to miss if we're not paying careful enough attention. We always have to make sure we read the prompt and all the answer choices carefully!

Page 621, Question 26

Again, the Red Book solution on page 710 is decent—it correctly points out that the key element of the question is that giant planets like Jupiter affect the orbital periods of some comets, and that Saturn is the only giant planet in the answer choices, which makes (J) correct.

But I wanted to discuss this question because it's one of the relatively rare ACT Science questions that actually does require outside scientific knowledge. As always in these situations, the required outside knowledge is relatively basic—we needed to know that Saturn was the only giant planet in the answer choices. This concept is also fairly unlikely to be tested on the ACT ever again, so don't bother memorizing facts about the planets for future ACT Science questions.

If you happened to study the solar system a little bit at some point and you remembered that Saturn is a giant planet, great. If not, don't worry about it, and don't worry about which basic fact will be tested on the real ACT when you take it. There's simply no way to predict what it will be. Instead, just focus on refining your approach to the ACT Science section so you can make sure you get questions right when the answer is directly on the page—since that will be the case for the vast majority of ACT Science questions. (For example, on this particular test, you could still score a 34 on the Science section if you only missed this question, question 31, and question 38, which are the three questions from this test that require outside knowledge. With a 34 on the Science section, you could still technically score a 36 on the ACT overall.)

Page 622, Question 31

This question describes osmosis as water moving through a barrier, and then asks us through which structure the osmosis occurs in the passage. So we need to look at the text to find the "osmosis" referred to in the passage.

If we do that, we'll see that the first bullet point in the passage describes "a net movement of H_2O between the cytoplasm of the plants' cells and the environment via osmosis."

We can tell that "the cytoplasm of the plants' cells" must be something inside the cell, and we know that "the environment" must be outside the cell. If something moves from inside the cell to outside the cell, it *must* pass through the cell membrane, which is the barrier between the inside of the cell and the environment. That means the correct answer is choice (C).

This is another question that requires a small amount of outside knowledge—as we trained test-takers know, there might be three or so questions like this on average per test. But notice how basic this fact was, really. We didn't need to know anything about the rough endoplasmic reticulum, or about how chromosomes work, or about the plant *Arabidopsis thaliana*. We only needed to know that the cell membrane separates what's inside the cell from what's outside the cell. (Actually, if we just know that the word "membrane" refers to a biological structure that serves as a boundary, we can probably answer the question from that alone.)

As I always say when we talk about an ACT Science question that requires outside knowledge, it's important not to get too worried if you didn't happen to know the answer to this one. Hopefully you'll get the next one, but, whether you do or not, it's far more important to work on the ACT Science questions that provide the answers directly on the page, because those questions will make up the vast majority of the Science section. As I just mentioned in our discussion of question 26, it would still technically be possible to score a 34 on this Science section and a 36 on this ACT overall if we missed all three questions on this section that require actual scientific knowledge, but still answered the other 37 Science questions correctly.

Page 625, Question 38

In order to answer this question, we have to understand how heat is transferred from one end of a rod to another. The word "conduction" refers to the process of heat moving along an object (from one end to the other), or from one solid object to another through direct contact. The word "convection" refers to the process of heat moving through a gas or a liquid that's in motion. The word "radiation" refers to the process of heat being released through electromagnetism.

In this case, since the heat is moving through solid objects themselves, we know that most of the heat being transferred must be moving by way of conduction. That means (H) is the correct answer.

Once more, we see a question that requires a little outside scientific knowledge—one big hint that this is the case is that the words "radiation," "convection," and "conduction" from the question aren't mentioned anywhere in the passage.

If we're not sure which is the correct answer, we might realize that when something conducts electricity, the electricity is moving along an object, or a string of objects, in a way that's similar to the way the passage describes the heat moving from one rod to another.

If you're dealing with one of the few questions per Science section that does require some actual scientific knowledge, and if you've got nothing else to go on, you can try looking for some simple, basic connection like this, mark your answer, and move on. There's no benefit to sitting and staring at one of the few questions that require outside scientific knowledge when the majority of the questions on the ACT Science section can be answered with information on the page in front of you.

So don't let this question bother you too much—your goal is still to master answering the questions that have answers directly on the page. Again, as I explained in our discussion of questions 26 and 31 from this section, you would still score a 34 on this particular ACT Science section if you only missed the three questions that require outside scientific knowledge. And that score would actually still allow you to make a perfect 36 overall on the entire ACT, if you scored 36s on the other three sections.

Page 625, Question 39

This question asks us which of the answer choices will have the highest value of R, assuming they all have the same ΔT. The differences among the answer choices seem to relate to the total length of the arrangement, and the number of rods, so we should look back into the passage to see if we can find something that relates R to the number of rods or the total length.

The challenge of this question comes primarily from the fact that the question doesn't tell us which part of the passage to look at for the answer. But since the question is asking about R, we can focus on the parts of the passage that mention R and see which ones are relevant to our answer choices.

Table 1 doesn't seem to be relevant, because it shows different R values with different ΔT values, but the question tells us that all of the rods in the answer choices have the same ΔT.

Figure 2 seems relevant, because it relates R to length, and we can see that the answer choices show identical rods arranged at different lengths.

Figure 3 doesn't look relevant to our answer choices, because it relates R to cross-section, and the rods in the answer choices all have the same cross-section, since we're told they're identical.

So Figure 2 is where we want to focus our attention. It shows a graph relating the R value to the lengths of different rods. We can see that R gets smaller as the length gets larger. That means that the answer choice with the greatest R value will be the one with the shortest length. In this case, that's choice (A), which is the correct answer.

Of course, we want to make sure we read very carefully to make certain that the question did indeed ask for the highest value of R, as opposed to the lowest value, as this kind of mistake is very common for test-takers who aren't in the habit of paying constant attention to the test.

Page 757, Question 2

In order to answer this question, we need to know what the question means when it talks about the concentration of LiCl increasing. In this context, concentration is the ratio between the amount of LiCl and the amount of H_2O in the sample.

So the concentration of LiCl can increase in two different ways, for our purposes:

1. The amount of LiCl can increase while the amount of H_2O remains the same.
2. The amount of H_2O can decrease while the amount of LiCl remains the same.

(Notice that this conclusion comes from the definition of the word "concentration," which is a common English word, not a technical scientific term.)

With that in mind, let's consider Figure 1. It shows three trials, each involving 20 g of LiCl dissolved in different amounts of H_2O. So which trial has the higher concentration? Well, if the amount of LiCl is the same in each sample, then the sample with the least amount of H_2O will have the highest concentration of LiCl.

So the highest concentration of LiCl occurs in the trial with 50 g of H_2O, and the lowest concentration of LiCl occurs in the sample with 100 g of H_2O.

We can see in Figure 1 that the curve representing the highest concentration of LiCl always has the highest ΔT values associated with it for any given mass, while the curve representing the lowest concentration of LiCl always has the lowest ΔT values. So we know that the correct answer is (F).

This question presents the usual assortment of traps that the ACT likes to use on the Science section. One of the wrong answers is the exact opposite of the correct answer, and the question gives us several opportunities to misread or misunderstand things and end up choosing (H). We might misread the prompt and think that it asks what happens as the LiCl concentration *decreased*, or we might misunderstand the concept of concentration and think that the sample with 50 g H_2O had the *lowest* concentration. As we've seen over and over again, these types of small mistakes are the ACT's main tactic to use against us. This is why we must always read carefully and pay attention!

Page 759, Question 6

The Red Book's explanation for this question starts on page 840, and it's much longer and more complicated than necessary.

That explanation tells us to look at Table 1 for the map distances between certain pairs of genes, and then to notice that the models referred to in the question observe those distances, and then to do a couple of other things. This approach can lead to the correct answer, but it's much easier to look at Figure 3 and work through the answer choices.

We know that Figure 3 is the proper place to look because the question refers to "4 models," and Figure 3 is the only place where we see four models.

The figure doesn't have any markings or anything to help us measure the distances, so we're going to have to eyeball them and go from there—we can trust that this approach will work because we know that the ACT Science section doesn't require us to make extremely precise readings that would require any kind of measuring device. So the differences among the distances must be obvious enough for us to come to a clear conclusion if we just look at them.

Let's take it one answer choice at a time.

If we look at the distances between A and B in each model, they appear to be pretty consistent. So choice (F) looks good, but we'll need to take a look at the other choices to be sure we're understanding the question correctly.

The distances between A and C in the first two models look pretty similar, but in 3 and 4 the distances are much shorter, so (G) is obviously not correct.

The distances between B and D are very short in models 2 and 4, and clearly longer in the other models. So (H) is also not correct.

Finally, the distance between C and D is very long in model 1, and very short in model 3, so that's enough for us to say that (J) is wrong as well.

Since we can clearly see that the models don't agree about the distances between the gene pairs in choices (G), (H), and (J), and because the distances between A and B seem to be consistent from model to model, we know that choice (F) must be the correct answer.

Notice that we were able to reach this conclusion without knowing anything about genes, models, RF, or anything else in the passage. Remember that the ACT Science section doesn't require us to know any advanced or obscure scientific facts.

Page 759, Question 10

This is one of those rare ACT Science questions that require outside scientific knowledge to answer. As is always the case with these questions, we just need general, basic knowledge of the subject matter in order to answer this question correctly—even though the ACT does its best to make the question seem complicated and difficult. Let's take a look.

This question asks which of the answer choices contains the name of the thing that's formed directly after the process that includes crossing over, which is discussed in the beginning of the passage. That sounds pretty scientific and scary, right?

Well, let's think about it a little bit. If we go back to the passage, we see that crossing over is related to chromosomes. If there's one thing we remember about chromosomes, it's probably that they're related to reproduction in some way, right?

Many test-takers who've had a biology class will remember that gametes play a role in the process of reproduction and are related to concepts like meiosis, chromosomes, and genes, which all appear in the passage. That will be enough for them to realize that (J) is the correct answer.

But some test-takers may not recognize the term "gamete," so they'll need to try to eliminate some other answer choices.

We might remember that neurons have to do with the nervous system (or we may be able to guess that from the "neuro-" part of the word). The nervous system isn't directly related to reproduction and chromosomes, so (F) is incorrect.

Skin cells aren't particularly relevant to reproduction, either, so (G) is incorrect.

It might be hard to figure out what an erythrocyte is if we don't already know the term (it's a red blood cell, by the way). If we happen to know what the word means, then we can tell that (H) is also not directly related to chromosomes and gene exchanges, which means it must also be wrong.

Even if we don't know the terms in (H) or (J), we can at least make a quick guess between the two choices and then move on.

Don't be alarmed if you wouldn't be able to answer this question on test day! As we've seen in every test from the Red Book (and in every other real ACT you'll ever see), each ACT Science section contains a handful of questions at most that actually require us to know some kind of basic scientific fact that isn't present on the page. Those basic scientific facts aren't repeated from test to test, so there's no point in studying meiosis to try to raise your ACT score, because it's very unlikely that any material from this question will appear on a future ACT. Instead, it's important to focus on mastering the correct approach to the ACT Science questions that require you to find the answer on the page, because those questions make up the vast majority of each ACT Science section. In fact, this question and number 22 are the only two questions on this particular ACT Science section that require outside knowledge. If you miss them both but answer everything else correctly, you'll actually still make a perfect 36 scaled score on the Science section, as you can see on page 924 in the Red Book, which has the conversion table for this practice test.

Page 762, Question 18

This question looks pretty scary to most test-takers—in fact, the entire passage does.

But, as always, we trained test-takers know that the ACT can't require us to know advanced, highly technical facts about something like the radioactive decay of a particular isotope. So if the ACT is asking us a question about something like that, then it must be possible to find the answer somewhere in the passage—without actually knowing any chemistry.

There are a few different ways we can figure out the answer to this question. The Red Book's approach, which appears on page 846, requires us to put together information from a few different places within the passage. The Red Book would have us find the Ra element on the top horizontal axis of Figure 1, and notice that the point on the curve underneath Ra corresponds to values of 88 on the horizontal axis of the figure and 226 on the vertical axis. From there, we need to notice that the horizontal axis is labeled with a Z, and the vertical axis is labeled with an A. Then we go hunting in the beginning of the passage and find that the proper notation for an atomic nucleus, according to the passage, takes this form:

$$^A_Z X$$

In our situation, the X represents the element (Ra), while A and Z correspond to the values we found for Ra in Figure 1: those values are 226 and 88, respectively.

So we can see that choice (J) puts everything in the proper format.

But, as often happens, there are other approaches we might take.

Notice that all of the answer choices feature the same chemical symbol, which is Ra, and they all restrict themselves to the same numbers: 226 and 88.

So if we check out the answer choices, we actually know for sure that we're working with Ra as the chemical symbol (because it's our only option), and now we just need to figure out how to arrange the 226 and/or 88.

If we glance around the passage, we find that several elements are presented in the $^A_Z X$ format throughout the passage:

- $^{12}_{6}C$

- $^{14}_{6}C$
- $^{238}_{92}U$
- $^{4}_{2}He$

In each case, there are two different numbers next to the chemical symbol, and the bigger number is written above the smaller number. If we look at the passage, we see that the number on the top is equal to the bottom number plus some other number, which explains why the number on top is always bigger. That in itself is also enough for us to know that (J) is the correct answer, and we never even have to look at Figure 1.

The wrong answer choices for this question follow a typical ACT Science pattern: every possible combination of 226 or 88 for the top number and for the bottom number. So we just double-check that we haven't made any mistakes, mark (J), and move on.

Notice that neither of these approaches requires us to know anything at all about radioactive decay, Radium, isotopes, nuclei, or anything else. Keep this kind of thing in mind the next time you see an ACT Science question that seems scary and technical!

Page 762, Question 20

This question asks us what would be produced if a nucleus of $^{230}_{90}Th$ underwent something called "beta decay." You might be thinking, "I don't know what beta decay is!" Don't worry—you can still find the correct answer without knowing the term "beta decay" in advance. All you have to do is look at Figure 1 and use all the information it provides, and compare Figure 1 to the answer choices.

Where is "beta decay" mentioned in Figure 1? It's in the key, and the key says that the β symbol indicates beta decay. So let's look at Figure 1 and see what we can learn from that.

Look at the beginning of the sequence, near the top left corner. There's a point at (92, 238). Then the line moves diagonally 2 units to the right, and 4 units down (in terms of Z and A, respectively). The line segment corresponding to that move is marked with an α, which the key tells us means "alpha decay."

From this new spot, the point moves to the left 1 unit, without moving vertically at all. That movement of 1 unit to the left is marked with a β, so we know it's an example of beta decay. Then it moves left one more unit, and that segment is also marked with a β.

Next the line segment moves diagonally 2 units to the right and 4 units down again, and that move is marked with another α.

We can keep going through the rest of Figure 1, but it seems pretty clear that the β symbol, which corresponds to beta decay, just means that the line moves one unit to the left.

So let's get back to the original question. We're asked what would be produced if a nucleus of $^{230}_{90}Th$ underwent beta decay. In terms of Figure 1, beta decay is just moving one space to the left. So let's find the point where $^{230}_{90}Th$ should be on the figure. It's at the intersection of the vertical line corresponding to 90 and the horizontal line corresponding to 230.

From that point, we move one unit to the left. Where are we now? We're at a Z value of 91, and the same A value of 230. When we move our eyes up the vertical line at $Z=91$, we see that the element has changed to Pa. The A value remains unchanged, so the result is $^{230}_{91}Pa$, which matches up with (G). So (G) is the correct answer.

That approach is pretty similar to the Red Book's explanation on page 847. But there's another approach we can use if we just focus on the answer choices, and it doesn't require us to understand the graphical representation of beta decay that appears in Figure 1.

As we saw when we looked at question 18 from this passage, the top number in the ^4_2X format must be larger than the bottom number, because the top number is the sum of the bottom number and some other number. So answer choices (F) and (J) must be wrong because they don't have top numbers that are larger than their bottom numbers.

Between choice (G) and choice (H), the only difference is whether the chemical symbol is Pa or Th. So now we have to figure out which of those symbols is correct. Since they only appear on Figure 1 in the passage, we can look there and see that Pa corresponds to a Z value of 91, while Th corresponds to a Z value of 90. Since we know that 91 must be part of the correct answer (because it's common to both (G) and (H), and one of them must be correct), we also know that Pa is the appropriate chemical symbol. So we can figure out that (G) must be correct even if we don't really understand how beta decay relates to Figure 1. This is one more good example of the importance of considering the similarities and differences among answer choices when you approach an ACT question!

Page 763, Question 22

The Red Book's explanation for this question on page 848 actually refers to the formula that a physicist would use to relate kinetic energy to mass and velocity. If you happen to know that formula off the top of your head, you could use it, of course, but it's ridiculous to assume that most ACT-takers will have that formula memorized when they take the test. I wouldn't recommend that you bother to learn that formula for future ACT questions, because it's extremely unlikely that a future ACT question will test it. As we've seen throughout our discussion of the ACT Science section, the ACT seems to find a new area of basic scientific knowledge to incorporate with each new test.

So let's talk about how we might approach this question even if we don't know the formula to relate kinetic energy to mass and velocity.

The first thing I would do in this situation, as in so many other situations on the ACT, is to look at the answer choices and see how they relate to one another. We see that the answer choices follow a common pattern on the ACT Science section: they offer every possible combination of the idea that either ^4_2He or e⁻ is moving at a higher speed, and the idea that either ^4_2He or e⁻ is more massive. So all we have to do is focus on those two issues.

It's probably easier to figure out which particle is larger first.

If we've ever taken a chemistry class, we probably know that electrons are smaller than nuclei or atoms (the e⁻ symbol represents an electron, as we can see from Table 1). Even if we're not familiar with the relative sizes of electrons and nuclei, we could probably guess that the ^4_2He nucleus is larger than the electron because we know that the ^4_2He nucleus is made up of at least 4 particles, while the electron is only one particle.

So the correct answer will have to include the idea that the electron is smaller than the ^4_2He nucleus. That idea is reflected in choices (F) and (J).

Now we need to figure out which particle should be moving faster—the smaller one, or the bigger one.

The prompt says that both particles would "have the same kinetic energy." (Let's proceed as though we don't know what the word "kinetic" means, for purposes of this discussion.)

Imagine that we have two everyday objects of different masses—say, a bowling ball and a golf ball. If we apply the same amount of energy to each ball, which one will roll away faster? We can probably tell that the smaller object will roll faster. It makes sense, if you think about it: if the amount of energy is constant, the smaller object should be affected by the energy more, because it has less "stuff" to bear the impact of the energy.

Following that idea, we can tell that the electron should move faster than the nucleus, because it has less mass for the energy to work on, which means that the energy should be able to drive the mass away more quickly. (Again, think of pushing a golf ball or a bowling ball with the same amount of power—wouldn't the less massive golf ball move faster?)

So (J) is the correct answer.

Don't worry if you weren't able to reason through this question with a little basic knowledge of physics. On this particular ACT Science section, if you only missed this question and number 10, which are the two questions on this test that require a little outside scientific knowledge, you would still score a perfect 36 on the Science section. (You can find the score conversion table for this ACT Science section on page 924 in the Red Book.)

Page 765, Question 26

This question asks us whether P3 molecules or P4 molecules diffused more easily into the pores of the beads while in the column of the SEC apparatus. What does the passage tell us about molecules diffusing easily into the pores of the beads?

Well, if we read the text of Passage V just below Figure 1, we see this: "smaller molecules easily diffuse into the pores. Larger molecules do not as easily diffuse into the pores." Now we know that whichever of the P3 or P4 molecules is smaller diffused more easily, so we just have to find out their relative sizes.

We can see data about these molecules listed in Table 1. The block of text under Figure 1 tells us that AMM stands for "average molecular mass," which confirms that we are looking at their sizes, as measured in amu, or "atomic mass units," as the bottom of the table tells us.

When we check the table, we see that P3 is the smaller of the two molecules, which means it should diffuse more easily into the pores. That means the correct answer is (G), since it correctly identifies which molecule would diffuse more easily *and* correctly compares the molecules' AMMs.

Note that we could also have ruled out (F) and (J) based on the fact that they make incorrect statements about the relative AMMs of the molecules.

Page 765, Question 27

In order to answer this question correctly, we need to think about what we know about molecules that measure 200,000 amu. If we look through the passage, we'll see in Table 1 that P5 molecules measure 200,000 amu. We can also see that Figure 2 shows all the molecules from Table 1 analyzed in the same way as the molecules in Figure 3.

When we look at Figure 2, we can see that the larger the molecule is, the lower its RT is. Molecule P5 is present in the figure at just under 5 minutes of RT. We can also see that all of the molecules smaller than P5 have higher values for RT. Along the same lines, we can see that larger molecules in Table 1 have lower RT values is in Figure 2.

With that in mind, we can look at M1, M2, and M3 in Figure 3 to decide which, if any, are probably larger than 200,000 amu. Only M1 has an RT that's lower than the RT of P5, so we know that M1 must have a size larger than the size of P5, which was 200,000 amu. That means (A) is the correct answer.

Notice that this question required us to combine information from three different places in the passage (Table 1, Figure 2, and Figure 3). Remember that this happens sometimes on the ACT Science section but, as always in these situations, we were able to find the relevant information by looking through the passage and the data for unusual technical terms from the question and the answer choices—in this case, those concepts from the question included things like 200,000 amu and M1, and then locating those things in the data led us to realize that concepts like P5 and RT were also relevant. It's all about careful reading and paying attention to details!

Page 765, Question 28

A lot of people aren't sure what to do with this problem because it feels like it might require some kind of outside information, but it's actually just testing a very simple idea based on data from the passage.

We're asked if a 1 gram sample of P2 would have more molecules or fewer molecules then a 1 gram sample of P4. If we check the answer choices, we can see that they all mention which molecule has a greater or lesser AMM, which is a big hint that we need to consider that in our answer.

We know from the passage that AMM is a measurement of molecular mass, and we can see in Table 1 that P4 has a greater AMM then P2, which means it has larger molecules.

So we can eliminate (F) and (H) because they include incorrect statements about the relative sizes of the molecules.

That means the question boils down to this: if you have a 1 gram sample of bigger things, and a 1 gram sample of smaller things, do you have a higher number of the bigger things or of the smaller things?

Well, you must have more of the smaller things, because they're smaller, which means it would take more of them to make up a given amount of mass. So the correct answer is (J).

Do you see how this doesn't really have anything to do with molecules, or really even with science? It's really just about counting. (It would be like if the question said, "If you have 10 pounds of 5-pound weights, and 10 pounds of 1-pound weights, do you have more 5 pound weights or 1 pound weights?" Of course, the answer would be that you have more 1 pound weights, because it would take more of them to reach a given weight.)

The ACT just found a more scientific-sounding way to ask this question so it could confuse a lot of people, which is exactly what the test is pretty much always trying to do.

Page 767, Question 30

In order to answer this question, we need to refer to Figure 1, where we can find the data about the mass lost by the leaves at 35% O_2. The key above the figure is critical for this, because there are four different lines in Figure 1, and we have to make sure we're paying attention to the right one. Since we're answering a question about leaves in an atmosphere of 35% O_2, we need to track the solid black line.

Now let's check the ranges of each answer choice. (F) and (G) both show drops in the percent of mass remaining. Choice (H) shows a drop as well, but less of one. Choice (J) corresponds to a much steeper drop than any of the other choices, so we know that (J) must be the correct answer.

Notice that choice (G) corresponds to a very steep drop in the lines corresponding to the data for paper—*not* for leaves! I'm sure you can imagine that lots of test-takers will make some kind of careless mistake that leads them to pick (G) because they misread the data, the key, or the question. Always make sure you look at the key so you know you're working with the right information!

Page 767, Question 31

The Red Book's solution to this question on page 851 neglects to explain a crucial step that many test-takers have problems with, and I'd just like to explain what that step is.

The question talks about the idea of a tree "burn[ing] completely" or not, but Table 1 doesn't specifically mention the idea of a complete burn.

But when we look at Table 1, we see a lot of data points that appear as the letter F, even though the table doesn't have a key that explains what the Fs mean. So we'll need to find some other explanation for the letter F. When we turn to the passage, we see in the paragraph above Table 1 that the F corresponds to a "failed burn," which is a trial in which the sample doesn't burn completely.

So now we know that the F values in Table 1 indicate that a sample didn't burn completely.

With that in mind, we need to determine whether a tree with a water content above 65% would burn in an atmosphere of 28% O_2, and in an atmosphere of 35% O_2.

We can see from the data in Table 1 that, as the water content increases, the samples are more likely to fail to burn completely. In fact, once the water content hits 61% for either kind of sample, all the samples fail to burn completely, no matter the level of oxygen in the atmosphere (including both 28% and 35% O_2).

If the samples all fail to burn at 61% water content, we know that similar material would also fail to burn at an even higher water content. The question refers to a water content greater than 65%, which is greater than the 61% shown in Table 1. So we know (B) is correct, because it says the sample would fail to burn at either percentage of O_2.

Notice here that we don't need to know anything at all about the Paleozoic era, or about modern *Pinus* trees. We know the ACT loves to throw in irrelevant scientific words to intimidate us when it can. Don't let it intimidate you!

Conclusion

By now, you've seen a lot of real ACT Science questions, and I hope you're getting used to the idea that you need to know very little actual science for the ACT. This part of the test is really a lot like the ACT Reading section, except that it involves tables and figures, and scientific subject matter.

The most important skill you need to develop is the ability to read the question and use the key terms in the question and the answer choices to find the information you need in the passage. If you can just do that over and over again, you'll get a great score on the ACT Science section.

Using The Question Explanations In *The Real ACT Prep Guide, 3rd Edition*

There is some value in the question discussions in *The Real ACT Prep Guide, 3rd Edition*, as long as you use them appropriately. First of all, you want to ignore any phrasing about "the best answer." For every question, there is one correct answer choice and there are three incorrect answer choices. You'll never have to choose a "best" answer from among several "good" answers—choices are always either right or wrong, and each question only has one answer that could be correct according to the ACT's rules.

Also, you'll generally find that explanations in the Red Book tend to be more formal than necessary, and they also tend to bring up outside knowledge you don't actually need when you're answering a question. They also often fail to point out ways you could eliminate incorrect answer choices based on how they contradict the passage, or are not supported by the passage.

So if you find yourself stuck on a question that we didn't walk through in this Black Book, you may want to take a look at the explanation for that question in the Red Book to get an idea of one way to solve that question. Just bear in mind that there's probably a quicker, less scientific way to solve that question, and/or that you may be able to eliminate some answer choices in ways that aren't mentioned in the walkthroughs in that book.

Video Demonstrations

If you'd like to see videos of some sample solutions like the ones in this book, please visit www.ACTprepVideos.com, where a selection of free videos is available for readers of this book.

ACT Science Quick Summary

This is a one-page summary of the major concepts for the ACT Science section. Use it to evaluate your comprehension or jog your memory. For a more in-depth treatment of these ideas, see the rest of the section.

The Big Secret: Almost all ACT Science questions reward you for reading the passage and finding the correct answer spelled out on the page. ACT Science is a lot like ACT Reading, except that it involves charts and graphs and scientific terminology.

Don't freak out when you see scientific terms you don't know. They'll either be explained in the passage somewhere, or you won't need to know them to answer the question.

Use the right data. Many passages involve multiple tables, graphs, etc., with similar information. Check to make sure you're using the right data to answer a given question.

Pay close attention to the labels on graphs, charts, and diagrams. These will tell you whether the data you're looking at is relevant to the question you're trying to answer.

There will be very few questions that require you to know any science on your own—plan on 3 to 4 questions like this at most. These questions are often designed to seem like they're advanced to an untrained test-taker, but they really hinge on basic ideas. You'll know you're dealing with one of these questions when it involves terms that aren't in the passage.

Answer choices are important because they can tell you what you'll need to think about to answer the question. They're as important as any other part of the question, so always read them carefully.

Here are some of the common answer choice patterns you'll see:

- Answer choices contain all the answers of a certain type that are relevant to the question—this could mean every date range on a chart, every type of metal used in an experiment, each temperature on a graph, and so on. This will tell you to focus on the part of the passage that deals with this concept.
- Wrong-answer choices are often the exact opposite of the correct answer.
- Wrong-answer choices contains two versions each of two possible answers with different supporting statements. Eliminate supporting statements that aren't supported by the text, or are irrelevant.

Here's the general ACT Science process:

1. Read, skim, or skip the passage depending on your preference.
2. Read the question carefully, noting key scientific terms.
3. Read the answer choices carefully.
4. Look at the relevant part of the passage.
5. Find the correct answer, or eliminate three wrong answers.
6. Double-check your answer, mark it, and move on.

Go back through the ACT Science walkthroughs and follow along in your copy of *The Real ACT Prep Guide, 3rd Edition* to see demonstrations of these ideas.

ACT English

"Thus I got into my bones the essential structure of the ordinary British sentence, which is a noble thing."
- Winston Churchill

Overview and Important Reminders For ACT English

At this point, we've definitely seen that the ACT is a highly standardized, highly repetitive test. This is just as true on the English section as it is everywhere else on the test. Of course, before you can learn to take advantage of the repetition and the standardization that make the ACT so beatable, you have to take the time to familiarize yourself with the specific ideas and patterns that keep appearing on each section of the test. The English section is no exception.

The ACT English section repeatedly tests a specific set of concepts related to the grammar and style conventions of written American English. Unfortunately for our purposes, most test-takers don't really know very much about the grammar and style of American English, because those things are almost never taught in American high schools—and even when teachers do try to cover those topics, they almost never teach them in a way that agrees with the ACT, because the ACT English section is based on the rules of written grammar that were popular in the middle of the 20th century.

So here's the bottom line: most test-takers who want to do well on the ACT English section will need to learn some grammar concepts, even if their English teachers have praised their writing ability in class.

But don't panic!

There aren't very many grammar concepts on the ACT, and the few concepts that do appear on the test aren't very advanced. Also, the ACT English section itself often gives you clues to help you identify the right answer to a question, if you know where to look for them.

On top of that, there are three general ways to learn the grammar you need for the ACT:

1. You can read through the test-taking advice in this Black Book, take a look at the walkthroughs in this Black Book and the explanations in the Red Book, and just sort of "get the hang of it" without obsessing over rules.

2. You can study all the strategies, rules, and principles in this book (which are found in this section and in the "Writing Toolbox" in the Appendix of this Black Book) until you have complete and total mastery of them, and the entire English section of the ACT cowers before you.

3. You can take a sort of middle path, which involves making a conscious effort to learn a few of the major concepts that the ACT tests, and then relying on practical experience with walkthroughs and sample tests to fill in the rest.

Any of those three approaches can work great, depending on your personality and the type of score you need.

In general, most of the students I've worked with prefer the more informal approach of reading through some question walkthroughs from this Black Book and trying some practice questions from the Red Book to develop an intuitive understanding of how the ACT English section works. Some prefer the middle approach of deliberately learning a few concepts in detail and then soaking up the rest through a relatively short period of trial and error.

One important note, though: if you're shooting for a 34 or higher on the ACT English section, you'll have very little room for error, which means you'll probably need to make a conscious decision to master the ACT's grammar rules. If you want to score in that range, you basically have to go through all 75 questions on the entire English section and only miss about 2 or 3 questions at most, and it's very hard to reach that level of accuracy without being consciously aware of the ACT's idea of grammar rules. (And even if you think you already have a perfect understanding of modern English grammar, I want to caution you gently that the ACT will probably disagree with you on at least a few issues.)

By the way, the ACT will never test you on the specific names of grammatical terms like "participle," "gerund," "nominative," and so on, so don't worry if you can't keep those terms straight (or if you've never even heard of them). Instead, the ACT tests your awareness of its principles of grammar and style by having you choose the form of a phrase that it considers superior within the context of a passage. So even if you choose to learn all the rules and principles in the Appendix of this Black Book, you'll never have to answer direct questions about grammatical terminology on the ACT.

Now that we've addressed some of the important preliminary issues with the ACT English section, let's talk about the section's big secret.

The Big Secret Of ACT English

The big secret of the ACT English section is that it doesn't follow the same rules and conventions that many educated people follow when they write or speak in American English today. Instead, it follows a set of rules that might loosely be described as the rules that governed standard written American English in the early-to-mid 20th century.

Most test-takers don't realize this. Whenever they come across a new ACT English question, they just think, "Which choice would make this phrase sound best *to me*?"

This is a huge mistake. By now we should realize that the ACT doesn't care what sounds good to you, or to me, or to anybody else who doesn't write the ACT. So instead of looking at an ACT question and answering based on what sounds good to us, we should be answering based on what the ACT consistently rewards. That's all. What you and I think sounds good or bad isn't important if it disagrees with the ACT's rules and patterns.

Let me say it again: when you're faced with an ACT English question, you should immediately ask yourself, "Which answer satisfies the ACT's standards and patterns for this type of question?"

When we talked about the ACT Reading section earlier in this Black Book, we talked about how one of the biggest reasons people struggle with those questions is that they're used to classroom discussions in which almost any interpretation of a text has some value, while the ACT Reading section only rewards a literal reading of each text. Well, a lot of test-takers have a similar issue when it comes to ACT English, because most English teachers have very loose standards for grammar and writing style. This means that most test-takers find the ACT penalizes them for things that their English teachers would accept.

For example, many people are taught in school that a comma can be placed almost anywhere in a sentence, whether to indicate that a reader would take a breath at that point in the sentence if it were being read out loud, or just to break up a lot of text, or for any number of other reasons. But the ACT Writing section doesn't reward us for using commas like that—instead, it has its own rigid rules about comma usage. Similarly, many test-takers would also naturally use apostrophes, participles, and pronouns in ways the ACT doesn't reward.

(By the way, don't be nervous if you don't know what a participle is, or if there are other technical grammatical terms you're not familiar with! Remember that the ACT never requires us to know the name of a grammatical concept; it only requires us to identify the form of a phrase that it considers to be correct, or to describe something in the passage the same way we might describe it on the ACT Reading section.)

Just as we learned to attack the questions on the Reading, Math, and Science sections in a systematic and dependable way—even though they mostly ask us to do things we don't normally do in school—we can learn to beat ACT English questions in a reliable way. As we did with the other sections, we'll use an approach that's tailored to the repetitive patterns and issues that come up in this part of the test. We'll see that most of the questions in the ACT English section test only a handful of concepts over and over again.

Commas In The ACT English Section

Before we get into all the details of the ACT English section, let's talk about how the ACT tests comma usage on that section.

I'll keep this discussion brief—we won't touch on all the hows and whys of proper comma usage on the ACT, but we'll cover a few simple rules that will help you understand what kind of comma usage the ACT English section rewards.

The majority of ACT English questions don't really have anything to do with commas, but comma-related issues appear in a significant portion of the questions that most test-takers have trouble with.

It's relatively easy to learn about exclamation points and quotation marks and periods, because each of those punctuation marks is really only used for one thing. Commas, on the other hand, are used in a variety of different situations, and that can make it harder to learn how the ACT wants us to use them.

One of the first steps in understanding commas on the ACT is correcting the misconceptions that many students have about commas. Here are the two main comma "myths" that I encounter when working with my clients:

1. MYTH: Commas should be used to show that a person would take a breath if the sentence were read out loud.
2. MYTH: When a sentence contains too many words in a row with no punctuation, you should put a comma in there to break up the sentence.

I want to make two things clear:

1. FACT: The ACT doesn't reward comma placement based on where a speaker would pause if reading the sentence aloud.
2. FACT: The ACT doesn't care how many words appear in a row without punctuation.

Instead, the ACT English section rewards comma usage that correctly demonstrates the relationships among concepts in a sentence.

Let me also make the broader point that we should approach questions that involve comma placement with the attitude that it's better to *avoid* commas unless we have an actual, concrete reason to put one in a particular part of a sentence. (We'll talk about what those concrete reasons are in the next section, and in the Writing Toolbox in the Appendix of this Black Book.) In other words, if a phrase would be acceptable without commas, then the ACT wants us to leave out commas.

It's also very important that you read the walkthroughs at the end of this training section so you can see what these comma placement questions are actually like.

In the next section, we'll take a look at the different issues that can come up in the ACT English section, including the various appropriate ways for commas to be used in ACT English questions. Students often find that the correct usage of commas on the ACT differs (at least somewhat) from what they've been taught about commas in school.

Remember that when we take the ACT, we must focus on the rules and patterns that the ACT rewards, even if those rules and patterns don't agree with the rules and patterns we'd expect in a classroom setting. In this Black Book, we'll just focus on doing what the ACT English section actually rewards when it comes to commas (or any other topic, for that matter).

Now that we've briefly addressed those important comma issues, let's take a look at the question types that we'll encounter on the ACT English section.

ACT English Question Types

I generally encourage test-takers to think of the questions on the ACT English section as falling into two rough types. These types are my own personal classifications, not official classifications from the ACT, so you won't see them listed or described this way on the actual test, or in the Red Book.

These types are pretty self-explanatory:

- "Reading Comprehension" questions
- Grammar/Style/Punctuation questions
- Questions that combine grammar/style/punctuation elements with reading comprehension elements

Training yourself to recognize these broad question types will make it easier for you to focus on the concepts that might be tested in a particular question. This, in turn, will make the ACT English section easier to approach.

Don't get stressed out at the thought of learning to recognize these different question types! It'll become second nature pretty quickly, and it's not really something that can lead you to a wrong answer if you do it wrong; it'll usually just save you some time if you do it right. As I said, it's more about helping you focus your mind on the specific tricks the ACT is trying to play on you with any particular question.

Now let's talk about each question type in more detail, and about some of the major issues that the ACT will test with each question type.

Reading Comprehension Questions

The second major type of question is what I call a "Reading Comprehension" question. These questions are relatively easy to spot because ACT English questions with prompts involve reading comprehension somehow (as opposed to questions that simply offer a set of answer choices, which usually focus on grammar, style, or punctuation).

The correct answers to these questions generally reward the same kind of literal approach to the text that we've already seen in the Reading and Science sections of the ACT: they directly restate or reflect the concepts and relationships from the relevant part of the passage.

As you might imagine, we'll also find that the wrong-answer choices on these kinds of questions are frequently similar to the types of wrong answers we'll encounter on the ACT Reading section: some wrong answers will directly contradict the text, some will confuse the relationships among concepts from the text, and so on.

There are a few different specific forms that these questions can take. We'll look at them now.

"Most relevant information"

You'll encounter questions that ask which of the answer choices provides the "most relevant information" regarding something. To find the answer to this type of question, you want to look for the choice that only talks about what the question asks about.

For example, if the question asks for the "most relevant information" regarding ice cream cones, then you want to pick the answer that only talks about ice cream cones—not about popsicles, or movies, or parties, or anything else.

To build on that example, you might see answer choices that talk about ice cream cones, but that throw in other information as well. Those choices would be wrong—you just want to find the one that focuses only on the relevant topic.

For a real life example of this type of question, let's look at question 5 on page 152 of your copy of *The Real ACT Prep Guide, 3rd Edition*. The question asks which version of the sentence provides "the most relevant information" about the "narrator's familiarity" with an exchange student named Ligia.

All four versions of the sentence (the given version in the passage and the three variations) mention that the narrator saw Ligia at school events and/or read a story about her in the school paper. Three of them also add extra information that isn't related to anything else in the passage:

(A) mentions that school events are "sometimes supported financially by local businesses."

(B) mentions that the school paper "is written by students interested in journalism."

(D) says something about the narrator checking for local movie listings.

These three answers must all be wrong because they introduce new information that's unrelated to the "narrator's familiarity" with Ligia.

Only the correct answer, (C), focuses exclusively on information that tells us about "the narrator's familiarity with Ligia," which is what the prompt asked us for.

Let me take a minute to remind you also that every one of those answer choices was grammatically and stylistically acceptable—the concern is purely for the content of the sentences and whether they stick to the topic that the question is asking about.

"Best conclusion"

Some questions will offer different sentences and ask which one is the "best conclusion" for the passage. The best conclusion will be the one that focuses on the main topic of the passage, often on something that's mentioned in the title of the passage itself.

If more than one answer choice mentions ideas from the passage, then we want to pick the answer choice with the idea that comes up most frequently in the passage.

A question of this type might even ask something like, "Which sentence would best conclude this essay while tying the end of the essay back to the beginning?" In this case, you just want to find the choice that talks about the main topic of the passage, and also mentions something related to the beginning of the essay.

For a real-life example of a "best conclusion" question, look at question 15 on page 154 of the Red Book. This question asks us which sentence, if true, would best conclude the essay.

We know the correct answer will be the one that's related to the main topic of the passage; according to the ACT's reading comprehension principles, the answer choice with the main topic from the passage will be the one that mentions the greatest number of concepts from the passage. In this case, we can eliminate (A), (B), and (D), because each choice only deals with one concept (at most) from the last paragraph. Choice (C) is correct because it mentions two concepts from the passage: "Spanish" and "dance steps."

For these reasons, we can be sure (C) is the correct answer.

"Most effective introduction"

Along similar lines, the ACT might also ask which sentence is the "most effective" introduction, usually to a paragraph. The answer will be the sentence that discusses the same topics that are discussed in the other sentences in that paragraph. If more than one answer choice mentions a topic that's already in the paragraph, then the correct answer will be the one that mentions the largest number of concepts from the paragraph.

You might see wrong-answer choices related to the previous paragraph, or wrong-answer choices that make some broad statement related to the passage as a whole, but that don't restate any ideas from the paragraph being introduced. The correct answer choice will include ideas from the paragraph being introduced.

Let's look at an example. Question 56 on page 445 asks us which answer choice "would most effectively introduce" the paragraph it would appear in. The paragraph is about the beltway, which is a massive expressway in the Washington, D.C., area. The correct answer choice mentions the idea of the beltway, and also mentions that the speaker planned to avoid the beltway; both of these concepts are restated in the rest of the paragraph when the author talks about asking people for help with other routes.

Two or the wrong answers to this question don't mention anything directly from the paragraph. One other wrong-answer choice, (J), does mention the beltway, but it also includes the idea of "official Washington" and "an island," and neither of those concepts appears in the rest of the paragraph. So the correct answer is the one that mentions the most concepts from the rest of the paragraph, just as we would expect.

"Most effective transition"

When you see a question that asks which answer choice would make the "most effective transition" from one paragraph to another, you just need to find the answer choice that mentions or refers to something from each of the two paragraphs.

If the first paragraph is about wooden roller coasters, and the second paragraph is about carousels, then you should pick the answer choice that refers to both wooden roller coasters and carousels.

If one paragraph is about kickball and the next paragraph is about lifting weights, then you want the answer choice that refers to both kickball and lifting weights. You get the idea.

We can see a real-life example of a "most effective transition" question in question 24 on page 155 of the Red Book. This question asks which choice "most effectively guides the reader from the preceding paragraph into this new paragraph." We know the correct sentence will be the one that mentions something from the preceding paragraph, and something from this paragraph.

The only answer choice that does this is (H). That choice mentions "friendly service," which appears in the beginning of the first paragraph, and "machines," which are mentioned in the second paragraph. That means (H) is correct.

Choice (F) only mentions concepts from the second paragraph, so it's wrong. Choice (G) mentions a concept from the first paragraph but doesn't mention anything from the second paragraph, so it's also wrong. Choice (J) might trick a lot of people who don't read carefully, because it mentions "service," from the first paragraph, and "*washing* machines [emphasis mine]"—but the machines in the second paragraph aren't washing machines, so (J) doesn't actually restate any concept from the second paragraph, which means it's wrong.

Sentence or paragraph placement

You'll sometimes encounter questions that ask where a sentence or paragraph should best be placed. In a question like this, the ACT wants sentences and paragraphs to appear in a sequence that makes them refer to each other in a logical order.

For example, if one sentence says, "My brother had a dog named Snowflake," then that sentence needs to come before a sentence that says, "That dog would follow him everywhere." It wouldn't make sense to use the word "that" to refer to the dog unless there's already a previous sentence that introduces the dog.

Also, if one sentence refers to something in another sentence, then the ACT will want those sentences to appear as close together as possible.

Let's look at a real-life example: question 21 on page 154 of *The Real ACT Prep Guide, 3rd Edition*. The question asks about the placement of Sentence 5.

If you read the paragraph, you'll see that sentence 4 mentions "the threats." Up to that point in the passage, no threat has been mentioned. The sentence that actually introduces the threats is sentence 5, which includes the phrase "threatening every sort of drastic action." So, according to the ACT's rules of sentence ordering, sentence 5 must be moved so that it comes before sentence 4, so that sentence 4's use of the word "the" in the phrase "the threats" will make sense.

Choices (B), (C), and (D) would all result in sentence 5 appearing before sentence 4, so they all satisfy the ACT's rule about a sentence referring to something appearing after the sentence that first introduces that thing. Now we look at the other half of that rule, which says that when a sentence refers to something in another sentence, those two sentences should appear as close together as they can.

With that in mind, we know that choice (D) is correct, because it puts the sentences together, and it puts the introduction of the "threatening" signs before the reference to "the threats."

Precision Vocabulary

A few times per test, you might see a question with an underlined word and three alternatives for that word. There won't be any punctuation involved, or different forms of the same word—just four different words with somewhat similar meanings.

Even though these questions don't have any prompts, they're basically reading comprehension questions. The words in the answer choices will often be words you could probably use interchangeably in a classroom discussion, but their specific meanings won't be quite the same, and one will clearly be a better choice than the others when you think carefully about the meaning of each word and the sentence they'll be inserted into.

Typically, these words aren't unusual—they tend to be words that test-takers are familiar with, but whose precise meanings might not be something the average test-taker normally pays any attention to.

The key to answering these questions correctly is to think in a precise way about what each relevant word actually means, and what it can be used to describe. For a real-life example, look at question 67 on page 302 of your copy of *The Real ACT Prep Guide, 3rd Edition*. That question asks us whether the word "intense," "cunning," "acute," or "vivid" is the best word to use in a sentence about wolves' hearing abilities.

All of these words might seem to be vaguely appropriate, but we know by now that the ACT isn't satisfied if we just pick an answer choice that's vaguely appropriate. Instead, we need to think about what each word actually means, and how it fits into the sentence.

The first choice says wolves have "intense" hearing. Does that really make sense? We might say that a scary experience is "intense," or even that a flavor is "intense," but does it make sense to call hearing "intense?" Not really. The word "intense" is used to describe an *experience* that we *perceive* with our senses, but it can't really be used to describe those senses *themselves*.

What about the word "cunning?" Maybe this is a word we associate with wolves, but it has to do with being clever or tricky. It doesn't make much sense to describe hearing as "cunning," since the hearing itself can't trick anyone.

How about the word "acute?" This means something like "finely tuned" or "sharp." It could makes sense to call hearing "acute," so this will be the correct answer. (Keep reading to see what we might need to do with this question if we don't know the word "acute.")

Finally, let's consider the word "vivid." You might describe a picture as "vivid" if it seems very real to you, but it doesn't make sense to use this word to describe "hearing." "Hearing" is a sense, but "vivid" things involve images. So this choice is no good either.

(If we don't know the word "acute," it may still be possible to answer this question correctly if we can realize that the other three answer choices can't be used to describe hearing, for the reasons we just went over. We can often work around words we don't know on the ACT, and this question is an example of that. I wouldn't recommend that you memorize the word "acute" as part of your ACT preparation, though—it's very unlikely that the word will come up on test day, at least not in such a way that you couldn't answer a question correctly unless you knew what it meant.)

Again, if you just skimmed these words, or if you heard any of them used in this context in a classroom discussion, you'd probably think any of them could be adequate. But if you take the time to think carefully about each one, you'll find that only one can actually describe "hearing" in a way that makes sense.

We'll often see something in the context of the sentence that gives us a pretty specific idea of what the correct answer should mean. In the Red Book example we just discussed, the sentence included the phrase "which makes it possible for them to pick up the sound of howling from as far away as ten miles." This phrase tells us that the correct answer should have something to do with being able to hear things from a long way off, which goes along with the word "acute."

So when you see a precision vocabulary question, be sure to check the context, including the sentences before and after the one in question, to see which key phrases you can find.

One more thing—the way to prepare for questions like these isn't to memorize thousands of vocabulary words. Most of the words in the answer choices are ones that test-takers are already familiar with, and the real issue is being very particular about the meanings of those words.

And if you run into a question with words you don't know, you may well be able to work around them. In the Red Book example we just used, for instance, some test-takers might not know the word "acute." But if they have decent ideas of the meanings of the other three words and they insist on finding a good match, they can realize that the three words they know are all wrong, which means that "acute" must be correct.

Adding or deleting a phrase or sentence

Sometimes the question will tell you that the author is considering adding or deleting a particular sentence. Then you'll be asked in one way or another what the impact of that change would be on the passage.

The answers to these types of questions depend on all the same principles of reading comprehension that we've been discussing for other ACT questions. You won't have to interpret anything—you'll just need to pick the answer that plainly describes what the sentence or phrase is doing.

Let's look at an example from the Red Book. Question 26 on page 155 of that book says the author is considering deleting the phrase "mostly older people from around the neighborhood" from a sentence in the passage, and asks what the essay would lose without that phrase.

The first answer choice says it would lose "specific descriptive material." Since the phrase "mostly older people from around the neighborhood" specifically describes the "regular customers" in the rest of the sentence, this is the correct answer.

The next answer choice says the phrase "mostly older people from around the neighborhood" is a "detail providing a logical transition," but this phrase isn't a transition, because it doesn't discuss any concepts that appear in the next sentence of the passage. So that choice is wrong.

The next choice says the phrase is "foreshadowing . . . the conclusion" of the passage, but the passage's ending has no particular connection with the idea of "mostly older people from around the neighborhood." So this choice is also wrong.

Finally, the last choice calls the phrase "an understatement of important information," but there's nothing in the rest of the passage that gives us any reason to call it an understatement (or an overstatement, for that matter) or to think of it as important information. This choice is wrong, too.

As you can see here (and as you'll see in the question walkthroughs in a few pages), only the correct answer choice will accurately describe the relationships of the phrases in the prompt and the passage in a literal way.

"Would this essay fulfill the writer's goal?"

Sometimes, at the end of a passage, you'll see a question that states a possible goal of the writer in writing the essay, and then asks you if that goal was fulfilled by the essay. The answer choices for this type of question will typically demonstrate the "yes yes no no" pattern we saw in our discussion of the ACT Science section; in this case, two answer choices will say the writer's goal was fulfilled, and two will say it was unfulfilled, and each choice will offer a different reason for its conclusion.

Like the other reading comprehension question types on the ACT English section, the correct answer will be the one that directly and literally describes the passage, and is relevant to the goal mentioned in the prompt.

You can often eliminate all of the wrong answers simply by getting rid of the ones that make statements that aren't supported by the text. If you do eliminate unsupported answer choices and find that you've still got more than one answer choice left, just eliminate any choice that isn't relevant to the question, and you'll be left with the correct answer.

For a real-life example of this question type, look at question 30 on page 297 of the Red Book. This question asks us to suppose that the writer wanted "to write a brief essay focusing on the history and development of Tejano music," and it asks us whether this essay would fulfill that goal.

Choice (F) is correct because it accurately says the passage "describes the origins of Tejano music and one of its early important figures." This is consistent with the passage: the first two paragraphs of the passage describe how Tejano music was created, and the third paragraph talks about "the first Tejano musician to gain star status." Since the passage definitely talks about "the history and development of Tejano music," as the prompt describes, choice (F) is correct.

We know (G) must be wrong because it makes a false statement about the passage—the essay doesn't mention contributions that Tejano music has made to other folk music traditions. (The passage does say that other folk traditions contributed to Tejano music, but it doesn't say Tejano music contributed to them. Remember that the ACT likes to include wrong-answer choices that reverse relationships from the text, like this one does!)

Choice (H) is wrong because whether the essay refers to other musical forms is irrelevant to the stated goal in the question. Choice (J) is wrong for the same reason; the issue of focusing only on one Tejano musician isn't necessarily relevant to the goal of successfully writing "a brief essay focusing on the history and development of Tejano music."

Grammar/Style/Punctuation Questions

These questions test your ability to identify the form of a phrase or sentence that sounds the most pleasing, according to the ACT's rules.

These questions can often test rule-based concepts like proper verb conjugations, the proper use of punctuation, the formation of possessives, and so on. They also sometimes offer us more than one answer choice that's grammatically acceptable, and ask us to indicate which one sounds the most appropriate according to the ACT. (I know that may sound like a pretty subjective exercise, and like exactly the kind of thing the ACT would never ask. But we'll find that the correct answers to these questions are just as predictable as the correct answer to any other ACT question, because the ACT consistently rewards the same attributes in the correct answers to English questions.)

You'll typically be able to identify these questions because of the following attributes:

- The question won't have a separate prompt—it's just a list of answer choices.
- The first answer choice will say, "NO CHANGE."

These grammar/style/punctuation questions can cover a lot of different areas of grammar, style, and punctuation, but don't worry—you may already know some or most of the subject matter that they'll test. We'll just need to highlight the important things that will come up in ACT English questions. Furthermore, most individual questions will only cover one or two topics each.

We'll look at the main grammar/style/punctuation issues one-by-one.

Also, because of the ways that different parts of a sentence interact with each other, there will be some overlap among the concepts we talk about—so don't worry if some of these ideas run together a little bit in your mind. As long as you can understand the right answer when you're practicing, you're in good shape.

One more thing—if you're feeling confused as you're reading through any one of these topics, just finish reading all the way through it. I'll always follow up with examples when necessary, and the examples will tend to clear things up.

It's often a lot harder to understand a description of these issues than it is just to look at an example and see what we're talking about. So just keep at it, even if things don't seem clear right away.

This is also a good time for me to bring up the importance of the question walkthroughs you'll see after this training. We'll cover a lot of stuff in this training section, but you'll really get the best sense of how to beat ACT English questions by following along in your copy of *The Real ACT Prep Guide, 3rd Edition* with the walkthroughs in this Black Book. That way, you can see all of this material in action, which will really help you recognize these concepts when you see them on test day.

And after that, of course, the most important thing is always for you to do some real practice ACT English questions on your own after you've learned the material in this Black Book.

We'll start with the first skill, which may sound pretty basic, but is actually really important.

NOTE: The following section will involve a lot of both good and bad examples of the concepts we'll be talking about. Just to keep things clear, I'll start any bad example with an asterisk (*). So if you see an example that begins with an asterisk, you'll know that it shows something you should avoid on the ACT English section.

Sentence Fragments

On the ACT, a proper sentence isn't just any group of words with a period after it. Some groups of words are acceptable sentences, and some are missing key elements. These are all sentences:

My sister loves to play basketball.

The dog is barking in the front yard.

If I don't hurry, I'm going to be late for work.

All of these groups of words describe someone or something doing something. They express a complete thought.

These are NOT sentences:

*The man driving in the car next to me.

*While I was waiting in line at the bank.

*Because I was too tired to stand up anymore.

These groups of words are called "sentence fragments" because they aren't complete sentences by ACT standards. They might describe things, but they aren't complete in the way that a correct sentence is complete. These fragments leave questions unanswered, like the following:

- What *about* the man driving in the car next to you—what did he do, apart from just driving next to you?
- What happened *while* you were waiting in line at the bank?
- What happened *because* you were too tired to stand up anymore?

Notice that the problem with these fragments isn't just that it's possible to ask questions about them. The problem is that the fragment itself invites a question without offering an answer. Take another look at this fragment:

*While I was waiting in line at the bank.

The word "while" specifically indicates the idea of some other thing that also happened during the period when "I was waiting in line at the bank." Without the word "while," we'd have a complete sentence, which would look like this:

I was waiting in line at the bank.

There are a lot of specific things that can turn a sentence into a fragment, and it's not really necessary to go over them all right now (see the Appendix if you're really interested in a technical description of what makes a complete sentence). As a speaker of English, you should have a basic understanding of what makes something a sentence, and any major gaps in your understanding should be filled in by this training section, the question walkthroughs, and your own practice.

It's very important for you to be able to tell the difference between a complete sentence (which is acceptable on the ACT) and a fragment (which isn't). You might see a question about some text that looks like this:

*I had the radio playing so I could listen to some <u>music. As</u> I was gardening.

The problem with this example is that "as I was gardening" is just a fragment, not a sentence. The word "as" implies a connection with something else that needs to be in the same sentence. In this case, the phrase about the gardening needs to be joined with the sentence "I had the radio playing so I could listen to some music."

When you look at the answer choices (as you would if this were a real ACT question), you should be able to recognize that the underlined portion needs to be changed to this:

> **I had the radio playing so I could listen to some <u>music as</u> I was gardening.**

There's a real-life example of a sentence fragment issue in question 63 on page 302 of the Red Book. The original version of this sentence is "<u>One of these,</u> self-defense, which includes protecting territory." This is a fragment because there's no main verb that ever says anything about "one of these." (If you'd like to learn more about the differences between sentence fragments and complete sentences, take a look at the section on clauses and phrases in the Writing Toolbox at the end of this book.)

We need to put a verb in there that completes the thought that started with the phrase "one of these" in order to make this a complete sentence. The only choice that offers one is (B), the correct answer, which provides the verb "is" after the phrase "one of these," so that the sentence would read, "One of these is self-defense, which includes protecting territory."

Run-On Sentences

You may also see something like this:

> ***I grabbed my umbrella on my way out the <u>door it was</u> raining outside and I didn't want to get wet.**

In this case, you want to recognize that you're actually looking at two groups of words that could each be independent sentences on their own—only there's no punctuation separating them. We call this situation a "run-on sentence," and it's not acceptable on the ACT.

On the ACT, there are two acceptable types of punctuation for separating two groups of words that could be complete sentences on their own:

- the period
- the semicolon

That means that either of the two following versions would be acceptable on the ACT:

> **I grabbed my umbrella on my way out the <u>door. It was</u> raining outside and I didn't want to get wet.**

> **I grabbed my umbrella on my way out the <u>door; it was</u> raining outside and I didn't want to get wet.**

The first version adds a period and capitalizes the letter "I" in the word "it." The second version just adds a semicolon between "door" and "it."

Again, these are both equally acceptable ways to divide the two sentences. Neither version is better or worse than the other on the ACT. If you see a situation like this on the ACT, you won't have to choose between a period or a semi-colon to separate the two sentences, since both are acceptable. Either you'll see only one of the two in the answer choices, or—if you *do* see both—there will be some other difference between the options that makes one or both of them wrong.

The issue of run-on sentences comes up in Question 1 on page 292 of the Red Book. The original version of the underlined portion splits the two chunks of text with a period. The other three options remove the period, and two of them add a comma and change the wording slightly.

When we look at the original text, we see that both of the original sentences can, indeed, stand on their own as sentences. Choice (B), which removes the period, would create a run-on sentence. Because the original text results in two complete sentences separated by a period, we can correctly pick choice (A) and leave the whole thing unchanged.

Verb Conjugation

The ACT English section will sometimes ask you to recognize when a verb is conjugated correctly. The following is a correctly conjugated verb:

My favorite sandwich <u>takes</u> a long time to make.

Here is the same sentence with an incorrectly conjugated verb:

*My favorite sandwich <u>take</u> a long time to make.

In the second version, the verb "take" is in the third-person plural form instead of the third-person singular form. Because the noun "sandwich" is singular, the verb must be in the appropriate singular form, "takes."

There are two primary ways the ACT will try to trick you into not noticing that a verb is conjugated incorrectly. The first one we'll talk about is something I call the "intervening phrase."

Just as the name suggests, the intervening phrase is a phrase that the ACT sticks between a noun and its verb. The test does this because it's hoping you'll get confused and think the verb should match up with a word in the inserted phrase, instead of matching up with the main noun that actually does the action of the verb.

Let's look at an example of the mistake that the ACT wants you to make:

*<u>A sandwich</u> with tomatoes and onions <u>take</u> a long time to make.

The above sentence has exactly the same verb error in it that the previous example had: incorrectly matching the singular noun "sandwich" with the plural verb-form "take." The difference is that this sentence includes the phrase "with tomatoes and onions" in between the words "sandwich" and "take." That phrase can be confusing if you're not careful. If you just look at the words right around the verb, you'll see the phrase "onions take a long time," which looks okay by itself at first glance. You'll only realize the subject of the verb should be the word "sandwich" if you stand back and look at the whole sentence. Then you can see that the thing doing the taking is actually the sandwich, so the correct form of the sentence should look like this:

<u>A sandwich</u> with tomatoes and onions <u>takes</u> a long time to make.

So whenever you see answer choices that involve different forms of a verb, the first thing you want to do is read the whole sentence and make sure you find out which noun is actually doing the action of that verb. Once you know that, you can mentally remove any intervening phrases from the sentence to make sure the subject and verb match each other—in this case, you'd get the sentence "A sandwich takes a long time to make." With a shorter, clearer sentence like this, it's easier to check if a verb is in the proper form.

We can see a real-life example of this issue in question 74 on page 303 of the Red Book. The question includes the phrase "*the collective sound of the wolves howling in various keys also <u>make</u> the pack seem larger." In this example, the phrase "of the wolves howling in various keys" comes between the noun "sound" and its verb. Once we mentally remove that intervening phrase, we realize the noun that the verb must agree with is the singular noun "sound," and not the plural nouns "wolves" or "keys." Then we know that we need the singular verb form "makes," which is choice (J), the correct answer.

Sometimes, the ACT uses a question's answer choices to try to confuse us about the proper form of a verb. You might see something like this:

The oldest person in the Twin Cities <u>has swept</u> the kitchen floor.

(A) NO CHANGE

(B) have been sweeping

(C) sweep

(D) are sweeping

If you scan through the answer choices, it might look like the question is asking which tense the verb should be in, since the answer choices all present different tenses and aspects of the verb "to sweep." That can be confusing, especially when the sentence doesn't give us any clues about a particular time-frame.

If you look more closely, though, you'll notice that choices (B), (C), and (D) are all *plural* verb-forms, but the word "person" is *singular*, so the correct answer should actually be a singular verb-form. The original phrase is the only singular one, so (A) would be the correct answer if this were an ACT question.

This is another reason why it's so important to read the whole sentence and figure out which noun actually goes with an underlined verb.

There's a real-life example of this issue in question 22 on page 155 of the Red Book. This question involves the phrase "the paneling on the walls <u>has been</u> painted to match." The answer choices include three plural verb forms: two are different past-tense forms, and one is in the present tense. To the untrained test-taker, it might seem like we need to figure out which tense is appropriate. But, in reality, the noun that should go with the verb is the singular noun "paneling." This singular noun needs a singular verb form, and the only answer choice with a singular verb form is the correct answer, choice (F).

There's one more important verb issue that you might see, and it looks like this:

*When he left to go to the bathroom, he <u>given</u> up his seat.

This sentence is wrong because "given" isn't the correct form of the verb "to give" in this case. The word "given" is a past participle of the verb "to give;" it can only be used with a version of a helping verb like "is" or "has." (You don't have to know what the phrase "past participle" means to answer an ACT English question correctly—you just have to be able to recognize that this verb-form is inappropriate.)

There are at least two ways to fix a phrase like this: we can either add in the missing helping verb, or we can change the word "given" to a form that doesn't need a helping verb. So here are two corrected versions of this sentence:

When he left to go to the bathroom, he <u>had given</u> up his seat.

When he left to go to the bathroom, he <u>gave</u> up his seat.

Either of those two versions of the sentence could be grammatically acceptable on the ACT.

We can see a real-life example of this issue in question 13 on page 153 of the Red Book. The sentence mentions "the days before two teenagers <u>taken</u> over the phone." In this example, "taken" is an inappropriate conjugation of the verb "to take." The appropriate form would be "two teenagers <u>took</u> over," which means the correct answer is (B).

Possessives

Luckily, the ACT's rules for possessives are actually pretty simple, even if they differ from today's common usage.

There are three things you need to know if you want to form possessives on the ACT.

First, you need to know how possessive pronouns are formed. Most people are comfortable with these possessive pronouns:

- my
- your
- his
- her

The ones that sometimes cause trouble tend to be these:

- its
- whose
- their

People often mix up those possessive pronouns with these contractions:

- The possessive pronoun "its" is confused with the contraction "it's," which is short for "it is."
- The possessive pronoun "whose" is confused with the contraction "who's," which is short for "who is."
- The possessive pronoun "their" is confused with the contraction "they're," which is short for "they are."

So here's the rule to remember for these three troubling possessive pronouns: these possessive pronouns contain no apostrophes. If you're in a position where you have to choose between "its" and "it's," or "whose" and "who's," or "their" and "they're," remember that the choice with the apostrophe is a contraction, and the other is a possessive form. Whenever you see these contractions in a sentence or an answer choice, imagine them in their "un-contracted" state, and you should be able to tell if they're appropriate.

- "It's" with an apostrophe can always be read as "it is"
- "Who's" with an apostrophe can always be read as "who is"
- "They're" with an apostrophe can always be read as "they are"

Many people are unsure about sentences like these:

> *She sat in the car and honked <u>it's</u> horn.

> *<u>Who's</u> house is this?

But if we imagine the contractions in their "un-contracted" forms, the grammatical errors become a lot more obvious:

> *She sat in the car and honked <u>it is</u> horn.

> *<u>Who is</u> house is this?

When you get into the habit of reading "it's" as "it is," "who's" as "who is," and "they're" as "they are," you won't be tricked by that kind of sentence.[1]

---

[1] One more bonus mistake: People sometimes confuse the word "there," which indicates a place, with the possessive pronoun "their," which indicates that something belongs to a group of people. In this case, the easiest thing to remember is probably that the word "there" has a spelling very similar to the spellings of the words "here" and "where," and all of those words are related to physical positions.

So, one more time, just to be clear:

The second thing to remember about possessives is that a PLURAL noun ending in "-s" will always form its possessive with a single apostrophe, and nothing more. Here are some examples:

> **This toy belongs to the cats. It is the <u>cats'</u> toy.**

> **Those are the <u>girls'</u> bikes. Those bikes belong to the girls.**

> **That lawn mower belongs to the neighbors. It is the <u>neighbors'</u> lawn mower.**

In each of these three situations, there's a plural noun that ends in "-s:"

- cats
- girls
- neighbors

To form a plural for each of those words, you just add an apostrophe, and don't change anything else:

- cats'
- girls'
- neighbors'

So that's the second rule: to form the possessive of a plural noun ending in "-s," just add an apostrophe to the end.

The third rule is that EVERY OTHER KIND OF NOUN forms its possessive by adding an apostrophe AND an "s." That's right: with the exception of pronouns, and plural nouns ending in "-s," every noun on the ACT forms its possessive with an apostrophe and an "s."

Here are a few examples of words that get an apostrophe and an "s" on the ACT. Note that many of these possessive forms differ from modern usage (and that includes the things your teachers might write):

> **This ball belongs to my dog. It is my <u>dog's</u> ball.**

> **The game belongs to the children. It is the <u>children's</u> game.**

> **Jess has a car. It is <u>Jess's</u> car.**

> **The abacus has wooden beads. They are the <u>abacus's</u> wooden beads.**

> **The geese live on a pond. It is the <u>geese's</u> pond.**

> **The mice live in the wall. That is the <u>mice's</u> home.**

So let's do a quick review of the three possessive rules you need to know for the ACT:

The word "their" is a possessive pronoun and indicates that a group of people own something: "They invited me to <u>their</u> house."

The word "they're" is always interchangeable with the phrase "they are:" "They said <u>they're</u> going to decide tomorrow."

The word "there" has a similar spelling to the words "here" and "where," and it always indicates position: "The car isn't here; it's over <u>there</u>."

---

1. The possessive pronouns "their," "whose," and "its" don't include apostrophes.

2. The possessive form of a plural noun ending in "-s" is formed by adding an apostrophe and nothing else.

3. The possessive form of EVERY OTHER KIND OF NOUN is formed by adding an apostrophe and an "-s," no matter what letter or sound the base noun ends in.

Once you learn these rules and see them in action on some real ACT practice questions, they'll become second nature.

For a real-life example of a question involving possessives, take a look at question 31 on page 156. The text mentions "*a company <u>who's</u> slogan is," and we're given the opportunity to change "who's" to "whose." Let's think about what's being said here. Are we saying, "*a company who is slogan is?" No, we're saying that the slogan belongs to the company—that this is the company's slogan. That means we need the possessive form of "who," which is choice (B), "whose."

Who Versus Whom

You'll occasionally see ACT English questions that require you to choose between "who" and "whom." For example, you may see a sentence like this:

> **This is the man <u>who</u> taught me how to ride a bike.**

Then, you may have to decide whether "who" or "whom" (or something else) is appropriate in this space. In the case above, "who" is the correct choice. You use the word "who" to describe something or someone doing an action. Here, the word "who" refers to "the man," and "the man" does the action indicated by the word "taught."

You use "whom" to describe someone who's being acted upon, like in this sentence:

> **He is also the man <u>whom</u> I accidentally hit with my bike before I knew how to ride it.**

In this sentence, the word "whom" is correct because it refers to someone receiving the action of getting hit. "Whom" refers to "the man," and in this sentence "the man" receives the action of being "hit with my bike."

Here's another way to think about it that's simpler for most people. It involves turning a sentence into a question, and then figuring out how that question would be answered. Let's take a look.

Imagine you need to evaluate a sentence like this:

> **This is the man <u>who</u> taught me how to ride a bike.**

Turn it into a question:

> ***(Who/whom) taught me how to ride a bike?**

Then answer it:

> **<u>He</u> taught me how to ride a bike.**

If you'd use the word "he" to answer the question, then "who" is the proper form.

If you'd use the word "him" to answer the question, then "whom" is the proper form (you can remember this because they both end in "m").

Let's do it with the other sentence:

> He is also the man <u>whom</u> I accidentally hit with my bike before I knew how to ride it.

Turn it into a question:

> *(Who/whom) did I accidentally hit with my bike?

Then answer it:

> I hit <u>him</u> with my bike.

Since we'd answer the question with "him," we know the proper form in the original sentence would be "whom."

So remember that "who" corresponds with "he," and "whom" corresponds with "him" (again, you can remember that because both "whom" and "him" end with the letter "m").

Of course, if the sentence has to do with a girl or a woman, you can just mentally switch out "she" for "he," and "her" for "him," or you can always think of it in terms of female pronouns if you want to. I just prefer to teach it in terms of "he" and "him" because "he" and "who" sound kind of similar, and so do "him" and "whom," which usually makes it easier for people to remember the correct usages of the words.

Let's look at this in one more example. Imagine we had to choose the correct version of this sentence:

> *That's the boy to (who/whom) I gave all my toys.

When we read that, we might ask ourselves, "To who/whom did you give all your toys?" The answer to this question would be "I gave all my toys to him." Because I'd answer with "him" (or "her" if it were a girl), I know that the correct form in the original sentence is "whom:"

> That's the boy to whom I gave all my toys.

There's a real-life example of this in question 3 on page 152 of the Red Book. The original question mentions "Ligia Antolinez, <u>who</u> came from Bucaramanga, Columbia." We have the option of changing "who" to "whom." But if we look at the sentence, we can see that "who" is correct, because the sentence describes Ligia doing the action in the verb "came." Since the person being described by who/whom is *doing* an action in this case, not receiving the action, we know that we need the "who" form, as in choice (A).

If we wanted to turn the sentence into a question, we would say "Who came from Bucaramanga, Columbia?" The answer would be "She came from Bucaramanga, Columbia." Since we know that "she" corresponds to "he" and "who," we can again see that the "who" form is needed, which we find in choice (A).

Much Versus Many

You may also encounter situations on the ACT that test you on the difference between "much" and "many." These are two words that a lot of people use interchangeably in normal speech, and even in the classroom, but they actually have two different purposes and meanings.

"Many" is used to describe a number of separate things that you could count on your fingers (or on your friends' fingers, if you ran out of your own). Here are a few examples:

> There are <u>many</u> cats in my neighborhood.
>
> You have too <u>many</u> bags to carry.
>
> <u>Many</u> people came to see her play.

We know that when we talk about things like "cats," "bags," and "people," we're talking about sets of individual things that can be counted.

On the other hand, "much" is used to describe things that can't be counted separately:

> You gave me too <u>much</u> milk.
>
> After the lights went out, there was <u>much</u> confusion.
>
> Near the equator there is <u>much</u> sunshine.

In context, "milk," "confusion," and "sunshine" can't be counted with your fingers, so you have to use the word "much" instead of "many" to describe them.

This is the sort of thing that many English speakers would already just "get" on an intuitive level, but actually thinking about the distinction requires an attention to detail beyond what most English teachers require in a classroom setting. Because we don't normally think about things like the difference between "much" and "many," it can be difficult to feel sure about that difference on test day—unless we've been trained properly ahead of time.

We can see a real-life example of this issue in question 25 on page 155 of the Red Book. The original version of the sentence involves the phrase "too much or too few quarters." We know this version must be incorrect, because it uses the word "much" to modify the countable noun "quarters," and we know that countable nouns must be modified with "many," not "much." The correct answer is (C), which fixes this problem without creating any new problems.

"Would of"

This doesn't come up too often on the ACT, but you still need to be aware of it.

When people speak, they often pronounce the phrase "would have" so it sounds just like the nonsense phrase "*would of." This is such a widespread error that some test-takers will read a sentence like this one and never notice a mistake:

> *I <u>would of</u> done that sooner if I were you.

The sentence should read:

> I <u>would have</u> done that sooner if I were you.

You can see a real-life example of this issue in question 47 on page 727. The underlined portion of the text is "would of been," which needs to be changed to "would have been," so choice (B) is correct.

Comparatives And Superlatives

Comparatives and superlatives are types of words that are used to describe how some things relate to other things.

The comparative version of an adjective or adverb either ends in "-er" or begins with the word "more" or "less." Here are some examples of comparatives:

>   **smarter**
>
>   **bigger**
>
>   **happier**
>
>   **more intelligent**
>
>   **less disgusting**
>
>   **more quickly**

The superlative version of an adjective or adverb either ends in "-est" or begins with the word "most" or "least." Here are some examples of superlatives:

>   **smartest**
>
>   **biggest**
>
>   **happiest**
>
>   **most intelligent**
>
>   **least disgusting**
>
>   **most quickly**

Some words have irregularly-formed comparatives and superlatives, but luckily they're very common, well-known forms. Here are a couple of examples:

>   **better, best**
>
>   **more, most**

Also, remember that we use the word "than" to compare two things—not the word "then." This doesn't come up much on the ACT, but it does come up occasionally, so it's something to watch out for.

There's one more important note we need to cover on this topic. Comparative forms are created using EITHER "-er" OR "more/less," and superlative forms are created using EITHER "-est" OR "most/least." You NEVER form a comparative using both "-er" AND "more/less," or a superlative using both "-est," AND "most/least." That means phrases like these are wrong on the ACT:

>   ***more happier**
>
>   ***most biggest**

Like a lot of concepts that come up in ACT English questions, this is something you're probably already basically familiar with on an unconscious level, but you might not be sure which version is correct when someone asks you about it—so make sure you're comfortable with this idea.

There's an example involving a comparative phrase in question 51 on page 445 of the Red Book. The underlined portion of the sentence is "far more busier." Choices (B) and (C) offer other versions of a comparative phrase, and (D) is a superlative phrase.

Some people might think they need to choose between a comparative form and a superlative form to answer this question. But because we know that comparatives are formed using *either* the word "more" *or* the "-er" ending, and we know that superlatives are formed using *either* the word "most/least" *or* the "-est" ending, we can see that only choice (B) offers a grammatically acceptable version of the underlined phrase. That means (B) is correct.

"Comma Sandwich"

Commas are tested pretty heavily on the ACT, but many test-takers intuitively sense some of the situations when commas are okay on the test. In just a moment, I'll explain one of the comma scenarios that test-takers aren't always familiar with . . . but, before I do that, I want to make something extremely clear:

I'M NOT SUGGESTING THAT THE "COMMA SANDWICH" IS THE ONLY WAY THAT COMMAS ARE USED ON THE ACT. Commas can be used in a variety of ways on the ACT, and you should take a look at the Writing Toolbox in the Appendix of this Black Book if you're interested in a technical description of the proper ways to use commas on the ACT English section. I'm not including that full discussion right now because experience has shown me that most students aren't interested in it—most students prefer to fill in any gaps in their knowledge of comma use by looking through question walkthroughs and having a few of the more challenging concepts spelled out concretely. So that's what I'm doing here :)

Again, if you'd like to see a full, detailed treatment of all the ways that commas can be used on the ACT, please see the Writing Toolbox in the Appendix of this Black Book.

Now, let's talk about the specific comma issue I wanted to address here. It's something I like to call a "comma sandwich." ("Comma sandwich" is not a technical grammatical term. It's something I made up to help test-takers remember this concept.) As the name implies, a "comma sandwich" is a phrase "sandwiched" between two commas, or between a comma and a period. This particular type of phrase isn't a complete sentence or a part of a list. Instead, it's a descriptive phrase that provides additional information about something that's going on in a sentence.

One thing the ACT often likes to do on the English section is to underline a part of a sentence and give you several answer choices that feature commas in different places within the underlined phrase.

In the case of a proper "comma sandwich," the commas need to be placed on either end of the phrase in such a way that the entire "sandwich" (the phrase and the commas) could be removed, leaving behind a complete sentence.

Let's look at a couple of examples of this so you can actually see what I'm talking about. In these examples, I'll underline the "comma sandwich."

> **The man next door, who told us we could borrow his lawn mower, was always very helpful.**

In that case, removing the "comma sandwich" gives us this:

> **The man next door was always very helpful.**

Here's another example. Imagine we start with this sentence:

> **The orange shirt, which is the one I wanted to wear, isn't clean right now.**

Removing the "comma sandwich" gives us this:

> **The orange shirt isn't clean right now.**

In each case, you can see that when the commas and the phrase between them are removed, what's left is still a complete sentence.

There are a few different ways that the ACT might present a sentence like this. Sometimes the entire phrase might be underlined, and it'll be your job to find the right comma placement for the whole phrase, as in the examples above. Sometimes there might be an underlined portion that only overlaps with one half of the comma sandwich. Either way, you need to be able to recognize this type of phrase and make sure the commas are placed in such a way that the comma sandwich can be removed from the sentence and still leave behind a complete sentence. Let's look at our two examples again, this time with the commas placed incorrectly.

> ***The man next door, who told us we, could borrow his lawn mower was always very helpful.**

Removing the phrase between the commas would give us this unacceptable fragment:

> ***The man next door could borrow his lawn mower was always very helpful.**

Here's another example of an improper use of commas:

> ***The orange shirt, which is the one I wanted to wear isn't clean, right now.**

Removing the phrase between the commas would give us this unacceptable fragment:

> ***The orange shirt right now.**

In these examples, we can see that removing the "comma sandwich" leaves behind an incomplete sentence, which would be unacceptable on the ACT.

What if the commas are correctly placed on either end of the "comma sandwich," but there's another comma in the middle? Well, then we'd have two "comma sandwiches," and we'd have to be able to remove either one (or both) and be left with a complete sentence. Here are two examples that each involve two comma sandwiches; after each one, you'll see two more versions of the sentence, each with one of the two sandwiches removed.

> Here's an example of a sentence with a couple of bad "comma sandwiches:"

> ***The man next door, who told us we, could borrow his lawn mower, was always very helpful.**

This is what we would get if we removed the first bad "sandwich:"

> ***The man next door could borrow his lawn mower, was always very helpful.**

This is what we would get if we removed the second bad "sandwich:"

> ***The man next door, who told us we was always very helpful.**

> Here's another example of a sentence with a couple of bad "comma sandwiches:"

> ***The orange shirt, which is the, one I wanted to wear, isn't clean right now.**

This is what we would get if we removed the first bad "sandwich:"

> ***The orange shirt one I wanted to wear, isn't clean right now.**

This is what we would get if we removed the second bad "sandwich:"

> ***The orange shirt, which is the isn't clean right now.**

In both of these examples the resulting phrases aren't complete sentences, which means these comma placements wouldn't be acceptable on the ACT.

(Again, for a full treatment of all the ways that commas can be used on the ACT, please see the Writing Toolbox in the Appendix. But most students prefer to learn most of the other comma-related concepts on the ACT by looking at walkthroughs and trying some real practice questions from the Red Book on their own.)

For a real-life example of the comma sandwich, take a look at question 53 on page 159 of the Red Book. In this example, choices (A), (C), and (D) all create comma sandwiches that, when removed, leave behind an incoherent sentence. For example, if you selected choice (D) and then removed the phrase "and a ball you thought was lost will," you would be left with "Then again, you can sometimes get lucky, inexplicably bounce back into play."

All of these comma placements break the ACT's rules for comma usage by creating bad comma sandwiches, so the correct answer is (B), which takes out the comma entirely.

One last note: you may see the "comma sandwich" concept on the test with dashes around the phrase, instead of commas. They don't show up too often, but "dash sandwiches" function just like "comma sandwiches" on the ACT.

List Of Two Things

Sometimes you'll encounter an underlined phrase on the ACT that involves a list of two things—in other words, just any two nouns joined by the word "and."

It's important to remember there should NOT be a comma immediately before or after the word "and" in a list of two things on the ACT English section.

Let's look at an example of this in the Red Book.

Question 7 on page 293 involves the underlined phrase "time, and the channel." In this example, the list of two things as it originally appears in the passage is the phrase "the time, and the channel."

Since we know a list of two things shouldn't include a comma either immediately before or after the word "and," we need to find an answer choice that follows this rule. Only choice (C) follows the rule without creating any other problems, so (C) is correct.

(**NOTE:** It can be acceptable to put a comma directly before "and" when it's not being used to connect two nouns in a list of two things. For example, in the sentence "I saw the play last week, and I thought it was great," the word "and" isn't connecting two nouns in a list of two, so the comma before "and" is acceptable according to the rules of the ACT English section. Also, in a list or series of *more than two* things, the ACT wants us to put a comma immediately before the word "and," as in the sentence "She took her briefcase, cellphone, and laptop computer to work with her." We can see an example of this type of list in question 27 on page 580 of the Red Book.)

Idioms

We need to take a minute to talk about prepositional idioms for two main reasons: they occasionally come up on the ACT, and they involve a concept that many test preparation resources explain poorly.

The word "idiom" has two different meanings. In a loose sense, the "idiom of a language" is the natural way that native speakers of that language communicate. In a stricter sense, an idiom is an individual phrase that's considered to be grammatically correct for reasons that can't be predicted or explained by a grammatical rule. In other words, this second type of idiom is an expression that's simply right because it's right, even though it has no detectable similarity to any other correct phrase.

This second type of idiom is the type I'm referring to when I talk about idioms on the ACT. Let's consider a quick example. You're probably familiar with the phrase "to fall in love." Why isn't it "*to fall *with* love" or "*to fall *to* love?" There's no logical reason for one of those phrases to be acceptable while the other two aren't—love isn't a physical substance or location, so people can't literally fall "in" love any more than they can literally fall "to" love or "with" love. This phrase just uses the preposition "in" because that's how English-speakers have spoken for a long time.

In other words, if you weren't already familiar with this phrase and you had to pick which preposition to use with it, there would be no rule you could follow that would predict the right answer. You'd just have to guess and hope you were right. And that's what makes this phrase's use of "in" truly idiomatic in the strict sense of that word—it's a truly one-of-a-kind expression in the sense that it doesn't follow any rule that applies to any other use of the word "in."

Luckily, on the ACT we only need to think about things being strictly "idiomatic" in a limited number of questions.

These questions will often involve prepositional phrases you've probably heard before, like "to fall in love." Prepositions are short words like "in," "at," "to," "by," "with," "for," and so on. (Not all short words are prepositions, and not all prepositions are short words, but prepositions are usually short words.) Many languages use prepositions idiomatically, and English is one of them. Here are a few more phrases that depend on idiomatic usage of prepositions, with those prepositions underlined:

> to be <u>on</u> time
>
> to depend <u>on</u> something
>
> to jump <u>to</u> a conclusion
>
> to be all <u>for</u> something

In these phrases, the only way to know which preposition is correct is to be familiar with each phrase beforehand. If you've never heard the phrase before, there's no way to predict the correct preposition to go with it.

Some students have asked me if they should try to memorize a list of idioms in the hope that something from the list might show up on test day, but the odds are very much against that, and the energy you'd spend on that would definitely be better spent somewhere else. For one thing, there are thousands upon thousands of idioms in English, and there doesn't seem to be any restriction on the ones the ACT occasionally tests; for another thing, you probably already know a lot of idioms if you're halfway decent at speaking English; for a third thing, there aren't very many ACT English questions that rely on idioms anyway.

So if you see a question that seems to be asking about an idiom, you should go with your gut instinct about which version of the phrase sounds right to you. There's no point in wasting time trying to figure something out that literally can't be figured out, because it doesn't follow any rules by definition.

Remember that most ACT English questions *do* follow rules and patterns, so you should be able to answer almost every ACT English question you see with certainty and confidence if you know the test's rules. If you feel like you're encountering lots of idiomatic phrases (in the strict sense) when you practice with the Red Book, then you're misunderstanding or misreading the passages and/or the questions.

(By the way, a lot of test-prep resources like to describe almost any acceptable word usage as "idiomatic," using the loose sense of the term. This is basically like saying that something is correct because it's correct—which isn't very helpful if you're trying to learn *why* a phrase is acceptable or unacceptable. Look out for that. On the ACT, the only strictly idiomatic phrases you'll encounter are similar to the ones we just talked about. When talking about ACT English questions, this Black Book will only use the word "idiomatic" in its strict sense, to describe the few phrases on the ACT that can't be predicted by rules.)

Question 64 on page 447 of the Red Book asks about an idiom that involves a preposition. The sentence says that certain gardens are "modeled <u>for</u>" certain other gardens. The correct phrase in this context is "modeled <u>on</u>." So the right answer is choice (G).

As we've discussed, there's no rule that would tell us which preposition should be used in this phrase. You just have to be familiar with the usage in question. Since there is no real rule governing this type of question, and since it appears rarely, I suggest you spend your energies working on other issues. If you do see a question like this on the test, go with your gut instinct and move on.

Redundancy

Redundancy is an important concept in ACT English questions. Basically, we want to avoid any answer choice that contains a word or phrase that restates something that's already clearly stated somewhere else in the sentence.

For example, imagine we have a choice between these two sentences:

> ***My house is in the space next to the library.**

> **My house is next to the library.**

The ACT would reward the second sentence, because the first sentence contains the unnecessary phrase "in the space." When we say that something is "next to" something else, it's already understood that we're talking about physical spaces, so the phrase "in the space" would need to be avoided if this were a sentence on the ACT English section.

> Here's another example:

> ***John always chose the aisle seat every time he flew.**

> **John chose the aisle seat every time he flew.**

In this example, the second sentence would be preferred on the ACT. The original sentence already contains the phrase "every time he flew," so the word "always" isn't necessary, and the ACT would reward you for avoiding it in this situation.

Notice that the example about the seat requires us to notice more of the sentence than the example about the house did, because the sentence about the seat included some other words between the redundant phrases.

The ACT likes to look for opportunities to separate important phrases from one another on the English section, to decrease the likelihood that test-takers will notice the key elements in a question. This is why it's always important for us to pay attention!

Still, our job won't be to read through every single sentence in every single ACT English passage and look out for redundant phrases, so please don't try to do that—it would be far too time-consuming. Instead, when we see an answer choice that allows us to get rid of a phrase (or part of a phrase) altogether, we just need to remember to take a look at the whole sentence and see whether that phrase is redundant and should be removed.

There's a real-life example of this kind of redundancy in question 35 on page 156 of the Red Book. The underlined portion describes something as "prestigiously acclaimed." Both of these words mean that something is respected or well-regarded; there is no reason to use both words to express that idea. Choice (B), which would change that portion to "famed, renowned, and notable," has the same problem—all of those words mean the same thing. Choice (C) introduces a word that would change the meaning entirely. Only choice (D), the correct answer, solves the problem by getting rid of one of the original words and leaving behind the word "prestigious."

Remember that if two words or phrases in one sentence on the ACT English section express the same idea, one of them needs to go (assuming we're given the option).

Irrelevant Information

We just saw that answer choices on the ACT English section can be wrong if they supply information that's already elsewhere in the same sentence.

It turns out that answer choices can also be wrong if they supply information that has no relevance to the discussion in the passage. Let's look at an example.

Imagine you're reading a passage that talks about a student getting ready for school, and you see this sentence:

> *After I brushed my teeth, I put my things into my backpack, which is the same color as my cat's eyes.

Unless the rest of the passage indicates that the cat's eye-color is somehow related to the student's morning routine, the phrase "which is the same color as my cat's eyes" is completely irrelevant.

Let's look at another example. Imagine that we're reading a passage that describes a dinner at home, and we see this sentence:

> *The grilled vegetables were laid out on a platter that my mom bought in 1973.

Unless there's some direct indication in the passage that knowing when the dinnerware was purchased is important, the phrase "that my mom bought in 1973" is irrelevant and should be removed.

When it comes to irrelevant information, we want to keep in mind the same idea we talked about regarding redundancy: the point is NOT that we should read through every passage in the ACT English section looking for irrelevant phrases. Instead, if we're asked about an underlined phrase, and we notice that one or more answer choices would let us chop out the phrase entirely, then we should think for a moment about whether the phrase is actually relevant.

For a real-life example of an ACT question that involves irrelevant information, take a look at question 46 on page 158 of the Red Book. The underlined portion of this question is an entire sentence, which reads, "Afterwards, I went to the movies." The first answer choice would leave this sentence unchanged, and the next two offer different versions of the sentence. But the correct answer is the last one, choice (J), which says to omit the sentence entirely. There's nothing else in the passage about the author going to the movies, and it's simply not relevant to the rest of the text, so the ACT's rules and patterns say this sentence needs to go.

Whenever you see an option to omit something, always consider the possibility that the thing in question isn't relevant to the passage (or that it's redundant, as discussed in the previous section) and should be removed.

Proximity

When a phrase on the ACT English section describes or refers back to another phrase, we want those two phrases to be as close to each other as possible, to keep the meaning clear. Let's look at a couple of examples.

This is an example of poor phrase placement on the ACT:

> ***Tomorrow I'll get that report done, which is when it's due.**

This is an example of good phrase placement on the ACT:

> **I'll get that report done tomorrow, which is when it's due.**

The phrase "which is when it's due" refers to "tomorrow," so we want the word "tomorrow" to be moved over so the two phrases are next to each other.

Here's another example of poor phrase placement on the ACT:

> ***As the event coordinator, flower arrangements are the main thing I worry about.**

This is an example of good phrase placement on the ACT:

> **As the event coordinator, I mainly worry about flower arrangements.**

The person who is the event coordinator is the one saying "I," so the word "I" needs to be positioned right next to the phrase "as the event coordinator." According to the rules of the ACT, the first version of the sentence makes it sound like "flower arrangements" is the event coordinator, since it comes immediately after the phrase "as the event coordinator."

You can see an example of this issue in question 36 on page 156 of your copy of *The Real ACT Prep Guide, 3rd Edition*. In this question, the underlined portion is immediately followed by the phrase "a time when . . .," which describes the time mentioned in the underlined portion.

The only time period mentioned in the underlined portion is the phrase "in 1989." Every answer choice features the phrase "in 1989," but only one choice has this phrase last, so that the phrase "in 1989" would come immediately before the phrase "a time when . . .". That choice is (G), which is correct. The resulting sentence reads, "He came up with his idea . . . in 1989, a time when . . .".

So remember—if a phrase refers back to another phrase in this way on the ACT, we want to put those phrases right next to each other if we can.

Relationship Words

This is an issue that has a little to do with style, and a little to do with reading comprehension.

Basically, there are a lot of instances in ACT English passages in which you'll see what I call "relationship words." This isn't a formal grammatical concept—it's just an easy way to think about this idea in the context of the ACT.

"Relationship words" are just words that indicate some type of relationship between things or ideas in a sentence. Here are some examples of the kinds of words I'm talking about:

unless

during

while

because

except

but

since

The ACT likes to ask us to select the "relationship word" that appropriately links two halves of a sentence. For example, the ACT would consider this sentence to be acceptable:

> **My brother likes to watch soccer on TV <u>because</u> he enjoys sports programming in general.**

In this case, the word "because" correctly indicates a causative relationship between the two halves of the sentence: the reason my brother likes watching soccer is that it's a specific example of something that he generally likes, according to the sentence.

But a sentence like the following would be unacceptable on the ACT English section:

> ***My brother likes to watch soccer on TV; <u>nevertheless,</u> he enjoys sports programming in general.**

In this case, the word "nevertheless" is supposed to indicate a contradiction between two ideas, but the two halves of this sentence don't contradict each other.

There's an example of a real ACT question involving relationship words in question 62 on page 161. That question refers to the following sentence:

> **The computer is probably sick, <u>unless</u> the diagnosis may be that the computer has a virus.**

The word "unless" indicates that the second part of the sentence would stop the first part of the sentence from being true. But the first part of the sentence talks about the computer being "sick," and the second part talks about the computer having a "virus." The two parts of the sentence seem to go together, not to contradict each other.

For that reason, we know that "unless" is an inappropriate relationship word in this context. We need a word that indicates that the second part of the sentence goes along with the first part. That means choice (H), "and," is the correct answer.

Shorter Is Better

This is an idea that overlaps with some of what we've already talked about, but it's worth mentioning on its own: in questions of style on the ACT English section, shorter is better, all else being equal.

This would be an example of an unnecessarily long sentence on the ACT:

> ***If I were the one who had the choice about going, I would choose to stay home.***

This would be an improved version of the sentence, according to the ACT:

> **If it were up to me, I would stay home.**

Technically speaking, there isn't anything grammatically *wrong* with the first choice: all the words in the sentence agree grammatically with the words they should agree with. But the ACT English section would prefer the second version, because it's the shorter version and also has no grammatical issues of its own.

I want to make it clear that shortness has nothing to do with grammar in real life. It's just something the ACT English section has arbitrarily decided to reward on the test.

We can see a real-life example of this "shorter is better" principle in question 34 on page 443. Each answer choice is grammatically acceptable, so the shortest choice is the correct answer: choice (G).

"Which Would Be Least Acceptable?"

This is a special type of style question that has a prompt. The prompt will ask which answer choice is the LEAST acceptable alternative to the underlined portion of the sentence. Three of the choices will be acceptable according to the ACT, and one will not.

First and foremost, let me stress the importance of noticing the word LEAST in all capital letters. You'd be surprised how often test-takers ignore this word and pick one of the three acceptable options instead of the one unacceptable option. Always read each question carefully!

Let's look at a real-life example so you know what I mean.

Question 8 on page 577 of the Red Book asks which answer choice is the LEAST acceptable alternative to the underlined phrase in the sentence.

Notice that three of the four choices are essentially identical with respect to the sentence. The only one that would result in an unclear sentence is choice (J), because the word "these" by itself could refer to any plural noun. Each of the other phrases clearly indicates that the two women did the sailing. Only (J) is ambiguous, so (J) is an unacceptable version of the underlined phrase, according to the ACT—which makes it the CORRECT answer to the question.

Parallelism

The term "parallelism" is used much too loosely when it comes to standardized test prep, in my opinion, but it's actually useful on ACT English questions if you understand what it really means and you use it in the proper context.

Ultimately, in order to use parallelism as a tool to beat the ACT, we should think of it as looking at the text surrounding the underlined portion when we're trying to find clues about what to do with the underlined portion. This often helps on the ACT English section because the test sometimes does us a favor by structuring a nearby part of the passage in the same way that it wants us to structure the correct answer to a question.

That probably sounds confusing, so let's look at an example.

Question 51 on page 159 of your copy of *The Real ACT Prep Guide, 3rd Edition* asks us about the underlined phrase "he or she learns." Our other options, from the answer choices, are "we learn," "you learn," and "people learned."

At first, just from looking at this sentence, we might have trouble deciding which choice is correct. Each would result in a grammatically acceptable sentence, technically speaking. We might also have trouble deciding if we should use the present tense or the past tense.

But if we look at the rest of the paragraph, we can see that it repeatedly uses the word "you" with present-tense verbs: ". . . you guide . . . you come . . . you never know . . . you can sometimes get . . .". Once we see that pattern, we know the sentence in our question should have the same structure, so the ACT English section wants us to pick "you learn." This means (C) is the correct answer.

Unfortunately, it's not possible to use this technique on every single question, simply because the ACT doesn't structure its texts in a way that makes this possible on every question. Depending on the context, though, we might use this technique to determine something like the appropriate form of a verb, or even the right punctuation for a phrase, as long as something in the surrounding text is similar and there's an answer choice to match it.

Of course, you shouldn't double-check every sentence in every passage for these kinds of parallel structures—that would take up a lot of time, for one thing, and the test doesn't include parallelism on every question, as we just discussed. Instead, keep this parallelism idea in mind for situations where multiple answer choices seem equally good—it may be that the correct answer becomes clear when you compare the underlined phrase to other phrases in the surrounding sentences, as we just did in the example above.

Questions that combine grammar/style/punctuation elements with reading comprehension elements

We'll occasionally see questions that mix elements from both grammar/style/punctuation questions and reading comprehension questions. They'll typically look like grammar/style/punctuation questions, with one key difference: more than one answer choice will be grammatically and stylistically acceptable to the ACT, but one of those choices will change the meaning of the original sentence. Let's take a look an example so you can see what I mean.

Question 35 on page 156 makes reference to this phrase from the passage: "the prestigiously acclaimed Culinary Institute of America."

When we look at the text and the answer choices, this seems to be a classic question about redundancy (as we saw in our discussion of redundancy a few pages ago). The original version of the text includes the phrase "prestigiously acclaimed." This is redundant because "prestigious" and "acclaimed" mean the same thing, so the ACT doesn't want us to use both words. Choice (B) is also redundant: "famed," "renowned," and "notable" all mean the same thing, so we shouldn't have all three words describing the same thing in an ACT sentence.

Now look at the remaining choices. Neither (C) nor (D) is redundant. These choices feature two words with two different meanings, and we have to use our reading comprehension skills to choose between them. At this point, the question is kind of like the "precision vocabulary" questions we discussed a few pages ago.

We know that we can eliminate (C) because it changes the original meaning of the sentence, and there's no indication in the passage that this is justified—the word "luscious" can be applied to a food, but it can't be applied to an Institute in this sentence. Only "prestigious," choice (D), solves the problem of redundancy *and* uses a word that can appropriately modify the word "Institute" from the passage.

Notice that we eliminated (A) and (B) because of stylistic considerations—but the remaining choices, (C) and (D), had no problems related to grammar, style, or punctuation. To choose between them, we had to look at the actual meanings of the original sentence and the words in the answer choices, which is a skill we would normally associate with reading comprehension questions on the ACT English section.

If you look carefully at a grammar/style/punctuation question and end up concluding that more than one answer choice is acceptable according to the normal rules of that question type, take a look to see whether the remaining answer choices violate the reading comprehension rules of the ACT English section. If one does, eliminate it. (If considering the reading comprehension aspect of the answer choices still doesn't make it clear which one is correct, then you should consider the possibility that you've misread the question or the answer choices.)

How To Read Passages On The ACT English Section

Earlier in this Black Book, we talked about the best ways to read passages on the ACT Reading and ACT Science sections. I said there were three main ways to approach those passages—reading, skimming, or skipping—and that you should experiment with them and pick the approach you're most successful with.

But my advice for the passages on the ACT English section is different. This section is structured differently from the way those other two sections are structured.

For the ACT English section, my recommendation is that you just start reading the passage from the very beginning (including the title). Every time you see an underlined, numbered portion of text, or a number with a square around it in the text, finish the sentence, and then look to the right of the text to find the question that corresponds to the text you've just read. In most cases, you'll be able to answer that question based on the text you've read so far; you may sometimes need to read a little further, especially if a question involves one of the following elements (which were all discussed in the preceding "ACT English Question Types" section):

- parallelism
- placing a set of sentences in the right order
- redundancy
- the option to eliminate a phrase or sentence
- introducing a paragraph, or providing a transition between paragraphs or sentences

You may also see questions at the end of a passage that ask about the passage as a whole; these will usually involve some kind of reading comprehension, which means the correct answer will restate or directly reflect the text. You should be able to answer these questions after answering the other questions about the passage, without needing to re-read the entire passage. Still, make sure you check back over the relevant portions of the passage before deciding on your answer.

You'll get used to this general approach as you look through the walkthroughs in this Black Book and do some practice of your own.

The General Process For Answering ACT English Questions

Now that we've learned all the basics, let's take a look at the general process I recommend for answering this type of question.

1. Read the passage until you come to a question.

The questions will appear to the right of the passage, and they'll either correspond to a certain portion of the passage (which will be underlined or marked with a number in a box), or they'll appear at the end of the passage and ask about that passage as a whole. When you come to a question, finish the sentence you're on, then stop reading the passage and shift your attention to the question.

2. Carefully read the prompt (if there is one) and the answer choices, and determine which type of question it is.

Not all questions will have a prompt; some will only offer four answer choices as possible versions of an underlined portion of the text. Either way, read the prompt if there is one, and carefully read the answer choices. Determine whether you're dealing with a grammar/style/punctuation question, or a reading comprehension question.

3a. For grammar/style/punctuation questions, look for any of the relevant issues we discussed in the section on ACT English question types.

Look at the words in the underlined portion, and see how they relate to the other words in the sentence. Do pronouns and agree in number with the words they relate to? Are verbs in the right number and tense? Are possessives formed correctly? Are periods, commas, and semicolons in the right place according to the ACT's grammar rules?

Consider all the answer choices. Are any choices functionally equivalent in the context of the passage, and therefore both wrong? Can any choices be eliminated for being unnecessarily long? Are there any relationship words that don't make sense?

3b. For a reading comprehension question, look for any of the relevant issues we discussed in the section on ACT English question types.

There are several different issues we talked about regarding reading comprehension questions in ACT English, but they generally have to do with finding an answer choice that directly restates or reflects the concepts and relationships in the text.

4. Find the right answer, or eliminate three wrong answers.

Sometimes you can immediately see which concept the question is testing, and you can tell that a particular answer choice is correct. If not, you should still be able to start eliminating wrong-answer choices based on the issues we discussed for that question type. For example, on a grammar/style/punctuation question, you might be able to tell that an answer choice has a verb in the wrong tense, or a comma in the wrong place; on a reading comprehension question, you might be able to see that an answer choice differs from the passage. Keep considering answer choices until you've identified the one correct choice that follows the rules and patterns of the ACT English section, and the three wrong-answer choices that break those rules and patterns.

5. Take a second look to reconsider the question, the answer choices, and the passage.

Now that you've chosen a correct answer, take another look at the question, answer choices, and passage to make sure you haven't overlooked or misread anything. Did you miss an intervening phrase between a subject and its verb? Did you overlook a word like "NOT," "EXCEPT," or "LEAST?" Always remember that the ACT is trying to trick you into making a small mistake on every single question. Stay on your toes.

6. Mark your answer choice and move on.

Once you've gone through the process and double-checked your answer, mark your choice and move on. Keep going through the passage until you reach the next question.

ACT English Answer-Choice Patterns And Issues

The ACT deliberately positions wrong-answer choices to take advantage of the mistakes it believes test-takers are likely to make, as we've repeatedly seen in our discussion of wrong-answer choices for the Reading, Math, and Science sections of the test. We'll find many of the same general patterns at work in the English section that we've already seen in the other sections.

We already discussed a variety of answer-choice patterns when we talked about the question types you'll encounter on the ACT English section. For example, we saw that some reading comprehension questions on the ACT demonstrate a "yes yes no no" pattern in their answer choices, just like some ACT Science questions do.

But there are some other answer-choice patterns that apply more generally on this section, and we'll take a look at them now.

ACT English Answer-Choice Pattern 1: Most Like The Others

This answer-choice pattern works more or less the same way as the pattern with the similar name that we discussed for the ACT Math section.

The ACT often likes to incorporate elements of the correct answer in the incorrect answers, so that test-takers who figure out part of a question will still have to work to figure out the rest of it, instead of being able to choose the only answer choice that includes the part of the question they've worked out. When the ACT does this on the English section, it often generates a set of answer choices that are highly similar to one another, such as choices that include identical wording with different punctuation. We'll often find that the right answer is the one that combines the elements that appear most frequently throughout the set of answer choices.

For an example of this pattern in action, take a look at question 20 on page 295 of the Red Book. All of the answer choices for the question contain the same four words: "style developed based on." The only differences among the answer choices are the locations and types of punctuation marks in the phrase. When we compare and contrast them, we observe the following:

- 3 of the 4 choices have no punctuation after the word "style."
- 3 of the 4 choices have no punctuation after the word "developed."
- 4 of the 4 choices have no punctuation after the word "based."
- 3 of the 4 choices have no punctuation after the word "on."

So the majority of the answer choices have no punctuation after any of the words in the phrase. In light of the "most like the others" pattern, we'd expect the correct answer to be the choice that has no punctuation after any of the words—and it is, because (G) is correct.

While the ACT English section follows it frequently, this pattern should never be the only factor in determining your answer (unless you've given up on a question and decided to guess—see the section on guessing in "The General Game Plan For Attacking A Section Of The ACT On Test Day" earlier in this Black Book for more on that). Instead, we should use this pattern to help us identify which concepts are being tested in a question, to predict which answer choice is *likely* to be correct, and to help us re-evaluate our answer to a question after we've decided on it.

You'll see these ideas in action when we go through the ACT English walkthroughs together in a few pages.

ACT English Answer-Choice Pattern 2: Functionally Identical Answer Choices

As you go through the ACT English section, you'll find many questions in which 2 or 3 of the choices are basically the same, in the context of the question.

Because there can only be one correct answer choice for every ACT question, if you find two or three answer choices that are effectively the same, they must all be wrong, since they can't all be right. This can be a helpful pattern to notice, especially if you're having trouble picking out a correct answer otherwise.

You can see an example of this concept in *The Real ACT Prep Guide, 3rd Edition* in question 68 on page 302.

In this example, the underlined phrase from the passage is "frequently, common." The next two choices to replace this are the phrases "quite regularly, common" and "many times, common." In context, all three of these answer choices functionally identical, since "frequently," "quite regularly," and "many times" all have the same meaning here. So each choice is a phrase indicating that something happens a lot, then a comma, and then the word "common."

Since these choices are all basically the same, we know they must all be wrong. The only answer choice that's different is the correct answer, (J), which is just the word "common" without any extra phrase before it.

(Incidentally, this is an example of a question that tests the "redundancy" issue we talked about earlier in this chapter. It could also be seen as an example of the "shorter is better" principle on the ACT English section. As you can see, these concepts can overlap a bit, but that's fine as long as you're able to use them to select the correct answer consistently.)

ACT English Answer-Choice Pattern 3: No Special Consideration For "NO CHANGE"

Don't be afraid to select "NO CHANGE" on a grammar/style/punctuation question if you think the original version of the phrase is correct according to the rules and patterns of the ACT English section.

A lot of people start to worry if they think they've chosen "NO CHANGE" too many times (or too few times). But those answer choices aren't any more or less likely to be correct than any other answer choices are.

On school tests, teachers often use trick answer choices like "none of the above" to make multiple-choice questions seem harder. But the ACT doesn't do that with the "no change" answer choice. On some days the "no change" choice is correct a little more often than other answer choices are, and on other days it's correct a little less often. So there's no magical number of times that this kind of answer choice has to be correct.

ACT English Answer-Choice Pattern 4: When To "OMIT The Underlined Portion"

Sometimes a question on the ACT English section will include an answer choice that allows you to omit an underlined phrase or sentence.

If the ACT English section gives you the option to omit a phrase or sentence, you should choose to omit it UNLESS it meets both of the following criteria:

- It must restate a concept from the surrounding text.
- It must also contribute a new concept not found in the surrounding text.

These criteria are really just extensions of the ACT English section's rules about relevance and redundancy. If an underlined phrase doesn't restate a concept from the surrounding text, the ACT considers it to be irrelevant; if it doesn't also contribute a new concept, the ACT considers it to be redundant. If that's confusing, take a look at the walkthroughs for this section so you can see this idea (and all the others) in action. They start on the next page.

Walkthroughs: The ACT English Process In Action Against Real Questions

Of course, now that we've learned everything we need to know to beat the ACT English section, we're going to use these techniques to solve some real ACT English practice questions. You'll want to follow along in your copy of *The Real ACT Prep Guide, 3rd Edition* (otherwise known as the Red Book).

These particular test items were selected either because they're questions that my one-on-one tutoring clients tend to have the most trouble with, or because they're good representations of the ideas we've talked about in the ACT English training section.

This is the last walkthrough section in this Black Book, so I'll say this one last time—going over these walkthroughs is every bit as important as reviewing the rest of the training. If you want to be able to use these techniques on real ACT English questions, you really need to follow along with these walkthroughs to see how they work against real questions.

(If you'd like to see some video demonstrations of these ideas, go to www.ACTprepVideos.com for a selection of demonstration videos that are free to readers of this book.)

Page 153, Question 7

The Red Book's explanation for this question on page 213 is essentially correct, but I want to talk about some elements of this question's setup that should be particularly interesting to us as trained test-takers.

First, we want to realize that each answer choice uses identical wording, and only the punctuation differs. This means, of course, that we're being tested on whether we can recognize the punctuation usage that the ACT finds acceptable. So we can focus on that completely, and ignore any issues we might think we have with the words themselves.

From a grammatical standpoint, we want to recognize that this sentence contains an example of the "comma sandwich" we talked about in the training. A "comma sandwich" is a phrase between two commas (or between a comma and the end of a sentence) that still leaves behind a complete sentence if we remove it. (We know that we're dealing with a potential "comma sandwich" because most of the phrases have at least one comma, and those commas aren't used with any series, adjectives, conjunctions, or anything else like that. See the Writing Toolbox in the Appendix of this Black Book for more on comma usage on the ACT English section.)

If we consider (A), we find that there would be two phrases in comma sandwiches: "who had volunteered to move," and "to those bedrooms for a year." The ACT requires us to be able to remove either of them separately and leave behind a complete sentence. If we were to remove the first phrase, the result would be this:

"The two 'little brothers' of Ligia's host family to those bedrooms for a year, had to be moved upstairs to the room Ligia was using."

We can probably tell this is an incomplete sentence, so (A) must be the wrong answer. (If you're not sure why that's not a complete sentence, please check out the Writing Toolbox in the Appendix.)

(B) has no comma at the end. That means this "comma sandwich" wouldn't end until the end of the sentence. If we took out everything in this "comma sandwich," we'd be left with just this:

"The two 'little brothers' of Ligia's host family."

That's also not a sentence, since it has no verb. So we know that (B) isn't the correct answer.

(C) creates a valid "comma sandwich" because we can remove the entire phrase between these two commas and still be left with a complete sentence:

"The two 'little brothers' of Ligia's host family had to be moved upstairs to the room Ligia was using."

That means (C) is the correct answer, since we know there can only be one grammatically acceptable answer when the question is only testing punctuation or grammar. But, as always, we have to make sure we consider all of the answer choices to make sure we haven't made a mistake.

(D) creates a "comma sandwich" around the phrase "who had volunteered." If we remove the first "comma sandwich," we get this:

"The two 'little brothers' of Ligia's host family to move to those bedrooms for a year, had to be moved upstairs to the room Ligia was using."

This isn't a complete sentence, so (D) is wrong.

But there's another way to look at this question, too. Because this is an ACT question with highly similar answer choices, we trained test-takers will want to see which elements appear most frequently in the answer choices, because we know that those elements are likely to be correct. (This is the same kind of analysis we'd make on any other section of the ACT if we saw a question with highly similar answer choices.)

We see that one choice has a comma after the word "volunteered," while three choices don't. So the correct answer probably doesn't include a comma after "volunteered."

One choice has a comma after the word "move," while three don't. So the correct answer probably doesn't have a comma there, either.

Three out of the four choices have a comma after the word "year," while only one choice doesn't. So the correct answer probably contains a comma after the word "year."

That means the correct answer choice is likely to have a comma after the word "year," but nowhere else. Sure enough, choice (C) fits that pattern, and is the correct answer. As I always say, there's no guarantee that an answer choice will be correct just because it fits this pattern, but when a choice fits this pattern it's very likely to be correct.

Page 155, Question 22

Of all the questions in the entire Red Book, this is one of the ones that people ask me about most consistently. And it's usually because they don't read carefully enough, or they forget the rule that each ACT question must have exactly one correct answer choice.

If we look at the three answer choices after "NO CHANGE," we see 3 different verb forms: "have been," "were," and "are." If we stick any of these choices back into the *immediate* context of the underlined portion of the sentence, we end up with phrases like these:

- "walls have been painted"
- "walls were painted"
- "walls are painted"

At this point, we may think we've run into a problem. We know the question is testing us on the proper verb form, because each answer choice is a different form of the helping verb "to be." But we also know that a verb tense can only be incorrect on the ACT if it creates an impossible scenario (like saying that a future event happened before an event in the past). And, in this case, each tense in those three answer choices is a possibility, because no other phrase in the sentence or the passage would contradict any of those tenses.

Once they realize that, most test-takers make a fatal mistake: they assume that the question must have been written badly, and they just cross their fingers and pick the choice that sounds best to them. That means they end up missing the question and getting a lower score for no good reason.

But a trained test-taker knows there always has to be a clear, distinct reason for one answer choice to be correct on an ACT question. So a trained test-taker would realize that he'd made a mistake if he found himself thinking that three answer choices were all equally correct, and there was no way to distinguish among them.

So it would be wise to revisit the whole question from the very beginning, and look for the mistake or misreading that led us to the impossible conclusion that all three answer choices were right.

It turns out that the real issue here has nothing to do with *tense* whatsoever. Instead, the question is all about the *number* of the verb form (that is, whether the verb is singular or plural). The underlined verb isn't supposed to agree with the word "walls," but with the word "paneling"—grammatically speaking, the thing in the sentence receiving the action of being painted is the "paneling," and the phrase "on the walls" is just an intervening prepositional phrase describing the paneling. Since "paneling" is a singular noun, the correct answer choice must be the singular form of a verb. The only option that works is "has been," which means that (F), NO CHANGE, is the correct answer.

This is a great example of the importance of reading carefully at all times. Remember, especially, that any time you're looking at an answer choice with different verb forms, you need to go back and read enough of the sentence to know for sure which noun the verb has to agree with. Anyone who did that on this question would realize that a singular verb form was required, which means only (F) can be correct.

Also try to keep this question in mind the next time you get frustrated by an ACT question that seems to have more than one correct answer. Remember that there's *always* exactly one distinctly correct answer—if you can't find it, you've misread something in the question, the answer choices, or the accompanying material (if there is any).

Page 155, Question 23

The Red Book's explanation for this question on page 218 is, frankly, pretty bad. It correctly states that we need to find an answer choice that describes the paneling, but then it says that only choice (A) is a description of the paneling, which is quite clearly incorrect. (A) and (B) both mention some aspect of the paneling directly, while (C) and (D) provide descriptions of the paint that's on the paneling, which is arguably another way to describe the paneling. The Red Book simply refers to the description in (B) as "irrelevant," without bothering to explain why the detail in (A) is relevant—especially since (B) is the only answer choice that actually mentions the paneling directly. If someone were to argue that (C) and (D) aren't talking about the paneling directly, the same argument should apply equally to (A), which talks about the brush strokes in the varnish on the paneling, and not about the paneling itself. (Or, again, if we say that talking about the brush strokes in the varnish on the paneling is the same thing as talking about the paneling, then talking about the paint on the paneling should also be the same thing as talking about the paneling—the ACT can't expect to have it both ways.)

I feel bad for test-takers who go to the trouble of studying the Red Book and then occasionally come across explanations like this one. The logic (or lack of logic) in the Red Book's description of the wrong answers could very easily lead people to conclude that the ACT is unpredictable, illogical, and arbitrary. Test-takers who read the Red Book explanation of this question would probably feel that their best chance of success on future questions is simply to go with their gut instincts. That might be good enough for some people who don't really care about the ACT, but it's not good enough for me—and I hope you'll decide it's not good enough for you.

Instead, we need to attack this question with precision and certainty, which requires us to know how the test actually works. As trained test-takers, we know that this question is essentially a reading comprehension question masquerading as an English question. That means the correct answer to this question will be the one that sticks as closely as possible to the concepts in the original paragraph, adding as little new material as possible.

Once we adopt that approach, it becomes clear why (A) is correct: (A) talks about "brush strokes" and "wood grain," and both of those concepts reflect ideas that appear elsewhere in the paragraph. The phrase "brush strokes" reflects the idea of the painting and varnishing that has been done to the paneling (because both of those processes require a brush), and the phrase "resemble wood grain" in the answer choice directly echoes the phrase "wood grain finish" in the previous sentence.

(B) is incorrect because it introduces the idea of "protection," which isn't directly reflected anywhere in the passage.

(C) is incorrect because it mentions the idea that lime green is "bizarre." We may have already thought that lime green was a bizarre choice, based on personal preference, but the passage itself never actually says so. Since we need to find an answer choice that restates ideas that are already in the passage, we know this choice is wrong.

(D) is wrong because the uniqueness of the person who chose the color scheme isn't directly mentioned anywhere in the passage. Now, if we read between the lines a little bit, we might detect that this answer choice seems a little sarcastic, and the last sentence in the paragraph might also seem like a sarcastic dig at the interior designer. So we might be tempted to say that this choice restates a concept from the passage, but it actually doesn't, if we read in the literal-minded way that the ACT requires. The sentence in this answer choice mentions the designer's uniqueness, while the sentence in the passage mentions the designer's competence. It's possible to be unique (or not unique) with or without being competent, so the idea of uniqueness in this answer choice would be a new concept if we added it into the passage. So (D) is wrong.

Let this question remind you, once more, of the importance of knowing how the ACT actually works, instead of always taking the Red Book at face value! Every question on the ACT can be approached in a logical, consistent way if you know what the ACT consistently rewards and punishes—and that's what you learn in this Black Book.

Page 155, Question 25

This question comes down to two important grammar ideas. The first is the correct use of "much" versus "many."

As we discussed in the training, if a noun is plural and countable, then you use the word "many" to describe it, as in the phrase "there are too many cars." Cars are countable—they're separate, distinct things that you can count.

If a noun isn't plural or countable, then you use the word "much" to describe a lot of it, as in the phrase "there's too much sunshine."

Because the passage is talking about the plural noun "quarters," which describes a bunch of distinct individual things that can be counted, we need to modify it with the word "many," not the word "much," so we can eliminate (A) and (D), which leaves just (B) and (C).

Between (B) and (C), the only difference is between saying "too fewer" or "too few." There are a lot of reasons why the phrase "too fewer" is wrong, but the easiest way to explain it might be to say that the word "fewer" requires us to *compare* two things, as in "this machine has fewer quarters than that machine does." Another way to describe the problem with the phrase "too fewer" might be to say that the word "too" has to be used with the basic form of an adjective, not the comparative form. If you're a native speaker of American English, you might also just be able to think about this phrase in your head and realize that it sounds unnatural, no matter which part of America you live in.

So (C) is correct.

As trained test-takers, we have another way to be pretty sure that "fewer" is incorrect: it only appears once in all the answer choices, while "few" appears three times and "too" also appears three times, strongly suggesting that both "too" and "few" should be part of the correct answer.

We may very well see other ACT English questions on test day that target the difference between "much" and "many," so make sure you keep those two things straight.

Page 156, Question 31

If we remember the discussion earlier in this book about possessive pronouns, then right away we know that "who's" is wrong. The pronoun "who" doesn't use an apostrophe to form a possessive on the ACT.

On the ACT, the form "who's" would only be acceptable as a contraction of the phrase "who is," as in "who's responsible for this mess?"

If we stick "who is" back in the sentence in place of "who's," we get the phrase "a company who is slogan is," which isn't correct.

(B) is a correctly formed possessive of the word "who," so it's the right answer here. The word "whose" can be used to refer to inanimate concepts like companies, as this sentence does, or in a sentence like "that's the car whose tires are new."

We can also eliminate choice (C), "that's" (or "that is") for basically the same reason as (A). (There is no possessive form of the word "that," by the way—at least, not on the ACT.)

(D) is something that a lot of test-takers might say in everyday speech, but the ACT requires a traditional possessive form in a case like this—the word "that" can only be used on the ACT in three ways:

1. to indicate a particular object (as in "that hat is the one I like")

2. to show that a previously mentioned noun is doing an action (as in "this is a company that loves its employees")

3. to turn a verb phrase into a noun phrase (as in "I want to demonstrate that peace is possible," where "that peace is possible" acts as a noun phrase that is the direct object of the verb "to demonstrate")

Another way we can tell that (D) is very unlikely to be correct is that three of the answer choices involve a possessive form (or things that many untrained test-takers will think are possessive forms, anyway). This typically indicates the correct answer will be one of those (apparently) possessive forms.

Page 157, Question 40

This question asks us if deleting a couple of phrases ("whenever possible" and "much of") from the previous sentence will change the meaning of that sentence. So let's take a look at the sentence without those phrases:

"The firm also employs African American [sic] professional advisers and subcontractors and contracts African American [sic] farmers to grow the produce that goes into Glory Foods."

Choice (F) says there is a change, because eliminating those phrases would make it sound like *all* the subcontractors and farmers were African-American. If we read the original sentence and the changed version, we can see that this observation is true. "Whenever possible" and "much of" are the only phrases in the sentence that indicate that it's talking about some portion of the subcontractors and farmers, as opposed to all of them. So (F) is the correct answer.

(G) also says there's a change, but incorrectly says the change would be that readers wouldn't know the company made an effort to employ African-American contractors. But we can see that the altered sentence would still contain that information.

(H) says there would be no change because these phrases don't provide extra information. But that's not accurate, as we discussed above for choice (F).

(J) says there would be no change because these phrases provide detail but "are not essential to the meaning of the sentence." Again, we saw in our discussion of (F) that these phrases do change the meaning of the sentence.

We know this question is testing our reading comprehension because it has a prompt, and because it asks about the impact of particular phrases, instead of offering us different versions of a phrase. That means the correct answer must accurately describe the passage in a literal way, which is exactly what (F) does.

Page 159, Question 49
In order to answer this question, we'll have to read Paragraph 2 and see how Sentence 4 relates to the other sentences in the paragraph.

The key element in Sentence 4 is the phrase "on the other hand," which indicates that Sentence 4 needs to appear after a sentence that contradicts it in some way. This fits perfectly with Sentence 3, because Sentence 3 talks about the wide variety of video games, while Sentence 4 says that pinball machines have no real variety. If we put Sentence 4 after any other sentence in the paragraph, the phrase "on the other hand" would make no sense.

We can also tell that Sentence 4 belongs where it does because Sentence 5 talks about pinball in a way that indicates the sentence before it must also talk about pinball. The phrase "some machines" at the beginning of Sentence 5 shows that the idea of machines has already been mentioned in the paragraph, and the only machines in the paragraph are pinball machines. But if we put Sentence 4 in any other position, Sentence 5 would be introducing (or re-introducing) the idea of pinball machines after the sentence that's currently Sentence 3, and the phrase "some machines" at the beginning of Sentence 5 wouldn't make any sense.

We can conclude that this sentence belongs right where it is, because of the key phrases "on the other hand" in Sentence 4 and "some machines" in Sentence 5. So the correct answer is choice (A).

Page 159, Question 53
As trained test-takers, we can tell that this question is testing our ability to recognize punctuation that conforms to the ACT's rules. We know this because all the phrases in the answer choices contain exactly the same two words, and the only differences among them are the placements of the commas.

The Red Book's explanation for the question on page 228 is the kind of vague discussion that relies on subjective words like "clearest" and "distracting," instead of explaining which choice is correct in terms of concrete rules that we could actually use to find the correct answers to future questions.

So let's talk about this question in a useful way that will help us understand how to approach future questions. That way, our scores won't be determined by how well we can guess what the ACT thinks is "distracting."

It's pretty clear that the issue in this question is whether the commas are being used in a way that creates a valid "comma sandwich." (In case you've forgotten, a "comma sandwich" is basically a phrase surrounded by commas that can be removed from the sentence and still leave behind a grammatically valid sentence.)

So now we have to figure out if any of the choices would create a legitimate "comma sandwich." (Just in case you haven't read the discussion of "comma sandwiches" earlier in this Black Book, I want to point out, again, that the term "comma sandwich" isn't a proper technical grammatical term. It's just the term I often use to help students remember that this type of phrase has to be surrounded by punctuation.)

Let's see what happens if we test the different answer choices to see if any of them create a valid "comma sandwich." We'll do this by removing the potential "comma sandwiches" and seeing if they leave behind complete sentences.

With choice (A), we'd get either of these two options:

- "Then again, you can sometimes get lucky, will inexplicably bounce back into play." (This version assumes that the phrase "and a ball you thought was lost" is the "comma sandwich.")
- "Then again, you can sometimes get lucky, and a ball you thought was lost." (This version assumes that the comma before "and" is okay by itself because "and" is a conjunction, and "will inexplicably bounce back into play" is the "comma sandwich" phrase.)

Neither of those two options is a complete sentence.

Choice (B) does give us a complete, grammatically correct sentence, so it's the correct answer:

"Then again, sometimes you get lucky, and a ball you thought was lost will inexplicably bounce back into play."

In this sentence, the action is "bounce back into play," and the thing doing the bouncing is "a ball you thought was lost."

But we should always check out the other choices as well, to make sure we haven't made a mistake.

Choice (C) would give us these options:

- "Then again, you can sometimes get lucky, will, inexplicably bounce back into play."
- "Then again, you can sometimes get lucky, and a ball you thought was lost, inexplicably bounce back into play."

Again, neither of those options is a complete sentence, so (C) is wrong.

For (D), our options would be the following:

- "Then again, you can sometimes get lucky, inexplicably bounce back into play."
- "Then again, you can sometimes get lucky, and a ball you thought was lost will."

If we really wanted to stretch the possibilities here, we might argue that both options in (D) could be construed as sentences. But even if we take that view, the first option for (D) would indicate that the thing inexplicably bouncing back was "you," instead of the ball; the second option would indicate that a ball will be lucky, just like "you." Neither sentence bears any relevance to the paragraph. So (D) is wrong no matter how we look at it.

Some test-takers will feel uncomfortable without a comma between "lost" and "will," because they'll feel like the phrase "a ball you thought was lost" is just too long to be the subject of a sentence without a comma to set it off. But this feeling is, unfortunately, the result of having been taught incorrectly in school. It's perfectly acceptable to write something like the phrase "a ball you thought was lost will bounce," with "will bounce" as the verb phrase and "a ball you thought was lost" as the noun phrase.

(Again, you don't really need to know all of these grammatical concepts to do well on the ACT—I'm only mentioning this stuff in case some readers are confused by the lack of a comma in the correct version of the phrase in this question.)

Remember that comma questions on the ACT will never depend on subjective concepts like "distract[ion]," even though those kinds of concepts frequently appear in the Red Book's explanations.

Page 160, Question 57

The official explanation for this question appears on page 229 of the Red Book, and relies on vague, subjective concepts like "clarity," instead of clearly setting out why the correct answer is correct in black and white. If you try to attack future ACT questions by thinking about "clarity," or about what seems "confusing" or "inappropriate" (to borrow more empty terms from the Red Book's discussion), you'll probably end up missing those questions unless you get lucky.

But we trained test-takers know exactly how to address questions like this with precision and confidence, in a way that will be repeatable against all real ACT English questions in the future. So let's take a look at this question.

First we'll talk about the question from a grammatical standpoint, and then we'll address it from a purely strategic point of view.

(Before I explain the grammar in this question, I want to point out that most test-takers don't really need to know this in order to reach their target ACT scores, because this particular issue doesn't come up very often on the ACT. But some test-takers will be interested in understanding this question—and test-takers who want to score in the 34+ range *will* need to know how a question like this works. So please feel free to skip the next paragraph if you'd rather focus on approaching these kinds of questions from a more strategic standpoint, or if you don't feel like you need to answer every single question correctly to hit your target score.)

Grammatically speaking, the original version of the sentence is bad because of the phrase "which is sometimes your enemy sometimes your ally," which is a type of run-on. Let's take the phrase apart word-by-word and see how everything ties together (or doesn't). The word "which" is a relative pronoun that refers back to the word "chance," and indicates that "chance" is the subject of the following phrase. The word "is" is the verb that goes with the subject "which" (or "chance," depending on how you'd like to look at it). The phrase "sometimes your enemy" is the thing that "which" or "chance" is being equated to—"enemy" is the noun, "your" is the possessive pronoun indicating whose enemy it is, and "sometimes" is an adverb indicating how often this takes place. But the next few words after "which is sometimes your enemy" can't be part of the same grammatical phrase, because the next word after "enemy," which is "sometimes," doesn't modify any of the words in the phrase "which is sometimes your enemy." So there needs to be some sort of punctuation after the word "enemy," or else the wording needs to be changed; either way, the phrase is ungrammatical the way it's originally presented.

Whew! That was probably a tedious explanation to read, but once you get used to the grammatical rules of the ACT you'll be able to identify these kinds of things pretty quickly if you want to. (Refer to the Writing Toolbox in the Appendix of this Black Book for more on the ACT's grammar rules if you'd like.) Now let's take a look at the other answer choices to see which one corrects the original version of the phrase.

(B) is the correct answer. If we insert a comma after the word "enemy," we can divide the problematic phrase about chance into two separate phrases with parallel structures. We also create two "comma sandwich" phrases that can each be removed individually (or even removed at the same time), leaving a full sentence behind in every case:

- ". . . you have three factors to consider: you, the machine, and chance, which is sometimes your enemy."
- ". . . you have three factors to consider: you, the machine, and chance, sometimes your ally." (In this version, the phrase "sometimes your ally" is an appositive describing the word "chance.")
- ". . . you have three factors to consider: you, the machine, and chance."

So (B) seems to be correct so far. As always, though, we need to look at the other choices to make sure we haven't made a mistake anywhere.

Choice (C) introduces a semicolon after the word "enemy." The ACT English section only allows us to use a semicolon in two situations:

1. To replace a period.
2. As part of a "super series" (see the Writing Toolbox in the Appendix of this Black Book for more on that).

We can't place a period after the word "enemy" because we would create the sentence fragment "sometimes your ally" after it, which wouldn't be an acceptable sentence on the ACT English section because it has no verb. And there's no series of any kind in the phrase "sometimes your enemy, sometimes your ally," even though there is a series earlier in the sentence that's unrelated to the phrase we're being asked about. So (C) is wrong.

(D) is also wrong because of the comma after the word "and." It's fine to put a comma between "enemy" and "and," because we know that commas can be used to introduce a conjunction like "and" in a situation like this on the ACT English section. But the ACT wouldn't let us put a comma directly after the word "and" in this case, because that wouldn't fit any of the valid uses for commas on the ACT English section. For example, we know it doesn't create an acceptable "comma sandwich" because removing either of the potential "sandwiches" would result in these phrases:

- "*. . . you have three factors to consider: you, the machine, and chance, which is sometimes your enemy sometimes your ally."
- "*. . . you have three factors to consider: you, the machine, and chance, which is sometimes your enemy, and."

That's the grammatical explanation for the question. Now let's talk about approaching the question from the standpoint of strategy, rather than relying purely on subject matter.

Since we know that the ACT often likes to create wrong answers that imitate the correct answer as closely as possible, we'd want to notice that 3 of the 4 answer choices in this question have some kind of punctuation after the word "enemy." We'd also want to notice that 2 of those 3 options use a comma for that piece of punctuation. Finally, we'd want to notice that 3 of the 4 choices only include one word. So the most popular elements in the answer choices are having a comma after the word "enemy," and having only one word in the answer choice. If there's a single answer choice with both of those elements, we'd expect it to be correct most of the time on the ACT. Sure enough, that's choice (B), and (B) is correct.

So that's the test-design approach to the question. As I've mentioned before, these kinds of patterns and tendencies will *tend* to lead to correct answers in most situations, but they're not guaranteed to do so. (If every single ACT question used this pattern with perfect consistency, then I wouldn't even bother explaining the grammar of any of these questions—I'd just show you the pattern and be done with it. But the pattern isn't 100% accurate, which is why test-takers who want to score a 34+ will need to know the actual grammar in the questions if they don't want to be at the mercy of chance when they take the ACT.)

So there are a variety of ways we could approach this question, but they all require us to know the ACT's rules and patterns, and to pay attention to small details. These things—not intelligence or college-readiness—are what the ACT rewards consistently.

(Have you noticed how I say that after almost every explanation? It must be important . . .)

Page 161, Question 61

This is one more question in which the ACT tries to confuse you with a lot of commas in different positions. Not surprisingly, it's also a question for which the Red Book's explanation makes repeated reference to vague concepts like confusion and appropriateness, instead of actually explaining how the ACT's rules for commas apply to the question.

The underlined phrase doesn't contain a series of things separated by commas, or any conjunctions, or anything else that would justify the presence of a comma on the ACT English section. So the issue is whether one of these answer choices includes a "comma sandwich," which is my made-up term for a phrase that's surrounded by commas and leaves behind a grammatically acceptable sentence when it's removed.

If we look for a "comma sandwich" in the original version of the sentence and remove it, we're left with this:

"Suddenly, without warning, in front of you tumbles to the bottom of the screen."

This isn't a complete sentence, so the original version of the phrase is grammatically unacceptable to the ACT.

Choice (B) would give us the following result if we tried removing the phrase surrounded by commas:

"Suddenly, without warning, to the bottom of the screen."

(C) would create this:

"Suddenly, without warning, tumbles to the bottom of the screen."

Neither of these is a complete sentence according to the ACT, so (C) is also wrong.

(D) is the option without any commas, and it creates a perfectly acceptable sentence. The subject of the sentence is the noun phrase "each of the letters in front of you," the verb is "tumbles," and the phrase "to the bottom of the screen" tells us the direction of the tumbling. No commas are necessary in, or between, any of those phrases.

So the choice without any commas is grammatically correct, and that's (D).

As often happens, we could also find the correct answer to this question by exploiting the patterns that frequently appear in ACT English questions. In this case, the correct answer is the one with the most similarity to the most other choices. Looking at the answer choices, we can see that 3 out of the 4 choices don't have a comma after the word "letters." Similarly, 3 of the 4 choices don't have a comma after the word "you," and 3 out of the 4 don't have a comma after "tumbles." So if there's a single choice that has no commas in those 3 positions, then it's probably going to be correct, according to the ACT's patterns. Sure enough, (D) is the only choice that has no commas in those positions, and (D) is the correct answer.

Page 161, Question 63

There are two main ways we can approach a question like this, as is often the case on the ACT English section: we can think about the grammar the ACT likes (and be totally sure we'll get the question right), or we can focus more on the test-design patterns that the ACT tends to incorporate (and be likely, but not guaranteed, to get the question right).

Of course, we can also consider *both* aspects of the question if we want to—that's what I would do.

From a grammatical standpoint, the word "however" needs to be in a "comma sandwich" in this case, because the surrounding commas indicate that the word can be removed from the sentence. So (D) is correct here, because it creates the "comma sandwich" around the word "however."

From the standpoint of the ACT's design patterns, we'd want to notice that the answer choices are highly similar to one another, which often indicates the correct answer will be the choice that has the most similarity to the greatest number of other choices. In this case, we'd want to notice that 3 out of the 4 choices have punctuation after the word "viruses," and 2 of those 3 choices have a comma. This would suggest that the correct answer probably has a comma after the word "viruses." We'd also want to notice that 3 of the 4 choices have a comma after the word "however," which would suggest that the correct answer probably has a comma in that position.

So if there's a single answer choice that incorporates the two most popular options (having a comma after "viruses" and a comma after "however"), then it's probably the correct choice. Again, that's choice (D).

Remember that these test-design patterns are things that work *most* of the time on the test, not *all* the time. If you read a question carefully and you're sure that only one answer choice is grammatically correct according to the ACT, then you should pick that choice, even if it doesn't incorporate all of the most popular options from the other answer choices. On the other hand, if you have no idea what's going on in a sentence and you notice that one of the answer choices fits this pattern and sounds okay, then you can probably pick that choice with a high degree of confidence that your guess is correct. (Of course, if you're serious about scoring high on the ACT, then it's best to answer questions based on the actual rules the test follows, and use the patterns to provide another perspective on the questions and help you check your work. You can find a detailed description of the ACT's rules for the English section in the Writing Toolbox in the Appendix of this Black Book.)

Page 162, Question 72

This question relies on our understanding of a certain American English idiom, in which the phrase "had better" is used as a rough synonym for the word "should."

If we're familiar with that idiom, we should be able to recognize that (H) is the only option that works here, so it must be correct.

But what if we're not familiar with that idiom? After all, the frustrating thing about idioms is that it's hard to figure them out—remember from our earlier discussion that an idiom is a phrase that doesn't follow the normal rules of grammar or meaning.

We might try to attack this question by seeing if we can rule out answer choices that sound ridiculous. It *might* be easy for some test-takers to see that option (G), for instance, creates a strange phrase that really isn't relevant to the passage at all: "your better system." But most test-takers who were unfamiliar with the idiom would still have a hard time wrestling with options (F) and (J) in addition to option (H).

So this could end up being a question that eats up a lot of time for a lot of test-takers, without leaving them any more certain of the correct answer in the end. It's important that we develop the ability to recognize these kinds of situations, so that we don't invest our time in questions where it's unlikely to pay off for us.

One other note on this question: after attempting it, you may decide that it's important to learn to use the idiomatic phrase "had better" as it's used in this passage. Knowing that phrase may help your studies in the future, but it's pretty unlikely to show up on the ACT on test day, because the ACT doesn't seem to repeat the idioms it tests very often, as we discussed earlier in the section on ACT English question types. I'm not discouraging you from learning the phrase for use in real life, if you want to—I'm just cautioning you not to expect to see this phrase on the ACT on test day. You might be tested on it again someday, but you probably won't.

Page 292, Question 4

This question brings up the issue of "extra" words on the ACT. In this context, (F) and (G) convey the same relationship that appears in (H). Since (H) is the shortest of these three functionally equivalent answer choices, the ACT will reward (H) as the correct answer.

Let's also talk for a moment about the difference between (H) and (J), because some test-takers may not pay careful enough attention to that difference. If you put each one back in the context of the original sentence, you'll probably see the difference:

- "Because" indicates the grandfather bought a television *as a result of* his old television quitting.
- "So" would indicate an impossible cause-effect relationship. We'd be saying the cause was the grandfather buying a new TV, and the effect was the old TV breaking. But the tenses of the phrases "had finally quit" and "went to buy" indicate that the quitting happened before buying—and it's not possible for an effect to happen before its cause.)

In other words, if we write a phrase with the structure "*X because Y*," we're saying that *Y* is the reason for *X*. But if we write a phrase with the structure "*X so Y*," we reverse the relationship, and we end up saying that *X* is the reason for *Y*.

This may seem pretty obvious once I point it out, but it's exactly the kind of unnecessary mistake that many test-takers make when they're hurrying through a section. Many people would realize the words "because" and "so" both generally refer to the idea of one thing causing another, but they might not stop to realize that the words indicate opposite causative relationships from one another. This is one more example of the extreme importance of paying careful attention to everything you read on test day!

The Red Book's explanation for this question, which appears on page 352 of that book, uses subjective words like "clunky," "empty," and "pretentious," and says that some phrases aren't "consistent with the style of the rest of this essay." These kinds of remarks might lead an untrained test-taker to think the ACT English section rewards us for making subjective assessments of style or tone. But trained test-takers like us know that the correct answer to every ACT question is always objectively predictable if we know the rules—in this case, (H) is the correct answer simply because it's the shortest choice that expresses the only possible relationship between two phrases in the original sentence.

Page 294, Question 16

The Red Book's explanation on page 356 correctly indicates that (F) is the correct answer because it pairs a singular subject ("one") with a correctly formed superlative ("the liveliest"). But I want to point out some of the mistakes that could easily be made on a question like this if we don't pay careful attention, so you'll be reminded once more how important it is to pay close attention on the ACT English section.

(G) is a grammatically impossible phrase, because we can't pair the word "most" with an "-est" form of an adjective. We might be able to write the phrase "the liveliest," or "the most lively," but the phrase "the most liveliest" is never acceptable.

On the other hand, (H) *could be* an acceptable phrase in some contexts, but it's not acceptable here, because of the mismatch between the word "forms" and the word "is." Either of these sentences would have been acceptable on the ACT:

- "The most lively folk music *form* to develop in the twentieth century is Tejano music."

- "The most lively folk music forms to develop in the twentieth century *are the ones that comprise* Tejano music."

Can you see how easy it would be for a test-taker in a hurry to misread the actual sentence and choose (H) because he thought it would be similar to one of the versions above?

(J) would also be grammatically acceptable except for the word "is" in the sentence—if the sentence had said, "The liveliest folk music forms to develop in the twentieth century *are the ones that comprise* Tejano music," it would have been acceptable. Again, notice how easily an untrained test-taker could have overlooked that small word, especially if she were in a hurry!

These kinds of small issues are the crux of most people's difficulties with the ACT English section. If you want to raise your score significantly, you need to get in the habit of reading carefully and making sure you consider the full context of an underlined phrase before you choose an answer!

Page 295, Question 21

The Red Book explanation for this question on page 357 rightly points out that choice (B) is correct because it's the only one that avoids the pronoun "it;" in this case, the word "it" might logically refer to any of the singular nouns in the previous sentence: "bass guitar," "upright bass," "accordion," "instrumentation," et cetera.

But I want to call your attention to this question to point out that some test-takers might accidentally choose something like (A) or (D) if they were unaware of the ACT's unwritten rule about the pronoun "it." As trained test-takers, we know that the word "it" is only acceptable on the ACT English section if it clearly refers to a specific singular noun. If there's confusion about what the word "it" could refer to, then we need to avoid using it. This is one more clear example of how knowing the ACT's rules can allow us to answer questions with confidence even though other test-takers might struggle with them.

Page 296, Question 26

The Red Book's explanation for this question, which appears on page 359, doesn't give a very technical explanation of proper comma usage on the ACT. Instead, it relies on vague words like "unnecessary" and "distracting." So I thought this might be a good moment to revisit proper punctuation on the ACT English section.

We can tell this question is going to focus on punctuation because the only differences among the choices are differences of punctuation. The only answer choice that's 'punctuated' correctly is choice (F), because no punctuation is necessary here.

This question requires us to consider certain phrases with colons and commas. As trained test-takers, we need to know that the ACT only allows us to use colons to introduce a phrase that demonstrates a previously mentioned concept (see the Writing Toolbox in the Appendix of this Black Book for more on using colons on the ACT English section).

Choice (G) places a colon after the word "popularity," which is unacceptable on the ACT because the phrase "in the Spanish-speaking regions of North and South America" isn't a demonstration of the previous concept in the sentence. Instead, it's a phrase that tells us where the action of the sentence took place. So (G) is wrong.

(An acceptable way to rephrase this sentence so it could feature a colon would be something like this:

"Her . . . style . . . gained her popularity *in some of the world's fastest-growing music markets:* the Spanish-speaking regions of North and South America."

In that example, the phrase "the Spanish-speaking regions of North and South America" is a specific example of the general concept "some of the world's fastest-growing music markets," which I added to the sentence in order to provide an example of acceptable colon use.)

Choices (H) and (J) place commas in different locations within the sentence. As trained test-takers, we know the ACT allows us to use commas to introduce a conjunction (unless the conjunction is in a "list of two things" like the kind we discussed earlier in this section), to divide things in a series, and so on. There are no conjunctions being introduced here, and no series of things being separated, so it looks like these answer choices are testing our understanding of the "comma sandwich." A correctly formed "comma sandwich" is a phrase that's surrounded by commas, and that can be removed from a sentence while still leaving a complete sentence behind.

 (H) doesn't work because it would try to create a "comma sandwich" around the phrase "in the Spanish-speaking regions," which would be inappropriate here because removing the phrase between the commas creates a nonsense phrase after the word "popularity:" "Her . . . style . . . gained . . . popularity of North and South America."

(J) is wrong because it has a similar problem to the one in (H). It unnecessarily inserts a comma between the word "regions" and the phrase "of North and South America," which tells where the regions are. With the comma inserted, we'd be trying to create a "comma sandwich" around the phrase "of North and South America," indicating that the phrase could be grammatically removed from the sentence. But removing that phrase would leave the phrase "the Spanish-speaking regions" without explaining *which* Spanish-speaking regions are referred to by the word "the."

So we can see that the correct answer is (F), the one with no punctuation, because none of the punctuation options in the answer choices conforms to the ACT's standards for punctuation.

Notice, also, that (F) is "tied" with (J) as the answer choice that has the most features in common with the most other answer choices:

- 2 out of the 4 choices have no punctuation after "popularity," while 1 choice has a colon and 1 has a comma.
- 2 out of the 4 choices have no punctuation after "regions," and 2 choices have a comma there.

We might expect that the correct answer would probably have no punctuation after the word "popularity," based on the ACT's similarity pattern; unfortunately, the pattern doesn't help us predict whether there should be a comma after "regions," since half the choices have one and half don't. Still, it's reassuring to see that (F) is at least in the majority when it comes to not having a comma after the word "popularity."

Page 296, Question 28

This question is essentially a Reading Comprehension question. It asks us which answer choice "would most effectively tie together the two main subjects of this essay," so we know the correct answer needs to restate a "main subject" of the essay. (It doesn't need to restate the ideas of two main subjects because Lydia Mendoza is already a subject of the essay, and her name already appears in the beginning of the sentence we're being asked to correct.)

If we read through the choices, we should be able to eliminate (H) and (J) easily, because they mention the concepts of "Santiago Jiménez and his son Flaco," and signing "large recording contracts." Neither of these topics appears anywhere in the passage, so the ACT English section won't consider them to be subjects of the essay.

That leaves us with (F) or (G). One mentions immigration; the other mentions Tejano music. If we read the essay, we see that both Tejano music and immigrating to America are mentioned somewhere in the passage. So we need to figure out which subject the ACT will say is the "main" one.

We know that if the ACT English section asks us to identify a main subject of a passage and more than one answer choice appears in the passage, then the correct answer choice will be the one that appears more times. So that makes (G) correct, because the idea of Tejano music and its influence appears more times in the passage than the idea of immigrating, which only appears once.

Some test-takers won't like the way (G) sounds because it would force the sentence it appears in to repeat the word "have," but we have to remember that this question isn't testing grammar, punctuation, or style—it's purely a matter of choosing the sentence that contains the right concepts from a reading comprehension perspective. As trained test-takers, we know that not every question on the ACT English section will be about grammar, punctuation, or writing style.

Page 299, Question 41

This question is clearly testing our ability to form possessive pronouns correctly; we can tell this because the only differences among the answer choices are found in the words "they're," "their," "it's," and "its." We've discussed the importance of understanding how to form the possessive versions of the pronouns "they" and "it," and we said they're not formed with apostrophes.

If we keep that in mind, and if we can tell that the sentence is referring to two possessive relationships, then we can tell right away that the correct answer is (C), because it has two properly formed possessive pronouns, without apostrophes.

If we're not sure about that, we can try sorting out which choice is correct by putting each contraction into its original, uncontracted form. The result would look like this:

(A) "they are attempt to reduce its"

(B) "they are attempt to reduce it is"

(C) "their attempt to reduce its"

(D) "their attempt to reduce it is"

In context, it becomes clear that only (C) uses the correct forms of both possessive pronouns, "their" and "its"—which, again, don't need any apostrophes.

This question is a fairly simple one that many people miss because they don't stop to read it carefully enough. Make sure you pay attention to what you see on test day so you don't end up costing yourself points unnecessarily!

Page 300, Question 49

Many test-takers will struggle with this question unnecessarily, and perhaps even answer it incorrectly, simply because they don't read it carefully enough.

Most ACT English questions ask us to pick the answer choice that follows the ACT's rules, but this is one of those questions that asks us to single out the only choice that doesn't follow those rules. We can see that plainly if we read the prompt carefully.

 Go to www.ACTprepVideos.com.

But most test-takers go into a sort of trance on the ACT English section, and when they see a set of answer choices that each contain a single word, they automatically assume they need to pick the word that would create the best version of the sentence.

If you make that mistake, you'll end up struggling to single out (B), (C), or (D) as the correct answer, because each of these choices makes an equally acceptable version of the sentence.

On the other hand, if you read the question carefully, and realize you're looking for the one word that doesn't fit in the sentence, it becomes clear that the word "among," in choice (A), is the correct answer.

We can only use the word "among" in situations involving a group of three or more. Since this sentence would be using the word "among" in combination with the singular phrase "Miami land," we know it's not appropriate here, and (A) is the correct answer.

Of course, if we misread the sentence and think the word "land" is plural, we might be frustrated for a different reason, because the phrase "among Miami lands" would be okay on the ACT.

So we see, once more, that the key issue in this question isn't really a deep knowledge of grammar, but a very precise awareness of what the question is actually asking, and of what the text actually says. Always make sure you take note of words like "NOT" and "EXCEPT." And if you ever run into an ACT question that seems to have two or three answer choices that are equally correct, make sure you go back and re-read things—you may well find that you've misread the question.

Page 300, Question 51

As trained test-takers, we know the ACT prefers phrases to be as short as possible without sacrificing grammar. So we could easily trick ourselves into choosing (A) if we're not careful, because (A) is the shortest answer choice and the following phrase would be fine on the ACT if it ended with a period:

"For years I had seen other Miami's pictures[.]"

The problem is that we can't just stop reading after the word "pictures" when we look at this sentence, because the sentence doesn't stop there. The rest of the sentence uses the word "them," and equates the word "them" with the word "ancestors," so we know the word "them" must refer to people. This means that (A) is actually not okay, from an ACT standpoint, because it would make the word "them" refer to the word "photos," and photos can't be ancestors. (In (A), the word "them" can't refer to the word "Miami" because the word "Miami" doesn't actually appear in the sentence—the word that appears in the sentence is the possessive form "Miami's," which creates a grammatically unacceptable phrase when plugged in for the word "them.")

The other answer choices all include the word "Miami," which means that the word "them" could refer back to the word "Miami" in these answer choices. Of these choices, we can see that (C) must be correct, because it's the shortest grammatically correct option that does allows the word "them" to refer to "Miami."

(By the way, this issue can be confusing for some people, because they see "Miami" as the name of a city in Florida. But the essay makes it clear the word "Miami" in this context refers to a tribe of Native Americans, and that the form "Miami" can be either singular or plural.)

The reason I wanted to discuss this question is to drive home the importance of considering all of the relevant context for a particular phrase when you answer a question.

Page 300, Question 52

This is another of those punctuation-based questions that can be answered by focusing on "comma sandwiches." It's also an example of a question that follows the ACT's similarity pattern, because the correct answer choice has the most in common with the greatest number of other answer choices.

From a grammatical standpoint, each choice except (J) would create an inappropriate "comma sandwich" that would result in an incomplete sentence if it were removed—for instance, removing the sandwiched phrase in (F) would result in leaving behind the nonsense phrase "ancestors of the people to the longhouse that summer evening."

If we wanted to consider the test-design aspect of this question, we'd notice that 3 out of the 4 choices have no comma after "who," 3 out of the 4 have no comma after "along," and 3 out of 4 have no comma after "me." So if there's a single choice that has no commas in each of those positions—in other words, if there's a single choice that incorporates all of the most popular options in each of those positions—then we'd expect that choice to be correct, since we know the ACT has a strong preference for making incorrect answers have a lot in common with correct answers. Sure enough, (J) is the only answer choice that incorporates all of those elements, and (J) is correct.

Page 302, Question 68

In this question we see the ACT testing the issue of redundancy. On the ACT English section, we want to eliminate words or phrases that repeat things that already appear elsewhere in the same sentence.

So the key here is reading enough of this sentence to realize that three of the answer choices are redundant, because the word "often" is already present in the sentence, so we don't need any words or phrases that mean the same thing as "often," such as "frequently, "quite regularly," or "many times."

Instead, we need the one answer choice that doesn't include a redundant element, so the correct answer is (J).

Remember that we should always consider the entire sentence when we're trying to pick the ideal version of a phrase on the ACT, so we can find the reason that one answer choice is right and the others are wrong. This can be especially true in questions like this one, which includes several answer choices that are basically the same.

Speaking of that, this is also an example of a question with "functionally identical" answer choices that must all be wrong. In this context, (F), (G), and (H) are all essentially the same answer choice: they each include a phrase that means something happens a lot, then a comma, and then the word "common." Since they're all grammatically the same, and they can't all be right (because there can only be one right answer), they must all be wrong.

Once more, we see the extreme importance of reading the text and the question carefully.

Page 303, Question 72

In this question, we need to choose the answer that makes an appropriate "comma sandwich," or a phrase between two commas that can be completely removed while still leaving behind a grammatically correct sentence. The only answer choice that does this is (G), because if we remove the phrase "or dominant" and both commas, we're still left with a good phrase:

"Usually begun by the alpha pair of wolves, . . . [blah blah blah]."

This question is also worth noting because it *doesn't* follow the ACT's "most like the others" pattern—that pattern would predict that (G) would probably be wrong, because it's the only choice with a comma after the word "or." Remember that the similarity pattern is only a strong tendency that we'll encounter in a lot of ACT questions—it's not an ironclad rule that's always true in every single question. This is why we should only use the similarity

Go to www.ACTprepVideos.com.

pattern as an indication of what is *likely* to be true in *most* cases, not of what is *always* true. If we know the rules of ACT grammar require a particular answer choice to be correct, we should choose that answer whether it fits the similarity pattern or not. (Of course, if we think an answer choice is correct and it doesn't really follow the similarity pattern, we might be wise to double-check the question and the passage and make sure we haven't misread something.)

Page 438, Question 2

This question can give untrained test-takers a lot of trouble—but if we know how to approach the test, we should be able to find the correct answer pretty easily.

If we quickly read through the answer choices and the context of this question, we might get the mistaken impression that we're supposed to pick the right tense of the verb "to keep," and also to make some kind of decision about using the passive voice. (If you don't know what the passive voice is, don't worry. It's not something the ACT tests).

But even if we make that mistake, we should be able to tell that the sentence doesn't really give us any basis for preferring one particular tense or voice in the answer choices. That should bother us, because we know that every question has exactly one correct answer—if this question seems to have several answer choices that are equally valid, then we know that we've made a mistake somewhere.

So we should double-check the question. Since we're asked to choose the correct version of a verb, the first thing we need to do is read the entire sentence to see which noun the verb should agree with.

In this case, that noun is "editors," which is plural. The ACT has tried to trick us by sticking the singular word "magazine" right before the underlined verb, in the hope that we'll think the verb should be agreeing with the word "magazine" instead of with the word "editors."

Once we know the real subject is "the editors," we see that the only possible right answer is (H), because it's the only choice that can go with a plural noun. So it turns out we don't need to think about tense or voice, because the real issue is that "editors" can only go with "are," not with "is," "keeps," or "has."

Unfortunately, most test-takers don't realize that every question must have one definitively correct answer, so they often miss relatively simple questions like this. They struggle to invent some small distinction among three wrong answers, instead of realizing their mistake and noticing that one answer is clearly right once the question is understood correctly.

So don't forget to re-evaluate your assumptions about a question if you find yourself unable to identify a single answer choice that's clearly correct. It may be that you've misread or misunderstood the question from the very beginning.

Page 441, Question 22

The Red Book explanation for this question on page 502 is accurate in terms of grammar, but I want to point out the mistake that people often make on this question, and on questions like it.

Many test-takers read the original version of the underlined phrase and correctly realize that it needs another comma after the word "hunters," so we can form a "comma sandwich" around the phrase "most of them filed by hunters." But then most people make a crucial mistake: they let their eyes jump straight to (H) or (J), and pick one of those choices because they each seem to solve the original comma problem if we don't read them carefully enough.

Of course, if we *do* read them carefully, we see that (H) doesn't form a "comma sandwich" because it changes the punctuation after "reports" to a semicolon. We also see that (J) maintains a "comma sandwich" but changes "filed" to "filing," and the phrase "having been filing" doesn't work in this context.

So the two answer choices that might seem like they solve the initial comma problem actually create other problems that still keep them from being correct.

The correct answer is (G), which uses dashes instead of commas to show that the phrase "most of them filed by hunters" can be removed and still leave behind a grammatically intact sentence. (G) creates what we might call a "dash sandwich." (Since "comma sandwich" is already a ridiculous-sounding phrase, I guess we might as well go ahead and call this a "dash sandwich," right?)

So one of the key lessons we can take away from this question is that it can be dangerous to anticipate what the correct answer must look like instead of patiently reading each choice as it actually is, and evaluating the options that the test gives us. Many people miss this question because their eyes jump straight to (H) and they never realize that a comma from the original phrase has been changed to a semicolon.

This, again, is just one more indication of the extreme importance of reading very carefully on the ACT! The only thing that makes (H) wrong is a little dot above a comma.

Page 442, Question 28

This question lets us choose from four different versions of the verb "to throw," so we know that we may need to think about which verb form can fit in with the surrounding text. Remember that on this question, as on any real ACT question, there must be a concrete reason that one answer choice is right and the others are wrong.

If we look at the original sentence, we can see it describes a set of actions that "they" have done: "they have flown . . . ridden . . . and [the verb that we choose]."

This question is an example of the parallelism we talked about on the ACT English section. When we see multiple things listed like this and joined with a conjunction like "and," the ACT will want all of those things to be in the same form.

The other two verbs being listed are "flown" and "ridden." We want a verb in the same form, so we know the correct verb form must be "thrown," which appears in choice (J).

What about the word "even?" Some people who look at this question wonder how they're supposed to know the word "even" should be in the correct answer. But in this question, the word "even" isn't relevant—only one answer choice uses the correct verb form, and that's all that matters in this question.

Page 443, Question 38

As trained test-takers, we know that a question like this on the ACT English section—a question that isn't concerned with grammar, style, or punctuation—should be treated like a Reading Comprehension question. In other words, we need to choose an answer that directly restates some relevant portion of the text.

In this case, we're asked which phrase would create "the most effective link between Sentences 4 and 6." If we read the context, we see that Sentence 4 is about children developing communication skills, and sentence 6 is about Suzuki's "philosophy of music education." We also see that sentence 5 already includes the phrase "these realizations," which is a reference to the concepts from the previous four sentences in the paragraph.

Because we need to link Sentences 4 and 6, and because part of Sentence 5 already refers back to concepts in Sentences 1 through 4, we need the underlined portion of the sentence to incorporate an element of Sentence 6.

(F) doesn't work, because it just makes another reference back to Sentences 1 through 4, without any connection to Sentence 6.

(G) is the correct answer, because the phrase "unique approach to violin studies" directly parallels the phrase "philosophy of music education" in Sentence 6: "philosophy" can be a synonym for "approach," and "violin studies" are a specific type of "music education."

(H) and (J) make general comments about Suzuki using his understanding of language-learning in some other way, but neither choice says anything that appears directly in Sentence 6.

The Red Book's explanation for this question on page 507 never directly explains why (G) is correct: it's the only choice that directly restates an element of Sentence 6. Instead, the Red Book uses unclear terms like "effective link" and "unnecessarily wordy." But trained test-takers like us know that these questions should be treated like Reading Comprehension questions, and "Reading Comprehension" questions on the ACT require us to think in terms of phrases that directly restate the relevant portion of the text.

Page 444, Question 42

This question involves an underlined portion in a sentence that features two phrases joined by a semicolon. As trained test-takers, we need to know the ACT English section only allows a semicolon in two situations (see the Writing Toolbox in the Appendix of this Black Book for more on colons and semicolons):

- for a "super series," which is rare on the ACT, and which requires the presence of a comma in at least one sub-series
- to divide a set of words into two phrases that could each stand on their own as a sentence (in other words, to "replace" a period)

There's clearly no super series in this sentence, since there are no commas in it. That means that the semicolon must indicate that all the words before it can be a sentence on their own, and all the words after it can be a sentence on their own. So we can eliminate (J), because choice (J) would leave the second phrase without a main verb.

That leaves us with (F), (G), and (H), which are three different tenses of the verb "to reward." We need to decide which tense is appropriate—remembering, of course, that every ACT English question has exactly one answer choice that is objectively correct.

If we check the rest of the sentence, we see the verb "provide," which is in the present tense. That means the ACT will also want the word "reward" to be in the present tense, since there's no word or phrase in the sentence that indicates the two verbs are happening in different timeframes. This is another example of the "parallelism" we'll sometimes encounter on the ACT English section, as we discussed in the section on ACT English question types.

For that reason, we know (F) is the correct answer.

It's technically true that each of the following would be grammatically acceptable on its own, if it were removed from the context of the question:

- "Group sessions and concerts rewarded students with opportunities to share music."
- "Group sessions and concerts had rewarded students with opportunities to share music."

But, as trained test-takers, we need to know that the ACT must always have a clear reason for crediting one answer choice; in these situations, we want to look at the context provided by the rest of the sentence to determine which form of the verb is appropriate—in this case, it's the simple present-tense form "reward."

Page 445, Question 54

This question is frustrating for many test-takers because it's very easy to miss if we just apply the comma rules without considering the context of the preceding sentences. It's also another example of a question that the Red Book explains in vague terms, using words like "unnecessary" and "distracting" (on page 512) without describing what would actually make a comma necessary or non-distracting.

Let's see what's really going on here, and what we can learn from it.

Without the preceding sentences, the original version of the underlined phrase would probably work as an example of a "comma sandwich" on the ACT, because we can remove the word "redeeming" and still be left with a sentence that would probably be okay by ACT standards:

"The one feature of the beltway is that it's impossible to get lost on it."

But the preceding sentences in this paragraph of the passage make it clear there are other features of the beltway—we see that it's large, busy, and fast, among other things. So we can't say that the impossibility of getting lost is "the one feature" of the beltway, because the paragraph just described at least three other features.

So the context provided by the other sentences in the paragraph makes it clear that we need to include the word "redeeming." And that means we can't put the word "redeeming" in a "comma sandwich," because the ACT would only let us use a comma sandwich if the phrase in the sandwich could be removed, which is contextually unacceptable in this case. This is an example of the way reading comprehension elements can sometimes be involved with questions that only seem to be testing grammar, style, or punctuation at first.

The correct answer is (J) because the commas in the different answer choices don't satisfy the ACT's comma rules—they don't form acceptable comma sandwiches, they don't appear in a series, et cetera. That means we need to pick the only answer choice without commas, which is (J).

Most untrained test-takers would stop reading the answer choices after they finished with (F) and decided it sounded okay. But trained test-takers know that we always need to look at each answer choice before coming to a conclusion, so we can see if we've made a mistake somewhere.

When we see that both (F) and (J) are grammatically acceptable, we know something else must be going on in the question, because we can never forget that each question can only have one correct answer choice, which must be beyond dispute. So we might go through the answer choices again to make sure we haven't misread something. After that, we should look at the context of the passage to see which answer choice is called for. When we do that in this case, we see that the word "redeeming" is necessary to the sentence in order to prevent the paragraph from contradicting itself. That means we can't place the word "redeeming" in a "comma sandwich," because doing so would indicate that it could be safely removed from the sentence.

Remember that every ACT question has a single correct answer choice that follows the test's rules—if a question seems to have more than one correct answer, then we've missed something.

Page 577, Question 7

The Red Book explanation for this question on page 637 is grammatically accurate, but I want to address a specific mistake that many test-takers make because they don't pay attention, not because they don't know grammar.

The underlined phrase is never an acceptable form of the verb "to blow" in any context, because the past participle of "to blow" is "blown."

If we're rushing through the ACT English section, we might think the question wants us to provide the correct past participle of "to blow," rather than the correct *tense* of "to blow."

Go to www.ACTprepVideos.com.

In that case, we might quickly read through the answer choices and accidentally pick (D), "blown," as our answer.

But there are two problems with that conclusion, of course. The first is that the question requires a verb-form that matches the tense of the word "sailed," so we need the simple past-tense form, which is "blew." That's why (C) is correct. The second problem is that both words in the phrase "had blew" are underlined, so, even if we inserted choice (D), we'd create the phrase "strong winds blown daily," which doesn't work here.

Both of these problems can be easily caught if we read the question carefully and keep the test's rules in mind. Still, you'd be surprised how often people miss this question, and others that are similar to it, because they rush through the section and don't pay enough attention.

(By the way, this is one more question that follows the similarity pattern with its answer choices: more choices include the word "blew" than any other word, and more choices have one word instead of two. So if there's a one-word choice with the word "blew" in it, we'd expect it to have a high probability of being correct according to the pattern—and it is.)

Page 578, Question 13

The Red Book's explanation for this question appears on page 639. It's a decent description, but it's missing one key element that I want to make sure I emphasize: (B) is the correct answer because it directly restates the phrase "became the first women to climb and ski across the continent of Antarctica," which appears back in the first paragraph. (The Red Book says that this paragraph "explain[s]" why the correct answer is correct, but I want to make sure my students know that the correct answer is correct because it *explicitly restates* something from elsewhere in the essay.)

Notice that we had to go back to the beginning of the essay to find the relevant portion of the text for this question. Most ACT English questions won't require us to jump so far back in a passage in order to answer a question correctly, but some will, as we can see here. If you ever find yourself unable to locate the relevant text for a question that refers to the entire passage like this, remember that it must be in there somewhere, and don't be too lazy to look all the way back at the beginning of the essay—or anywhere else in the essay, if necessary.

Page 578, Question 14

The key difficulty that most test-takers encounter with this question is the meaning of the word "prudently"—we need to know what it means so we can tell which word in the sentence it's modifying.

If we know that the word "prudent" means something along the lines of "sensible" or "wise," we see that it can only make sense in this sentence if it modifies the word "called," because calling a ski plane to avoid being stranded is a prudent decision. So (J) would have to be correct.

But what if we don't know the word "prudently?"

If we don't know what "prudently" means, it's much harder to tell which idea in the sentence it should describe— in fact, it's probably impossible for most people. (The only way I can think of would be to get lucky and realize that "prudently" has a similar root to the word "Prudential," which is the name of a big financial company. We'd know that "Prudential" and "prudently" must have positive meanings, because it would be very unlikely for a large, successful company to give itself a name with a negative meaning. All of that would suggest that "prudently" can't really refer to being stranded. But that's a difficult connection to make for a lot of people.)

We can probably at least tell that "prudently" doesn't belong where it is now. If it were modifying the idea of the call, we'd expect it before "called;" if it were modifying the idea of the airlift, we'd probably expect it after the word "them." (Technically, it wouldn't be totally incorrect in its current place if it were modifying the infinitive "to airlift," but that phrasing would sound a bit clunky to most modern English speakers.)

So most test-takers who don't know the word "prudently" will be torn between the phrases "becoming prudently stranded" and "the women prudently called." It would be hard to make much progress beyond that (again, unless you happened to get lucky and realize that "prudent" is probably a positive-sounding word). At this point, we'd probably have to guess and hope for the best (see the discussion on "Guessing On The ACT" in "The General Game Plan For Attacking A Section Of The ACT On Test Day" for more on that).

The ACT doesn't make any effort to incorporate particular words on the English section, so don't worry too much if you ended up missing this question because of the word "prudently." There's a small chance it might randomly make another appearance on test day, but the odds are much better that it won't. Instead, you might run into a question or two with other words you're not familiar with. Just try to work around those unknown words if you can, and guess if you have to.

It's because of the occasional question like this that we have to make sure we don't miss questions when they're completely within our control! Don't waste your energy worrying about exotic words that might or might not show up in the future—instead, invest your energy in making sure you never miss a question due to sloppiness or misreading.

Page 582, Question 41

This question asks us to pick the answer choice that would be "most relevant." As trained test-takers, we know that means we need to think in terms of the ACT's reading comprehension rules: the "most relevant" answer choice will be the one that mentions concepts from the surrounding text.

The sentence before mentions bats being "useful to humans, especially farmers." The following sentence mentions some ways that bats help farmers.

With that in mind, let's take a look at the answer choices.

(A) doesn't say anything about bats helping anyone, so it can't be the right answer.

(B) mentions something bats do that's good for "fruits we eat." This is a specific way that bats are "useful to humans, especially farmers," as mentioned in the previous sentence. So (B) is the correct answer. Of course, we always have to check out all the answer choices, because we want to make sure we're not making any mistakes.

(C) says that some plants have special ways to attract bats. This choice might seem tempting to some test-takers because it mentions concepts that are vaguely related to the paragraph, but in the end it's wrong, because it doesn't explicitly provide an example of a way that bats are useful to humans. (Note the subtle difference between the word "plants" in the answer choice and the word "crops" in the original text. While all crops are plants, it isn't true that all plants are crops, which means that the statement about "plants" in this answer choice isn't necessarily relevant to the concept of "crops" in the passage. Believe it or not, the ACT frequently requires us to split hairs like this.)

(D) refers to bats, but it doesn't say anything about them helping anyone, so it's wrong.

The Red Book explanation for this question, which appears on page 648, is decent, but it relies on words like "relevant" and "fit" without really clarifying what they mean, so I wanted to use this opportunity to reiterate that trained test-takers approaching a question like this one must look for an answer choice with specific phrases that specifically parallel phrases in the key part of the text. We don't want to scratch our heads and wonder if

Go to www.ACTprepVideos.com.

something feels "relevant," which is what the Red Book solution would have us do. Instead, we want to realize that "pollinat[ing] . . . fruits we eat" is a specific way that "bats are useful to humans, especially farmers."

Page 582, Question 45

Some test-takers will be tempted by choices (A) and (B), and the Red Book's explanation of the question (which is on page 649) doesn't really do a good job of explaining why those two choices are wrong, so I want to make sure I address it for you.

(A) is wrong because the passage never actually says humans are "the *greatest threat of all* to bat survival [emphasis mine]," as choice (A) says. The passage says that humans are destroying bats' habitats, but it doesn't specifically rank humans against other threats to bats. (A) is also wrong because it talks about the "many enemies" of bats, but the essay never mentions any threats beside humans.

(B) is wrong because exploring people's misconceptions about bats (which is what the essay does) isn't the same thing as "focusing on the various ways . . . people are causing the extinction of some bat species," which is what the prompt of the question describes.

(C) correctly says the essay "primarily focuses on people's mistaken ideas about bats." This is correct because the passage mentions people's ideas about bats more times than it mentions the idea of bats facing extinction, and the ACT English section's unwritten reading comprehension rules tell us that the concept that's mentioned the most times is the primary focus of the passage. It's also important to point out that the prompt says the author wanted to write about "the ways in which people are causing the *extinction*" of bats, but the essay doesn't actually say bats have become fully extinct; it only says some bat species "*face* extinction [emphasis mine]." This answer choice correctly points out that the passage doesn't focus on the ways "people are *causing the extinction* of some bat species [emphasis mine]." These kinds of small differences—like the difference between actually being extinct and only facing extinction—are exactly the kind of thing we have to look out for on the ACT.

(D) is wrong because the text never says that only those bats who feed on livestock are at risk.

Once more, we see that ACT questions based on reading comprehension require us to stick very carefully to a literal interpretation of the words on the page.

Page 586, Question 70

We know that the phrase "for children" is supposed to describe something in this sentence. We also know from the previous sentence that we're talking about a "304-acre sports, counseling, and education center" for "youths."

With that in mind, we can see that the only thing in this sentence that can be "for children" is the "sports complex." So the ACT will want us to put the phrase "for children" right after the phrase "sports complex," which means (H) is correct.

Notice that the sentence itself sounds out of place—question 71 is about to ask us to fix that. Still, we can tell that the sports complex must be the thing for children when we look elsewhere in the paragraph for context. Remember that it's often important to consider more than just the sentence we're asked about!

Page 586, Question 71

In order to figure out where to put this sentence, we should read the sentence and the paragraph as a whole. If we do that, we'll notice that the sentence starts with the phrase "one of them." That means the sentence needs to come after something that "one of them" could logically refer to.

The word "them" is a plural pronoun, which means it can only refer to a plural noun. The plural nouns in the paragraph are "projects," "years," "sports," "thousands," and "youths." If we look at sentence 4 in its entirety, we see that the phrase "one of them" is being equated with "a sports complex," and that it's something "for children." So the phrase "one of them" can only be referring to the word "projects," because none of the other plural words in the paragraph can be a sports complex for children.

The phrase "long-term humanitarian projects" only appears in the first sentence. As trained test-takers, we know the ACT English section will want the word "them" to appear after the noun it's referring to, but as close to that noun as possible (see our discussions of proximity and sentence placement in the section on ACT English question types for more on this). We can also see that placing the sentence after Sentence 1 will allow it to be followed by two sentences that elaborate on the idea of a "sports complex" mentioned in this sentence.

So we know the correct answer must be (C), according to the ACT's rules.

(My explanation for the question is essentially the same as the one in the Red Book on page 657, but I wanted to go through this question since it's kind of related to Question 70, which we just talked about.)

Page 587, Question 73

This is another one of the relatively few ACT English questions that require us to use "precision vocabulary" like we talked about in the section on ACT English question types. As I've mentioned before, these questions aren't usually worth worrying about, even if you can't answer them, because it's very unlikely that this specific vocabulary issue will show up on test day, and because there's no way to know beforehand which words will be tested like this.

In this case, we pretty much need to know that when we see the word "principals," with the "-pals" spelling at the end, it refers to people. (Many people remember this with the phrase "The principal is your 'pal,'" if that helps. But, again, you'll probably never see this exact vocabulary issue on the ACT ever again.)

Realizing that the "-pals" spelling refers to people would allow us to see that the "-ples" spelling must be the one that refers to abstract concepts. So the "-ples" spelling is the one we want here, because we're referring to the abstract concepts of sportsmanship and community service.

We also have to choose the right preposition, of course. If we're familiar with American English, we may naturally feel that "of" is the correct preposition in this case, so we can confidently pick choice (D). But even if we're not native American English speakers, we can tell that "of" is probably going to be correct because it appears in the answer choices more often than "for" or "in," and we know the ACT often likes to incorporate elements of the correct answer choice in the wrong answers.

So even if we didn't know the proper spelling of the word "principles" in this context, we could at least realize that we probably want to be guessing between (A) and (D), because those two choices include the word "of," which appears more than any other one preposition in the answer choices for this question.

Remember not to get too worried about questions like this! Instead, focus on making sure you never miss an ACT English question when you know everything necessary to answer it. If you can focus on correctly answering the 70+ questions on each ACT English section that don't require some kind of relatively obscure knowledge like this, then the few questions like this one won't make a noticeable dent in your overall ACT score.

Page 721, Question 5

As trained test-takers, we know that the ACT will want us to choose a sentence that restates concepts in the rest of the paragraph on a reading comprehension-based English question like this. With that in mind, let's look at the answer choices in more detail.

(A) is the correct answer. The original version of the sentence mentions two main concepts: the idea of "it," and the idea of being "difficult . . . to grasp." We can see that the word "it" refers to "Miami time," and we can see that the idea of being "difficult . . . to grasp" is reflected in the fact that the grandmother "tried to explain" it, and how the "meaning" had only recently "started to sink in." Of course, we still need to look at all the other answer choices to help make sure we haven't misread or misunderstood something.

(B) is wrong. It mentions being late for a doctor's appointment, which doesn't come up anywhere else in the paragraph. It's true that the *previous* paragraph mentions the idea of sometimes "running late for an appointment," but we need a sentence that's relevant to the current paragraph, since the question asks us to introduce "this paragraph."

(C) is also wrong, because this paragraph doesn't talk about the grandmother living with the narrator. It may be true that they lived together, and it does seem as though the narrator likes the grandmother, but neither idea is directly stated in the paragraph, so the ACT won't give credit for this answer.

(D) is also wrong. The son and grandmother are both mentioned in the paragraph, but the paragraph doesn't say anything about the son asking about the grandmother, or about his never meeting her.

Remember that it's not enough to find a sentence that's vaguely related to the topic of the passage as a whole—we need a sentence that ties in directly to the rest of the paragraph. Since (A) mentions something being difficult to understand, and the rest of the paragraph is about the narrator trying to understand that thing, we know that (A) is the correct answer.

Page 721, Question 10

We often talk about how the people who write the ACT love to confuse test-takers who aren't paying close attention to what's going on in a question. Notice that the underlined phrase in this question starts with the word "does." That by itself isn't too unusual, but in this case it's a plural form of the noun "doe," not a conjugation of the verb "to do." Little unexpected things like this can get you flustered and confused on test day, so always make sure to read carefully.

This question deals with comma placement. We know right away that there shouldn't be a comma immediately before or after the word "and," because we're dealing with a list of two things, and the ACT doesn't allow us to use a comma in that situation. That means we can eliminate (G) and (J).

But wait a minute—how can this be a list of two things if we're talking about a group of five animals? This is yet another example of the ACT trying to trick students who aren't paying attention. Even though there are five animals being described in the question, there are still two noun phrases: one is the phrase "two does," and the other is the phrase "three fawns." If the phrase had been "two does, three fawns, and a moose," then there would have been three noun phrases, and we would have needed to insert commas. But as the passage is written, this is a list of two things, which means there should be an "and" and no commas between the two nouns.

That leaves us with the original underlined phrase, which contains no commas, and choice (H), which puts a comma after "fawns." Choice (H) would create a "comma sandwich" around the phrase "two does and three fawns." If you took out that phrase, you'd be left with the fragment "There stood watching us." Since you can't remove the phrase "two does and three fawns" and leave behind an acceptable sentence, we can rule out (H) as well, which leaves us with the correct answer, (F).

Page 724, Question 27

The Red Book explanation for this question on page 786 is technically correct, but it uses grammatical jargon that will probably only make sense to someone who already knows the answer to the question anyway. In other words, the Red Book's explanation is unlikely to help someone who actually has difficulty with the question.

Let's break down what's happening here and describe it in simpler terms.

On the ACT, when we have a phrase at the beginning of a sentence that starts with an "-ing" word or an "-ed" word and is joined to the rest of the sentence by a comma, the first noun after the comma must be the noun that's doing the action of the "-ing" or "-ed" word (this is related to the idea of proximity that we discussed in the section on ACT English question types).

In this case, the sentence begins with the words "establishing her own hair products business in the first decade of the twentieth century." This phrase starts with an "-ing" word ("establishing") and is joined to the rest of the sentence by a comma. So the noun phrase that comes immediately after the comma must indicate who or what did the "establishing" at the beginning of the phrase.

In this case, the noun phrase that did the "establishing" was "Madam C. J. Walker," and the only choice that starts with "Madam C. J. Walker" is (B). So (B) is correct.

Page 726, Question 43

Many test-takers incorrectly choose (A) for this question because they don't know what it means, and they assume its meaning must be related to the word "wet."

These types of vocabulary issues come up pretty rarely on the ACT. But when we do encounter an unknown word, we can't assume that it must be inappropriate in a given sentence—instead, we have to focus on getting the most advantage we can from the words that we *do* know in the question.

In this case, we can probably tell that the sentence doesn't make any sense with the word "disturb" in it, both because the idea of disturbing someone's curiosity makes no sense in English, and because it doesn't make sense for the word "fantasy" to be disturbing in the context of the passage. So we can know that (D) is correct because we know its meaning would be unacceptable.

Don't worry if you didn't know the word "whet," and don't expect it to come up on a future ACT, because it probably won't. Instead, the next time you see an ACT English question with a challenging word or two, remain calm and try your best to work around any holes in your vocabulary if you can. If you can't do that, then skip the question or guess on it as described in "The General Game Plan For Attacking A Section Of The ACT On Test Day" earlier in this Black Book. Remember that if we can focus on the questions where we know enough words to answer with certainty, and get all of those questions right, the occasional question with challenging vocabulary won't matter much.

Page 731, Question 75

As trained test-takers, we know that a question like this will give credit for the answer that maintains the focus of the paragraph—in other words, we should choose to add the statement to the paragraph if it talks about the same concepts that are already in the paragraph, and we should choose to leave it out if it talks about stuff that's not in the paragraph.

On top of that, we need to find an answer choice that correctly describes the paragraph (and perhaps the passage) in explaining whether the sentence should be added or not.

So let's take a look:

(A) is wrong because the paragraph doesn't mention any particular "emotion" as "the basis for . . . space exploration."

(B) is also wrong. The previous sentence just said that the issue of money should be "carefully considered." That means that a sentence about ignoring the issue of money contradicts the paragraph, rather than reinforcing it as the ACT would want.

(C) is wrong because it refers to a "chronological history of people who traveled in space," but there is no such history in the essay. (A chronological history of space-travelers would be a list of individuals who have been in space, arranged in order from the first mission to the last.)

(D) is the correct answer. It accurately says that the essay's focus is "on Mars and the cost of sending humans there," and we can see that very issue reflected in the sentence before the number 75. It's also true that the sentence being considered for addition doesn't mention concepts from the paragraph where it would be inserted, which breaks the ACT's rule about how sentences added to a passage should repeat concepts from the surrounding text.

Conclusion
That concludes the ACT English section walkthroughs. By this point, you should be developing a feel for the right way to apply the training in this Black Book to actual ACT English questions from the Red Book. The best thing to do now is to continue to work with real ACT English practice questions, and to try to apply these methods in the same way that we just did in the walkthroughs.

Using The Explanations In *The Real ACT Prep Guide, 3ʳᵈ Edition*
As we've seen in our discussions of other parts of the ACT, you'll find that the Red Book's explanations for ACT English questions can sometimes be helpful—as long as you approach them with the right mindset. First of all, as always, you want to ignore any phrasing about "the best answer" that you find in the Red Book explanations. As trained test-takers, we know that every real ACT English question has exactly one correct answer choice and three incorrect answer choices; the correct choice will be the only one that follows the ACT's established rules, which you've learned in this Black Book.

Beyond that, you may find that some of the explanations for the ACT English practice questions in *The Real ACT Prep Guide, 3ʳᵈ Edition* can point you in the right general direction on a question if you're lost. Those explanations tend to be longer and more technical than necessary, and they often miss shortcuts and/or simpler ways to understand the question and the text.

So when you refer to solutions from the Red Book, try to keep these things in mind and look for the simpler, quicker kinds of approaches that we've been talking about in this Black Book.

Video Demonstrations
If you'd like to see videos of some sample solutions like the ones in this book, please visit www.ACTprepVideos.com, where a selection of free videos is available for readers of this book.

ACT English Quick Summary

This is a one-page summary of the major concepts you'll need to know for the ACT English section. Use it to evaluate your comprehension or jog your memory. For a more in-depth treatment of these ideas, see the rest of this section in this Black Book.

The Big Secret: ACT English is all about learning the ACT's standards and then applying them, rather than relying on your own sense of what sounds good to you personally.

There are 3 main types of ACT English questions: reading comprehension questions, grammar/style/punctuation questions, and questions that combine elements of both.

Reading comprehension questions will tend to include a prompt. Generally speaking, the correct answers to reading comprehension questions on the English section will involve reading the prompt, the answer choices, and the passage literally, and then picking the answer choice that directly restates or reflects the concepts in the passage and/or the prompt.

Depending on the context, the correct answer might also be the one that keeps related ideas together, or that restates the idea that comes up most frequently in a given selection of text, or that places sentences or paragraphs in a logical order, or that uses a particular word in a precise way.

Grammar/style/punctuation questions will tend not to include a prompt. They'll usually ask you to pick which version of an underlined phrase fits with the ACT's rules.

- Common grammatical issues for these kinds of questions include agreement in tense and number between/among verbs and nouns, agreement in number between pronouns and their nouns, idiomatic usage of prepositions, parallel structures of phrases, and similar topics.
- Common style issues will include the idea of avoiding redundancy, irrelevancy, and unnecessary length.
- Common punctuation issues will include comma placement, the formation of possessives, and the proper use of semicolons and colons.

Questions that include elements of both reading comprehension and grammar/style/punctuation will tend to look like pure grammar/style/punctuation questions at first. But you'll find that more than one answer is grammatically acceptable according to the ACT, and then you'll have to choose the answer that doesn't contradict other concepts in the surrounding text. These kinds of questions are relatively rare.

Here's the general ACT English process:

1. Read the passage until you come to a question.
2. Carefully read the prompt (if there is one) and the answer choices and determine whether the question is primarily based on reading comprehension or on grammar/style/punctuation.
3. Look for any of the issues we discussed in the training according to the question type.
4. Find the right answer, or eliminate three wrong answers.
5. Take another look at the question and answer choices.
6. Mark your answer choice and move on.

Go back through the ACT English walkthroughs in this Black Book, and follow along in your copy of *The Real ACT Prep Guide, 3rd Edition* to see demonstrations of these ideas.

If you want a more detailed description of the ACT's rules for grammar, style, and punctuation, see the Writing Toolbox in the Appendix of this Black Book.

ACT Writing Test (The ACT Essay)

"Have something to say, and say it as clearly as you can. That is the only secret of style."
- Matthew Arnold

Two Important Notes!

Before you spend your valuable time preparing for the ACT Essay, you should make sure that the schools you're applying to will require you to submit an ACT Writing score (the ACT Writing score is the essay score). The ACT Writing test is an optional part of the ACT. Some schools don't require an ACT Writing score; some schools recommend you submit, but don't require it; some schools require it. If you're not sure whether your target schools will require you to submit an ACT Writing score, contact them directly to find out. There's no reason to prepare for the ACT Essay if you aren't going to submit the ACT Writing score to anybody.

It's also important for us to clear something up about the scoring of the ACT Essay. Your final score on the ACT Essay will be on a scale of 2 to 12, but each individual grader who reviews your ACT Essay will give you a score from 1 to 6, and those scores will ultimately be combined to arrive at your final score on the 12-point scale. This means a perfect overall score on the ACT Writing test is 12, but each grader can only give a maximum score of 6. For some reason, the sample essays that appear on pages 123 to 139 of the Red Book are discussed as though they were only reviewed by one grader and given a score out of 6. So keep in mind that a perfect ACT Writing score is a 12 out of 12, but the Red Book sometimes refers to it as a 6 out of 6.

Overview And Important Reminders For The ACT Essay

At this point, you probably won't be shocked to learn that the ACT Essay has very little in common with the essays you normally write in school—after all, nothing else on the ACT is the same as what we do in school.

Let's take a minute to understand why the ACT Essay is so different from a school essay.

One of the most important differences between the two essays is that the person who grades your ACT essay will spend far less time on it than your teachers spend on your school essays. This is because ACT Essay-graders have to evaluate a much larger number of essays, and they have to do it in a standardized, repetitive, reliable way. (Remember that the results of the ACT must be standardized to be valuable, and that goes for the ACT essay just as much as it does for the multiple-choice sections.)

What does that mean? For one thing, graders can't spend any time confirming any factual claims you make in your essay. Since it isn't possible to evaluate all the factual claims in the nearly 2 million ACT essays written each year, and since all the essays have to be held to the same standard, the ACT graders can't evaluate ANY of the factual claims made in ANY of the essays they grade—that's the only way to treat all factual claims equally in the grading process.

That means you don't have to worry about being penalized for saying something that's factually incorrect on your ACT essay. In other words, your essay could be completely full of factual errors, and the grader wouldn't be allowed to penalize you for it.

On the other hand, if you wrote an essay for history class and it contained factual errors, your teacher would certainly penalize you.

For similar reasons, you shouldn't try to amuse or inform the reader of your ACT Essay; nor should you try to do anything else creative. Your grader isn't going to be sitting in a cafe, having a leisurely look over your paper for an hour or so while drinking a latte and contemplating life. Instead, she'll read your essay in a minute or so, with the goal of identifying key features of your essay that indicate which score it should receive, based on her training. So you really won't have an opportunity to write an essay that stands out from the others in a positive way, as you might try to do with an admissions essay or a scholarship essay. On the contrary, you want your essay to blend in with all the other top-scoring essays by imitating the characteristics that all of those essays have (which is what you'll learn about in this section of this Black Book, of course).

We may not be used to thinking about essay tests in terms of rules. The processes involved in writing and grading essays might seem like they're too subjective for that. But we know the ACT Essay must follow regular, predictable rules in order to be part of a standardized test.

But those regular, predictable rules are probably not the rules you'd expect—for one thing, the actual characteristics of top-scoring ACT Essays don't really reflect the Red Book's guidelines for the ACT essay. ACT, Inc. doesn't just come out and say, "Well, we're going to have a lot of essays to grade, so yours probably won't be looked at for more than a couple of minutes. A couple of overworked essay graders are going to read it once each really quickly and assign it a score based on a few key things like length, and then move on. Just make the essay more than two pages long and do a couple of other things, and you should score high." Instead, the Red Book says things like, "the ACT Writing Test is designed to measure . . . those writing skills taught in rigorous high school English and writing classes and expected of students entering first-year college composition courses."

So what should you do?

I recommend you approach this part of the test the same way we've approached every other part of the test: by exploiting the standardized nature of the ACT and doing the things that are consistently rewarded on this section, instead of believing what ACT, Inc. claims the section is about.

This section of this Black Book will teach you the unwritten rules of the ACT Essay, and then it will show you how those rules apply to real student essays that appear in the Red Book.

Unwritten Test Design Rules Of The ACT Essay (ACT Writing Test)

You're probably not used to thinking of essay tests as having "rules" the way a multiple choice test would. But, as trained test-takers, we know that every part of a standardized test like the ACT must follow predictable guidelines, or else the results from different days' tests wouldn't be comparable to each other, and the test would have no purpose.

In this brief section, we'll learn the unwritten rules of the ACT Essay.

ACT Essay Rule 1: Make It To The Third Page

The single most important factor affecting the score of your ACT Essay is its length: the longer it is, the higher it can potentially score. If you want to be assured of having the possibility of scoring a perfect 12, I recommend you try to make it to the third page of writing space provided on the test; taking up any more space than that doesn't seem to have any further impact on your score.

Don't get me wrong: it's certainly *possible* to write a high-scoring essay and not make it onto the third page. But *most* high-scoring essays will make it to the third page, and pretty much all of them will come very close to that—and you want your essay to be as much like other high-scoring essays as possible. That way, your essay grader can glance at your work, see that it looks like the other high-scoring essays, and feel comfortable giving you a good score if the actual writing is halfway decent. Remember that the grader isn't going to spend much more than a minute evaluating your essay, and may even spend less time than that.

But this doesn't mean you can just write two-and-a-half pages of gibberish and expect to get a good score. You still need to articulate a clear position, and support that position with relevant examples and reasoning, as we'll discuss in this section of this Black Book.

But this length guideline *does* mean that if you write a short essay (say, a page-and-a-half or shorter) then you have very little chance of getting out of the middle score range, no matter how splendid your writing is.

As we've already discussed, the ACT will probably never be up-front with us about the impact of an essay's length on its score, but we'll see solid proof that length really is the most important single aspect of your essay in a few pages. So be prepared to write more than two pages in the 30 minutes that the ACT provides on the Writing Test.

ACT Essay Rule 2: High School-Related Prompts

Every ACT Essay prompt will be focused on the everyday lives of high-school students in some way. In many cases, the prompts will ask your opinion of some hypothetical policy that would affect high-school students; for example, the prompt on page 204 of the Red Book asks whether teenagers should be "required to maintain a 'C' average in school before receiving a driver's license." So you know that the prompt will be directly relevant to your life experience in some way.

ACT Essay Rule 3: The Grader Doesn't Care What You Talk About, As Long As It's Relevant

If we were writing an essay for a particular teacher in school, or for a scholarship or college application, we'd want to consider the personal biases and preferences of the people who were likely to read those essays, because those readers would make decisions about our work based on their personal feelings.

But the people who read the ACT Essay aren't allowed to punish us for saying something just because they find it boring, or because they disagree with it. The graders of the ACT Essay are only allowed to lower your grade if you use examples and reasoning that aren't actually relevant to your thesis.

For example, let's imagine you were trying to support the opinion that high-school students shouldn't have to maintain a "C" average in order to be allowed to drive, and part of your argument was that many high-school teachers are incompetent and petty, and they might deliberately give a student bad grades to keep him from driving if they didn't like him. This could be a pretty offensive thing for an ACT Essay-grader to read, because a lot of those graders are high-school teachers themselves, and they know how hard high-school teachers have to work, and how most of them try to do a good job. But the grader wouldn't be able to punish you for using this in your argument, because it's directly relevant to the question—the question asked if a person's grades should affect his driving privileges, and this part of the argument would be discussing where those grades come from and how they might be manipulated.

The reason that graders for the ACT Essay aren't allowed to consider their personal feelings when grading your essay is the same reason behind most of what the ACT does: standardization. Since different readers will have different feelings about different subjects, ACT, Inc. instructs the readers to ignore their personal feelings and only consider whether an argument is relevant to its thesis.

So we shouldn't spend any time trying to guess what the essay-grader wants to hear. You aren't trying to interest your reader, nor do you need to worry about offending her. You just need to pick a position that answers the question in the prompt, and then write an essay with the same key elements that appear in other high-scoring essays, which we'll continue to talk about in this section.

Again, if your goal is to get a high score on the ACT Writing test, all you need to think about is cranking out an essay that follows the rules we're talking about here. Don't waste any time trying to do anything else—it won't help your score, and it might really hurt your score.

ACT Essay Rule 4: There's No Set Format (But You Should Probably Use The 6-Paragraph One Anyway)

In theory, you can use any type of essay format to write a top-scoring ACT Essay. In my experience, though, the top-scoring essays do tend to have a certain similarity in their structures. They usually include an introductory paragraph and a closing paragraph, and they tend to have around three body paragraphs, each dedicated to an individual reason or example in support of the thesis. When you add in another paragraph dedicated to counter-arguments (as we'll discuss below), you're looking at an essay with 6 paragraphs, which is what I generally recommend.

Of course, it's possible to get a great score without writing exactly 6 paragraphs! The exact number of paragraphs can vary. But if you want to maximize your chances of blending in with the other top-scoring essays, then you'll want to have paragraphs for an introduction, a conclusion, a consideration of counterarguments, and a few examples or reasons to support your thesis, all of which will almost definitely work out to about 6 paragraphs in total.

In *The Real ACT Prep Guide, 3rd Edition*, the number of paragraphs in the example essays goes up as the scores go up; the last two essays (with scores of 5 and 6 out of 6) use 6 and 7 paragraphs, respectively.

In a moment, we'll look at the recommended ACT essay structure in more detail, so you'll know how and when to vary it if you really want to. Again, though, this 6-paragraph format is generally what I recommend:

- intro paragraph (with thesis statement—see below)
- first example/reason paragraph
- second example/reason paragraph
- third example/reason paragraph

- counterargument paragraph
- conclusion paragraph

While we're on this topic, you may notice that the Red Book's descriptions of sample essays occasionally use the word "predictable" to describe them, which may make some readers want to avoid any kind of set essay format. But on page 132 of the Red Book, the analysis specifically says, "no credit is earned or lost specifically for using a familiar writing formula." Further, the rubric on page 141 of the Red Book says that, for a perfect-scoring essay, "the organization may be somewhat predictable or it may grow from the writer's purpose."

But most importantly, we can see in the two highest-scoring example essays from the Red Book that the "predictable" format (an introduction, some sample paragraphs, a paragraph considering counterarguments, and a conclusion) is effective and can get you a 5 or 6 out of 6. These two examples of real-world essays that have been graded by the ACT are the best kind of proof we could ask for.

ACT Essay Rule 5: State Your Thesis Clearly (Preferably In The First Paragraph)

After the length of your essay, the second-largest factor affecting your ACT Essay score is the degree to which your reasoning and examples support your thesis. (In a moment, we'll talk about what the words "reasoning" and "examples" mean on the ACT Essay.)

This means that your thesis needs to be clearly stated in a conspicuous way, so the reader can locate it quickly and easily. After all, if the reader can't identify your thesis statement, she has no way of knowing whether the rest of your essay supports that thesis statement; if she can't tell whether the rest of the essay supports your thesis, then she can't give you a good score. This is probably why most high-scoring ACT Essays contain clear and conspicuous thesis statements.

Most top-scoring ACT Essays place the thesis statement in the first paragraph, often as the very last sentence of that paragraph. That's sort of the classic position for the thesis statement that's taught in most high-school English classes, so it makes sense that lots of test-takers are comfortable placing the thesis there, and that most graders are conditioned to expect the thesis to appear there.

Now, in the sample essay from the Red Book that scored a perfect 6, the thesis doesn't appear until the beginning of the second paragraph. This only reinforces what I've been saying about my ACT Essay advice in general: it's not the *only* way to get a top score on the essay—it's just the way I recommend as the most reliable, teachable way to get a high score. The vast majority of top-scoring ACT Essays that I've seen have placed the thesis in the first paragraph, so that's what I recommend. (It's also worth noting that the only "perfect" ACT Essay in the Red Book still does include a clear thesis, even if it's not in the most common position, which further reinforces the general value of including a thesis in your ACT Essay.)

Again, it's possible to get a great score on your essay without stating your thesis in the first paragraph, but your best bet to make yourself clear on test day is still to put it there. That way, your grader is sure to know from the beginning what your stance is.

ACT Essay Rule 6: Your Position Must Be Supported With Reasons Or Examples, But They Can Be Made-Up If You Want, And They Don't Have To Be Academic

As we just discussed when we talked about including a thesis, the second-most important factor in your ACT Essay score seems to be how well you support your thesis with examples and reasoning. So each supporting paragraph you write needs to focus on an example or a reason that's directly relevant to your thesis.

For purposes of this discussion, a "reason" is an abstract principle or concept that supports your thesis. An "example" is a description of a specific instance in which something happened that supports your thesis.

So if we were trying to defend the position that students shouldn't be required to maintain a "C" average in order to have a driver's license, the following points would be *reasons* to support our position:

- A person's performance in school should have nothing to do with his rights in society.

- Requiring a student to maintain a "C" average to keep a driver's license would discourage students from attempting more challenging courses.

- Making people maintain a "C" average in order to be able to drive would give students an incentive to cheat in school.

As you can see, the above reasons are basically abstract principles that support our position.

But an *example* in support of our position would be a description of a concrete instance in which something happened that demonstrated the validity of our position. So statements like the following would be examples if they appeared in an ACT Essay:

- In the novel *High School Tragedy*, the character Isolde loses her driver's license when she fails to maintain her grades. As a result, she's unable to get to her job on time, which causes her to lose it, and creates a financial hardship for her family.

- A recent article on the Huffington Post described a riot at a school that had tried to interfere with students' driving privileges.

- I have a friend whose parents require him to maintain good grades to keep his driving privileges, and it just makes him more willing to cheat on his assignments so he can make sure he doesn't lose his privileges.

Don't worry if you're not quite sure of the difference between examples and reasons; the important thing is just to understand that ACT Essay graders will accept either kind of support. You can even use a mix of both, if you want: some of your supporting paragraphs can feature abstract reasons, while others rely on concrete examples.

Some people wrongly assume that it's better to rely on academic examples that draw from history, literature, or science. This might sound like a reasonable assumption to an untrained test-taker, because academic examples would probably impress a real teacher or professor more than non-academic examples would.

But we trained test-takers know the ACT often differs from school assignments, so it shouldn't really surprise us that academic examples don't receive any preference on the ACT Writing section. As it turns out, ACT, Inc. doesn't want to put test-takers who have less academic material to draw from at an unnecessary disadvantage on the ACT Writing test, so it instructs its essay-graders to give equal consideration to academic and non-academic examples: this way, test-takers aren't penalized simply for being less familiar with certain academic subjects, since the way those subjects are taught can vary greatly from school to school.

It might also surprise an untrained test-taker to learn that the ACT doesn't care if the examples we cite in our essays are even *true*.

Standardization is the reason for this quirk of the ACT Essay, just as it's the reason for so many others. Because the ACT Writing test must apply the same standards to all test-takers, and because it would be impossible to fact-check every single claim in every single essay, the only possible solution for ACT, Inc. is to instruct its graders to ignore whether statements in ACT essays are true or false. So you can make up examples for your ACT Essay if you want—you can even make up the titles of books and other works, as I did above with the book *High School Tragedy*. You can also be wrong about the details of things that actually did happen—for instance, you wouldn't be penalized for saying that the American Civil War happened in the 1200s, as long as whatever you were saying about the war was relevant to your thesis.

So let's summarize all of this stuff about supporting examples and reasons in a few simple sentences:

1. Your ACT Essay needs to include supporting paragraphs that use reasoning and/or examples to back up your thesis statement.
2. If you decide to use examples to support your position, they don't have to be academic. They only have to be relevant to the thesis.
3. If you decide to use examples to support your position, your examples don't have to be true.

ACT Essay Rule 7: Address Counterarguments!

We've already seen that the most important factor in your ACT Writing score is the length of your essay, and the second-most important factor is how well your examples and/or reasoning support your thesis. The third-most important factor is whether you address possible counterarguments in your essay.

A counterargument is something that somebody might say if she disagrees with your argument. The ACT will penalize us for not discussing possible counterarguments. This requirement of the ACT Essay can be especially challenging for trained test-takers to remember because it isn't required on a lot of other standardized tests, or in a lot of high-school classrooms.

I find the simplest way to address counterarguments is to dedicate your next-to-last paragraph to the task. One way to do this is to start with something like, "Some critics of my position might point out that . . ." and then list one or two counterarguments in a couple of sentences. Then you can finish the paragraph by addressing those counterarguments in another sentence or two, explaining why you still believe in your original position even though you're aware of these counterarguments.

If we're writing an ACT Essay defending the position that students shouldn't have to maintain a "C" average to keep their licenses, then our counterarguments paragraph might look like this:

> Some supporters of a mandatory "C" average for student drivers might say that the requirement would be good for society because it communicates the importance of being a responsible driver. Those supporters might also claim that people who can't maintain a "C" average can't be trusted to drive safely. But those people fail to realize that the job of deciding who can drive should belong to the department of motor vehicles, not to schools. If people are worried that student drivers aren't serious or cautious enough, then they should work to make the driving tests more rigorous, instead of getting schools involved in the process of licensing drivers.

You probably won't have a difficult time thinking of counterarguments—in fact, when you first read the prompt and you're deciding how to respond, you might even think of a couple of arguments for either side of the question automatically. If so, you can just save the arguments you thought of for the side you didn't take, and use them as counterarguments when the time comes.

For further examples and discussion of counterarguments, see my sample ACT Essay later in this section, and my analyses of the exemplar essays from the Red Book.

ACT Essay Rule 8: A Little Imperfect Grammar Is Okay

The high-scoring sample essays in *The Real ACT Prep Guide, 3rd Edition,* contain a few grammatical mistakes, so we know that an ACT essay can make a perfect score even if its grammar isn't perfect. That doesn't mean you should go out of your way to make mistakes, or that you shouldn't try to use proper grammar. But it does mean that grammar shouldn't be your main concern when you write your ACT Essay.

Don't waste time trying to proof your essay thoroughly to catch and fix every grammatical error—just write your ideas down in a clear and direct way. As we've discussed, it's much more important to focus on length, supporting your thesis with relevant examples and/or reasoning, and addressing counterarguments.

ACT Essay Rule 9: Vocabulary Isn't A Big Deal.

Untrained test-takers often hope to impress their graders by using big words in their ACT Essays. Please don't do this on test day. Your ACT Essay graders won't reward you for using a big word—but they might penalize you if they notice you using words incorrectly, which often happens when test-takers try to incorporate words they're not actually familiar with.

When we look at the sample essays from the Red Book, we'll see that top-scoring essays don't make any particular effort to incorporate impressive vocabulary words. You shouldn't, either. Instead, remember to focus on length, matching your examples and/or reasoning to your thesis, and addressing counterarguments. Those are the things that will impact your score on the ACT Essay.

Recommended Step-By-Step Approach To The ACT Essay

The whole challenge of the ACT essay is to write an essay in 30 minutes that includes the features that tend to appear in top-scoring ACT Essays. As I've said repeatedly, there are a few different ways to do this, but I find the following approach to be the easiest and most straightforward. After we go over this process, I'll write a sample essay using these guidelines in the next section. Finally, we'll finish our discussion of the ACT Essay by analyzing the example essays from the Red Book, to see how they demonstrate the concepts we've discussed.

1. Watch The Clock.

You only have 30 minutes, so losing focus for just a few minutes could really harm your score. Do your best to stay focused and keep writing until you've made it onto the third page of writing room and finished your essay—for most people, that will take up practically all of your 30 minutes.

2. Read The Prompt And Pick A Side.

The prompt will address some issue related to the everyday lives of high-school students, so it shouldn't be too hard for you to decide how you feel about it—or at least to pick a side that you can support.

Of course, there's no right or wrong answer to the prompt, and the grader isn't allowed to penalize you or reward you based on whether she agrees with your position. So just choose the side that seems easiest to support.

3. Come Up With 3 Reasons And/Or Examples To Support Your Side.

You'll need these reasons or examples to fill out your essay and support your thesis. Remember that one of the most important things about your essay is that your reasons or examples must clearly support your position. Also remember that the reasons and examples don't have to be true or academic—they *can* be true or academic, or both, if you want, but the graders aren't allowed to care either way. The only thing that matters is that your reasoning and examples would support your thesis if they were true.

4. Write Your Introduction, Including Your Thesis Statement.

Now that you've picked a side and thought of some ways to support it, start writing.

Remember that this is a 30-minute essay test, and length counts more towards your score than any other single thing. You don't want to waste time.

Your introductory paragraph should include your thesis statement. In addition to your thesis statement, you just want a few sentences related to the topic to fill out your essay.

You can fill out the rest of your opening paragraph by referring to the examples you'll be using, like the 5-scoring essay does on page 133 of your copy of the Red Book. Or you can just write filler material on the general topic of the prompt, like the 6-scoring essay on page 137 of the same book does in its opening paragraph. The most important goal to accomplish with the introductory paragraph is to state your thesis clearly.

5. Write Your Supporting Paragraphs, Using Examples And/Or Reasoning.

Once you've finished your introduction, you're ready to write your supporting paragraphs. This is the bulk of your essay, and length counts. I recommend one paragraph per example or reason, so if you have three examples to write about, you'll end up writing three paragraphs.

Three isn't necessarily the magic number of supporting paragraphs. You could do just two if you expanded on them enough to fill out more than two pages in total, or you could do four or five if you could think of that many ways to support your position, and if you could write about all of them quickly enough to finish on time. In general, though, I find that three supporting examples or reasons is the best number for most people.

Each support paragraph should more or less follow this structure:

- General statement that introduces what that paragraph will be about
- 3-5 sentences describing your reason or example
- 1-2 sentences relating this reason or example to the thesis.

Once you've written a paragraph like this for each example, I recommend you address counterarguments.

6. Address Counterarguments.

You've got most of your essay written by now, and you should be around halfway down the second page, or possibly even further along than that. Now you need to address counterarguments.

Your counterarguments paragraph should indicate that you're aware of reasons why someone might disagree with your answer to the prompt, but that people who disagree with you simply aren't aware of something that makes your position best. For examples of this type of paragraph, see my sample ACT Essay on the next page, as well as the sixth paragraph of the "perfect" 6-scoring ACT Essay that starts on page 137 of the Red Book.

7. Conclude The Essay.

At this point, you should be near the bottom of page 2, or even starting on page 3. It's time to write your conclusion and finish your essay.

Start with a couple of sentences reasserting the position you took in the beginning of the essay. Then, in another couple of sentences, re-summarize your reasons and examples, and wrap up your thoughts. If necessary, you can draw this summary out to get to the third page (remember that the length of your essay is the single most reliable indicator of its score).

Now that we've discussed this process in the abstract, let's take a look at some examples! On the next page, you'll see me construct a sample ACT Essay using this process. After that, we'll analyze the exemplar essays in the Red Book to see how the top-scoring ones follow the principles we've been talking about.

Example ACT Essay

In this exercise, I'll walk you through the process of writing a sample ACT Essay for a made-up prompt. This isn't a prompt I've ever seen before, but it's the sort of thing the ACT likes to ask about, and it'll create an opportunity for you to see this process in action. We'll go through it step by step.

Of course, there's no way for me to have this sample ACT Essay graded by an official grader, but when we look at the sample ACT Essays in the Red Book you'll see that the top-scoring essays demonstrate the same key features you'll see in this sample.

So here we go! I'll include the steps from the recommended process we just discussed on the previous pages. My made-up prompt will be, in a nutshell, "Should students have to do homework over their summer vacations?"

1. Watch The Clock.

We'll need to remember that we only have 30 minutes to write more than two pages of material. For most test-takers, that will mean starting to write early, and quickly.

2. Read The Prompt And Pick A Side.

My answer to the made-up question "Should students have to do homework over the summer?" will be "No, they shouldn't have to."

3. Come Up With 3 Reasons And/Or Examples To Support Your Side.

If I were taking the test, I wouldn't bother jotting these down—I'd just remember them. (If you forget one, you can always just make up another one later.)

1. The school year is stressful enough without adding work over the summer.

2. Time off from school in the summer is important because it allows students to pursue other interests.

3. My cousin needs to work during the summer to save money for college, and homework would get in the way of that.

4. Write Your Introduction.

Here's my intro paragraph. Notice that my thesis is the very last sentence in this paragraph, which is where most high-scoring ACT Essays will have it:

> We live in a very competitive world, and the workload of the average high school student is increasing every year. Some people even think that students should have to do homework over the summer, so that they are able to spend at least some of that time on their school subjects. However, the normal school year is already too stressful for students, and doing schoolwork over the summer would take up valuable time that students could otherwise use to pursue non-academic interests, or even to work summer jobs. Students shouldn't have to do homework over their summer vacations.

5. Write Your Supporting Paragraphs, Using Examples And/Or Reasoning.

Here are my three supporting paragraphs. Again, you don't need to have exactly three of these—you just need enough supporting material to allow you to reach the third page, while still remaining on-topic. For most people, using three supporting paragraphs (as opposed to two, or four, or five) will be the easiest way to do that.

There is no need to add more work to a high school student's life, because there is already plenty of work to get done during the year. I have to get up before 7 AM to take a bus across town to get to school. Often, I am doing homework or cramming for a test or quiz during that bus ride. Then I have to spend the rest of the day in class until after 3 PM. At that point, I usually have an after school activity—either swimming or drama. I don't get home until almost 6 PM, and then I have dinner and spend most of the night working on homework and preparing for the next day. The life of a high school student is already completely packed with work, and there is no need to add more to do over the summer.

Furthermore, time off in the summer is important because it gives students the opportunity to pursue interests outside of school. Some students might want to take up a musical instrument, or learn to fix cars. They might also be interested in playing in a recreational sports league over the summer, or in trying hiking or mountain biking. Students might even want to catch up on reading for pleasure, which is often not possible during the school year due to time constraints. School is important, but not everything important is part of school, and the summer provides valuable time for students to do things that are not necessarily academic.

My cousin is a good example of a person who would be negatively impacted if she had to do homework over the summer. She has two summer jobs she needs to work so she can save money for college, and throwing homework into the mix might possibly prevent her from earning the money she needs. Many other teenagers are in similar positions. Working to earn money during the summer is an important experience for them, and it would be hard to have that experience if they had to do homework during their summer vacations.

6. Address Counterarguments.

Here's my sample counterarguments paragraph:

Of course, people who like the idea of summer homework would probably point out that not everyone uses their time off in the summer wisely. It's also true that if students did work over the summer, they might be able to do less work during the year, which might make their lives easier overall. Still, I think that students should be given the choice of how to use their time in the summer, and I think it's unlikely that adding work over the summer would really mean there would be less work to do during the year. Time off in the summer is valuable, and once it starts to be used for homework, there will only be less and less time for summer jobs or other activities.

7. Conclude The Essay.

Now, all we have left is the conclusion:

With all of this in mind, I think it's very important not to give students homework over the summer. Normal high school life is already very stressful, and if we start getting assignments over the summer, we may never get a break from it. Also, those assignments will take up time that students could be using to pursue interests outside of school, or even to work at summer jobs. These are valuable experiences that will be threatened if students lose time to summer homework assignments.

Thoughts On This Sample Essay

Take a few minutes to recall the guidelines in this book for each part of the ACT Essay, and then look at how I used those guidelines to create the content I needed. Think about how you could apply this process to the sample prompts at the end of each of the practice tests in your copy of the Red Book, and to the prompt you'll see on test day.

As far as length is concerned, the word count for this essay exceeds the word count for the sample essay that got a "perfect" 6 on page 137 of the Red Book, so it would almost certainly exceed 2.5 pages if it were handwritten. (If I were writing it out by hand on test day and I realized that I had already taken up a lot of space by the time I got ready to start my third example paragraph, I could always choose to skip it and go right into my counterarguments paragraph if I was feeling tight on time.)

Notice how I consistently connected the points that I was making back to the prompt and to my thesis, so that it would be clear to the grader that I was addressing the prompt and supporting my position.

Also, notice that several of the personal details in my essay didn't need to be true—for example, that I get up before 7 AM each day. All that matters is that those details *would* support my position *if they were true*. Along similar lines, note that my essay makes no use of historic or literary examples—again, there's nothing wrong with those kinds of examples, but we don't get any special credit for using them.

Analysis Of Sample Essays In *The Real ACT Prep Guide, 3rd Edition*

Now let's take a look at the six sample essays provided in the Red Book. We'll talk briefly about the most important aspects of these essays and what you can learn from them to make sure you write your best essay on test day.

Essay 1, Page 123

Score: 1

Length: 1/2 page

Thesis: This writer says, "I don't think they should have a dress code because, [sic] it takes away from the kids."

Support: This essay contains a lot of sentences that seem to support the thesis, all crammed into one paragraph. None of those ideas are ever really developed or explained.

Counterarguments: This essay doesn't consider counterarguments.

Errors: There are some grammatical errors in this essay, such as the sentence fragment "If they start to control how we dress."

Vocabulary: The essay doesn't use any unusual or advanced vocabulary words.

Overview: Above all else, this essay is far too short, and it crams too many ideas into one paragraph without developing any of them. Don't write an essay like this one.

Essay 2, Page 125

Score: 2

Length: 3/4 page

Thesis: This writer says, "I agree with parents and teachers who say dress codes is [sic] needed." The thesis is elaborated with another sentence that also has grammatical issues.

Support: The student says that uniforms "encourage equality" and "helps [sic] stops [sic] rivalry between groups and clicks [sic]." These ideas are followed by a few sentences each, although a lot of those sentences say almost exactly the same thing, and they don't really explain how these ideas tie in to the prompt and the thesis.

Counterarguments: This essay doesn't consider counterarguments.

Errors: This essay contains a lot of errors in verb conjugation, among other errors.

Vocabulary: The essay doesn't use any unusual or advanced vocabulary words.

Overview: This essay has several failings. There's really nothing in it that should be imitated.

Essay 3, Page 127

Score: 3

Length: 1.5 pages

Thesis: This thesis statement is the first sentence in the essay: "In my opinion, teenagers should not have to have a dress code, because it restricts them and takes away a freedom they should have." The thesis is expanded with a few more sentences.

Support: The first supporting paragraph says teenagers have "the right to express ourselves." The next supporting paragraph makes a similar point by saying that a dress code "is a clear violation of the basic rights America was built upon." The third supporting paragraph says dress codes are bad because some students wouldn't be able to afford new clothes to meet the standards of a new dress code.

Counterarguments: This essay doesn't consider counterarguments.

Errors: This essay contains a few errors, including the misspelled word "kahkies [sic]," a couple of punctuation errors, and the phrase "that kind of clothes," which should be either "those kinds of clothes" or "that kind of clothing."

Vocabulary: The essay doesn't contain any unusual or advanced vocabulary words.

Overview: The main difference between this essay and the first two is that it's a bit longer and it offers a little actual development of the supporting ideas, although not much.

Essay 4, Page 130
Score: 4

Length: just under 2 pages

Thesis: This thesis is the first sentence in the essay, and is pretty well developed in the rest of the introductory paragraph: "I believe that it would be beneficial for our schools to adopt dress codes."

Support: The writer says that adopting a dress code would create "a better learning environment," that it will "prepare students to dress properly for different places," and that it will help students who "worry about fitting in." These are three separate reasons that each support the thesis, and they're reasonably developed, although the last one is in a paragraph that's a bit short.

Counterarguments: Counterarguments are considered only briefly in the introduction ("Although some may argue that this action would restrict the individual student's freedom of expression . . .").

Errors: There are no noteworthy grammatical errors in this essay.

Vocabulary: The essay does misuse the word "risky" to describe images on t-shirts; an appropriate word would be "risqué." But it's unlikely that this small mistake had any impact on the essay's score.

Overview: In terms of actual writing quality, I'd say this is the best sample essay in the Red Book. There are two main reasons this sample essay was a 4 and not a "perfect" 6:

- It was less than two pages long, and high-scoring essays should be at least two pages long.
- Counterarguments were only considered *extremely* briefly.

Adding a paragraph dedicated to counterarguments would have solved both problems.

Essay 5, Page 133
Score: 5

Length: 2.75 pages

Thesis: This essay's thesis statement appears as the first two sentences of the essay, and is developed in the rest of the introductory paragraph: "Many teachers and parents are now debating whether or not a dress code should be adopted. They think that it will improve the learning environment in our schools, and I agree."

Support: This essay says that a dress code "will substantially reduce distractions in the classroom," that dressing nicely "improves the school esthetically," and that a dress code "would prepare the youth of today for the workforce of tomorrow." These ideas are developed in turn, each in its own paragraph.

Counterarguments: This essay mentions one counterargument in the beginning of the fifth paragraph, and then addresses that counterargument. The counterargument is mentioned in only half of a sentence, though, and the rest of the paragraph comes off as a restatement of earlier ideas without necessarily making a clear connection between those ideas and the counterargument.

Errors: This essay has a couple of minor errors, such as when the author spells the possessive pronoun "its" with an apostrophe.

Vocabulary: The essay doesn't contain any unusual or advanced vocabulary words.

Overview: The only real issue with this essay, from the standpoint of the ACT's unwritten essay rules, is the lack of a more focused treatment of counterarguments.

Essay 6, Page 137

Score: 6

Length: 2.5 pages

Thesis: This essay's thesis appears in its second paragraph: "Freedom of expression is important, but when inappropriate attire begins to interfere with the educational process, something needs to be done." The thesis is thoroughly prefaced in the first paragraph and developed in the second paragraph, and it's summed up in the sentence "I think the answer is school uniforms."

Support: This essay says that "school uniforms could help even the playing field between poor and rich students," that "they could help curb some of the gang-related violence in our schools," and that the author "would enjoy the sheer effortlessness of not having to rummage through [her] closet each morning." All of these ideas are thoroughly fleshed out and clearly related back to the thesis.

Counterarguments: The sixth paragraph of this essay is dedicated to counterarguments. The student explains the counterarguments in several sentences, and then explains why she still thinks her solution to the dress code problem (school uniforms) is the right one in spite of those arguments.

Errors: This essay contains several spelling errors ("inuendo" instead of "innuendo," "descrimination" instead of "discrimination," et cetera) and a couple of awkward sentences ("We live in a materialistic world and, for some, it is all about the label"). These errors were clearly not serious enough to keep the essay from receiving a 6 out of 6.

Vocabulary: This essay contains a couple of words that might be considered slightly advanced, such as "arbitrary" and "defray." But it also contains misspelled words, as noted above.

Go to www.ACTprepVideos.com.

Overview: This essay is obviously an example of what ACT Essay-graders want to see, since it received a "perfect" 6 out of 6. This essay is well over two pages long, it takes a clear stance on the issue, and it supports that stance with multiple reasons and examples. It also devotes a paragraph to addressing counterarguments thoroughly. The presence of a few awkward sentences and misspellings had no effect on the score.

ACT Writing Test (The ACT Essay) Quick Summary

This is a one-page summary of the major concepts you'll need to keep in mind when addressing the ACT Essay. Use it to evaluate your comprehension or jog your memory. For a more in-depth treatment of these ideas, see the rest of this section.

The Big Secret: The ACT Essay is just as standardized as the rest of the ACT, and if we can imitate other high-scoring essays, we can get a high score, too. It's all about giving the graders exactly what they're trained to look for in a high-scoring essay.

The prompt will be related to things the average teenager deals with on a regular basis, such as school. Keep this in mind on test day so you're ready to come up with related material to support your position.

You need to make it to the third page. The length of an ACT Essay is the single most reliable indicator of its score. If you can make it onto the third page, you greatly increase the likelihood of scoring a 10 or higher on the essay out of 12.

Your thesis must be stated clearly. After the length of your essay, one of the most important factors in your score is how well your examples and reasons support your thesis. If your thesis isn't stated clearly, it's difficult for the grader to tell if you did a good job supporting it.

Support your position with reasons or examples (even made-up ones). All that matters is that your examples and reasons would support your position *if they were true*. So you can use examples and reasons that actually *are* true, or you can just make them up.

Some imperfect grammar is okay. Don't waste time on thorough proofreading. You'll probably need to spend almost all of the allotted time on writing in order to make it to the third page.

Don't go out of your way to use obscure vocabulary words. Stick with words you feel comfortable using; if you try to inject a big word you're not comfortable with, you run the risk of sounding awkward, which can hurt your score if the grader notices it. Remember that the top-scoring example essays from the Red Book don't tend to use advanced vocabulary words.

Consider counterarguments! You must address possible counterarguments if you want a high score.

There's no required format, but you should probably follow the 6-paragraph format we talked about.

Don't worry about being interesting or funny. The grader has to read your essay no matter how boring it is, and top-scoring ACT Essays are rarely interesting. Instead, focus on including the key features we've discussed in this Black Book: length, a clear thesis, relevant reasoning and examples, and so on.

Here's the general ACT Essay process that I recommend:

1. Watch the clock.
2. Read the prompt and pick a side.
3. Come up with 3 reasons or examples to support your side.
4. Write your Introduction.
5. Write your three supporting paragraphs.
6. Write a paragraph that considers counterarguments.
7. Write your conclusion.

Go back through this section of the Black Book to see demonstrations of these ideas, especially in my analyses of the sample essays from the Red Book, and in my sample ACT Essay.

You Have To Practice

"Being busy does not always mean real work. The object of all work is production or accomplishment and to either of these ends there must be forethought, system, planning, intelligence, and honest purpose, as well as perspiration. Seeming to do is not doing."
- Thomas Edison

This is an idea that's come up a few times already, but now that you've actually read through all the training material, we need to talk about it one more time.

You've got to practice.

You've learned my approach to every part of the ACT. Hopefully you feel like you've got a much better handle on the whole thing, and hopefully you're less worried than you were when you started, and hopefully you're going to get the score you need.

But before that happens, you've got to practice.

I always like to say that getting better at the ACT is a lot more like training for a sport or learning to play a musical instrument than like preparing for a "normal" high school test.

You're not just memorizing a list of facts or concepts that you have to spit back out on test day. You're developing a skill, and that means you actually have to sit down and do it for a while before you can expect to execute properly when it counts.

Would you feel comfortable suiting up for a football game, or walking out on stage for a piano recital, just because you read a book about football, or about playing the piano? Of course not! You wouldn't do either of those things unless you'd spent some time honing your skills. The ACT is the exact same way.

Most people who are getting ready to take a standardized test have at least a few important misconceptions about the test. Often, when I work with people, and I explain what's wrong with those misconceptions, and then we talk about how the test really works, it's like a light bulb turning on in their heads—things that didn't make any sense before suddenly do make sense.

That's great, but it can create a false sense of confidence. It's easy to look at a couple of examples from real ACT questions and feel like you understand what's going on, but that doesn't necessarily mean you'll automatically answer every future ACT question correctly without practicing.

In fact, the first practice questions you look at after you read this book might seem *more* challenging than you expect, because you'll have to work them out on your own, instead of just reading and understanding my analysis. You're probably going to get frustrated. But you simply have to stick with it. Just keep at your practice, analyze your mistakes until you understand them, and re-read parts of this Black Book (or even the whole thing) as necessary. You have to put in the time so you can learn to recognize the patterns we've talked about without me pointing them out to you for each new question, because I won't be able to do that for you on test day :)

Of course, learning the approach in this Black Book will take a lot less time and cause much less aggravation than following the typical approach to the ACT, and your results should also be better if you apply the methods correctly—but you'll still need to spend *some* time practicing.

You are now armed with the knowledge you need to beat the ACT. So make sure you invest the time to apply that knowledge to the real ACT practice questions in your copy of the Red Book, so you'll be able to give your best possible performance on test day.

When Things Go Wrong

"If things go wrong, don't go with them."
- Roger Babson

Everyone makes mistakes on the ACT at some point, because the test is long and repetitive, and we're only human.

Of course, one major goal of your training should be to minimize those mistakes in the first place as much as possible. But another major goal should be to develop the habit of looking out for mistakes *after* you've made them, so you can correct them.

When your training tells you something about a question just doesn't feel quite right, it's important not to ignore that instinct. Instead, you should re-evaluate your approach to the question until you understand how it follows the rules and patterns of the ACT's design that you've learned in this Black Book. Of course, this is what you should do during your practice—if it's test day, you should skip the question, work on the rest of the section, and come back to it later.

Here are some guidelines to help remind you what you might have overlooked when you can't figure out the answer to a question. I've broken them up by section. (If you'd like more a detailed refresher on the best ways to approach a given section of the ACT, you should refer back to that part of this Black Book for instructions and examples.)

Reading
- Are you reading the wrong part of the passage?
- Did you remember to eliminate answer choices that aren't supported by the text?
- Have you misunderstood, misread, or overlooked a word or phrase in the question, answer choice, or passage?
- Have you made an assumption that isn't actually supported by the text?

English
- Did you misread or overlook part of the underlined portion of the text?
- What are differences among the answer choices? How long are the answer choices? Based on the lengths of the answer choices and their degree of similarity, does the question seem to be more about reading comprehension, or about grammar, style, and/or punctuation?
- Did you misread or overlook part of an answer choice?
- Is it possible that the question involves a grammar or punctuation rule you haven't considered?
- Is it possible that a sentence before or after the underlined part of the passage might contain a parallel phrase that indicates which answer choice is correct?
- Is this one of the ACT English questions that involves reading comprehension rules?

Math
- Did you misread the question, answer choice, or diagram?
- Did you make any calculation mistakes? (Remember that it's still possible to make a mistake when you use a calculator—you might mis-key something or leave the calculator in radians mode when it should be in degrees mode, for example.)

- Could the question involve a math concept you haven't considered? (Remember that the question might involve concepts that are directly related to the concepts in the question and the answer choices, but the question can't require you to know calculus or advanced trigonometry or statistics.)

Science

- Did you misread the question, answer choice, or data?
- Did you overlook a label on an axis or column heading?
- Did you overlook the information you need somewhere in the passage?
- Have you made an assumption that isn't supported in the passage?
- Have you tried to rely on your own advanced scientific knowledge, rather than drawing your answers from the data? (Remember that a small number of questions on the ACT Science section might require relatively basic knowledge of science, but nothing too sophisticated.)

4 ACT Myths

"The occurrence of mysteries is always by word of mouth."
- *Yamamoto Tsunetomo*

We've discussed at length the fact that there's a lot of bad information out there about the ACT. This information doesn't just come from other students who aren't familiar with the test—it can also come from well-meaning teachers and guidance counselors.

But don't blame them. As we've seen, the ACT likes to perpetuate a lot of these myths because they distract students from the predictable, repetitive nature of the test's standardization. People who spread bad information about the ACT often do it without meaning to.

I thought it would be a good idea to cover some of the biggest ACT myths in this section, so you won't be tempted to fall for any of them.

Myth 1: The ACT tests the skills you'll need in college.

This is the big one—it's what most proponents of the ACT come back to over and over again. These people especially point out that the ACT has questions on trigonometry, as well as an entire "Science" section.

But the ACT really doesn't reward the skills you'll use in college.

We've learned that the ACT requires attention to detail in a way that high school (and college) classes do not. A lot of interpretations that would be rewarded in a high school or college English class are dead wrong on the ACT Reading section, and sentences that would be acceptable in a lot of college papers would be wrong on the ACT English section. ACT Science requires almost no outside scientific knowledge, and ACT Math often tests basic math in ways that are unlike anything you'd see in a high school or college math class.

So in most cases, the skills you need in a college classroom have very little do with the skills involved in getting ready for the ACT.

The ACT requires its own skillset. If you approach the ACT the same way a good student approaches college, you'll find the test very difficult.

Myth 2: Colleges don't care about the ACT.

There's a lot of controversy surrounding standardized tests like the ACT. For that reason, many colleges like to pretend that the ACT and similar tests aren't that important when it comes to the admissions process.

But this isn't true.

If you look into any highly competitive college, and you find out the average ACT and SAT scores of the people who go there, you'll pretty much always find that those scores are well above average—for some schools, the average scores are in the top few percent nationwide.

It would have to be a pretty big coincidence for a school that doesn't care about standardized test scores to keep selecting students for admission who tend to have exceptionally high scores on standardized tests.

Think about it: if schools didn't care about your ACT scores, they wouldn't ask for those scores, and they wouldn't spend the time necessary to consider them. The ACT certainly isn't the only piece of the admissions puzzle, especially for more competitive schools, but standardized test scores matter a lot, whether we like it or not.

Myth 3: ACT Reading is for literary people, ACT Math is for math people, ACT Science is for science people . . .

In high school, people tend to get better grades in classes that they're naturally more interested in. For similar reasons, people also tend to think they'll do better on the sections of the ACT that correspond to their interests or abilities.

Of course, by now we know that these subjects aren't tested on the ACT the same way they're tested in school. For example, we know we can't approach the ACT Essay the same way we would write a great essay in an English class or a History class. We also know the unwritten rules in the Math, Science, English, and Reading sections of the ACT are very different from the things we'd see on tests in high school or college.

So don't get stuck on the idea that you can only do well on a section of the ACT that's named after a class you're good at in high school. If you learn the rules of the test and practice them, you can do well on any section of the test.

Myth 4: Answer choices are evenly distributed within a section.

Students often tell me they get worried when they're working on a section of the ACT and they notice they've marked a lot of (B)s, or (F)s, or whatever.

Don't spend any time worrying about this! There's no way to know what the answer choice distribution should be in any one section. (And, even if there were, what good would it do you? If you found out you'd marked too many (A)s, for instance, how would you know which ones to change, and which ones to keep?)

All you should ever do—and all you *can* ever do—is attack one ACT question at a time. So just do that, and don't try to figure out if you're picking any particular letter more or less frequently than any other letter.

Conclusion

One of the things that makes the ACT so hard for most people is that they're distracted by all the misinformation they receive about the test. Don't fall for these myths! Practice, stay focused on what you know is true, and remember to test out any ACT advice you receive on real test questions from the Red Book. If you do that, you should have no trouble separating fact from fiction.

Shooting For A 36

"Trifles make perfection, and perfection is no trifle."
- Michelangelo Buonarroti

If you've read the whole Black Book up to this point, you've already seen all the material you'll need to master in order to score a 36 on the ACT. In other words, as I've said before, there are no special, "secret" techniques or strategies for a perfect score—getting a perfect score is just a matter of refining and perfecting the ACT strategies we've already discussed until you execute them almost flawlessly.

Still, there are a few topics we can discuss that can help you to have the right attitude in your preparation if you hope to get a perfect score on the ACT. Let's talk about them now.

Confront Problem Areas

Imagine you're looking at a list of 100 ACT questions, and you have to answer any one question on the list correctly. Almost anyone could do that—if you only had to answer one question correctly, you could just look through them until you found the one you were most comfortable with, and then answer that one.

Even if you had to answer any 10 ACT questions from the list correctly, you could probably do that without much difficulty, because you'd have the freedom to choose the 10 questions you found easiest.

But what if you'd already answered 90 out of those 100 ACT questions? At that point, you probably would have picked all the easy ones already. That means that answering each of the remaining 10 questions correctly would become increasingly hard, because the questions that are left will be the more challenging ones for you—the ones you chose to avoid earlier.

The bottom line here is that answering every single ACT question (or nearly every question) correctly will require you to confront every single weakness and problem area you have when it comes to the ACT. Even students who only want to score well above average can still miss a handful of challenging questions and do quite well—but you won't have that option if you want a perfect score.

As I said earlier, there's no special way to approach this issue except to use the same strategies we've already discussed. It's just useful to be aware of this challenge ahead of time—most people have to work harder to improve from a 33 to a 36 than they do to improve from a 23 to a 26.

Practice Intelligently

If you're serious about getting a 36, you're probably a pretty good student. Often, being a good student involves long hours and an ability to keep working when your assignments get tedious.

When you train for the ACT, though, you need to keep in mind that just putting in long hours won't cut it (in fact, for some students, long hours of ACT preparation are neither necessary nor helpful). Instead, you need to focus on making your practice time count. That means paying careful attention to your mistakes, and trying to figure out why they happen, so you can avoid them in the future. Look out for the issues that give you trouble, and think about ways to improve in those areas.

There are some academic situations where large quantities of mindless work can be beneficial. The ACT isn't one of them. Make sure you're actively engaged in your ACT practice (especially when you *review* your practice), or else you'll probably be wasting your time.

Review Your Practice

This concept of review is so critical that it still deserves its own separate heading, even though it just came up in the previous sentence. You simply must review your practice work if you want to get a perfect score. Analyze your practice questions—especially the ones you missed—and keep thinking about them until you've figured out why you got them wrong. Otherwise, your practice won't count for much.

Have The Right Attitude

If you want a perfect score on the ACT, you've got to have the right mindset. Decide ahead of time to keep your frustration to a minimum, and not to blame other people when you run into difficulty. If you really are committed to this challenge, then you also need to accept full responsibility for the results. Don't make excuses—even if they're valid, they don't change anything.

Summary

Getting a perfect score on the ACT is hard. Executing flawlessly on the test doesn't really require any advanced knowledge or extreme intelligence, but it does require you to go through several hours of tedious test-taking without letting more than maybe a couple of mistakes get past you.

In this Black Book, you have all the information you need to get any score you want on the ACT, if you'll pay enough attention to detail and apply yourself diligently enough. All that's left is for you to train and practice with real ACT practice questions until you can apply these strategies consistently and without error. Commit to your goal and maintain a good attitude.

Good luck!

If American English Isn't Your First Language . . .

"The conquest of learning is achieved through the knowledge of languages."
- Roger Bacon

Reading is the single most important ACT skill, so if American English isn't your native language, you could run into some difficulty on the test. Here's a general approach I recommend for my foreign clients, to help them make the most of the situation if their English isn't perfect.

1. Start With The Questions You Can Already Answer.

If you're able to read this book, and you're planning to take the ACT, you obviously have some English ability already. Start by using that existing ability to answer as many questions as possible without focusing specifically on improving your American English skills. These questions could potentially be on any section of the ACT, so just try out some different kinds of practice questions and figure out where you can already succeed with your current level of English.

It's not going to be worthwhile for you to put significant effort into improving your English until you're getting the most out of what you already know, so do your best to learn the strategies from this Black Book and apply them as best you can before you start focusing on your language skills.

2. Next, Learn "Testing" Vocabulary.

When you're ready to focus on your American English, try to learn the words the ACT uses to frame the actual questions you have to answer, because you're likely to see those words come up frequently on the test in the future.

The "testing" vocabulary words on the Reading and English sections could include things like "infer," "characterize," "conclusion," "context," and "describe."

The "testing" vocabulary on the Math and Science sections could include words like "average," "experiment," "equivalent," "variable," and "axis."

These are only examples; I'm not saying you should only learn the specific words I listed. To figure out which words to study, just work with a lot of real ACT practice questions from the Red Book and make a note of the words you don't know that frequently appear in the prompts of ACT question. These are the words you need to learn, because you're more likely to see them on test day.

3. Don't Worry—Nobody Else Knows All The Science Vocabulary Either.

As you prepare for the ACT Science section, you'll probably notice a lot of large words and unusual phrases that you're not familiar with. But the odds are good that native speakers of American English don't know them, either.

As we discussed in the section of this Black Book on training for the ACT Science section, one thing the ACT loves to do is to include scientific-sounding terms like "stratopause" and "blackbody radiation"—phrases that are either explained in the text, or irrelevant to the question. So when an ACT question actually asks about one of these obscure scientific terms, check to see if it's defined in the passage, or if it matches up with a label on a chart, graph, or table. In either situation, you can answer the question correctly without knowing the phrase beforehand.

Other than that, handle the Science section like any other part of the ACT, and just take note of the words that come up over and over again from section to section. Don't focus on learning the specialized words that only come up in a particular passage and then never get repeated in other passages. (Of course, if you want to learn them to enrich your English, you should feel free to do that—I'm just saying that you shouldn't waste time on those words if your only goal is to improve on the ACT, because your time would be better spent elsewhere.)

4. Take A Look At ACT Style And ACT Grammar.

Once you've improved your ACT-taking skills, and then learned the ACT-specific vocabulary you need, you should spend some time learning ACT style and grammar for the English section.

(It's important to make a distinction between the rules of modern American English and the things that are rewarded on the ACT English section, because the rules that sentences need to follow on the ACT aren't necessarily the rules that today's students learn when they study English.)

Most American students don't spend much time studying English grammar, so you might actually be able to do better on the English section than many native speakers if you put in a little work. Just make sure you use this Black Book to learn what the ACT likes, and you should be fine.

5. Find Out If You Need To Write The ACT Essay.

A lot of colleges don't care about the ACT Essay (also known as the ACT Writing Test), so you'll probably want to contact someone in the admissions departments of your target schools to find out if they require you to submit an ACT Essay score. If your target colleges do consider that part of the test, you'll need to write the best ACT Essay you can.

If you need to write the ACT Essay, one of the most important things you can do is to try to avoid awkward phrases. Stick with sentence structures that you feel comfortable with, and use words whose meanings you're sure of. A lot of people try to impress the ACT Essay graders with big words or fancy sentences, but that doesn't work, as we discussed earlier in this Black Book. It's much more important to stick with what you know and write in a way that sounds as natural and native as possible. That way, you can avoid sounding like you can't write coherent English.

Conclusion

I know it's frustrating to look at an ACT question and feel like the only reason you can't answer it is that it has words you don't know. But you have to remember that the ACT isn't like other tests, which means you can't prepare for it the same way you'd prepare for other tests. If your goal is to get the highest ACT score you possibly can—and that really should be your goal, of course—then you'll probably have the easiest time picking up extra points by prioritizing things the way I've laid out here.

The ACT is very repetitive and relatively simple once you know what to look for. Try to follow the advice in this section, and the strategies in this Black Book, to make the most of the English you know. Good luck!

Parting Advice

"There is nothing impossible to him who will try."
- Alexander The Great

By now you know everything you need to know to be able to get a great score on the ACT. At this point, you just need to practice these techniques and get comfortable using them against real ACT questions from the Red Book.

Let me offer you an important piece of advice to keep in mind as you do that practice.

The ACT is a highly detail-oriented test. It's much more detail-oriented than other aspects of your educational experience, and that's why so many people struggle with it. Paying careful attention to repetitive, detailed questions for hours at a time just isn't something most test-takers are used to doing.

Because of this, even trained test-takers will have lapses sometimes. I even do it myself, occasionally. When my students make these kinds of mistakes, I often hear something like this:

"I found a question that doesn't follow the ACT rules you told me about. What should I do?"

The first thing you need to check is that you're working with an actual ACT question written by ACT, Inc. Of course, what we've learned in this Black Book can only be reliably applied to real ACT questions, not fake questions written by other test-prep companies. Fake questions you get from other companies may not follow the same rules as official ACT questions.

But if you are indeed looking at a real ACT question, and if you are indeed familiar with the concepts in this Black Book, then the explanation for your difficulty is that you've overlooked or misunderstood some detail from the question, or the answer choice, and that's the reason the question doesn't seem to follow the normal ACT rules.

I know it can be frustrating to hear this, and it can be even more frustrating to spend a lot of time trying to hunt down your mistake on a question, but it's important not to forget the ACT's rules when you feel stuck. Don't give up!

Of course, it's also important to remember that you may be better off temporarily skipping a question if you're stuck on it, so you can focus on other questions in the section that are easier for you. Then you can come back for the troublesome questions later and see if you can figure out which detail you've missed.

So please, when you're practicing these methods on real ACT practice questions, and you see something that makes you doubt the training I've given you, don't worry. It happens to everybody once in a while. The important thing—and it's very, very important—is that you take the time to figure out what's going on in that question, so you can choose an answer that correctly follows the ACT's rules.

On the ACT, as with most things in life, you tend to make the best progress when you're faced with the biggest challenges, and you overcome them. You can do it.

Thanks For Reading!

I hope you've enjoyed learning my strategies for beating the ACT, and that you feel much better prepared for test day. Please be sure to spend some time practicing what you've learned in this Black Book on real ACT practice questions from the Red Book!

I know that preparing for a test like the ACT is a huge deal, and it means a lot to me that thousands of students over the years have trusted me at such an important and stressful time in their lives.

I wish you the best of luck on test day.

Appendix: Writing Toolbox

I decided to create this appendix for readers who feel like they need a little refresher course in some aspects of English grammar. Like everything else in this Black Book, this section is designed to help you *on the ACT, specifically*—you may find that some of the "rules" we cover in this Writing Toolbox don't agree with some things you've learned elsewhere about grammar in general. That's fine—just remember that the rules in this Writing Toolbox are the ones you need to follow when it comes to the ACT.

Because of the standardized nature of the test, ACT English questions tend to test the same concepts over and over again. That means we don't need to study all of English grammar to do well on the ACT; we only need to study the things that actually show up in real ACT questions.

Most people don't spend any real time formally studying English grammar in school, so they end up being a little uncomfortable when they think about things like verb conjugation, semicolons, prepositional idioms, and so on.

Don't worry! We can attack these issues as intelligently and efficiently as we attack any other part of the test.

How We'll Do This

We'll need to start by talking about some basic concepts that you won't actually need to know on the test. For example, we'll review the names of basic parts of speech, like nouns and verbs, even though ACT English questions don't require you to know the meanings of the words "noun" and "verb."

We're going to start with these basic terms because we'll need to refer to them in order to discuss the things that actually *will* be on the test.

You might feel like you're already familiar with some of this material, but if you really want to understand all the concepts on the ACT English section, then you should read through this entire Appendix. In fact, I'd strongly recommend that you read the whole thing *twice*, because you'll probably get a lot more out of it the second time around.

Important Note

This section will contain a lot of good and bad examples of ACT grammar, so you'll know which kinds of phrases to choose on the test, and which ones to avoid. To keep things straight, I'll put an asterisk (*) at the beginning of any example that would be considered *incorrect* on the ACT. (Remember that we only care about what the ACT considers to be correct or incorrect, for the purposes of this Appendix.)

Let's get started by looking at some basic grammar concepts.

Nouns

Nouns are words that describe objects or ideas, essentially. The easiest nouns to understand are words that describe objects, like these:

apple	bicycle	toy	umbrella
watch	computer	shoe	train
mall	sign	book	car

Any object you can touch or point to is a noun.

But nouns can also refer to abstract concepts or ideas, like these:

happiness	anger	weather	peace
hope	idealism	love	election
talent	operation	biology	speed

These aren't things you can touch or point to, but they're still nouns. Often, you can recognize nouns like these because they have suffixes like "-ness", "-ism," "-ion," "-ology," "-hood," "-ence/-ance," and so on.

Nouns can be singular or plural. We typically form a plural of a noun by adding "-s" or "-es" to the singular version of the noun, but some nouns have irregular plurals that are formed differently. Here are some examples of regular and irregular nouns in their singular and plural forms:

Nouns with regular plural forms:

houses	clouds	foxes

Nouns with irregular plural forms:

geese	children	mice

Pronouns are a particular type of noun that we use to refer to a noun we've already mentioned. These are pronouns:

I	you	he	she	it	we	they	which
me	him	her	us	them	one	that	

(**NOTE:** the words "that" and "which" are special types of pronouns called "relative pronouns." Both words can also be used in other ways that aren't related to pronouns, depending on the context. Don't worry about those other usages right now—just know that the words "that" and "which" are often, but not always, pronouns.)

Pronouns are useful because they save us from having to say the same noun over and over again.

Example:

Ashley says she has to leave by Monday.

In the above sentence, we use the pronoun "she" to replace the word "Ashley." That way, we don't have to say this:

Ashley says Ashley has to leave by Monday.

When a pronoun appears on the ACT, it must agree in number with the noun it's replacing.

Example:

> **Last week I saw an antique car. It was over 100 years old.**

In the above example, the singular pronoun "it" is correctly used to refer to the singular noun "car."

Let's look at a sentence that breaks this rule:

> ***Last week I saw an antique car. At over 100 years old, they were in great shape.**

The above sentence incorrectly uses the plural pronoun "they" to refer to the singular noun "car."

Subjects and objects

In the traditional view of English grammar, every sentence must have a main verb. The main verb is the word (or phrase) that describes an action being performed in the sentence.

The thing that performs the action is called the "subject" of the sentence (or the subject of the verb). If there's a noun that receives the action in the sentence, that noun is called the "object" in the sentence (or the object of the verb). Sentences don't have to have objects.

Example:

> **John grabbed the pencil.**

In the above sentence, the word "John" is the subject, because "John" is the thing doing the action—in this case, the action is described by the word "grabbed." The word "pencil" is the object of the verb, because "pencil" is the thing receiving the action of being grabbed.

Some pronouns are subject pronouns, and some are object pronouns.

The following pronouns are subject pronouns, because they can be used to replace words that serve as subjects of verbs:

I	We
You	They
He	Who
She	What
It	

The following pronouns are object pronouns, because they can be used to replace words that serve as objects of verbs:

Me	Us
You	Them
Him	Whom
Her	What
It	

Notice that the words "you," "it," and "what" each have identical subject and object forms.

Subject pronouns can only be used as subjects; they must be the thing in the sentence that does an action.

Object pronouns can only be used as objects; they must be the thing in a sentence that receives an action.

So the following sentences would be acceptable sentences on the ACT English section:

He gave her a present.

They sent a letter to us.

In the above sentences,

- "He" and "they" are subject pronouns that are doing the actions in the sentences.
- "Her" and "us" are object pronouns that are receiving the actions in the sentences.

The following sentences would be unacceptable on the ACT English section:

*He gave she a present.

*Them sent a letter to us.

In the above sentences,

- "She" is a subject pronoun that can't properly receive the action of the verb "gave."
- "Them" is an object pronoun that can't properly do the action of the verb "sent."

Personal pronouns

Personal pronouns are pronouns that can be used to replace a noun that describes a person. When a pronoun is used in place of a noun that describes a person, that pronoun must be a personal pronoun.

The following would be an acceptable sentence on the ACT English section:

This is my uncle, who got me interested in physics.

In the above sentence, the word "who" is a personal pronoun that takes the place of the personal noun "uncle."

The following would be an unacceptable sentence on the ACT English section:

*This is my uncle that got me interested in physics.

In this sentence, the word "that" isn't a personal pronoun, so it can't be used to refer to the word "uncle" on the ACT English section.

Verbs

Generally speaking, a verb is a word that describes an action.

One way to test whether a word is a verb is to try to think of a sentence that places that word immediately after the word "cannot." If you can do that with the word, then that word is a verb.

Examples:

run	do	make	swim
cook	imagine	follow	think

You can see that any of these words can be placed into a logical sentence after the word "cannot."

Examples:

> I cannot run far.
>
> He cannot do that for very long.
>
> They cannot make a sports car.
>
> We cannot swim here.

Verbs can be "conjugated," which means they change their forms according to how they're used in a sentence. On the ACT, we need to pay attention to two different things when it comes to conjugating verbs:

1. We sometimes need to know whether the verb should be singular or plural (to match its subject).
2. We sometimes need to know who is doing the action of the verb—whether the verb is in the first, second, or third person.
3. We sometimes need to know the verb's tense (whether it describes an action in the past, present, or future).

Singular verbs versus plural verbs

When a present-tense verb goes with a third-person, singular noun, that verb needs to end in "-s" or "-es." (A third-person, singular noun is any noun that can be replaced by the pronouns "he," "she," or "it.")

Other forms of verbs don't require "-s" or "-es."

Examples:

> Rhonda drives to the dentist.
>
> My friends drive downtown.

In these sentences,

- The singular noun "Rhonda" requires the singular verb form "drives." (Again, note that the present-tense, third-person singular form of a regular verb ends in "-s" or "-es.")
- The plural noun "friends" requires the plural verb form "drive."

A verb must always agree in number with the noun or nouns it modifies. This would be an acceptable sentence on the ACT English section:

> Charles and Adam speak German.

In this sentence,

- The phrase "Charles and Adam" requires a plural verb form, because it describes more than one person.
- The word "speak" is a plural verb form to match the plural subject.

This would be an unacceptable sentence on the ACT English section:

> *Charles and Adam speaks German.

In this sentence, the singular verb form "speaks" is incorrect, because it's being used with the plural phrase "Charles and Adam." The phrase "Adam speaks" may sound correct on its own, but when we read the whole sentence we can see that the subject is actually the noun phrase "Charles and Adam," not just the word "Adam."

Here is the verb "to speak" conjugated in the present tense. Note that the third-person singular form ends in -s:

I speak	We speak
You speak	You speak
He/She/It speaks	They speak

The ACT English section has a lot of questions that mix up singular nouns with plural verbs, or plural nouns with singular verbs. When you see a verb form being tested in a question, always figure out which noun phrase is its subject, and then see whether the verb is in the correct form.

Verb tenses

Verbs are actions that take place at a certain time. The action described by a verb can take place in the past, present, or future, and the form of a verb phrase changes according to the time frame when the verb's action takes place. We call these different forms of the verb "tenses."

Examples:

I enjoyed elementary school.

In the above sentence, the verb form "enjoyed" is in the past tense, which shows that the act of enjoying elementary school happened in the past. We can tell this because of the "-ed" suffix on the verb.

I enjoy high school.

In the above sentence, the verb form "enjoy" is in the present tense, showing that the act of enjoying high school is happening now.

I will enjoy college.

In the above sentence, the verb form "will enjoy" is in the future tense, which shows that the act of enjoying college will happen in the future.

You'll see some other verb forms on the test as well. We don't need to know the names of these forms, but we do need to be able to tell whether they describe actions in the past or present. These verb forms involve forms of the verbs "to have" and "to be," which are often called "helping verbs" in this context.

On the ACT English section, any verb-form that uses the helping verb "to have" describes a completed action:

Examples:

We have gone there.

Brian had considered studying Spanish before he went to Madrid.

In the above sentences, the verb forms "have gone" and "had considered" both involve the helping verb "to have," so we know they both describe completed actions:

- The phrase "we have gone" emphasizes that the action of going is completed at the time the sentence is being spoken.
- The phrase "had considered" shows that the action of considering was completed before Brian went to Madrid.

Verb forms that use a past-tense form of the helping verb "to be" describe an action in the past.

Example:

She was looking for a computer.

In this sentence, the verb form "was looking" involves the word "was," which is a past-tense form of the helping verb "to be," so we know it describes an action taking place in the past.

On the ACT English section, any verb-form that uses a present-tense form of the helping verb *to be* describes an action in the present.

Example:

She is thinking about buying a computer.

In the above sentence, the verb form "is thinking" involves the word "is," which is the present-tense form of the helping verb "to be," so we know it describes an action taking place in the present.

On the ACT English section, verbs in a sentence should generally describe actions in the same time frame whenever possible—that is, unless the passage involves words like "before" or "after," which specifically indicate that verb phrases are taking place in different time frames.

This would be an acceptable sentence on the ACT English section:

I was making dinner when my parents arrived.

In the above sentence, all the verb forms ("was making" and "arrived") take place in the same time frame (the past).

This would be an unacceptable sentence on the ACT English section:

*I was making dinner when my parents will arrive.

In the above sentence, the word "when" tells us that the two events happen simultaneously, but the verb forms "was making" and "will arrive" are in different tenses (past and future, respectively).

The ACT English Section can be very tricky about verb tenses, so always make sure that any verb you encounter is in a tense that makes sense in context.

Conjugating irregular verbs

English verbs are conjugated in ways that show their tenses. The ACT particularly likes to test your familiarity with irregular verbs (in this case, verbs whose past-tense forms end in something other than "*-ed*").

Example:

The manager has left for the day.

"Has left" is the past participle conjugation of the verb "to leave."

Sometimes you'll see a verb-form on the ACT English section that isn't conjugated correctly. For example, this would be an unacceptable sentence on the ACT English section:

*The wind had blew the leaves everywhere.

"*Had blew" is an incorrect conjugation of the verb "to blow." The correct conjugation would be "had blown," as in the following version of the sentence:

The wind had blown the leaves everywhere.

Verb-forms used as nouns

There are two verb forms that can be used as nouns: the "-ing" form of a verb, and the "to" form of a verb.

Examples:

I love to dance.

Running is her hobby.

In these sentences, the verb phrase "to dance" is the object of the verb "love," and the verb form "running" is the subject of the verb "is."

Adjectives and adverbs

Adjectives are single words that describe nouns. You'll usually find an adjective right before the noun it describes, or as part of a list of other adjectives describing that noun.

Example:

Bowser is a tiny dog.

In this sentence, the word "tiny" is an adjective that describes the noun "dog."

If you want to modify something that isn't a noun, you'll need to use the adverb form of the adjective. The adverb form of an adjective almost always ends in "-ly."

Example:

I quickly ran across the street to see what was happening.

In this sentence, the adverb "quickly" is used to modify the verb "ran." Notice that "ran" isn't a noun, so we must use an adverb to modify it.

On the ACT English Section, you'll sometimes see incorrect sentences that involve adjectives modifying words that are not nouns, or adverbs modifying words that are nouns. Watch out for this!

This would be an unacceptable sentence on the ACT English section:

*I walked slow through the halls so no one would hear me.

In the above sentence, the adjective "slow" is being incorrectly used to modify the verb "walked," which is not a noun. That means we should use the adverb form "slowly."

This would be an acceptable sentence on the ACT English section:

I walked slowly through the halls so no one would hear me.

In the above sentence, the adverb "slowly" is correctly being used to modify the verb "walked."

Adjectives with copular verbs: an exception

For copular verbs like "to be" and "to become," we have to use adjective forms, even when those adjectives don't come right before a noun.

This would be an acceptable sentence on the ACT English section:

I was quiet as I walked through the halls.

In the above sentence,

- The pronoun "I" is being modified by the adjective "quiet."
- The word "was" is a copular verb that equates the words "I" and "quiet."
- The word "quiet" is an adjective that appears after a correctly used copular verb.

Conjunctions

Conjunctions are words that we use to link ideas to each other.

Examples:

and	**but**	**yet**	**either**
or	**nor**	**because**	**neither**

On the ACT English section, two or more ideas that are linked by a conjunction must appear in the same form. This is one example of something called "parallelism."

This would be an acceptable sentence on the ACT English section:

We like reading, learning, and thinking.

In the above sentence, the words "reading," "learning," and "thinking" are connected by the conjunction "and," and they're all in the same form (the "-ing" form), so this would be a good sentence on the ACT English section.

This would be an unacceptable sentence on the ACT English section:

*We like to read, learning, and thinking.

In the above sentence, the phrases "to read," "learning," and "thinking" are all connected with the conjunction "and," but they're not all in the same form (one is in the "to" form, and two are in the "-ing" form), so this wouldn't be a good sentence on the ACT English section.

Prepositions

Prepositions are words that tell us where concepts in a sentence are physically located relative to one another, or where they come from.

Example:

The mirror is in the living room on the wall near the door.

In the above sentence,

- "In the living room" is a prepositional phrase in which the preposition "in" shows the location of the mirror relative to the living room.
- "On the wall" is a prepositional phrase in which the preposition "on" shows the location of the mirror relative to the wall.
- "Near the door" is a prepositional phrase in which the preposition "near" shows the location of the mirror relative to the door.

Prepositional idioms

There are also idioms that involve certain prepositions. Sometimes the ACT will test your knowledge of these "prepositional idioms" in the ACT English section.

This would be an acceptable sentence on the ACT English section:

I am capable of finding the information you need.

In the above sentence, "capable of" is a correctly used prepositional idiom in this context, because speakers of American English routinely use the preposition "of" after the word "capable."

But this would be an unacceptable sentence on the ACT English section:

*I am capable with finding the information you need.

In the above sentence, "capable with" is NOT a correctly used prepositional idiom, because speakers of American English don't use the preposition "with" after the word "capable."

The rules that govern which preposition is used in a prepositional idiom aren't predictable—this is just something that the ACT expects you to be able to recognize. There's no logical reason for the phrase "capable of" to be correct, and no logical reason for the phrase "capable with" to be incorrect; that's just how this specific phrase has evolved.

For that reason, and because these types of issues doesn't come up often on the ACT, and because we can't predict which prepositional idioms might appear on any given test anyway, it's not a good use of your time to try to prepare for questions about prepositional idioms. Just keep in mind that this is something that might come up, so you'll be able to recognize when a question might be testing this concept.

Intervening prepositional phrases

Sometimes questions on the ACT English section will place a prepositional phrase between a subject and its verb. This makes it difficult to tell which noun is really the subject of the verb in question.

This would be an acceptable sentence on the ACT English section:

The best gardeners in the neighborhood are going to receive a prize.

In the above sentence, the verb form "are going" agrees in number with its subject, the noun "gardeners."

This would be an unacceptable sentence on the ACT English section:

*The best gardeners in the neighborhood is going to receive a prize.

In the above sentence, it might seem like the phrase "the neighborhood is going" would be acceptable by itself, because the placement of the prepositional phrase "in the neighborhood" makes it seem like "neighborhood" is the subject of the verb phrase "is going." But if we read the whole sentence, we know that the plural noun "gardeners" is actually the subject of the verb form "is going," which means the singular form "is going" is incorrect. The correct form is "are going," as we saw in the previous version of this sentence.

Comparatives

A comparative is a phrase that compares one concept to another concept. A comparative phrase can be created using the "-er" form of an adjective with the word *than* to compare two things. Sometimes, instead of the "-er" version of the adjective, we use the word *more* or *less* before that adjective (still using the word *than* after the adjective).

Example:

These tomatoes are bigger than the ones at the store.

In the above sentence, the phrase "bigger than" is a comparative phrase that compares these tomatoes to the ones at the store.

Example:

This book is more interesting than the last one we read.

In the above sentence, the phrase "more interesting than" is a comparative phrase that compares this book to the last one we read.

We can also create comparatives with phrases that use the word "as" twice.

Example:

This cookie is as big as my face.

In the above sentence, the phrase "as big as" is a comparative phrase that compares this cookie to my face.

Superlatives

Superlatives are like comparatives, except they are used to compare one thing to more than one other thing. A superlative is formed either by adding "-*est*" to an adjective, or by adding the word *most* or *least* before an adjective.

Examples:

That's the fastest cat in the neighborhood.

In the above sentence, the word "fastest" is a superlative that compares the cat to all the other cats in the neighborhood.

Matthew, Lauren, and I discussed our summer vacations, and we decided that Lauren's was the most exciting.

In the above sentence, the phrase "most exciting" is a superlative phrase that compares Lauren's summer vacation to Matthew's summer vacation and my summer vacation.

Whenever you see a comparative or a superlative on the ACT English section, make sure that the comparative or superlative is appropriate to the number of things involved.

Also, note that comparatives and superlatives use *either* the "-*er*"/"-*est*" form of the adjective, *or* the word "*more*"/"*less*"/"*most*"/"*least*" before the adjective, but not both. These sentences would be unacceptable on the ACT, because they break this rule:

*That was the most tastiest meal I ever had.

*Try to be more quieter next time.

Possessives

Possessives are words that show ownership. There are possessive pronouns and possessive nouns. These are possessive pronouns:

my	its	your
their	his	our
hers	whose	one's

People often have difficulty with "its," "whose," and "their" in particular, and confuse them with the contractions "it's," "who's," and "they're." Remember that when you see "it's," "who's," and "they're," those contractions are the same as the phrases "it is," "who is," and "they are," respectively.

Once you're comfortable with possessive pronouns, you need to understand how to form possessive nouns. There are two rules to remember when forming possessive nouns.

The first rule is that plural nouns ending in "-s" form their possessives by adding a single apostrophe to the end of the word.

Examples:

Plural nouns	Possessive plural nouns
dogs	dogs'
brothers	brothers'
schools	schools'
houses	houses'

The other rule is that *all other nouns* form their possessives by adding an apostrophe and an "-s."

Examples:

Nouns	Possessive nouns
girl	girl's
geese	geese's
horse	horse's
children	children's
Agnes	Agnes's

A lot of people are unclear on these rules, so the ACT English section often features incorrectly formed possessives—watch out for those.

Clauses and phrases

A phrase is a group of words that serves a particular function in a sentence. A phrase can include one word, or multiple words.

We refer to phrases based on the what they do in a given sentence—such as "noun phrases," "verb phrases," "prepositional phrases," etc.

Example:

> **My new neighbor really likes to build wooden furniture in his spare time.**

In the above sentence,

- "My new neighbor" is a noun phrase.
- "Likes to build" is a verb phrase.
- "Wooden furniture" is a noun phrase.
- "In his spare time" is a prepositional phrase.

It's possible to pick out other phrases from this sentence, but I think you get the idea.

The ACT won't directly ask about names or roles of phrases, so don't worry if you're not totally comfortable with this concept. I'm just talking about it because it will make this appendix easier to understand, especially on your second time reading it (and you should definitely read it twice).

A clause is a group of words that includes a subject noun phrase, a verb phrase, and an object noun phrase (if necessary).

Example:

> **The gorilla doesn't like you.**

This is a clause, because it includes a subject noun phrase ("the gorilla"), a verb phrase ("doesn't like"), and an object noun phrase ("you").

Clauses are either "dependent" or "independent." Dependent clauses often begin with conjunctions, but independent clauses don't.

Example:

> **I fell down because I wasn't paying attention.**

In the above sentence,

- The phrase "I fell down" is an independent clause because it's a clause that doesn't start with a conjunction.
- The phrase "because I wasn't paying attention" is a dependent clause that starts with a conjunction (the word "because").

We also often see dependent clauses on the ACT that start with a comma and then the word "which."

Example:

> **Gerald went back to bed, which is what he wanted to do in the first place.**

In the above sentence,

- The phrase "Gerald went back to bed" is an independent clause because it's a clause that doesn't start with a conjunction.
- The phrase "which is what he wanted to do in the first place" is a dependent clause that starts with the word "which" immediately after a comma.

Every complete sentence in the ACT English section must include at least one independent clause; that clause can be as simple as a subject and a verb. (It may include an object, but it doesn't have to.)

Example:

I am.

This is a complete sentence, because it consists of one independent clause.

Clauses and commas

Independent clauses on the ACT English section cannot be separated from each other by a comma. They can only be separated by a period or by a semicolon.

So this would be an unacceptable sentence on the ACT English section:

*I went to the store to buy a flashlight, the power came back on before I got home.

In the above sentence, "I went to the store to buy a flashlight" and "the power came back on before I got home" are both independent clauses, so they can't be separated by a comma. They have to be separated by a period or a semicolon.

These are acceptable sentences on the ACT English section:

I went to the store to buy a flashlight; the power came back on before I got home.

I went to the store to buy a flashlight. The power came back on before I got home.

In the above sentences, the phrase "I went to the store to buy a flashlight" and "the power came back on before I got home" are both independent clauses, so they can be separated by either a period or a semicolon on the ACT.

A period or a semi-colon is equally correct in this situation; one isn't preferable to the other on the ACT. You won't be asked to choose between two answer choices on the test where one has a period separating two independent clauses and the other has a semi-colon separating the same two independent clauses. If it seems like you *are* asked to do that, there must be some other difference between the two choices beside the semi-colon or period, or they must both be wrong for some other reason.

Conditionals

A "conditional" is a statement that use the conjunction "if." A conditional sentence that's properly written avoids the word "would" in the clause that begins with the conjunction "if."

This would be an unacceptable sentence on the ACT English section:

*If they would have seen you walking by, they would have said hello.

The above sentence would be unacceptable on the ACT English section because the word "would" is in the clause that starts with the word "if."

This would be an acceptable sentence on the ACT English section:

> **If they had seen you walking by, they would have said hello.**

The above sentence would be acceptable on the ACT English section because it doesn't use the word "would" in the clause that starts with the word "if."

Your/you're/yore

"Your" is the possessive form of the pronoun "you."

>   Example:

> **This is your suitcase.**

In this sentence, the word "your" tells us that the suitcase belongs to "you."

The word "you're" is a contraction of the phrase "you are."

>   Example:

> **You're right on time.**

In this sentence, the word "you're" is the same as the phrase "you are."

The word "yore" is a somewhat rare noun that describes a time long in the past.

>   Example:

> **People rode on horses in days of yore.**

In this sentence, the word "yore" describes a time from long ago.

These words sound the same, and a lot of students confuse them, so you need to make sure you know the differences among them. The ACT loves to test whether you know which version of your/you're/yore belongs in a sentence.

Their/they're/there

The word "their" is the possessive form of the pronoun "they."

>   Example:

> **Here is their car.**

In this sentence, the word "their" tells us that the car belongs to them.

The word "they're" is a contraction of the words "they" and "are."

>   Example:

> **They're standing in the back.**

In this sentence, the word "they're" is equivalent to the phrase "they are."

The word "there" tells us where something is.

>   Example:

> **The building is over there.**

In this sentence, the word "there" tells us where the building is.

This is another set of words that sound the same. Watch out for them, because the ACT loves to test whether you know which version of their/they're/there belongs in a sentence.

Much versus many

The word "much" is a word you use to describe a large amount of an uncountable noun.

> Examples:
>
> > **We have much work to do.**
> >
> > **Holidays bring much happiness.**

We use the word "much" in these sentences because the nouns involved ("work" and "happiness") aren't individually countable.

The word "many" is used to describe a large quantity of a countable noun.

> Examples:
>
> > **There are many houses in our neighborhood.**
> >
> > **You have many toys to put away.**
> >
> > **She has many leaves to rake up outside.**

We use the word "many" in these sentences because it's possible to count the nouns involved. "Houses," "toys," and "leaves" are all things that we can count individually.

When you see the words "much" and "many" in an ACT English question, make sure they're being used appropriately.

Misplaced modifiers

A misplaced modifier often shows up as a participle that modifies the wrong part of a sentence. A participle is a form of a verb that can end in "*-ing,*" "*-ed,*" or "*-en.*" Participles at the beginning of a sentence are understood to refer to the first noun phrase in the independent clause of the sentence in which they appear.

> This would be an acceptable sentence on the ACT English section:
>
> > **Crushed by his defeat, the wrestler sat motionless in the gym.**

In the above sentence, the word "crushed" is the past participle of the verb "to crush." The independent clause is "the wrestler sat motionless in the gym." This is correct because the verb form "crushed" describes "the wrestler," which is the first noun phrase in the independent clause.

On the ACT English section, we often see this order changed in unacceptable sentences. So this would be an unacceptable sentence on the ACT English section:

> > ***Crushed by his defeat, the gym was where the wrestler sat motionless.**

This sentence is unacceptable because the first noun phrase in the independent clause is now "the gym," which means the sentence is technically saying that the gym is "crushed by his defeat."

Whenever you see a participle at the beginning of a sentence on the ACT English section, make sure that it correctly describes the first noun phrase in the independent clause of that sentence.

Redundancy

Redundancy is when two parts of a sentence give the same information, making one of those parts unnecessary.

This would be an unacceptable sentence on the ACT English section:

> ***I frequently go on walks in the countryside often.**

In this sentence, the words "frequently" and "often" express the same idea, which makes one of them unnecessary on the ACT English section.

These are acceptable sentences on the ACT English section:

> **I frequently go on walks in the countryside.**

> **I go on walks in the countryside often.**

Notice that it doesn't matter whether we get rid of "frequently" or "often" as long as we get rid of one of them.

Watch out for sentences that include redundant phrases on the ACT English section.

Semicolons

Semicolons are acceptable in two situations on the ACT English section. They can separate two independent clauses, or they can separate listed items in a "super series."

Two independent clauses on the ACT can be separated by a semicolon. So this would be an acceptable sentence on the ACT English section:

> **I wonder what time it is; I'll go check the clock.**

In the above sentence, the phrases "I wonder what time it is" and "I'll go check the clock" are both independent clauses, so they can be correctly separated by a semicolon.

This would be an unacceptable sentence on the ACT English section:

> ***They decided to stay home; because it was raining.**

In the above sentence, the phrase "they decided to stay home" is an independent clause, and the phrase "because it was raining" is a dependent clause. Since these aren't both independent clauses, we can't separate them with a semicolon on the ACT English section.

The ACT English section also allows semicolons to be used to separate items in a "super series." A super series is a series of things that includes another series of things. The items in the sub-series are separated by commas, and the items in the super series are separated by semicolons. That might sound confusing, so let's look at an example.

Example:

> **I like indoor sports; water sports, including water skiing, kneeboarding, and surfing; and outdoor sports.**

In the above sentence, the sub-series is "water skiing, kneeboarding, and surfing." The super series is "indoor sports; water sports . . . ; and outdoor sports."

Colons

Colons can be used on the ACT to introduce a phrase that demonstrates a previously mentioned concept.

Example:

There's one thing I love about going to the movies: buttered popcorn.

In this sentence, the phrase "buttered popcorn" demonstrates the previously mentioned concept "one thing I love about going to the movies."

Marian brought three things with her to the beach: a towel, some sunscreen, and a hat.

In this sentence, the phrase "a towel, some sunscreen, and a hat" demonstrates the previously mentioned concept of Marian bringing "three things with her to the beach."